04/0X    #2

KV-194-417

# Harden's

in association with

RÉMY MARTIN
FINE CHAMPAGNE COGNAC

# UK
# Restaurants
## 2006

# A Taste for the Finest

Founded in 1724, Rémy Martin is renowned for producing Fine Champagne Cognacs of the highest quality. Whether you are enjoying a cocktail or long drink based on Rémy Martin Grand Cru, a glass of the world's favourite V.S.O.P, the smooth and spicy X.O. Excellence, the elegant Extra or the ultimate cognac, Louis XIII de Rémy Martin, each cognac in the range reflects the brand's philosophy of excellence.

Rémy Martin has a passion for creating exceptional taste experiences. The very best grapes are selected from the finest growing areas of Cognac and expensive traditional methods of production are still used to ensure that Rémy Martin cognacs remain the finest in the world.

In the same way, talent, passion, good judgement of taste and a dedication to creating excellence are the characteristics of a truly outstanding chef. These are the qualities that we reward in the fourth year of the Restaurant Rémy awards.

## Paying Tribute to Excellence

Rémy Martin launched the Restaurant Rémy awards in 2003 to recognise the emerging talent of the UK restaurant scene – those restaurants that were receiving consistently excellent reviews from British diners and setting new exacting standards for the whole industry.

These awards are won not through the ratings of restaurant critics or panels of judges but through the reviews of ordinary people who love dining out and understand what it takes to make that experience a real pleasure.

In our fourth year we are once more delighted to announce that twenty establishments from all over the UK have achieved an outstanding level of excellence and have been awarded a 2006 Restaurant Rémy award.

The diversity of cuisines and the variety of styles amongst this year's winners provide an insight into the rapidly changing landscape of the UK restaurant scene. In each and every winner we are witness to a commitment to delivering excellence and new taste experiences to our tables.

# WINNER OF THE 2006 EXCELLENCE AWARD

## BLACK DOOR RESTAURANT – NEWCASTLE

David Kennedy built up an extensive knowledge of the Newcastle dining scene after a decade's experience at leading local restaurant 21 Queen Street (later Café 21). When it came to opening Black Door, both he and business partner David Ladd recognised the need for upmarket and adventurous, yet accessible dining in Newcastle.

Their dedication to providing high-quality food and drink in a relaxed and inviting atmosphere has won them extensive praise from diners, who are thrilled to find this gem of a restaurant in the North East. It is this outstanding and consistent level of service and finesse that has earned them this year's Excellence award in the 2006 Restaurant Rémy awards.

Described by David Kennedy as "a fresh twist on classic French techniques", Black Door's elegant menu is all about getting the best, freshest local produce and combining it with quality ingredients from abroad. Menu items range from Northumberland smoked cheese soufflé with pickled girolles and pears, to roasted foie gras with caramelised mango, honey and cracked pepper.

David Ladd is responsible for creating the truly illuminating drinks selection – which includes a range of classic cocktails with a contemporary touch.

Fresh and exciting talent found at the now award-winning Black Door is contributing to the North East's emergence as a gastronomic destination for foodies all over the UK.

## RÉMY MARTIN
FINE CHAMPAGNE COGNAC

# 2006 Restaurant Rémy Awards
## Regional Winners

### Q Restaurant – Fowey, Cornwall

Set in a beautiful estuary in Cornwall, Q Restaurant blends a picturesque setting with innovative menus, excellent service and chic décor. Head chef Ben Bass creates innovative and tempting modern menus with an eclectic mix of influences from France, Italy and Cornwall.

### Russell's – Broadway, Worcestershire

Owners Barry Hancox and Andrew Riley have pooled more than 30 years' experience in the hotel and restaurant industry to create this 'restaurant-with-rooms', nestled at the heart of the picturesque village of Broadway. Local produce and seasonal dishes take centre stage.

### Wing's – Manchester

This city-centre restaurant serves up great-tasting contemporary Cantonese cuisine, including dim sum and seafood specialities, in a sleek, modern setting. Its good food and friendly staff have made it popular with the city's movers and shakers.

# 2006 Restaurant Rémy Awards

## Regional Winners

### Secco Ristorante Salentino
### Newcastle Upon Tyne

Cristina, Aldo and Joseph De Giorgi have injected their own blend of 'la dolce vita' into Secco Ristorante Salentino. The menu mirrors the cooking styles of the Salento region of Italy, with fresh fish, seafood dishes and hearty, rustic food cooked simply and slowly.

### Baraset Barn
### Alveston, Stratford-Upon-Avon

Set in a stylishly converted barn, Paul Hales and Paul Salisbury's Baraset Barn follows in the footsteps of their other successful ventures – The Boot, Orange Tree Stable and Crabmill. The wide-ranging menu has won a host of local fans.

### Abstract – Inverness

With a team of award-winning chefs working under head chef Loic Lefebvre, Abstract combines traditional high quality French-style cooking with local ingredients such as spring Scottish lamb, North Sea turbot and West Coast scallops.

# 2006 Restaurant Rémy Awards
## Regional Winners

### The Cabinet
### Reed, Nr Royston, Hertfordshire

With the help of head chef Paul Maguire, new owners Simon Smith and Mark Hagger have managed to maintain the excellent standards of food and great service expected by local fans of this stunningly converted 16th-century inn.

### Forbury's – Reading

Chef José Cau and fellow patron Xavier Le-Bellego are used to winning accolades, having spent time at The Waterside Inn at Bray and Le Gavroche respectively. This winning combination has led to an innovative menu, delivered with flair, earning Forbury's a reputation as a real Thames Valley gem.

### The Priory Inn
### Tetbury, Gloucestershire

Tanya and Dave Kelly set out to create a family-friendly hotel and restaurant without compromising on quality. The result is a gastropub dining experience with a glowing reputation. Great-tasting food is served from a simply executed and flexible menu.

# 2006 Restaurant Rémy Awards
## London Winners

## Salt Yard – Fitzrovia

It's a gutsy move to offer a menu composed of an assortment of Spanish and Italian tapas dishes, but head chef Brian Villahermosa has already wowed Londoners with his top-quality charcuterie boards, cheese selections and sharing-dishes, straight from the Mediterranean.

## The Ledbury – Notting Hill

Owners Nigel Platts-Martin and Philip Howard are used to success and The Ledbury is no exception, having proved popular with the Notting Hill locals since its opening. The menu features an exciting blend of flavours, presented with style.

## Camerino – Fitzrovia

Camerino is an elegant restaurant that explores the regional cuisines of Italy through a classic yet thoroughly modern menu. Head chef Valerio Daros has a wealth of culinary experience, including four years as sous-chef for Giorgio Locatelli. Regulars are fans of both the food and the friendly, intimate atmosphere.

**RÉMY MARTIN**
FINE CHAMPAGNE COGNAC

# 2006 Restaurant Rémy Awards

## London Winners

### The Gun – Docklands

The Gun is the latest gastropub offering from Tom and Ed Martin, whose past ventures include the White Swan in Fetter Lane. Head chef Scott Wade creates an elegant and indulgent menu which features fish purchased daily from nearby Billingsgate market.

### Nuovi Sapori – Fulham

Nuovi Sapori means 'new tastes' in Italian, which is precisely what owner Carlo Petitto and head chef Fernando Estrella have created. Their menu takes some of the best-known Italian dishes and makes them new with inventive touches and creative combinations.

### Ottolenghi Upper St – Islington

Following on from its successful sister restaurant in Notting Hill, Ottolenghi has been causing a stir in Islington since its opening. Part deli, part pâtisserie, part restaurant, Ottolenghi boasts an inventive Mediterranean menu with Arabic and Greek tones.

# 2006 RESTAURANT RÉMY AWARDS

## LONDON WINNERS

### KOBA – FITZROVIA

Koba offers a zesty, enticing Korean menu in a very 'now' setting. Its varied menu includes pancakes, casseroles and rice dishes, and its speciality 'table bbq' is fast becoming a favourite amongst North Soho diners.

### ARTURO – BAYSWATER

This chic and modern restaurant serves traditional Italian food with a gourmet touch, at reasonable prices. Fans praise its simple and beautifully executed dishes, along with its cosy atmosphere and friendly, accommodating staff.

### FRATELLI LA BUFALA – HAMPSTEAD

The food philosophy at Fratelli La Bufala is based on simple cooking methods, and authentic and nutritional ingredients. Dishes are cooked in a traditional rural Italian way, with an emphasis on quality and freshness.

### SABOR – ISLINGTON

The Nuevo Latino menu at Sabor is inspired by owner Esnayder Cuartas' time spent travelling in South America. Diners are treated to delicious, authentic dishes in a lively atmosphere.

# RÉMY MARTIN
FINE CHAMPAGNE COGNAC

# THE SECRETS OF EXCELLENCE

At Rémy Martin we insist on adhering to the most exacting production methods in our pursuit of the finest taste.

Cognac, as distinct from any other brandy, can only be produced in the specified area surrounding the town of Cognac, consisting of six crus (growing areas). At Rémy Martin we select only grapes from the two finest crus of the Cognac region – Grande Champagne and Petite Champagne – to ensure the aromatic richness of our cognacs. The combination of grapes from these two prestigious areas leads to the name Fine Champagne Cognac.

Our wines undergo a double distillation on the lees in small copper stills to impart a wonderful texture and rich complexity of flavour.

Rémy Martin uses only the highest quality Limousin oak barrels for the long ageing of its eaux-de-vie, ensuring the natural, warm amber colour and delicious aromas and flavours that characterise Rémy Martin cognacs.

The skill of the Cellar Master is central to the crafting of our sublime spirit. The Cellar Master's art lies in combining selected eaux-de-vie to create the perfect combination of aromas and flavours in each of our cognacs.

Our passion for excellence ensures that you can enjoy the quality of Rémy Martin however you choose to drink your cognac – served neat, frozen, over ice, mixed in a long drink or savoured with food.

**RÉMY MARTIN**

FINE CHAMPAGNE COGNAC

# DISCOVER PERFECT TASTE MATCHES WITH RÉMY MARTIN

While you sample the diversity of cuisine represented by the twenty Restaurant Rémy award winners, why not embark on a journey of new taste discoveries with Rémy Martin Fine Champagne Cognacs?

Cognac has an incredible flexibility beyond traditional digestifs and the smooth texture and richness of flavours and aromas found in the Rémy Martin range can create some stunning partnerships with food. Instead of waiting for a glass to cap the end of a great meal, why not enjoy a serving as you dine?

# FROZEN RÉMY MARTIN V.S.O.P. WITH SUSHI

When served frozen, Rémy Martin V.S.O.P. takes on a wonderful viscosity and intensity of flavours, which complement the oily texture of raw fish. Enjoy the spicy vanilla flavours and aromatic hints of violet and apricot in Rémy Martin V.S.O.P. – a perfect match for sushi.

# DISCOVER PERFECT TASTE MATCHES WITH RÉMY MARTIN

## RÉMY MARTIN X.O. EXCELLENCE WITH DARK CHOCOLATE

Indulge yourself by partnering a glass of Rémy Martin X.O. Excellence with your favourite chocolate dessert. The cognac's rich velvet texture and aromatic notes of candied fruit, fig and juicy prunes marry beautifully with the bitter-sweet flavours of rich, dark chocolate.

## RÉMY MARTIN V.S.O.P. AND ROQUEFORT CHEESE

Strongly flavoured and aromatic cheeses like Roquefort can overwhelm a wine, but the depth of flavour and texture found in Rémy Martin V.S.O.P. make this the ideal accompaniment. A glass served at room temperature can really enhance Roquefort's indulgent creamy texture and intense flavours.

## Publisher's announcements

### Other Harden's titles

*London Restaurants*
*London Party & Corporate Event Guide*
*Good Cheap Eats in London*
*London Bars & Pubs*
*London Baby Book*
*UK Baby Book – NEW*
*London for Free*

### The ideal corporate gift

*Harden's London Restaurants*, *Harden's UK Restaurants*,
*Harden's Hotel Guide* and *Harden's London Bars & Pubs*
are available in a range of specially customised corporate
gift formats.

For further information on any of the above, please call
(020) 7839 4763 or visit www.hardens.com.

© Harden's Limited 2005

ISBN 1-873721-73-0

British Library Cataloguing-in-Publication data:
a catalogue record for this book is available from
the British Library.

Printed and bound in England by Polestar Wheatons

Research manager: Frances Gill
Research assistants: Lois Lee, Shannon Doubleday,
Joanne Nonkoh, Sarah Ashpole

Harden's Limited
14 Buckingham Street
London WC2N 6DF

The views expressed in the editorial section of this guide are
exclusively those of Harden's Limited.

The contents of this book are believed correct at the time of
printing. Nevertheless, the publisher can accept no responsibility
for errors or changes in or omissions from the details given.

No part of this publication may be reproduced or transmitted in
any form or by any means, electronically or mechanically, including
photocopying, recording or any information storage or retrieval
system, without prior permission in writing from the publisher.

# CONTENTS

# RATINGS & PRICES

We see little point in traditional rating systems, which generally tell you nothing more than that expensive restaurants are 'better' than cheap ones because they use costlier ingredients and attempt more ambitious dishes. You probably knew that already. Our system assumes that, as prices rise, so do diners' expectations.

## £ Price

The cost of a three-course *dinner* for one person.
We include half a bottle of house wine, coffee and service (or a 10% tip if there is no service charge).

## Food

The following symbols indicate that, ***in comparison with other restaurants in the same price-bracket***, the cooking at the establishment is:

★★ **Exceptional**
★ **Very good**

We also have a category for places which attract a notably high proportion of adverse comment:

✗ **Disappointing**

## Ambience

Restaurants which provide a setting which is very charming, stylish or 'buzzy' are indicated as follows:

𝔸 **Particularly atmospheric**

## Restaurant Rémy awards

 A bold Restaurant Rémy symbol signifies this year's winners – see front colour section

 A faded Restaurant Rémy symbol signifies a former year's winner

## Small print

**<u>Telephone number</u>** – *All numbers in the London section are (020) numbers. Dublin numbers are shown for dialling within the Republic (the international code for which is + 353).*

**<u>Sample dishes</u>** – *these dishes exemplify the style of cooking at a particular establishment. They are merely samples - it is unlikely that these specific dishes will be available at the time of your visit.*

**<u>Details</u>** – *the following information is given where relevant:*

**Directions** – *to help you find the establishment.*

**Website** – *if applicable.*

**Last orders time** – *at dinner (Sun may be up to 90 mins earlier).*

**Opening hours** – *unless otherwise stated, restaurants are open for lunch and dinner seven days a week.*

**Credit and debit cards** – *unless otherwise stated, Mastercard, Visa, Amex and Maestro are accepted.*

**Dress** – *where appropriate, the management's preferences concerning patrons' dress are given.*

**Smoking** – *cigarette smoking restrictions are noted. Pipe or cigar smokers should always check ahead.*

**Children** – *if we know of a specified minimum age for children, we note this.*

**Accommodation** – *if an establishment has rooms, we list how many and the minimum price for a double.*

# FROM THE EDITORS

To an extent we believe to be unique, this guide is written 'from the bottom up'. That is to say, its composition reflects the restaurants, pubs and cafés which people across the country – as represented by our diverse reporter base – talk about. It does not, therefore, concentrate on hotel restaurants (as does one of the major 'independent' guides whose publisher also does big business in paid-for hotel inspections). Nor does it 'overweight' European cuisines. Most restaurants in this country fall in the category usually called 'ethnic', but most guidebooks would lead you to think that such places are generally unworthy of serious commentary. It seems to us that this approach is positively wrong-headed in a country where the diversity of restaurant types is one of the most notable (and positive) features.

The effects of London's restaurant revolution of the '90s are now becoming apparent across the whole of the UK. Most major conurbations, for example, now have several ambitious restaurants good enough to be of note to visitors. The areas that are still truly 'culinary deserts' are becoming both smaller and more dispersed. Much as this is to be applauded, it does not make our task any easier, and we are keenly aware – as any honest publisher must acknowledge – that all guide books are imperfect. There will be deserving places missing, and opinions will be repeated that the passing of time has rendered redundant. However, we believe that our system – involving the careful processing of tens of thousands of reports – is the best available.

We are very grateful to each of our thousands of reporters, without whose input this guide could simply not have been written. Many of our reporters express views about a number of restaurants at some length, knowing full well that – given the concise format of the guide – we can seemingly never 'do justice' to their observations. We must assume that they do so in the confidence that the short – and we hope snappy – summaries we produce are as fair and as well-informed as possible. You, the reader, must judge – restaurant guides are not works of literature, and should be assessed on the basis of utility. This is a case where the proof of the pudding really is in the eating.

Given the growing scale of our task, we are particularly grateful for the continuing support we have received from Rémy Martin Fine Champagne Cognac in the publication of this guide. With their help, this is now well on the way to becoming the most comprehensive – as well as the most democratic and diverse – guide available to the restaurants of the UK.

All restaurant guides are the subject of continual revision. This is especially true when the restaurant scene is undergoing a period of rapid change, as at present. **Please help us to make the next edition even more comprehensive and accurate: sign up to join the survey by following the instructions overleaf.**

**Richard Harden**                                    **Peter Harden**

# HOW THIS BOOK IS ORGANISED

This guide begins in *London*, which, in recognition of the scale and diversity of its restaurant scene, has an extensive introduction and indexes, as well as its own maps. Thereafter, the guide is organised strictly alphabetically, without regard to national divisions – Ballater, Beaumaris, Belfast and Birmingham appear together under 'B'.

For *cities and larger towns*, you should therefore be able to turn straight to the relevant section. Cities which have significant numbers of restaurants also have a brief introductory overview, as well as entries for the restaurants themselves.

In *less densely populated areas*, you will generally find it easiest to start with the map of the relevant area at the back of the book, which will guide you to the appropriate place names.

# HOW THIS BOOK IS RESEARCHED

This book is the result of a research effort involving thousands of 'reporters'. These are 'ordinary' members of the public who share with us summary reviews of the best and the worst of their annual dining experiences. This year, some 8,000 people gave us approximately 93,000 reviews in total.

The density of the feedback on London (where many of the top places attract several hundred reviews each) is such that the ratings for the restaurants in the capital included in this edition are almost exclusively statistical in derivation. We have, as it happens, visited almost all the restaurants in the London section, anonymously, and at our own expense, but we use our personal experiences only to inform the standpoint from which to interpret the consensus opinion.

In the case of the more commented-upon restaurants away from the capital, we have adopted an approach very similar to London. In the case of less-visited provincial establishments, however, the interpretation of survey results owes as much to art as it does to science.

In our experience, smaller establishments are – for better or worse – generally quite consistent, and we have therefore felt able to place a relatively high level of confidence in a lower level of commentary. Conservatism on our part, however, may have led to some smaller places being underrated compared to their more visited peers.

# HOW YOU CAN JOIN THE SURVEY

Register on our mailing list at www.hardens.com and you will be invited, in the spring of 2006, to participate in our next survey. **If you take part you will, on publication, receive a complimentary copy of *Harden's UK Restaurants 2007*.**

# LONDON INTRODUCTION & SURVEY RESULTS

# LONDON INTRODUCTION

### How does London compare internationally?

London is not Paris, Rome or Madrid. As the capital of a country which, for at least two centuries, has had no particular reputation for its gastronomy, its attractions are rarely indigenous. By-and-large, only tourists look for 'English' restaurants.

Where London does score – and score magnificently – is in the range and quality it offers of other national styles of cooking. Always an entrepot, London is now a culinary melting pot, too: in terms of scale *and* variety, its only obvious competitor is New York.

In one area, London may claim worldwide supremacy. As a paradoxical legacy of empire, it is in the cuisine of the Indian subcontinent. For a combination of variety, quality and innovation, London's 'Indian' (including Pakistani and so on) restaurants are without peer.

### Which is London's best restaurant?

However much we may speak of melting pots and diversity, when people talk about the very best cooking, they tend – rightly or wrongly – to mean the best French cooking. In that sense, the capital's best restaurant is where you can find the capital's best Gallic cooking, and that is clearly *Gordon Ramsay* – the Chelsea flagship of the UK's leading chef. Offering French cooking a whisker behind Ramsay's, there's quite a group of low-key places which – in total contrast – never make the headlines. These comprise the *Capital*, *Pied à Terre* (assuming, post-relaunch, it lives up to its old standards), *Roussillon*, *Aubergine* and *1880*. Particularly for its 'all-round', if rather 'period', charms, *Le Gavroche* – London's longest-established grand French restaurant – remains of note. For Gallic fish dishes, *Restaurant One-O-One* is still the capital's top place.

Even traditions change, though, and the idea that French is Best is increasingly under attack…

### What's 'in' at the moment?

The obvious question is: "in with whom?" The all-purpose business-to-media in-place of recent times has been the famous *Ivy*. It may now – for the first time in ten years – no longer be the survey's favourite, but it remains a hard place to book.

Sharing some of the same cachet, but easier to reserve, are siblings *J Sheekey* and *Le Caprice*. The *Wolseley* – launched by Christopher Corbin and Jeremy King who used to own all the above – was hailed on its launch a couple of years ago as the obvious competitor to the Ivy. It has certainly stolen some of the latter's celebrity custom, but has yet to become the total 'wow' which some expected.

Mayfair continues to (re-)emerge as an international in-crowd destination. If that's what you're looking for, *Cipriani* is certainly something of a 'scene'. For those in search of somewhere a little more traditional, new arrival *Bellamy's* is a discreet haven, in a quiet mews. Fresh-out-of-the-wrapper *Automat* seems to be emerging as the NyLon place of the moment.

Hip, young-at-heart types, with money to burn, increasingly opt for oriental places. It was *Nobu* which set the trend, but it now has plenty of competition such as *Hakkasan, Taman gang, Roka, Yauatcha* and *Zuma*. As we go to press, *Nobu Berkeley* looks set to make more than a few waves.

## I'm not fussed about fashionable scenes – where can I find a really good meal without spending the earth?

*J Sheekey* and *Le Caprice* are not that expensive, and, if you want a bit of glamour plus a decent meal in the heart of town, are hard to beat. In Knightsbridge, *Racine* is now well-established as a top quality all-rounder.

The name Nigel Platts-Martin has become a by-word for value amongst those who know about London's restaurant-scene. *Chez Bruce,* his Wandsworth restaurant was the survey's favourite this year. *La Trompette* in Chiswick, *The Glasshouse* in Kew and, now, Notting Hill's *Ledbury* also win raves.

For sheer consistency over years, few restaurants match *Clarke's* in Kensington.

## What if I want the best of British tradition?

Because Britain is a 'pub culture', there are very few traditional restaurants of note (and fewer which can be recommended). *The Dorchester Grill* is currently the grandest of the native flag bearers (though some changes are afoot as this guide goes to press). The venerable *Rules* combines generally good cooking with charming period style. Nearby, the famous *Simpsons-in-the-Strand* has been too variable to recommend in recent years. The City preserves some extraordinary olde-worlde places such as *Sweetings*.

For foodies, Smithfield's *St John* continues to be an inspiration with its exploration of traditional British cooking, including lots of offal: uncompromising food in an uncompromising setting. South Bank gastropub, the *Anchor & Hope* has created a big name – it topped the survey's list of favourite pubs for the first time this year– by offering similar (but perhaps less 'threatening') fare, in a rather similar vein.

For afternoon tea, *The Wolseley* or *The Ritz* are best.

## Isn't London supposed to be a top place for curry?

London is the world's leading Indian restaurant city: the days are long gone when a pint and a curry were seen as the height of culinary adventure. At the top end, names such as *Amaya, Chutney Mary, Vama, Zaika, Tamarind, The Cinnamon Club* and *Rasoi Vineet Bhatia* are 'pushing back the frontiers'.

To eat well on a budget, the capital's inexpensive Indians offer a great deal of choice in almost all areas. Such names as *Rasa, Mirch Masala* and *New Tayaabs* stand out, but the number of interesting places is large and growing. The very best Indian restaurants are invariably not to be found in the West End, but competent names to look out for include *Chowki* and *Mela*.

## What are gastropubs?

Many pubs have re-invented themselves as informal restaurants in recent years. *The Eagle* was the original (1991). The trend goes from strength to strength. There are now almost no affluent suburbs which lack pubs serving food of a quality that even five years ago would have been inconceivable. Outlying examples include *The Earl Spencer* and *St Johns*.

Generally the pub tradition of ordering at the bar is kept, but some of the grander establishments offer full table service and have really become restaurants in all but name.

**Can't we just grab a bowl of pasta?**

Italian cooking remains the 'default' choice for relaxed neighbourhood dining, especially in the more affluent parts of town, and there is an enormous variety of trattorias and pizzerias. In recent years, some excellent high-level Italians have emerged. At the mid-level, good Italian newcomers seem to be much more common than good French ones.

**What about these orientals we've heard so much of?**

Japanese restaurants are finally being accepted in London, as in New York, amongst the city's top dining rooms. *Umu* now has the distinction of offering London's most expensive menu, though it has failed to impress all but a few aficionados of Kyoto cuisine. *Tsunami* in Clapham offers a Japanese-fusion experience similar to that at many 'in'-places, but at a fraction of the cost.

Traditional Chinese restaurants remain a far cry from the Hakkasans and Yauatchas of the world. The very best are not in fact in or near Chinatown. *Hunan* and *Phoenix Palace* are both excellent and on the periphery of the West End. The biggest concentration of very good restaurants is in Bayswater – the most prominent/listed example being *Mandarin Kitchen*.

Thai cooking is also widespread, but strongest in west London. Fulham's grand *Blue Elephant* has been amazingly consistent over the years, as has Notting Hill's *Churchill Arms* – that curious London formula of Thai-in-a-pub.

**You said diverse: what about other cuisines?**

A major hit of recent years has been the cuisines of North Africa and the Eastern Mediterranean. These cuisines lend themselves well to good budget experiences – the *Tas* chain and *Haz* are among the good, less expensive places.

See the lists on pages 26 and 27 for the top exponents of each type of cuisine by nationality.

**Any suggestions for 'something completely different'?**

How about *Archipelago, Champor-Champor, LMNT,* the *Lobster Pot, Les Trois Garçons* or *MVH*?

**Are there any sharp practices I should look out for?**

Yes: the 'blank credit card slip trick'. If you are presented with a credit card slip with a blank line for a gratuity, do **not** assume that a tip is appropriate. Often, 10% or (more usually) 12.5% service has already been included in the sum you are being asked to pay, but the restaurant is hoping that you will inadvertently 'double up'. With 'chip & pin' technology, there is a new variant of this ploy: you are handed the portable credit card terminal, with the option to amend the total for a tip, when service has already been included.

# SURVEY – MOST MENTIONED

These are the restaurants which were most frequently mentioned by reporters. (Last year's position is given in brackets.) An asterisk* indicates the first appearance in the list of a recently-opened restaurant.

1   J Sheekey (1)
2   Hakkasan (4)
3   The Ivy (2)
4   Gordon Ramsay (3)
5   The Wolseley (11)
6   Bleeding Heart (7)
7   Nobu (5)
8   Gordon Ramsay at Claridge's (9)
9   Chez Bruce (8)
10   Oxo Tower (6)

11   La Poule au Pot (12)
12   Andrew Edmunds (10)
13   Le Gavroche (17)
14   Yauatcha*
15   The Cinnamon Club (19)
16   Le Caprice (14)
17   Locanda Locatelli (13)
18   Zuma (26)
19   Tom Aikens (24)
20   La Trompette (22)

21   The Square (19)
22   Mirabelle (16)
23   Pétrus (21)
24   Club Gascon (15)
25   The River Café (27)
26   Blue Elephant (23)
27   Connaught (Angela Hartnett) (35)
28   Le Pont de la Tour (28)
29   Chutney Mary (34)
30   The Don (-)

31   Racine (31)
32   Moro (30)
33=  The Anchor & Hope*
33=  Savoy Grill (28)
35   Coq d'Argent (25)
36   Zafferano (32)
37   Café du Marché (37)
38   Sketch (Gallery) (18)
39   Amaya*
40   St John (-)

**sign up for the survey at www.hardens.com**

# LONDON - HIGHEST RATINGS

These are the restaurants which received the best average food ratings (excluding establishments with a small or notably local following).

Where the most common types of cuisine are concerned, we present the results in two price-brackets. For less common cuisines, we list the top three, regardless of price.

---

## British, Modern

| *£45 and over* | *Under £45* |
| --- | --- |
| *1* Chez Bruce | *1* St John |
| *2* 1880 | *2* Mosaica |
| *3* The Glasshouse | *3* The Palmerston |
| *4* Clarke's | *4* Lamberts |
| *5* Notting Hill Brasserie | *5* The Anglesea Arms, W6 |

## French

| *£45 and over* | *Under £45* |
| --- | --- |
| *1* Gordon Ramsay | *1* Racine |
| *2* Capital Hotel | *2* Le Cercle |
| *3* Pied à Terre | *3* Le Vacherin |
| *4* Aubergine | *4* Petit Max |
| *5* Roussillon | *5* Café du Marché |

## Italian/Mediterranean

| *£45 and over* | *Under £45* |
| --- | --- |
| *1* Assaggi | *1* Ottolenghi |
| *2* Quirinale | *2* Latium |
| *3* Zafferano | *3* Arancia |
| *4* Tentazioni | *4* A Cena |
| *5* Locanda Locatelli | *5* The Oak |

## Indian

| *£45 and over* | *Under £45* |
| --- | --- |
| *1* Rasoi Vineet Bhatia | *1* Rasa |
| *2* Amaya | *2* New Tayyab |
| *3* Tamarind | *3* Mirch Masala |
| *4* Chutney Mary | *4* Vijay |
| *5* Zaika | *5* Lahore Kebab House |

## Chinese

| £45 and over | Under £45 |
|---|---|
| 1 Hakkasan | 1 Hunan |
| 2 Kai Mayfair | 2 Mandarin Kitchen |
| 3 Ken Lo's Memories | 3 Phoenix Palace |
| 4 Ken Lo's Memories W8 | 4 Good Earth |
| 5 Taman gang | 5 Yauatcha |

## Japanese

| £45 and over | Under £45 |
|---|---|
| 1 Zuma | 1 Café Japan |
| 2 Nobu | 2 Tsunami |
| 3 Tatsuso | 3 Jin Kichi |
| 4 Sumosan | 4 K10 |
| 5 Ubon | 5 Kulu Kulu |

---

**British, Traditional**
1 Dorchester Grill
2 Two Brothers
3 St John Bread & Wine

**Vegetarian**
1 The Gate
2 Blah! Blah! Blah!
3 Mildred's

**Burgers, etc**
1 GBK
2 Wolfe's
3 Lucky Seven

**Pizza**
1 Pizza Metro
2 Made in Italy
3 Il Bordello

**Fish & Chips**
1 Nautilus
2 Faulkner's
3 Toff's

**Thai**
1 Patara
2 Amaranth
3 Churchill Arms

**Fusion**
1 Tsunami
2 Nobu
3 Ubon

**Fish & Seafood**
1 One-O-One
2 J Sheekey
3 Mandarin Kitchen

**Greek**
1 Vrisaki
2 Lemonia
3 The Real Greek

**Spanish**
1 Moro
2 Fino
3 Tapas Brindisa

**Turkish**
1 Haz
2 Gallipoli
3 Kazan

**Lebanese**
1 Beirut Express
2 Ranoush
3 Maroush

*sign up for the survey at www.hardens.com*

# SURVEY – NOMINATIONS

Ranked by the number of reporters' votes.

## Top gastronomic experience

1  Gordon Ramsay (1)
2  Gordon Ramsay at Claridge's (3)
3  Chez Bruce (2)
4  Tom Aikens (4)
5  Le Gavroche (5)
6  Nobu (6)
7  La Trompette (9)
8  The Ivy (8)
9  Pétrus (-)
10  Locanda Locatelli (10)

## Favourite

1  Chez Bruce (2)
2  The Ivy (1)
3  The Wolseley (8)
4  J Sheekey (3)
5  Le Caprice (4)
6  Gordon Ramsay (5)
7  La Trompette (6)
8  Hakkasan (7)
9  Nobu (-)
10  Zuma (10)

## Best for business

1  Bleeding Heart (3)
2  The Don (5)
3  The Wolseley (-)
4  The Square (2)
5  Coq d'Argent (1)
6  The Ivy (7)
7  1 Lombard Street (4)
8  Rhodes 24*
9  Savoy Grill (6)
10  Bank Aldwych (9)

## Best for romance

1  La Poule au Pot (1)
2  Andrew Edmunds (2)
3  Bleeding Heart (3)
4  Chez Bruce (4)
5  The Ivy (6)
6  Le Caprice (5)
7  Julie's (7)
8  Café du Marché (-)
9  Oxo Tower (Bras') (8)
10  Blue Elephant (9)

# OPENINGS

Restaurants in **bold** are included in the London section of this guide - for the full selection, see *Harden's London Restaurants 2006* (£10.99), available in all good bookshops.

## OPENINGS

**Abeno Too**
Abingdon Road
Addendum
Albannach
**Arturo**
As Greek As It Gets
**Automat**
The Aviary
Awana
Babes 'n' Burgers
Bankside, *EC2*
The Bar & Grill
Bastille
Beauberry House
Beaufort House
**Bellamy's**
Blue Lagoon, *SW1*
**Bombay Bicycle Club**,
*W11 & NW3*
**Broadway Bar & Grill**
The Bull
**La Buvette**
Chakalaka
China Tang
**The Chinese Experience**
**Chisou**
Christopher's In The City
Coco
Comptoir Gascon
**Crazy Homies**
The Cross Bar
Cube & Star
Dans le Noir
Deep
dim T, *W1*
Epicurean Pizza Lounge
EV
Evo
Fairuz, *W2*
Fiore
Fire & Stone
**Firezza**
**Fish Club**
Food@TheMuse
43 South Molton
Frankie's
**Fratelli la Bufala**
**Freemasons Arms**
Galvin
**The Garden Café**

Giardinetto
Glas
Graze
The Green
Greenwich Park
**The Greyhound**, *SW11*
Grocer on Warwick Café
**The Gun**
Haché
Hadley House
Hole in the Wall
Homage
Iniga
Isarn
Ishtar
**Kisso**
**Koba**
Kurumaya
**Laureate**
**The Ledbury**
**Leon**
**Lilly's**
Little Earth Cafe
Louvaine
Love India
Luna Rossa
Mamounia
Matilda's
Matriciano
maze
Menier Chocolate Factory
Messanges
**Mestizo**
Metro
Michiaki
**Missouri Grill**
Morel
Moti Mahal
**Nobu Berkeley**
Noura, *three branches*
Nozomi
**Nuovi Sapori**
Occo
**OQO Bar**
**Ottolenghi**
Le Pain Quotidien
Pengelley's
The Penthouse
The Pig's Ear
**Ping Pong**

## OPENINGS (cont'd)

Pomino
Portal
The Princess
Pucci Pizza
The Pumphouse
Putney Station
Real Burger World
Relais de Paris
Le Relais de Venise
Rhodes W1
Roast
Rodizio Rico, *N1*
Rowley's, *W1*
Ruby Lounge &
   Sequoia Bar
**Sabor**
**Le Saint Julien**
**Salt Yard**
Sam's Brasserie
San Frediano *(yet again)*
Santa Maria de Buen Ayre
**Sarkhel's**, *SW14*
Savarona
The Sea Cow, *SW4*
Shanghai Blues
Shikara
Silk
Sketch (Glade)
**La Superba**
**Tapas Brindisa**
Taqueria
Tartine, *TW9*
The Tea Palace
**Thai on the River**
3G
Throgmorton
Tobia
**Tugga**
W'sens
Whole Hog Canteen
Wizzy
**Yelo**, *W11*
**Yi-Ban**, *SW6*

# LONDON DIRECTORY

**A Cena TW1** £40 A★
418 Richmond Rd 8288 0108
This "professional yet informal" St Margarets Italian – with its
"simple" but "extremely well-cooked" food – is one of the top
places to eat around Richmond; lunch in particular is "excellent
value". / **Value tip:** set weekday L £25 (FP). **Details:** 10.30 pm; closed Mon &
Sun D; booking: max 6, Fri & Sat.

**Abeno WC1** £33
47 Museum St 7405 3211 1–1C
This "authentic" okonomi-yaki (Japanese omelette) café
in Bloomsbury offers a "novel" experience that's customarily well-
rated; this year saw the odd "slight disappointment", though –
perhaps the strain of opening Abeno Too. / **Details:** www.abeno.co.uk;
11 pm.

**L'Accento Italiano W2** £38
16 Garway Rd 7243 2201 5–1B
"A good, consistent neighbourhood place", in Bayswater, serving
an "unpretentious" menu of "well-cooked" Italian fare.
/ **Details:** 11.15 pm; closed Sun.

**Adam Street WC2** £53 A
9 Adam St 7379 8000 3–4D
"Discreet surroundings", "reliable" cooking and an "interesting"
wine list make the "cosy vaults" of this "informal" members' club
– open to all at lunch – a "great business venue", just off the
Strand. / **Details:** www.adamstreet.co.uk; L only (open for D to members only),
closed Sat L & Sun.

**Admiral Codrington SW3** £42 A
17 Mossop St 7581 0005 4–2C
This "upmarket" pub has long been a "buzzy" watering hole near
Brompton Cross, and offers "enjoyable" (if undemanding) cooking;
the dining room's retractable roof enables "outside eating
indoors". / **Details:** www.admiralcodrington.co.uk; 11 pm.

**Aglio e Olio SW10** £28 ★
194 Fulham Rd 7351 0070 4–3B
It may be "very noisy" and "canteen"-like, but this Chelsea
trattoria has won many fans with its "reliable" and "down-to-
earth" charms; the menu – with "fabulous" pasta a highlight –
is "reasonably-priced", too. / **Details:** 11.30 pm.

**Al San Vincenzo W2** £45 ★
30 Connaught St 7262 9623 5–1D
"Now back on form", the Borgonzolo family's tiny Bayswater
establishment offers "a good choice of real Italian specialities",
in a "quiet", "comfortable" and "friendly" setting. / **Details:** 9.30 pm;
closed Sat L & Sun; no Amex; no smoking.

**Ali Baba NW1** £20 ★
32 Ivor Pl 7723 5805 1–1A
"You feel like you have been welcomed into an Egyptian family",
when you visit this BYO Marylebone dining room, which offers
"very good" food. / **Details:** 11.30 pm; no credit cards.

## Alloro W1          £46    A★

19-20 Dover St    7495 4768    2–3C

*"Fantastic Italian cooking", "warm service", and "just the right balance of formality and glamour" are ingredients which win very consistent praise for this Mayfair all-rounder. / Details: 10.30 pm; closed Sat L & Sun.*

## The Almeida N1          £47

30 Almeida St    7354 4777

*"Devoid of the usual Conran condescension", this "comfortable" Islington venture dispenses "enjoyable" Gallic fare (from "an abundance of retro trolleys"); it is "not cheap", though, and critics find it "uninspired". / Value tip: set weekday L & pre-theatre £33 (FP). Details: www.almeida-restaurant.co.uk; 11 pm; no smoking area.*

## Amano Café SE1          £26    A★

Victor Wharf, Clink St    7234 0000

*A "busy" café, near Borough Market, well worth knowing about for its "great coffee", and "healthy" wraps and sandwiches. / Details: www.amanocafe.com; 10.30 pm; no smoking; no booking.*

## Amaranth SW18          £22    A★★

346 Garratt Ln    8871 3466

*"Absolutely wonderful" Thai food – and at "bargain prices" – wins local adulation for this BYO Wandsworth spot; it has recently added a take-away, and a shop. / Details: 10.30 pm; D only, closed Sun; no Amex; no smoking area.*

## Amaya SW1          £50    A★★

Halkin Arc, 19 Motcomb St    7823 1166    4–1D

*This "exciting" new Belgravia Indian (from the Chutney Mary team) is "one of the year's top openings", offering a "novel" grazing concept that has gone down very well with reporters; service, though, can be "patchy". / Value tip: set weekday L £32 (FP). Details: www.realindianfood.com; 11 pm; smoking in bar only.*

## The Anchor & Hope SE1          £30    ★

36 The Cut    7928 9898

*"Inventive, original and reasonably-priced" English dishes – in a "hearty" style reminiscent of St John – have made a huge name for this "most sociable of gastropubs", near the Old Vic; "if only you could book…" / Details: 10.30 pm; closed Mon L & Sun; no Amex; no smoking; no booking.*

## Andrew Edmunds W1          £30    A★

46 Lexington St    7437 5708    2–2D

*"Cramped and uncomfy", it may be, but this candlelit Soho townhouse has a "special" vibe and remains wildly popular, not least for a "perfect date" – "lovely" staff serve up "homely" food and a "real gem" of a wine list at admirably "sensible" prices; sit on the ground floor if you can. / Details: 10.30 pm; no Amex; booking: max 6.*

## (Angela Hartnett's Menu) The Connaught W1          £78

Carlos Pl    7592 1222    2–3B

*Many reporters still find it a "very classy" experience to visit this "sumptuous" bastion of old Mayfair (reformatted three years ago by Gordon Ramsay); the overall verdict on Angela Hartnett's cooking remains distinctly middling, though, and the setting "lacks the character it had of old". / Value tip: set always available £50 (FP). Details: www.angelahartnett.co.uk; 11 pm; no smoking; booking: max 8.*

## The Anglesea Arms W6 £32 A★★

35 Wingate Rd 8749 1291 6–1B

*The "startlingly good" cooking at this "cramped" fixture near Ravenscourt Park "never disappoints" – for many reporters, this remains "London's best gastropub"; "you can't book", though, and service (while "improved") is still "slow".* / **Value tip:** set weekday L £22 (FP). **Details:** 10.15 pm; no Amex; no booking.

## Anglo Asian Tandoori N16 £23 A★

60-62 Stoke Newington Church St 7254 3633

*"Welcoming, unassuming and great value" – this Stoke Newington curry house is "as consistent as ever"; well, not quite – "they no longer give flowers to the ladies".* / **Details:** www.angloasian.co.uk; 11.30 pm; no smoking area.

## Annie's £33 A

162 Thames Rd, W4 8994 9080
36-38 White Hart Ln, SW13 8878 2020

*"Beautiful decoration that's both cosy and sumptuous" – plus "extremely welcoming" staff – helps create a "relaxing" vibe at these west London "gems"; "wonderful brunch" is a highlight of the "hearty" (and sometimes heavy-handed) cooking.* / **Details:** 10 pm, Thu-Sat 10.30 pm.

## Antipasto e Pasta SW4 £31

31 Abbeville Rd 8675 6260

*"Cheerful" and "incredibly hospitable", this Clapham trattoria is praised for its "solid" and "dependable" fare.* / **Details:** 11.30 pm.

## Aperitivo W1 £30

41 Beak St 7287 2057 2–2D

*A "reliable Soho option", offering "delicious, good-value Italian tapas" in "slightly cramped" surroundings; the Camden Town branch is no more.* / **Details:** www.aperitivo-restaurants.com; 11 pm; closed Sun; no smoking area.

## Apostrophe £12 ★

23 Barrett St, W1 7355 1001 2–1A
20/20 Opt' Store, Tottenham Ct Rd, W1 7436 6688 1–1C
215 Strand, WC2 7427 9890 3–2D
42 Gt Eastern St, EC2 7739 8412
3-5 St Bride St, EC4 7353 3704

*"Putting Starbucks and Co. to shame", these "funky" coffee shop/pâtisseries are a "real step up from the norm", and are particularly notable for the "tastiest" sandwiches and "excellent" pastries.* / **Details:** www.apostropheuk.com; L & afternoon tea only, Barrett St 8pm; no smoking; no booking.

## Arancia SE16 £25 A★

52 Southwark Park Rd 7394 1751

*"Very fairly-priced, traditional, rustic Italian food" is just part of the formula that makes this "hidden jewel" – a "front room type place" set "in the middle of nowhere" – a continuing, Bermondsey success story.* / **Details:** www.arancia-london.co.uk; 11 pm; closed Mon & Sun.

### Archipelago W1 £49 &#x1D49;

110 Whitfield St   7383 3346   1–1B

*It's not just the "bric-à-brac shop-meets-witch-doctor's hut" décor which makes a visit to this Fitzrovia spot a "total one-off" – the menu is also "bizarre" (locusts, peacock and so on), but "it works" (and at least "you're never short of conversation on a date"). / **Details:** 10.30 pm; closed Sat L & Sun; no smoking area.*

### Armadillo E8 £34 &#x1D49;★

41 Broadway Mkt   7249 3633

*"Not just great food, but great food the likes of which you've never tasted before" – this "genuine" and "unique" Hackney South American offers an experience which satisfies almost all reporters. / **Details:** www.armadillorestaurant.co.uk; 10.30 pm; closed Mon.*

### Arturo W2 £40 ★

23 Connaught St
7706 3388   5–1D

*"Very good" Italian cooking is making this small, smart Bayswater newcomer quite a hit locally; its set lunch menu is particularly worth seeking out. / **Details:** www.arturorestaurant.co.uk; 10.30 pm; no smoking area.*

### Assaggi W2 £53 ★★

39 Chepstow Pl   7792 5501   5–1B

*"Simple dishes from supreme ingredients", served by "passionate and attentive" staff, make this "stripped-down" and "ordinary"-looking Bayswater dining room – over a pub – once again the survey's "best Italian"; it can be "ludicrously hard to get a table". / **Details:** 11 pm; closed Sun; no Amex.*

### The Atlas SW6 £29 &#x1D49;★

16 Seagrave Rd   7385 9129   4–3A

*"Good" (sometimes "outstanding") Mediterranean grub, in "large portions", has won a big fan club for this "hard-to-find" boozer, near Earl's Court II; it can get "horribly noisy". / **Details:** www.theatlaspub.co.uk; 11 pm; no Amex; no booking.*

### Aubergine SW10 £90 ★★

11 Park Wk   7352 3449   4–3B

*"Exquisite" cooking (by William Drabble), "outstanding" service and "a refreshing lack of pretension" feature in many reports on this "discreet" Chelsea "haven"; it's hardly inexpensive, of course, and the atmosphere can sometimes seem rather "hushed". / **Value tip:** set weekday L £38 (FP). **Details:** 11 pm; closed Sat L & Sun.*

### Aurora W1 £38 &#x1D49;

49 Lexington St   7494 0514   2–2D

*A "romantic", "cosy" ("cramped") Soho bistro, which "feels like a secret hide-away"; the food and service are "good, but nothing to shout about". / **Details:** 10.30 pm; closed Sun; no Amex.*

### Aurora
### Great Eastern Hotel EC2 £61 ★

40 Liverpool St   7618 7000

*Chef Allan Pickett has seriously bucked-up the cooking at Conran's "spacious" and "impressive" ("if rather cold") City dining room; some reporters still find it "horrendously overpriced", but perhaps that's just part of being a "power scene". / **Details:** www.great-eastern-hotel.co.uk; 10 pm; closed Sat & Sun; booking: max 8.*

**Automat W1**　　　　　　　　£38　　　A

33 Dover St　7499 3033　2–3C

*There is nothing especially high-tech about this straightforward new American brasserie in Mayfair, but it had already established a strong local following on our early visit (June 2005); it looks nondescript from the street, but the interior is striking, and surprisingly spacious.* / **Details:** I am; no smoking area.


**L'Aventure NW8**　　　　　　£49　　　A

3 Blenheim Ter　7624 6232

*"You could be in France" ("apart from the prices", of course), at this "enchanting" St John's Wood fixture (whose "ultra-romantic" terrace is a particular summer attraction); this year's reports, however, were more mixed than usual.* / **Value tip:** set weekday L £30 (FP). **Details:** I I pm; closed Sat L & Sun.


**Babur Brasserie SE23**　　　£30　　　A★

119 Brockley Rise　8291 2400

*"Special themes add interest" to the menu at this "bustly" Brockley Indian whose "very welcoming" staff and "excellent" cooking have made it a "south east London favourite"; the restaurant re-opens after a three-month revamp in late-2005.* / **Details:** www.babur-brasserie.com; 11.15 pm; closed Fri L; no smoking area.


**Back to Basics W1**　　　　£40　　　★★

21a Foley St　7436 2181　1–1B

*"Just fabulous fresh fish" – that's the formula that wins rave reviews for this "noisy and cramped" Fitzrovia "treasure"; "booking is a must" (ideally for an early table, as "the food goes very quickly") – for a "perfect summer lunch, sit outside".* / **Details:** www.backtobasics.uk.com; 10.30 pm; closed Sun.


**Balans**　　　　　　　　　　£34　　　X

34 Old Compton St, W1　7439 3309　3–2A
60 Old Compton St, W1　7439 2183　3–3A
239 Old Brompton Rd, SW5　7244 8838　4–3A
214 Chiswick High Rd, W4　8742 1435　6–2A
187 Kensington High St, W8　7376 0115　4–1A

*Though avowedly "gay-friendly", these "camp and energetic" diners have become institutions of universal appeal – especially for brunch; the cooking, however, is "very uneven" nowadays.* / **Details:** www.balans.co.uk; varies from midnight to 24 hours; no smoking area; some booking restrictions apply.


**Baltic SE1**　　　　　　　　£38　　　A

74 Blackfriars Rd　7928 1111

*A "groovy, cavernous and moodily-lit" setting, "unexpectedly tasty food" and "a vast range of fantastic vodka cocktails" have made this unlikely Polish bar/restaurant Borough's coolest destination; it can get "very noisy".* / **Value tip:** set weekday L & pre-theatre £24 (FP). **Details:** www.balticrestaurant.co.uk; I I pm.


**Bam-Bou W1**　　　　　　　£41　　　A★

1 Percy St　7323 9130　1–1C

*"Dark and mysterious" décor helps lend a "beautiful and romantic" air to this "confusingly rambling" Fitzrovia townhouse, which serves "delicately-flavoured" Vietnamese cuisine; there are also "great cocktails" in the "evocative" bar.* / **Details:** www.bam-bou.co.uk; I I pm; closed Sat L & Sun; booking: max 8.


**sign up for the survey at www.hardens.com**　　　　　36

**Bangkok SW7** £31 ★

9 Bute St 7584 8529 4–2B
*"Good food, terrible décor" – that's the formula which has long
sustained the UK's oldest Thai, near South Kensington tube.*
/ **Details:** *10.45 pm; closed Sun; no Amex.*

**Bank Aldwych WC2** £49

1 Kingsway 7379 9797 1–2D
*This "cavernous" and "noisy" '90s-mega-brasserie "lacks sparkle,
but is still OK"; its business-friendly location ensures it's often
"full of suits", and it's also handy for breakfast, brunch and pre-
theatre.* / **Value tip:** *set weekday L & pre-theatre £29
(FP).* **Details:** *www.bankrestaurants.com; 11 pm; closed Sun.*

**Banners N8** £30 𝔸

21 Park Rd 8348 2930
*"Book in advance for weekend breakfast", which is the star turn
at this "funky" and "chaotic" Crouch End phenomenon; the said
meal comprises "a massive range of dishes, from Continental
to American, cooked to perfection".* / **Details:** *11.30 pm; no Amex.*

**Bar Capitale** £31 ★

The Concourse, 1 Poultry, EC2 7248 3117
Bucklersbury Hs, 14 Walbrook, EC4 7236 2030
*"Modestly-priced but tasty pizzas" make these "very buzzy"
diners useful City stand-bys (in the evening, as well as for lunch).*
/ **Details:** *www.mithrasbars.co.uk; 9 pm; closed Sat & Sun; EC2 no smoking area.*

**Beirut Express W2** £22 ★★

112-114 Edgware Rd 7724 2700 5–1D
*"Great shwarmas", "the best falafel wraps" and "awesome fresh
juices" help make this "fab little Lebanese" a top "cheap and
cheerful" choice.* / **Details:** *www.maroush.com; 1 am; no credit cards.*

**Bellamy's W1** £55

18-18a Bruton Pl 7491 2727 2–2B
*Ex-Annabel's manager Gavin Rankin has helped create an instant
"buzz" at this "discreet" Gallic brasserie-style newcomer, on the
Mayfair mews site formerly occupied by Caviar Kaspia (RIP);
its "assured" cooking is "expensive" for what it is, though,
and some tables are "squashed".* / **Details:** *10.15 pm; closed Sat L & Sun.*

**Belvedere W8** £55 𝔸

Holland Pk, off Abbotsbury Rd 7602 1238 6–1D
*Given its "idyllic" location and "beautiful" Art Deco style, it is easy
to assume that this Holland Park destination will be of most
interest for its "romantic" charms; this is probably true,
but reports on Billy Reid's MPW-inspired cuisine are improving,
and service is "attentive".* / **Value tip:** *set weekday L & pre-theatre £32
(FP), set Sun L £35 (FP).* **Details:** *www.whitestarline.org.uk; 10 pm; closed Sun D.*

**Benares W1** £55 ★

12 Berkeley Hs, Berkeley Sq 7629 8886 2–3B
*Ex-Tamarind chef Atul Kochar's "stylish" (if slightly "soulless")
Mayfair two-year-old is slowly growing in stature; his "elegant,
if expensive" nouvelle Indian cuisine won more applause this year,
as did the the "attentive" service.* / **Value tip:** *set weekday L £39
(FP).* **Details:** *www.benaresrestaurant.com; 10.30 pm; closed Sat L & Sun L;
no smoking.*

**Bengal Clipper SE1** £29 &#x1F4C4;

Shad Thames   7357 9001

*"An Indian restaurant with a pianist" is a bit of a rarity, and the latter adds to the stylish impression made by this large South Bank subcontinental; the cooking is "reliable" too – service a little less so. / **Details:** www.bengalclipper.co.uk; 11.30 pm.*

**Bevis Marks EC3** £45 ★

4 Heneage Ln   7283 2220

*"Interesting, because it's so distinctive" – this "hidden oasis", attached to a City synagogue, offers some "excellent" kosher dishes, in an "airy" and "historic" setting. / **Details:** www.bevismarkstherestaurant.com; 7.15 pm; closed Fri D, Sat & Sun; no smoking.*

**Bibendum SW3** £66 &#x1F4C4;

81 Fulham Rd   7581 5817   4–2C

*"Classy" styling helps maintain the allure of this airy modern classic, in Brompton Cross's landmark Michelin Building; the "epic" wine list is arguably a greater attraction than the slick cuisine, though, and both come with "a big price tag". / **Value tip:** set weekday L £47 (FP). **Details:** www.bibendum.co.uk; 11.30 pm; booking: max 12.*

**Bistrothèque E2** £36 &#x1F4C4;

23-27 Wadeson St   8983 7900

*"Hard to find, but a gem when you do!" – this "interesting" Bethnal Green warehouse-conversion has won quite a following with its "original" menu. / **Details:** 10.30 pm.*

**Blah! Blah! Blah! W12** £25 ★

78 Goldhawk Rd   8746 1337   6–1C

*"Imaginative" fare has long made it worth braving the "uninspiring" frontage and "noisy" interior of this BYO veggie, near Goldhawk Road tube; this year's reports were a fraction less rapturous than usual, though. / **Details:** 11 pm; closed Sun; no credit cards.*

**Blakes Hotel SW7** £101 &#x1F4C4;

33 Roland Gdns   7370 6701   4–2B

*If you're "hell bent on a luxurious romantic experience", this "sexy", if "dated", South Kensington basement is happy to oblige; prices for its "oriental-inspired" cuisine are, however, "simply outrageous". / **Details:** www.blakeshotels.com; 11.30 pm.*

**Bleeding Heart EC1** £45 &#x1F4C4;★

Bleeding Heart Yd, Greville St   7242 8238

*"All occasions are covered" – from a smoochy dinner to a client lunch – at this "superb" and seriously popular all-rounder, off Holborn; a semi-subterranean "warren" of a place, it comprises a tavern, wine bar and restaurant, where "helpful" staff serve up "old-school Gallic cuisine" (and "a good range of wines"). / **Details:** www.bleedingheart.co.uk; 10.30 pm; closed Sat & Sun.*

**Blue Elephant SW6** £47 &#x1F4C4;★

3-6 Fulham Broadway   7385 6595   4–4A

*"Getting lost in the foliage" brings on a "holiday mood", at this "wonderful", "OTT" Fulham "old favourite" (which comes complete with "waterfalls, streams and Koi carp"); the Thai food, if not the main point, is "simply delicious" (and the "Sunday buffet is recommended"). / **Value tip:** set always available £30 (FP). **Details:** www.blueelephant.com; midnight; closed Sat L.*

**Bluebird SW3**                                    £50          ✗

350 King's Rd   7559 1000   4–3C

*Conran's cavernous Chelsea landmark "fails on every level" –
given its food ("average", but "outrageously pricey"),
its surroundings ("clinical") and its service ("incredibly bad"),
it's "amazing that it's still trading".* / **Details:** www.conran.com; 11 pm.


**Bombay Bicycle Club**                             £35          ★

128 Holland Park Ave, W11   7243 1106   5–2A
3a Downshire Hill, NW3   7435 3544
95 Nightingale Ln, SW12   8673 6217

*The mass roll-out "hasn't affected quality", at the original
Wandsworth branch – long popular for its "light" and
"interesting" Indian dishes – of this growing chain; reports on its
new West Hampstead and Holland Park siblings (and the take-
aways) are similarly upbeat.* / **Details:** www.bombaybicycleclub.co.uk;
11 pm; D only ex NW3 Sun open L & D.


**Bombay Brasserie SW7**                            £55          𝔸★

Courtfield Close, Gloucester Rd   7370 4040   4–2B

*"My boss from Mumbai takes me here" – one endorsement
of the ever-more "reliable" standards at this grand South
Kensington subcontinental, where the large conservatory,
in particular, has "a great ambience, reminiscent of the Raj".*
/ **Value tip:** set weekday L & Sun L £30
(FP). **Details:** www.bombaybrasserielondon.com; 11.30 pm; D only;
no smoking area.


**Bombay Palace W2**                                £38          ★★

50 Connaught St   7723 8855   5–1D

*"High-quality" cooking and "the highest standards of service"
make this grand (if "slightly clinical") subcontinental, just north
of Hyde Park, well worth seeking out; it remains too little-known.*
/ **Details:** www.bombay-palace.co.uk; 11.30 pm; no smoking area.


**Il Bordello E1**                                  £36          𝔸★

75-81 Wapping High St   7481 9950

*Wapping's "perfect neighbourhood joint" is "always full, always
buzzing"; its "beaming" staff deliver "massive" portions of "well-
priced and genuine Italian fare", which includes some
"memorable" pizza.* / **Details:** www.ilbordello.com; 11 pm; closed Sat L.


**Boudin Blanc W1**                                 £43          𝔸

5 Trebeck St   7499 3292   2–4B

*"Cosy inside, and just as good outside on a balmy summer
evening" – this rustic Shepherd Market restaurant makes
a "romantic" destination for some "straightforward" Gallic fare;
it's "cramped and noisy", though, and "not cheap".* / **Value tip:** set
weekday L £26 (FP). **Details:** www.boudinblanc.co.uk; 11 pm.


**The Brackenbury W6**                              £37          𝔸★

129-131 Brackenbury Rd   8748 0107   6–1C

*A "short but imaginative" menu and "friendly" staff help make
this "cosy" spot in a Hammersmith backstreet a "perfect
neighbourhood restaurant"; two years into her proprietorship,
Lisa Inglis "has improved standards considerably".*
/ **Details:** 10.45 pm; closed Sat L & Sun D; no smoking.


**sign up for the survey at www.hardens.com**

## Brady's SW18 £22 ★
513 Old York Rd   8877 9599
*As ever, "superb fresh fish and great chips" ensure a huge local
following for Mr Brady's "lively" and "comfortable" Wandsworth
bistro. / Details: 10.30 pm; D only, closed Sun; no credit cards; no booking.*

## Brasserie St Quentin SW3 £43
243 Brompton Rd   7589 8005   4–2C
*"Classic French dishes" in a "comfy", "traditional" setting still
draw a "refined" following to this Knightsbridge stalwart; although
it's been totally eclipsed by its neighbour, Racine, in recent years,
diehard fans insist it's "much better".
/ Details: www.brasseriestquentin.co.uk; 10.30 pm.*

## Brilliant UB2 £33 ★
72-76 Western Rd   8574 1928
*"Bollywood on the screens" and "large parties of locals" set the
scene at this famous Punjabi (in the middle of suburban Southall);
it offers an authentically "different" menu, executed to a
"consistently good" standard. / Details: www.brilliantrestaurant.com;
11 pm; closed Mon, Sat L & Sun L; no smoking area; booking: weekends only.*

## Broadway Bar & Grill SW1 £32
11 Haymarket   7976 1313   3–4A
*This prominent Theatreland site was home to the ambitious but
short-lived Osia (RIP); under the same owner, it's now a useful,
if uninspired, grand American diner; the hidden-away rear bar
remains the star attraction. / Details: 11 pm; no smoking area.*

## Brula TW1 £36 A★
43 Crown Rd   8892 0602
*"You could have been transported to the suburbs of Paris", at this
"great local favourite" in St Margarets; it offers "super", "above-
bistro" cooking and "friendly" service, in a cosy (if "slightly
curious") room. / Value tip: set weekday L £23 (FP). Details: 10.30 pm;
no Amex.*

## Buona Sera £28 A
289a King's Rd, SW3   7352 8827   4–3C
22 Northcote Rd, SW11   7228 9925
*"Surprisingly good food, and surprisingly good value" maintain the
appeal of these "buzzy" budget Italians; the "fun" and "novel"
Chelsea branch (with 'double-decker' seating) has a particularly
"cosy" atmosphere. / Details: midnight; SW3 closed Mon; SW11 no Amex.*

## Busaba Eathai £27 A★
106-110 Wardour St, W1   7255 8686   2–2D
8-13 Bird St, W1   7518 8080   2–1A
22 Store St, WC1   7299 7900   1–1C
*"A cheap eat that makes you feel you are somewhere special" –
Alan Yau's "communal" Thais seem like a "posher Wagamama";
they serve "tasty" dishes at "very good-value" prices in "stylish",
low-lit surroundings. / Details: 11 pm, Fri & Sat 11.30 pm; no smoking;
no booking W1.*

## Bush Garden Café W12 £12 A★
59 Goldhawk Rd   8743 6372   6–1C
*In the grotty environs of Goldhawk Road tube, this "charming,
neighbourhood café" – with a small garden – makes
an unexpected find; it serves "good coffee", nice cakes and "lovely
breakfasts". / Details: 5 pm; L only; no smoking.*

### La Buvette TW9 £32 A★

6 Church Walk   8940 6264

*On the "bland" Richmond scene, this new Brula-sibling – "a small bistro, set in a churchyard in the heart of the town" – has been "a most welcome arrival"; it delivers "simple, but well-executed" Gallic cooking at good prices. / Details: 10.30 pm; no Amex; no smoking.*

### Café du Marché EC1 £40 A★

22 Charterhouse Sq   7608 1609

*Many regulars are "never disappointed" with this "little corner of France", in a former Clerkenwell warehouse; it serves "honest, affordable fare of high quality", and – though "superb for a relaxed business lunch" – is most popular for romance. / Details: 10 pm; closed Sat L & Sun; no Amex.*

### Café Japan NW11 £27 ★★

626 Finchley Rd   8455 6854

*"The freshest sushi and sashimi in town" is the highlight of the "great Japanese food" served (at "super prices") at this "cheerfully busy" Golder's Green café; no one minds that it's "a bit of a dive". / Details: 10 pm; closed Mon & Tue; no Amex; no smoking.*

### Café Spice Namaste E1 £37 ★

16 Prescot St   7488 9242

*It may have "an unprepossessing location", near Tower Bridge, but the "sensationally different" Parsi cooking at Cyrus Todiwala's "brightly decorated" (going-on "garish") subcontinental remains well worth seeking out. / Details: www.cafespice.co.uk; 10.45 pm; closed Sat L & Sun.*

### Cambio de Tercio SW5 £45 ★

163 Old Brompton Rd   7244 8970   4–2B

*Cooking with "passion and imagination" is returning this "buzzy" Earl's Court fixture – sometimes regarded as London's leading Spanish restaurant – to its previous eminence; service, though, can be "erratic". / Details: www.cambiodetercio.com; 11.30 pm.*

### Camerino W1 £42 ★

16 Percy St
7637 9900   1–1C

*"Unpretentious and very enjoyable", this year-old Italian, off Tottenham Court Road, offers "well-conceived" dishes and "interesting" wines in a "simple but pleasing" setting; the "characterful" staff are "helpful", too. / Details: www.camerinorestaurant.com; 11 pm; closed Sat L & Sun.*

### Il Cantuccio di Pulcinella SW11 £26 ★

143 St John's Hill   7924 5588

*"Excellent antipasti" and "custom-made wood-fire pizzas" are highlights of the "consistently good-quality food" at this Wandsworth yearling; owners and staff are "real characters", too. / Details: www.ilcantucciodipulcinella.co.uk; 11 pm; closed Tue; no Amex.*

### Capital Hotel SW3 £79 ★★

22-24 Basil St   7589 5171   4–1D

*The "real subtlety" of Eric Chavot's "wonderful" Gallic cuisine makes him "a match for any of the celebrity chefs"; service – in this "quiet" and "formal" small dining room, by Harrods – is often "excellent", too. / Value tip: set weekday L £49 (FP). Details: www.capitalhotel.co.uk; 11 pm; no smoking.*

**sign up for the survey at www.hardens.com**

**Le Caprice SW1**  £50  A★

Arlington Hs, Arlington St  7629 2239  2–4C

"Slick... but not showy" – this "perennial favourite", "'80s time-warp" brasserie, behind the Ritz, is still "a place to impress", thanks to its "assured" service, "always-buzzing" atmosphere and "honest" food. / **Details:** midnight.

**Caraffini SW1**  £44  A★

61-63 Lower Sloane St  7259 0235  4–2D

"Staff always have a smile for you", at this "jovial" Italian, near Sloane Square; "for straightforward food in a buzzy atmosphere, it's hard to beat". / **Details:** www.caraffini.co.uk; 11.30 pm; closed Sun.

**Carluccio's Caffè**  £28

8 Market Pl, W1  7636 2228  2–1C
St Christopher's Pl, W1  7935 5927  2–1A
236 Fulham Road, SW10  7376 5960  4–3B
1-7 Old Brompton Rd, SW7  7581 8101  4–2C
5-6 The Grn, W5  8566 4458
305-307 Upper St, N1  7359 8167
32 Rosslyn Hill, NW3  7794 2184
60 St John's Wood High St, NW8  7449 0404
Putney Wharf, Brewhouse St, SW15  8789 0591
Reuters Plaza, 2 Nash Court, E14  7719 1749
12 West Smithfield, EC1  7329 5904

"I thought it was brilliant when it opened, now it's not so good" – ratings on Antonio and Priscilla Carluccio's burgeoning chain of "bright", "busy" and "very noisy" Italian deli-cafés have slipped from pretty good to very average over the years; ("great kids' menu", though). / **Details:** www.carluccios.com; 11 pm; no smoking area; no booking weekday L.

**Cây Tre EC1**  £26  ★★

301 Old St  7729 8662

"Brilliant" and "reasonably priced" food wins acclaim for this year-old Hoxton Vietnamese, where service is "pleasant" and the décor is in "simple café-style". / **Details:** 11 pm.

**Cellar Gascon EC1**  £41  A★

59 West Smithfield Rd  7796 0600

"A tremendous variety of SW French wine" ("stuff they don't usually send here") and "quality" tapas – as at Club Gascon – make this "busy" Clerkenwell outfit "perfect for a light bite". / **Details:** midnight; closed Sat L & Sun.

**Le Cercle SW1**  £38  A★★

1 Wilbraham Pl
7901 9999  4–2D

"Perfect execution" of an "excellent French-tapas concept" (plus "many wines by the glass") has won instant acclaim for this year-old Belgravia-fringe sibling to Club Gascon; the ambience is "stylish and sophisticated", too, ... "for what's essentially a basement". / **Details:** 10.45 pm; closed Mon & Sun; smoking in bar only.

### Champor-Champor SE1 £39 A★★

62 Weston St
7403 4600
An "incredible" oriental-fusion menu – "with delicate, well-judged flavours that can't be matched anywhere else in town" – helps make it a "wonderful" and "stimulating" experience to visit this "cave of Eastern exotica", tucked-away behind London Bridge station. / Details: www.champor-champor.com; 10.15 pm; closed L (unless receive a booking for 6+), closed Sun; booking: max 12.

### The Chancery EC4 £44 ★

9 Cursitor St   7831 4000
This "small but perfectly-formed" yearling has been a big hit with the Chancery Lane business/legal crowd, thanks to its "great-value", "beautifully-presented" food, and its "always-attentive" service; it can, however, seem "devoid of atmosphere".
/ Details: www.thechancery.co.uk; 9 pm; closed Sat & Sun; no smoking area.

### Chelsea Bun Diner SW10 £23

9a Lamont Rd   7352 3635   4–3B
"A wonderful place for a lazy, full-works breakfast" – this "cramped" World's End diner remains west London's most famous hangover recovery point (with an "overwhelming choice" of "interesting" breakfast menus).
/ Details: www.chelseabunrestaurant.co.uk; 11 pm; no Amex; no booking, Sat & Sun.

### Chez Bruce SW17 £50 A★★

2 Bellevue Rd   8672 0114
Bruce Poole's "perfect neighbourhood spot", by Wandsworth Common, has finally edged out The Ivy as reporters' No 1 London-wide favourite; "time and time again", it delivers "terrific" cuisine, "exceptional" service and a "staggering" wine list, and all at eminently "reasonable" prices. / Details: 10.30 pm, Sun 10 pm; no smoking; booking: max 6 at D.

### Chez Kristof W6 £39 A

111-115 Hammersmith Grove   8741 1177   6–1C
This "very decent neighbourhood place" – on the Hammersmith site of Maquis (RIP) – serves "hearty", if slightly "hit-and-miss" Gallic country fare in "simple" but "convivial" surroundings; there also a very nice terrace for sunny days. / Details: www.chezkristof.co.uk; 11 pm.

### Chez Liline N4 £34 ★

101 Stroud Green Rd   7263 6550
"You're mad", if you let yourself be put off by the "awful location" of this Finsbury Park fixture, as it offers "outstanding fish, with a unique Mauritian flavour"; last year's revamp, however, has been double-edged – "it's made the place more popular, but they can't cope". / Details: 10.30 pm; closed Sun L; no smoking area.

### Chez Lindsay TW10 £35 ★

11 Hill Rise   8948 7473
Some reporters feel "as if in Brittany", when they visit this "cosy" and "friendly" bistro, near Richmond Bridge; the "excellent seafood and crêpes" are just as you'd hope, and there's also an interesting list of ciders. / Details: 10.45 pm; no Amex.

**Chez Marcelle W14**  £23  ★★
34 Blythe Rd  7603 3241  6–1D
*"Stuff yourself with delicious food, and still get change from £20"*
*– that's the proposition at the "charming" Marcelle's "excellent"*
*Olympia Lebanese; it is pretty "basic", though.* / **Details:** 10.30 pm;
closed Mon, Tue-Thu D only; no credit cards; no smoking area.

**The Chinese Experience W1**  £32  ★
118-120 Shaftesbury Ave  7437 0377  3–3A
*"A great new Chinese, in hideous Shaftesbury Avenue!", where*
*the "most welcoming" staff deliver "very competent" cooking*
*(including "excellent dim sum") in "clean and modern" café-style*
*surroundings.* / **Details:** 11 pm.

**Chisou W1**  £38  ★
4 Princes St  7629 3931  2–1C
*"Delicious" sushi and sashimi – plus an "interesting" range*
*of other "quality" dishes – win high praise for this low-key ("no-*
*ambience") Japanese, near Hanover Square.* / **Value tip:** set
weekday L £23 (FP). **Details:** 10.15 pm; closed Sun.

**Chor Bizarre W1**  £42  Ⓐ
16 Albemarle St  7629 9802  2–3C
*"It's expensive, but you get what you pay for", at this "high-*
*quality", but little-known Mayfair Indian, where*
*a "very interesting" menu is served in a room wittily decorated*
*with subcontinental bric-à-brac.* / **Details:** www.chorbizarre.com; 11 pm;
closed Sun L; no smoking area.

**Chowki W1**  £24  ★
2-3 Denman St  7439 1330  2–2D
*"Regularly-changing regional menus" which are "always reliable,*
*and good value-for-money" help make this "pleasant" and*
*"bustly" modern Indian, near Piccadilly Circus, a very handy West*
*End stand-by.* / **Details:** www.chowki.com; 11.30 pm; no smoking area.

**Churchill Arms W8**  £17  Ⓐ★
119 Kensington Church St  7792 1246  5–2B
*"Fantastic, basic Thai food at unbeatable prices", served in a*
*"traditional pub" setting, has become a "classic combination"*
*at this well-known Kensington hostelry (with conservatory dining*
*annex) – it's "always packed".* / **Details:** 10 pm; closed Sun D;
no smoking area.

**Chutney Mary SW10**  £52  Ⓐ★
535 King's Rd  7351 3113  4–4B
*Having taken on a "sleek" new look a couple of years ago,*
*this "professional"Chelsea/Fulham-fringe Indian offers*
*a "deservedly popular" all-round formula, which includes*
*"consistently very good" and "subtly-spiced" cuisine.* / **Value tip:** set
brunch £31 (FP). **Details:** www.realindianfood.com; 10.30 pm; closed weekday
L; no smoking area; booking: max 12.

**Cibo W14**  £42  ★
3 Russell Gdns  7371 6271  6–1D
*"Big plates" (literally) of "great" Italian cooking win nothing but*
*praise for this "charming" – if sometimes "noisy" – Olympia*
*fixture; despite apparently being a favourite of Michael Winner,*
*it has unaccountably fallen from fame in recent years.*
/ **Details:** www.ciborestaurant.com; 11 pm; closed Sat L & Sun D.

### Cicada EC1 £34 A★

132-136 St John St 7608 1550

*This always "buzzy" bar/restaurant – Will Ricker's original venture – remains a "funky" Clerkenwell linchpin, serving "delicious", "Asian-fusion" dishes. / Details: www.cicada.nu; 10.45 pm; closed Sat L & Sun; no smoking area.*

### Cinnamon Cay SW11 £36 ★

87 Lavender Hill 7801 0932

*"Outstanding cooking at reasonable prices" makes this Battersea Antipodean "everything a neighbourhood restaurant should be"… and arguably more. / Details: www.cinnamoncay.co.uk; 10.30 pm; closed Sun.*

### The Cinnamon Club SW1 £55 ★

Gt Smith St 7222 2555 1–4C

*This "top-notch" Indian – with its "innovative" and "unusual" modern cuisine – draws a crowd rich with "media-types, politicos and luvvies" to its swish premises (a converted library, near Westmin███████bbey). / Value tip: set weekday L & set D £36 (FP). Details: w██████onclub.com; 10.45 pm; closed Sat L & Sun; no smoking area.*

### Cipriani W1 £67 ✕

25 Davies Street 7399 0500 2–2B

*"Great people-watching" ("you can check out trends in plastic surgery") is the only justification for visiting this year-old Mayfair outpost of Venice's Harry's Bar – otherwise it's an "arrogant" operation, where "average" cooking is dished up at "criminal" prices. / Details: www.cipriani.com; 11.45 pm; booking: max 6.*

### City Miyama EC4 £43 ★★

17 Godliman St 7489 1937

*"The quality of the sushi more than makes up for the total lack of ambience", at this "excellent" City Japanese; there's also a good teppan-yaki. / Details: 9.30 pm; closed Sat D & Sun.*

### Clarke's W8 £62 ★★

124 Kensington Church St 7221 9225 5–2B

*"First-rate" ingredients, "simply" but "beautifully" prepared, are a hallmark of Sally Clarke's "phenomenally consistent" Kensington fixture (whose dinner menu offers zero choice); its setting is "romantic" to some, but "dull" to others (especially downstairs). / Details: www.sallyclarke.com; 10 pm; closed Mon D & Sun; no smoking; booking: max 14.*

### Club Gascon EC1 £56 A★★

57 West Smithfield 7796 0600

*"Foie-gras-tastic" food combinations (served tapas-style) and a "knockout" wine list – both rooted in SW France – create some "stunning" gastronomic experiences at this "slightly cramped" City-fringe fixture; aficionados tip the tasting menu as the way to go. / Details: 10 pm; closed Sat L & Sun.*

### Coach & Horses EC1 £33 ★

26-28 Ray St
7278 8990

*"Simple but excellent traditional fare" and a "genuine" approach again wins high praise for this "unpretentious" pub, near The Guardian. / Details: www.thecoachandhorses.com; 9.30 pm; closed Sat L & Sun D.*

### Le Colombier SW3 £44 &#x1F2B6;
145 Dovehouse St 7351 1155 4–2C
*A new chef is injecting a bit of (much-needed) 'élan' into the
cooking at Didier Garnier's "elegant" and "personal" bourgeois
restaurant, on a quiet Chelsea corner, which is on the verge
of becoming a "great all-rounder"; a superb terrace is a feature.*
/ **Value tip:** *set weekday L £31 (FP).* **Details:** *10.30 pm.*

### Il Convivio SW1 £42 ★
143 Ebury St 7730 4099 1–4A
*"Really improved" over the past couple of years, this "attractive"
Belgravia Italian wins praise for the "high-quality" realisation of its
"interesting" menu, and its "stylish presentation and service".*
/ **Details:** *www.etruscarestaurants.com; 10.30 pm; closed Sun.*

### Coq d'Argent EC3 £53
1 Poultry 7395 5000
*Not many sites in the heart of the City have "fantastic gardens"
and "wonderful views" – with these 'natural' advantages, it's all
too predictable that this sixth-floor Conran establishment should
charge "sky-high" prices for a "dull" overall experience.*
/ **Details:** *www.conran.com; 10 pm; closed Sat L & Sun D.*

### Cotto W14 £30 ★
44 Blythe Rd 7602 9333 6–1D
*"Shame about the obscure location", say fans of James Kirby's
Olympia local, which offers "outstanding" but "affordable"
contemporary cuisine; the "chilly" décor does little to help the
cause, though.* / **Details:** *10.30 pm; closed Sat L & Sun.*

### The Cow W2 £36 &#x1F2B6;★
89 Westbourne Park Rd 7221 0021 5–1B
*"Great oysters and Guinness" are the classic choice at Tom
Conran's "trendy" but "unpretentious" Irish bar, on the fringe
of Notting Hill (where service is "at best unhurried"); the "cosy" –
less commented-on – upstairs room serves "more elaborate" fare.*
/ **Details:** *10.30 pm; no Amex.*

### Crazy Bear W1 £45 &#x1F2B6;
26 Whitfield St 7631 0088 1–1C
*The "funkiest" décor – "especially the loos!" – helps make a visit
to this Fitzrovia yearling an "enjoyable" occasion, for most
reporters; surprisingly good-quality oriental fare comes as a
"bonus".* / **Details:** *www.crazybeargroup.co.uk; 10.30 pm; closed Sat L & Sun.*

### Crazy Homies W2 £35 &#x1F2B6;
127 Westbourne Park Rd 7727 6771 5–1B
*"Good Mexican food (by London standards)" has won applause –
if from a modestly-sized fan club – for the snacks at Tom
Conran's small new bar, on the fringe of Notting Hill.*
/ **Details:** *10.30 pm; closed weekday L; no Amex.*

### Da Mario SW7 £30
15 Gloucester Rd 7584 9078 4–1B
*"Cheerful" and "buzzy", this Kensington veteran maintains its
reputation for "great pizza and pasta"; it's one of the few places
handy for the Albert Hall.* / **Details:** *www.damario.co.uk; 11.30 pm.*

### Daphne NW1 £23 Ⓐ
83 Bayham St 7267 7322
*"Always the same menu and staff"* help induce a sense of well-being at this *"comforting"* and *"cosy"* Camden Town Greek, which serves *"good-value"*, *"straightforward"* dishes. / **Details:** 11.30 pm; closed Sun; no Amex.

### Delfina Studio Café SE1 £36 Ⓐ★★
50 Bermondsey St 7357 0244
*"Great space, great experience"* – this *"light and airy"* Bermondsey art gallery is universally hailed for its *"amazingly interesting"* food and its *"smiley"*, *"professional"* staff; *"pity it's only open for lunch"* (except Fridays). / **Details:** www.delfina.org.uk; 10 pm; L only, except Fri when open L&D, closed Sat & Sun.

### Devonshire House W4 £39
126 Devonshire Rd 8987 2626 6–2A
*"Consistently good"* cooking and *"interesting"* wines win strong local support for this slightly *"sombre"* gastropub, five minutes' walk from Chiswick High Road. / **Details:** www.thedevonshirehouse.co.uk; 10.30 pm; closed Mon.

### Deya W1 £41 ★★
34 Portman Sq 7224 0028 1–2A
*"A surprise, just north of Oxford Street"* – this *"nice-despite-being-part-of-an-hotel"* Indian delivers *"impressively subtle"* cooking from a *"very innovative"* menu; despite Michael Caine's backing, however, it remains almost unknown.
/ **Details:** www.deya-restaurant.co.uk; 10.45 pm; closed Sat L & Sun.

### Dish Dash SW12 £31 Ⓐ★
11-13 Bedford Hill 8673 5555
There's *"always a party atmosphere"*, at this Balham Persian, where *"delicious mezze"* and *"fab kebabs"* are the menu stars.
/ **Details:** www.dish-dash.com; 11 pm.

### Ditto SW18 £38 Ⓐ
55-57 East Hill 8877 0110
*"Things have improved a lot"*, under the new régime at this *"pleasant"*, *"relaxed"* and *"easy"* Wandsworth local; *"very good"* service is a particular highlight, and the menu – if still *"fairly standard"* – is *"well-executed"*. / **Details:** www.doditto.co.uk; 11 pm; no Amex; no smoking area.

### The Don EC4 £47 Ⓐ★
20 St Swithin's Ln 7626 2606
*"A hidden gem"*, *"right in the heart of the City"*, this *"efficient and friendly"* Gallic restaurant is as close as the Square Mile gets to a *"perfect"* business destination – either the *"cosy"* cellar bistro, or the more formal ground-floor; the wine list is *"brilliant"*, too.
/ **Details:** www.thedonrestaurant.com; 10 pm; closed Sat & Sun.

### The Duke of Cambridge N1 £37 ★
30 St Peter's St 7359 3066
*"North London trendies predominate, but you do get great organic food"* – *"all the way down to the Cola!"* – at this *"airy"* and *"lively"* gastropub favourite, on the fringe of Islington.
/ **Details:** www.singhboulton.co.uk; 10.30 pm; no Amex; no smoking area.

## E&O W11 £40 A ★★

14 Blenheim Cr
7229 5454 5–1A
*"Cracking" – "I mean, wow!" – fusion tapas are the lead attraction at Will Ricker's "oh-so-trendy" Notting Hill celeb-haunt; the service – "without W11 attitude" – is "charming", too.*
/ **Details:** www.eando.nu; 10.45 pm; booking: max 6.

## The Eagle EC1 £25 A
159 Farringdon Rd 7837 1353
*Still always "packed", this Clerkenwell boozer – which, in 1992, was London's first gastropub – is still hailed as "the original and best" by legions of reporters; overall, however, this year's ratings support those who say it's "resting on its laurels".*
/ **Details:** 10.30 pm; closed Sun D; no Amex; no booking.

## Earl Spencer SW18 £30
260-262 Merton Rd 8870 9244
*"Arrive early", to nab a table at this large gastropub on an "ugly" bit of road in Southfields, as its "great-value pub food" has made it a smash hit locally; however, like its sibling (the Havelock Arms), it risks getting "smug".* / **Details:** www.theearlspencer.co.uk; 10 pm; no booking.

## Edokko WC1 £30 ★
50 Red Lion St 7242 3490 1–1D
*This "Japanese lunchtime favourite", just by Gray's Inn, is a "traditional" and "charming" establishment, attracting uniform praise for its "authentic" and "affordable" cuisine.* / **Details:** 10 pm; closed Sat & Sun; no Amex.

## Eight Over Eight SW3 £44 A ★★
392 King's Rd 7349 9934 4–3B
*"It's not quite as exhaustingly trendy as its big sister E&O", but Will Ricker's Chelsea outpost offers a similar blend of "amazing" Asian fusion dishes in a "chic" setting that's "always humming".* / **Value tip:** set weekday L £26 (FP). **Details:** www.eightovereight.nu; 10.15 pm; closed Sun L.

## 1880
### The Bentley Hotel SW7 £67 ★★
27-33 Harrington Gdns
7244 5555 4–2B
*Andrew Turner's "technically brilliant" cooking is "among the capital's best", and his "fantastic 9-course grazing menus" offer an "enjoyable, educational and truly memorable gastronomic experience"; the setting – in a South Kensington basement – is "opulent" going on "OTT".* / **Details:** www.thebentley-hotel.com; 10 pm; D only, closed Sun; no smoking; booking: max 8.

## El Rincón Latino SW4 £28 A
148 Clapham Manor St 7622 0599
*"You're teleported to Spain", at this "treasure" of a tapas bar, off Clapham High Street – staff are "so welcoming" and its "fresh-tasting" dishes offer "good value".* / **Details:** 11.30 pm.

## Electric Brasserie W11 £45 A
191 Portobello Rd 7908 9696 5–1A
*"The place to be seen on lazy weekends", this "really buzzy" and "funky" Notting Hill in-crowd brasserie is especially popular as a brunch destination… and for a "fantastic" burger at any time.*
/ **Value tip:** set weekday L £30 (FP). **Details:** www.the-electric.co.uk; 10.45 pm.

**sign up for the survey at www.hardens.com**

### Elena's L'Etoile W1 £49 &#x1D538;
30 Charlotte St 7636 7189 1–1C
*This "old-fashioned" Fitzrovia "stalwart" draws a large following, thanks to its "elegantly faded" charm and "cosseting" service (still presided over by octogenarian Elena Salvoni); the traditional Gallic fare can be "hit-and-miss", but "the experience usually transcends the food".* / **Details:** *www.simplyrestaurants.com; 10.30 pm; closed Sat L & Sun.*

### Elephant Royale
### Locke's Wharf E14 £34 &#x1D538;
Westferry Rd 7987 7999
*A "lovely" riverside location, with gorgeous views of Greenwich, is the high-point at this Isle of Dogs Thai (whose interior strikes some reporters as a bit "Basildon-esque"); the food is "tasty", if "pricey" for what it is.* / **Details:** *www.elephantroyale.com; 10.30 pm; no smoking area.*

### Emile's SW15 £30 &#x1D538;★
96-98 Felsham Rd 8789 3323
*Now thoroughly "back on form", this rambling Putney bistro is "a lovely place for supper with friends" – "welcoming", and "very relaxed", it offers "great food at bargain prices".* / **Details:** *emiles-restaurant.co.uk; 11 pm; D only, closed Sun; no Amex.*

### The Engineer NW1 £40
65 Gloucester Ave 7722 0950
*"Lovely" but "too popular", this "casual" Primrose Hill gastropub (which benefits from "the best garden") "trades on its reputation" a bit these days; that said, the food "seems to have improved" of late.* / **Details:** *www.the-engineer.com; 11 pm; no Amex.*

### Enoteca Turi SW15 £45 ★
28 Putney High St 8785 4449
*It's the "very interesting and educational" Italian wine list which has made a big name for the Turi family's simple venture by Putney Bridge, but the "genuine" cooking is "consistently good", too.* / **Value tip:** *set weekday L £28 (FP).* **Details:** *www.enotecaturi.com; 11 pm; closed Sun; no smoking area.*

### Eriki NW3 £30 ★
4-6 Northways Pde, Finchley Rd 7722 0606
*"Not your usual Indian" – this "upscale" Swiss Cottage subcontinental, with its "original" cooking and "excellent" décor, makes quite a "find"; service is generally good, too, but the occasional "snotty" reception is not unknown.* / **Details:** *www.eriki.co.uk; 11.15 pm; closed Sat L.*

### L'Escargot W1 £45
48 Greek St 7437 2679 3–2A
*The "complex" cuisine in the "romantic" upstairs Picasso Room of this Soho veteran (formula price £60) scored well this year, but the "traditional" fare in the "elegant" main brasserie also won consistent praise; chef Jeff Galvin, however, left post-survey to set up on his own account.* / **Details:** *www.whitestarline.org.uk; 11.30 pm; closed Sat L & Sun (Picasso Room also closed Mon).*

## L'Etranger SW7 £61 ★
36 Gloucester Rd   7584 1118   4–1B
*Jerome Tauvron's "imaginative" and "prettily-presented" Franco-Japanese cuisine is winning more consistent acclaim for this "understated" South Kensington two-year-old, which is also noted for its "outstanding" wine list. / Value tip: set weekday L & pre-theatre £27 (FP). Details: www.etranger.co.uk; 11 pm; closed Sat L & Sun.*

## Fakhreldine W1 £49
85 Piccadilly   7493 3424   2–4C
*"Friendly" staff add to the upbeat vibe of this "buzzy", first-floor Mayfair Lebanese, recently rejuvenated, which enjoys "fine views" of Green Park; the food's "not cheap", but "very good". / Details: www.fakhreldine.co.uk; midnight.*

## La Famiglia SW10 £45
7 Langton St   7351 0761   4–3B
*"Still one of the buzziest Italians in London", this age-old World's End trattoria exerts a curiously timeless appeal, even if it is "too noisy", and certainly "not cheap" – key selling points include "characterful" staff and a "magical" garden. / Details: www.lafamiglialondon.com; 11.45 pm; no smoking area.*

## Faulkner's E8 £26 ★
424-426 Kingsland Rd   7254 6152
*"Pure chippie heaven, worth driving out of your way for" – this "jovial" institution ("long a feature of Dalston Market", and recently refitted) serves "excellent fish", "big bags of chips", and "mushy peas like they used to make 'em". / Details: 10 pm; no smoking area; need 8+ to book.*

## Ffiona's W8 £38 𝔸
51 Kensington Church St   7937 4152   4–1A
*"Ffiona is the key" to this "warm and cosy" Kensington bistro, whose "retro", "comfort food" adds to the impression of a "dinner party" ("just with someone else doing all the work"). / Details: www.ffionas.com; 11 pm; D only, closed Mon.*

## La Figa E14 £33
45 Narrow St   7790 0077
*A Wapping sibling to Docklands' Il Bordello, similarly tipped for its "top pizza" and other hearty Italian dishes; relatively speaking, however, it attracts very little commentary from reporters. / Details: 11 pm; no smoking area.*

## Fino W1 £42 ★
33 Charlotte St
7813 8010   1–1C
*"Tapas taken to a new, more exciting level" – plus "superlative" wines and "superb" service – have won fame for this Fitzrovia basement yearling (which is done out "in defiantly non-Spanish style"); even some fans, though, note that "prices seem stuck on the 'up' escalator". / Details: www.finorestaurant.com; 10.30 pm; closed Sun; booking: max 12.*

## Firezza SW11 £23 ★★
40 Lavender Hill   7223 5535
*"Surpassing all expectations of how a pizza should look and taste", this "unbeatable" new south London mini-chain is off to a cracking start; primarily the branches are take-out, but there are a few (mainly alfresco) tables at the outlet listed. / Details: 11.15 pm.*

## Fish Club SW11 £30 ★

189 St John's Hill   7978 7115

*"Fresh fish served simply, cooked skillfully, and priced right"* has made a local hit of this Battersea newcomer – a *"very modern take"* on the classic chippie formula. / **Details:** www.thefishclub.com; 10 pm, Sun 9 pm; closed Mon; no Amex; no smoking.


## Five Hot Chillies HA0 £23 A★★

875 Harrow Rd   8908 5900

*"Explosive flavours, bargain prices and total authenticity"* win unanimous raves for this *"packed"* BYO cantina, in Sudbury – *"as good as Indian food gets anywhere in the world!"* /


## Flâneur EC1 £44 A★

41 Farringdon Rd   7404 4422

An *"unusual situation"* (within a *"beautiful"* food hall) contributes to the appeal of this Farringdon 'one-off' – be it for a *"tasty"* brunch, for *"superb"* cakes, or for a *"very good"* light lunch. / **Details:** www.flaneur.com; 10 pm; closed Sun D; no smoking.


## Foliage
## Mandarin Oriental SW1 £67 A★

66 Knightsbridge   7201 3723   4–1D

*"Complex dishes, with brilliant clarity of flavour"* (from chef Chris Staines) have helped push this *"extremely professional"* Knightsbridge dining room to new heights this year; some reporters still discern a *"lack of ambience"*, though – get a table with a *"lovely park view"* if you can. / **Value tip:** set always available £39 (FP). **Details:** www.mandarinoriental.com; 10.30 pm; booking: max 6.


## The Fox & Hounds SW11 £29 A★

66 Latchmere Rd   7924 5483

This *"fantastic"* Battersea gastropub is acclaimed for its *"delicious"*, largely Mediterranean cuisine, and its *"good selection of wines by the glass"*. / **Details:** 10.30 pm; no Amex.


## Franklins SE22 £40 A★

157 Lordship Ln   8299 9598

*"The best for miles around"* – this *"fantastic local eatery"* wins a hymn of praise from East Dulwich folk for its *"simple"* but *"delicious"* fare, *"great"* service and *"relaxed"* atmosphere. / **Value tip:** set weekday L £22 (FP). **Details:** www.franklinsrestaurant.com; 10.30 pm.


## Fratelli la Bufala NW3 £27 ★★

45a South End Rd
7435 7814

This *"splendid"* new south Hampstead Italian occupies the former site of Cucina (RIP); *"fantastic"* pizzas are complemented by *"excellent buffalo meat and cheese"*, and served in a setting that's *"warm"*, *"welcoming"* and *"very lively"*. / **Details:** www.fratellilabufala.com; 11 pm; no smoking area.


## Frederick's N1 £47 A

106 Camden Pas   7359 2888

With its *"beautiful high-ceilinged conservatory"*, this grand but *"friendly"* Islington *"favourite"* has long been *"a lovely place for special occasions"* (in *"an area still surprisingly short of high-quality options"*). / **Value tip:** set weekday L & pre-theatre £26 (FP). **Details:** www.fredericks.co.uk; 11.30 pm; closed Sun; no Amex; no smoking area.

**The Freemasons SW18** £32 A

2 Wandsworth Common Northside  7326 8580
*"Superbly presented"* and *"flavoursome"* dishes are already
beginning to make quite a name for this *"casual"* and
*"comfortable"* new Wandsworth gastropub. / **Details:** 10 pm;
*no smoking.*


**Fresco W2** £18 ★

25 Westbourne Grove  7221 2355  5–1C
*"Delicious juices squeezed before your very eyes"* (and other
*"freshly-prepared"* snacks) win rave reviews for this small
Lebanese café, *"tucked-away"* in Bayswater – *"the queues outside
speak for themselves"*. / **Details:** 11 pm; no smoking area.


**La Fromagerie Café W1** £29 A★★

2-4 Moxon St  7935 0341  2–1A
*"You're lucky if you can get a seat at the single trestle table"*,
at this *"divine"* Marylebone cheese shop/food emporium, which
offers *"gorgeous"* soups and salads, as well as dairy products;
there's an *"interesting wine list"*, too.
/ **Details:** www.lafromageriecafe.co.uk; 6.30 pm; L only; no smoking; no booking.


**Fuzzy's Grub** £ 9 ★

6 Crown Pas, SW1  7925 2791  2–4D
10 Well Ct, EC4  7236 8400
62 Fleet St, EC4  7583 6060
*"The best roast meat sandwiches in the world"* (*"with crackling
even better than mum's!"*) and *"charming"* service make it well
worth truffling out these *"brilliant"* British cafés.
/ **Details:** www.fuzzysgrub.com; EC4 3 pm, SW1 4 pm; closed Sat & Sun; no credit
cards; EC4 no smoking.


**Galicia W10** £27 A★

323 Portobello Rd  8969 3539  5–1A
*"Plenty of Spaniards"* add authenticity to this no-nonsense North
Kensington veteran, where the tapas are *"good-quality, and good-
value, too"*. / **Details:** 11.30 pm; closed Mon.


**Gallipoli** £21

102 Upper St, N1  7359 0630
*107 Upper St, N1  7226 5333*
120 Upper St, N1  7359 1578
*"For a fun night out at low prices"*, these trio of neighbouring
*"warm"*, and *"boisterous"* Turkish bistros are an Islington
*"mainstay"*; constantly *"oversubscribed"*, though, they risk
becoming *"slapdash"*. / **Details:** www.gallipolicafes.com; 11 pm, Fri & Sat
midnight; 107 Upper St closed Mon.


**The Garden Café NW1** £29 A

Inner Circle, Regent's Pk  7935 5729
*With its beautiful location and large garden, this attractive
(if rather '70s) park café has long cried out for investment;
it finally got it this year, with the introduction of a simple menu
that's both well-realised and good value; summer sees a regular
programme of lunchtime jazz.* / **Details:** www.thegardencafe.co.uk; 9 pm;
no Amex; no smoking.

### The Gate W6     £32     A★★

51 Queen Caroline St    8748 6932    6–2C

*"Almost enough to make you a veggie" – the "colourful" and "enticing" creations at this "un-preachy" Hammersmith fixture (in a converted church hall) make it "the best vegetarian in town"; "lovely courtyard in summer".* / **Details:** www.thegate.tv; 10.45 pm; closed Sat L & Sun.

### Le Gavroche W1     £118     A★

43 Upper Brook St    7408 0881    2–2A

*"Exemplary" service (under Silvano Giraldin) and a wine list of "biblical" proportions help set the scene at this "old-fashioned" Mayfair basement (which is London's oldest temple of Gallic gastronomy); prices are "dizzying", but Michel Roux Jr's "classic" cuisine almost invariably "delivers the goods".* / **Value tip:** set weekday L £50 (FP). **Details:** www.le-gavroche.co.uk; 10.45 pm; closed Sat L & Sun; jacket required; smoking in bar only.

### Geeta NW6     £16     ★

57-59 Willesden Ln    7624 1713

*"Grim"-looking Kilburn veteran, long known for its "dependably excellent" south Indian food, super-"friendly" service and "impressive value-for-money"; the occasional report this year, though, was a fraction less rapturous than usual.* / **Details:** 10.30 pm, Fri & Sat 11.30 pm; no Amex.

### Le Gifto's Lahore Karahi & Tandoori £18     ★

162-164 Broadway    8813 3669

*"The best competitively-priced, authentic tandoori food" is the draw to this vast, "canteen-like-but-fun" suburban fixture, as the presence of "many happy Indian families" confirms; unlicensed, but you can BYO.* /

### Giraffe     £29

6-8 Blandford St, W1    7935 2333    1–1A
270 Chiswick High Rd, W4    8995 2100    6–2A
7 Kensington High St, W8    7938 1221    4–1A
29-31 Essex Rd, N1    7359 5999
46 Rosslyn Hill, NW3    7435 0343
Royal Festival Hall, Riverside, SE1    7928 2004    1–3D
27 Battersea Rise, SW11    7223 0933

*"A fine variety" of "scrumptious" breakfast items make these "colourful" diners a great brunch choice (even if they do get "knee-deep in kids"); the 'proper' menu is "unexciting", though, and "expensive for what it is".* / **Details:** www.giraffe.net; 11 pm; no smoking; no booking at weekends.

### The Glasshouse TW9     £47     ★★

14 Station Pde    8940 6777

*"Well worth the trek to Kew", this "light and airy" neighbourhood fixture – sibling to the legendary Chez Bruce – maintains all-round "admirable" standards, not least of "immaculate" cuisine and "knowledgeable" service.* / **Value tip:** set weekday L £31 (FP). **Details:** www.glasshouserestaurant.co.uk; 10.30 pm; no smoking.

### Golden Hind W1     £16     ★

73 Marylebone Ln    7486 3644    1–1A

*"Just eat, don't worry about the cafeteria-style ambience" – this "age-old, BYO chippie" in Marylebone, serves "superb fish 'n' chips" (with "all the trimmings"), and it's "much better than the nearby Seashell".* / **Details:** 10 pm; closed Sat L & Sun; no smoking area.

**Good Earth** £38 ★★

233 Brompton Rd, SW3  7584 3658  4–2C
143-145 The Broadway, NW7  8959 7011
*"Keeping up their standards", these "smart" veterans offer a "fail-safe" formula of "wonderful" Chinese food at "fair" prices.
/ Details: 10.45 pm.*

**Gordon Ramsay SW3** £91 A★★

68-69 Royal Hospital Rd  7352 4441  4–3D
*Head chef Mark Askew's "peerless" cuisine and maître d' Jean-Claude's "seamless" service combine to make Gordon Ramsay's Chelsea flagship once again London's undoubted number one dining room; if there is a quibble, it's that – for some tastes – the cooking is just too "clean and classic". / Value tip: set weekday L £58 (FP). Details: www.gordonramsay.com; 11 pm; closed Sat & Sun; jacket required; no smoking; booking: max 8.*

**Gordon Ramsay at Claridge's
Claridge's Hotel W1** £83

55 Brook St  7499 0099  2–2B
*This "luxurious" Art Deco dining room may have Gordon Ramsay's name over the door, but it's "not a patch on the Chelsea flagship" (and not much cheaper, either); Mark Sargeant's cuisine can certainly scale "sublime" peaks, but too many reports of "pretty ordinary" meals undercut the rating overall. / Value tip: set weekday L £50 (FP). Details: www.gordonramsay.com; 11 pm; jacket required; no smoking; booking: max 8.*

**Goring Hotel SW1** £59 A

15 Beeston Pl  7396 9000  1–4B
*Being "a trifle staid" is "part of the appeal" of this "splendid" family-owned hotel, near Victoria, where "good, rather traditional food" is served by staff versed in "traditional courtesies"; let's hope their mid-2005 revamp doesn't wreck it! / Value tip: set Sun L £41 (FP). Details: www.goringhotel.co.uk; 10 pm; closed Sat L; no smoking area; booking: max 12.*

**Gourmet Burger Kitchen** £20 ★

49 Fulham Broadway, SW6  7381 4242  4–4A
50 Westbourne Grove, W2  7243 4344  5–1B
131 Chiswick High Rd, W4  8995 4548  6–2A
200 Haverstock Hill, NW3  7443 5335
*331 West End Ln, NW6  7794 5455*
44 Northcote Rd, SW11  7228 3309
*333 Putney Bridge Rd, SW15  8789 1199*
*This "relentlessly busy" chain – the survey's most often mentioned – does "exactly what it says on the tin", offering "the best burgers on the planet", in "monster" portions, and with "every topping imaginable"; "great shakes", too ("if you still have room"). / Details: www.gbkinfo.co.uk; 11 pm; no Amex; no smoking; no booking.*

**The Grapes E14** £39 A

76 Narrow St  7987 4396
*"It's a challenge to get a table", at this "cracking" old pub in Docklands, whose "brilliant" seafood and "top fish 'n chips" continue to please (nearly) all reporters; it has "amazing views over the Thames", too. / Value tip: set Sun L £22 (FP). Details: 9.15 pm; closed Sun D; no smoking.*

**sign up for the survey at www.hardens.com** 54

### Great Eastern Dining Room EC2 £34 A★

54 Gt Eastern St   7613 4545

*Quite a veteran, by Shoreditch standards, Will Ricker's "friendly" local linchpin offers "cheaper Nobu-ish fare" that's often "just as good"; what really distinguishes it, though, is its "great buzz".*
/ **Details:** www.greateasterndining.co.uk; 10.45 pm; closed Sat L & Sun.

### Great Nepalese NW1 £23 ★

48 Eversholt St   7388 6737

*"A gem, by Euston station" – this "really friendly" fixture has dished up "interesting" Nepalese specials (plus more standard subcontinental fare) for over 20 years.*
/ **Details:** www.great-nepalese.co.uk; 11.30 pm; no smoking area.

### Green's SW1 £55 A

36 Duke St   7930 4566   2–3D

*The "clubby" ambience "lends gravitas" to a meal at this "comfortable" St James's fixture, where "good, plain dishes" (with much seafood) are served up by "friendly" staff.*
/ **Details:** www.greens.org.uk; 11 pm; closed Sun, May-Sep.

### The Greenhouse W1 £84

27a Hays Mews   7499 3331   2–3B

*Last year, Marlon Abela set out to turn this Mayfair mews "old favourite" into "a serious temple of gastronomy"; with its "intricate" cuisine and "overwhelming" wine list, he's succeeded, in a way, but the 'feel' is now "very corporate", and prices can seem "off the scale".* / **Value tip:** set weekday L £53
(FP). **Details:** www.greenhouserestaurant.co.uk; 11 pm; closed Sat L & Sun; booking: max 4.

### The Greyhound SW11 £39 ★

136 Battersea High St   7978 7021

*"A phenomenally good wine list" (actually there are two!) has helped win instant popularity for this "keen" Battersea newcomer – a restaurant "posing as a gastropub", serving some "really good" food; a fair number of reporters, however, rail at the "toppish" prices.* / **Value tip:** set weekday L £25
(FP). **Details:** www.thegreyhoundatbattersea.co.uk; 9.30 pm; closed Mon & Sun D; no smoking in dining room; booking: max 6.

### (Grill Room)
### Dorchester Hotel W1 £73 A

53 Park Ln   7629 8888   2–3A

*For British "tradition at its finest", this "luxurious", Spanish Baronial dining room has been hard to beat in recent years; a new chef (Olivier Couillaud, from La Trompette) was appointed in mid-2005 – let's hope he keeps the best of the old as well as installing a little of the new.* / **Value tip:** set weekday L £44 (FP), set Sun L £52
(FP). **Details:** www.dorchesterhotel.com; 11 pm.

### The Guinea W1 £52 ★

30 Bruton Pl   7499 1210   2–3B

*"Some of the best steak you'll find", "world-renowned" steak 'n' kidney pies and "a good range of clarets" – that's the "no-frills" formula which sustains the popularity of this "dated" dining room (attached to an "olde-worlde" Mayfair pub).*
/ **Details:** www.theguinea.co.uk; 11 pm; closed Sat L & Sun; booking: max 8.

## The Gun E14

£44    A★

27 Coldharbour Ln
7515 5222

*"A cracking addition to Dockland's dining", this "brilliant nautical gastropub" – with a "nice" waterside location, opposite the Dome – has certainly "hit the ground running"; it combines "a proper pub feel on one side" (the view side) with "crisp white tablecloths" on the other. / Details: www.thegundocklands.com; 10.30 pm.*

## Gung-Ho NW6

£30    A★

328-332 West End Ln   7794 1444

*"Consistently good" cooking helps make this West Hampstead Chinese a "popular local favourite"; it's usually "packed to the gills". / Details: 11.30 pm; no Amex.*

## Hakkasan W1

£75    A

8 Hanway Pl   7927 7000   3–1A

*"Hip, happening and simply great" – this "clubby" basement, tucked away off Tottenham Court Road, serves some of "the best Chinese food in London" (including "stunning" dim sum), and has become the second most talked-about place in town; the service, though, can be "appalling", and prices increasingly seem "way too high". / Value tip: set weekday L £53 (FP). Details: midnight, Mon & Sun 11 pm.*

## Harbour City W1

£25

46 Gerrard St   7439 7859   3–3B

*A Chinatown canteen where the "absolutely fresh" and "very reasonably-priced" dim sum "continues to be a delight"; in other respects it's unremarkable. / Details: 11.30 pm.*

## Harry Morgan's NW8

£20    ★

31 St John's Wood High St   7580 4849

*"Salt beef sandwiches to die for" and "chicken soup as good as mother makes" help ensure that this age-old kosher deli in St John's Wood is "always busy". / Details: www.harryms.co.uk; 10 pm.*

## The Havelock Tavern W14

£31    A★★

57 Masbro Rd   7603 5374   6–1C

*Olympia's "fantastic local secret" is well and truly out nowadays, and – thanks to its "gutsy" and "excellent-value" cooking – this "super-gastropub" is always "chaotically busy"; none of this, however, excuses the "graceless" service. / Details: www.thehavelocktavern.co.uk; 10 pm; no credit cards; no booking.*

## The Haven N20

£32    A

1363 High Rd   8445 7419

*For its many fans, this "lovely" Whetstone restaurant lives up to its name, offering "everything you might expect to find in the West End"; the food is "not inspirational", but it is "consistently good", and "getting a table can be difficult". / Details: www.haven-bistro.co.uk; 11 pm; no smoking.*

## Haz E1

£29    ★

9 Cutler St   7929 7923

*"A stone's throw from Liverpool Street", this "energetic" ("noisy") modern Turkish restaurant offers a winning package of "fresh, simple and tasty" food, "super" service and a "light" and "airy" setting; the set meals offer especially "good value". / Details: www.hazrestaurant.com; 11.30 pm.*

**Home EC2** £38   𝔸

100-106 Leonard St   7684 8618
*"One of the 'original' Shoreditch venues", this "hip" but "friendly"*
*basement bar and ground-floor restaurant wins unanimous praise*
*for its "buzzing" ambience and "very good" food; "I've known*
*it since it was a quarter of the size, and it's still consistent".*
/ **Details:** www.homebar.co.uk; 10.30 pm; closed Sat L & Sun.


**Hot Stuff SW8** £14   ★

19 Wilcox Rd   7720 1480
*"Awesome Indian and West African food... and so cheap!" –*
*this "cramped" BYO destination looks "like a greasy spoon",*
*but doesn't cook like one; "you have to book".*
/ **Details:** www.eathotstuff.com; 9.45 pm; closed Sun.


**Hunan SW1** £39   ★★

51 Pimlico Rd   7730 5712   4–2D
*"Let Mr Peng order for you", when you visit this "bustling" Pimlico*
*spot, where almost all reporters are "bowled over" by the "varied,*
*very fresh, and original" cooking – for some, "the best Chinese*
*food in London".* / **Details:** 11 pm; closed Sun; no smoking area.


**Ikkyu W1** £28

67a Tottenham Court Rd   7636 9280   1–1C
*"No-frills, 'proper' Japanese food" helps maintain the consistent*
*popularity of this basement veteran, near Goodge Street tube –*
*"language difficulties with the staff only add to the authenticity".*
/ **Details:** 10 pm; closed Sat & Sun L; no Maestro; no smoking area.


**Imperial China WC2** £36   𝔸★

25a Lisle St   7734 3388   3–3B
*This "tucked-away" Chinatown venture is a "pleasant" place that*
*"doesn't feel like all the others" thereabouts; it's "reliable" all-*
*round, but the "fantastic dim sum" has a particular following.*
/ **Details:** www.imperial-china.co.uk; 11.15 pm.


**Imperial City EC3** £39   𝔸★

Royal Exchange, Cornhill   7626 3437
*"Well-executed and presented" Chinese dishes have made these*
*"tightly-packed" cellars (under the Royal Exchange) a "long-*
*running favourite for business dining".*
/ **Details:** www.orientalrestaurantgroup.co.uk; 10.30 pm; closed Sat & Sun; smoking
in bar only.


**Indian Ocean SW17** £22   ★

216 Trinity Rd   8672 7740
*"Every year we try loads of curry houses, but this is still one of the*
*best" – for "solid" subcontinental fare, this Wandsworth veteran*
*is hard to beat.* / **Details:** 11.15 pm; no smoking area.


**Indigo**
**One Aldwych WC2** £51

1 Aldwych   7300 0400   1–2D
*"Tables overlooking the bar are best", at this "light and airy"*
*mezzanine dining room, whose "consistent" cooking and*
*"comfortable" setting make it a "classy" venue for business*
*(and also pre-theatre, or for brunch).* / **Details:** www.onealdwych.com;
11.15 pm; no smoking at breakfast.

## Ishbilia SW1 £38 ★

9 William St 7235 7788 4–1D

*"Very fresh"* and *"subtle"* dishes make this *"friendly"* Knightsbridge café a *"top Lebanese"* for the few reporters who comment on it. / **Details:** www.ishbilia.com; 11.30 pm.

## The Ivy WC2 £57 Ⓐ

1 West St 7836 4751 3–3B

This legendary Theatreland haunt may not – for the first time in a decade – be voted reporters' No 1 favourite, but its *"magical"* charm, egalitarian staff, and reliable *"comfort"* food still make *"hard to beat"*; (the new owner, rag trade millionaire Richard Caring, seems to plan no sweeping changes). / **Value tip:** set weekday L £41 (FP). **Details:** www.the-ivy.co.uk; midnight; booking: max 6.

## Jashan £21 ★

1-2 Coronet Pde, Ealing Rd, HA0 8340 9880

19 Turnpike Ln, N8 8340 9880

*"They look like bog-standard curry houses, but they aren't"* – these suburban Indian restaurants provide *"really friendly"* service and *"varied and deeply tasty"* south Indian cuisine. / **Details:** www.jashanrestaurants.co.uk; 10.30 pm; N8 D only, closed Mon; no Amex; HA0 no smoking.

## Jenny Lo's Tea House SW1 £23 ★

14 Eccleston St 7259 0399 1–4B

For a *"delicious"* bowl of rice or noodles that's *"so fresh and cheap"*, Jenny Lo's *"efficient"* Belgravia venture *"always hits the spot"*; *"fluorescent lighting, stark walls and communal tables"*, however, is a combination that *"doesn't make you linger"*. / **Details:** 10 pm; closed Sat L & Sun; no credit cards; no booking.

## Jin Kichi NW3 £33 ★★

73 Heath St 7794 6158

*"Always packed, for a reason"*, this *"cramped"* but *"great-value"* Hampstead Japanese is again applauded by reporters for its *"very authentic, fresh and tasty"* fare – this includes *"the best yakitori"*, as well as *"outstanding sushi"*. / **Details:** www.jinkichi.com; 11 pm; closed Mon & weekday L.

## K10 EC2 £27 ★★

20 Copthall Ave 7562 8510

*"A well-stocked conveyor-belt brings an interesting array of dishes"* (*"not just traditional sushi"*), at this *"excellent"* City basement – it gets *"very busy"*, so *"arrive early"*. / **Details:** www.k10.net; L only, closed Sat & Sun; no smoking; no booking.

## Kai Mayfair W1 £50 Ⓐ★

65 South Audley St 7493 8988 2–3A

A zillion spiritual miles from Chinatown, this *"comfortable"* and *"quiet"* Mayfair oriental offers *"impeccable"* service and a wine list strong in first-growth clarets; the food is *"imaginative"* and *"interesting"*, too... but *"be prepared for a huge bill"*. / **Details:** www.kaimayfair.com; 10.45 pm.

## Kaifeng NW4 £45 ★

51 Church Rd 8203 7888

*"The best Kosher Chinese food in town"* wins uniform praise for this Harrow stalwart; that said, even if it's a style of cooking that rarely comes cheap, it can seem *"unnecessarily expensive"* here. / **Details:** 10.30 pm; closed Fri; no smoking.

**kare kare SW5** £33 ★
152 Old Brompton Rd 7373 0024 4–2B
*"Fresh and light" cuisine and "exceptional" service are generating
a devoted local following for this "innovative" Earl's Court Indian.*
/ **Value tip:** *set weekday L £19 (FP).* **Details:** *www.karekare.co.uk; 11.30 pm;
no smoking area.*

**Kastoori SW17** £21 ★★
188 Upper Tooting Rd 8767 7027
*"Outstanding" Gujarati/East African veggie "delicacies" make
it "worth the trek" to this family-run Tooting spot, where "lovely"
service enlivens the rather "drab" environment.* / **Details:** *10.30 pm;
closed Mon L & Tue L; no Amex or Maestro; booking: max 12.*

**Kazan SW1** £31
93-94 Wilton Rd 7233 7100 1–4B
*With its "nice Turkish food" and "good atmosphere",
this (much smarter) spin-off from the Sofra group is emerging
as one of Pimlico's few "good evening-out" destinations.*
/ **Details:** *www.kazan-restaurant.co.uk; 10.45 pm; no Amex; no smoking area.*

**Ken Lo's Memories SW1** £46 ★
67-69 Ebury St 7730 7734 1–4B
*"Amazing consistency over the years" makes this "pricey"
Belgravia veteran "London's top Chinese" for many reporters;
after a "modern" facelift, the room feels "bright" and "livelier",
too.* / **Details:** *11.15 pm; closed Sun L.*

**Ken Lo's Memories of China W8** £47 ★
353 Kensington High St 7603 6951 6–1D
*"It feels like a neighbourhood Chinese", but fans go wild about the
"excellent-quality" cooking at this low-key oriental, near Olympia;
it doesn't wow everyone, though (and some find prices
"extortionate").* / **Value tip:** *set weekday L & set D £24 (FP).* **Details:** *11 pm.*

**Kisso SW5** £35
251 Old Brompton Rd 7584 9920 4–3A
*"A welcome addition to Earl's Court", this "fusion-type" Japanese
(replacing Bar Japan, RIP) offers "carefully prepared" and
"reasonably-priced" dishes in a modern setting.* /

**Koba W1** £38 ★
11 Rathbone St
7580 8825 1–1C
*A new Fitzrovia Korean with a stylish "modern" look; we very
much agree with the early reporter who thought the food –
cooked at your table – "lovely", and the service "charming".*
/ **Details:** *11 pm; closed Sun L.*

**Kovalam NW6** £23 ★
12 Willesden Ln 7625 4761
*"Excellent food for the price" and "amazingly friendly" service
help make this "naff"-looking subcontinental (with a south Indian
bias) a top Kilburn-fringe destination.*
/ **Details:** *www.kovalamrestaurant.co.uk; 11 pm, Fri & Sat midnight;
no smoking area.*

**sign up for the survey at www.hardens.com**

**Kulu Kulu** £21 ★

76 Brewer St, W1   7734 7316   2–2D
51-53 Shelton St, WC2   7240 5687   3–2C
39 Thurloe Pl, SW7   7589 2225   4–2C

*"Very tasty and amazingly cheap sushi" wins acclaim for this duo of 'kaiten' (conveyor-belt-style) Japanese cafés; the Regent Street site is a bit of "a dive", though (and "don't expect to linger"). / Details: 10 pm, SW7 10.30 pm; closed Sun; no Amex; no smoking area, WC2 no smoking; no booking.*

**Kwan Thai SE1** £37 ★

Unit 1, Hay's Galleria   7403 7373

*It's testament to the 'plain vanilla' charms of this attractive Thai (with river views towards the City), that although it's voted a 'top oriental' by some reporters, no one actually wastes any words on it! / **Value tip:** set weekday L £24 (FP). **Details:** www.kwanthairestaurant.co.uk; 10 pm; closed Sat L & Sun; no smoking area.*

**The Ladbroke Arms W11** £37 A★

54 Ladbroke Rd   7727 6648   5–2B

*With its "delicious, imaginative and fairly-priced cooking", this ever-popular Notting Hill gastroboozer offers standards "well above its peers"; get there early, especially if you want a table on the "lovely" terrace. / **Details:** www.capitalpubcompany.co.uk; 9.45 pm; no booking after 7.30 pm.*

**Lamberts SW12** £38 A★★

2 Station Pde   8675 2233

*"Book early", if you want a table at this "outstanding local", behind Balham station, which a number of locals note "is only beaten around here by Chez Bruce!" / **Details:** www.lambertsrestaurant.com; 10.30 pm; closed Mon, Tue-Fri D only, Sat & Sun open L & D; no Amex; no smoking area.*

**Lanes**
**East India House E1**  £44

109-117 Middlesex St
7247 5050

*"Well-executed" food, "accommodating" service and an air of "easy sophistication" have come together to make this City-fringe yearling "a good safe choice, particularly for a business lunch". / **Details:** www.lanesrestaurant.co.uk; 10 pm; closed Sat L & Sun.*

**The Lanesborough SW1** £93 A

Hyde Park Corner   7259 5599   4–1D

*"You can't beat the setting" – a "delightful and airy" conservatory – in the dining room of this "splendid" hotel; "breakfasts and afternoon teas are its forte", though – "lunch and dinner are less impressive" (and arguably "way overpriced"). / **Value tip:** set weekday L £37 (FP), brunch £57 (FP), set D £62 (FP). **Details:** www.lanesborough.com; 11.30 pm.*

**Lansdowne NW1** £39 A★

90 Gloucester Ave   7483 0409

*Despite having The Engineer down the road, this "laid-back" gastropub is, for many reporters, "first choice in Primrose Hill"; "cramped" and "always busy", it serves "fresh" and "interesting" dishes to a "lively meedja crowd". / **Details:** 10 pm; closed Mon L; no Amex or Maestro.*

**La Lanterna SE1**                                          £32

6-8 Mill St   7252 2420

*"The smell of garlic hits you as you go in" to this "lively" Italian joint, near Butlers Wharf; it serves "simple" and "dependable" grub, with pizza a highlight.* / **Details:** www.millstreetcafe.co.uk; 11 pm; closed Sat L; no smoking area.

**Latium W1**                             £40        ★

21 Berners St

7323 9123   1–1C

*"The best value in the West End?" – perhaps not quite, but "consistently interesting" and "accomplished" Italian cooking is putting this "reliable" yearling, north of Oxford Street, firmly on the map; it's equally good for "a corporate lunch or a relaxed dinner with friends".* / **Details:** www.latiumrestaurant.com; 10.30 pm; closed Sat L & Sun.

**Laughing Gravy SE1**                                       £39        𝔸

154 Blackfriars Rd   7721 7055

*"Eclectic" décor and "lovely" service help create a "cosy" ambience at this family-run Southwark outfit, where the cooking is somewhere between "inexpert" and "distinctive".* / **Details:** 10 pm; closed Sat L & Sun; no Amex.

**Laureate W1**                                              £27

64 Shaftesbury Ave   7437 5088   3–3A

*On the fringe of Chinatown, this pleasant new corner Chinese is already gathering something of a following, not least for its "quality dim sum".* / **Details:** 11.15 pm.

**The Ledbury W11**                       £58        𝔸★

127 Ledbury Rd

7792 9090   5–1B

*"Finally, a proper grown-up restaurant in Notting Hill"; this "calmly-decorated" newcomer (sibling to The Square, Chez Bruce, etc) – where "knowledgeable" staff serve up Brett Graham's "original" (if rather ornate) cuisine – has emerged as the 'high-end' opening of the year.* / **Details:** www.theledbury.com; 11 pm; no smoking.

**Lemonia NW1**                                              £27        𝔸

89 Regent's Park Rd   7586 7454

*This "large", "loud" and "lively" Primrose Hill taverna has long been a north London institution – its Greek fare may be "nothing special", but the atmosphere is "unbeatable".* / **Details:** 11.30 pm; closed Sat L & Sun D; no Amex.

**Leon W1**                                                  £18        ★

35-36 Gt Marlborough St   7437 5280   2–2C

*"Wholesome" victuals – salads, wraps, grills, juices – with "vibrant" tastes have made this "superior organic take-away-with-tables", by Liberty's, a great hit with most reporters; "why hasn't it been done before?"* / **Details:** www.leonrestaurants.co.uk; 10 pm; no smoking.

**Lilly's E1**                                               £33        𝔸★

75 Wapping High St   7702 2040

*"Much more sophisticated than it needs to be", this "relaxing" all-day brasserie (with boothed seating) has been a "top-class" addition to the "Wapping scene".* / **Value tip:** set weekday L £18 (FP). **Details:** www.lillysrestaurant.co.uk; 11 pm; smoking in bar only.

**Lindsay House W1**  £74  A

21 Romilly St  7439 0450  3–3A

*On most accounts, Richard Corrigan's "gorgeous" Soho townhouse offers "sublime" and "faultless" meals; support is still undercut, however, by the minority of reporters which complains of "astronomical" bills for cooking that's "good, but not outstanding".* / **Value tip:** *set weekday L & pre-theatre £48 (FP).* **Details:** *www.lindsayhouse.co.uk; 11 pm; closed Sat L & Sun; no smoking area.*


**LMNT E8**  £25  A

316 Queensbridge Rd  7249 6727

*"Amazing", "totally mad" décor ("like an Egyptian boudoir") has won fame for this "quirky" Hackney venture; the food is surprisingly "innovative", too, and it comes at "great-value" prices.* / **Details:** *www.lmnt.co.uk; 10 pm; no Amex.*


**Lobster Pot SE11**  £41  ★★

3 Kennington Ln  7582 5556

*"The sound of seagulls and fog-horns" transports you from an ugly Kennington junction to the "weird and wonderful world" of this "bizarre" Breton venture; "ten minutes in, you forget the absurdity", allowing you to focus on the "superb" Gallic fish cooking.* / **Value tip:** *set weekday L £24 (FP).* **Details:** *www.lobsterpotrestaurant.co.uk; 11 pm; closed Mon & Sun; no smoking area; booking: max 8.*


**Locanda Locatelli**
**Churchill InterCont'l W1**    £56  A★

8 Seymour St
7935 9088  1–2A

*Giorgio Locatelli's "swish" modern Italian on Portman Square delivers "straightforward cooking of the highest calibre"; it is, for many reporters, simply London's top Italian.* / **Details:** *www.locandalocatelli.com; 11 pm, Fri & Sat 11.30 pm; closed Sun; booking: max 8.*


**Locanda Ottoemezzo W8**  £58  A

2-4 Thackeray St  7937 2200  4–1B

*The "rustic" cooking is "very good" and staff "will do anything to help" at this "down-to-earth" Kensington Italian; some reporters still feel it's "ludicrously overpriced", though.* / **Value tip:** *set weekday L £34 (FP).* **Details:** *10.45 pm; closed Sat L & Sun.*


**Lola's N1**  £46

359 Upper St  7359 1932

*Given the comings-and-goings of numerous chefs over the years, reporters' loyalty to this "calm" and "classy" Islington venture – above the Antiques Market – is impressive ; perhaps the (post-survey) return of a Juliet Peston protégée to the stove will herald an era of greater stability.* / **Details:** *11 pm; closed Sun D; booking: max 14.*


**Lucio SW3**  £46  A★

257 Fulham Rd  7823 3007  4–3B

*"Suddenly very fashionable" – this Chelsea yearling is a "happy" sort of place, where "really tasty" Italian dishes are served by "very sweet" staff.* / **Details:** *10.45 pm; no smoking area.*

## Lucky Seven W2　　　　　　£31　　　A

127 Westbourne Park Rd　7727 6771　5–1B

Tom Conran's "fun", "faux-American" diner, in Bayswater, serves "burgers straight off the set of 'Grease'" (and milkshakes "which make your straw stand to attention"). / **Details:** 11 pm; closed Mon L; no credit cards; no booking.

## Lundum's SW7　　　　　　£45　　　A★

119 Old Brompton Rd　7373 7774　4–2B

"Beautiful and romantic" décor and "attentive" staff win the highest praise for the Lundum Family's "elegant" but "homely" South Kensington restaurant, where a "classic" menu comes with a "Scandinavian twist" – highlights include seafood and the Sunday buffet brunch. / **Value tip:** set weekday L £29 (FP). **Details:** www.lundums.com; 11 pm; closed Sun D.

## Ma Goa SW15　　　　　　£31　　　★

244 Upper Richmond Rd　8780 1767

"Sumptuous" and "genuine" Goan cuisine is served by "lovely people", at this "cosy", if "slightly poky", Putney "gem". / **Details:** www.ma-goa.com; 11 pm; D only, ex Sun open L & D; no smoking.

## Made in China SW10　　　　£35　　　★

351 Fulham Rd　7351 2939　4–3B

"Freshly-prepared" food at "reasonable prices" is making this Chelsea two-year-old a bit of a "local favourite"; it's "a bit canteen-like", though – "they need to turn the lights down or something". / **Details:** 11.30 pm.

## Made in Italy SW3　　　　　£34　　　★

249 King's Rd　7352 1880　4–3C

"It's a bit of a squeeze", but "great fun", at this "loud" Chelsea fixture, which is known for its "fabulous" and "very authentic" pizza; service, though, is "useless". / **Details:** 11.30 pm; closed weekday L; no Amex.

## Madhu's UB1　　　　　　£29　　　★★

39 South Rd　8574 1897

With its "great smells, textures and ingredients" the food "takes some beating for authenticity", at this pleasant Southall Indian – the best all-rounder in this curry-dominated suburb. / **Details:** www.madhusonline.com; 11.30 pm; closed Tue, Sat L & Sun L.

## Maggie Jones's W8　　　　£43　　　A

6 Old Court Pl　7937 6462　4–1A

"Like the '90s never happened" (or the '80s, for that matter), this "cheesy" rustic Kensington veteran can still make a "lovely" destination for those with romance in mind; it offers "simple" going-on "basic" English fare. / **Value tip:** set Sun L £28 (FP). **Details:** 11 pm.

## Maggiore's WC2　　　　　£49　　　A★

33 King St　7379 9696　3–3C

"In the midst of Covent Garden's tourist hell", this "wonderfully romantic" venture (complete with "magical" inside courtyard) comes as a "very nice surprise"; but that's not all – the food is "very competent", and the "massive" wine list is "simply stunning". / **Value tip:** set weekday L £30 (FP), set pre-theatre £22 (FP), set Sun L £20 (FP). **Details:** www.maggiores.uk.com; 10.45 pm; no smoking.

## Malabar W8 £30 ★
27 Uxbridge St   7727 8800   5–2B
*"Standards never slip", at this "old-favourite" curry house,
off Notting Hill Gate; it has a big fan club, thanks to its
"sophisticated" and "slightly different" curries, which offer "great
value". / **Details:** www.malabar-restaurant.co.uk; 11.15 pm.*

## Malabar Junction WC1 £30
107 Gt Russell St   7580 5230   1–1C
*A very "civilised" and "spacious" – if slightly "characterless" –
Bloomsbury venture, where "courteous" staff dish up some
notably "delicate" south Indian dishes (including a "wide veggie
selection"). / **Details:** 11.30 pm; no smoking area.*

## Malmaison EC1 £41 Ⓐ
18-21 Charterhouse St   7012 3700
*"Elegant" décor and a slightly "secluded" feel make this
Clerkenwell design-hotel dining room a surprise 'hit' on the
ambience front; the food – though a less reliable attraction –
is generally "good value". / **Value tip:** set weekday L £27
(FP). **Details:** www.malmaison.com; 10.30 pm; no smoking area.*

## Mandalay W2 £18 ★★
444 Edgware Rd   7258 3696
*"The friendliest restaurant in London" may be this "drab" shop-
conversion, near Edgware Road tube, where "truly enthusiastic"
proprietors serve up "delicious" Burmese dishes ("a cross between
Indian and Chinese") at "very reasonable prices"; book ahead.
/ **Details:** 10.30 pm; closed Sun; no smoking.*

## Mandarin Kitchen W2 £27 ★★
14-16 Queensway   7727 9012   5–2C
*It's "a complete zoo" – and "booking doesn't seem to make any
difference" – but this "scruffy" Queensway oriental remains
a "brilliant" choice for seafood; "you mustn't miss the lobster"
(of which they claim to serve more than anywhere else in the
UK!). / **Details:** 11.15 pm.*

## Mangal E8 £15 ★★
10 Arcola St   7275 8981
*"A lesson in how to do simple things well" – this "fantastic-value"
Turkish caff, in Dalston, offers "wonderful" kebabs and
"good mezze"; "try to spend over 20 quid, without having to be
wheeled home". / **Details:** midnight; no credit cards.*

## Mao Tai £38 ★
96 Draycott Ave, SW3   7225 2500   4–2C
58 New King's Rd, SW6   7731 2520
*With their "classic" Chinese cuisine, these "consistent" orientals –
in Parson's Green and at Brompton Cross – continue to please;
they're "certainly not cheap", though, and some reporters feel
that they "need to re-invent themselves". / **Details:** www.maotai.co.uk;
11.30 pm; no smoking area.*

## Marine Ices NW3 £26 Ⓐ
8 Haverstock Hill   7482 9003
*Seventy-five this year, the Mansi family's "really atmospheric"
Belsize Park veteran remains every north London child's dream,
thanks to "Britain's best ice cream"; "the mains are worth a look,
too", in particular the "reliable" pizza. / **Details:** www.marineices.co.uk;
11 pm; no Amex; no smoking.*

**Maroush** £40 ★

I) 21 Edgware Rd, W2   7723 0773   5–1D
II) 38 Beauchamp Pl, SW3   7581 5434   4–1C
III) 62 Seymour St, W1   7724 5024   1–2A
IV) 68 Edgware Rd, W2   7724 9339   5–1D
V) 3-4 Vere St, W1   7493 3030   2–1B
"Garden") 1 Connaught St, W2   7262 0222   5–1D
*"Consistent, high-quality Lebanese food"* has long made this
upmarket Middle Eastern group a London benchmark; branches
vary in style and appeal, but most are open till late –
the (cheaper) café sections of I, II and V offer good-value early-
hours re-fuelling. / **Details:** www.maroush.com; 11.30 pm-3.30 am.

**Matsuri** £60 ★

15 Bury St, SW1   7839 1101   2–3D
Mid City Place, 71 High Holborn, WC1   7430 1970   1–1D
*"Particularly great sushi"* is a mainstay of the often-*"stunning"*
cuisine of these *"bland"*-looking St James's and Holborn
Japaneses; service comes *"with a smile"*, and , in SW1, you also
get *"lots of whirling knives"* at the *"fabulous"* teppan-yaki. / **Value
tip:** set D £35 (FP). **Details:** www.matsuri-restaurant.com; 10 pm;
WC1 closed Sun.

**Medcalf EC1** £32 Ⓐ★

40 Exmouth Mkt   7833 3533
The *"deliberately basic"* look and *"very British"* menu go down
well with a *"hip"* clientèle at this *"bustling"*, *"café-style"*
Clerkenwell yearling; by night, it's much more of a bar.
/ **Details:** www.medcalfbar.co.uk; 10 pm; closed Fri D & Sun D; no Amex.

**Mehek EC2** £30 ★

45 London Wall   7588 5043
Notably consistent standards make this smart Indian, near the
Barbican, a handy City stand-by. / **Details:** www.mehek.co.uk; 11 pm;
closed Sat & Sun; no smoking area.

**Mela WC2** £33

152-156 Shaftesbury Ave   7836 8635   3–2B
*"Different"* and *"tasty"* dishes at *"good-value prices for the West
End"* have made quite a name for this *"reliable"* Indian,
by Cambridge Circus; over the years, though, its standards have
drifted noticeably. / **Details:** www.melarestaurant.co.uk; 11.30 pm;
no smoking area.

**Mestizo NW1** £27 ★

103 Hampstead Rd   7387 4064
*"High-quality food at good prices"* makes this new Mexican
restaurant – five minutes' walk north of Warren Street tube –
a *"gem"*, according to one early reporter; we didn't find
it especially atmospheric, but it's certainly interesting.
/ **Details:** www.mestizomx.com; midnight; no smoking area.

**Metrogusto N1** £42 Ⓐ

13 Theberton St   7226 9400
When it's on form – which has become much more the norm
again of late – this Islington side street spot can be a *"terrific
local"*, offering *"imaginative"* cooking, *"personable"* service and
an *"excellent"* wine list. / **Details:** www.metrogusto.co.uk; 10.30 pm, Fri &
Sat 11 pm; Mon-Thu D only; smoking in bar only; booking: max 8, Sat & Sun.

**Mildred's W1**                                    £27    ★

45 Lexington St   7494 1634   2–2D

*"Proof that veggie food isn't all mung beans!" – this "cramped"
Soho stalwart generates "queues out the door", thanks to its
"diverse" and "really tasty" fare; the veggie-burger is especially
recommended.* / Details: www.mildreds.co.uk; 11 pm; closed Sun; only Maestro;
no smoking area; no booking.

**Mint Leaf SW1**                                   £50    A★

1 Suffolk Pl   7930 9020   1–2C

*"Not at all the triumph of style over substance you might expect"
– this "smooth" and "dimly-lit" basement, near Trafalgar Square,
offers "beautifully-presented" Indian dishes "of high quality";
there's a "good bar", too.* / Details: www.mintleafrestaurant.com; 11 pm;
closed Sat L & Sun.

**Mirabelle W1**                                    £65    A

56 Curzon St   7499 4636   2–4B

*Fans still see MPW's "grand Art Deco dame" as a "great"
Mayfair "all-rounder", serving "classic Gallic cuisine"
(complemented by a "cellar to die for"); its ratings continue
to drift, though, with critics finding it "dated", "tired" and
"impersonal".* / **Value tip:** set Sun L £40 (FP), set weekday L £39
(FP). Details: www.whitestarline.org.uk; 11.15 pm.

**Miraggio SW6**                                    £30    A★

510 Fulham Rd   7384 9774   4–4A

*The Aiello family now run this modest-looking, Parson's Green
Italian, which is universally hailed for its "fantastic", "authentic"
cuisine at "very reasonable" prices.* / Details: 11 pm.

**Mirch Masala**                                    £22    ★★

1416 London Rd, SW16   8679 1828
213 Upper Tooting Rd, SW17   8672 7500
171-173 The Broadway, UB1   8867 9222

*"Unbelievable", "home-style" Indian cooking "at great prices" puts
branches of this "basic" south London chain among the capital's
top budget destinations.* / Details: midnight; no Amex; SW17 no smoking,
SW16 no smoking area.

**Missouri Grill EC3**                              £40    ★

76 Aldgate High St   7481 4010

*"Simple and satisfying" cooking – not especially American in style
– and exceptional service have helped make this bravely-sited
newcomer (opposite Aldgate tube) quite a "classy" City lunching
destination; it's not inexpensive, though, and the evenings can
be "dead".* / Details: www.missourigrill.com; 11 pm; closed Sat & Sun.

**Mitsukoshi SW1**                                  £53    ★

Dorland Hs, 14-20 Lower Regent St   7930 0317   2–3D

*The "excellent" sushi is amongst the best in town at this West
End department store basement (even if it does badly "need a
make-over") – "sit at the counter, and let the chef sort out your
order".* / **Value tip:** set weekday L £25
(FP). Details: www.mitsukoshi-restaurant.co.uk; 10 pm; no smoking area.

**Miyama W1**                                       £55    ★

38 Clarges St   7499 2443   2–4B

*The sushi is "excellent", at this long-established Mayfair Japanese,
but the "cold" décor perennially "needs a re-design".*
/ Details: 10.30 pm; closed Sat L & Sun L.

## Mju

### Millennium Knightsbridge SW1 £70 ★

16-17 Sloane St 7201 6330 4–1D

*Despite Tom Thomson's "delicious", "experimental" fusion fare, this Knightsbridge dining room has never gathered much of a following among reporters – the airport-lounge style doesn't help. / **Value tip:** set weekday L £41 (FP). **Details:** www.milleniumhotels.com; 10.30 pm; closed Sun; no smoking area.*

### Mohsen W14 £25 ★

152 Warwick Rd 7602 9888 6–1D

*"Brilliant fresh Persian dishes" and "an honest welcome" help ensure this "modest" BYO café, opposite Olympia's Homebase, is usually "filled with local Iranians". / **Details:** 11.30 pm; no credit cards.*

### Mon Plaisir WC2 £40 🄰

19-21 Monmouth St 7836 7243 3–2B

*"Like stumbling into a bit of France", this "romantic" Covent Garden "stalwart" of half a century's standing can still weave its magic (not least for "the best-value pre-theatre menu in town"); there's a slight feeling that the food "is not as good as it used to be", but, for most reporters, it's "still worth a go". / **Value tip:** set weekday L £24 (FP), set pre-theatre £22 (FP). **Details:** www.monplaisir.co.uk; 11.15 pm; closed Sat L & Sun.*

### Monmouth Coffee Company £10 ★★

27 Monmouth St, WC2 7645 3560 3–2B
2 Park St, SE1 7645 3560

*For "top-class caffeine kicks", this micro-chain – with its "wonderful selection of coffees" – is London's "absolute best"; the Borough Market branch – with its larger range of "yummy cakes, pastries and savouries" – has more of an 'on-trade' than the smaller Covent Garden shop. / **Details:** www.monmouthcoffee.co.uk; L & afternoon tea only; closed Sun; no Amex; no smoking; no booking.*

### Monza SW3 £41

6 Yeomans Row 7591 0210 4–2C

*This "intimate", lesser-known Italian, in a Knightsbridge backstreet, is "not especially cheap, but is reliably good". / **Value tip:** set weekday L £25 (FP). **Details:** www.monza.co.uk; 11 pm; closed Mon L & Sun.*

### Morgan M N7 £46 ★★

489 Liverpool Rd
7609 3560

*Many reporters leave "awe-struck" by the cuisine at Monsieur Meunier's Islington/Holloway-fringe yearling; the ambience of his pub-conversion is "chilly", though, and we can personally vouch for the advice staff now give customers: "don't park in a side street". / **Details:** www.morganm.com; 10 pm; closed Mon, Tue L, Sat L & Sun D; no Amex; no smoking; booking: max 6.*

### Moro EC1 £40 🄰★★

34-36 Exmouth Mkt 7833 8336

*Samantha and Samuel Clark's "innovative" and "delicious" Spanish/North African cuisine makes a visit to this "buzzy" Clerkenwell hotspot "a sublime gastronomic experience"; service – after an 'iffy' patch – "has improved", too. / **Details:** www.moro.co.uk; 10.30 pm; closed Sun; booking essential ex Sat L.*

## Mosaica
### The Chocolate Factory N22        £37    A★★
Unit C005, Clarendon Rd    8889 2400
*A Wood Green wonder, where the food is "superb" and the
service "unsurpassed"; the fact this it has an "unsettling" location
(a converted factory, "in the middle of an industrial estate") only
boosts its appeal.* / **Details:** *www.mosaicarestaurant.com; 9.30 pm; closed
Mon, Sat L & Sun D; no smoking area.*

## Mr Jerk        £18    ★★
189 Wardour St, W1    7287 2878    2–1D
19 Westbourne Grove, W2    7221 4678    5–1C
*"Food this good for this price is hard to find in central London" –
these "cramped", "friendly" Caribbean cafés (in Soho and
Bayswater) offer "huge" portions of "scrummy" curries, fried
plantains and BBQ dishes; "queue early".* / **Details:** *www.mrjerk.co.uk;
10 pm, Sun 8 pm.*

## Mr Wing SW5        £45    A★
242-244 Old Brompton Rd    7370 4450    4–2A
*This pricey 'party-Chinese', in Earl's Court, has always had its
"peaks and troughs foodwise"; for most reporters, though,
it offers a "fabulous" experience, "time and time again".*
/ **Details:** *www.mrwing.com; 11.30 pm.*

## MVH SW13        £46    A★
5 White Hart Ln    8392 1111
*Michael von Hruschka's "unusual" – and, for some, "over-
complicated" – cuisine is delivered "with panache" at this brave,
Barnes venture; the upstairs bar ('Hell') is "dark and sinful",
the ground-floor restaurant ('Heaven') is light and "serene".*
/ **Details:** *11 pm; Mon-Wed D only; no smoking area.*

## Nanglo SW12        £23    ★
88 Balham High Rd    8673 4160
*A modern Nepalese on Balham's main drag; its curries are "of a
very high standard" and, for the staff, "nothing is too much
trouble".* /

## Nautilus NW6        £26    ★★
27-29 Fortune Green Rd    7435 2532
*"Still good, despite the change of management" –
this "traditional", kosher chippie in West Hampstead continues
to serve "brilliant fish in matzo meal", with "loads of chips".*
/ **Details:** *9.30 pm; closed Sun; no Amex; mainly non-smoking.*

## Navarro's W1        £25    A
67 Charlotte St    7637 7713    1–1C
*Central London's leading traditional tapas bar – a Fitzrovia
veteran, where "fresh and delicious" dishes are served in a
"very pretty" and "authentic" tiled setting.* / **Details:** *www.navarro.co.uk;
10 pm; closed Sat L & Sun.*

## New Tayyabs E1        £16    ★★
83 Fieldgate St    7247 9543
*"Insanely busy, but worth the wait"; "poshed-up" décor (and more
space) has done nothing to change the basic appeal of this
"astounding" Pakistani East End caff, which serves "fabulous"
grills, naans and dry curries at "rock bottom" prices; BYO.*
/ **Details:** *www.tayyabs.co.uk; 11.30 pm; no smoking area.*

**sign up for the survey at www.hardens.com**       

**Nobu**
**Metropolitan Hotel W1**                                      **£84**          ★
Old Park Ln   7447 4747   2–4A
*"Still amazing after all these years"* – this *"slick"* (*"Manhattan-vibe"*) Mayfair star-magnet continues to maintain a towering reputation for its *"divine"* Japanese-fusion cuisine; the bill is an *"arm and a leg job"*, though, and service can be *"arrogant"*.
/ **Details:** www.noburestaurants.com; 10.15 pm, Fri & Sat 11 pm; no smoking area; booking: max 12.

**Nobu Berkeley W1**                                           **£84**
15-16 Berkeley St   7290 9222   2–3C
*As this guide goes to press, the latest opening from Matsuhisa Nobu's legendary international group is poised to launch in extraordinarily swanky premises, near the Ritz; it looks likely that this will be THE 'hot ticket' of late-2005.* / **Details:** D only, closed Sun; need 6+ to book.

**Noor Jahan**                                                 **£30**          ★
2a Bina Gdns, SW5   7373 6522   4–2B
26 Sussex Pl, W2   7402 2332   5–1D
*"Superb"* dishes – there's *"never an off night"* – and *"professional"* (if sometimes *"humourless"*) service have made this South Kensington curry house a local *"favourite"* for many years; its Bayswater spin-off is also *"excellent"*, if rather *"dull"*. / **Details:** 11.30 pm.

**The Northgate N1**                                           **£33**      𝔸★
113 Southgate Rd   7359 7392
*"Food above gastropub expectations"* – with dishes that are *"uniformly well thought-out and executed"* – is winning much local acclaim for this *"tasteful"* De Beauvoir boozer; service is *"very friendly"*, too. / **Details:** 11 pm; closed weekday L; no Amex.

**Notting Hill Brasserie W11**            **£46**      𝔸★
92 Kensington Park Rd
7229 4481   5–2B
*This "secret" townhouse "gem" has "gone from strength to strength" since its 2003 relaunch; it offers "perfect romantic dining" (complete with "excellent but not intrusive live music"), as well as Mark Jankel's "sophisticated" cuisine – "'brasserie' doesn't really do it justice".* / **Value tip:** set weekday L £32 (FP). **Details:** 11 pm; closed Sun D; no smoking area.

**Nuovi Sapori SW6**                                           **£33**          ★
295 New King's Rd
7736 3363
*A Fulham newcomer which hides a notably "friendly" heart behind a rather unpromising façade; that's not the only surprise – the reasonably-priced Italian cuisine is "great", too.* / **Details:** 11 pm; closed Sun.

**O'Conor Don W1**                                             **£34**      𝔸★
88 Marylebone Ln   7935 9311   2–1A
*Back on form, this "special" Irish pub in Marylebone boasts a "quiet" dining room serving hearty scoff, which is "perfect for a bowsie sort of lunch"; ('bowsie', Irish English, adj: raffish, drunken).* / **Details:** www.oconordon.com; 10 pm; closed Sat & Sun.

### The Oak W2

£38    A★

137 Westbourne Park Rd
7221 3355   5–1B
"Thin, crisp and perfectly-formed" pizza and an "attractive and buzzy" setting have helped make this former boozer "one of the trendier Notting Hill hang-outs"; (the upstairs room is also now open again — an early report says it's "effortlessly cool, with an eclectic tapas-style menu"). / **Details:** 10 pm; Mon-Thu closed L; no booking.

### Odette's NW1

£50    A

130 Regent's Park Rd   7586 5486
"Mirrors all around" and "subtle" lighting create a "fantastic", ultra-"romantic" atmosphere at this "posh" Primrose Hill "favourite"; in the first full year of the new régime, however, ratings for its "lovely" cuisine slipped rather, and there was the occasional incident of "grumpy" service. / **Value tip:** set weekday L & Sun L £34 (FP). **Details:** 10.30 pm; closed Sat L & Sun D; no smoking.

### Odin's W1

£45    A★

27 Devonshire St   7935 7296   1–1A
This "tranquil" Marylebone "old faithful" — adorned with the late Peter Langan's "gorgeous" art collection — offers a "classic", "time-warped" experience; the reasonably-priced cooking "doesn't bowl you over, but is much better than average and always dependable". / **Details:** www.langansrestaurants.co.uk; 11 pm; closed Sat & Sun; no smoking area; booking: max 10.

### (Ognisko Polskie)
### The Polish Club SW7

£37    A

55 Prince's Gate, Exhibition Rd   7589 4635   4–1C
For "faded glory", it's hard to beat this "quiet" South Kensington émigrés' club dining room, with its "old-fashioned" service and its "robust" Polish cooking; in summer, you can "eat outside, overlooking the garden". / **Details:** www.ognisko.com; 11 pm.

### Olley's SE24

£29    ★★

67-69 Norwood Rd   8671 8259
This "converted railway arch overlooking Brockwell Park" is an unlikely setting in which to enjoy "some of the very best fish and chips in the capital" — "worth the above-par prices".
/ **Details:** www.olleys.info; 10.30 pm; closed Mon L.

### 1 Lombard Street EC3

£65

1 Lombard St   7929 6611
"A perfect location for City lunches" — plus "reliable" standards overall — make for a "buzzy" atmosphere at this former banking hall, by Bank; it can seem a touch "overpriced", though, and "the brasserie is better value than the dining room".
/ **Details:** www.1lombardstreet.com; 10 pm; closed Sat & Sun; no smoking in dining room.

### One-O-One
### Sheraton Park Tower SW1

£73    ★

101 Knightsbridge
7290 7101   4–1D
Pascal Proyart's "sublime" seafood is hailed by fans as "the best in town" — "it doesn't even seem that expensive when it tastes this good"; the "airport-lounge" décor of this Knightsbridge hotel dining room, however, is "so bad it's funny". / **Value tip:** set weekday L £47 (FP). **Details:** www.oneoonerestaurant-luxurycollection.com; 10.15 pm; no smoking area.

### OQO Bar N1 £33 A★
4-6 Islington Grn   7704 2332
*Incomparably better than your typical Islington bar/restaurant,
this stylish newcomer serves up top-quality, light oriental dishes
in a stylishly understated setting; good-looking cocktail list, too.
/ Details: www.oqobar.co.uk; 10.45 pm, Thu-Sat 11.45 pm.*

### L'Oranger SW1 £77
5 St James's St   7839 3774   2–4D
*A "safe" St James's choice – this "expensive but impressive"
establishment offers an "enjoyable all-round" experience,
comprising "rich" modern French cuisine and "attentive" service,
in an "intimate" and "clubby" setting that can suit both business
and romance. / Value tip: set weekday L £52 (FP). Details: 10.45 pm; closed
Sat L & Sun; no smoking area; booking: max 8.*

### Orrery W1 £68
55 Marylebone High St   7616 8000   1–1A
*Often hailed as "the best Conran", this "spacious" room,
overlooking a Marylebone churchyard, impresses many reporters
with its "knowledgeable" staff, "stylish" cuisine and "incredibly
diverse" wine list; prices are "sky high", though, and the setting
strikes some as "dull". / Value tip: set weekday L £40 (FP), set Sun L £46
(FP). Details: www.orrery.co.uk; 11 pm; no smoking area; booking: max 12.*

### Oslo Court NW8 £48 ★
Charlbert St, off Prince Albert Rd   7722 8795
*"It'll never win any style awards" – its "greying" clientèle would
be horrified if it did – but this "unfailing" St John's Wood
"time warp" almost invariably wows reporters with its "gigantic"
portions of "creamy" scoff ("leave room for the sweet trolley"),
and its "amazing", "old-fashioned" service. / Details: 11 pm;
closed Sun.*

### Osteria Basilico W11 £42 A★
29 Kensington Park Rd   7727 9957   5–1A
*"Great bustle" has helped make this "cramped" Italian – where
"humorous" staff deliver "solid" cooking (and "great pizza") –
a Notting Hill "institution"; "do all you can to avoid the
basement!" / Details: www.basilico.co.uk; 11.30 pm; no booking, Sat L.*

### Osteria dell'Arancio SW10 £37 A
383 King's Rd   7349 8111   4–3B
*"Decent and affordable" cooking (from a "limited" menu) and
a wine list "with many interesting finds" win support from most
reporters for this "creative" new Chelsea Italian; it's not for
everyone, though, and sceptics say "it'll have to work hard, in the
face of so much local competition". / Value tip: set weekday L £23
(FP). Details: www.osteriadellarancio.co.uk; 11.30 pm; closed weekday
L; no smoking area.*

### Ottolenghi £36 A★★
63 Ledbury Rd, W11
7727 1121   5–1B
287 Upper St, N1
7288 1454

*"Out-of-this-world" salads and cakes have made this "effortlessly
cool" deli-duo an instant smash-hit with Notting Hill and
(especially) Islington trendies; "they're up there as contenders for
best breakfast, too". / Details: www.ottolenghi.co.uk; W11 8 pm, Sat 7 pm,
Sun 6 pm, N1 11 pm; W11 L only; N1 no Amex; no smoking; W11 no booking,
N1 booking for D only.*

**(Brasserie)**
**Oxo Tower SE1**                    £47          ✗
Barge House St   7803 3888
*"At least they can't screw up the view", from the eighth floor
of this South Bank landmark; just as well, as – with its "severely
overpriced" food and "amateur" service – it's now topped the
survey's 'most disappointing' nominations for five years in a row!*
/ **Details:** www.harveynichols.com; 11 pm; booking: max 8.


**Page in Pimlico SW1**              £29
11 Warwick Way   7834 3313   1–4B
*Reports on the Thai cuisine at one of Pimlico's nicer boozers were
more upbeat this year; staff are "mainly Aussie, and 100%
smiley".* / **Details:** www.frontpagepubs.com; 10 pm; closed Sat L & Sun L;
no smoking.


**The Painted Heron**                £40          ★★
112 Cheyne Walk, SW10
7351 5232   4–3B
205-209 Kennington Ln, SE11
7793 8313
*"Not your generic Indian"* – thank to its *"exquisite"*
(and *"very different"*) cuisine, and *"first-class"* service, this *"posh"*
Chelsea and Kennington mini-chain is at last making quite a name
for itself. / **Details:** www.thepaintedheron.com; SE11 10.30 pm, SW10 11 pm;
SW10 closed Sat L; SE11 no smoking area.


**The Palmerston SE22**              £36          ★★
91 Lordship Ln   8693 1629
*"Top-quality cooking"* – from *"an inventive menu which changes
regularly"* – is creating a growing reputation for this East Dulwich
gastropub. / **Value tip:** set weekday L £24
(FP). **Details:** www.thepalmerston.co.uk; 10 pm; no Amex; no smoking area.


**Papageno WC2**                     £36          𝔸
29-31 Wellington St   7836 4444   3–3D
*"Great decoration"* and a *"fun atmosphere"* have made this new
Theatreland son-of-Sarastro a worthy chip off the old block;
the food (*"fine"*) is actually something of an improvement!
/ **Details:** www.papagenorestaurant.com; 11.45 pm.


**Pappa Ciccia**                     £26          ★
105-107 Munster Rd, SW6   7384 1884
41 Fulham High St, SW6   7736 0900
90 Lower Richmond Rd, SW15   8789 9040
*"Fresh and well-cooked"* Italian dishes – with *"massive pizzas"*
a speciality – have made this *"squashed"* but *"fun"* chain a local
institution (aided, at SW6 branches, by the BYO policy).
/ **Details:** www.pappaciccia.com; 11 pm; Fulham High St no smoking area.


**Pappagallo W1**                    £45
54-55 Curzon St   7629 2742   2–4B
*"A real find for Mayfair"* – this year-old relaunch of Ristorante
Italiano wins praise for its *"upmarket"* décor, *"efficient"* service
and *"good prices"*; it's still little-known, though, which can make
for a lack of atmosphere in the evenings. / **Details:** 11 pm; closed
Sat L & Sun L.

## Pasha SW7 £43 Ⓐ

1 Gloucester Rd 7589 7969 4–1B

*"Ask for one of the hidden nooks", if you visit this "exotic" South Kensington Moroccan – the "romantic" décor is a much stronger attraction that the "OK" food and service. / **Value tip:** set weekday L £21 (FP). **Details:** www.pasha-restaurant.co.uk; 10.45 pm; closed Sun L; booking: max 10 at weekends.*

## Passione W1 £55 ★

10 Charlotte St 7636 2833 1–1C

*"The highest-quality ingredients prepared with love and care" still win raves for Gennaro Contaldo's "busy" and "noisy" Fitzrovian; this year's feedback was a bit up-and-down though, with one or two reporters finding the place "overrated". / **Details:** www.passione.co.uk; 10.15 pm; closed Sat L & Sun.*

## Patara £46 ★★

15 Greek St, W1 7437 1071 3–2A
3-7 Maddox St, W1 7499 6008 2–2C
181 Fulham Rd, SW3 7351 5692 4–2C
9 Beauchamp Pl, SW3 7581 8820 4–1C

*"The most delicious Thai food" – "perfumed to perfection" – underpins the high popularity of this small group; its "serene" charms are perhaps best appreciated at the spacious new Soho branch. / **Value tip:** set weekday L £31 (FP). **Details:** 10.30 pm; no smoking area.*

## Pâtisserie Valerie £22

17 Motcomb St, SW1 7245 6161 4–1D
Hans Cr, SW1 7590 0905 4–1D
105 Marylebone High St, W1 7935 6240 1–1A
162 Piccadilly, W1 7491 1717 2–3C
44 Old Compton St, W1 7437 3466 3–2A
215 Brompton Rd, SW3 7823 9971 4–1C
Duke of York Sq, SW3 7730 7094 4–2D
27 Kensington Church St, W8 7937 9574 4–1A
37 Brushfield St, E1 awaiting tel

*"Yummy breakfast pastries" are still done very well by this expanding café/pâtisserie chain which claims to have introduced croissants to London in the '30s – go to the Soho original for maximum authenticity; other light fare (availability varies from branch to branch) is reliable, too. / **Details:** www.patisserie-valerie.co.uk; 6.30 pm; no booking.*

## Patterson's W1 £51 ★

4 Mill St
7499 1308 2–2C

*Raymond Patterson's "impressive" cooking, and service "that genuinely cares" make this family-run Mayfair two-year-old a "value-for-money" package of a type "rare in central London"; unsurprisingly, it's beginning to gather quite a following. / **Details:** www.pattersonsrestaurant.com; 11 pm; closed Sat L & Sun; no smoking area.*

## The Pepper Tree SW4 £19 ★★

19 Clapham Common S'side 7622 1758

*"Fresh and tasty" food that's "quick, easy and reliable" – and "unbeatable at the price" – keeps on packing 'em in at this "squashed" refectory-style Clapham Thai; the former Earlsfield branch is no more. / **Details:** 11 pm; no Amex; no smoking area; no booking at D.*

**Pescador Too NW3** £32

108 Heath St   7443 9500

*A "very good" and "friendly" Portuguese fish and seafood restaurant, regarded by some reporters as "Hampstead's bright point". / Details: 10.30 pm.*

**Le Petit Max SW11** £34 ★

Riverside Plaza, Chatfield Rd   7223 0999

*Those in search of "a superb French bistro experience" will find it "worth discovering" this "out-of-the-way" Battersea riverside spot, where "good, old-fashioned, well-priced" food is set off by Max Renzland's "welcoming" (and perhaps slightly "OTT") service. / Details: 10.30 pm; closed Sun D; no Amex; smoking in bar only.*

**Pétrus**
**The Berkeley SW1** £84 🅐★

Wilton Pl   7235 1200   4–1D

*Marcus Wareing is now fully settled in to this "pampering" year-old Knightsbridge dining room, and his "stunning" cooking – served by "unhurried" staff – is "firing on all cylinders"; a "superlative" wine list ("on which not everything is wildly-priced") remains a stand-out attraction. / Value tip: set weekday L £44 (FP). Details: www.marcuswareing.com; 10.45 pm; closed Sat L & Sun; jacket required; no smoking; booking: max 10.*

**Pham Sushie EC1** £22 ★★

155 Whitecross St   7251 6336

*"The standard of the sushi is superb", at this "tiny", "bargain" café, near the Barbican (which relocated to this site a year or two ago). / Details: 10 pm; closed Sat L & Sun; no smoking area.*

**Phoenix Bar & Grill SW15** £39

162-164 Lower Richmond Rd   8780 3131

*A new chef seems to have revitalised this Putney "favourite", where "lovely" staff serve some "splendid" Italian cooking. / Details: www.sonnys.co.uk; 11 pm; no smoking area.*

**Phoenix Palace NW1** £29 ★★

3-5 Glentworth St   7486 3515   1–1A

*"Always full of Chinese families", this Cantonese two-year-old, "tucked-away near Baker Street", provides "high-quality" cooking, and notably "fabulous" dim sum. / Details: 11.15 pm; no smoking area.*

**Pied à Terre W1** £77

34 Charlotte St   7636 1178   1–1C

*As this guide goes to press, a total post-fire revamp of David Moore's hallowed Fitzrovian is nearing completion; Shane Osborne is an exceptional chef, so let's hope the new décor provides – at last! – the setting his cooking deserves. / Value tip: set weekday L £50 (FP). Details: www.pied.a.terre.co.uk; 11 pm; closed Sat L & Sun; no smoking area; booking: max 8.*

**Ping Pong W1** £26 🅐★

45 Gt Marlborough St   7851 6969   2–2C

*This friendly newcomer, near Liberty's, offers good-value dim sum in a stylish and impressive setting, and was already deservedly busy on an early visit in June 2005; a further site, in Bayswater, has already been acquired – the first of many planned for the next few years. / Details: www.pingpongdimsum.com; midnight, Sun 10.30 pm; no smoking.*

### Pizza Metro SW11 £29     𝔸★
64 Battersea Rise   7228 3812
*"It sure helps if you speak Italian", at this "immensely popular"
and "chaotic" Battersea pizza-by-the-metre spot; since it enlarged,
some regulars feel it's "not quite as good as it was", but even so,
many reporters still tip it as "the best pizza joint in town".*
/ **Details:** 11 pm; no Amex; no smoking area.

### Pizzeria Castello SE1 £27
20 Walworth Rd   7703 2556
*"Down-to-earth" Elephant & Castle veteran, which remains
a favourite pizzeria for some reporters thanks to its "fun" style
and "reasonable prices"; (n.b. it's got no connection with the
similarly-named – and quite similar – venture at 192 Jamaica
Road, SE1).* / **Details:** 11 pm, Fri & Sat 11.30 pm; closed Sun.

### Poissonnerie de l'Avenue SW3 £53     ★
82 Sloane Ave   7589 2457   4–2C
*"Professional" – if "old-fashioned" and "rather stuffy" –
this Brompton Cross veteran particularly appeals to an "older
clientèle", for whom its "top-quality" dishes "still set the standard
in fish cooking".* / **Details:** www.poissonnerie.co.uk; 11.30 pm; closed Sun.

### Le Pont de la Tour SE1 £60
36d Shad Thames   7403 8403
*An "unbeatable location" (near Tower Bridge) and an "incredible"
wine list draw expense-accounters in droves to Conran's riverside
flagship; perhaps that's why – with its "run-of-the-mill cooking,
indifferent service and eye-watering bills" – it can seem
"astoundingly complacent".* / **Details:** www.conran.com; 11 pm; closed
Sat L.

### La Porchetta Pizzeria £23
33 Boswell St, WC1   7242 2434   1–1D
141-142 Upper St, N1   7288 2488
147 Stroud Green Rd, N4   7281 2892
74-77 Chalk Farm Rd, NW1   7267 6822
84-86 Rosebery Ave, EC1   7837 6060
*"They can hardly find plates big enough", for the "massive"
pizzas at these "noisy" and "brightly-lit", family-run Italians;
"it's hard to spend a lot of money", and "there's often a queue",
especially at the Finsbury Park original.* / **Details:** midnight,
WC1 10.30 pm; WC1 closed Sat L & Sun, N1 Mon-Thu closed L, N4 closed
weekday L, EC1 closed Sat L; no Amex; no smoking area; need 5+ to book.

### Il Portico W8 £42
277 Kensington High St   7602 6262   6–1D
*"An old-fashioned, family-run gem", by the Kensington Odeon;
the Italian food "has its ups and downs", but fans insist
"it's currently on an up".* / **Details:** www.ilportico.co.uk; 11.15 pm; closed
Sun, & Bank Holidays; mainly non-smoking.

### La Poule au Pot SW1 £43     𝔸
231 Ebury St   7730 7763   4–2D
*"For lovers and Francophiles", nowhere beats this "timeless"
Pimlico survivor – yet again reporters' romantic No 1 destination
– where "authentic" bourgeois cuisine is delivered
by "nonchalantly Gallic" staff in a "dark" and "rustic" setting
that's "ever so slightly louche".* / **Value tip:** set weekday L £29
(FP). **Details:** 11 pm.

**Princess Garden W1**  £54  ★

8 North Audley St  7493 3223  2–2A

*This rather "inscrutable" Mayfair oriental is, as ever, hailed by its small fan club as "London's best smart Chinese"; partly because it's so "expensive", though, it leaves sceptics stone cold.*
/ **Details:** www.princessgardenofmayfair.com; 11.30 pm.

**Quaglino's SW1**  £51  ✗

16 Bury St  7930 6767  2–3D

*Even by Conran standards, this "loud" and "tawdry" St James's mega-brasserie is "outrageously bad" – it offers "all the enjoyment of eating ready meals in an aircraft hangar" (and expensively, too).* / **Value tip:** set weekday L & pre-theatre £32 (FP). **Details:** www.conran.com; midnight, Fri & Sat 1 am.

**Quilon SW1**  £45  ★

41 Buckingham Gate  7821 1899  1–4B

*"A mainly business clientèle" frequents this smart dining room, off Victoria Street; it wins high praise for its "extremely helpful" staff and for its "haute-cuisine, Indian-style".* / **Value tip:** set weekday L £26 (FP). **Details:** www.thequilonrestaurant.com; 11 pm; closed Sat L & Sun; no smoking area.

**Quirinale SW1**  £46  ★★

North Ct, 1 Gt Peter St  7222 7080  1–4C

*"Streets ahead of anything else in Westminster", this rather "serious" basement operation offers "some of the best high-end Italian food in town"; service is notably "attentive", too.*
/ **Details:** 10.30 pm; closed Sat L & Sun.

**Racine SW3**  £44  ★

239 Brompton Rd
7584 4477  4–2C

*Henry Harris delivers "no culinary fireworks" – just cooking that's "robust and bursting with flavour" – at this "very Parisian" brasserie, in Knightsbridge; its huge success also owes much to its "incredibly smooth and professional" service.* / **Value tip:** set weekday L & pre-theatre £30 (FP). **Details:** 10.30 pm; no smoking area.

**Ragam W1**  £30  ★★

57 Cleveland St  7636 9098  1–1B

*"Still superb after all these years", this south Indian restaurant, by the Telecom Tower, serves "remarkable-value" dishes "to die for"; the setting is "pretty awful", though ("but not so much as to put you off").* / **Value tip:** set weekday L £16 (FP). **Details:** www.mcdosa.com; 11 pm.

**Rajasthan EC3**  £28  ★

49 Monument St  7626 1920

*"The best curry in the Square Mile" helps ensure that this City Indian is "always busy"; "very good service", too.*
/ **Details:** www.rajasthan.co.uk; 11 pm; closed Sat & Sun.

**Randall & Aubin**  £34  𝔸★

16 Brewer St, W1  7287 4447  2–2D
329-331 Fulham Rd, SW10  7823 3515  4–3B

*"A haven in the sex quartier" – the "cramped" stools at the "always-buzzing" Soho original of this mini-chain provide prime people-watching, as well as "excellent" seafood snacks; the "fun" but less funky Chelsea brasserie offers a more standard "staples" menu.* / **Details:** www.randallandaubin.co.uk; 11 pm; SW10 no smoking area; W1 no booking.

## Rani N3 £24 ★
7 Long Ln 8349 4386
*"A good-value buffet" and some "unusual" dishes contribute
to the ongoing success of this "nice" and "utterly reliable" Gujarati
vegetarian, in North Finchley. / Details: www.raniuk.com; 10 pm; D only,
ex Sun open L & D; no smoking.*

## Ranoush £25 ★
22 Brompton Rd, SW1 7235 6999 4–1D
338 Kings Rd, SW3 7352 0044 4–3C
43 Edgware Rd, W2 7723 5929 5–1D
86 Kensington High St, W8 7938 2234 4–1A
*"Good food at amazingly low prices" – not least "fantastic
shwarmas" and "fresh juices to die for" – make these "crowded"
Lebanese cafés brilliant stand-bys, especially "for a late-night
snack". / Details: www.maroush.com; midnight-2.30 am; no credit cards.*

## Ransome's Dock SW11 £44
35 Parkgate Rd 7223 1611 4–4C
*The "encyclopaedic but unintimidating" wine list crops up in over
half of the many reports on Martin Lam's "casual" but "well-
managed" Battersea fixture; "consistent" cooking and "wonderful"
outdoor tables play respectable supporting rôles.
/ Details: www.ransomesdock.co.uk; 11 pm; closed Sun D; no smoking area.*

## Rapscallion SW4 £37 𝔸
75 Venn St 7787 6555
*"Inventive" cooking and an "interesting" cocktail menu make this
"buzzy" Clapham bar a leading local destination of its type;
it's also popular for breakfast. / Details: www.therapscalliononline.com;
10.30 pm, Fri & Sat 11 pm; booking: max 6.*

## Rasa N16 £20 𝔸★★
55 Stoke Newington Church St 7249 0344
*"Worth the trip to Stokey!" – the "intriguing" south Indian veggie
dishes on offer at the "cramped" but "friendly" cradle of the Rasa
empire offer "a new taste experience". / Details: 10.30 pm, Fri & Sat
11 pm; closed weekday L; no smoking area.*

## Rasa £35 ★★
5 Charlotte St, W1 7637 0222 1–1C
6 Dering St, W1 7629 1346 2–2B
Holiday Inn Hotel, 1 Kings Cross, WC1 7833 9787
56 Stoke Newington Church St, N16 7249 1340
*The "plate-lickingly good" Keralan cuisine at these spin-off
ventures is impressively faithful to that at the famed Stoke
Newington original (see also); Dering Street and N16
(Travancore) serve meat, while Charlotte Street (Samudra) also
offers some "gorgeous" seafood dishes.
/ Details: www.rasarestaurants.com; 10.45 pm; N16 Mon-Thu closed L, W1 closed
Sun L; N16 no smoking area.*

## Rasoi Vineet Bhatia SW3 £70 ★★
10 Lincoln St 7225 1881 4–2D
*An "extraordinary range of subtle flavours" leads reporters on a
"rare journey of gastronomic discovery" when they visit Vineet
Bhatia's "haute Indian" yearling, in a Chelsea townhouse; the high
prices make it "a rare treat", though, and the setting is on the
"cramped" side. / Details: www.vineetbhatia.com; 10.30 pm; closed Sat L &
Sun; no smoking.*

**The Real Greek N1** £38

15 Hoxton Market   7739 8212

*Many reporters perceive an ongoing "slacking-off" at this "lively" Hoxton fixture – the "Greek-with-a-twist" cooking here was once outstanding, but now it's just "dull", and service is so-so in the extreme. / Details: www.therealgreek.com; 10.30 pm; closed Sun; no Amex.*


**Rebato's SW8** £27   A★

169 South Lambeth Rd   7735 6388

*"Magic, such a find"; this "Vauxhall stalwart" offers "a great buzzing atmosphere" and "unbeatably friendly service", plus "real" Spanish food – both in the tapas bar, and the amusingly cheesy restaurant. / Details: www.rebatos.com; 10.45 pm; closed Sat L & Sun.*


**Red Fort W1** £47   ★

77 Dean St   7437 2525   3–2A

*"Modern minimalist decor, a water feature and a groovy basement bar" set the tone at this Soho subcontinental veteran, which was revamped a couple of years ago; its "delicious" cooking is currently on a high, but even fans find it "fully priced". / Details: www.redfort.co.uk; 11 pm; closed Sat L & Sun L.*


**Redmond's SW14** £45   ★

170 Upper Richmond Rd West   8878 1922

*"Courteous and friendly service" is a hallmark of this "slightly old-fashioned" East Sheen "favourite"; other attractions include "consistently high-quality" food and a "short but fine" selection of wines. / Value tip: set pre-theatre £27 (FP). Details: www.redmonds.org.uk; 10 pm; D only, ex Sun L; no Amex; no smoking.*


**Rhodes 24 EC2** £59   A★

25 Old Broad St   7877 7703

*"Stunning" views and "wonderful" British classic dishes (from a "short" menu) make Gary Rhodes's City eyrie "more than just a business haunt"; rents can't be cheap up on the 24th floor, so it's all the more pleasing how "well-spaced" the tables are. / Details: www.garyrhodes.co.uk; 9 pm; closed Sat & Sun; booking essential.*


**Rick's Café SW17** £31   A★

122 Mitcham Rd   8767 5219

*"Just what you want from a local" – this "busy and cramped" outfit ("Tooting's top place!", say fans) is always "buzzing", and serves an "adventurous" menu prepared to a "surprisingly good" standard. / Details: 11 pm; no Amex; no smoking area.*


**The Ritz W1** £89   A

150 Piccadilly   7493 8181   2–4C

*Promoters of this "staggeringly beautiful" Louis XVI chamber say new chef John Williams is leading an "inspirational revolution" there; service is certainly more "motivated" these days, but the "traditional" cuisine still has a way to go to banish recollections of the "tragic" standards of former years. / Value tip: set weekday L & pre-theatre £60 (FP). Details: www.theritzlondon.com; 11.30 pm; jacket & tie required; no smoking.*

### The River Café W6 £60 ★
Thames Wharf, Rainville Rd 7386 4200 6–2C
*This Thames-side legend, in the backstreets of Hammersmith (and with a "beautiful" summer terrace), achieved renewed acclaim this year for its "flavour-packed" Italian cooking, using "the finest seasonal ingredients"; the question remains, though: "how do they get away with such mind-blowing prices?"*
/ **Details:** www.rivercafe.co.uk; 9 pm; closed Sun D; no smoking.

### The Rivington Grill Bar Deli EC2 £44 ★
28-30 Rivington St 7729 7053
*A "cool place in cool Shoreditch", where the "British classic" fare – including pies and fish-fingers – is "not cheap" but "fulfills its promise".* / **Details:** www.rivingtongrill.co.uk; 11 pm.

### Rocket £30 🄐
4-6 Lancashire Ct, W1 7629 2889 2–2B
Putney Wharf, Brewhouse St, SW15 8789 7875
*It's hard not to be won over by these "very buzzy" joints, where you can "catch up with friends" over a drink or some "super" pizza or a "really nice salad"; Mayfair is "fairly-priced for somewhere so central" – Putney has "great Thames views".*
/ **Details:** www.rocketrestaurants.co.uk; 10.45 pm; W1 closed Sun; no smoking area.

### Rosemary Lane E1 £41 ★
61 Royal Mint St 7481 2602
*Though "cheerlessly-located", this East End pub-conversion is hailed by most (if not quite all) reporters as a "gem", where Christina Anghelescu's cooking shows "good attention to detail".*
/ **Details:** www.rosemarylane.btinternet.co.uk; 10 pm; closed Sat L & Sun.

### Roussillon SW1 £62 ★★
16 St Barnabas St 7730 5550 4–2D
*Alexis Gauthier's "flamboyant but thoughtful" Gallic cuisine may be well and truly "in the top tier", but this Pimlico backstreet "gem" – with its "fantastic" wine and "wonderful" service – is still known mainly "by foodies, rather than the fashionable".*
/ **Details:** www.roussillon.co.uk; 10.30 pm; closed Mon L, Sat L & Sun; no smoking area.

### Rules WC2 £53 🄐
35 Maiden Ln 7836 5314 3–3D
*"Irresistible for entertaining foreign guests" – London's oldest restaurant (1798) is a "unique" destination which generally satisfies the natives too; the meaty English cuisine (with much game) is "good", but it's the wonderful Victorian interior which "really shines".* / **Details:** www.rules.co.uk; 11.30 pm; no smoking.

### Rusticana W1 £31
27 Frith St 7439 8900 3–3A
*"A good find in Soho" – a "great-value", family-run corner Italian, with notably "friendly" service; it remains curiously little-known.*
/ **Details:** www.rusticanasoho.co.uk; 11.15 pm; no smoking area.

### Sabor N1 £32 🄐★
108 Essex Rd
7226 5551

*It's hard not to be won over by the "very enthusiastic" and "well-informed" service at this new Islington Latin American... especially when it offers "interesting" food at "unfathomably low" prices!* / **Details:** www.sabor.co.uk; 10.45 pm.

**Sagar W6**  £23  ★★

157 King St  8741 8563  6–2C

*"A surprise find" – even if it looks "sterile", this simple Hammersmith café produces "wonderful, intensely-flavoured" veggie dishes that are among the best south Indian food in town; staff are "always charming", too.* / **Details:** *10.45 pm; no smoking area.*


**St John EC1**  £44  ★★

26 St John St  7251 0848

*Fergus Henderson is wooing ever more reporters to his "unique" Smithfield ex-smokehouse – "a haven of British culinary lore" – which serves "terrific" and unusual dishes (in which offal often figures); the bright white interior is "beautifully utilitarian" to some, but "cold and clinical" to others.* / **Details:** *www.stjohnrestaurant.com; 11 pm; closed Sat L & Sun; no smoking area.*


**St John Bread & Wine E1**  £40  ★

94-96 Commercial St  7247 8724

*"Apparently simple" English dishes from "truly outstanding" ingredients can make it an "exciting culinary experience" to visit this "canteen-like" Spitalfields spin-off from St John; "perfect bacon sarnies" and "stunning Eccles cakes" rated particular mention.* / **Details:** *www.stjohnbreadandwine.com; 10.30 pm; closed Sun D; need 10+ to book..*


**St Johns N19**  £33  Ⓐ★

91 Junction Rd  7272 1587

*The "comfortably faded grandeur" of the "huge dining hall" of this Archway gastropub can come as a "delightful surprise" to first-timers – so can the "well-cooked" grub (from a "regularly-changing blackboard menu") and the "incredibly welcoming" staff.* / **Details:** *11 pm, Sun 9.30 pm; closed Mon L; booking: max 12.*


**Le Saint Julien EC1**  £30

62-63 Long Ln  7796 4550

*It always astonishes us how few authentic and straightforward Gallic brasseries there are in London, so let's hope for more arrivals like this good all-round Smithfield newcomer (which would make a useful destination for a low-key business lunch).* / **Details:** *10.15 pm; closed Sat L & Sun.*


**St Moritz W1**  £40  Ⓐ★

161 Wardour St  7734 3324  2–1D

*It may look like a tourist trap, but this Soho veteran – with its "homely" and "cosy" chalet décor – is a "romantic" spot, serving sound Swiss cooking; highlights include the "great, if pricey, fondue", and some "fantastic Swiss wines".* / **Details:** *www.stmoritz-restaurant.co.uk; 11.30 pm; closed Sat L & Sun.*


**Sale e Pepe SW1**  £45

9-15 Pavilion Rd  7235 0098  4–1D

*"If you don't mind sitting in someone else's lap", this "real '70s trattoria survivor", near Harrods, is "always a laugh"; the food is "OK", too.* / **Details:** *11.30 pm; closed Sun.*

**Salt Yard W1**  £31 ★★
54 Goodge St
7637 0657 1–1B
*"Fantastic" tapas (Italian, as well as Spanish) and "interesting"*
*wines – all at "good-value" prices – have helped make*
*an "exciting" start for this plain but "buzzy" Fitzrovia newcomer.*
*/ Details: 11 pm; closed Sat L & Sun; no smoking.*

**Sardo W1** £43 ★
45 Grafton Way 7387 2521 1–1B
*"Great" and "gutsy" Sardinian fare is helping to win growing*
*acclaim for this "delightful family-run restaurant, tucked-away*
*in north Fitzrovia"; it's usually "full of doctors from UCH, plotting*
*against the management". / Details: www.sardo-restaurant.com; 11 pm;*
*closed Sat L & Sun; no smoking area.*

**Sardo Canale NW1** £40
42 Gloucester Ave 7722 2800
*Sardinian cooking "with gusto" has won instant applause for this*
*"airy", year-old Primrose Hill sibling to Sardo; it still doesn't*
*impress everyone, though, with "small" portions attracting*
*particular flak. / Details: www.sardocanale.com; 10 pm; closed Mon L;*
*no smoking area.*

**Sargasso Sea N21** £45 Ⓐ★
10 Station Rd 8360 0990
*"West End ambience and quality" have made this suburban five-*
*year-old world-famous in Winchmore Hill; it serves "excellent"*
*(if quite "pricey") seafood in a "contemporary" setting;*
*"book early". / Value tip: set weekday L £23 (FP), set Sun L £30*
*(FP). Details: www.sargassosea.co.uk; 10.30 pm; closed Mon, Tue L, Wed L, Sat L &*
*Sun D.*

**Sarkhel's** £28 ★
199 Upper Richmond Road West, SW14 8876 6220
*199 Replingham Rd, SW18 8870 1483*
*Udit Sarkhel's "stunning" food (and his "friendly" staff) have won*
*a London-wide reputation for his Southfields curry house; a new*
*more "intimate" branch opened in East Sheen last winter –*
*one early reporter found it "still with some shaking down to do".*
*/ Details: www.sarkhels.com; 10.30 pm; closed Mon; no Amex.*

**Sarracino NW6** £32 ★
186 Broadhurst Gdns 7372 5889
*A "lovely" West Hampstead Italian, applauded for its "tasty"*
*pasta and "fabulous" pizzas. / Details: 11 pm; closed weekday*
*L; no smoking area.*

**Savoy Grill**
**Savoy Hotel WC2** £77
Strand 7592 1600 3–3D
*Marcus Wareing "has improved the food", at this famous power*
*scene, making it again a "perfect all-rounder for business"; ratings*
*waned this year, though, putting the place in line with the good-*
*but-no-more standards which now characterise most of the*
*Ramsay empire. / Value tip: set weekday L & pre-theatre £50 (FP), set Sun L*
*£44 (FP). Details: www.marcuswareing.com; 11 pm; jacket required; no smoking;*
*booking: max 12.*

### Scalini SW3 £54 A★
1-3 Walton St 7225 2301 4–2C
*"Bellissimo" – this "loud", "lively" and "cosmopolitan"*
*Knightsbridge spot is "your classic, full-on Italian job"; with its*
*"happy" and "consistent" charms, it is – for many reporters –*
*simply "the best". / Details: 11.45 pm.*

### Shampers W1 £34 A
4 Kingly St 7437 1692 2–2D
*"Always welcoming", this "dependable" Soho-fringe wine bar "still*
*has the same old '70s atmosphere", and still dishes up fare that's*
*"simple", but generally "well-executed". / Details: 10.45 pm; closed Sun*
*(& Sat in Aug).*

### Shanghai E8 £26 ★
41 Kingsland High St 7254 2878
*This striking former Dalston pie & eel shop has been "lovingly*
*restored" and turned into this "pretty good" oriental (where dim*
*sum is a speciality); "other than sometimes ear-splitting Karaoke,*
*it's a perfect local". / Details: www.wengwahgroup.com; 10.45 pm.*

### J Sheekey WC2 £55 A★★
28-32 St Martin's Ct 7240 2565 3–3B
*This "olde-worlde" star-magnet once again inspired more*
*commentary than anywhere else in town, thanks to its "divine"*
*fish, and the "exciting buzz" that permeates its "snug"*
*Theatreland premises – "the only problem is getting in".*
*/ Details: www.caprice-holdings.co.uk; midnight.*

### Shogun W1 £50 ★★
Adam's Row 7493 1255 2–3A
*"One of the better-priced top Japanese" – this estimable Mayfair*
*basement "gem" still offers "excellent" food, and retains its "loyal*
*expat following". / Details: 11 pm; D only, closed Mon.*

### Signor Sassi SW1 £50 A
14 Knightsbridge Grn 7584 2277 4–1D
*"Entertaining" staff help create a "memorable" experience at this*
*"buzzy" Knightsbridge Italian; the food is not the main thing,*
*but is consistently good nonetheless. / Details: 11.30 pm; closed Sun.*

### Simpsons-in-the-Strand WC2 £56
100 Strand 7836 9112 3–3D
*For "classic British old style", this roast beef "bastion" may*
*be unrivalled, but – aside from the "wonderful, full works*
*breakfast" – its lacklustre cooking has caused it to fall into*
*relative obscurity in recent years; new management (Fairmont*
*Hotels) took over in 2005, though, so let's hope that change*
*is afoot... / Value tip: set always available £37*
*(FP). Details: www.simpsons-in-the-strand.com; 10.45 pm, Sun 9 pm; no jeans*
*or trainers.*

### Singapore Garden NW6 £33
83-83a Fairfax Rd 7328 5314
*A long-time reputation for "authentic" Singaporean/Malay cuisine*
*ensures that this "suburban"-style Swiss Cottage spot is usually*
*"packed"; declining ratings, however, support those who feel*
*it "has deteriorated" in recent times. / Value tip: set weekday L £20*
*(FP). Details: 10.45 pm.*

**(Gallery)**
**Sketch W1** £60 ✗

9 Conduit St   0870 777 4488   2–2C

*"Go to be seen, not to eat" and you may enjoy a visit to this "'70s"-sci-fi-style "scene", in Mayfair; prices for the "poncy" food, though, are "from another planet", and the service is "from Mars". / **Details:** www.sketch.uk.com; 10.30 pm; D only, closed Sun; booking: max 12.*


**(Ground Floor)**
**Smiths of Smithfield EC1** £23 🄰

67-77 Charterhouse St   7251 7997

*"What better place for a hazy start to Sunday morning" than this large and "buzzing" bar, which is renowned for its "bacon butties" and other "perfect" breakfast fare; service, though, is sometimes "really terrible" (and the non-breakfast fare is much less of an attraction). / **Details:** www.smithsofsmithfield.co.uk; L only.*


**(Top Floor)**
**Smiths of Smithfield EC1** £56 🄰

67-77 Charterhouse St   7251 7950

*"The best steak in London" and "spectacular City views" – plus, in summer, a "great" terrace – make this top-floor Smithfield dining room an "impressive place to take clients"; those paying their own way, however, can find it "very expensive" for what it is. / **Value tip:** set Sun L £40 (FP). **Details:** www.smithsofsmithfield.co.uk; 10.45 pm; closed Sat L; booking: max 10.*


**Snows on the Green W6** £36

166 Shepherd's Bush Rd   7603 2142   6–1C

*"For unpretentious food at reasonable prices", Sebastian Snow's Brook Green fixture (est. 1991) offers "all you could want from a local"; it's quite "kind on the wallet", too. / **Details:** www.snowsonthegreen.co.uk; 10.45 pm; closed Sat L & Sun.*


**Sophie's Steakhouse SW10** £34 🄰

311-313 Fulham Rd   7352 0088   4–3B

*"The bar is a lively place to wait for a table" – there are no reservations – at this "young" and "always-overcrowded" joint on the Chelsea 'Beach', which serves up "good-value" grills and burgers, in a "party" atmosphere. / **Value tip:** set weekday L £23 (FP). **Details:** www.sophiessteakhouse.com; 11.45 pm; no booking.*


**Sotheby's Café W1** £39 🄰★

34 New Bond St   7293 5077   2–2C

*"For a quick and delicious lunch" in Mayfair, this "elegant", small café – off the foyer of the auction house – is hard to beat; it offers "simple" but "interesting" dishes, and "good people-watching", too. / **Details:** www.sothebys.com; L only, closed Sat & Sun; no smoking.*


**Le Soufflé**
**Inter-Continental Hotel W1** £68 ★

1 Hamilton Pl   7318 8577   2–4A

*Jeff Haviland's "outstanding modern cuisine" is really beginning to "find its way", say fans of this "comfortable" Mayfair "haven", which deserves to be better known; service is "exemplary", too. / **Value tip:** set weekday L £44 (FP). **Details:** www.london.interconti.com; 10.30 pm, Sat 11.15 pm; closed Mon, Sat L & Sun; no smoking area; booking: max 12.*

## South EC2 £34 ★

128 Curtain Rd 7729 4452
*"Simple French dishes, expertly prepared"* make this Shoreditch bistro well worth remembering (especially at lunchtime); if only they could sort out the *"cold"* ambience... / **Details:** 10.30 pm; closed Sun; no Amex; no smoking area.

## Spread Eagle SE10 £44 A

1-2 Stockwell St 8853 2333
*"So cosy and romantic"*, this *"beautiful"* old Greenwich inn offers *"rather rich"* Gallic cooking in a *"professional"* (*"old-fashioned"*) manner. / **Details:** www.spreadeagle.org; 10.30 pm; no Amex; no smoking area.

## The Square W1 £76 ★

6-10 Bruton St 7495 7100 2–2C
Philip Howard realises his *"creative"* cooking *"with aplomb"*, at this *"polished"* Mayfair business-favourite (and the *"substantial"* wine list would gladden the heart of any wine buff); the place looks rather like a *"swanky conference room"* (but a 'new look' is apparently on the cards).
/ **Details:** www.squarerestaurant.com; 10.45 pm; closed Sat L & Sun L.

## Sree Krishna SW17 £19 ★★

192-194 Tooting High St 8672 4250
*"Still excellent after all these years"*, this *"dreary"*-looking Tooting veteran is well worth seeking out for its *"wonderful, fresh and inventive"* south Indian cooking (including meat dishes).
/ **Details:** 10.45 pm, Fri & Sat midnight; no smoking area.

## Sri Thai Soho W1 £37 ★

16 Old Compton St 7434 3544 3–2A
A handy location (*"at the less cruisy end of Old Compton Street"*) contributes to the charm of this long-established Soho Thai, and its *"above-average"* cuisine offers some *"fabulous"* flavours.
/ **Details:** www.orientalrestaurantgroup.co.uk; 11 pm; closed Sun L; no smoking area.

## Stratford's W8 £38 ★

7 Stratford Rd 7937 6388 4–2A
*"A best-kept secret"* – this *"charmingly old-fashioned"* Kensington backwater seafood-specialist may have a slightly *"quiet"* (*"teashop"*) ambience, but it offers *"individual"* service, and *"very good food at reasonable prices"*. / **Value tip:** set D £25 (FP). **Details:** www.stratfords-restaurant.com; 11.30 pm.

## Sumosan W1 £60 ★★

26b Albemarle St
7495 5999 2–3C
Food *"on a par with Nobu's"* hasn't won this minimalist Mayfair Japanese nearly the following it deserves; it would help if they improved the *"sterile"* décor. / **Details:** www.sumosan.com; 11.30 pm; closed Sun L; no smoking area.

## La Superba NW1 £30

17 Princess Rd 7483 0192
The *"unpretentious"* charms of the Primrose Hill Italian formerly called Vegia Zena – with its *"rustic"* cuisine, and its *"secluded"* garden – seem little changed by the adoption of a new name; *"the menu has a bit less choice, but the restaurant is as good as ever"*. / **Details:** 11 pm.

### Sushi-Hiro W5 £25 ★★
1 Station Pde 8896 3175
*"Always chock full of Japanese expats", this small and "clinical"-looking spot, near Ealing Common, is a real "rarity"; its "beautifully fresh sushi" (at "really cheap prices") are hailed – by a number of oriental reporters – as arguably "the best in London".* / **Details:** 9 pm; no credit cards.

### Sushi-Say NW2 £33 ★
33b Walm Ln 8459 7512
*"A wonderful little Japanese oasis in not very epicurean Willesden" – this "authentic" ten-year-old offers "very fresh" sushi and sashimi, with "charming" service that helps to enliven the "basic" setting.* / **Details:** 10.30 pm; closed Mon, Tue-Fri D only, Sat & Sun open L & D; no smoking.

### The Swan W4 £33 𝔸★
119 Acton Ln 8994 8262 6–1A
*"Great, if you're lucky enough to get a table" – this "excellent little gastropub, on the Chiswick/Acton border" has "interesting" food, "diverse" wine, and "service that stays on top of its game"; "the garden is heaven in summer".* / **Details:** 10.30 pm; closed weekday L; no Amex; no booking.

### Sweetings EC4 £43 𝔸★
39 Queen Victoria St 7248 3062
*It may be "an anachronism" but "they've got the basics right", at this "immortal" City "institution" – a "quaint" Victorian parlour serving fish and seafood of "outstanding quality".* / **Details:** L only, closed Sat & Sun; no booking.

### Talad Thai SW15 £25 ★
320 Upper Richmond Rd 8789 8084
*"Great authentic Thai food" – and "at bargain prices", too – makes this café-cum-supermarket a top Putney destination; the queue, though, can be "horrible".* / **Details:** 10.30 pm; no Amex; no smoking.

### Taman gang W1 £71 𝔸
141 Park Ln 7518 3160 1–2A
*"Sexy" décor helps create an "intimate but cool" vibe at this swanky Mayfair basement oriental; the food is "better than you'd expect" for such a "footballer-tastic" venue, but it can also seem "incredibly pricey" for what it is.* / **Details:** www.tamangang.com; 11.30 pm; closed Sun; booking: max 6.

### Tamarind W1 £52 ★
20 Queen St 7629 3561 2–3B
*"One of the first posh Indians", and still one of the best – this "sophisticated" Mayfair basement has many fans, thanks to Alfred Pasad's "fantastic" and "sensitively-spiced" subcontinental dishes (with a "twist").* / **Value tip:** set weekday L & Sun L £33 (FP). **Details:** www.tamarindrestaurant.com; 11.15 pm; closed Sat L.

### Tandoori Nights SE22 £25 𝔸★★
73 Lordship Ln 8299 4077
*Local reporters in particular are unstinting in their praises for this "excellent" and "inexpensive" East Dulwich curry house, where the food is "fresh" and "fabulous", and service "friendly" and "professional".* / **Details:** www.tandoorinights.co.uk; 11.30 pm; closed weekday L & Sat L; no smoking area.

**(Tapa Room)**
**The Providores W1**  £32  A★

109 Marylebone High St  7935 6175  1–1A
*You may have to queue to enjoy "the best light lunch in town",
at this "interesting" Marylebone café/bar – its "terrific" weekend
brunches have a particular following.* / **Details:** www.theprovidores.co.uk;
10.30 pm; no smoking.

**Tapas Brindisa SE1**  £30  A★

18-20 Southwark St  7357 8880
*This simple newcomer by Borough Market is run by the
eponymous Spanish food importers, and has won instant foodie
raves for its "lovely" tapas (using the "outstanding" ingredients
you'd hope for); it's "not cheap", though, and "tables are close".*
/ **Details:** 11 pm; closed Sun L; no Amex; no smoking in dining room.

**Tas**  £26

33 The Cut, SE1  7928 2111
72 Borough High St, SE1  7403 7200
*"Dependable" mezze and other dishes at "great-value" prices
make these "hustling and bustling" Turkish establishments
"invaluable" stand-bys; they're especially suited to large parties
on a budget.* / **Details:** www.tasrestaurant.com; 11.30 pm; no smoking area.

**Tas Pide**  £29  A

20-22 New Globe Walk, SE1  7928 3300
37 Farringdon Rd, EC1  7430 9721
*These notably "welcoming" and "cosy" Turkish restaurants dish
up "flavoursome" dishes at prices that represent "impressive
value-for-money"; they also feature "something different" – pide is
Anatolian flat-bread 'pizza'.* / **Details:** www.tasrestaurant.com; 11.30 pm.

**Tatsuso EC2**  £80  ★

32 Broadgate Circle  7638 5863
*"Make sure you're not paying", if you visit this "outstanding" –
but very "corporate" – City Japanese, where "the freshest and
best sushi and sashimi" and "top-quality" teppan-yaki come
at "absurd" prices; the basement is a bit "grim".* / **Details:** 9.45 pm;
closed Sat & Sun; no smoking area.

**Tawana W2**  £29  ★

3 Westbourne Grove  7229 3785  5–1C
*"Staple and authentic dishes" make this Bayswater Thai veteran
(near Queensway) a handy stand-by; it has "no atmosphere"
though.* / **Details:** www.tawana.co.uk; 11 pm.

**Teca W1**  £51  ★

54 Brooks Mews  7495 4774  2–2B
*"Out-of-the-way" (by Mayfair standards), this "quiet", modern
Italian has never found the fame its "sophisticated" cooking,
distinctive wine list, and "polished" service deserve; its "anodyne"
interior doesn't help.* / **Details:** www.atozrestaurants.com; 10.30 pm; closed
Sat L & Sun.

**Tendido Cero SW5**  £28  A★

174 Old Brompton Rd  7370 3685  4–2B
*"Fabulous tapas, wonderful presentation and BYO... and all
on the fringe of South Kensington!" – that's the deal at this
"lively" and "intimate" sibling to Cambio de Tercio (opposite).*
/ **Details:** 11 pm; no credit cards.

**sign up for the survey at www.hardens.com**

**Tentazioni SE1**  £49  ★

2 Mill St   7237 1100

*"Tucked-away from the madding crowd", this quirky Italian
(five minutes from Butler's Wharf) is winning renewed support
as an "under-rated" location, with "excellent", genuine cooking,
"interesting" wine and "enthusiastic" service; "the only thing
lacking on occasion is diners".* / **Details:** *www.tentazioni.co.uk; 10.45 pm;
closed Mon L, Sat L & Sun.*


**Thai on the River SW11**  £40  A

2 Lombard Rd   7924 6090   4–4B

*Part of the team from SW10's Thai on the River (RIP) has crossed
the Thames to the old Battersea premises of La Na Thai (RIP);
the new set-up offers "really good" (if "pricey") dishes in a
"beautiful" riverside setting; (n.b. a rival spin-off has also opened
under the same name, at 92-94 Waterford Road – no reports
as yet).* / **Details:** *www.thaiontheriver.com; 11 pm.*


**Thailand SE14**  £26  ★★

15 Lewisham Way   8691 4040

*"Outstanding" Thai/Laotian cooking has long been acclaimed
at this "unassuming" Lewisham "gem", run by a "pleasant"
husband (Scottish) and wife (Laotian) team; it also boasts
"an excellent selection of malt whiskies".* / **Details:** *11.30 pm; no Amex;
no smoking.*


**The Thatched House W6**  £31  A

115 Dalling Rd   8748 6174   6–1B

*There's some "surprisingly good", if simple, food to be had –
and in "huge portions" – at this lesser-known Hammersmith
gastropub, which boasts a "bubbly" atmosphere and a brilliant
garden.* / **Details:** *www.thatchedhouse.com; 10 pm; no Amex; no smoking area.*


**Toff's N10**  £27  ★

38 Muswell Hill Broadway   8883 8656

*A "very crowded" and "wonderfully friendly" Muswell Hill
institution, where many north Londoners insist you get
"the capital's best fish 'n' chips".* / **Details:** *10 pm; closed Sun; no smoking
area; no booking, Sat.*


**Tom Aikens SW3**  £77

43 Elystan St   7584 2003   4–2C

*Most reporters are "blown away" by the cooking at Tom Aikens's
much-fêted Chelsea two-year-old, lauding "exquisite
combinations" that look "worthy of an art gallery"; there are
increasing concerns, though, about "too much 'going on' on the
plate" – "I couldn't find my food for foams, jellies and mousses!"*
/ **Value tip:** *set weekday L £42 (FP).* **Details:** *www.tomaikens.co.uk; 11 pm; closed
Sat & Sun; no smoking; booking: max 6.*


**Tom's W11**  £26

226 Westbourne Grove   7221 8818   5–1B

*"If you're willing to wait in line, you get the best brunch in town",
say fans of Tom Conran's "cramped" and "pricey" deli/café
favourite, in the heart of Notting Hill.* / **Details:** *L only; no Amex;
no smoking; no booking.*

**Toto's SW1**                          £60          A★

Lennox Gardens Mews   7589 0075   4–2C

A "dreamy" Knightsbridge mews setting and "excellent" staff help
make this glamorous Italian a firm "favourite" for some reporters
(and one that's "perfect for a date", probably of a more mature
sort); prices can seem "stupendous", but the food is usually hailed
as "delicious". / **Value tip:** set weekday L £35 (FP). **Details:** 11 pm.


**Les Trois Garçons E1**                £63          A

1 Club Row   7613 1924

An "amazing camp interior" (complete with "stuffed animals
wearing jewellery") pulls in punters by the limo-load to this
"eccentric" but "seductive" East End pub-conversion; its "totally
overpriced" Gallic cuisine is rather beside the point. / **Value tip:** set
D £46 (FP). **Details:** www.lestroisgarcons.com; 10.30 pm; D only, closed Sun.


**La Trompette W4**                     £48          A★★

5-7 Devonshire Rd
8747 1836   6–2A

"Lucky Chiswick residents" have "west London's best restaurant"
in one of their backstreets – it mixes "memorable" modern
French cuisine, with "intelligent" service, "stylish" décor and
an "extensive" wine list; the chef recently moved on to the
Dorchester – let's hope for a smooth succession!
/ **Details:** www.latrompette.co.uk; 11 pm; no smoking; booking: max 6


**La Trouvaille W1**                    £43          A

12a Newburgh St   7287 8488   2–2C

"Like being whisked to Paris for the evening"; "passionate" service
contributes much to the "intimate" and "quirky" charms of this
candlelit Soho bistro, where "unfussy" cooking comes
at "reasonable" prices. / **Details:** www.trouvaille.co.uk; 11 pm; closed Sun.


**Tsunami SW4**                         £35          ★★

5-7 Voltaire Rd
7978 1610

"The location's odd, but who's complaining" given the
"sensational" ("especially for the money"), "Nobu-esque" cooking
at this "startling" Clapham oriental; "…and not a pretentious
wannabe in sight". / **Details:** www.tsunamirestaurant.co.uk; 11 pm,
Sat 11.30 pm; D only, closed Sun; no smoking area.


**Tugga SW3**                           £39          A

312-314 King's Rd   7351 0101   4–3C

London's only trendy Portuguese – this new Chelsea
bar/restaurant boasts a lot of style (from the man who did Paris's
Buddha Bar); we thought the food pleasant rather than
spectacular on our May 2005 visit, but service tries hard.
/ **Details:** www.tugga.com; 10.30 pm.


**Two Brothers N3**                     £25          ★

297-303 Regent's Park Rd   8346 0469

"It IS worth the queue", for this "deserving North London
stalwart", whose "wonderful fresh fish and chips" are hailed
by many as "the best in town". / **Details:** www.twobrothers.co.uk;
10.15 pm; closed Mon & Sun; no smoking at D; no booking at D.


**sign up for the survey at www.hardens.com**

## Ubon E14 £80 ★

34 Westferry Circus   7719 7800
*You don't just get "Nobu food minus the waiting list", at its less hip Canary Wharf sibling – the room itself (with its "cracking Thames-views") is "more attractive than the Park Lane original"; prices are equally "outrageous". / Details: www.noburestaurants.com; 10.15 pm; closed Sat L & Sun; no smoking.*

## Uli W11 £29 🅰★

16 All Saints Rd   7727 7511   5–1B
*"The friendliest host in London" adds an extra dimension to this "perfect" Notting Hill local, which serves an "excellent mixed bag of oriental dishes". / Details: www.uli-oriental.co.uk; 11 pm; D only, closed Sun; no Amex.*

## Umu W1 £100

14-16 Bruton Pl   7499 8881   2–2C
*A few cognoscenti eulogise the "authentic Kyoto cooking" ("with truly the best ingredients") at this "luxurious" Mayfair newcomer; even they concede prices are "steep", though, and most reporters find that the "extortionate" bill – and "suffocating" service – mar the whole experience. / **Value tip:** set weekday L £53 (FP). **Details:** www.umurestaurant.com; 11 pm; closed Sun; no smoking; booking: max 14.*

## Le Vacherin W4 £38 ★

76 South Pde   8742 2121   6–1A
*"Terrific French country cuisine", served in a very "authentic" style, has already won a more-than-local fan club for this "excellent neighbourhood spot" – "a great find in a grim bit of Chiswick". / Details: www.levacherin.co.uk; 10.30 pm; closed Mon L; no Amex; no smoking.*

## The Vale W9 £34 ★

99 Chippenham Rd   7266 0990
*"What every good local should be like" – this Maida Hill stalwart offers a "simple, but interesting" menu that's "very good value-for-money"; the service is "always friendly", too. / Details: 11 pm; closed Mon L, Sat L & Sun D; no Amex; no smoking area.*

## Vama SW10 £40 ★★

438 King's Rd   7351 4118   4–3B
*"Tantalising", "light" dishes make this very popular Chelsea "jewel" one of "the most 'authentic' of the contemporary curry houses". / Details: www.vama.co.uk; 11 pm.*

## Vasco & Piero's Pavilion W1 £42 ★

15 Poland St   7437 8774   2–1D
*"Friendly staff with a personal touch" add much to the slightly "eccentric" appeal of this Soho "stalwart", which "feels like someone's living room" ("in a good way"); its "honest" Italian cooking is "good value", too. / Details: www.vascosfood.com; 11 pm; closed Sat L & Sun.*

## El Vergel SE1 £16 🅰★★

8 Lant St   7357 0057
*"Unsurpassed" Latin American fare – with "terrific flavours and freshness", and at "knockdown" prices – makes this hidden Borough gem an "absolutely wonderful" light lunch venue; "it's just a crying shame they aren't open evenings or weekends". / Details: www.elvergel.co.uk; breakfast & L only, closed Sat & Sun; no credit cards; no smoking.*

**sign up for the survey at www.hardens.com**

## Vertigo
### Tower 42 EC2 £46     Ⓐ
20-25 Old Broad St    7877 7842
*"What a place! – shame about the food"; "fantastic views"
of "the sun setting over St Paul's"* help make the 42nd floor of the
former NatWest tower *"an excellent spot to strike a deal"* – be it
of a business or romantic nature. / **Details:** www.vertigo42.co.uk;
9.15 pm; closed Sat & Sun; booking essential.

## Vijay NW6 £28    ★★
49 Willesden Ln    7328 1087
*"Brilliant south Indian food"* (at *"very low prices"*) and *"really
friendly"* service combine to make this *"low-key"* Kilburn curry
house an *"unbeatable-value"* destination. / **Details:** 10.45 pm, Fri & Sat
11.45 pm.

## Vivat Bacchus EC4 £43
47 Farringdon St    7353 2648
*"A treat for oenophiles"* – this City-fringe basement offers
a distinctive, business-friendly formula which mixes *"phenomenal"*
wine (*"with a South African bent"*) with *"not-stunning-but-good"*
food and *"superb"* cheese (chosen in an *"impressive, walk-in
room"*); notably *"warm and attentive"* service enlivens the plain
setting. / **Value tip:** set weekday L £28 (FP). **Details:** www.vivatbacchus.co.uk;
9.30 pm; closed Sat & Sun.

## Vrisaki N22 £29    ★
73 Myddleton Rd    8889 8760
The *"mega-mezze"* – *"a huge variety of dishes, in leisurely
procession"* – is the culinary star turn at this *"charmingly tacky"*
Bounds Green taverna; *"don't even try to eat most of the cold
starters, or you'll run out of steam long before the end"*.
/ **Details:** midnight; closed Sun.

## Wapping Food E1 £46    Ⓐ
Wapping Power Station, Wapping Wall    7680 2080
A *"bizarre"*, *"über-cool"* setting – in a former hydraulic power
station – makes this *"amazing"* Wapping spot quite
a *"destination"*; a wine list that *"challenges pre-conceptions about
Australia"* is a further plus, and it's complemented by food *"which
varies from average to excellent"*. / **Details:** 10.30 pm; closed Sun D.

## The Wells NW3 £41
30 Well Walk    7794 3785
A *"lovely"* dining room, overlooking the Heath, helps underpin the
high popularity of this *"stylish"* Hampstead gastropub (which
is *"more a restaurant"*, really); the food, however – which started
off here so well – *"slipped"* further this year. / **Value tip:** set weekday L
£29 (FP). **Details:** www.thewellshampstead.co.uk; 10.15 pm; booking: max 8.

## Weng Wah House NW3 £30
240 Haverstock Hill    7794 5123
Belsize Park's long-established *"local-favourite"* Chinese
is *"particularly popular for weekend dim sum"*; it's *"a bit
variable"*, but performance is generally good across the board.
/ **Details:** www.wengwahgroup.com; 11.30 pm.

**sign up for the survey at www.hardens.com**       

### The White Swan EC4 £39 ★
108 Fetter Ln 7242 9696
*This second-floor dining room on the fringe of the City is "classy"
(for somewhere over a pub), and serves "surprisingly good" food;
now in its second year, it's "proving very popular".*
/ **Details:** www.thewhiteswanlondon.com; 10 pm; closed Sat & Sun.

### Wiltons SW1 £74
55 Jermyn St 7629 9955 2–3C
*Nowhere are the "traditional" values of "real old English dining"
enshrined more faithfully than at this "impeccably consistent" and
"rather stiff" clubland legend; Jerome Ponchelle's fish dishes
(in particular) may be "simple", but they're "perfect"… as long
as you don't mind them being "vastly overpriced".*
/ **Details:** www.wiltons.co.uk; 10.30 pm; closed Sat & Sun; jacket required.

### Winkles E2 £38 ★★
238 Roman Rd 8880 7450
*"Lovely fish", "superb seafood", "shame about the ambience" –
that's the whole story on this "brave" modern café, in Bethnal
Green.* / **Details:** www.winkleseafood.com; 10.30 pm; closed Mon L;
no smoking area.

### Wódka W8 £44 Ⓐ
12 St Alban's Grove 7937 6513 4–1B
*"Forget the food, just go for the amazing vodkas" – that's long
been the standard advice on this "quietly-situated", "fun" and
rather "romantic" Kensington Pole; its "hearty" cooking, however,
was more often deemed "delicious" this year.* / **Value tip:** set always
available £28 (FP). **Details:** www.wodka.co.uk; 11.15 pm; closed Sat L & Sun L.

### Wolfe's WC2 £32
30 Gt Queen St 7831 4442 3–1D
*"Wonderful Kobe beefburgers" star in a number of reports on this
long-established, genuinely American-feeling fixture, on the fringe
of Covent Garden.* / **Details:** www.wolfes-grill.net; 11.45 pm, Sun 8.45 pm;
no smoking area.

### The Wolseley W1 £50 Ⓐ
160 Piccadilly 7499 6996 2–3C
*Messrs Corbin & King's star-studded Continental-style café, by the
Ritz, is a "dramatic" location for any occasion (including
"the ultimate breakfast" or "a perfect tea"); its "comfort" dishes
– from the long main menu – "can border on average", though,
and a few reporters find the place plain "over-hyped"; (n.b. it lost
its head chef and head pastry chef post-survey).*
/ **Details:** www.thewolseley.com; midnight; no smoking area.

### Woodlands £28 ★
37 Panton St, SW1 7839 7258 3–4A
77 Marylebone Ln, W1 7486 3862 1–1A
12-14 Chiswick High Rd, W4 8994 9333 6–2B
*"Great south Indian food" wins many fans for these "reliable" and
"good-value" veggies; their ambience is somewhere between
"serene" and "depressing".* / **Details:** www.woodlandsrestaurant.co.uk;
10.45 pm.

**sign up for the survey at www.hardens.com**

**Yatra W1**  £42
34 Dover St   7493 0200   2–3C
"It's lost some of its initial wow-factor, but the food and service are still excellent", at this funky Mayfair Indian, which never quite seems to get the following it deserves. / **Value tip:** set weekday L £22 (FP). **Details:** www.yatra.co.uk; 11 pm; closed Sat L & Sun.

**Yauatcha W1**  £38  A★★
Broadwick Hs, 15-17 Broadwick St
7494 8888   2–2D
"Exquisite" dim sum and "hip" décor make Alan Yau's Soho yearling a sort of "Hakkasan at half the price"; sometimes "under-whelming" service (including assiduous table-turning) can grate, though, and some reporters "prefer the ground-floor tea room" (with its "stunning pastries") to the "cramped" main dining area in the basement. / **Details:** 11.30 pm; no smoking.

**Yelo**  £24  A
136a Lancaster Rd, W11   7243 2220   5–1A
8-9 Hoxton Sq, N1   7729 4626
"Hip" but "reliable", this Thai diner has some great alfresco tables on Hoxton Square; there are no reports yet on its new sibling, near Ladbroke Grove tube. / **Details:** www.yelothai.com; 11 pm; no booking.

**Yi-Ban**  £29  A★
Imperial Wharf, Imperial Rd, SW6   7731 6606   4–4B
Regatta Centre, Dockside Rd, E16   7473 6699
The original branch of this Chinese duo (near Royal Albert DLR) boasts Thames and City Airport views, and is especially worth seeking out for its "top dim sum"; it's early days for its (more expensive) offshoot, in a development near Chelsea Harbour. / **Details:** www.yi-ban.co.uk; 11 pm; closed Sun; SW6 no smoking area.

**Yming W1**  £30  ★★
35-36 Greek St   7734 2721   3–2A
"Unusual" Chinese dishes – "better than any in Chinatown" – lead many reporters to seek out this "unassuming" Soho fixture (whose "exterior gives no hint of the quality within"); the staff are "so helpful and polite" – "let them tell you what to order".
/ **Details:** www.yminglondon.com; 11.45 pm; closed Sun; no smoking area.

**Yoshino W1**  £38  ★
3 Piccadilly Pl   7287 6622   2–3D
This "pure Japanese" – a tiny, "minimalist" "bolt hole", a "stone's throw from Piccadilly Circus" – often has a majority of oriental diners; "helpful" staff serve "excellent-quality sushi at reasonable prices". / **Details:** www.yoshino.net; 10 pm; closed Sun.

**Yuzu NW6**  £36  ★★
102 Fortune Green Rd   7431 6602
"A great 'neighbourhood' contemporary Japanese" – this "cramped" West Hampstead oriental is hailed for its "excellent" food (including "always-fresh" sushi), and "stylish" presentation. / **Details:** www.yuzu-restaurants.com; 10.30 pm; closed Mon, Tue-Fri D only, Sat & Sun open L & D; no smoking.

**Zafferano SW1**  £51  A★★
15 Lowndes St  7235 5800  4–1D
*"Still the best Italian in town", for many reporters, this "hype-free"*
*Belgravian offers "perfectly-flavoured" food and "great*
*(unobtrusive) service"; the only real gripe is that the tables "are a*
*bit too close". / Details: www.atozrestaurants.com; 11 pm.*


**Zaika W8**  £48  ★
1 Kensington High St  7795 6533  4–1A
*Still "towards the top of the premier league of London's nouvelle*
*Indians" – new chef Sanjay Dwivedi has more than ably picked*
*up where Vineet Bhatia left off, at this "smart" former banking*
*hall, opposite Kensington Gardens. / Value tip: set weekday L &*
*pre-theatre £32 (FP). Details: www.zaika-restaurant.co.uk; 10.45 pm; closed Sat L.*


**ZeNW3 NW3**  £37  ★
83 Hampstead High St  7794 7863
*"Perhaps not the best in London, but as a local it can't be faulted"*
*– this glazed-fronted venue, in the heart of Hampstead serves*
*"reliable, upper-end" Chinese cooking, in a "dated", '80s-*
*minimalist setting. / Details: www.zenw3.com; 11 pm; no Amex.*


**Zero Degrees SE3**  £25  A
29-31 Montpelier Vale  8852 5619
*"Very decent" brews help fuel the "very lively buzz" at this stylish*
*(if slightly "echoey") Blackheath microbrewery; the "simple" food*
*– especially "large pizzas, with interesting toppings" – gives "little*
*cause for complaint". / Details: www.zerodegrees.co.uk; 11 pm;*
*no smoking area.*


**Ziani SW3**  £39  A
45-47 Radnor Walk  7352 2698  4–3C
*"You play sardines", at this "hectic" Chelsea Italian, but – with the*
*help of its "amusing" staff – it "always lifts the spirits". / Value*
*tip: set Sun L £24 (FP). Details: 11 pm.*


**Zuma SW7**  £60  A★★
5 Raphael St  7584 1010  4–1C
*"You can see the Chelsea football team, Penelope Cruz and Robin*
*Williams…all in one night!", at this "painfully hip" Knightsbridge*
*Japanese, whose "fantastic" food "rivals Nobu", and whose*
*"always-buzzing" setting makes for "a better all-round*
*experience". / Details: www.zumarestaurant.com; 11 pm; no smoking; booking:*
*max 8.*

# LONDON
# AREA OVERVIEWS

## CENTRAL

### Soho, Covent Garden & Bloomsbury
### (Parts of W1, all WC2 and WC1)

| Price | Name | Cuisine | Rating |
|---|---|---|---|
| £70+ | Lindsay House | British, Modern | A |
| | Savoy Grill | British, Traditional | - |
| | | | |
| £60+ | Matsuri | Japanese | ★ |
| | | | |
| £50+ | Adam Street | British, Modern | A |
| | The Ivy | " | A |
| | Indigo | " | - |
| | Simpsons-in-the-Strand | " | - |
| | Rules | British, Traditional | A |
| | J Sheekey | Fish & seafood | A ★★ |
| | | | |
| £40+ | Bank Aldwych | British, Modern | - |
| | Maggiore's | French | A ★ |
| | Mon Plaisir | " | A |
| | La Trouvaille | " | A |
| | L'Escargot | " | - |
| | Vasco & Piero's Pavilion | Italian | ★ |
| | St Moritz | Swiss | A ★ |
| | Red Fort | Indian | ★ |
| | Patara | Thai | ★★ |
| | | | |
| £35+ | Aurora | British, Modern | A |
| | Papageno | International | A |
| | Yauatcha | Chinese | A ★★ |
| | Imperial China | " | A ★ |
| | Rasa Maricham | Indian, Southern | ★★ |
| | Sri Thai Soho | Thai | ★ |
| | | | |
| £30+ | Andrew Edmunds | British, Modern | A ★ |
| | Randall & Aubin | French | A ★ |
| | Shampers | International | A |
| | Balans | " | - |
| | Aperitivo | Italian | - |
| | Rusticana | " | - |
| | Wolfe's | Burgers, etc | - |
| | Yming | Chinese | ★★ |
| | The Chinese Experience | " | ★ |
| | Malabar Junction | Indian | - |
| | Mela | " | - |
| | Edokko | Japanese | ★ |
| | | | |
| £25+ | Mildred's | Vegetarian | ★ |
| | Harbour City | Chinese | - |
| | Laureate | " | - |
| | Ping Pong | Chinese, Dim sum | A ★ |
| | Busaba Eathai | Thai | A ★ |
| | | | |
| £20+ | La Porchetta Pizzeria | Italian | - |
| | Pâtisserie Valerie | Sandwiches, cakes, etc | - |
| | Chowki | Indian | ★ |
| | Kulu Kulu | Japanese | ★ |
| | | | |
| £15+ | Leon | Mediterranean | ★ |
| | Mr Jerk | Afro-Caribbean | ★★ |

| | | | |
|---|---|---|---|
| £10+ | Monmouth Coffee Company | *Sandwiches, cakes, etc* | ★★ |
| | Apostrophe | " | ★ |

## Mayfair & St James's (Parts of W1 and SW1)

| | | | |
|---|---|---|---|
| £110+ | Le Gavroche | *French* | 𝔸★ |
| £100+ | Umu | *Japanese* | - |
| £80+ | The Ritz | *French* | 𝔸 |
| | G Ramsay at Claridges | " | - |
| | The Greenhouse | " | - |
| | Nobu | *Japanese* | ★ |
| | Nobu Berkeley | " | - |
| £70+ | Dorchester Grill | *British, Traditional* | 𝔸 |
| | Wiltons | " | - |
| | The Square | *French* | ★ |
| | L'Oranger | " | - |
| | Connaught (Angela Hartnett) | *Mediterranean* | - |
| | Hakkasan | *Chinese* | 𝔸 |
| | Taman gang | " | 𝔸 |
| £60+ | Le Soufflé | *British, Modern* | ★ |
| | Mirabelle | *French* | 𝔸 |
| | Sketch (Gallery) | " | - |
| | Cipriani | *Italian* | - |
| | Sumosan | *Japanese* | ★★ |
| | Matsuri | " | ★ |
| £50+ | Le Caprice | *British, Modern* | 𝔸★ |
| | Patterson's | " | ★ |
| | The Wolseley | " | 𝔸 |
| | Bellamy's | " | - |
| | Quaglino's | " | - |
| | Green's | *British, Traditional* | 𝔸 |
| | Teca | *Italian* | ★ |
| | The Guinea | *Steaks & grills* | ★ |
| | Kai Mayfair | *Chinese* | 𝔸★ |
| | Princess Garden | " | ★ |
| | Mint Leaf | *Indian* | 𝔸★ |
| | Benares | " | ★ |
| | Tamarind | " | ★ |
| | Shogun | *Japanese* | ★★ |
| | Mitsukoshi | " | ★ |
| | Miyama | " | ★ |
| £40+ | Boudin Blanc | *French* | 𝔸 |
| | Alloro | *Italian* | 𝔸★ |
| | Pappagallo | " | - |
| | Fakhreldine | *Lebanese* | - |
| | Chor Bizarre | *Indian* | 𝔸 |
| | Yatra | " | - |
| | Quilon | *Indian, Southern* | ★ |
| | Patara | *Thai* | ★★ |
| £35+ | Automat | *American* | 𝔸 |
| | Sotheby's Café | *British, Modern* | 𝔸★ |
| | Rasa | *Indian* | ★★ |
| | Chisou | *Japanese* | ★ |

*sign up for the survey at www.hardens.com*

|       | Yoshino              | "                       | ★   |
|-------|----------------------|-------------------------|-----|
| £30+  | Broadway Bar & Grill | American                | -   |
|       | Rocket               | Mediterranean           | A   |
| £25+  | Woodlands            | Indian                  | ★   |
|       | Busaba Eathai        | Thai                    | A★  |
| £20+  | Pâtisserie Valerie   | Sandwiches, cakes, etc  | -   |
| £5+   | Fuzzy's Grub         | "                       | ★   |

### Fitzrovia & Marylebone (Part of W1)

|       |                         |                         |      |
|-------|-------------------------|-------------------------|------|
| £70+  | Pied à Terre            | French                  | -    |
| £60+  | Orrery                  | "                       | -    |
| £50+  | Locanda Locatelli       | Italian                 | A★   |
|       | Passione                | "                       | ★    |
| £40+  | Odin's                  | British, Traditional    | A★   |
|       | Back to Basics          | Fish & seafood          | ★★   |
|       | Elena's L'Etoile        | French                  | A    |
|       | Archipelago             | Fusion                  | A    |
|       | Camerino                | Italian                 | ★    |
|       | Latium                  | "                       | ★    |
|       | Sardo                   | "                       | ★    |
|       | Fino                    | Spanish                 | ★    |
|       | Maroush                 | Lebanese                | ★    |
|       | Deya                    | Indian                  | ★★   |
|       | Crazy Bear              | Thai                    | A    |
|       | Bam-Bou                 | Vietnamese              | A★   |
| £35+  | Rasa Samudra            | Indian                  | ★★   |
|       | Koba                    | Korean                  | ★    |
| £30+  | Tapa Room (Providores)  | Fusion                  | A★   |
|       | O'Conor Don             | Irish                   | A★   |
|       | Salt Yard               | Mediterranean           | ★★   |
|       | Ragam                   | Indian, Southern        | ★★   |
|       | Abeno                   | Japanese                | -    |
| £25+  | Giraffe                 | International            | -    |
|       | Carluccio's Caffè       | Italian                 | -    |
|       | Navarro's               | Spanish                 | A    |
|       | La Fromagerie Café      | Sandwiches, cakes, etc  | A★★  |
|       | Woodlands               | Indian                  | ★    |
|       | Ikkyu                   | Japanese                | -    |
| £20+  | Pâtisserie Valerie      | Sandwiches, cakes, etc  | -    |
| £15+  | Golden Hind             | Fish & chips            | ★    |
| £10+  | Apostrophe              | Sandwiches, cakes, etc  | ★    |

## Belgravia, Pimlico, Victoria & Westminster (SW1, except St James's)

| | | | |
|---|---|---|---|
| £90+ | The Lanesborough | *British, Modern* | 𝔸 |
| £80+ | Pétrus | *French* | 𝔸★ |
| £70+ | One-O-One | *Fish & seafood* | ★ |
| | Mju | *Fusion* | ★ |
| £60+ | Roussillon | *French* | ★★ |
| | Foliage | *"* | 𝔸★ |
| | Toto's | *Italian* | 𝔸★ |
| £50+ | Goring Hotel | *British, Traditional* | 𝔸 |
| | Zafferano | *Italian* | 𝔸★★ |
| | Signor Sassi | *"* | 𝔸 |
| | Amaya | *Indian* | 𝔸★★ |
| | The Cinnamon Club | *"* | ★ |
| £40+ | La Poule au Pot | *French* | 𝔸 |
| | Quirinale | *Italian* | ★★ |
| | Caraffini | *"* | 𝔸★ |
| | Il Convivio | *"* | ★ |
| | Sale e Pepe | *"* | - |
| | Ken Lo's Memories | *Chinese* | ★ |
| £35+ | Le Cercle | *French* | 𝔸★★ |
| | Ishbilia | *Lebanese* | ★ |
| | Hunan | *Chinese* | ★★ |
| £30+ | Kazan | *Turkish* | - |
| £25+ | Ranoush | *Lebanese* | ★ |
| | Page in Pimlico | *Thai* | - |
| £20+ | Pâtisserie Valerie | *Sandwiches, cakes, etc* | - |
| | Jenny Lo's | *Chinese* | ★ |

## WEST

### Chelsea, South Kensington, Kensington, Earl's Court & Fulham (SW3, SW5, SW6, SW7, SW10 & W8)

| | | | |
|---|---|---|---|
| £100+ | Blakes Hotel | *International* | 𝔸 |
| £90+ | Gordon Ramsay | *French* | 𝔸 ★★ |
| | Aubergine | " | ★★ |
| £70+ | Capital Hotel | " | ★★ |
| | Tom Aikens | " | - |
| | Rasoi Vineet Bhatia | *Indian* | ★★ |
| £60+ | Clarke's | *British, Modern* | ★★ |
| | 1880 | *French* | ★★ |
| | Bibendum | " | 𝔸 |
| | L'Etranger | *Fusion* | ★ |
| | Zuma | *Japanese* | 𝔸 ★★ |
| £50+ | Bluebird | *British, Modern* | - |
| | Poissonnerie de l'Avenue | *Fish & seafood* | ★ |
| | Belvedere | *French* | 𝔸 |
| | Scalini | *Italian* | 𝔸 ★ |
| | Locanda Ottoemezzo | *Mediterranean* | 𝔸 |
| | Bombay Brasserie | *Indian* | 𝔸 ★ |
| | Chutney Mary | " | 𝔸 ★ |
| £40+ | Admiral Codrington | *British, Modern* | 𝔸 |
| | Maggie Jones's | *British, Traditional* | 𝔸 |
| | Lundum's | *Danish* | 𝔸 ★ |
| | Racine | *French* | ★ |
| | Le Colombier | " | 𝔸 |
| | Brasserie St Quentin | " | - |
| | Lucio | *Italian* | 𝔸 ★ |
| | La Famiglia | " | - |
| | Monza | " | - |
| | Il Portico | " | - |
| | Wódka | *Polish* | 𝔸 |
| | Cambio de Tercio | *Spanish* | ★ |
| | Pasha | *Moroccan* | 𝔸 |
| | Maroush | *Lebanese* | ★ |
| | Mr Wing | *Chinese* | 𝔸 ★ |
| | Ken Lo's Memories | " | ★ |
| | The Painted Heron | *Indian* | ★★ |
| | Vama | " | ★★ |
| | Zaika | " | ★ |
| | Eight Over Eight | *Pan-Asian* | 𝔸 ★★ |
| | Patara | *Thai* | ★★ |
| | Blue Elephant | " | 𝔸 ★ |
| £35+ | Ffiona's | *British, Traditional* | 𝔸 |
| | Stratford's | *Fish & seafood* | ★ |
| | Osteria dell'Arancio | *Italian* | 𝔸 |
| | Ziani | " | 𝔸 |
| | Polish Club (Ognisko Polskie) | *Polish* | 𝔸 𝔸 |
| | Tugga | *Portuguese* | 𝔸 |
| | Good Earth | *Chinese* | ★★ |

| | | | |
|---|---|---|---|
| | Made in China | *"* | ★ |
| | Mao Tai | *"* | ★ |
| | Kisso | *Japanese* | - |
| £30+ | Randall & Aubin | *French* | 𝔸★ |
| | Balans West | *International* | - |
| | Balans | *"* | - |
| | Miraggio | *Italian* | 𝔸★ |
| | Made in Italy | *"* | ★ |
| | Nuovi Sapori | *"* | ★ |
| | Da Mario | *"* | - |
| | Sophie's Steakhouse | *Steaks & grills* | 𝔸 |
| | kare kare | *Indian* | ★ |
| | Malabar | *"* | ★ |
| | Noor Jahan | *"* | ★ |
| | Bangkok | *Thai* | ★ |
| £25+ | Giraffe | *International* | - |
| | Aglio e Olio | *Italian* | ★ |
| | Pappa Ciccia | *"* | ★ |
| | Buona Sera | *"* | 𝔸 |
| | Carluccio's Caffè | *"* | |
| | The Atlas | *Mediterranean* | 𝔸★ |
| | Tendido Cero | *Spanish* | 𝔸★ |
| | Ranoush | *Lebanese* | ★ |
| | Yi-Ban | *Chinese* | 𝔸★ |
| £20+ | Chelsea Bun Diner | *International* | - |
| | Gourmet Burger Kitchen | *Burgers, etc* | ★ |
| | Pâtisserie Valerie | *Sandwiches, cakes, etc* | - |
| | Kulu Kulu | *Japanese* | ★ |
| £15+ | Churchill Arms | *Thai* | 𝔸★ |

## Notting Hill, Holland Park, Bayswater, North Kensington & Maida Vale (W2, W9, W10, W11)

| | | | |
|---|---|---|---|
| £50+ | The Ledbury | *French* | 𝔸★ |
| | Assaggi | *Italian* | ★★ |
| £40+ | Notting Hill Brasserie | *British, Modern* | 𝔸★ |
| | Electric Brasserie | *International* | 𝔸 |
| | Osteria Basilico | *Italian* | 𝔸★ |
| | Al San Vincenzo | *"* | ★ |
| | Arturo | *"* | ★ |
| | Café Maroush | *Lebanese* | ★ |
| | Maroush | *"* | ★ |
| | Maroush Garden | *"* | ★ |
| | E&O | *Pan-Asian* | 𝔸★★ |
| £35+ | The Ladbroke Arms | *British, Modern* | 𝔸★ |
| | The Cow | *Fish & seafood* | 𝔸★ |
| | Ottolenghi | *Italian* | 𝔸★★ |
| | The Oak | *"* | 𝔸★ |
| | L'Accento Italiano | *"* | - |
| | Crazy Homies | *Mexican/TexMex* | 𝔸 |
| | Bombay Palace | *Indian* | ★★ |
| | Bombay Bicycle Club | *"* | ★ |
| £30+ | Lucky Seven | *American* | 𝔸 |

|       | The Vale                 | British, Modern         | ★    |
|       | Noor Jahan               | Indian                  | ★    |
| £25+  | Galicia                  | Spanish                 | A★   |
|       | Tom's                    | Sandwiches, cakes, etc  | -    |
|       | Ranoush                  | Lebanese                | ★    |
|       | Mandarin Kitchen         | Chinese                 | ★★   |
|       | Uli                      | Pan-Asian               | A★   |
|       | Tawana                   | Thai                    | ★    |
| £20+  | Gourmet Burger Kitchen   | Burgers, etc            | ★    |
|       | Beirut Express           | Lebanese                | ★★   |
|       | Yelo Thai Canteen        | Thai                    | A    |
| £15+  | Mr Jerk                  | Afro-Caribbean          | ★★   |
|       | Fresco                   | Lebanese                | ★    |
|       | Mandalay                 | Burmese                 | ★★   |

## Hammersmith, Shepherd's Bush, Olympia, Chiswick & Ealing (W4, W5, W6, W12, W14)

|       | The River Café           | Italian                 | ★    |
| £60+  |                          |                         |      |
| £40+  | La Trompette             | French                  | A★★  |
|       | Cibo                     | Italian                 | ★    |
| £35+  | The Brackenbury          | British, Modern         | A★   |
|       | Devonshire House         | "                       | -    |
|       | Snows on the Green       | "                       | -    |
|       | Le Vacherin              | French                  | ★    |
|       | Chez Kristof             | "                       | A    |
| £30+  | The Anglesea Arms        | British, Modern         | A★★  |
|       | The Havelock Tavern      | "                       | A★★  |
|       | Cotto                    | "                       | ★    |
|       | The Thatched House       | "                       | A    |
|       | Annie's                  | International           | A    |
|       | Balans                   | "                       | -    |
|       | The Swan                 | Mediterranean           | A★   |
|       | The Gate                 | Vegetarian              | A★★  |
|       | Brilliant                | Indian                  | ★    |
| £25+  | Giraffe                  | International           | -    |
|       | Carluccio's Caffè        | Italian                 | -    |
|       | Blah! Blah! Blah!        | Vegetarian              | ★    |
|       | Mohsen                   | Persian                 | ★    |
|       | Madhu's                  | Indian                  | ★★   |
|       | Woodlands                | "                       | ★    |
|       | Sushi-Hiro               | Japanese                | ★★   |
| £20+  | Gourmet Burger Kitchen   | Burgers, etc            | ★    |
|       | Chez Marcelle            | Lebanese                | ★★   |
|       | Mirch Masala             | Indian                  | ★★   |
|       | Sagar                    | Indian, Southern        | ★★   |
| £15+  | Gifto's Lahore Karahi & Tandoori | Pakistani       | ★    |
| £10+  | Bush Garden Café         | Organic                 | A★   |

## NORTH

### Hampstead, West Hampstead, St John's Wood, Regent's Park, Kilburn & Camden Town (NW postcodes)

| | | | |
|---|---|---|---|
| £50+ | Odette's | British, Modern | A |
| £40+ | The Engineer | " | - |
| | The Wells | " | - |
| | Oslo Court | French | ★ |
| | L'Aventure | " | A |
| | Sardo Canale | Italian | - |
| | Kaifeng | Chinese | ★ |
| £35+ | Lansdowne | British, Modern | A★ |
| | Good Earth | Chinese | ★★ |
| | ZeNW3 | " | ★ |
| | Bombay Bicycle Club | Indian | ★ |
| | Yuzu | Japanese | ★★ |
| £30+ | Sarracino | Italian | ★ |
| | La Superba | " | - |
| | Pescador Too | Portuguese | - |
| | Gung-Ho | Chinese | A★ |
| | Weng Wah House | " | |
| | Eriki | Indian | ★ |
| | Jin Kichi | Japanese | ★★ |
| | Sushi-Say | " | ★ |
| | Singapore Garden | Malaysian | - |
| £25+ | The Garden Café | British, Modern | A |
| | Lemonia | Greek | A |
| | Giraffe | International | - |
| | Fratelli la Bufala | Italian | ★★ |
| | Marine Ices | " | A |
| | Carluccio's Caffè | " | - |
| | Nautilus | Fish & chips | ★★ |
| | Mestizo | Mexican/TexMex | ★ |
| | Phoenix Palace | Chinese | ★★ |
| | Vijay | Indian | ★★ |
| | Café Japan | Japanese | ★★ |
| £20+ | Daphne | Greek | A |
| | La Porchetta Pizzeria | Italian | - |
| | Gourmet Burger Kitchen | Burgers, etc | ★ |
| | Ali Baba | Egyptian | ★ |
| | Harry Morgan's | Kosher | ★ |
| | Five Hot Chillies | Indian | A★★ |
| | Great Nepalese | " | ★ |
| | Jashan | " | ★ |
| | Kovalam | Indian, Southern | ★ |
| £15+ | Geeta | Indian | ★ |

## Hoxton, Islington, Highgate, Crouch End, Stoke Newington, Finsbury Park, Muswell Hill & Finchley (N postcodes)

| £40+ | Frederick's | British, Modern | 𝔸 |
| | Lola's | " | - |
| | Sargasso Sea | Fish & seafood | 𝔸★ |
| | Morgan M | French | ★★ |
| | The Almeida | " | - |
| | Metrogusto | Italian | 𝔸 |
| | | | |
| £35+ | Mosaica | British, Modern | 𝔸★★ |
| | The Duke of Cambridge | " | ★ |
| | The Real Greek | Greek | - |
| | Ottolenghi | Italian | 𝔸★★ |
| | Rasa Travancore | Indian, Southern | ★★ |
| | | | |
| £30+ | The Northgate | British, Modern | 𝔸★ |
| | The Haven | " | 𝔸 |
| | St Johns | British, Traditional | 𝔸★ |
| | Chez Liline | Fish & seafood | ★ |
| | Banners | International | 𝔸 |
| | Sabor | South American | 𝔸★ |
| | OQO Bar | Chinese | 𝔸★ |
| | | | |
| £25+ | Vrisaki | Greek | ★ |
| | Giraffe | International | - |
| | Carluccio's Caffè | Italian | - |
| | Toff's | Fish & chips | ★ |
| | Two Brothers | " | ★ |
| | | | |
| £20+ | La Porchetta Pizzeria | Italian | - |
| | Gallipoli | Turkish | - |
| | Rasa | Indian | 𝔸★★ |
| | Anglo Asian Tandoori | " | 𝔸★ |
| | Jashan | " | ★ |
| | Rani | " | ★ |
| | Yelo | Thai | 𝔸 |

## SOUTH

### South Bank (SE1)

| | | | |
|---|---|---|---|
| £60+ | Le Pont de la Tour | *British, Modern* | - |
| £40+ | Oxo Tower (Bras') | *International* | - |
| | Tentazioni | *Italian* | ★ |
| £35+ | Champor-Champor | *Fusion* | 𝔸★★ |
| | Delfina Studio Café | *International* | 𝔸★★ |
| | Laughing Gravy | *"* | 𝔸 |
| | Baltic | *Polish* | 𝔸 |
| | Kwan Thai | *Thai* | ★ |
| £30+ | The Anchor & Hope | *British, Traditional* | ★ |
| | La Lanterna | *Italian* | - |
| | Tapas Brindisa | *Spanish* | 𝔸★ |
| £25+ | Giraffe | *International* | - |
| | Amano Café | *Pizza* | 𝔸★ |
| | Pizzeria Castello | *"* | - |
| | Tas Pide | *Turkish* | 𝔸 |
| | Tas | *"* | - |
| | Bengal Clipper | *Indian* | 𝔸 |
| £15+ | El Vergel | *South American* | 𝔸★★ |
| £10+ | Monmouth Coffee Company | *Sandwiches, cakes, etc* | ★★ |

### Greenwich, Lewisham & Blackheath (All SE postcodes, except SE1)

| | | | |
|---|---|---|---|
| £40+ | Franklins | *British, Modern* | 𝔸★ |
| | Lobster Pot | *Fish & seafood* | ★★ |
| | Spread Eagle | *French* | 𝔸 |
| | The Painted Heron | *Indian* | ★★ |
| £35+ | The Palmerston | *British, Modern* | ★★ |
| £30+ | Babur Brasserie | *Indian* | 𝔸★ |
| £25+ | Arancia | *Italian* | 𝔸★ |
| | Olley's | *Fish & chips* | ★★ |
| | Zero Degrees | *Pizza* | 𝔸 |
| | Tandoori Nights | *Indian* | 𝔸★★ |
| | Thailand | *Thai* | ★★ |

### Battersea, Brixton, Clapham, Wandsworth Barnes, Putney & Wimbledon (All SW postcodes south of the river)

| | | | |
|---|---|---|---|
| £50+ | Chez Bruce | *British, Modern* | 𝔸★★ |
| £40+ | MVH | *"* | 𝔸★ |
| | Redmond's | *"* | ★ |
| | Ransome's Dock | *"* | - |
| | Enoteca Turi | *Italian* | ★ |

**sign up for the survey at www.hardens.com**          *105*

| | | | |
|---|---|---|---|
| | Thai on the River | *Thai* | Ⓐ |
| £35+ | Cinnamon Cay | *Australian* | ★ |
| | Lamberts | *British, Modern* | Ⓐ★★ |
| | The Greyhound | " | ★ |
| | Ditto | " | Ⓐ |
| | Rapscallion | " | Ⓐ |
| | Phoenix | " | - |
| | Bombay Bicycle Club | *Indian* | ★ |
| | Tsunami | *Japanese* | ★★ |
| £30+ | The Freemasons | *British, Modern* | Ⓐ |
| | Earl Spencer | " | - |
| | Fish Club | *Fish & seafood* | ★ |
| | Emile's | *French* | Ⓐ★ |
| | Le Petit Max | " | ★ |
| | Annie's | *International* | Ⓐ |
| | Rick's Café | *Italian* | Ⓐ★ |
| | Antipasto e Pasta | " | - |
| | Rocket Riverside | *Mediterranean* | Ⓐ |
| | Dish Dash | *Persian* | Ⓐ★ |
| | Ma Goa | *Indian* | ★ |
| £25+ | Giraffe | *International* | - |
| | Il Cantuccio di Pulcinella | *Italian* | ★ |
| | Pappa Ciccia | " | ★ |
| | Buona Sera | " | Ⓐ |
| | Carluccio's Caffè | " | |
| | The Fox & Hounds | *Mediterranean* | Ⓐ★ |
| | Rebato's | *Spanish* | Ⓐ★ |
| | El Rincón Latino | " | Ⓐ |
| | Pizza Metro | *Pizza* | Ⓐ★ |
| | Sarkhel's | *Indian* | ★ |
| | Talad Thai | *Thai* | ★ |
| £20+ | Gourmet Burger Kitchen | *Burgers, etc* | ★ |
| | Brady's | *Fish & chips* | ★ |
| | Firezza | *Pizza* | ★★ |
| | Kastoori | *Indian* | ★★ |
| | Mirch Masala SW16 | " | ★★ |
| | Indian Ocean | " | ★ |
| | Nanglo | " | ★ |
| | Amaranth | *Thai* | Ⓐ★★ |
| £15+ | Sree Krishna | *Indian* | ★★ |
| | The Pepper Tree | *Thai* | ★★ |
| £10+ | Hot Stuff | *Indian* | ★ |

## Outer western suburbs
## Kew, Richmond, Twickenham, Teddington

| | | | |
|---|---|---|---|
| £40+ | The Glasshouse | *British, Modern* | ★★ |
| | A Cena | *Italian* | Ⓐ★ |
| £35+ | Brula | *French* | Ⓐ★ |
| | Chez Lindsay | " | ★ |
| £30+ | La Buvette | " | Ⓐ★ |

## EAST

### Smithfield & Farringdon (EC1)

| | | | |
|---|---|---|---|
| £50+ | Smiths (Top Floor) | *British, Modern* | 𝔸 |
| | Club Gascon | *French* | 𝔸★★ |
| £40+ | Moro | *British, Modern* | 𝔸★★ |
| | Malmaison | *"* | 𝔸 |
| | St John | *British, Traditional* | ★★ |
| | Bleeding Heart | *French* | 𝔸★ |
| | Café du Marché | *"* | 𝔸★ |
| | Cellar Gascon | *"* | 𝔸★ |
| | Flâneur | *Mediterranean* | 𝔸★ |
| £30+ | Medcalf | *British, Modern* | 𝔸★ |
| | Coach & Horses | *"* | ★ |
| | Le Saint Julien | *French* | - |
| | Cicada | *Pan-Asian* | 𝔸★ |
| £25+ | Carluccio's Caffè | *Italian* | - |
| | The Eagle | *Mediterranean* | 𝔸 |
| | Tas Pide | *Turkish* | 𝔸 |
| | Cây Tre | *Vietnamese* | ★★ |
| £20+ | Smiths (Ground Floor) | *British, Modern* | 𝔸 |
| | La Porchetta Pizzeria | *Italian* | - |
| | Pham Sushie | *Japanese* | ★★ |

### The City (EC2, EC3, EC4)

| | | | |
|---|---|---|---|
| £80+ | Tatsuso | *"* | ★ |
| £60+ | 1 Lombard Street | *British, Modern* | - |
| | Aurora | *French* | ★ |
| £50+ | Rhodes 24 | *British, Modern* | 𝔸★ |
| | Coq d'Argent | *French* | - |
| £40+ | Missouri Grill | *American* | ★ |
| | The Don | *British, Modern* | 𝔸★ |
| | The Chancery | *"* | ★ |
| | The Rivington Grill | *"* | ★ |
| | Sweetings | *Fish & seafood* | 𝔸★ |
| | Vertigo | *"* | 𝔸 |
| | Vivat Bacchus | *International* | - |
| | Bevis Marks | *Kosher* | ★ |
| | City Miyama | *Japanese* | ★★ |
| £35+ | The White Swan | *British, Modern* | ★ |
| | Home | *"* | 𝔸 |
| | Imperial City | *Chinese* | 𝔸★ |
| £30+ | South | *French* | ★ |
| | Bar Capitale | *Pizza* | ★ |
| | Mehek | *Indian* | ★ |
| | Gt Eastern Dining Room | *Pan-Asian* | 𝔸★ |
| £25+ | Rajasthan | *Indian* | ★ |

|        | K10                  | Japanese                | ★★ |
| ------ | -------------------- | ----------------------- | -- |
| £10+   | Apostrophe           | Sandwiches, cakes, etc  | ★  |
| £5+    | Fuzzy's Grub         | "                       | ★  |

## East End & Docklands (All E postcodes)

|        |                        |                        |     |
| ------ | ---------------------- | ---------------------- | --- |
| £80+   | Ubon                   | Japanese               | ★   |
| £60+   | Les Trois Garçons      | French                 | 𝔸   |
| £40+   | The Gun                | British, Modern        | 𝔸★  |
|        | Wapping Food           | "                      | 𝔸   |
|        | Lanes                  | "                      | -   |
|        | St John Bread & Wine   | British, Traditional   | ★   |
|        | Rosemary Lane          | French                 | ★   |
| £35+   | Winkles                | Fish & seafood         | ★★  |
|        | The Grapes             | "                      | 𝔸   |
|        | Bistrothèque           | French                 | 𝔸   |
|        | Il Bordello            | Italian                | 𝔸★  |
|        | Café Spice Namaste     | Indian                 | ★   |
| £30+   | La Figa                | Italian                | -   |
|        | Lilly's                | Steaks & grills        | 𝔸★  |
|        | Armadillo              | South American         | 𝔸★  |
|        | Elephant Royale        | Thai                   | 𝔸   |
| £25+   | LMNT                   | British, Modern        | 𝔸   |
|        | Carluccio's Caffè      | Italian                | -   |
|        | Faulkner's             | Fish & chips           | ★   |
|        | Haz                    | Turkish                | ★   |
|        | Yi-Ban                 | Chinese                | 𝔸★  |
|        | Shanghai               | "                      | ★   |
| £20+   | Pâtisserie Valerie     | Sandwiches, cakes, etc | -   |
| £15+   | Mangal                 | Turkish                | ★★  |
|        | New Tayyabs            | Pakistani              | ★★  |

# LONDON INDEXES

# INDEXES

## BREAKFAST
### (WITH OPENING TIMES)

#### Central
Apostrophe: *all branches*••••• *(7)*
Automat *(Sat & Sun 11)*
Balans: *all branches (8)*
Bank Aldwych *(Mon-Fri 7, Sat 8, Sun 11.30)*
Carluccio's Caffè: *all branches (10)*
The Cinnamon Club *(Mon-Fri 7.30)*
Connaught (Angela Hartnett) *(7)*
Dorchester Grill *(7)*
La Fromagerie Café *(8)*
Fuzzy's Grub: *SW1 (7)*
Giraffe: *all branches (7.45, Sat & Sun 9)*
Goring Hotel *(7)*
Indigo *(6.30)*
The Lanesborough *(7)*
Leon *(8 am)*
Mju *(7)*
Monmouth Coffee Company: *WC2 (8)*
One-O-One *(7)*
Pâtisserie Valerie: *all branches (7.30)*
Tapa Room (Providores) *(9, Sat & Sun 10)*
The Ritz *(7, Sun 8)*
Simpsons-in-the-Strand *(Mon-Fri 7.15)*
Sotheby's Café *(9.30)*
The Wolseley *(Sat & Sun 9)*
Yauatcha *(10)*

#### West
Annie's: *all branches (Tue-Sun 10)*
Balans West: *all branches (8)*
Beirut Express *(7)*
Bibendum *(8)*
Blakes Hotel *(7.30)*
Capital Hotel *(7, Sun 7.30)*
Carluccio's Caffè: *all branches (10)*
Chelsea Bun Diner *(7)*
Electric Brasserie *(8)*
Fresco *(8)*
Giraffe: *all branches (7.45, Sat & Sun 9)*
Lucky Seven *(8)*
Lundum's *(9)*
Maroush: *I) 21 Edgware Rd W2 (10)*
Pâtisserie Valerie: *all branches (7.30)*
Ranoush: *W2 (9)*
Sophie's Steakhouse *(Sat & Sun 11)*
Tom's *(8, Sun 9)*

#### North
The Almeida *(9, summer only)*
Banners *(9, Sat & Sun 10)*
Carluccio's Caffè: *all branches (10)*
Gallipoli: *Upper St N1, Upper St N1 (10.30)*
Giraffe: *all branches (7.45, Sat & Sun 9)*
Harry Morgan's *(11.30)*

#### South
Amano Café *(7)*
Annie's: *all branches (Tue-Sun 10)*
Carluccio's Caffè: *all branches (10)*
Ditto *(Sat & Sun 9.30)*

Giraffe: *all branches (7.45, Sat & Sun 9)*
Monmouth Coffee Company: *SE1 (7.30)*
Rapscallion *(10.30)*
Tapas Brindisa *(Fri & Sat 9)*
El Vergel *(8.30)*

#### East
Apostrophe: *all branches (7)*
Carluccio's Caffè: *all branches (10)*
Coq d'Argent *(Mon-Fri 7.30)*
Flâneur *(Sat & Sun 9)*
The Gun *(Sat & Sun 10.30)*
Lilly's *(Sat & Sun 11)*
Malmaison *(7, Sat & Sun 8)*
1 Lombard Street *(7.30)*
Pâtisserie Valerie: *all branches (7.30)*
St John Bread & Wine *(9, Sat & Sun 10)*
Smiths (Ground Floor) *(7)*
Wapping Food *(10.30, Sat & Sun 11)*

## BRUNCH MENUS

#### Central
Aurora
Balans: *all branches*
Bank Aldwych
Le Caprice
La Fromagerie Café
Fuzzy's Grub: *SW1*
Giraffe: *all branches*
Indigo
The Ivy
The Lanesborough
Pâtisserie Valerie: *Marylebone High St W1, Old Compton St W1*
Tapa Room (Providores)
The Wolseley

#### West
Admiral Codrington
Balans West: *all branches*
Blue Elephant
Bluebird
Chelsea Bun Diner
Chutney Mary
Electric Brasserie
L'Etranger
Giraffe: *all branches*
Lucky Seven
Lundum's
Notting Hill Brasserie
The Oak
Ottolenghi: *all branches*
Sophie's Steakhouse
Tom's
The Vale
Zuma

#### North
Banners
The Engineer
Giraffe: *all branches*
Ottolenghi: *all branches*

#### South
Chez Lindsay

**sign up for the survey at www.hardens.com**

Cinnamon Cay
Giraffe: *all branches*
Lamberts
Ransome's Dock
Rapscallion

**East**
Armadillo
Flâneur
Smiths (Ground Floor)
Wapping Food
Winkles

## BUSINESS

**Central**
Adam Street
Alloro
Amaya
Automat
Bank Aldwych
Bellamy's
Le Caprice
The Cinnamon Club
Connaught (Angela Hartnett)
Dorchester Grill
Elena's L'Etoile
L'Escargot
Foliage
Le Gavroche
Gordon Ramsay at Claridge's
Goring Hotel
Green's
The Greenhouse
The Guinea
Indigo
The Ivy
Ken Lo's Memories
The Lanesborough
Lindsay House
Locanda Locatelli
Matsuri: *all branches*
Mirabelle
Miyama
Mon Plaisir
O'Conor Don
Odin's
One-O-One
L'Oranger
Orrery
Patterson's
Pétrus
Pied à Terre
Quilon
Rules
Savoy Grill
J Sheekey
Simpsons-in-the-Strand
Le Soufflé
The Square
Tamarind
Teca
Wiltons
The Wolseley
Zafferano

**West**
Aubergine
Bibendum
Bluebird
Capital Hotel
Clarke's
1880
Gordon Ramsay
The Ledbury
Poissonnerie
de l'Avenue

**North**
Frederick's
Odette's
Yuzu

**South**
Delfina Studio Café
Oxo Tower (Bras')
Le Pont de la Tour

**East**
Bevis Marks
Bleeding Heart
Café du Marché
The Chancery
City Miyama
Coq d'Argent
The Don
Imperial City
Lanes
Malmaison
Moro
1 Lombard Street
Rhodes 24
Sweetings
Tatsuso
Vertigo
Vivat Bacchus

## BYO
*(BRING YOUR OWN WINE AT MINIMAL CORKAGE. NOTE FOR £5-£15 PER BOTTLE, YOU CAN NORMALLY NEGOTIATE TO TAKE YOUR OWN WINE TO MANY, IF NOT MOST, PLACES.)*

**Central**
Golden Hind
Ragam

**West**
Blah! Blah! Blah!
Chelsea Bun Diner
Five Hot Chillies
Gifto's Lahore Karahi &
    Tandoori
Mohsen
Pappa Ciccia: *Munster Rd SW6*
Tendido Cero

**North**
Ali Baba
Geeta
Vijay

# INDEXES

Da Mario *(hpm)*
Devonshire House *(pm)*
E&O *(heo)*
Electric Brasserie *(hp)*
L'Etranger *(h)*
La Famiglia *(hp)*
Fresco *(h)*
Galicia *(p)*
The Gate *(h)*
Giraffe: *all west branches (hme)*
Gourmet Burger Kitchen: *all branches (hp)*
The Havelock Tavern *(hp)*
kare kare *(hp)*
Lucio *(hp)*
Lucky Seven *(h)*
Lundum's *(hp)*
Made in Italy *(hp)*
Madhu's *(h)*
Maggie Jones's *(h)*
Malabar *(h)*
Mandalay *(hp)*
Mandarin Kitchen *(h)*
Maroush: *all branches (h)*
Miraggio *(h)*
Mohsen *(h)*
Monza *(p)*
Noor Jahan: *all branches (p)*
Notting Hill Brasserie *(h)*
Nuovi Sapori *(hp)*
The Oak *(p)*
Osteria Basilico *(hp)*
Osteria dell'Arancio *(h)*
The Painted Heron: *SW10 (hp)*
Pappa Ciccia: *all branches (hme)*
Poissonnerie
  de l'Avenue *(p)*
Ognisko Polskie *(hp)*
Il Portico *(p)*
Racine *(h)*
Randall & Aubin: *SW10 (h)*
Ranoush: *all branches (hp)*
Rasoi Vineet Bhatia *(p)*
The River Café *(hpo)*
Sagar *(h)*
Scalini *(hp)*
Snows on the Green *(hp)*
Sophie's Steakhouse *(hmo)*
Tendido Cero *(p)*
The Thatched House *(hp)*
Tom's *(h)*
La Trompette *(h)*
Le Vacherin *(hp)*
The Vale *(hp)*
Vama *(hp)*
Wódka *(h)*
Woodlands: *all branches (h)*
Yi-Ban: *all branches (hp)*
Zaika *(h)*
Ziani *(p)*
Zuma *(he)*

**North**
Ali Baba *(h)*
The Almeida *(h)*
Anglo Asian Tandoori *(h)*
L'Aventure *(hp)*

Banners *(hm)*
Carluccio's Caffè: *all branches (h)*
Chez Liline *(hp)*
Daphne *(hp)*
The Duke of Cambridge *(hp)*
The Engineer *(hm)*
Fratelli la Bufala *(hp)*
Frederick's *(hm)*
Gallipoli: *Upper St N1, Upper St N1 (h)*
The Garden Café *(hm)*
Geeta *(hp)*
Giraffe: *all north branches (hme)*
Good Earth: *NW7 (h)*
Gourmet Burger Kitchen: *all branches (hp)*
Great Nepalese *(p)*
The Haven *(hp)*
Jashan: *all branches (hp)*
Lansdowne *(h)*
Lemonia *(p)*
Lola's *(hpo)*
Marine Ices *(hp)*
Mestizo *(hm)*
Metrogusto *(hpm)*
Morgan M *(p)*
Mosaica *(hp)*
Nautilus *(hp)*
Ottolenghi: *N1 (h)*
Pescador Too *(hp)*
Phoenix Palace *(h)*
La Porchetta Pizzeria: *all branches (hp)*
Rani *(hm)*
Rasa Travancore: *N16 (h)*
Rasa *(h)*
The Real Greek *(hp)*
Sabor *(hp)*
St Johns *(hp)*
Sardo Canale *(h)*
Sargasso Sea *(hm)*
Sarracino *(h)*
Singapore Garden *(h)*
La Superba *(hp)*
Toff's *(hm)*
Two Brothers *(hm)*
Vijay *(p)*
The Wells *(p)*
Weng Wah House *(hp)*
Yuzu *(hm)*
ZeNW3 *(h)*

**South**
A Cena *(hp)*
Amano Café *(p)*
Annie's: *all branches (hm)*
Antipasto e Pasta *(h)*
Arancia *(hp)*
Babur Brasserie *(hp)*
Baltic *(hm)*
Bengal Clipper *(h)*
Buona Sera: *SW11 (h)*
Il Cantuccio di Pulcinella *(h)*
Carluccio's Caffè: *all branches (h)*
Champor-Champor *(h)*
Chez Bruce *(h)*
Chez Lindsay *(h)*
Cinnamon Cay *(h)*

Dish Dash (p)
Ditto (hpm)
Earl Spencer (hp)
El Rincón Latino (hp)
Enoteca Turi (h)
Fish Club (hme)
Franklins (hp)
The Freemasons (hp)
Giraffe: SW11 (hme); SE1 (hpme)
The Glasshouse (hpm)
Gourmet Burger Kitchen: all branches (hp)
The Greyhound (h)
Indian Ocean (hp)
Kastoori (p)
Kwan Thai (h)
Lamberts (hpm)
La Lanterna (h)
Laughing Gravy (hp)
Lobster Pot (hp)
Ma Goa (hm)
Mirch Masala: all branches (h)
MVH (hp)
Olley's (hm)
Oxo Tower (Bras') (hm)
The Painted Heron: SE11 (p)
The Palmerston (hp)
Pappa Ciccia: all branches (hme)
The Pepper Tree (h)
Le Petit Max (hp)
Phoenix (hm)
Pizza Metro (hp)
Pizzeria Castello (hp)
Le Pont de la Tour (h)
Ransome's Dock (hp)
Redmond's (m)
Rick's Café (hp)
Rocket Riverside: SW15 (hpe)
Sarkhel's: SW18 (hm)
Spread Eagle (hp)
Sree Krishna (h)
Tandoori Nights (h)
Tas: all branches (h)
Tas Pide: all branches (h)
Tentazioni (p)
Tsunami (h)
El Vergel (o)
Zero Degrees (hp)

### East

Aurora (h)
Il Bordello (h)
Café Spice Namaste (hp)
Carluccio's Caffè: all branches (h)
Cây Tre (hm)
The Chancery (hpm)
Club Gascon (p)
Coach & Horses (hp)
Coq d'Argent (h)
The Eagle (p)
Faulkner's (hm)
La Figa (hp)
The Gun (h)
Haz (h)
Lilly's (hp)
Malmaison (h)
Missouri Grill (hm)

Moro (h)
New Tayyabs (h)
La Porchetta Pizzeria: all branches (hp)
The Rivington Grill (p)
St John (h)
St John Bread & Wine (h)
Shanghai (hp)
Smiths (Top Floor) (h)
Smiths (Ground Floor) (hp)
Tas Pide: all branches (h)
Ubon (h)
Wapping Food (h)
Winkles (hp)
Yi-Ban: all branches (hp)

## ENTERTAINMENT
*(CHECK TIMES BEFORE YOU GO)*

### Central
Bank Aldwych
*(jazz, Sun)*
Camerino
*(jazz, Mon)*
Le Caprice
*(pianist, nightly)*
Connaught (Angela Hartnett)
*(pianist, nightly)*
Foliage
*(jazz, Mon-Sat)*
Goring Hotel
*(pianist, nightly)*
Hakkasan
*(DJ, nightly)*
Imperial China
*(pianist, Thu-Sat)*
Indigo
*(film brunches, Sun)*
Ishbilia
*(live music, Thu-Sat)*
Kai Mayfair 113
*(harpist, Sat)*
The Lanesborough
*(dinner dance, Fri & Sat; jazz, Sun brunch)*
Maroush: V) 3-4 Vere St W1
*(music & dancing, nightly)*
Mirabelle
*(pianist, Tue-Sat & Sun L)*
O'Conor Don
*(DJ, Thu)*
Quaglino's
*(jazz, nightly; pianist, Sat & Sun brunch)*
Red Fort
*(DJ, Thu-Sat)*
The Ritz
*(band, Fri & Sat )*
Simpsons-in-the-Strand
*(pianist, nightly)*
Le Soufflé
*(pianist, Tue-Sat)*
Taman gang
*(DJ, nightly)*

### West
Belvedere
*(pianist, nightly)*
Bluebird
*(DJ , Fri & Sat)*
Bombay Brasserie
*(pianist & singer, nightly)*
Chutney Mary
*(jazz, Sun)*
Da Mario
*(disco, Wed-Sat; magician, Wed)*
Maroush: I) 21 Edgware Rd W2
*(music & dancing, nightly)*

Mr Wing
*(jazz, Fri & Sat)*
Notting Hill Brasserie
*(jazz, nightly)*
Tugga
*(DJ, Tue-Sun)*
Vama
*(jazz, Sun)*

### North
The Garden Café
*(live jazz, Wed & Thu; DJ, Fri & Sun)*
Lola's
*(pianist, Thu-Sat)*
Weng Wah House
*(karaoke, nightly)*

### South
Baltic
*(jazz, Sun)*
Bengal Clipper
*(pianist, nightly)*
La Lanterna
*(live music, Fri)*
Laughing Gravy
*(jazz, Thu)*
Oxo Tower (Bras')
*(Jazz, nightly)*
Rocket Riverside: *SW15*
*(live music, Sun, Sept-June only)*
Tas: *Borough High St SE1*
*(guitarist, nightly); The Cut SE1*
*(live music, nightly)*
Tas Pide: *SE1*
*(guitarist, nightly)*

### East
Aurora
*(pianist, nightly)*
Bistrothèque
*(transvestite show Wed)*
Café du Marché
*(pianist & bass, nightly)*
Coq d'Argent
*(pianist, Sat; jazz, Fri & Sun L)*
Elephant Royale
*(live music, Wed-Sat)*
Home
*(DJ, Thu-Sat)*
LMNT
*(opera, Sun)*
Medcalf
*(DJ, Fri )*
1 Lombard Street
*(pianist, Mon & Fri)*
Le Saint Julien
*(live jazz, Thu)*
Smiths (Ground Floor)
*(DJ, Thu-Sat)*
Yi-Ban: *E16*
*(band, Fri & Sat)*

## LATE
*(OPEN TILL MIDNIGHT OR LATER AS SHOWN; MAY BE EARLIER SUNDAY)*

### Central
Automat *(1 am)*
Balans: *Old Compton St W1 (24 hours); Old Compton St W1 (5 am, Sun 1 am)*
Le Caprice
Fakhreldine
Hakkasan *(midnight, ex Mon & Sun)*
The Ivy
Maroush: *V) 3-4 Vere St W1 (12.30 am)*
Ping Pong

Quaglino's *(midnight, Fri & Sat 1 am)*
Ranoush: *SW1*
J Sheekey
The Wolseley

### West
Balans: *W4, W8 ; SW5 (2 am)*
Beirut Express *(1 am)*
Blue Elephant
Buona Sera: *all branches*
Maroush: *I) 21 Edgware Rd W2 (1.45 am); IV) 68 Edgware Rd W2 (12.30 am); SW3 (3.30 am)*
Ranoush: *SW3 ; W8 (1.30 am); W2 (2.30 am)*

### North
Gallipoli: *all branches (Fri & Sat midnight)*
Kovalam *(Fri & Sat midnight)*
Mestizo
La Porchetta Pizzeria: *all north branches*
Vrisaki

### South
Buona Sera: *all branches*
Mirch Masala: *all branches*
Sree Krishna *(Fri & Sat midnight)*

### East
Cellar Gascon
Mangal
La Porchetta Pizzeria: *EC1*

## NO-SMOKING AREAS
*(* COMPLETELY NO SMOKING)*

### Central
Apostrophe: *all branches**
Archipelago
Balans: *all branches*
Benares*
Broadway Bar & Grill
Busaba Eathai: *Wardour St W1, WC1**
Carluccio's Caffè: *all central branches*
Le Cercle*
Chor Bizarre
Chowki
The Cinnamon Club
Connaught (Angela Hartnett)*
La Fromagerie Café*
Giraffe: *all branches**
Golden Hind
Gordon Ramsay at Claridge's*
Goring Hotel
Hunan
Ikkyu
Indigo*
Kazan
Kulu Kulu: *WC2*; W1*
Leon*
Lindsay House
Maggiore's*
Malabar Junction
Mela
Mildred's*
Mitsukoshi
Mju

# INDEXES

Kwan Thai
Lamberts
La Lanterna
Lobster Pot
Ma Goa*
Mirch Masala: *SW17**
Monmouth Coffee Company: *all branches**
MVH
The Painted Heron: *SE11*
The Palmerston
The Pepper Tree
Le Petit Max*
Phoenix
Pizza Metro
Ransome's Dock
Redmond's*
Rick's Café
Rocket Riverside: *SW15*
Sarkhel's: *SW18*
Spread Eagle
Sree Krishna
Talad Thai*
Tandoori Nights
Tas: *Borough High St SE1*
Thailand*
Tsunami
El Vergel*
Zero Degrees

### East
Apostrophe: *all branches**
Bevis Marks*
Carluccio's Caffè: *all east branches*
Cicada
Elephant Royale
Faulkner's
La Figa
Flâneur*
The Grapes*
K10*
Malmaison
Mehek
New Tayyabs
Pâtisserie Valerie: *all branches*
Pham Sushie
La Porchetta Pizzeria: *EC1*
St John
South
Tatsuso
Ubon
Winkles

## OUTSIDE TABLES
### (* PARTICULARLY RECOMMENDED)

### Central
Apostrophe: *Barrett St W1, WC2*
Archipelago
Aurora*
Back to Basics
Boudin Blanc*
Busaba Eathai: *WC1*
Camerino
Caraffini
Carluccio's Caffè: *Market Pl W1**
Il Convivio

Giraffe: *all branches*
The Greenhouse
Imperial China
Ishbilia
Jenny Lo's
Leon
Mela
Mirabelle*
Nobu
L'Oranger
Orrery
Page in Pimlico
Papageno
Pâtisserie Valerie: *Motcomb St SW1, Piccadilly W1, Marylebone High St W1*
La Poule au Pot*
Tapa Room (Providores)
The Ritz*
Salt Yard
Sardo
Toto's*
La Trouvaille
Wolfe's

### West
Admiral Codrington*
The Anglesea Arms
Annie's: *all branches*
Arturo
The Atlas*
Balans: *W4*
Belvedere*
Bombay Brasserie
Bombay Palace
The Brackenbury*
Bush Garden Café
Chez Kristof*
Le Colombier*
Cotto
Devonshire House
E&O
Electric Brasserie
La Famiglia*
The Gate*
Giraffe: *all branches*
Gourmet Burger Kitchen: *W4*
The Havelock Tavern
kare kare
The Ladbroke Arms*
The Ledbury
Lundum's
Made in Italy
Mao Tai: *SW3*
Mohsen
Monza*
Noor Jahan: *W2*
The Oak
Osteria dell'Arancio
The Painted Heron: *all branches*
Pappa Ciccia: *all branches*
Pâtisserie Valerie: *all west branches*
Poissonnerie
  de l'Avenue
Ognisko Polskie*
Il Portico
Randall & Aubin: *SW10*
The River Café*

Stratford's
The Swan*
Tendido Cero
The Thatched House*
Tom's*
La Trompette
Tugga
Uli*
Le Vacherin
Vama
Yi-Ban: all branches

### North
L'Aventure*
Daphne*
The Duke of Cambridge
The Engineer*
Fratelli la Bufala
Frederick's*
Gallipoli: all branches
The Garden Café*
Giraffe: all branches
Gourmet Burger Kitchen: all north branches
Harry Morgan's
Jashan: HA0
Lansdowne
Lemonia
Metrogusto
Mosaica
The Northgate
Ottolenghi: N1
La Porchetta Pizzeria: NW1
Rasa
The Real Greek
St Johns
Sardo Canale
Sargasso Sea
Singapore Garden
La Superba*
The Wells*
Yelo: N1
Yuzu

### South
Amano Café*
The Anchor & Hope
Annie's: all branches
Antipasto e Pasta
Arancia
Baltic
Brula
Buona Sera: SW11
La Buvette
Il Cantuccio di Pulcinella
Cinnamon Cay
Earl Spencer
Firezza
Fish Club
The Fox & Hounds
Franklins
The Freemasons
Giraffe: all branches
Gourmet Burger Kitchen: SW11
The Greyhound
Hot Stuff
Kwan Thai*

La Lanterna
MVH
Oxo Tower (Bras')*
The Painted Heron: all branches
The Palmerston
Pappa Ciccia: all branches
The Pepper Tree
Le Petit Max
Phoenix
Pizza Metro
Le Pont de la Tour*
Ransome's Dock*
Rapscallion
Rocket Riverside: SW15*
Spread Eagle
Tandoori Nights
Tas: The Cut SE1
Tas Pide: SE1
Thai on the River*
El Vergel

### East
Apostrophe: EC2
Armadillo
Bar Capitale: all branches
Bevis Marks*
Bleeding Heart*
Café Spice Namaste*
Carluccio's Caffè: all east branches
Cicada
Coach & Horses
Coq d'Argent*
The Eagle
Elephant Royale*
La Figa
The Gun
Lilly's
LMNT
Medcalf
Moro
New Tayyabs
Pâtisserie Valerie: E1
La Porchetta Pizzeria: EC1
Smiths (Top Floor)*
Smiths (Ground Floor)
Wapping Food
Winkles
Yi-Ban: all branches

## ROMANTIC

### Central
Andrew Edmunds
Archipelago
Aurora
Bam-Bou
Boudin Blanc
Le Caprice
Chor Bizarre
Il Convivio
Crazy Bear
Dorchester Grill
Elena's L'Etoile
L'Escargot
Le Gavroche
The Greenhouse
Hakkasan

The Ivy
The Lanesborough
Lindsay House
Locanda Locatelli
Maggiore's
Mirabelle
Mon Plaisir
Nobu
Odin's
L'Oranger
Orrery
La Poule au Pot
The Ritz
Roussillon
Rules
St Moritz
J Sheekey
Taman gang
Toto's
La Trouvaille
Zafferano

### West
Assaggi
Belvedere
Bibendum
Blakes Hotel
Blue Elephant
The Brackenbury
Cambio de Tercio
Chez Kristof
Clarke's
Le Colombier
E&O
Eight Over Eight
La Famiglia
Gordon Ramsay
The Ledbury
Lundum's
Maggie Jones's
Mr Wing
Notting Hill Brasserie
Osteria Basilico
Pasha
Ognisko Polskie
The River Café
La Trompette
Tugga
Wódka
Zuma

### North
Anglo Asian Tandoori
L'Aventure
The Engineer
Frederick's
Lola's
Odette's
OQO Bar
Oslo Court

### South
Arancia
Brula
Champor-Champor
Chez Bruce
Cinnamon Cay

Ditto
The Glasshouse
MVH
Oxo Tower (Bras')
Le Pont de la Tour
Ransome's Dock
Spread Eagle

### East
Bleeding Heart
Café du Marché
Club Gascon
Elephant Royale
LMNT
Moro
Les Trois Garçons
Vertigo

## ROOMS WITH A VIEW

### Central
Fakhreldine
Foliage
Orrery

### West
Belvedere

### South
Carluccio's Caffè: SW15
Kwan Thai
Oxo Tower (Bras')
Rocket Riverside: SW15

### East
Coq d'Argent
Elephant Royale
The Grapes
Rhodes 24
Smiths (Top Floor)
Ubon
Vertigo
Yi-Ban: E16

## NOTABLE WINE LISTS

### Central
Adam Street
Andrew Edmunds
Camerino
Le Cercle
Connaught (Angela Hartnett)
L'Escargot
Fino
Foliage
La Fromagerie Café
Le Gavroche
Gordon Ramsay at Claridge's
The Greenhouse
The Ivy
Kai Mayfair
Locanda Locatelli
Maggiore's
Mirabelle
Orrery
Pétrus
Pied à Terre
Roussillon

St Moritz
Savoy Grill
Shampers
Sotheby's Café
Le Soufflé
The Square
Teca
Zafferano

**West**
Bibendum
Clarke's
Le Colombier
L'Etranger
Gordon Ramsay
Osteria dell'Arancio
Racine
The River Café
Tom Aikens
La Trompette

**North**
Lola's
Metrogusto
Odette's
The Real Greek

**South**
Chez Bruce
Enoteca Turi
The Glasshouse
The Greyhound
Le Pont de la Tour
Ransome's Dock
Redmond's
Tentazioni

**East**
Bleeding Heart
Cellar Gascon
Club Gascon
Coq d'Argent
The Don
Moro
Vivat Bacchus
Wapping Food

# LONDON MAPS

## MAP 1 - WEST END OVERVIEW

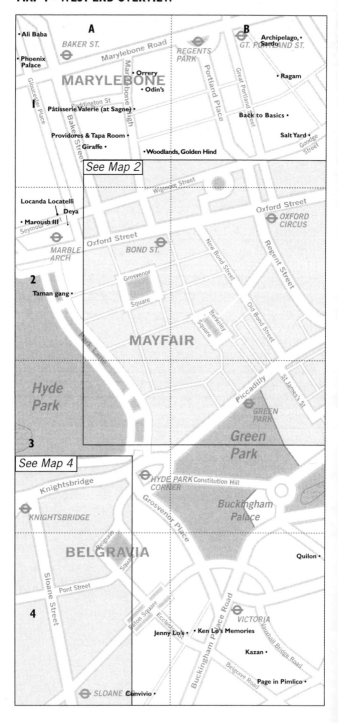

**MAP 1 - WEST END OVERVIEW**

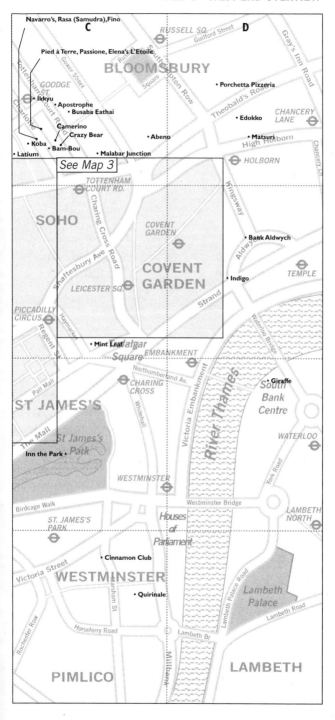

# MAP 2 - MAYFAIR, ST JAMES'S & WEST SOHO

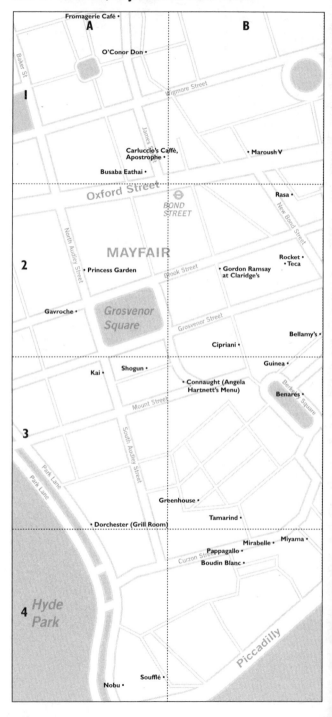

# MAP 2 - MAYFAIR, ST JAMES'S & WEST SOHO

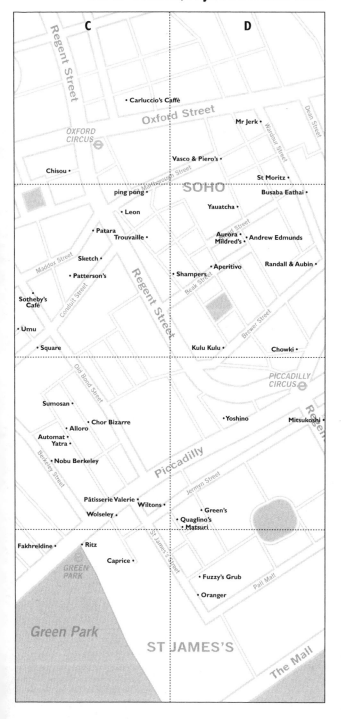

# MAP 3 - EAST SOHO, CHINATOWN & COVENT GARDEN

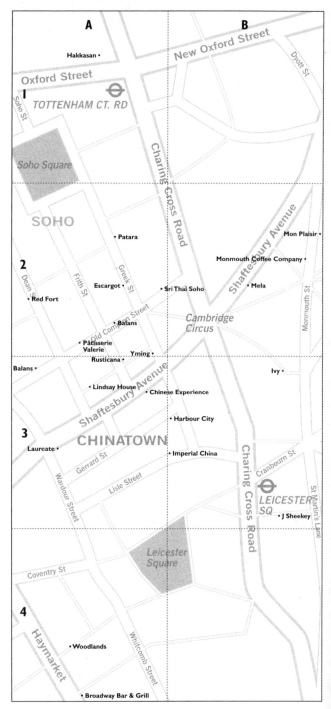

# MAP 3 - EAST SOHO, CHINATOWN & COVENT GARDEN

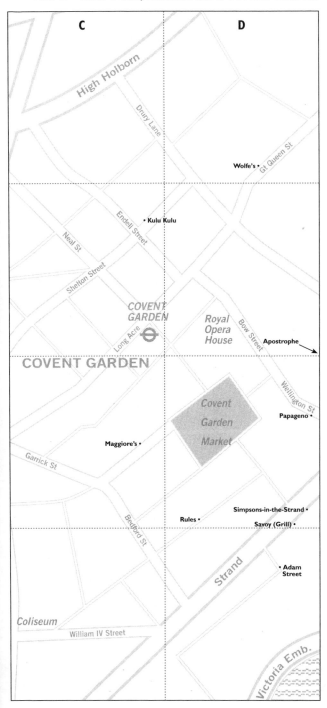

# MAP 4 - KNIGHTSBRIDGE, CHELSEA & SOUTH KENSINGTON

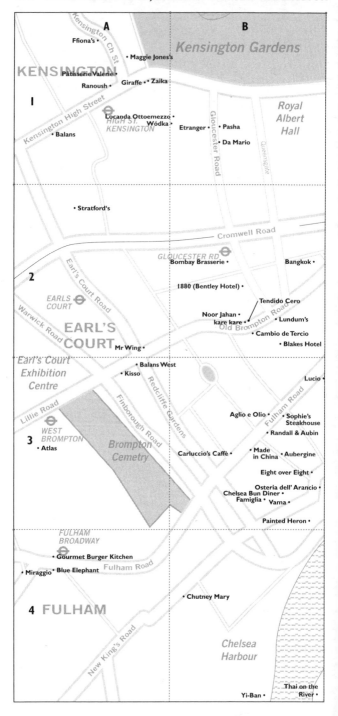

**A**

**B**

Kensington Ch St

Kensington Gardens

Ffiona's •

• Maggie Jones's

KENSINGTON

Pâtisserie Valerie •

Ranoush •  Giraffe • • Zaika

Kensington High Street

**1**

Royal
Albert
Hall

HIGH ST.
KENSINGTON

Locanda Ottoemezzo •
Wódka

• Balans

Etranger •  • Pasha

• Da Mario

Gloucester Road

Queensgate

• Stratford's

Cromwell Road

GLOUCESTER RD

Bombay Brasserie •

Bangkok •

**2**

Earl's Court Road

EARLS
COURT

Warwick Road

EARL'S
COURT

1880 (Bentley Hotel) •

Tendido Cero
•

Noor Jahan •
kare kare •

Old Brompton Road

• Lundum's

• Cambio de Tercio

• Blakes Hotel

Mr Wing •

Earl's Court
Exhibition
Centre

• Balans West

• Kisso

Redcliffe Gardens

Finborough Road

Lucio •

Lillie Road

WEST
BROMPTON

• Atlas

Brompton
Cemetery

Fulham Road

Aglio e Olio •  • Sophie's
Steakhouse

• Randall & Aubin

**3**

Carluccio's Caffè •

• Made
in China  • Aubergine

Eight over Eight •

Osteria dell' Arancio •
Chelsea Bun Diner •
Famiglia •  • Vama

Painted Heron •

FULHAM
BROADWAY

• Gourmet Burger Kitchen

• Miraggio • Blue Elephant

Fulham Road

**4** FULHAM

• Chutney Mary

New King's Road

Chelsea
Harbour

Yi-Ban •

Thai on the
River •

## MAP 4 - KNIGHTSBRIDGE, CHELSEA & SOUTH KENSINGTON

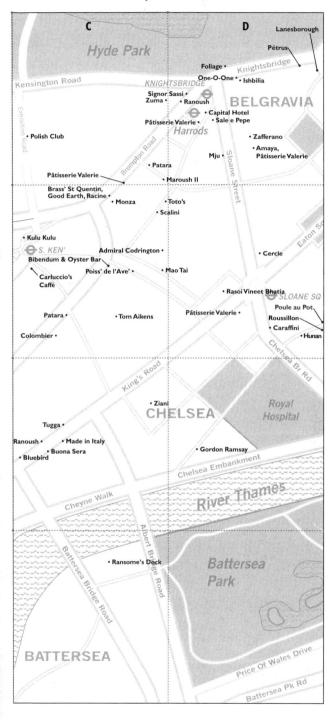

**MAP 5 - NOTTING HILL & BAYSWATER**

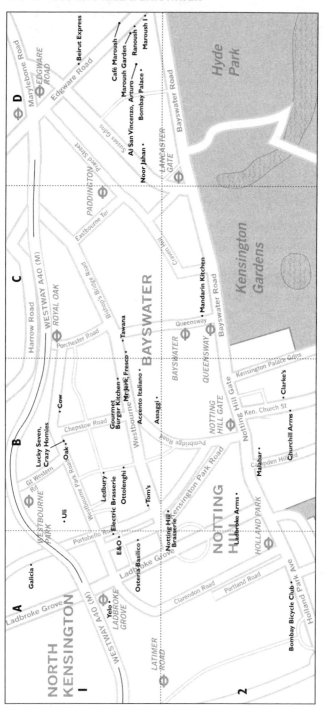

## MAP 6 - HAMMERSMITH & CHISWICK

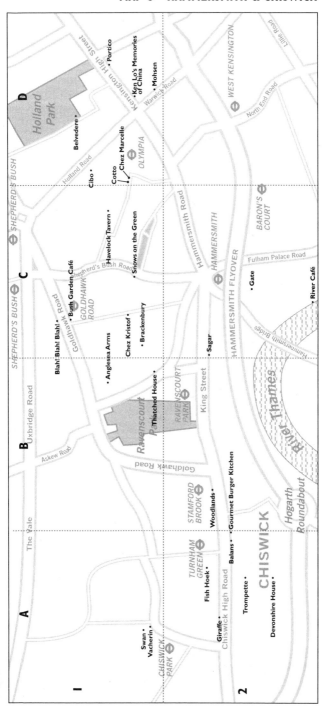

# UK SURVEY RESULTS
# & TOP SCORERS

# PLACES PEOPLE TALK ABOUT

*These are the restaurants outside London that were mentioned most frequently by reporters (last year's position is shown in brackets). For the list of London's most mentioned restaurants, see page 25.*

| | | |
|---|---|---|
| 1 | Fat Duck *(2)* | *Bray, Berks* |
| 2 | Manoir aux Quat' Saisons *(1)* | *Great Milton, Oxon* |
| 3 | Waterside Inn *(4)* | *Bray, Berks* |
| 4 | Seafood Restaurant *(3)* | *Padstow, Cornwall* |
| 5 | Yang Sing *(5)* | *Manchester* |
| 6= | Anthony's *(-)* | *Leeds* |
| 6= | Magpie *(7=)* | *Whitby, N Yorks* |
| 8 | Star Inn *(6)* | *Harome, N Yorks* |
| 9 | Vineyard/Stockcross *(13=)* | *Stockcross, Berkshire* |
| 10 | Auberge du Lac *(19=)* | *Lemsford, Hertfordshire* |
| 11= | Harts *(13=)* | *Nottingham* |
| 11= | The Witchery *(11=)* | *Edinburgh* |
| 13= | Chapter One *(9)* | *Locksbottom, Kent* |
| 13= | Croma *(11=)* | *Manchester* |
| 15 | Terre à Terre *(17)* | *Brighton* |
| 16 | The Angel *(13=)* | *Hetton, N Yorks* |
| 17 | Winteringham Fields *(18)* | *Winteringham, N Lincs* |
| 18 | The Olive Branch *(-)* | *Clipsham, Rutland* |
| 19 | Hotel du Vin et Bistro *(7=)* | *Brighton, E Sussex* |
| 20= | Rick Stein's Café *(9=)* | *Padstow, Cornwall* |
| 20= | Chiang Mai *(13=)* | *Oxford* |
| 20= | Lime Tree *(-)* | *Manchester* |

**sign up for the survey at www.hardens.com**

# TOP SCORERS

*All restaurants whose food rating is ★★; plus restaurants whose price is £50+ with a food rating of ★.*
*(Dublin restaurant prices have been converted to £.)*

| | | |
|---|---|---|
| £120+ | Waterside Inn *(Bray)* | ★★🄐 |
| £110+ | Le Manoir aux Quat' Saisons *(Great Milton)* | ★★🄐 |
| £90+ | The Fat Duck *(Bray)* | ★★ |
| | Restaurant Patrick Guilbaud *(Dublin)* | ★ |
| £80+ | Andrew Fairlie *(Auchterarder)* | ★🄐 |
| | Thorntons *(Dublin)* | ★ |
| £70+ | Lucknam Park *(Colerne)* | ★★🄐 |
| | Midsummer House *(Cambridge)* | ★★🄐 |
| | Harry's Place *(Great Gonerby)* | ★★ |
| | Hambleton Hall *(Hambleton)* | ★🄐 |
| | Longueville Manor *(Jersey)* | ★🄐 |
| | Cameron House *(Loch Lomond)* | ★ |
| | L'Ecrivain *(Dublin)* | ★ |
| | L'Ortolan *(Shinfield)* | ★ |
| £60+ | Northcote Manor *(Langho)* | ★★🄐 |
| | Samling *(Windermere)* | ★★🄐 |
| | Underscar Manor *(Applethwaite)* | ★★🄐 |
| | Champignon Sauvage *(Cheltenham)* | ★★ |
| | Mallory Court *(Bishops Tachbrook)* | ★★ |
| | Restaurant Martin Wishart *(Edinburgh)* | ★★ |
| | Auberge du Lac *(Lemsford)* | ★🄐 |
| | Bath Priory Hotel *(Bath)* | ★🄐 |
| | Champany Inn *(Linlithgow)* | ★🄐 |
| | Gravetye Manor *(East Grinstead)* | ★🄐 |
| | Holbeck Ghyll *(Windermere)* | ★🄐 |
| | Juliana's *(Chipping Campden)* | ★🄐 |
| | Kinnaird House *(Dunkeld)* | ★🄐 |
| | L'Enclume *(Cartmel)* | ★🄐 |
| | Seaham Hall *(Seaham)* | ★🄐 |
| | The Chesil Rectory *(Winchester)* | ★ |
| | Fisherman's Lodge *(Newcastle upon Tyne)* | ★ |
| | Manor House *(Chippenham)* | ★ |
| | Read's *(Faversham)* | ★ |
| | Seafood Restaurant *(Padstow)* | ★ |
| £50+ | The Black Door *(Newcastle upon Tyne)* | ★★🄐 |
| | Bohemia *(Jersey)* | ★★🄐 |
| | Mr Underhill's *(Ludlow)* | ★★🄐 |
| | The Three Chimneys *(Dunvegan)* | ★★🄐 |
| | Yorke Arms *(Ramsgill-in-Nidderdale)* | ★★🄐 |
| | Anthony's *(Leeds)* | ★★ |
| | Drakes *(Ripley)* | ★★ |
| | Hibiscus *(Ludlow)* | ★★ |

# TOP SCORERS

| | |
|---|---|
| JSW *(Petersfield)* | ★★ |
| Morston Hall *(Morston)* | ★★ |
| The Old Passage Inn *(Arlingham)* | ★★ |
| Le Poussin At Whitley Ridge *(Brockenhurst)* | ★★ |
| Albannach *(Lochinver)* | ★A |
| Ballathie House *(Kinclavan)* | ★A |
| Bodysgallen Hall *(Llandudno)* | ★A |
| Cavendish *(Baslow)* | ★A |
| Darroch Learg *(Ballater)* | ★A |
| George Hotel *(Yarmouth)* | ★A |
| Gilpin Lodge *(Windermere)* | ★A |
| Hartwell House *(Aylesbury)* | ★A |
| Hintlesham Hall *(Hintlesham)* | ★A |
| Llangoed Hall *(Llyswen)* | ★A |
| Ockenden Manor *(Cuckfield)* | ★A |
| Plas Bodegroes *(Pwllheli)* | ★A |
| Raemoir House *(Banchory)* | ★A |
| Samuel's *(Masham)* | ★A |
| Seafood Restaurant *(St Andrews)* | ★A |
| Sharrow Bay *(Ullswater)* | ★A |
| Silver Darling *(Aberdeen)* | ★A |
| Starr *(Great Dunmow)* | ★A |
| Sundial *(Herstmonceux)* | ★A |
| The Buttery *(Glasgow)* | ★A |
| The Glasshouse *(Chandlers Cross)* | ★A |
| The Mirabelle *(Eastbourne)* | ★A |
| The Oak Room *(Egham)* | ★A |
| Thornbury Castle *(Thornbury)* | ★A |
| Treacle Moon *(Newcastle upon Tyne)* | ★A |
| Wesley House *(Winchcombe)* | ★A |
| Adlards *(Norwich)* | ★ |
| Drakes On The Pond *(Abinger Hammer)* | ★ |
| Fischers at Baslow Hall *(Baslow)* | ★ |
| Juniper *(Manchester)* | ★ |
| La Potinière *(Gullane)* | ★ |
| La Rive at Castle House *(Hereford)* | ★ |
| Le Mont *(Manchester)* | ★ |
| Off The Wall *(Edinburgh)* | ★ |
| Ripleys *(St Merryn)* | ★ |
| Seafood Restaurant *(St Monans)* | ★ |
| Simpson's *(Birmingham)* | ★ |
| Strawberry Tree *(Milton Ernest)* | ★ |
| The Vanilla Pod *(Marlow)* | ★ |
| Wordsworth Hotel *(Grasmere)* | ★ |
| Gamba *(Glasgow)* | ★ |
| Moss Nook *(Manchester)* | ★ |
| Old Post Office *(Cardiff)* | ★ |
| The Plumed Horse *(Castle Douglas)* | ★ |

| | | |
|---|---|---|
| £40+ | Braidwoods *(Dalry)* | ★★A |
| | Driftwood *(Rosevine)* | ★★A |
| | Fairyhill *(Reynoldston)* | ★★A |
| | Monachyle Mhor *(Balquhidder)* | ★★A |

# TOP SCORERS

| | | |
|---|---|---|
| | Ostlers Close *(Cupar)* | ★★Ⓐ |
| | Star Inn *(Harome)* | ★★Ⓐ |
| | Summer Isles *(Achiltibuie)* | ★★Ⓐ |
| | The Angel *(Hetton)* | ★★Ⓐ |
| | The Cellar *(Anstruther)* | ★★Ⓐ |
| | The Ebb *(Padstow)* | ★★Ⓐ |
| | The Foxhunter *(Nant-y-Derry)* | ★★Ⓐ |
| | Tyddyn Llan *(Llandrillo)* | ★★Ⓐ |
| | Terre à Terre *(Brighton)* | ★★ |
| | 22 Mill Street *(Chagford)* | ★★ |
| | Drewe Arms *(Broadhembury)* | ★★ |
| | The Wild Bergamot *(Glasgow)* | ★★ |
| | Bosquet *(Kenilworth)* | ★★ |
| £30+ | 22 Chesterton Road *(Cambridge)* | ★★Ⓐ |
| | Great House *(Lavenham)* | ★★Ⓐ |
| | Jeremy's at Borde Hill *(Haywards Heath)* | ★★Ⓐ |
| | Les Mirabelles *(Nomansland)* | ★★Ⓐ |
| | Margot's *(Padstow)* | ★★Ⓐ |
| | Pier House Hotel *(Port Appin)* | ★★Ⓐ |
| | Porthminster Café *(St Ives)* | ★★Ⓐ |
| | Riverside *(Bridport)* | ★★Ⓐ |
| | Rowan Tree *(Askrigg)* | ★★Ⓐ |
| | The King's Arms *(Stow-on-the-Wold)* | ★★Ⓐ |
| | Three Acres *(Shelley)* | ★★Ⓐ |
| | Wheeler's Oyster Bar *(Whitstable)* | ★★Ⓐ |
| | Wing's *(Manchester)* | ★★Ⓐ |
| | Aldens *(Belfast)* | ★★ |
| | Culinaria *(Bristol)* | ★★ |
| | Ee-Usk (Fish Café) *(Oban)* | ★★ |
| | Rick Stein's Café *(Padstow)* | ★★ |
| | Sportsman *(Whitstable)* | ★★ |
| | Crannog *(An Aird)* | ★★ |
| £20+ | Akbar's Balti *(Bradford)* | ★★Ⓐ |
| | Golden Palace *(Harrow)* | ★★ |
| | Great Kathmandu *(Manchester)* | ★★ |
| | Green's *(Manchester)* | ★★ |
| | Lucky Dragon *(Leeds)* | ★★ |
| | Magpie Café *(Whitby)* | ★★ |
| | Mumtaz Paan House *(Bradford)* | ★★ |
| | David Bann *(Edinburgh)* | ★★ |
| | Aagrah *(Wakefield)* | ★★ |
| | Hansa's *(Leeds)* | ★★ |
| | Village Bakery *(Melmerby)* | ★★ |
| | Tai Wu *(Manchester)* | ★★ |
| | The Mermaid Café *(Hastings)* | ★★ |
| £10+ | Chez Fred *(Bournemouth)* | ★★ |
| | The Company Shed *(West Mersea)* | ★★ |

# UK DIRECTORY

Comments in "double quotation-marks" were made
by reporters.

## ABERAERON, CEREDIGION                    4–3C

**Harbourmaster**                              £ 37      Ⓐ★

Quay Pde  SA46 0BA   (01545) 570755

"A top wine list" and "inspiring" views are not the only attraction
of this former harbour-side boozer; now "really into its stride", it is
hailed by pretty much all reporters for its "top-class" cooking
(which uses "first class ingredients, cooked to perfection").
/ **Sample dishes:** fishcakes; char-grilled beef fillet; lavender crème brûlée.
**Details:** www.harbour-master.com; 9 pm; closed Mon L & Sun D; no Amex;
no smoking. **Accommodation:** 9 rooms, from £95.

## ABERDEEN, ABERDEEN                         9–2D

**Silver Darling**                             £ 53      Ⓐ★

Pocra Quay, North Pier  AB11 5DQ   (01224) 576229

"It's stunning watching the ships come and go", at this converted
lighthouse at the harbour mouth; though some reporters still find
Didier Dejean's cooking "expensive" and "over-elaborate",
his "attention to detail" and "inventiveness" attracted more praise
this year. / **Sample dishes:** squid stuffed with ratatouille & cockles; roasted
monkfish with broccoli & asparagus; flavoured crème brûlée. **Details:** beside
harbour master's tower; 9.30 pm; closed Sat L & Sun; no smoking.

## ABERDYFI, GWYNEDD                          4–3C

**Penhelig Arms**                              £ 33         ★

LL35 0LT   (01654) 767215

"An oasis of quality food in mid-Wales", this estuary-side inn
is "very popular, with good reason" – namely its "varied", fresh
and "interesting" cuisine and its "great wine list".
/ **Sample dishes:** spinach & cream cheese lasagne; char-grilled lamb with roast
aubergines; raspberry frangipane tart. **Details:** www.penheligarms.com; 9.30 pm;
no Amex; no smoking. **Accommodation:** 14 rooms, from £118.

## ABERFORD, WEST YORKSHIRE                   5–1C

**Swan Hotel**                                 £ 23

Great North Rd  LS25 3AA   (0113) 281 3205

A 16th-century coaching inn, where solid nosh comes in "huge"
portions; "the menu is so varied, it makes choosing impossible!"
/ **Sample dishes:** queen scallops & king prawn tarlets; steak rossini, baby onions &
Madeira wine sauce; white & dark chocolate mousse.
**Details:** www.swanaberford.co.uk; 10 pm; closed Mon & Tue, Wed-Sat closed
L; jacket required; book only for restaurant.

## ABERGAVENNY, MONMOUTHSHIRE                 2–1A

**Clytha Arms**                                £ 35

NP7 9BW   (01873) 840206

"Out of the way, but well worth a visit" – this "authentic country
pub" (with a "separate smart dining room") is praised by all
reporters for its "good cooking, and value for money".
/ **Sample dishes:** smoked duck with tropical fruit & jasmine salad; roast hake with
herb salsa; Sauternes cream with spiced prunes. **Details:** www.clytha-arms.com;
on Old Abergavenny to Raglan Road; 9.30 pm; closed Mon & Sun D; no smoking.
**Accommodation:** 4 rooms, from £70.

**sign up for the survey at www.hardens.com**

**Walnut Tree** £41 ✕

Llandewi Skirrid NP7 8AW (01873) 852797

*"Such a shame to see a restaurant with such an amazing reputation fall away"; this rural stalwart inspires very limited (and mixed) feedback nowadays – a claim that it's "making a post-Ramsay-TV comeback" rings hollow, given the proportion of reporters who now find it "uninspired" and "lacking spirit".*

/ **Sample dishes:** scallops & saddle of rabbit wrapped in Parma ham; braised Welsh lamb shank; baked lemon cheesecake with raspberry coulis. **Details:** www.thewalnuttreeinn.com; 3m NE of Abergavenny on B4521; 10 pm; closed Mon & Sun D; no Amex; smoking in bar only.

---

## ABINGER HAMMER, SURREY 3–3A

**Drakes On The Pond** £59 ★

Dorking Rd RH5 6SA (01306) 731174

*In the sense that it has "no atmosphere", this townhouse-restaurant is in some ways the 'perfect' Michelin establishment; service is often "amateurish" too, but it's worth braving all the negatives for Jonathan Clarke's "cracking" cooking.*

/ **Sample dishes:** asparagus, rocket & pea purée salad; roast duck breast with potatoes & elderberry sauce; orange & almond savarin. **Details:** www.drakesonthepond.com; 9 pm; closed Mon & Sun; no Amex; no smoking; booking: max 6; children: 8+.

---

## ACHILTIBUIE, HIGHLAND 9–1B

**Summer Isles** £49 Ⓐ★★

IV26 2YG (01854) 622282

*Thanks to its "exquisite" food and its "beautiful" and remote location – overlooking the islands after which it is named – this celebrated hotel "repays every inch of the journey"; the bar is "wonderful" too (but, even there, you "need to book").*

/ **Sample dishes:** grilled wild mushrooms; breast of duck & baked spiced apple; amaretto, apricot & honey steamed pudding. **Details:** www.summerisleshotel.co.uk; 25m N of Ullapool on A835; 8 pm; no Amex; no smoking; children: 8+. **Accommodation:** 13 rooms, from £119.

---

## ADDINGHAM, WEST YORKSHIRE 5–1C

**Fleece** £26 Ⓐ

152-4 Main St LS29 0LY (01943) 830491

*"A thoroughly traditional Yorkshire pub that majors on atmosphere and superb local produce" – it may be the ambience (and the location in an "exquisite" village) that really 'sells' it, but the "wide-ranging" menu also gets the thumbs-up.*

/ **Details:** 9.15 pm; no Amex; smoking in bar only.

---

## ALDEBURGH, SUFFOLK 3–1D

**The Lighthouse** £29 ★

77 High St IP15 5AU (01728) 453377

*A "busy" bistro (the best-known place in town) where – thanks to the "lovely, fresh and well-cooked fish dishes" – "it's always a pleasure to eat"; customers are "crammed-in", though – this is certainly "not a place for a quiet night out".*

/ **Sample dishes:** half-dozen Irish oysters; lobster with chunky chips; boozy banana pancakes. **Details:** www.thelighthouserestaurant.co.uk; 10 pm; closed for 2 weeks in Jan & 1 week in Oct; no smoking.

### 152 £39
152 High St IP15 5AX (01728) 454594
*For most reporters, this is an "unpretentious, pleasing café"
offering "a warm welcome", "fresh" food and "some good wines
from Adnams list"; feedback, though, is still somewhat
inconsistent.* / **Sample dishes:** smoked chicken Caesar salad; dark chocolate cup
with chocolate ganache & mint curd. **Details:** www.152aldeburgh.co.uk; 10 pm;
closed Tue (& Mon in winter); no smoking.

### Regatta £30
171-173 High St IP15 5AN (01728) 452011
*"Very friendly" service, plus "excellent fish, simply and decently
cooked", makes this "consistent" café-style fixture popular with
almost all who report on it.* / **Sample dishes:** smoked prawns; duck with
French beans; crème brûlée. **Details:** www.regattaaldeburgh.com; 9.30 pm; closed
Sun D Nov-Feb; no smoking.

### Wentworth Hotel £27    A
Wentworth Rd IP15 5BD (01728) 452312
*The "plain" cuisine at this "gracious" and "comforting" hotel
(owned by the same family for over 80 years) is universally
approved by reporters, who say it offers "consistently good value".*
/ **Sample dishes:** platter of smoked salmon; oven-baked sea bream; raspberry
mousse cake. **Details:** www.wentworth-aldeburgh.com; 9 pm; no smoking.
**Accommodation:** 35 rooms, from £90.

---

## ALDFORD, CHESHIRE 5–3A

### The Grosvenor Arms £32    A
Chester Rd CH3 6HJ (01244) 620228
*"One of Cheshire's most popular country pub/restaurants";
this "pleasant" and "not-too-pricey" destination is praised for its
"good" food (albeit from a "rarely-changing" menu) and its
"very good" wine.* / **Sample dishes:** corned beef & black pudding hash cake;
pork chops with Stilton rarebit topping; chocolate bread & butter pudding.
**Details:** 6m S of Chester on B5130; 11 pm; no smoking area; children: 14+ at D.

---

## ALVESTON, WARWICKSHIRE 2–1C

### Baraset Barn  £33    A ★
Pimlico Ln CV37 7RF
(01789) 295510
*"More a top country restaurant than a gastropub" – this "lovely"
multi-level addition to a local mini-chain (in a "very stylishly
converted barn") has been instantly hailed by locals as "one of the
best places in Warwickshire".* / **Sample dishes:** asparagus with free range
duck egg; lamb rump, braised cabbage & dauphinoise potatoes.
**Details:** www.barasetbarn.co.uk; 9.30 pm; closed Sun D; no Amex;
no smoking area.

## AMBERLEY, WEST SUSSEX　　　　　　　3–4A
**Amberley Castle**　　　　　　　**£66**　　　Ⓐ
BN18 9ND　(01798) 831992
The "wonderful surroundings" of this ancient castle (which dates
back to the 12th century) make it a romantic destination par
excellence; eating here is "expensive", naturally, but a rising
number of reporters rate the cuisine as "very good".
/ **Sample dishes:** home-smoked Scottish salmon; loin of venison; kahlua marquise.
**Details:** www.amberleycastle.co.uk; N of Arundel on B2139; 9.30 pm; jacket or tie
required; no smoking; booking: max 8; children: 12+. **Accommodation:** 19 rooms,
from £155.

## AMBLESIDE, CUMBRIA　　　　　　　　7–3D
**Drunken Duck**　　　　　　　**£40**　　　Ⓐ
Barngates　LA22 0NG　(01539) 436347
"Eat outside, for fabulous views", at this celebrated pub-cum-
microbrewery, which enjoys an "idyllic" location, high above Lake
Windermere; prices are toppish, though, and some reporters feel
the place is "getting too big for its webbed boots".
/ **Sample dishes:** tempura battered okra; diver-caught seared king scallops with
pancetta; waffles with ice cream & maple syrup coffee sauce.
**Details:** www.drunkenduckinn.co.uk; 3m from Ambleside, towards Hawkshead;
8.30 pm; no smoking; booking: max 6. **Accommodation:** 16 rooms, from £95.

**The Glass House**　　　　　　**£34**　　Ⓐ★
Rydal Rd　LA22 9AN　(01539) 432137
Reports are not entirely consistent, but most reporters feel that
this former mill offers "excellent food and service" to match its
"lovely location". / **Sample dishes:** tomato & Parmesan tart; roast monkfish
with Parma ham & vegetable crêpes; mint chocolate chip soufflé.
**Details:** www.theglasshouserestaurant.co.uk; behind Little Bridge House; 9.30 pm,
Sat 10 pm; closed Tue (& all of Jan); no Amex; no smoking; children: 5+ at D.

**Lucy's on a Plate**　　　　　　**£32**　　Ⓐ★
Church St　LA22 0BU　(01539) 431191
"Delicious freshly-cooked delights" and a "fantastic range
of puddings" win warm reviews for this "rare" deli/wine
bar/restaurant; the place does get "very busy", though,
and standards can sometimes slip. / **Sample dishes:** confit of crisp duck
leg; Lakeland lamb steak; apple crumble tart. **Details:** www.lucys-on-a-plate.co.uk;
centre of Ambleside; 9 pm; no Amex; no smoking.

**Rothay Manor**　　　　　　　**£45**　　Ⓐ★
Rothay Bridge　LA22 0EH　(01539) 433605
This year, Jane Binns celebrates 30 years at the stoves of this
"very popular" Regency country house hotel – "a wonderful place,
with splendid food". / **Sample dishes:** fish terrine; rack of lamb, pea & mint
purée & rosemary jus; chocolate marquise. **Details:** www.rothaymanor.co.uk; 9 pm;
no smoking; no booking, Sat D; children: 7+ at D. **Accommodation:** 19 rooms,
from £135.

**Sheila's Cottage**　　　　　　**£32**
The Slack　LA22 9DQ　(01539) 433079
"Good for lunch or tea" – this tea shop-cum-restaurant doesn't
aim to push back culinary frontiers, but makes a very practical
stand-by in these parts. / **Sample dishes:** Westmoreland ramekin;
game sausage; sticky toffee pudding. **Details:** www.amblesideonline.co.uk; next to
Queen's Hotel; 9 pm; closed Tue D & Wed D in winter; no Amex; no smoking;
children: 8+ after 6 pm.

### Zeffirelli's £27 ★
Compston Rd LA22 9AD (01539) 433845

*"Since it moved to a larger space, it's lost magic"* (and *"service isn't as good"*), say fans of this stylish and popular eatery (part of a 4-screen cinema); reports remain generally upbeat, though, including about its *"amazing veggie dishes"*, and *"the best"* pizzas. / **Sample dishes:** *pesto & cherry tomato bruschetta; red chilli bean & Cheddar pizza; tiramisu.* **Details:** *www.zeffirellis.co.uk; 10 pm; no Amex; no smoking.*

---

## AMERSHAM, BUCKINGHAMSHIRE 3–2A

### Artichoke £45 ★
9 Market Sq HP7 0DF (01494) 726611

*Laurie Gear's "superb" Gallic cuisine is winning ever wider renown for this "small and intimate" restaurant – in a 16th-century building on the market square.* / **Sample dishes:** *saffron ravioli with rabbit & prunes; roast loin of monkfish; creamed vanilla rice pudding & gingerbread.* **Details:** *www.theartichokerestaurant.co.uk; 10 pm; closed Mon & Sun; no Amex; no smoking.*

### Famous Fish £36
11 Market Sq HP7 0DF (01494) 728665

*"Delicious fish and great home-made puds" again win praise for this informal seafood café in Old Amersham.* / **Sample dishes:** *grilled prawn tails with avocado; Cajun cod with tomato concassé; crème brûlée.* **Details:** *in Old Amersham; 10 pm; closed Sun; no smoking.*

### Gilbey's £38
1 Market Sq HP7 0DF (01494) 727242

*"Fairly standard brasserie food, but first-class wine" – that the formula that's made a long-running success of this "friendly" local stand-by, run by a scion of the eponymous distillers.* / **Sample dishes:** *crab cakes with lime pickle; braised lamb with mint mash & red wine jus; rhubarb oat crumble.* **Details:** *www.gilbeygroup.com; in Old Amersham; 9.30 pm; L & afternoon tea only.*

### Santhi £26
16 Hill Ave HP6 5BW (01494) 432621

*A handy Indian stand-by, near the end of the Metropolitan Line – "the food is consistently tasty, but the friendly staff and jungle-like atmosphere are the real draw".* / **Sample dishes:** *chicken tikka; murgh makhani; kulfi.* **Details:** *www.santhirestaurant.co.uk; 10.45 pm; no smoking area.*

---

## AN AIRD, HIGHLAND 9–3B

### Crannog
### The Underwater Center £35 ★★
at the Waterfront, The Underwater Centre PH33 6AN (01397) 705589

*As a result of storm damage, this famous "langoustine heaven" was displaced to its current location in early-2005; it was unclear as this guide went to press whether it would stay at these 'temporary' premises, or return to its old spot on the pier.* / **Sample dishes:** *clams & mussels; pistachio-crusted halibut with risotto; chocolate pudding.* **Details:** *www.crannog.net; 10 pm; no Amex; no smoking.* **Accommodation:** *20 rooms, from £56.*

## ANSTRUTHER, FIFE                                 9–4D

### Anstruther Fish Bar                    £16        ★
42-44 Shore St  KY10 3AQ   (01333) 310518
"It isn't just a fish 'n' chip shop – it's THE fish 'n' chip shop", for a
fair number of reporters; for the best ambience, "visit as the sun
sets over the harbour". / **Sample dishes:** prawns; home-made ice cream.
**Details:** www.anstrutherfishbar.co.uk; 9.30 pm; no Amex; no smoking.

### The Cellar                             £48      A★★
24 East Grn  KY10 3AA   (01333) 310378
"Superlative cooking of fish straight from the sea" – and "sheer
consistency, year after year" – makes the Jukes's friendly
basement fixture (in an historic building behind the Scottish
Fisheries Museum) an "unbeatable" destination.
/ **Sample dishes:** seared scallops; roast pesto-crusted cod; hazelnut praline parfait.
**Details:** in the harbour area; 9.30 pm; closed Mon L & Tue L; no smoking area.

## APPLECROSS, HIGHLAND                           9–2B

### Applecross Inn                         £27        A★
Shore St  IV54 8LR   (01520) 744262
This may be "one of the more inaccessible places to eat in the
UK" – the road was only built 30 years ago! – but, once you're
there, this waterside inn enjoys a "wonderful" location; it wins
almost universal praise from reporters for "the freshest and best
seafood". / **Sample dishes:** smoked salmon; venison sausages with mash &
onion gravy; chocolate brûlée. **Details:** www.applecross.uk.com; off A896, S of
Shieldaig; 9 pm; no Amex; no smoking; need 4+ to book. **Accommodation:** 7
rooms, from £60.

### Walled Garden & Café Restaurant    £32        A
IV54 8ND   (01520) 744440
It's the situation – "within the beautiful walled garden
of Applecross House" – that makes this café of most note, but its
"very tasty home-made soups, sandwiches and light lunches" also
rate mention. / **Sample dishes:** home-made chicken liver parfait; baked scallops
in the shell & garden lima beans; home-made profiteroles with ice cream &
chocolate sauce. **Details:** 8.30 pm; closed Mon D & Sun D; no credit cards;
no smoking.

## APPLETHWAITE, CUMBRIA                          7–3C

### Underscar Manor                        £60      A★★
CA12 4PH   (01768) 775000
"The most beautiful views" (of Derwent Water) are just part of a
package of "olde worlde charm" that makes this "first-class"
country house hotel universally popular – one reporter did find the
cuisine "rather dated", but all the others seem to like it that way!
/ **Sample dishes:** Swiss cheese soufflé with buttered spinach; roast lamb with
moussaka gâteau; mini chocolate desserts. **Details:** www.underscarmanor.co.uk;
on A66, 17m W of M6, J40; 8.30 pm; jacket required at D; no smoking; children:
12+. **Accommodation:** 11 rooms, from £180.

## ARLINGHAM, GLOUCESTERSHIRE 2–2B

### The Old Passage Inn £52 ★★
Passage Rd GL2 7JR (01452) 740547
*"Fabulous" fish and a "unique setting by the Severn" (with a "wonderful view") make this "oddly-located" ex-boozer a big hit with practically all who report on it.* / **Sample dishes:** *pan-fried scallops & foie gras; poached Cornish hake; glazed baked tarte citron.*
**Details:** *www.fishattheoldpassageinn.co.uk; 9 pm; closed Mon & Sun D; no Amex; no smoking.* **Accommodation:** *3 rooms, from £85.*

## ARMSCOTE, WARWICKSHIRE 2–1C

### Fox & Goose £33
CV37 8DD (01608) 682293
*"Varied and ever-changing food" helps win popularity for this "archetypal country pub", whose interior is decked out in a modern bistro style.* / **Sample dishes:** *goat's cheese with red onion marmalade; tagliatelle; panna cotta.* **Details:** *www.foxandgoose.co.uk; 10m S of Stratford-upon-Avon on the A4300; 9.30 pm; no Amex; booking: max 10.* **Accommodation:** *4 rooms, from £85.*

## ARUNDEL, WEST SUSSEX 3–4A

### Arundel House £45
11 High St BN18 9AD (01903) 882136
*Feedback on this recently revamped restaurant-with-rooms is still modest in volume, but it all suggests that this is now a "stylish", but "well-priced" place with a "creative menu" and "fabulous service".* / **Sample dishes:** *chicken, rabbit & pistachio terrine; local roebuck with a mushroom-stuffed tomato; iced vanilla & white chocolate mousse.*
**Details:** *www.arundelhouseonline.co.uk; 9 pm; closed Sun; no jeans or trainers; no smoking; children: 18+.* **Accommodation:** *5 rooms, from £65.*

## ASCOT, BERKSHIRE 3–3A

### Ascot Oriental £37 🅰★
London Rd SL5 0PU (01344) 621877
*"Excellent" cooking and "lovely" staff ensure pre-eminent local status for this "busy" Chinese restaurant, decked out in smart, if bare, modern style.* / **Sample dishes:** *tempura prawns; seared tuna with Asian greens; coconut & mango tart.* **Details:** *www.ascotoriental.com; 2m E of Ascot on A329; 10.30 pm.*

### The Thatched Tavern £39
Cheapside Rd SL5 7QG (01344) 620874
*This small thatched outfit "still feels pubby", despite the fact that it operates more as a restaurant nowadays, serving "good" modern bistro fare; service is "personal" too.* / **Sample dishes:** *crispy oriental duck salad; steak & kidney pudding; lemon & ginger crunch.*
**Details:** *www.thethatchedtavern.co.uk; 2m from Ascot, signed to Cheapside village; 9.30 pm; smoking in bar only.*

**sign up for the survey at www.hardens.com**

## ASENBY, NORTH YORKSHIRE                          8–4C

**The Crab & Lobster**                     £ 40        Ⓐ★
Dishforth Rd  YO7 3QL   (01845) 577286
*"Eclectic" décor helps lend a "really relaxed and intimate" feeling
to this "crowded" pub, just off the A1; most reporters say its fish
and seafood cooking is "amazing" too – compared to a few years
back, though, some long-term fans say "it's lost some of its old
excitement". / Sample dishes: Irish oysters; crab-crusted salmon with saffron
mash; chocolate torte. Details: www.crabandlobster.com; at junction of Asenby
Rd & Topcliffe Rd; 9 pm; no smoking. Accommodation: 14 rooms, from £150.*

## ASHBOURNE, DERBYSHIRE                            5–3C

**Dining Room**                            £ 49
33 St. John's St  DE6 1GP   (01335) 300666
*All reports suggest that this tiny town-centre spot delivers "great"
and "quirky" cooking (including from its 12-course tasting menu);
even some fans, though, feel prices risk becoming "ridiculous".
/ Sample dishes: asparagus served five ways; organic duck with carrot & red lentil
purée; tasting of plum. Details: www.thediningroomashbourne.co.uk; 7.45 pm;
closed Mon & Sun; no Amex; no smoking; children: 12+.*

## ASHBURTON, DEVON                                 1–3D

**Agaric**                                 £ 44        ★
30 North St  TQ13 7QD   (01364) 654478
*A restaurant of some note in an area where "eyebrow-raising"
menu combinations are a bit of a rarity; it offers "well-prepared
dishes" (sometimes in "small" portions), in an informal setting.
/ Sample dishes: fish soup with garlic croutons; iced ginger meringue with coffee
sauce. Details: www.agaricrestaurant.co.uk; 11.30 pm; closed Mon & Tue, Sat L &
Sun D; no Amex; no smoking area. Accommodation: 4 rooms, from £50.*

## ASKRIGG, NORTH YORKSHIRE                         8–4B

**Rowan Tree**                             £ 34        Ⓐ★★
Market Pl  DL8 3HT   (01969) 650536
*Derek Wylie's "intimate little restaurant", in the Dales, is a
"quirky" but accomplished destination; it continues to attract
glowing reviews for "personal" service, and "excellent",
"uncomplicated" cooking. / Sample dishes: Louisiana prawn & okra gumbo;
lamb cutlets; coffee, chocolate & cardamom truffle torte. Details: 4m from
Aysgarth falls; 8.30 pm; D only Wed-Sat, L only Sun; closed Mon & Tue; no credit
cards; no smoking; children: 12+.*

## ASTBURY, CHESHIRE                                5–3B

**Pecks**                                  £ 46
Newcastle Rd  CW12 4SB   (01260) 275161
*At lunch (less of an attraction) there's a brasserie menu,
but dinner at this bright contemporary-style venue sees one 8pm
sitting, with a 5- or 7-course menu – it's generally hailed as a
"good value-for-money" experience . / Sample dishes: broad bean &
goat's cheese risotto; braised lamb; rum & raisin cheesecake.
Details: www.pecksrest.co.uk; off A34; 8 pm; closed Mon & Sun D; no smoking
at D; booking essential.*

## AUCHTERARDER, PERTH & KINROSS    9–3C

**Andrew Fairlie**
**Gleneagles Hotel**    £85    A★
PH3 1NF   (01764) 694267
*"Very expensive, but still value for money"* – Andrew Fairlie's
*"perfect"* French cuisine combines with distinguished service and
*"sophisticated"* surroundings to deliver an *"excellent"* overall
experience at this famous hotel. / **Sample dishes:** foie gras terrine; roast
venison with wild mushrooms; chocolate orange pudding.
**Details:** www.gleneagles.com; 10 pm; L only, closed Sun; no smoking; children: 12+.
**Accommodation:** 273 rooms, from £320.

## AYLESBURY, BUCKINGHAMSHIRE    3–2A

**Hartwell House**    £59    A★
Oxford Rd  HP17 8NL   (01296) 747444
Given its fame and grandeur, this *"refined"* part-Jacobean country
house hotel continues to inspire less feedback than one might
expect, but it's generally to the effect that it's *"pricey, but worth
it"*. / **Sample dishes:** smoked chicken & spring onion sausage; sea bass with
spinach; mango mousse with pineapple crisps. **Details:** www.hartwell-house.com;
2m W of Aylesbury on A418; 9.45 pm; jacket required at D; no smoking; children:
6+. **Accommodation:** 49 rooms, from £260.

## AYLESFORD, KENT    3–3C

**Hengist**    £36
7-9 High St  ME20 7AX   (01622) 719273
Early reports on this modernised village restaurant – an offshoot
of Thackeray's in Tunbridge Wells – are too few in number to be
definitive; they tend to support the reporter who says it *"continues
the tradition"* of first-class cuisine. / **Sample dishes:** pan-fried sea
scallops; roast fillet of Scottish beef; hot chocolate fondant. **Details:** 10.30 pm;
closed Mon & Sun D; smoking in bar only.

## BABINGTON, SOMERSET    2–3B

**Babington House**    £42    A
BA11 3RW   (01373) 812266
The *"fantastic"*, *"original"* and *"laid-back"* style is the cornerstone
of the experience at this Soho-House-owned 'country' club;
the menu is *"varied"* rather than especially remarkable,
and strikes some reporters as *"a bit expensive"* (*"like the
clientele"*); you have to stay (or be a member) to eat.
/ **Sample dishes:** potted shrimp, watercress & toast; chocolate & milk ice cream.
**Details:** www.babingtonhouse.co.uk; 11 pm; open to residents & members only for
L & D all week; booking essential. **Accommodation:** 28 rooms, from £215.

## BAKEWELL, DERBYSHIRE    5–2C

**The Monsal Head Hotel**    £26
DE45 1NL   (01629) 640250
This *"busy"* inn enjoys a *"stunning"* Peak District setting
(overlooking an old railway viaduct), with *"fantastic seating outside
in summer"*; it serves a *"decent range"* of *"quality"* dishes, in both
its bar and more modern bistro. / **Sample dishes:** squid with spicy
dressing; chicken breast filled with Stilton & cream sauce; sticky toffee pudding.
**Details:** www.monsalhead.com; just outside the town; 9.30 pm; closed Mon-Wed
in Winter; no Amex; no smoking. **Accommodation:** 7 rooms, from £55.

**No. 4** £36

4 Buxton Rd DE45 1DA (01629) 813895

*Aitch's Wine Bar, the commendable former bistro-type operation on this site, is set to be re-formatted by the existing owners as this guide goes to press; an all-day café bar is promised for the ground floor – upstairs will be for fine dining.* / **Details:** *9.30 pm; closed Sun (open Sun D in summer); no Amex; smoking in bar only.*

**Renaissance** £31

Bath St DE45 1BX (01629) 812687

*This small family-owned spot inspired mixed feedback this year – fans again hail its "classical French cooking" and "friendly" style, but critics find it "middle-aged and dull".* / **Sample dishes:** *French onion soup; chicken stuffed with crab mousse; chocolate & pear terrine.* **Details:** *www.renaissance-restaurant.com; 9.30 pm; closed Mon & Sun D; Sun L only first 2 Sun in month; no smoking.*

---

## BALLATER, ABERDEEN 9–3C

**Darroch Learg** £51 A★

Braemar Rd AB35 5UX (01339) 755443

*It's not just the "consistently wonderful food and friendly service" which commend the Franks family's long-established country house hotel to all reporters – it also enjoys splendid views over the Dee Valley.* / **Sample dishes:** *roasted calf's sweetbread; pan-fried trout; hot chocolate tart.* **Details:** *www.darrochlearg.co.uk; 9.30 pm; D only, ex Sun open L & D; no smoking.* **Accommodation:** *17 rooms, from £100.*

**Green Inn** £48 ★

9 Victoria Rd AB35 5QQ (01339) 755701

*"Fresh, local ingredients" prepared with care, and "friendly service" win high praise for this superior inn, which styles itself a restaurant-with-rooms.* / **Sample dishes:** *duck with black pudding & sweet soy sauce; turbot with leek risotto & Arbroath smokie; treacle tart with liquorice ice cream.* **Details:** *www.green-inn.com; in centre of village, on the green; 9 pm; D only, closed Sun; no smoking.* **Accommodation:** *3 rooms, from £60.*

---

## BALQUHIDDER, PERTHSHIRE 9–3C

**Monachyle Mhor** £45 A★★

FK19 8PQ (01877) 384622

*"Produce, cooking, service, scenery: all A1" – this pithy summary typifies the ecstatic feedback on Angela and Tom Lewis's "relaxed" and remote former farmhouse, overlooking a loch.* / **Sample dishes:** *creamed spinach & quail tart; fillet of John Dory; creamed sago pudding on carmelised banana.* **Details:** *www.monachylemhor.com; 8.45 pm; no Amex; no smoking; children: 12+ at D.* **Accommodation:** *11 rooms, from £95.*

---

## BANBURY, OXFORDSHIRE 2–1D

**Thai Orchid** £29 A★

56 Northbar St OX16 0TL (01295) 270833

*This large, traditionally-styled Thai is again hailed as a "rare find" by locals, offering "a super experience in the Banbury dessert".* / **Details:** *www.thaiorchidbanbury.co.uk; 10.30 pm; no smoking area.*

**sign up for the survey at www.hardens.com**

## BANCHORY, ABERDEEN                        9–3D

### Raemoir House                    £51        A★
AB31 4ED   (01330) 824884
*"A lovely hotel with a lovely dining room", which attracts consistent praise, not least for its "top-quality" cuisine. / Details: www.raemoir.com; 9 pm; no Amex; no smoking. **Accommodation:** 20 rooms, from £137.*

## BANGOR, COUNTY DOWN                  10–1D

### Shanks                           £53
150 Crawfordsburn Rd  BT19 1GB   (028) 9185 3313
*Owing to the untimely death of chef Robbie Millar in a road accident, this stylish dining room beside a golf course is, as this guide goes to press, 'closed until further notice'; his cooking was the best in the Province. / **Sample dishes:** seared foie gras; fillet of beef; chocolate pastilla with caramelised bananas. **Details:** www.shanksrestaurant.com; A2 to Bangor, follow signs for Blackwood golf centre; 10 pm; closed Mon, Sat L & Sun; no smoking.*

## BANGOR, GWYNEDD                        4–1C

### The Fat Cat Café Bar              £24
161 High St  LL57 1NU   (01248) 370445
*The original of a small northern chain – this "friendly" café/bar is "pretty cheap" and only "rarely lets you down". / **Sample dishes:** chicken quesadillas; tuna with stir-fried vegetables in oyster sauce; Caribbean banana charlotte. **Details:** www.fatcat.to; 10 pm; no smoking area; children: 18+ only.*

## BARNET, HERTFORDSHIRE                    3–2B

### Emchai                           £23        ★
78 High St  EN5 5SN   (020) 8364 9993
*Arguably it's just "a good local", but this suburban oriental's fans say its "delicious" Malaysian cooking "would make it packed if it were more central". / **Details:** 11 pm; no smoking.*

## BARNSLEY, GLOUCESTERSHIRE               2–2C

### Barnsley House                   £60
GL7 5EF   (01285) 740000
*This boutique-hotel in a 17th-century house – where alfresco lunches may be taken "with a view of the Verey cottage garden" – splits reporters down the middle; fans say it's all-round "magnificent" (with "astounding attention to detail") – critics that it's a total "disappointment" (with service a real "let-down"). / **Sample dishes:** bresaola with goat's cheese; baked pasta with mushroom and truffles; Mascarpone & raspberry brûlée. **Details:** www.barnsleyhouse.com; 9.30 pm, Sat 10 pm; no smoking; children: 12+ at D. **Accommodation:** 10 rooms, from £270.*

**The Village Pub**                                          **£36**

GL7 5EF   (01285) 740421

*"Two Ferraris in the car park" hint at the style of this "buzzy"
gastropub (which is under the same ownership as Barnsley
House); some reports are of "very good food at reasonable
prices", but doubters find the place "over-rated" and "arrogant".*
/ **Sample dishes:** smoked duck-breast salad; John Dory, braised octopus, chick
peas, tomato & oregano; chocolate & espresso tart.
**Details:** www.thevillagepub.co.uk; 9.30 pm; no Amex; no smoking area.
**Accommodation:** 6 rooms, from £90.

---

## BARTON UPON HUMBER, N LINCS                      6–2A

**Elio's**                                          **£40**   ★

11 Market Pl  DN18 5DA   (01652) 635147

*"It's grown over the past two decades", but "standards are
maintained" at this marketplace Italian, where fresh fish is the
speciality.* / **Sample dishes:** cannelloni alla Romana; seafood risotto; amaretto
cheesecake. **Details:** A15 towards Humber Bridge, first exit into Barton upon
Humber; 9.30 pm; D only, closed Sun; smoking in bar only. **Accommodation:** 8
rooms, from £85.

**Rafters**                                          **£32**   ★

24 High St  DN18 5PD   (01652) 660669

*"Good food at silly-cheap prices" made this "delightful" market-
town bistro the "top find of the year" for one visitor to the area,
and the locals say it's "always good value".* / **Sample dishes:** antipasti
with avocado; pork medallions with cider & cream sauce; chocolate chip cheesecake.
**Details:** www.rafters.co.uk; just S of Humber Bridge off A15; 10 pm; closed Mon &
Sun D; no smoking area.

---

## BARTON-ON-SEA, HAMPSHIRE                         2–4C

**Pebble Beach**                                    **£38**   𝔸★

Marine Drive  BH25 7DZ   (01425) 627777

*"An interesting fish menu that changes daily" (from an ex-
Chewton Glen chef) and "nice sea views" are the features which
are beginning to make quite a name for this seaside
bar/café/restaurant.* / **Sample dishes:** salmon & crab with new potato;
char-grilled tuna tournedos; iced nougat & crunchy almonds with apricot purée.
**Details:** www.pebblebeach-uk.com; 9.30 pm; smoking in bar only.
**Accommodation:** 3 rooms, from £70.

---

## BARWICK VILLAGE, SOMERSET                        2–3B

**Little Barwick House**                            **£48**   ★

BA22 9TD   (01935) 423902

*"High-quality cooking" has created quite a reputation for this
family-owned country house hotel; an "arrogant" staff attitude,
however, has taken the edge off some recent visits.*
/ **Sample dishes:** pink-roast quail with mushroom risotto; brill with baby leeks &
girolles; hot plum soufflé. **Details:** www.littlebarwick.co.uk; 9.30 pm; closed Mon,
Tue L & Sun D; no Amex; no smoking. **Accommodation:** 6 rooms, from £94.

## BASLOW, DERBYSHIRE                                    5–2C

**Cavendish**                                           **£ 50**         Ⓐ ★

Church Ln  DE45 1SP   (01246) 582311

A "stunning" setting (overlooking the Chatsworth Estate) and "lovely" food make for all-round satisfaction with this ducally-owned hotel; for informal meals, the lounge/conservatory is "really good". / **Sample dishes:** roast garlic & potato soup; roast squab breast with potato rosti; treacle tart with butterscotch sauce & vanilla ice cream. **Details:** www.cavendish-hotel.net; 10 pm; no smoking. **Accommodation:** 24 rooms, from £135.

**Fischers at Baslow Hall**                             **£ 55**              ★

Calver Rd  DE45 1RR   (01246) 583259

"Faultless" food is hailed by many fans of Max Fischer's "formal but welcoming" manor house – on the fringe of the Chatsworth estate – which, they say, goes "from strength to strength"; there are some reservations, though, over "escalating prices". / **Sample dishes:** sea bream with butternut squash ratatouille; pan-fried sea bass; passion fruit soufflé. **Details:** www.fischers-baslowhall.co.uk; 9.30 pm; closed Mon L & Sun D; no jeans or trainers; no smoking; children: 12+at D. **Accommodation:** 11 rooms, from £140.

## BASSENTHWAITE LAKE, CUMBRIA                          7–3C

**Pheasant Hotel**                                      **£ 43**         Ⓐ

CA13 9YE   (01768) 776234

"Much improved in recent years" ("without any detriment to the ambience"), this "memorable" inn is unanimously hailed by reporters for its good-quality traditional cuisine. / **Sample dishes:** pan-fried breast of wood pigeon; roast rack of Lakeland lamb; Frangelico panna cotta with a plum & pawpaw salad. **Details:** www.the-pheasant.co.uk; 8.30 pm; no Amex; no smoking. **Accommodation:** 15 rooms, from £100.

## BATH, BATH & NE SOMERSET                             2–2B

Beautiful stone-built English cities seem to think their architectural riches will be enough to satisfy any visitor. How else to explain the fact that this affluent destination-city remains a culinary wilderness? There's a plethora of places to eat, of course, but pricey mediocrity seems to be the order of the day – even on the ambience front! For a very grand and traditional experience, the Bath Priory Hotel can be recommended, but when it comes to restaurants proper, the 'quality' pickings are very thin indeed. The 'all-purpose' choice of the moment is the Moon and Sixpence. For an 'experience', the Pump Rooms should not be overlooked.

**Bath Priory Hotel**                                   **£ 68**         Ⓐ ★

Weston Rd  BA1 2XT   (01225) 331922

"Fine dining" in "traditional surroundings" doesn't come much more "luxurious" than at this "outstanding" hotel (in "stunning" gardens) on the fringe of the city; its style can seem a bit "stuck in a bygone age" – including the cuisine – but most reporters hail its cooking as "wonderful". / **Sample dishes:** broad bean & pea risotto; pan-roasted salmon; vanilla panna cotta. **Details:** www.thebathpriory.co.uk; 1m W of city centre, past Victoria Park; 9.30 pm; no jeans or trainers; no smoking; children: not for D. **Accommodation:** 31 rooms, from £245.

### Beaujolais £39 Ⓐ
5 Chapel Row, Queen Sq  BA1 1HN  (01225) 423417
*"A lively French place, which just keeps on going"* – this *"genuine"*
*'70s bistro remains a useful "bolt hole".* / **Sample dishes:** *salad niçoise*
*with tuna; nougat glacé.* **Details:** *www.beaujolaisbath.co.uk; next to Francis Hotel;*
*10.30 pm; closed Sun; no smoking.*

### Café Fromage £15 Ⓐ★
1 John St  BA1 2JL  (01225) 313525
*"A lovely place for excellent coffee, a good breakfast or a delicious*
*light lunch"* – this *"cramped"* but *"pleasant"* café is somewhere
all visitors should know about.* / **Sample dishes:** *no starters; grilled*
*mushrooms with roast vegetables and goat's cheese; warm Belgian apple tart with ice*
*cream.* **Details:** *L & afternoon tea only; closed Sun & Mon, Tue-Sat L only; no credit*
*cards; no smoking; no booking.*

### Demuths £33
2 North Parade Pas  BA1 1NX  (01225) 446059
This 20-year-old vegetarian restaurant is still hailed by most
reporters for its *"consistently good"* and *"imaginative"* cuisine;
it's *"cramped"*, though, and can seem a bit *"overpriced"*.
/ **Sample dishes:** *Feta, mint & pea pâté with walnut bread; goat's cheese soufflé*
*with tomato salsa; Indonesian black rice pudding.* **Details:** *www.demuths.co.uk;*
*10 pm; no Amex; no smoking; booking: max 4 at D, Fri & Sat; children: 6+ after*
*7.30 pm.*

### The Eastern Eye £36 Ⓐ
8a Quiet St  BA1 2JS  (01225) 422323
An *"unusual"* and very popular destination, where *"grand Indian*
*food"* – claimed by some as *"Bath's best"* – is served in a
*"splendid Georgian setting"*. / **Sample dishes:** *chicken with coriander &*
*mint; lamb marinated in yoghurt with herbs & spices; kulfi.*
**Details:** *www.easterneye.com; 11 pm; no smoking area.*

### Firehouse Rotisserie £35
2 John St  BA1 2JL  (01225) 482070
*"Upmarket"* – and *"with prices to match"* – this *"easy-going"*
pizzeria is universally hailed by reporters as a *"pleasant"*
destination. / **Sample dishes:** *Brie & grape quesadillas; Pacific crab & smoked*
*salmon fishcakes; chocolate pecan pie.* **Details:** *www.firehouserotisserie.co.uk;*
*11 pm; closed Sun; no smoking area.*

### FishWorks £41
6 Green St  BA1 2JY  (01225) 448707
*"Well-prepared fish, let down by the café ambience"* –
this original branch typifies the strengths and weaknesses of the
chain (which also include *"a menu where everything seems*
*'extra', and bumps up the bill"*). / **Sample dishes:** *crab salad; spaghetti*
*with clams; Sicilian lemon tart.* **Details:** *www.fishworks.co.uk; 10.30 pm; closed*
*Mon & Sun; no smoking.*

### Hole in the Wall £37
16 George St  BA1 2EN  (01225) 425242
Reports on these quirky cellars – the site of one of the earliest
post-war restaurants of note – remain mixed; optimists insist that
it's *"greatly improved"* under its new (2004) régime, but the
consensus more supports those who record an *"open verdict"*.
/ **Sample dishes:** *scallop & bacon salad; guinea fowl with beetroot & garlic sauce;*
*caramelised pears with coffee ice cream.* **Details:** *www.theholeinthewall.co.uk;*
*10 pm; no Amex; no smoking.*

**The Hop Pole**  £35
7 Albion Buildings, Upper Bristol Rd  BA1 3AR
(01225) 446327
*"Off the beaten track but popular"*, this *"real-ale pub"* is praised
for its *"hearty"* cooking, and its *"stunning garden for alfresco
dining"*; *"the restaurant is becoming very well known, but the bar
may be more fun"*. / **Sample dishes:** carpaccio of beef; char-grilled Aberdeen
Angus fillet steak; chocolate & walnut brownie. **Details:** www.bathales.co.uk;
opp Victoria Park; 9 pm; closed Mon & Sun D; no smoking area.

**Loch Fyne**  £34
24 Milsom St  BA1 1DG  (01225) 750120
A *"light and airy"* branch of the national seafood chain;
its *"reliable"* charms help make it a popular choice for an *"easy-
going"* meal (especially lunch). / **Sample dishes:** lobster bisque with garlic
rouille; rosemary-infused bream with tomatoes & black olives; lemon sorbet.
**Details:** www.loch-fyne.com; 10 pm; smoking in bar only. **Accommodation:** 9
rooms, from £85.

**Mai Thai**  £27  ★
6 Pierrepont St  BA2 4AA  (01225) 445557
This *"cheap and cheerful"* Thai is *"always full, and deservedly
popular with both tourists and locals alike"*. / **Sample dishes:** Thai fish
curry; Thai green chicken curry with coconut; banana in coconut milk.
**Details:** www.maithai.co.uk; 10.30 pm; no smoking area.

**Moon & Sixpence**  £38  𝔸★
6a Broad St  BA1 5LJ  (01225) 460962
*"Hidden-away"* in a courtyard in the city-centre, this *"buzzing"*
bistro of 20 years' standing is going stronger than ever – feedback
is copious, and it all praises *"good food and atmosphere"*.
/ **Sample dishes:** guinea fowl & pistachio ballotine; sea bass with pak choy & sweet
chilli; dark chocolate mousse. **Details:** www.moonandsixpence.co.uk; 10.30 pm;
no smoking area.

**No 5 Bistro**  £39
5 Argyle St  BA2 4BA  (01225) 444499
This cute-looking French restaurant, near Pulteney Bridge, induced
more consistent feedback this year – all to the effect that it's
a *"reliable"* destination, and quite *"romantic"* too (*"especially for
lunch!"*). / **Sample dishes:** goat's cheese mousse; pan-fried sea bass with
aubergine caviar; chocolate truffle & pineapple cake.
**Details:** www.no5restaurant.uk.com; 10 pm, Sat 11 pm; no smoking.

**The Olive Tree**
**Queensberry Hotel**  £45
Russell St  BA1 2QF  (01225) 447928
It was recently revamped, but the (dwindling) feedback on this
basement dining room remains a bit up-and-down – fans say it's
a *"beautiful"* place with *"lovely"* food, whereas doubters just find
it *"overpriced and overpraised"*. / **Sample dishes:** red mullet & roast
aubergine salad; braised pork with morels & savoy cabbage; roast peach tart.
**Details:** www.thequeensberry.co.uk; 10 pm; closed Mon L; no smoking.
**Accommodation:** 29 rooms, from £105.

### Pimpernel's
### Royal Crescent Hotel                                £72                     A
16 Royal Cr  BA1 2LS   (01225) 823333
*The setting – the gardens of a luxurious hotel, in the famous crescent – is "so beautiful", and fans say a visit here is an experience "to die for"; doubters can find the place "somewhat tired", though, and it certainly generates far fewer reports than one might expect. / Sample dishes: smoked salmon; lamb Lyonnaise with white bean purée; Cointreau & pecan nougat parfait.*
***Details:*** *www.royalcrescent.co.uk; 9.30 pm; no jeans or trainers; no smoking; booking: max 8. **Accommodation:** 45 rooms, from £210.*

### Pump Rooms                                          £36
The Pump Room, Stall St  BA1 1LZ   (01225) 444477
*It's as "an excellent place for afternoon tea" (or perhaps for breakfast) that this "beautiful" Georgian room is most naturally suited; other meals can be "a waste of time". / Sample dishes: baked mackerel rarebits; grilled butternut squash with leeks, Stilton & cream spinach.*
***Details:*** *www.searcys.co.uk; by the Abbey; L only, open until 10 pm in July & Aug; no smoking; no booking, Sat & Sun.*

### Rajpoot                                             £33
4 Argyle St  BA2 2BA   (01225) 466833
*"Still out-performing its many neighbouring competitors", this Indian "warren" (in "dark" cellars, near Pulteney Bridge) maintains quite a reputation locally; as a result, it's often "very busy" – sometimes beyond the point of amusement. / Details: www.rajpoot.com; 11 pm, Fri & Sat 11.30 pm; no smoking.*

### Sukhothai                                           £23
90a Walcot St  BA1 5BG   (01225) 462463
*"Accept no imitations", say fans of "Bath's best Thai"; set lunches offer particular "value-for-money". / Sample dishes: tom yum soup; green curry; Thai panckae. Details: 10.30 pm; closed Sun L; no Amex; no smoking.*

### Thai Balcony                                        £25                     ★
1 Seven Dials  BA1 1EN   (01225) 444450
*"Great food at reasonable prices" is making a success of this "efficient" and "lively" new oriental, on the old Clos du Roy site, near the theatre. / Details: 10.30 pm.*

### Tilley's Bistro                                     £39                     A
3 North Parade Pas  BA1 1NX   (01225) 484200
*This "pleasant" bistro on a cute pedestrianised lane was more consistently rated this year for its "wide and good-value choice" of dishes, and its "friendly" service. / Sample dishes: ramekin of sauteed chicken livers; pork Roquefort; pear crème brûlée. Details: www.tilleysbistro.co.uk; 11 pm; closed Sun; no Amex; no smoking.*

### Woods                                               £34
9-12 Alfred St  BA1 2QX   (01225) 314812
*This "fading" Gallic favourite is "expensive" and "dated", but it has its good points ("especially if you're a regular") – it's "always congenial", and serves "straightforward" scoff of "OK-ish" quality. / Sample dishes: roast tomato & basil soup; lamb & roast garlic casserole; chocolate torte. Details: www.bathshopping.co.uk; 10 pm; closed Sun D; no Amex; smoking in bar only.*

**sign up for the survey at www.hardens.com**

## BATTLE, EAST SUSSEX                          3–4C
### The Pilgrims                        £ 33         𝔸
I High St  TN33 0AE   (01424) 772314
A "beautiful and comfortable old building", composed of "part of
Battle Abbey, tastefully turned into a restaurant"; this year's
reports foodwise were mixed, but hopefully will settle down
as new chef Howard Doran settles in.
/ **Details:** www.thepilgrimsrestaurant.co.uk; 9.30 pm; closed Sun D; no Amex;
no smoking area.

## BAWTRY, SOUTH YORKSHIRE                    5–2D
### China Rose                          £ 30         ★
16 South Pde  DN10 6JH   (01302) 710461
"Fantastic" Chinese food makes this mega-oriental quite
a destination in these parts; it's perhaps best enjoyed "in a party".
/ **Details:** 10 pm; D only; no jeans or trainers; no smoking.

## BEACONSFIELD, BUCKINGHAMSHIRE              3–3A
### Leigh House                         £ 36
53 Wycombe End  HP9 ILX   (01494) 676348
This "consistent", "comfortable" and "reliable" destination
is again hailed as "Bucks's best Chinese" – admittedly not in the
face of the hottest competition. / **Sample dishes:** sesame prawn toast;
crispy aromatic duck; toffee apples. **Details:** 10.30 pm; no smoking area.

## BEARSTED, KENT                             3–3C
### Soufflé                             £ 39         ★
31 The Green  ME14 4DN   (01622) 737065
"An oasis in the culinary dessert of mid-Kent", with "nice white
tablecloths, crystal glasses and an excellent view of the village
green"; "good food and service" too… but "unfortunately,
no soufflés!" / **Sample dishes:** tiger prawns with chilli sauce; fillet of beef with
red wine sauce; soufflé with ice cream. **Details:** off M20; 9.30 pm; closed Mon,
Sat L & Sun D.

## BEAUMARIS, ISLE OF ANGLESEY                4–1C
### Ye Olde Bull's Head                 £ 47         𝔸★
Castle St  LL58 8AP   (01248) 810329
This ancient coaching inn boasts a "bright and airy" brasserie
annex, which offers "very good, contemporary" food; there's also
a "small but charming restaurant", up in the eaves, which
is equally acclaimed (but only open at night).
/ **Sample dishes:** Thai-style scallops; loin of Welsh lamb; sticky stem ginger sponge.
**Details:** www.bullsheadinn.co.uk; 9.30 pm; D only, closed Sun; no smoking; children:
7+ at D. **Accommodation:** 13 rooms, from £97.

## BECKENHAM, KENT                            3–3B
### Mello                               £ 35         ★
2 Southend Rd  BR3 ISD   (020) 86630994
This "little gem" – not far from the railway station – is generally
hailed for offering "the best food for miles around", from its
"imaginative" modern European menu. / **Details:** www.mello.uk.com;
10 pm.

## BELFAST, COUNTY ANTRIM     ·   10–*1D*

Belfast is slowly developing a restaurant scene with more
to interest the visitor. Paul Rankin, of *Cayenne* and *Roscoff
Brasserie*, and Michael Deane are the 'big' names in these parts,
but reporters are not, generally speaking, very impressed
by their restaurants. There's not much doubt that the best-
value cooking in Belfast – and quite probably the whole
Province nowadays – is to be had at *Alden's*.

### Aldens     £ 38     ★★

229 Upper Newtownards Rd   BT4 3JF   (028) 9065 0079
*The area may be "grotty", and the ambience of this former
supermarket "a bit austere", but this is one of the Province's most
copper-bottomed culinary destinations; it may not have any
vaulting gastronomic ambitions, but all recent reports attest that
the food is "some of the best around".* / **Sample dishes:** pea risotto with
smoked salmon, crème fraiche & chives; lavender shortbread with honey roast figs.
**Details:** www.aldensrestaurant.com; 2m from Stormont Buildings; 10 pm, Fri & Sat
11 pm; closed Sat L & Sun; no smoking area.

### Cayenne     £ 35

7 Ascot Hs, Shaftesbury Sq   BT2 7DB   (028) 9033 1532
*Supporters still hail Paul Rankin's city-centre spot – the most
commented-on place in town – as a "professional" operation
that's "Belfast's best"; all aspects of its performance, however,
suffer mixed reviews, and some former fans fear the TV-chef has
"lost the plot".* / **Sample dishes:** seared foie gras; Cambodian seafood hotpot;
Indian mango and coconut cheesecake. **Details:** www.cayennerestaurant.com;
near Botanic Railway Station; 10.15 pm, Sat & Sun 11.15 pm; closed Sat L & Sun L;
no smoking area.

### Deanes     £ 40

34-40 Howard St   BT1 6PF   (028) 9056 0000
*Michael Deane is a 'grand fromage' locally, so it's surprising how
few reports his venues inspire; the upstairs fine-dining area of this
city-centre landmark is indeed sometimes hailed as "the best
restaurant in Belfast", but both the glitzy brasserie below and the
new all-day deli (at 44 Bedford Street) can be "disappointing".*
/ **Sample dishes:** goat's cheese with salami & asparagus; ground beef with onion
mash & spiced ketchup; steamed pineapple pudding.
**Details:** www.michaeldeane.co.uk; near Grand Opera House; 10.30 pm; closed Sun;
no smoking area.

### James Street South     £ 39

21 James Street South   BT2 7AG   (028) 9043 4310
*"A dash of metropolitan sophistication" – chef Niall McKenna
spent a decade in London – and an "excellent wine list" combine
to make this city-centre three-year-old "a good location for
business", in particular; its "white-walled" interior, however,
can sometimes feel a trifle "stilted".* / **Sample dishes:** smoked salmon &
crab beignet; roast loin of lamb with lemon & mint couscous; chocolate plate.
**Details:** www.jamesstreetsouth.co.uk; 10.30 pm; closed Sun L; smoking in bar only.

**sign up for the survey at www.hardens.com**     157

### Nick's Warehouse £ 37 ★
35 Hill St  BT1 2LB   (028) 9043 9690
"First-class" food helps ensure a constant crush at this long-
established central wine bar (and service can sometimes
be "slow"); this is "still the best place for lunch".
/ **Sample dishes:** mushroom velouté tempura; grilled sirloin steak with garlic & herb
cubed potatoes; white peach cheesecake. **Details:** www.nickswarehouse.co.uk;
behind St Anne's Cathedral; 9.30 pm; closed Mon D, Sat L & Sun; no smoking;
children: before 9 pm only.

### Roscoff Brasserie £ 42
7-11 Linhall St  BT2 8AA   (028) 903 1150
Opinions divide as to whether this city-centre yearling ("more a
'proper' restaurant than a brasserie") represents "a return to the
level of the original Roscoff" (local hero Paul Rankin's earlier
landmark) or is "not a patch" on it; even critics, though, concede
it's a "smart" place with "professional" standards.
/ **Sample dishes:** crab & avocado; rack & braised shoulder of lamb; lemon crème
brûlée with a blueberry compote. **Details:** www.rankingroup.co.uk; 11.15 pm; closed
Sat L & Sun; no smoking area.

### Zen £ 33 𝔸★
55-59 Adelaide St  BT2 8FE   (028) 9023 2244
It doesn't attract that many reports, but all feedback confirms
that this glamorous, "warehouse-style" oriental is "a winner".
/ **Sample dishes:** crispy king prawns; enoki mushroom; black sesame ice cream.
**Details:** www.theredpanda.com; 9.30 pm.

---

## BELTON, LEICESTERSHIRE 5–3D
### Queens Head £ 43
2 Long St  LE12 9TP   (01530) 222359
A "total refurbishment" was required to create this "high-quality"
gastropub – the resulting establishment comes "strongly
recommended" by an enthusiastic local fan club.
/ **Sample dishes:** pan-fried foie gras; fillet of beef; chocolate & orange tart.
**Details:** www.thequeenshead.org; 9.30 pm; closed Sun L; no Amex; smoking in bar
only. **Accommodation:** 6 rooms, from £100.

---

## BERKHAMSTED, HERTFORDSHIRE 3–2A
### Cape Fish £ 38 ★
(01442) 879988
"Good" and "unusual" fish ("from places like Australia and South
Africa") served "with enthusiasm" has won general popularity for
this recent offshoot of the Chalfont St Giles restaurant of the
same name. / **Details:** www.capefish.co.za.

---

## BIDDENDEN, KENT 3–4C
### Three Chimneys £ 38
Hareplain Rd  TN27 8LW   (01580) 291472
"A pleasant traditional country pub, now almost entirely given over
to dining" – opinions divide between reporters who say the food
is "varied and interesting" and those who say that "the menu's
too long", and yields "average" results. / **Sample dishes:** baked
mushrooms with goat's cheese; sea bass with sweet potato & coconut chowder;
lemon tart with plum compote. **Details:** A262 between Biddenden and Sissinghurst;
9.30 pm; no Amex; no booking, Sun L.

**sign up for the survey at www.hardens.com**

### West House £ 42 ★

28 High St TN27 8AH (01580) 291341

*"Still relatively undiscovered", this "traditional"-looking village restaurant is hailed by all of its (quite small) following for its "inventive" dishes, which offer "good value for money".*
/ **Sample dishes:** *samphire and lobster hollandaise; fillet of sea trout; grappa marinated peach.* **Details:** *9.30 pm; closed Mon, Sat L & Sun D; no Amex.*

---

## BIGBURY, DEVON 1–4D

### Oyster Shack £ 30 Ⓐ★

Millburn Orchard Farm, Stakes Hills TQ7 4BE
(01548) 810876

*Anywhere the shellfish is "just out of the sea, and you can BYO" tends to be a winner, and reporters rave about this "individual and charming" institution (with its "lovely estuary views"); it has been "much enhanced" by a recent revamp.* / **Sample dishes:** *grilled oysters with cream; smoked fish medley with salad; raspberry pavlova.*
**Details:** *www.oystershack.co.uk; L only, Fri & Sat 9 pm; L only, closed Mon; no smoking.*

---

## BIRCHOVER, DERBYSHIRE 5–3C

### Druid Inn £ 31

Main St DE4 2BL (01629) 650302

*"A different place, now Richard Smith (of Thyme, Sheffield) has taken over" – this "elegantly refurbished" boozer has had a positive reception from most early reporters; doubters, though, find the style "out of character with the building".*
/ **Sample dishes:** *parfait of foie gras; breast of chicken; dark chocolate mousse with home-made ice cream.* **Details:** *www.druidinnbirchover.co.uk; SW of Bakewell off B5056; 9 pm; closed Sun D; no smoking.*

---

## BIRMINGHAM, WEST MIDLANDS 5–4C

Birmingham – the major city which was until recently of note for having no interesting restaurants – now has at least two: *Jessica's* and *Simpson's*. At a slightly less ambitious level, the well-established *Toque d'Or* continues to put in a very creditable performance. As a rendezvous for a light meal, *Café Ikon* is well worth knowing about. Generally speaking, however, it remains the case that Brum – despite the huge improvements to the cityscape of recent years – is a notably also-ran culinary destination, with many of the new sites in the revitalised city-centre given over to large but bland operations (such as *Bank* and *Petit Blanc*). The city is also weak in ethnic appeal aside, of course, from its famous balti houses (which are mostly concentrated in Moseley and Sparkbrook).

### Adil £ 17 ★

148-150 Stoney Ln B12 8AJ (0121) 449 0335

*Brum's original Balti house, in Sparkbrook; it "still offers some of the best baltis".* / **Sample dishes:** *shish kebabs; kulfi.*
**Details:** *www.adilbalti.co.uk; 3m from city centre on A41; 11.30 pm; no smoking area.*

**sign up for the survey at www.hardens.com**

## Bank £ 42
4 Brindleyplace B1 2JB (0121) 633 4466
*Service can be "impersonal" and the setting is "noisy and bland", but the cooking is pretty "solid" at this large outpost of the London mega-brasserie group; it makes a "safe" business choice at any time, and in summer its canalside tables are "lovely".*
/ **Sample dishes:** five-onion soup with cheese croutons; calf's liver & bacon; rum & raisin cheesecake. **Details:** www.bankrestaurants.com; 10.30 pm, Fri & Sat 11 pm; no smoking area.

## Bar Estilo £ 29
110-114 Wharfside St B1 1RF (0121) 643 3443
*"A lively place with great service and a good range of tapas" – that's the whole story on this large bar in the Mailbox development; it's "particularly handy with children".*
/ **Sample dishes:** spicy chicken quesadilla; lime cheesecake.
**Details:** www.barestilo.co.uk; 11 pm; no smoking area.

## Café Ikon
## Ikon Gallery £ 32 ★
Oozells Sq, Brindleyplace B1 2HS (0121) 248 3226
*"A wonderful find" – an "unfailingly good" (if not hugely atmospheric) central rendezvous, where "very authentic and generous" tapas are served by "friendly young Spaniards".*
/ **Sample dishes:** cured Spanish meats; seared tuna; baked custard flan.
**Details:** www.ikon-gallery.co.uk; 10 pm; closed Sun D; no Amex; no smoking area; children: before 9 pm only.

## Chez Jules £ 28
5a Ethel St, off New St B2 4BG (0121) 633 4664
*"A cheap eatery with a good atmosphere and good-quality French food" – that's the whole story on this "barn-like" central bistro; "the lunch set menu is the best value around".* / **Sample dishes:** roast snails with beetroot juice & crispy salad; crème brûlée.
**Details:** www.chezjules.co.uk; 11 pm; closed Sun D; no smoking area; no booking, Sat L.

## Chung Ying Garden £ 29
17 Thorp St B5 4AT (0121) 666 6622
*The small level of commentary attracted by this Chinatown fixture is in contrast to its huge size, but praises it as a dependable all-rounder, with "top dim sum" a special attraction; the 'other' Chung Ying, rather similar, is not far away, at 16-18 Wrottesley Street (tel 622 5669).* / **Sample dishes:** crispy aromatic duck with pancakes.
**Details:** www.chungying.co.uk; 11.30 pm.

## Coconut Lagoon £ 28 ★
12 Bennetts Hill B2 5RS (0121) 643 3045
*South Indian cuisine "makes an enjoyable contrast to other Indian restaurants in the city", and this centrally-located yearling wins high praise for its "wonderful" dishes.* / **Sample dishes:** chicken drumsticks with cashews; stuffed pomfret; mango sorbet.
**Details:** www.coconutlagoon.com; 11 pm.

**Hotel du Vin et Bistro**                           £ 48

25 Church St  B3 2NR   (0121) 200 0600

*It's "hard to believe you're in central Birmingham", at this "calm"
and "civilised" local outpost of the boutique-hotel chain –
the most talked-about place in town; the food is "humdrum",
though, and service "patchy" – it "needs to up its game".*
/ ***Sample dishes:*** Mozzarella & avocado salad; duck with apple & foie gras;
butterscotch cheesecake with chocolate sauce. ***Details:*** www.hotelduvin.co.uk;
9.45 pm; no smoking; booking: max 10. ***Accommodation:*** 66 rooms, from £125.

**Jessica's**                           £ 45        ★

1 Montague Rd  B16 9HN
(0121) 455 0999

*Thanks to its "imaginative" cooking and "hospitable" surroundings
("best in the conservatory"), Glynn Purnell's Edgbaston villa vies
with Simpsons for the title of "Brum's best"; the occasional
doubter, however, discerns a tendency to "over-elaboration".*
/ ***Sample dishes:*** salted Cornish cod with smoked black olives; loin of veal with
pea & broad bean salad; white chocolate mousse, poached peach & raspberries.
***Details:*** www.jessicasrestaurant.co.uk; 10 pm; closed Mon, Sat L & Sun; no Amex;
no smoking.

**Jyoti**                           £ 16        ★

569-571 Stratford Rd  B11 4LS   (0121) 766 7199

*"Consistently good, consistently cheap, and BYO – what more
could you want?"* – this "interesting" Gujerati vegetarian,
in Sparkbrook, continues to please reporters. / ***Sample dishes:*** mogo
chips; kofta, paneer bhurji, aubergine & potatoes; rasmalai. ***Details:*** 9.15 pm;
closed Mon, Tue-Thu D only; no Amex; no smoking.

**Malmaison**                           £ 37        Ⓐ

Royal Mail St  B1 1XL   (0121) 246 5000

*In the Mailbox, a "very busy and buzzy" outpost of the "stylish
boutique hotel chain", whose "steady" cuisine is approved by all
reporters.* / ***Sample dishes:*** eggs Benedict; poached salmon with spinach &
sorrel; iced banana parfait. ***Details:*** www.malmaison.com; 10 pm; smoking in bar
only. ***Accommodation:*** 189 rooms, from £135.

**Metro Bar & Grill**                           £ 39        Ⓐ

73 Cornwall St  B3 2DF   (0121) 200 1911

*This "see-and-be-seen" dining room is a "buzzy" sort of joint,
attracting a "mixed" crowd – from "execs to Footballers' Wives
types"* – with its "consistently well-realised fusion fare"; it's often
noted as "Birmingham's best place for a business meal".
/ ***Sample dishes:*** masala squid with mango & avocado guacamole; braised lamb
shank; home-made tart with custard. ***Details:*** www.metrobarandgrill.co.uk;
9.30 pm; closed Sat L & Sun.

**Paris**                           £ 65        ✗

109-111 The Mailbox, Wharfside  B1 1RF   (0121) 632 1488

*"Sterile", "hushed" and "up-itself", this ambitious restaurant
in the Mailbox development is chastised by reporters for its
"not amazingly original" cuisine and its "slow and laborious"
service – all this might all be more forgivable if prices weren't
"a joke".* / ***Details:*** www.restaurantparis.co.uk; 9.30 pm; closed Mon & Sun;
no smoking.

**sign up for the survey at www.hardens.com**                           161

### Le Petit Blanc £ 30 ✕
9 Brindleyplace B1 2HS (0121) 633 7333
*Raymond Blanc's name stands for nothing at this "mediocre" and "disappointing" modern brasserie; it's gone from bad to worse since Loch Fyne took over the management.* / **Sample dishes:** smoked chicken & chilli linguine; Thai-baked sea bass with coriander rice; sticky toffee pudding. **Details:** www.lepetitblanc.co.uk; 10.30 pm; no smoking.

### Rajdoot £ 28
78-79 George St B3 1PY (0121) 236 1116
*"Good standards" across the board characterise feedback on this long-established ('70s) subcontinental.* / **Details:** www.rajdoot.co.uk; 11.15 pm; closed Sat L & Sun L.

### San Carlo £ 38
4 Temple St B2 5BN (0121) 633 0251
*This "flash" city-centre stalwart can still seem something of "find" (and it's often thought of as "a great place for a business lunch"); by night, though, sceptics think it "crowded" and "noisy", with "indifferent" Italian fare.* / **Sample dishes:** Parma ham & buffalo Mozzarella; saltimbocco alla Romana; panna cotta. **Details:** www.sancarlo.co.uk; near St Philips Cathedral; 10.45 pm.

### Shimla Pinks £ 31
214 Broad St B15 1AY (0121) 633 0366
*"Some unusual dishes" add interest to a visit to this trendy city-centre subcontinental; times have changed since when it was 'the hot place in town', though, and it can seem "expensive for what it is", nowadays.* / **Sample dishes:** lamb kebabs & chicken; lamb rogan josh; kulfi ice cream. **Details:** www.shimlapinks.com; 11 pm; closed Sat L & Sun L.

### Simpson's £ 55 ★
20 Highfield Rd B15 3du (0121) 454 3434
*Relocated from Kenilworth a year ago, Andreas Antona's Edgbaston yearling wins hearty praise for "sophisticated" cooking that's judged the best in town; the "reserved" feel of the "suburban conservatory" setting doesn't wow everyone, but "enthusiastic" staff help lighten things up.* / **Sample dishes:** seared foie gras; pavé of turbot & confit of chicken wings; délice of chocolate, coffee & milk ice cream. **Details:** www.simpsonsrestaurant.co.uk; 9.45 pm; no smoking. **Accommodation:** 4 rooms, from £140.

### Thai Edge £ 39
7 Oozells Sq B1 2HS (0121) 643 3993
*It's often "lively" and "entertaining" – and the Thai cooking is sometimes "very good" too – but inconsistency remains something of a theme in commentary on this large city-centre restaurant.* / **Details:** 11 pm, Fri & Sat 11.30 pm; no smoking.

### La Toque d'Or £ 39 ★
27 Warstone Ln B18 6JQ (0121) 233 3655
*Didier Philipot's "wonderful food" again wins praise for this notably "reliable" Gallic restaurant, occupying a converted mill in the Jewellery Quarter; the setting, though, can seem surprisingly "lacking in atmosphere".* / **Sample dishes:** Isle of Skye scallops; fillet of turbot & girolle mushrooms; toffee soufflé with chocolate ice cream. **Details:** www.latoquedor.co.uk; 9.30 pm; closed Mon, Sat L & Sun; closed 2 weeks in Aug; no smoking.

## BISHOPS STORTFORD, HERTFORDSHIRE          3–3D

### The Lemon Tree                    £ 37          ★
14-16 Water Ln  CM23 2LB  (01279) 757788
*An "intimate" and "relaxing" bistro, which is a "favourite locally";
it's nominated both for a date, and as "a good setting for
a business lunch".* / **Sample dishes:** *grilled calf's liver mash; duck breast;
sticky toffee pudding.* **Details:** *www.lemontree.co.uk; 9.30 pm; closed Mon &
Sun D; no Amex; smoking in bar only.*

## BISHOPS TACHBROOK, WARWICKSHIRE          5–4C

### Mallory Court                     £ 65          ★★
Harbury Ln  CV33 9QB  (01926) 330214
*Simon Haigh's "sensational" cooking helps make this Lutyens-
designed country house hotel a simply "brilliant" destination;
its wine list "ascends into the stratosphere", but "includes good
bottles at affordable prices".* / **Sample dishes:** *goat's cheese ravioli;
sea bass with tarragon mousse; raspberry soufflé.* **Details:** *www.mallory.co.uk; 2m S
of Leamington Spa, off B4087; 9 pm; no smoking.* **Accommodation:** *29 rooms,
from £135.*

## BISPHAM GREEN, LANCASHIRE                5–1A

### Eagle & Child                     £ 29
Maltkiln Ln  L40 3SG  (01257) 462297
*A "cosy country boozer" that's "always buzzing" – the odd slip
up is reported, but for the most part it's "great".*
/ **Sample dishes:** *deep-fried goat's cheese; toasted chicken & red pepper panini;
sticky toffee pudding.* **Details:** *M6, J27; 8.30 pm; no Amex; no smoking area.*

## BLACKPOOL, LANCASHIRE                    5–1A

### Kwizeen                           £ 30
47-49 King St  FY1 3EJ  (01253) 290045
*It may have "the worst name ever", but some – if not all –
reporters find the cooking at this "unexpected" restaurant "really
innovative" (with a "good range of wines" too).* / **Sample dishes:** *lime
curry chicken breast; glazed duck breast with plum & blackberry sauce; chocolate
fudge pudding.* **Details:** *www.kwizeen.co.uk; 9 pm; closed Sat L & Sun; no Amex.*

## BLAIRGOWRIE, PERTH & KINROSS             9–3C

### Kinloch House                     £ 42
PH10 6SG  (01250) 884237
*The Allen Family seems to be beginning to get to grips with this
formerly "slightly faded" hotel (which they bought a few years
ago), and its food can sometimes be "very good".*
/ **Sample dishes:** *wild mushroom, chicken & sweetbread terrine; fillet steak with
Lanark blue cheese; chocolate truffle cake with mint cream.*
**Details:** *www.kinlochhouse.com; past the Cottage Hospital, turn L, procede
3m along A923, (signposted Dunkeld Road); 9 pm; jacket required; no smoking;
children: 7+ at D.* **Accommodation:** *18 rooms, from £220.*

**sign up for the survey at www.hardens.com**

## BLAKENEY, NORFOLK  6–3C
**The White Horse Hotel**  £37  A★
4 High St  NR25 7AL  (01263) 740574
*"Lovely wholesome food, by the sea"* is the draw to this
*"welcoming"* inn; *"although they have separate kitchens, the bar
seems just as good as the restaurant"*. / **Sample dishes:** smoked cod,
leek & Parmesan tartlet; roast black bream with chilli & fennel dressing; chocolate
mousse. **Details:** www.blakeneywhitehorse.co.uk; 9 pm; D only; no Amex;
no smoking. **Accommodation:** 10 rooms, from £60.

## BOLTON ABBEY, NORTH YORKSHIRE  8–4B
**Devonshire Arms**  £73
BD23 6AJ  (01756) 710441
*Some meals at this grand and famous ducally-owned inn
"far outweigh expectations"* (and it boasts a *"superb"* wine list
too); portions can be *"miniscule"*, though, and service is up-and-
down, contributing to a strong minority view that the place
*"does not offer good value"*. / **Sample dishes:** goose, mango & smoked foie
gras salad; roast cod with fennel & olive sauce; chocolate & Turkish delight soufflé.
**Details:** www.devonshirehotels.co.uk; on A59, 5m NE of Skipton; 9 pm; closed Mon,
Tue-Sat D only, Sun open L & D; no jeans or trainers; no smoking.
**Accommodation:** 40 rooms, from £230.

## BOSHAM, WEST SUSSEX  3–4A
**Millstream Hotel**  £41
PO18 8HL  (01243) 573234
*"A warm welcome"* and generally *"super"* food is the gist
of commentary on this attractive contemporary hotel, set in a nice
riverside garden. / **Details:** www.millstream-hotel.co.uk; A259 from Chichister;
9 pm; no smoking. **Accommodation:** 35 rooms, from £139.

## BOUGHTON LEES, KENT  3–3C
**The Manor Restaurant**
**Eastwell Manor**  £59  A
Eastwell Pk  TN25 4HR  (01233) 213000
*This "sumptuous" country house is replete with "olde worlde
charm"* (to which notably *"warm"* and *"friendly"* staff make
no small contribution); the cooking *"does not disappoint"*,
but plays something of a supporting rôle. / **Sample dishes:** white bean
soup with langoustine & truffles; chicken supreme with mustard cream sauce;
apple & rhubarb crumble. **Details:** www.eastwellmanor.co.uk; 3m N of Ashford
on A251; 9.30 pm; jacket & tie required; no smoking; booking: max 8.
**Accommodation:** 62 rooms, from £220.

## BOURNEMOUTH, DORSET  2–4C
**Bistro on the Beach**  £33  A
Solent Promenade, Southbourne Coast Rd  BH6 4BE
(01202) 431473
*"The waves crash on the beach yards away"*, at this *"unusual"*
location at the foot of the cliffs in Southbourne – *"by day a sea-
front cafe, by night a candlelit bistro"*; fans say the food is *"lovely"*
and *"fairly-priced"*, but some reporters fear that the place has
*"lost the plot"*. / **Sample dishes:** ricotta & spinach ravioli; blueberry &
shortbread millefeuille. **Details:** www.bistroonthebeach.com; 2m E of town centre
in Southbourne; 9.30 pm; D only, closed Sun-Tue (open Tue in Summer); no smoking.

**sign up for the survey at www.hardens.com**

## Chez Fred                                    £16      ★★
10 Seamoor Rd  BH4 9AN   (01202) 761023
*"The best fish and chips on the planet" are – say fans – to be found at this Westbourne fixture, renowned locally as "the chippie of the stars!"* / **Sample dishes:** *no starters; cod & chips with mushy peas; treacle sponge & custard.* **Details:** *www.chezfred.co.uk; 1m W of town centre; 9.45 pm; closed Sun L; no Amex; no smoking; no booking.*

## Ocean Palace                                 £31
8 Priory Rd  BH2 5DG   (01202) 559127
*"A very good-quality Chinese, especially for seafood" which offers some of the best food near the BIC and pier; popularity is such that it can get "very busy and rushed" – "the noise level is just like Hong Kong!"* / **Sample dishes:** *deep-fried chicken in chilli sauce; crispy aromatic duck with pancakes; banana fritters.* **Details:** *www.oceanpalace.co.uk; 11 pm.*

## Red Panda                                    £32
Pier Approach  BH2 5AA   (01202) 298800
*This "very large" Chinese restaurant (part of a chain whose three other branches are in Belfast) serves "good" cooking, and has been a "welcome addition" to the local dining scene.* / **Details:** *www.theredpanda.com.*

## West Beach                                   £36      Ⓐ
Pier Approach  BH2 5AA   (01202) 587785
*For fans, this is a "stylish venue, with food to match" (and with "great fish" a highlight); sceptics say service can be "terrible", though, and fear the place is beginning to rely rather on its "to die for" seaside location.* / **Sample dishes:** *sauteed spiced crevettes; poached organic salmon; Valrhona chocolate & honeycomb terrine.* **Details:** *10 pm; no smoking area.*

---

## BOWNESS, CUMBRIA                             7–3D

## Linthwaite House                             £57      Ⓐ
Crook Rd  LA23 3JA   (01539) 488600
*"Fabulous views" of the lake (from the garden) help whet the appetites of diners at this "very special" country house hotel; limited feedback on the cuisine puts it somewhere between "pleasant" and "first-class".* / **Sample dishes:** *creamy scrambled duck egg; sea bass with hand-dived scallops; rice pudding with caramalised plum.* **Details:** *www.linthwaite.com; 9 pm; smoking in bar only; children: 7+ at D.* **Accommodation:** *27 rooms, from £140.*

## Miller Howe                                  £56      Ⓐ
Rayrigg Rd  LA23 1EY   (01539) 442536
*A "wonderful romantic location above Windermere" is the famous 'USP' of this "elegant" and "welcoming" country house hotel; some reporters say the food is "very good" too, but others say the place "survives on its reputation".* / **Sample dishes:** *chicken liver salad; roast halibut with sage mash; sticky toffee pudding.* **Details:** *www.millerhowe.com; on A592 between Windermere & Bowness; 8.45 pm; closed for 2 weeks in Jan; no smoking; children: 8+.* **Accommodation:** *15 rooms, from £200.*

**sign up for the survey at www.hardens.com**

### Porthole                                           £ 45
3 Ash St LA23 3EB   (01539) 442793
*After 30 years, this well-known Italian restaurant was bought
in 2004 by its chef and its sommelier; most reporters express all-
round satisfaction – not least with its "classy" wine list and quality
cooking, and even a critic who found the food "not what is was"
proclaims service "still exceptional".* / **Sample dishes:** seared king
scallops over mash; braised oxtail; sticky toffee pudding.
**Details:** www.potholeeatinghouse.co.uk; near Old England Hotel; 10.30 pm; D only,
closed Tue; no smoking.

---

## BRADFORD ON AVON, WILTSHIRE            2–3B

### Thai Barn                                          £ 32        ★
24 Bridge St BA15 1BY   (01225) 866443
*Locals who claim the food is "the best outside Thailand" may
be overdoing it a bit, but this "atmospheric" place attracts nothing
but praise, not least for its "attentive" service.* / **Sample dishes:** royal
platter; saute pork; pineapple ice cream. **Details:** opp Bridge St car park;
10.30 pm; closed Mon & Tue L; no Amex; no smoking.

---

## BRADFORD, WEST YORKSHIRE                5–1C

### Aagrah                                             £ 24        ★
483 Bradford Rd LS28 8ED   (01274) 668818
*Feedback is modest in volume, but confirms the continuing appeal
of this good Indian all-rounder – part of an outstanding Yorkshire
chain.* / **Details:** www.aagrah.com; on A647, 3m from city centre; 11.30 pm, Fri &
Sat midnight; D only; no smoking area.

### Akbar's Balti                                      £ 22      A★★
1276 Leeds Rd BD3 3LF   (01274) 773311
*Reporters really can't speak highly enough of the "terrific curries"
– not to mention the other "great" dishes – at this "always-
crowded" subcontinental; its setting is quite "trendy" and
"sophisticated" too.* / **Details:** www.akbars.co.uk; midnight; D only;
no smoking area.

### Clark's                                            £ 26
46-50 Highgate BD9 4BE   (01274) 499890
*"Consistently good value" – and the fact they don't sell curry! –
had made this modern brasserie a popular destination locally;
it moved into new ownership just as our surveying year was
drawing to a close, so we've left it unrated.* / **Sample dishes:** pea &
mint soup; bacon chop with Cheddar mash & parsley sauce; treacle tart. **Details:** 5
mins from city centre on A650 to Shipley; 9.30 pm; closed Sat L; smoking in bar only.

### Karachi                                            £ 8         ★
15-17 Neal St BD5 0BX   (01274) 732015
*"Smartened up a bit since Rick Stein visited, but still offering
excellent food at bargain prices" – "Bradford's oldest Indian
restaurant" (1974) continues to pack 'em in; no booze.*
/ **Sample dishes:** meat & spinach karahi; shamee & shish kebab; home-made
kulfi & barfi. **Details:** 1 am; no credit cards.

**sign up for the survey at www.hardens.com**

## Kashmir £ 10 ★

27 Morley St  BD7 1AG  (01274) 726513

*"Very basic in a way that's rare nowadays"* – this veteran curry house (the oldest in town) is, for many reporters, *"still the benchmark"*. / **Sample dishes:** *fish pakora; chicken karahi; home-made kulfi.* **Details:** *3 am; no smoking area.*

## Love Apple Cafe £ 23 Ⓐ★

34 Great Horton Rd  BD7 1AL  (01274) 744075

A *"really relaxed and mellow"* all-day café, with *"a fantastic cosmopolitan menu"* that's *"great for either a full meal or a snack"*. / **Sample dishes:** *nachos; chana massala with tomatoes & coriander; chocolate truffle cheesecake.* **Details:** *www.loveapplecafe.co.uk; 9 pm; no smoking area.*

## Mumtaz Paan House £ 25 ★★

Great Horton Rd  BD7 3HS  (01274) 571861

*"They've made it posher"* (and *"prices seem to have gone up a bit"*), but this *"extraordinary"* Kashmiri veteran continues to incite rave reviews for its *"top-quality"*, *"subtly-spiced"* dishes; it's *"great for families"* too; no alcohol. / **Sample dishes:** *spiced chicken & sweetcorn in pastry; spiced cod with pomegranate; mango ice cream.* **Details:** *www.mumtaz.co.uk; 1 am; no smoking area.*

## Nawaab £ 24 ★

32 Manor Row  BD1 4QE  (01274) 720371

*Recently remodelled "on more contemporary lines", this "upmarket curry house" continues to be an "all-round enjoyable" destination – service can be up-and-down, but fans insist that the place is "streets ahead of its competitors".* / **Details:** *www.nawaab.net; 11.30 pm; D only; no smoking area.*

---

## BRAMPTON, CUMBRIA 7–2D

### Farlam Hall £ 49 Ⓐ

CA8 2NG  (01697) 746234

*"Gourmet-quality"* dining attracts only positive reports on this Relais & Châteaux country house – the ambience and service attract higher ratings than the cooking, but the overall 'package' is usually judged as *"excellent"*. / **Sample dishes:** *cream of sweet potato & chive; slow-cooked spiced pork with carmelised apples; crème fraîche mousse with fruit coulis.* **Details:** *www.farlamhall.co.uk; 2.5m S.E of Brampton on A689, not in Farlam Village; 8.30 pm; D only; no smoking; children: 5+.* **Accommodation:** *12 rooms, from £260.*

---

## BRANCASTER, NORFOLK 6–3B

### White Horse £ 37 Ⓐ

Main Rd  PE31 8BY  (01485) 210262

*"Reliable"* fish and a *"superb"* setting with *"great coastal views"* have helped make a big name for this *"friendly"* inn; the occasional reporters fears that – *"like so many places in Norfolk"* – it's getting a bit *"expensive"* for what it is. / **Sample dishes:** *salmon & crab fishcakes; pan-fried skate wing; strawberry shortbread.* **Details:** *www.whitehorsebrancaster.co.uk; 9 pm; no Amex; no smoking.* **Accommodation:** *15 rooms, from £90.*

**sign up for the survey at www.hardens.com**

## BRANSCOMBE, DEVON                      2–4A
### Masons Arms                          £34
Main St  EX12 3DJ   (01297) 680300
*"A lovely pub, in a beautiful village, offering quality food" – let's
hope that new owners Collin and Carol Slaney are keeping up the
standards which have made it "very popular".*
/ **Sample dishes:** *steamed mussels with Thai green curry sauce; pan-fried peppered
skate wing; coffee torte & raspberry coulis.* **Details:** *www.masonsarms.co.uk; 9 pm;
D only; no Amex; no smoking.* **Accommodation:** *20 rooms, from £50.*

---

## BRAY, WINDSOR & MAIDENHEAD            3–3A
### The Fat Duck                         £99      ★★
1 High St  SL6 2AQ   (01628) 580333
*Hundreds of reports affirm the ever-growing stature of this world-
renowned shrine to the "outlandish" 'molecular gastronomy' which
Heston Blumenthal offers in this "unpompous" former village pub;
about one reporter in seven, though, still doesn't quite 'get it'.*
/ **Sample dishes:** *cuttlefish cannelloni with duck & maple syrup; slow-cooked lamb
with lamb's tongue; tarte Tatin.* **Details:** *www.fatduck.co.uk; 9.30 pm, Fri & Sat
10 pm; closed Mon & Sun D; closed 2 weeks at New Year; no smoking.*

### The Hind's Head                      £37      ★
High St  SL6 2AB   (01628) 626151
*This "lovely old pub" was recently purchased and "tastefully
revamped" by Heston Blumenthal; it's no Fat Duck, though,
delivering a menu of "traditional" dishes with "big English
flavours" in an "informal" setting.* / **Sample dishes:** *pea & ham soup;
oxtail & kidney pudding; treacle tart with milk ice cream.* **Details:** *9.30 pm; closed
Sun D; no smoking.*

### Jasmine Oriental                     £39      ★
Old Mill Ln  SL6 2BG   (01628) 788999
*This elegant Chinese two-year-old continues to win high all-round
ratings from a more-than-local fanclub.* / **Details:** *10 pm; no Amex.*

### Riverside Brasserie             £42
Monkey Island Ln, Bray Marina  SL6 2EB
(01628) 780553
*It's no longer associated with the Fat Duck, but this "cheerful"
place is still hailed as a great "informal" stand-by; it's only the
"fantastic waterside location" in Bray Marina (complete with
terrace), however, which could be said to give it anything
approaching 'destination' status.* / **Sample dishes:** *sardine tart; rib-eye
steak & chips; strawberry soup with butter biscuits.*
**Details:** *www.riversidebrasserie.co.uk; follow signs for Bray Marina off A308;
10 pm; closed Mon & Sun D; no Amex.*

### Waterside Inn                        £125     A★★
Ferry Rd  SL6 2AT   (01628) 620691
*Michel Roux's "faultless" temple of gastronomy – with son Alain
at the stoves – "represents the pinnacle of gastronomic
achievement" for most reporters; its prices may "border
on extortion", but it offers "sublime", "classically-rooted" cuisine,
"sensational" service and a "beautiful" Thames-side setting.*
/ **Sample dishes:** *spiced foie gras terrine; grilled rabbit with glazed chestnuts;
golden plum soufflé.* **Details:** *www.waterside-inn.co.uk; off A308 between
Windsor & Maidenhead; 10 pm; closed Mon & Tue (open Tue D Jun-Aug); booking:
max 10; children: 12+.* **Accommodation:** *9 rooms, from £160.*

## BREARTON, NORTH YORKSHIRE 8–4B

**The Malt Shovel** £23 A★
HG3 3BX (01423) 862929
*A popular boozer, in a former barn; under new ownership,
its "good, tasty and unpretentious food" and the attraction of its
"real fire in winter" combine to ensure that you need
to "book early".* / **Sample dishes:** Wensleydale blue & red onion tart; steak &
ale pie; hot chocolate brownie. **Details:** off A61, 6m N of Harrogate; 9 pm; closed
Mon & Sun D; no credit cards; no smoking area; need 8+ to book.

## BRECON, POWYS 2–1A

**Felin Fach Griffin** £40 A★
Felin Fach LD3 0UB (01874) 620111
*"Excellent hearty scoff" and "great service" are helping make
a big name for this "Brecon Beacons gem" – a "welcoming" and
"relaxed" gastropub-with-rooms, where the only occasional
complaint is that it's "getting too popular".* / **Sample dishes:** wild
mushroom tagliatelle; rib of Welsh black beef with chips; lemon tart.
**Details:** www.eatdrinksleep.ltd.uk; 20 mins NW of Abergavenny on A470; 9.30 pm;
closed Mon L; no Amex; no smoking area. **Accommodation:** 7 rooms,
from £92.50.

## BRIDPORT, DORSET 2–4B

**Riverside** £39 A★★
West Bay DT6 4EZ (01308) 422011
*"Perfection, on a sunny day"; thanks to its "brilliant" fish cooking
and its "enviable" waterside location, this "really excellent" but
"unflashy" restaurant – a 'destination' of four decades' standing –
is "always packed".* / **Sample dishes:** deep-fried calamari with lemon; local
line-caught plaice fillets; sweet jelly with lemon glazed pears & biscotti.
**Details:** www.thefishrestaurant-westbay.co.uk; 9 pm; closed Mon & Sun D;
no Amex; no smoking.

## BRIGHOUSE, WEST YORKSHIRE 5–1C

**Brook's** £37
6 Bradford Rd HD6 1RW (01484) 715284
*A former Savoy chef runs this quite ambitious venture –
a "romantic" converted pub – and the results from the "really
unusual" menu (certainly for these parts) can be "delicious";
it doesn't wow everyone, though.* / **Sample dishes:** confit of bacon,
potato & onion salad; chicken stuffed with cep & mushrooms; poached peaches
in pink champagne. **Details:** www.brooks-restaurant.co.uk; 11 pm; closed Sun;
smoking in bar only.

## BRIGHTON, EAST SUSSEX                      3–4B

In some ways, 'London by the Sea' mimics the restaurant scene
of the metropolis, offering some pretty decent dining options
at most levels. In the middle ground, restaurants of note
include *Due South*, *La Fourchette* and *Strand*. *Terre à Terre* heads
up a large veggie contingent, and is now re-established
as arguably the best restaurant of that type in the country. For
quintessential seaside seafood, the *Regency* remains hard
to beat. Diners on a budget (in particular) benefit from a very
good range of reasonably-priced ethnic restaurants, often
of good quality. However, the city is still in search of a true
champion – the relaunched *One Paston Place* has yet to achieve
the consistency to justify such a description.

### Al Duomo                              £ 24        ✕
7 Pavilion Building  BN1 1EE   (01273) 326741
*The major refit a couple of years ago has "done nothing" for this
well-established pizzeria which – despite a touristy location –
used to be a popular local stand-by; these days it's "less homely",
and its food is "very ordinary".* / **Sample dishes:** *calamari; fusilli with
tomatoes & anchovies; tiramisu.* **Details:** *www.alduomo.co.uk; near the Royal
Pavilion; 11 pm; no smoking area.*

### Blanch House                          £ 48
17 Atlingworth St  BN2 1PL   (01273) 603504
*There were somewhat better reports this year on this design-hotel
dining room; its ("Austin Powers meets Space 1999") ambience
can still seem "really cold", though, and views on the food are up-
and-down – "go for a cocktail" still seems the safest advice.*
/ **Sample dishes:** *loin of rabbit; Gressingham duck; apple tartlette & sorbet.*
**Details:** *www.blanchhouse.co.uk; 9.30 pm, Sat & Sun 10 pm; closed Mon, Tue L &
Sun D; smoking in bar only.* **Accommodation:** *12 rooms, from £125.*

### Bombay Aloo                           £ 13        ★
39 Ship St  BN1 1AB   (01273) 771089
*"Unbeatable for cheap and surprisingly good food",
this "welcoming", if "crowded", buffet-style veggie Indian "may not
be a gastronomic experience", but it is an "old faithful" par
excellence.* / **Details:** *www.bombay-aloo.co.uk; near the Lanes; midnight;
no Amex; no smoking area; need 6+ to book.*

### Casa Don Carlos                       £ 27        𝔸
5 Union St  BN1 1HA   (01273) 327177
*"You can eat really well for very little", at this "crowded but
intimate" Lanes tapas bar.* / **Details:** *11 pm.*

### China Garden                          £ 30        ★
88-91 Preston St  BN1 2HG   (01273) 325124
*Thanks to its "very good dim sum", this cheap 'n' cheerful
Chinese can get very "crowded" (and "smokey").* / **Details:** *opp West
Pier; 11 pm; no smoking area.*

**sign up for the survey at www.hardens.com**

**Donatello** £30

1-3 Brighton Pl BN1 1HJ (01273) 775477

*Fans insist you get "the best cheap pizzas", at this Lanes institution; its "rushed" and "buzzing" style, though, is a bit too "churn-and-burn" for some tastes. / **Sample dishes:** grilled sardines; tagliatelle with smoked salmon & cream; cherries in liqueur with ice cream.* **Details:** www.donatello.co.uk; 11.30 pm; no smoking area.

**The Dorset Street Bar** £29 Ⓐ

28 North Rd BN1 1YB (01273) 605423

*Staff "without the pretentiousness prevalent in these parts" add to the appeal of this North Laine ex-boozer – an all-day destination at its best for Sunday brunch. / **Sample dishes:** salmon fishcakes; grilled chicken with salami & Camembert; chocolate brioche.* **Details:** www.thedorset.co.uk; 10 pm; no smoking area; booking: max 12.

**Due South** £35 ★

139 King's Arches BN1 2FN
(01273) 821218

*A "superb sea-view from the terrace" and "a menu strong on local produce and fish" again win high praise for this "chilled" beach-side yearling; even fans can find the cooking "variable", though, and the setting of the non-window tables is a bit "tunnel"-like. / **Sample dishes:** pan-fried red mullet fillets; fish of the day; elderflower & vanilla panna cotta.* **Details:** www.duesouth.co.uk; 10 pm; no smoking.

**English's** £45

29-31 East St BN1 1HL (01273) 327980

*After 60 years in the same hands, this famously "quaint" Lanes fish parlour moved into new ownership just as our survey for the year was drawing to a close; a rating is therefore inappropriate, but initial signs seem positive. / **Sample dishes:** melon with honey-roasted salmon; Dover sole & prawns with lobster sauce; pear tatin.* **Details:** www.englishs.co.uk; 10 pm; smoking in bar only.

**Food for Friends** £29

17-18 Prince Albert St BN1 1HF (01273) 202310

*This "solid" Lanes veggie of long standing can still be "worth a visit"; it managed to be criticised for being both "too worthy" and "too commercial" – presumably that means they've got it about right? / **Sample dishes:** Jerusalem artichoke soup; Cheddar & mushroom risotto with spicy tomato sauce; Bramley & blackberry crumble.* **Details:** www.foodforfriends.com; 10 pm; no smoking.

**La Fourchette** £38 ★

105 Western Rd BN1 2AA (01273) 722556

*"On a good night, you get some of the best food anywhere in town", at this "very friendly" and "fairly-priced" Gallic restaurant, which wins warm words from practically all reporters. / **Sample dishes:** spinach, asparagus & Mozzarella lasagne; confit duck with mash & veal sauce; citron tart.* **Details:** www.lafourchette.co.uk; 10.30 pm; closed Sun D; no smoking area.

**sign up for the survey at www.hardens.com**

## The George £21 A★
5 Trafalgar St BN1 4EQ (01273) 681055
"An excellent veggie pub" – all reports paint a glowing picture
of this North Laine boozer, which manages "to create a friendly
'family' atmosphere, while still retaining a young and studenty
vibe". / **Sample dishes:** tomato & Mozzarella bruschetta; smoked Applewood
rarebit with leeks & salsa; tarte Tatin. **Details:** 9.30 pm, Fri-Sun 8.30 pm;
no smoking area; children: 16+ at D.

## Gingerman £37 ★
21a Norfolk Sq BN1 2PD (01273) 326688
The setting may be "small", "noisy" and "cramped", but this
popular Lanes venture more than compensates with its "cheerful"
and "competent" service, and Ben McKellar's often-"excellent"
cooking. / **Sample dishes:** beetroot & anchovy salad; swordfish with plum tomato
tart; passion fruit soufflé. **Details:** off Norfolk Square; 10 pm; closed Mon;
no smoking.

## The Gingerman
## Drakes Hotel £43
44 Marine Pde BN1 (01273) 696934
Ben McKellar's new venture "builds on the reputation of the
original, in a light, clean and uncluttered setting" – on limited
initial feedback most (but not quite all) reporters found it "equally
good".

## Havana £45 A
32 Duke St BN1 1AG (01273) 773388
This "lovely-night-out" venue in the Lanes was better supported
this year as a "different", "pricey-but-worth-it" destination;
the "limited" menu is vaguely Cuban in style, but the fare on offer
also includes a "great cheese-board"! / **Sample dishes:** haddock &
poached egg tartlet; roast venison; Bailey's parfait with biscuits.
**Details:** www.havana.uk.com; 10.30 pm; children: 6+ at D.

## Hotel du Vin et Bistro £48 A
Ship St BN1 1AD (01273) 718588
The "fabulous" wine list helps fuel the "lovely", "buzzy"
atmosphere at this South Coast outpost of the popular boutique-
hotel chain; the food is barely mentioned. / **Sample dishes:** moules
marinière; duck with apple & foie gras; chocolate tart. **Details:** www.hotelduvin.com;
9.45 pm; no smoking; booking: max 10. **Accommodation:** 37 rooms, from £125.

## Indian Summer £34 ★
69 East St BN1 1HQ (01273) 711001
In both Hove (since 2001, 5 Victoria Terrace, 773090) and
Brighton (2003), these "inventive new-wave Indian eateries" have
made quite a name for themselves; although they take pride
in being "different", it's the "authentic-sounding dishes" which are
most prized by reporters. / **Sample dishes:** masala dosa; mughal chicken;
mango brûlée. **Details:** www.indian-summer.org.uk; 10.30 pm; closed Mon L;
no smoking.

## One Paston Place £56

I Paston Pl BN2 IHA (01273) 606933

*For its fans, this grand Kemptown townhouse-restaurant has re-emerged as a "gem" under its new owners; it can still seem rather "staid", though, and even some who find the menu "interesting" also find it rather "overpriced".* / **Sample dishes:** seared halibut with lobster tortelli; free range Sussex lamb with herb mousse & saffron rice; pear William Charlotte. **Details:** www.onepastonplace.co.uk; between the pier & marina; 10 pm; closed Mon & Sun; no smoking; children: 7.

## Regency £20 ★

131 Kings Rd BN1 2HH (01273) 325014

*A reputation for "great fresh fish, right on the sea-front" has helped make this "very busy" café quite a "venerable institution"; the occasional reporter would recommend it "purely for the fish 'n' chips" – "they're so good, it's not worth paying more for anything else".* / **Sample dishes:** oysters; dressed crab salad; peach melba. **Details:** www.theregencyrestaurant.co.uk; opp West Pier; 11 pm; no smoking area. **Accommodation:** 30 rooms, from £65.

## The Saint £37

22 St James's St BN2 1RF (01273) 607835

*"Great little booths to cosy up in" add romantic interest to this "lively" Kemptown hang-out; the "interesting" food, however, was rated more variably this year.* / **Sample dishes:** smoked ham hock & foie gras terrine; rump of lamb; griottine tart with kirsch coulis. **Details:** www.thesaintrestaurant.co. uk; 10 pm, Fri & Sat 10.30 pm; closed Mon; no smoking area.

## Sanctuary Café £24 &#x24B6;

51-55 Brunswick Street East BN3 1AU (01273) 770002

*This "friendly" Brunswick veggie café maintains its reputation for "delicious" light meals (and top coffee).* / **Sample dishes:** pâté of the day; falafel with tahini & salads; vegan chocolate cake. **Details:** www.sanctuarycafe.co.uk; 10 pm; no Amex; no smoking.

## Seven Dials £38

1-3 Buckingham Pl BN1 3TD (01273) 885555

*The setting is a bit "barn-like" (and "out of the centre"), but this "decent" restaurant is generally hailed by reporters for its "inventive" and "well-executed" grub; lunch, in particular, offers "very good value".* / **Sample dishes:** crispy breast of lamb; pan-fried lemon sole fillets with sage ratatouille; strawberry sundae with passion fruit cream. **Details:** www.sevendialsrestaurant.co.uk; 10.30 pm; closed Mon; no smoking area.

## Strand £36 &#x24B6;★

6 Little East St BN1 1HT (01273) 747096

*"Great cooking" and an "intimate and romantic setting" win consistent praise for this "lovely little restaurant", just off the sea-front.* / **Sample dishes:** pan-fried scallops on vegetarian haggis; lamb en croûte; dark chocolate & pistachio terrine. **Details:** www.thestrandrestaurantbrighton.co.uk; 10 pm, Fri & Sat 10.30 pm; closed Mon L; no smoking area; booking: max 8, Fri & Sat.

**sign up for the survey at www.hardens.com**

## Terre à Terre                                    £ 40        ★★

71 East St  BN1 1HQ   (01273) 729051
First-timers can be "amazed and enchanted" by a visit to this
veggie "one-off" in the Lanes – the most commented-on place
in town; the "incredibly inventive and imaginative" menu
is "an experience in itself", and amongst the UK's best meat-free
cooking. / **Sample dishes:** wild garlic & goat's cheese risotto; asparagus tips &
piccalilli; chocolate brioche pudding. **Details:** www.terreaterre.co.uk; 10.30 pm;
closed Mon & Tue L; no smoking; booking: max 8 at weekends.

---

## BRIMFIELD, SHROPSHIRE                            5–4A

## The Roebuck Inn                                  £ 35        ★

SY8 4NE   (01584) 711230
A handsome pub, not far from Ludlow; it doesn't attract a huge
amount of feedback – such as there is tips it as a "relaxed" but
"professional" place, serving food to suit all tastes – "from pies
to pithiviers!" / **Sample dishes:** seared scallops with carrots & cumin curry; fillet
of sea bass on vegetable risotto; panna cotta. **Details:** www.roebuckinn.com;
9.30 pm; no Amex; no smoking. **Accommodation:** 3 rooms, from £80.

---

## BRINKWORTH, WILTSHIRE                            2–2C

## The Three Crowns                                 £ 32

The Street  SN15 5AF   (01666) 510366
"Near enough the M4 to stop en voyage", this large inn boasts
an "unusual variety of pub food"; it's very popular – "get there
early". / **Sample dishes:** grilled kangaroo, venison & ostrich; sticky toffee pudding.
**Details:** www.threecrowns.co.uk; 9.30 pm; no smoking area; no booking.

---

## BRISTOL, CITY OF BRISTOL                         2–2B

For such a pleasant and affluent city, Bristol remains
surprisingly short of restaurants of any note. Many of the city's
best-known places are good-looking but culinarily
undistinguished – this comment sadly applies not only to some
of the waterfront locations, such as *riverstation*, but also
to what should be the best place in town (*Michael Caines*). As a
general 'night-out' destination, the much improved *Severnshed*
stands out. Well-heeled Clifton has many places to go out,
but only one place of real note – local hero Stephen
Markwick's unpretentious *Culinaria*.

## Aqua                                             £ 29        ✕

Welsh Back  BS1 4RR   (0117) 915 6060
The "very attractive waterside location" is a "great spot for
alfresco eating", and makes it worth knowing about this
"very busy" bar/restaurant; the food can seem "perfunctory",
though, and the staff often "can't be bothered" either.
/ **Sample dishes:** crispy duck & noodle salad; sticky toffee pudding.
**Details:** www.aquarestaurant.com; 10 pm; L only, ex Mon open L & D; smoking
in bar only.

## Bell's Diner £41 🄰

1 York Rd BS6 5QB (0117) 924 0357

*Chris Wicks's Montpelier fixture has long divided locals; for the
majority it "can't be surpassed in Bristol", thanks to its
"imaginative" food and "charming" service – critics say it's now
"over-experimental".* / **Sample dishes:** *cannelloni of honey with truffle &
goat's cheese; strawberry & peanut butter sandwich.* **Details:** *www.bellsdiner.co.uk;
10 pm; closed Mon L, Sat L & Sun D; no smoking.*

## Bocanova £38

90 Colston St BS1 5BB (0117) 929 1538

*"Genuinely innovative and distinctive cooking" (and served in a
"great" atmosphere too) is hailed by enthusiastic local fans of this
"Brazilian-European fusion" joint; it displeased a couple
of reporters this year, though, who found it "tired"
or "overpriced".* / **Sample dishes:** *goat's cheese salad with raspberry dressing;
tagliatelle with red wine plum sauce; panna cotta with plums & whisky syrup.*
**Details:** *www.bocanova.co.uk; 10.30 pm, Fri & Sat 11 pm; closed Sun; no Amex;
no smoking.*

## Boston Tea Party £20 🄰★

75 Park St BS1 5PF (0117) 929 8601

*"The best coffee in the West Country, as well as delicious
sandwiches and salads" have made a big name for this "cosy"
and "laid-back" café (which benefits from a "summer sun-trap
garden"); the staff are "very helpful" too.* / **Sample dishes:** *carrot &
coriander soup; Spanish chicken; carrot cake.* **Details:** *www.thebostonteaparty.co.uk;
10 pm, Sun 7 pm; closed Mon D; no Amex; no smoking; no booking.*

## Budokan £26 ★

31 Colston St BS1 5AP (0117) 914 1488

*For "a quick and easy refuel" at "very cheap prices", this pan-
Asian mini-chain – which also has a branch in Whiteladies –
is popular with all reporters; early-evening menus offer special
value.* / **Sample dishes:** *steamed mussels in lemon grass & chilli; duck teriyaki;
chocolate marquise.* **Details:** *www.budokan.co.uk; 11 pm; closed Sun; no Amex;
no smoking; need 6+ to book.*

## Budokan £25 🄰

Whiteladies Rd BS8 2PH (0117) 949 3030

*"Pan-Asian food at very low prices" ("from good sushi to delicious
laksa") wins many fans for this duo of hard-benched diners –
both in Clifton and at the original city-centre branch at 31 Colston
Street (tel 914 1488).* / **Sample dishes:** *Thai fishcakes; mango sorbet.*
**Details:** *www.budokan.co.uk; 11 pm; closed Sun; no Amex; no smoking.*

## Byzantium £39 🄰✕

2 Portwall Ln BS1 6NB (0117) 922 1883

*"Crazy" and "wonderfully exotic", neo-Byzantine décor –
plus "a belly dancer", if you're lucky – set the party scene at this
lavish Moroccan, near Temple Meads; no great surprise, then,
that the cooking seems, at best, an afterthought.*
/ **Sample dishes:** *crab, chilli & coriander tart; smoked lamb with Swiss chard gratin;
chocolate & Grand Marnier mousse.* **Details:** *www.byzantium.co.uk; near Temple
Meads, opp St Mary's Redcliffe church; 11 pm; D only, closed Sun (open for L in
Dec); no Amex; no smoking area.*

**sign up for the survey at www.hardens.com**

### A Cozinha £34
40 Alfred Pl BS2 8HD   (0117) 944 3060
A "friendly" and "charming", family-run Portuguese bistro, praised
by most reporters for its "generous" portions of "rustic" fare.
/ *Sample dishes:* salt cod & chick pea salad; porco na cataplana; bitter orange
milk pudding. *Details:* 8.30 pm, Fri & Sat 9.30 pm; L only Tue-Fri, open Sat D;
no Amex; children: 14+ at D.

### Culinaria £39 ★★
1 Chandos Rd BS6 6PG   (0117) 973 7999
Star local chef Stephen Markwick used to run Bristol's swankiest
restaurant, so it's no great surprise that his "very small" and
informal Redland newcomer (with deli attached) has won instant
raves for its "beautifully simple and fresh" dishes; even with Mrs
B's "friendly" service, though, atmosphere can be elusive.
/ *Details:* www.culinariabristol.co.uk; 9.30 pm; closed Sun-Tue, Wed L & Thu L;
no Amex; no smoking.

### Fishers £34
35 Princess Victoria St BS8 4BX   (0117) 974 7044
Just like the Oxford original, this may be a "generally reliable" fish
bistro, but it still attracts slightly ambivalent reports; support for
the "very good low-cost early-evening menu", however,
is unanimous. / *Sample dishes:* grilled sardines with parsley & lemon;
beer battered fish & chips; banana fritters with amaretto ice cream.
*Details:* www.fishers-restaurant.com; 10.30 pm; no Amex; no smoking.

### FishWorks £39 ★
128 Whiteladies Rd BS8 2RS   (0117) 974 4433
Thanks to its "lovely fish, simply cooked", this outlet of the
national chain is very popular with reporters; "for what's basically
a cafe attached to a fishmongers", though, even fans can find
it "too expensive", especially when service is too often "sloppy".
/ *Sample dishes:* spaghetti with crab & chilli; grilled plaice with black butter; lemon
tart. *Details:* www.fishworks.co.uk; 10.30 pm; closed Mon & Sun; no smoking.

### Glasnost £28 A★
1 William St BS3 4TU   (0117) 972 0938
It may be "tucked-away off the beaten track", but it's still "difficult
to get a table" at this "very friendly" Totterdown spot, whose
"interesting" and "good-value" cuisine has won a dedicated
following. / *Sample dishes:* crab & ginger chopsticks; char-grilled kangaroo;
Bailey's & Maltesers cheesecake. *Details:* 9.45 pm; D only, closed Mon & Sun;
no Amex; no smoking.

### The Glass Boat £43
Welsh Back BS1 4SB   (0117) 929 0704
A "wonderful setting on the river" is acclaimed by all who opine
on this moored barge in the docks; reviews were mostly positive
all-round, this year, but there was still the odd report of "woeful"
food and "arrogant" service. / *Sample dishes:* goat's cheese with radish &
chive salad; roast duck with duck spring rolls & mango; Szechuan-peppered crème
brûlée. *Details:* www.glassboat.co.uk; below Bristol Bridge; 9.30 pm; closed Sat L &
Sun; no smoking.

### Hope & Anchor £23 A
38 Jacobs Wells Rd BS8 1DR   (0117) 929 2987
This "buzzy" city-centre boozer is "always on the money"
foodwise; its "beautifully overgrown back garden" is a star feature.
/ *Sample dishes:* crayfish tail & anchovy salad; lamb & rosemary pie; sticky toffee
pudding. *Details:* 10 pm; no smoking.

**Hotel du Vin et Bistro**                 £41          🄰

Sugar Hs, Narrow Lewins Mead  BS1 2NU   (0117) 925 5577

*This "imaginatively-converted" warehouse – "in the heart of the city" – has become the best-known place in town; it's primarily due to the "stylish" and "intimate" ambience and "very well-thought-out" wine list, though – the "rustic" cuisine can be "ordinary".* / **Sample dishes:** *gravlax with citrus oil; braised lamb shank with olive jus; banana tarte Tatin.* **Details:** *www.hotelduvin.com; 9.45 pm; no smoking; booking: max 10.* **Accommodation:** *40 rooms, from £130.*


**Howards**                               £34

1a-2a Avon Cr  BS1 6XQ   (0117) 926 2921

*This cosy Hotwells veteran changed owner in 2004, and chef in early-2005; a long-term customer notes (unsurprisingly) that it's become more "variable" of late, and we've left it unrated till the dust settles.* / **Sample dishes:** *chicken, asparagus & leek terrine; seafood tagliatelle; lemon meringue pie.* **Details:** *10.30 pm; no smoking.*


**Michael Caines**
**The Royal Marriott Bristol**            £59

College Grn  BS1 5TA   (0117) 910 5309

*A setting "like an Italian piazza with balconies and classical statues" commends the swankiest dining room in town to some reporters – others, though, find it "soulless" and "pretentious", and complain that it "continues to ride on the chef's Gidleigh Park reputation".* / **Sample dishes:** *Cornish lobster & Parmesan salad; turbot with cannelloni of scallops; raspberry parfait.* **Details:** *www.michaelcaines.com; 10 pm; closed Mon L, Sat L & Sun; no smoking.* **Accommodation:** *242 rooms, from £75.*


**Mud Dock Cafe**
**CycleWorks**                            £38          🄰

40 The Grove  BS1 4RB   (0117) 934 9734

*"Slow and generally rude" service can take the edge off a visit to this "trendy" first-floor waterside café; that's a shame, as it's a "fun" place, where the food – especially for brunch or a light lunch – is usually "fine".* / **Sample dishes:** *spinach, yoghurt & mint soup; grilled tuna; banoffi pie.* **Details:** *www.mud-dock.com; close to the Industrial Museum & Arnolfini Gallery; 10 pm; no smoking area; no booking.*


**Olive Shed**                            £36

Floating Harbour, Princes Whf  BS1 4RN   (0117) 929 1960

*"A lovely location" ("once you've found it") adds to the appeal of this waterside spot – which offers some "great tapas" and some "interesting fish and vegetarian dishes"; fans claim it's "a notch above some of the city's better-known trendy places".* / **Sample dishes:** *deep-fried deviled crab pancake; wood-roasted red pepper parcel; orange & star anise parfait.* **Details:** *www.therealolivecompany.co.uk; 9.40 pm; closed Mon; no Amex; no smoking.*


**One Stop Thali Cafe**                   £20          🄰★

12 York Rd  BS6 5QE   (0117) 942 6687

*This Montpelier veggie diner, decorated Bollywood-style, seems fairly modest in its aims – all reporters agree, however, that it's a "fabulous" destination on all fronts, and with "great atmosphere" too.* / **Sample dishes:** *veggie pakora; three-curry plate with rice; saffron & pistachio kulfi.* **Details:** *www.onestopthali.co.uk; 10 pm; D only, closed Mon; no credit cards; no smoking.*

### Primrose Café £ 34 A★
I Boyces Ave BS8 4AA (0117) 946 6577
*"The Sunday queue is testimony to the superb breakfasts" at this "buzzy" café in a Clifton backstreet; it also makes "a good place for lunch or dinner".* / **Sample dishes:** crab risotto with avocado ice cream; char-grilled smoked salmon fillet; brown sugar meringues with grilled bananas. **Details:** 9.30 pm; Sun D; no Amex; no smoking area; no booking at L.

### Quartier Vert £ 35
85 Whiteladies Rd BS8 2NT (0117) 973 4482
*Fans say that "quality shines through in every dish" at this "consistent" Clifton institution; doubters find its mostly organic cuisine "healthy, rather than exciting", though, and complain of "very full prices" – tapas in the bar offers a (relatively) budget option.* / **Sample dishes:** seared scallops; braised shank of lamb; chocolate & cranberry délice. **Details:** www.quartiervert.co.uk; 10.30 pm; Sun D only in summer; no Amex; no smoking.

### Rajpoot £ 33 ★
52 Upper Belgrave Rd BS8 2XP (0117) 973 3515
*Fans say the curries are "in a league of their own", at this "classy" old subcontinental fixture.* / **Sample dishes:** chicken tikka; chicken jalfrezi; hot jalabies. **Details:** www.rajpootrestaurant.co.uk; 11 pm; D only, closed Sun; no smoking.

### riverstation £ 37 A
The Grove BS1 4RB (0117) 914 4434
*A "lovely" waterfront location and "lively" atmosphere are key strengths of this "stylish" bar/brasserie/restaurant; its cuisine, however, attracts every flavour of opinion from "above-average", via "good but pricey", to "rather disappointing".* / **Sample dishes:** sauteed duck liver; monkfish with aubergine & courgette gallette; blueberry & almond cake. **Details:** www.riverstation.co.uk; 10.30 pm, Fri & Sat 11 pm; no Amex; no smoking.

### San Carlo £ 38
44 Corn St BS1 1HQ (0117) 922 6586
*"A good-value city-centre Italian" that's "always busy and noisy"; "booking is essential as it's a favourite for students and residents alike".* / **Sample dishes:** avocado, smoked trout & prawns; fillet steak in pepper verde; cheesecake. **Details:** 11 pm.

### Sands £ 28 A
95 Queens Rd BS8 1LW (0117) 973 9734
*"Massive" helpings of "yummy" cuisine put this "authentic" Lebanese firmly on the city's culinary map (not least on the last Thursday of each month, which is belly dancing night).* / **Sample dishes:** smoked aubergine purée with sesame seeds; slow-baked lamb shank; baklava. **Details:** www.sandsrestaurant.co.uk; 10.30 pm; no smoking area.

### Severnshed £ 37 A★
The Grove, Harbourside BS1 4RB (0117) 925 1212
*"Bristol's best venue for a one-stop night out", this "buzzy" waterside bar/restaurant is praised by most reporters for its "great" contemporary looks and its "stylish but unpretentious" food; cooking standards have notably improved under the new chef.* / **Sample dishes:** lobster risotto; fillet of beef; chocolate mousse. **Details:** www.severnshed.co.uk; 10.30 pm; no smoking area.

## Teohs £ 23 ★

26-34 Lower Ashley Rd  BS2 9NP   (0117) 907 1191
"Long shared tables" help create an "upbeat, if slightly school-
dinners, ambience" at these popular "cheap and cheerful" Pan-
Asian canteens; there's also a branch at The Tobacco Factory,
Raleigh Road (tel 902 1122) – "the locations are equally
appealing". / **Sample dishes:** green curry with prawns; coconut pancakes stuffed
with mango. **Details:** 100 yds from M32, J3; 10.30 pm; closed Sun; no Amex;
no smoking.

---

## BROAD HAVEN, PEMBROKESHIRE 4–4B

### Druidstone Hotel £ 32 Ⓐ

Druidston Haven  SA62 3NE   (01437) 781221
A "quirky" cliff-top hotel (with "fantastic views"), whose "family-
friendly" atmosphere one reporter likens to a "kibbutz"; the food
doesn't really seem to be the main point, but it's often
"very good" nonetheless. / **Sample dishes:** Polish meat soup; sea bass &
mullet with watercress cream; chocolate orange cheesecake.
**Details:** www.druidstone.co.uk; from B4341 at Broad Haven turn right, then left
after 1.5m; 9.30 pm; closed Sun D; no smoking. **Accommodation:** 11 rooms,
from £57.

---

## BROADHEMBURY, DEVON 2–4A

### Drewe Arms £ 42 ★★

EX14 3NF   (01404) 841267
"A lovely pub in a picturesque village", whose handy
(for travellers) location leads to lots of feedback from reporters –
this is pretty much all to the effect that it's a "cosy" place, serving
"fabulous fish and seafood". / **Sample dishes:** mixed seafood; grilled turbot;
bread pudding with whisky butter. **Details:** 5m from M5, J28, on A373 to Honiton;
9 pm; closed Sun D; no Amex; no smoking area.

---

## BROADSTAIRS, KENT 3–3D

### Marchesi £ 32

19 Albion St  CT10 1LU   (01843) 862481
"A well-established Italian restaurant, with superb sea views,
very good food and competent service" – since new chef Daniel
Rowe took over in 2004, feedback has been been notably upbeat.
/ **Sample dishes:** seared tuna loin; pan-fried calf liver with beetroot; chocolate tart
with raspberries. **Details:** www.marchesi.co.uk; 9.30 pm; closed Mon & Sun D;
no smoking. **Accommodation:** 19 rooms, from £92.

---

## BROADWAY, WORCESTERSHIRE 2–1C

### Buckland Manor £ 70 Ⓐ

WR12 7LY   (01386) 852626
"What a setting, what a house" – this romantic Cotswold country
house, now run by the Von Essen group, attracts very positive
(if limited) feedback. / **Sample dishes:** pan-fried scallops on a truffled
cauliflower purée; sauteed monkfish; souffléd chocolate pancakes.
**Details:** www.bucklandmanor.co.uk; 2m SW of Broadway on B4632; 9 pm;
jacket & tie required at D; no smoking in dining room; booking: max 8; children:
12+. **Accommodation:** 14 rooms, from £235.

**Lygon Arms** £55

High St WR12 7DU (01386) 852255

*The post-Savoy owners of this "amazing" ancient inn did nothing for its already poor standards, and it seemed likely as this guide went to press that it had been, or was about to be sold, yet again – those planning a pilgrimage here should proceed with caution!* / **Sample dishes:** leek & mushroom lasagne with truffle oil; sea bass with creamed leeks & chorizo; plum crumble soufflé with liquorice ice-cream. **Details:** www.thelygonarms.co.uk; just off A44; 9.30 pm; D only, ex Sun open L & D; no smoking. **Accommodation:** 69 rooms, from £240.

**Russell's**  £44 A ★

20 High St WR12 7DT

(01386) 853555

*Prices that are "very reasonable, for the Cotswolds", have helped make a big name for this buzzy and very contemporary brasserie, on the main street of this picture-postcard village; it helps that the food is of consistent "high quality" too.* / **Sample dishes:** salmon with Jersey potato salad; grilled fillet of Scottish beef; passion fruit pyramid filled with nougatine. **Details:** www.russellsofbroadway.co.uk; 9.30 pm; closed Sun D; no Amex; no smoking. **Accommodation:** 4 rooms, from £95.

---

BROCKENHURST, HAMPSHIRE 2–4C

**Le Poussin at Whitley Ridge** £54 ★★

Beaulieu Rd SO42 7QL (0238) 028 2944

*While the celebrated Poussin at Parkhill is closed for refurbishment (till 2007), this newly-acquired country house hotel offers the Aitkens's "excellent food at good prices"; when Parkhill re-opens, a continuing (if lower-key) operation is planned for here.* / **Details:** www.lepoussin.co.uk; 9.30 pm; no smoking; children: 8+ at D. **Accommodation:** 18 rooms, from £95.

**Simply Poussin** £35 ★

The Courtyard, Brookley Rd SO42 7RB (01590) 623063

*The 'original' Poussin – in a yard tucked off the main street – doesn't aim as high gastronomically as its more swankily-housed relatives; it wins consistent praise, though, for its "delightful food at reasonable prices".* / **Sample dishes:** twice-baked cheese soufflé; whole-roasted poussin; chocolate fondant. **Details:** www.simplypoussin.co.uk; behind Bestsellers Bookshop; 9.30pm; closed Mon & Sun; no smoking; children: 8+ in the evening.

---

BRODICK, ISLE OF ARRAN 7–1A

**Creelers Seafood Restaurant** £33 ★

Home Farm KA27 8DD (01770) 302810

*"The best seafood" is the point of this unpretentious but "very reliable" outfit (which has an offshoot in Auld Reekie).* / **Sample dishes:** smoked fish pâté with Arran oatcakes; sea bass; strawberry cheesecake. **Details:** www.creelers.co.uk; 9 pm; closed Mon; no Amex; no smoking.

---

BROMLEY, KENT 3–3B

**Tamasha** £35  A

131 Widmore Rd BR1 3AX (020) 8460 3240

*A regular says the standard of food has "wobbled" of late, but this unusually atmospheric Indian retains quite a following in an area without much competition.* / **Sample dishes:** mixed kebab; tamasha raja jhinga; gajjar halwa. **Details:** www.tamasha.co.uk; 10.30 pm; no smoking in bar. **Accommodation:** 7 rooms, from £65.

## BRUNDALL, NORFOLK 6–4D

**Lavender House** £49 A★

39 The St NR13 5AA (01603) 712215

"Just better each time we visit" – all aspects of Richard and Sue Hughes's "personal" thatched-cottage three-year-old are consistently praised for their "super attention to detail".

/ **Sample dishes:** goat's cheese tart with chilli ice cream; Sheringham lobster bisque & pasta; hot caramel soufflé with peanut butter ice cream. **Details:** www.thelavenderhouse.co.uk; 12.30 am; D only, ex Fri open L & D, closed Sun & Mon; no Amex; no smoking.

## BUCKLAND, OXFORDSHIRE 2–1C

**The Lamb at Buckland** £34

Lamb Ln SN7 8QN (01367) 870484

"An attractive country pub", where the food is "always of a high standard", if sometimes "pricey for what it is".

/ **Sample dishes:** lemon sole with chive butter sauce; pan-fried skate wing; peach & almond flan. **Details:** www.thelambatbuckland.co.uk; on A420 between Oxford & Swindon; 9.30 pm; closed Mon & Sun D; no Amex; no smoking. **Accommodation:** 1 room, at about £95.

## BUNBURY, CHESHIRE 5–3B

**The Dysart Arms** £34 A

Bowes Gate Rd CW6 9PH (01829) 260183

"One of Cheshire's best pub dining experiences" – this "beautiful" establishment may (like most of the Brunning & Price chain) not aim too high in the culinary stakes, but is consistently "well run".

/ **Sample dishes:** king prawns with provençale sauce; confit of duck leg; apple & blackberry crumble tart. **Details:** www.dysartarms-bunbury.co.uk; 9.30 pm; no Amex; no smoking area.

## BURFORD, OXFORDSHIRE 2–2C

**The Lamb** £44

Sheep St OX18 4LR (01993) 823155

An "exceptionally attractive setting" has long helped make this 15th-century inn of note; it changed hands as our survey for the year was drawing to a close, so we've left it unrated.

/ **Sample dishes:** haddock soufflé with quail egg salad; roast lamb loin; iced hazelnut & Bailey's parfait. **Details:** www.lambinn-burford.co.uk; A40 from Oxford toward Cheltenham; 9.30 pm; no Amex; no smoking. **Accommodation:** 15 rooms, from £130.

## BURNHAM MARKET, NORFOLK 6–3B

**Fishes** £48 ★

Market Pl PE31 8HE (01328) 738588

"Really interesting" dishes and "enthusiastic and polite" service have helped make a big name for the Owsley-Browns' "friendly" fish restaurant. / **Sample dishes:** foie gras and smoked eel terrine; tandoori monkfish; crabapple crème brûlée. **Details:** www.fishesrestaurant.co.uk; 9.30 pm; closed Mon & Sun L; no Amex; no smoking; children: 8+ after 8.30 pm.

## Hoste Arms £34  🅰

The Green  PE31 8HD  (01328) 738777

*Paul Whittome's "Chelsea-on-Sea" coaching inn draws ever more flak for being just too popular; the "variable" cooking can still sometimes be "excellent", but even some long-term fans speak in terms of a "slight decline". / **Sample dishes:** cullen skink; honey-glazed ham hock with minted mash; apple tart with cinnamon ice cream.* **Details:** www.hostearms.co.uk; 6m W of Wells-next-the-Sea; 8.45 pm; no Amex; no smoking area. **Accommodation:** 46 rooms, from £114.

---

## BURNSALL, NORTH YORKSHIRE 8–4B

## Red Lion £35  🅰

BD23 6BU  (01756) 720204

*All agree this remote riverside pub in the Dales has a "fine location", and most − if not quite all − reporters also praise its "good" scoff. / **Sample dishes:** seared scallops; medallions of beef, parsnip mash & black pudding; treacle tart with candied lemon.* **Details:** www.redlion.co.uk; off A59; 9.30 pm; no smoking. **Accommodation:** 15 rooms, from £120.

---

## BURY ST EDMUNDS, SUFFOLK 3–1C

## Ickworth Hotel £48

Horringer  IP29 5QE  (01284) 735350

*In a wing of a grand National Trust house, this 'Luxury Family Hotel' enjoys a "unique" setting; the food it offers can be "fantastic" too, but the odd reporter feels that flavour sometimes "comes second" to the "very stylish" presentation. / **Sample dishes:** pea & truffle soup; wild brill with baby artichoke & roast scallops; bitter chocolate tart.* **Details:** www.ickworthhotel.com; 9.30 pm; no smoking; booking: max 8; children: 18+ at D. **Accommodation:** 38 rooms, from £155.

## Maison Bleue £35  🅰★

30-31 Churchgate St  IP33 1RG  (01284) 760623

*"Fantastically fresh fish" is a menu highlight at this "bubbly", "entertaining" and "very Gallic" bistro, where the "wonderful" service is of particular note. / **Sample dishes:** fish soup with garlic croutons; Dover sole; white chocolate & lime mousse.* **Details:** www.maisonbleue.co.uk; near the Cathedral; 9.30 pm; closed Mon & Sun; smoking in bar only.

---

## BUSHEY, HERTFORDSHIRE 3–2A

## St James £40

30 High St  WD23 3HL  (020) 8950 2480

*"Good, for the area"; this "very friendly" family-run Italian restaurant has a surprisingly large fanclub for somewhere in the 'burbs, but − reflecting the lack of local competition − it can seem "rather expensive" for what it is. / **Sample dishes:** tian of smoked haddock & salmon; poached lemon sole fillets; chocolate fudge cake with orange anglaise.* **Details:** opp St James Church; 9 pm; closed Sun; no Amex; no smoking.

**sign up for the survey at www.hardens.com**

## CAMBER SANDS, EAST SUSSEX                3–4C

### Place                                          £ 35
New Lydd Rd  TN31 7RB   (01797) 225057
*"Good-value food and wine in an ugly, motel-like building" – that's
the deal at this "bright spot in a rather bleak resort", which is the
brasserie of a trendy (if relatively affordable) boutique-hotel;
the use of "lots of local produce" is a highlight.*
/ **Sample dishes:** *twice-baked goat's cheese & thyme soufflé; slow-cooked
marinated duck; chef's brûlée with organic cinnamon ice cream.*
**Details:** *www.theplacecambersands.co.uk; 9 pm; no smoking.*
**Accommodation:** *18 rooms, from £80.*

## CAMBRIDGE, CAMBRIDGESHIRE             3–1B

The truth of the sweeping generalisation that Cambridge is a
vile place to eat seems remarkably resilient. Oddly, however –
although the city-centre remains something of a void – there
are some places of note around the edges. *Midsummer House*
has now become a restaurant of true 'destination' status
(rather than merely being the best of a bad bunch), and the
hotel restaurant *Graffiti* is beginning to make something of a
name. For a good mid-range meal, *22 Chesterton Road* is clearly
the best choice.

### Browns                                        £ 28        ✗
23 Trumpington St  CB2 1QA   (01223) 461655
*A "cavernous" branch of the dismal English brasserie chain
"always seems to be busy", in spite of the fact that many
reporters just think it's "bad, bad… and bad".*
/ **Sample dishes:** *baked tiger prawns; pan-fried monkfish with beans & wild
mushrooms; chocolate fudge brownie.* **Details:** *www.browns-restaurants.com;
opp Fitzwilliam Museum; 11 pm; no smoking area; need 5+ to book.*

### Cazimir                                       £ 16
13 King St  CB1 1LH   (01223) 355156
*"A blessed relief from the chain sandwich bars"; this Polish-run
café wins praise for its "unusual" fillings and "friendly" service.*
/ **Sample dishes:** *roast vegetable bruschetta; Polish sausage & Mozzarella salad;
chocolate cake.* **Details:** *L & afternoon tea only; closed Sun; no credit cards;
no smoking area.*

### Curry Queen                                   £ 19
106 Mill Rd  CB1 2BD   (01223) 351027
*"Reliable curries" make this "traditional" 20-year-old the city's
only subcontinental of any note.* / **Sample dishes:** *fish Ayr; chicken tikka
masala.* **Details:** *midnight.*

### Dojo                                          £ 18
1-2 Millers Yd,  Mill Ln  CB2 1RQ   (01223) 363471
*In most places, this "nice, buzzy noodle-bar" might not be worthy
of special note, but in Cambridge…* / **Sample dishes:** *Siamese caviar
rolls; Thai suppard rice.* **Details:** *www.dojonoodlebar.co.uk; off Trumpington St;
11 pm; no Amex; no smoking; no booking.*

**sign up for the survey at www.hardens.com**              183

### Fitzbillies £35
52 Trumpington St CB2 1RG (01223) 352500
*An intimate dining room, next to the famous bakery of the same name that's "good for lunch" or a light bite at any time of day; "a decent choice of wines by the glass" is a feature.*
/ **Sample dishes:** shrimp & leek tart; pink bream on crab cake; fruit tart with Chantilly cream. **Details:** www.fitzbillies.com; 9.30 pm; closed Sun D; no smoking area.

### Graffiti
### Hotel Felix £43 ★
Whitehouse Ln CB3 0LX (01223) 277977
*"Super food" is winning quite a name for this "stylish" (going-on "weird") boutique hotel dining room, in a converted Victorian house, just outside the city-centre; service — which is sometimes "very slow" — still needs attention, though.* / **Sample dishes:** venison carpaccio with baby artichokes; tournedos of beef with gorgonzola mousse potatoes; honey & bourbon mousse with candied filo pastry. **Details:** www.hotelfelix.co.uk; 10 pm, Fri & Sat 10.30 pm; no smoking. **Accommodation:** 52 rooms, from £163.

### Loch Fyne £37
37 Trumpington St CB2 1QY (01223) 362433
*For fans, this is an "ever-reliable branch of the popular chain"; it certainly attracts a high volume of reports (the second highest in town), but middling ratings suggest it does well in the absence of much local competition.* / **Sample dishes:** smoked organic salmon with wasabi & soy sauce; poached smoked haddock with mash; sticky toffee pudding. **Details:** www.lochfyne.com; opp Fitzwilliam Museum; 10 pm, Sat 11 pm; no smoking area.

### Midsummer House £74 Ⓐ★★
Midsummer Common CB4 1HA (01223) 369299
*Daniel Clifford's "unforgettable" cuisine — in "innovative" modern style — is increasingly rated as "of the highest order", and this Victorian villa is now of national note; "high" wine mark-ups, though, remain a cause of some complaint.* / **Sample dishes:** sauteed snails with garlic soup; grilled Anjou pigeon; passion fruit & mango soufflé. **Details:** www.midsummerhouse.co.uk; facing University Boathouse; 9.30 pm; closed Mon & Sun, Tue-Thu L only; no smoking.

### Peking Restaurant £31
21 Burleigh St CB1 1DG (01223) 354755
*"Expensive, but with an impressive menu" — this long-established Chinese, near the Grafton Centre, remains comparatively well-rated in this still-underserved city.* / **Sample dishes:** deep-fried squid in chilli; Szechuan chicken; toffee bananas. **Details:** 10.30 pm; no Amex; no smoking area.

### 22 Chesterton Road £35 Ⓐ★★
22 Chesterton Rd CB4 3AX (01223) 351880
*This "very intimate" restaurant in an Edwardian house (on the fringe of the town-centre) is going from strength to strength; all feedback speaks in terms of "fine" cooking, and "good value".* / **Sample dishes:** pork & rabbit terrine with plum sauce; crab cakes with spring onion risotto; steamed marmalade pudding. **Details:** www.restaurant22.co.uk; 9.45 pm; D only, closed Mon & Sun; no smoking; children: 12+.

**sign up for the survey at www.hardens.com**

### Vaults Restaurant & Bar      £29
14a Trinity St  CB2 1TB   (01223) 506090
A "cosy cellar-restaurant and bar", where you can kick the
evening off with some "gorgeous cocktails"; on the food front,
there's a "wide choice" of "tasty" tapas-style dishes.
/ **Sample dishes:** pigeon breast; sticky toffee pudding.
**Details:** www.localsecrets.com; 10.30 pm, Sat 11 pm; no smoking area.

---

## CANTERBURY, KENT      3–3D

### Augustines      £36      Ⓐ★
1-2 Longport  CT1 1PE   (01227) 453063
"Smart but relaxed", Robert Grimer's Georgian townhouse –
with its "top-quality" food and its "attentive but unobtrusive"
service – would be an asset to any city; here it is of particular
note. / **Sample dishes:** provençale fish soup; marsh lamb with parsley mash;
lemon tart with raspberry sauce. **Details:** near the Cathedral; 9.30 pm; closed
Mon & Sun; smoking in bar only; booking: max 7.

### Café des Amis      £27
95 St Dunstan's St  CT2 8AD   (01227) 464390
In this under-served city, this "cheerful", "well-established"
Mexican – by Westgate Towers – is hailed year-in-year-out as an
"individual" destination where the food's "always good".
/ **Sample dishes:** antojitos; lamb with Merguez sausages; chocolate fundido.
**Details:** by Westgate Towers; 10 pm; no smoking area; booking: max 6 at D,
Fri & Sat.

### Goods Shed      £35      Ⓐ★
Station Road West  CT2 8AN   (01227) 459153
Most reports of this "restaurant within a farmers' market" (on the
mezzanine of "a converted railway shed") say that it's
"an outstanding location and a winning formula" (with "fresh food
from the market cooked to perfection"); on a cold day, though,
the setting can seem pretty "chilly". / **Sample dishes:** seared pigeon
breast with lentils; wild sea trout with grilled aspargus; shortbread.
**Details:** 9.30 pm; closed Mon & Sun D; no smoking area.

---

## CAPEL CURIG, GWYNEDD      4–1D

### Bryn Tyrch      £27
LL24 0EL   (01690) 720223
"The best sticky toffee pudding" is the sort of dish that delights
reporters who make the "hike" (often literally) to this "friendly"
and "unpretentious" Snowdonia inn; it's also noted as being
"excellent for vegetarians". / **Sample dishes:** salmon fishcake; sticky toffee
pudding. **Details:** www.bryntyrch-hotel.co.uk; on A5; 9.30 pm; no Amex; no smoking
area. **Accommodation:** 15 rooms, from £28.

**sign up for the survey at www.hardens.com**

## CARDIFF, CARDIFF 2–2A

The Welsh capital still has yet really to join the 21st century as far as eating out is concerned. The only places of any real standing are *Le Gallois Y Cymro* in the smart suburb of Canton and the (new) *Old Post Office* at St Fagans. In the city centre, the vast and long-established complex based on a pleasant but dated steak 'n' fish formula incorporating *La Brasserie*, *Champers* and *Le Monde* continue to dominate (the last-mentioned being perhaps the best). Trendy Cardiff Bay still continues to show more style than substance, with *Tides* the best-known culprit in that respect.

### Armless Dragon £34
97-99 Wyeverne Rd  CF2 4BG  (029) 2038 2357
*"Worth seeking out in the suburbs" (Cathays), this backstreet bistro attracts pretty consistent praise for its cooking, which is notably "imaginative" by local standards.* / **Sample dishes:** solaria fritter; sea bass with razor clams & roasted tomatoes; lemon tart with toffee cream. **Details:** www.thearmlessdragon.co.uk; 10 min outside city centre; 9 pm, Fri & Sat 9.30 pm; closed Mon & Sun; no smoking.

### La Brasserie £34  Ⓐ
60 St Mary St  CF10 1FE  (029) 2023 4134
*This "busy city-centre restaurant" – long a local linchpin – is particularly notable for a "wide range of fish and seafood" (selected at the counter), generally "well-cooked" and served in "huge portions"; "it's pleasant enough, but probably not the place for a dinner for two".* / **Sample dishes:** frogs legs with garlic mayonnaise; lemon sole with new potatoes; apple tart. **Details:** www.labrasserierestaurant.co.uk; midnight; closed Sun D; need 8+ to book.

### Champers £34
61 St Mary St  CF10 1FE  (029) 2037 3363
*An "utterly reliable" formula of steak-and-fish grilled to order wins enduring popularity for this similar – but smarter – sibling to La Brasserie (to which it is adjacent).* / **Sample dishes:** garlic prawns; stuffed chicken breast; chocolate truffle. **Details:** www.le-monde.co.uk; nr Castle; midnight, 10.30 pm for tapas; closed Sun L.

### Cibo £26
83 Pontcanna St  CF11 9HS  (029) 2023 2226
*"Great pizzas" and a "buzzy atmosphere" are among the features which make it "worth the drive" to this funky family-run Italian, in distant Poncanna.* / **Sample dishes:** vegetable antipasti; salami & Mozzarella ciabatta; lemon cheesecake. **Details:** 9 pm; no Amex; no smoking; booking: max 10.

### Da Vendittos £48
7-8 Park Pl  CF10 3DP  (029) 2023 0781
*"Bright", "modern" and "stylish", this city-centre Italian offers a style of dining not much found in the Welsh capital; it is priced accordingly, so those paying their own way may wish to seek out the lunch and pre-theatre menus.* / **Sample dishes:** tempura, tomato & Mozzarella stuffing; roasted monkfish; basil ice cream. **Details:** www.vendittogroup.co.uk; 10.45 pm; closed Mon & Sun; no smoking.

## Le Gallois Y Cymro £49 ★

6-10 Romilly Cr CF11 9NR (029) 2034 1264

*For "the best cooking in South Wales" ("food for foodies, from the bread to the pudding"), many reporters would tip this venture in the suburb of Canton – the best-known place in the Welsh capital; the-late-'90s interior, however, is a mite "bland".*

/ **Sample dishes:** Roquefort soufflé with poached pears; pan-fried John Dory with artichoke barigoule; spiced pineapple with pepper ice cream.
**Details:** www.legallois-ycymro.com; 1.5m W of Cardiff Castle; 10.30 pm; closed Mon & Sun; no smoking area.

## Happy Gathering £28

233 Cowbridge Road East CF11 9AL (029) 2039 7531

*It only attracts a tiny volume of feedback, considering, but fans say this well-established Chinese restaurant is "the best"; "for a family experience", Sunday dim sum can be recommended.*

/ **Sample dishes:** chicken satay & crispy seaweed; steamed duck in orange sauce; crispy toffee banana. **Details:** 10.45 pm, Fri & Sat 11.45 pm; no smoking area.

## Le Monde £34 &#x1D538;

62 St Mary St CF10 1FE (029) 2038 7376

*This more upmarket sibling to La Brasserie (situated below) continues to score highly for ambience; its "plain cooking of fresh raw materials" mostly finds favour, but feedback on the food this year was a little up-and-down.* / **Sample dishes:** marinated seafood salad; venison with port wine sauce; Welsh cheeses. **Details:** www.le-monde.co.uk; midnight; closed Sun; no jeans; no booking.

## Old Post Office £51 ★

Greenwood Ln CF5 6EL (029) 2056 5400

*Despite its name, there's nothing quaint about this bright and "minimalist" venture (by the Woods Brasserie people), which claims to be 'South Wales's first restaurant-with-rooms', in a village a few minutes' drive from the city-centre; the odd reporter finds it "pricey", but almost all feedback speaks in terms of the food's "exceptional quality and presentation".* / **Sample dishes:** terrine of ham hock & foie gras & pear; roast breast of duck; vanilla & raspberry mousse with pistachio ice cream. **Details:** www.old-post-office.com; 9 pm; closed Mon & Tue; smoking in bar only. **Accommodation:** 6 rooms, from £80.

## Scallops £36

Unit 2 Mermaid Quay CF10 5BZ (029) 2049 7495

*This "minimalist" fish café, on the Cardiff Bay waterfront, offers a "limited" menu – though mostly well-rated by reporters, it inspired a couple of unenthusiastic critiques.*

/ **Sample dishes:** pan-seared scallops; roasted sea trout, carrots, orange & tarragon; summer trifle. **Details:** www.scallopsrestaurant.com; 10 pm; no smoking.

## Tides
## St David's Hotel & Spa £46

Havannah St CF10 5SD (029) 2031 3018

*"The view deserves better"; Rocco Forte's "gloriously-located" modern landmark hotel, overlooking the Bay offers cooking which is "certainly not worthy of a five-star".* / **Sample dishes:** terrine of foie gras with toasted brioche; roast fillet of cod; coffee panna cotta with chocolate & hazelnut ice cream. **Details:** www.thestdavidshotel.com; in Cardiff Bay; 10.15 pm; no smoking. **Accommodation:** 132 rooms, from £165.

**sign up for the survey at www.hardens.com**

## Woods Brasserie £ 38

Pilotage Building, Stuart St CF10 5BW (029) 2049 2400
*Fans insist that this well-established brasserie is "the best place
to eat round the Bay by a mile", and it has a fair local following;
as ever, though, there are quite a few doubters, for whom
it "used to be better" or "just misses the mark".*
/ **Sample dishes:** tian of smoked trout & guacamole with balsamic jelly; char-grilled
ribeye of Aberdeen Angus; Bakewell tart & custard.
**Details:** www.woods_brasserie.com; in the Inner Harbour; 10 pm; closed Sun D;
smoking in bar only.

---

## CARLISLE, CUMBRIA 7–2D

## No 10 £ 35 Ⓐ

10 Eden Mount CA3 9LY (01228) 524183
*Modest commentary this year on this "friendly", family-run local
hotspot, in a cosy old townhouse – still all to the effect that its
cooking makes "great use of regional produce".*
/ **Sample dishes:** spinach & goat's cheese fritatta; baked fillet of sea bass; brandy
snap with coconut & Malibu ice cream. **Details:** 9.30 pm; D only, closed Mon &
Sun; no smoking.

---

## CARTMEL, CUMBRIA 7–4D

## Aynsome Manor £ 35 Ⓐ★

LA11 6HH (015395) 36653
*A "lovely setting", "hearty dishes" and "reasonable prices" are
a formula making for all-round satisfaction at this "gracious"
country house hotel.* / **Sample dishes:** risotto of asparagus & butternut
squash; pan-fried breast of guinea fowl with puy lentil.
**Details:** www.aynsomemanorhotel.co.uk; off A590,1/2m N of village; 8.30 pm;
D only, ex Sun open L only; no smoking; children: 5+ in restaurant.
**Accommodation:** 12 rooms, from £150.

## L'Enclume £ 60 Ⓐ★

Cavendish St LA11 6PZ
(01539) 536362
*Simon Rogan's "inspirational" and "risk-taking" cuisine ("with a
touch of humour and chemistry") continues to "thrill" most of the
many who report on this "fantastically-designed" former smithy;
the feedback increasingly includes far too many gripes, though,
about "parsimonious" portions or "OTT" prices.*
/ **Sample dishes:** pan-fried langoustine with sour grapefruit drops; poached brill
with English mace and wild tree spinach; upside down coconut soufflé, mango
mousse, raspberry jelly and test tube. **Details:** www.lenclume.co.uk; 9.30 pm; closed
Mon & Sun D; no jeans or trainers; no smoking; children: 12+ at D.
**Accommodation:** cottage, plus 7 rooms, from £125.

## Uplands £ 40 Ⓐ★

Haggs Ln LA11 6HD (01539) 536248
*"Consistent imaginative" cooking (in a "traditional" vein) inspires
only positive reports on this "lovely old house", which enjoys views
towards Morecambe Bay.* / **Sample dishes:** poached scallops in lime; braised
guinea fowl with prune & bacon roll; home-made praline ice cream in a brandy snap
basket. **Details:** www.uplands.uk.com; 8 pm; D only, ex Fri & Sun open L &
D, closed Mon; no smoking; no booking, Sat; children: 8+ at
D. **Accommodation:** 5 rooms, from £86.

**sign up for the survey at www.hardens.com**

## CASTLE DOUGLAS, DUMFRIES & GALLOWAY 7–2B

**The Plumed Horse** £ 52 ★

Crossmicheal DG7 3AU (01556) 670333
*On most accounts, Tony Borthwick's establishment achieves some
"outstanding French-influenced Scottish cooking"; feedback on the
service, though, is more mixed. / **Sample dishes:** seafood & fennel velouté;
pan-fried breast of corn-fed guinea fowl; whiskey & prailine bombe.*
***Details:*** *www.plumedhorse.co.uk; 9 pm; closed Mon, Sat L & Sun D; no Amex;
no smoking.*

## CAUNTON, NOTTINGHAMSHIRE 5–3D

**Caunton Beck** £ 35

Main St NG23 6AB (01636) 636793
*Open all day, like its Lincoln sibling the Wig & Mitre,
this "relaxed" country establishment remains an "ever-popular"
destination; fans say the food is "above-average", but a higher
number of "disappointing" meals were recorded this year.
/ **Sample dishes:** garlic-infused tiger prawns; Eton mess.*
***Details:*** *www.wigandmitre.com; 6m NW of Newark past British Sugar factory
on A616; 10 pm; no smoking.*

## CAVENDISH, SUFFOLK 3–1C

**The George** £ 34

The Green CO1 8BA (01787) 280248
*The "standard" gastropub cuisine is prepared "with flair" at this
converted pub ("more a restaurant-with-rooms nowadays");
"the courtyard is especially nice for lunch". / **Details:** 9.30 pm; smoking
in bar only. **Accommodation:** 4 rooms, from £60.*

## CHADDESLEY CORBETT, WORCESTERSHIRE 5–4B

**Brockencote Hall** £ 44 A★

DY10 4PY (01562) 777876
*A Gallic-run country house hotel, whose "beautiful" dining room,
with "lovely views", offers the culinary style of "a good provincial
French restaurant"; it's "great for a weekend away, or just dinner".
/ **Sample dishes:** scallops with juniper berry sauce; lemon tart with Earl Grey
sorbet. **Details:** www.brockencotehall.com; on A448, just outside village; 9.30 pm;
closed Sat L; no smoking; booking: max 6. **Accommodation:** 17 rooms,
from £116.*

## CHAGFORD, DEVON 1–3D

**Gidleigh Park** £ 90

TQ13 8HH (01647) 432367
*"So faultless!" – this "luxurious" Tudorbethan country house hotel
offers Michael Caines's "lovingly-prepared" cooking and a truly
"awesome" wine list; the property was sold this year to the
Brownswords (of Bath Priory, et al), and a major refurb is planned
for 2006 – in the circumstances, a rating seems inappropriate.
/ **Sample dishes:** ravioli of lobster with cabbage and girolle mushrooms; roast
grouse with celeriac puree; hot prune and Armagnac soufflé.
**Details:** www.gidleigh.com; from village, right at Lloyds TSB, take right fork to end
of lane; 9 pm; no smoking; children: 7+ at D. **Accommodation:** 14 rooms,
from £440.*

**22 Mill Street** £ 49 ★★
22 Mill St  TQ13 8AW   (01647) 432244
*"The passion shines through"*, in Duncan Walker's *"splendid seasonal cooking"*, and it's *"fairly-priced"* too; he's made quite a name for this *"calm"* venture in *"an attractive village"*, just down the road from the hotel where he used to work.
/ **Sample dishes:** saffron lasagne of crab & red pepper; roast pigeon with pea purée; hot raspberry soufflé. **Details:** www.22millstreet.co.uk; 9 pm; closed Mon L, Tue L & Sun; no Amex; no smoking; children: 14+. **Accommodation:** 2 rooms, from £75.

---

CHALFONT ST GILES, BUCKINGHAMSHIRE 3–2A

**Cape Fish** £ 38 ★
London Rd  HP8 4NL   (01494) 872113
This *"very good South African fish restaurant"* has made a big name locally, and it has already become a *"perennial favourite"* for a fair number of reporters; it can get *"noisy"*, though.
/ **Sample dishes:** Cape fishcakes; traditional melva pudding.
**Details:** www.capefish.co.za; 10 pm; closed Mon L & Sun D; no smoking.

---

CHANDLERS CROSS, HERTFORDSHIRE 3–2A

**Colette's**
**The Grove** £ 78
WD3 4TG   (01923) 296015
*"Superb food in a great setting"* wins high praise in most reports on this *"luxurious"* – and, of course, *"very expensive"* – modern venture; perhaps inevitably, though, this newish five star hotel's main dining room can also sometimes seem a bit *"pretentious"*.
/ **Sample dishes:** terrine of baby leeks with Scottish langoustines; pan-fried Dover sole; passion fruit soufflé. **Details:** www.thegrove.co.uk; J19 or 20 on M25; 10 pm; closed Sun D; no jeans or trainers; smoking in bar only. **Accommodation:** 227 rooms, from £250.

**The Glasshouse**
**The Grove** £ 53 A★
WD3 4TG   (01923) 296015
*"A fabulous buffet"* – *"you won't leave hungry!"*, and with *"a much better class of food than you'd expect"* – earns numerous enthusiastic reports for this *"buzzy"* venue; it is the largest eatery at this *"stunning"* hotel, *"beautifully set in the Hertfordshire countryside"*. / **Details:** www.thegrove.co.uk; 10 pm; no smoking. **Accommodation:** 227 rooms, from £250.

---

CHELMSFORD, ESSEX 3–2C

**Waterfront Place** £ 43
Wharf Rd  CM2 6LU   (01245) 252000
A *"light and airy"* canalside restaurant in a setting that reminded one reporter of the capital's Docklands; it offers *"well presented"* cooking in contemporary style. / **Sample dishes:** seared tuna steak; roasted venison on truffle mash with vine tomatoes; passion fruit & orange tart with vanilla ice cream. **Details:** www.waterfront-place.co.uk; 10 pm; closed Sun D; no smoking area.

CHELTENHAM, GLOUCESTERSHIRE                      2–1C

**Café Paradiso**
**Hotel Kandinsky**                              £ 40
Bayshill Rd  GL50 3AS   (01242) 527788
*Verdicts on the food at this hip-hotel dining room (specialising in pizza) range from "tasty" to "tasteless"; views on the atmosphere are also a bit mixed, but trendier reporters say it's "lovely".* / **Sample dishes:** seared scallops with black pudding; poached halibut fillet with a mixed salad; white chocolate fondue. **Details:** www.hotelkandinsky.com; 10 pm; no smoking. **Accommodation:** 45 rooms, from £75.

**Champignon Sauvage**          £ 61          ★★
24-28 Suffolk Rd  GL50 2AQ   (01242) 573449
*David Everitt-Matthias's "honest treatment of first-class ingredients" – creating "brilliant" dishes that are "to be eaten, not admired" – has created a huge foodie reputation for this "superb" dining room (where wife Helen presides); fingers crossed that the major summer-2005 expansion has only enhanced the experience.* / **Sample dishes:** eel tortellini with watercress cream; pan-fried cock's kidneys & langoustines; bitter chocolate & salted caramel délice. **Details:** www.lechampignonsauvage.co.uk; near Cheltenham Boys College; 9 pm; closed Mon & Sun; no smoking.

**Daffodil**                    £ 38          𝔸✕
18-20 Suffolk Pde  GL50 2AE   (01242) 700055
*It's the "sensational setting" – an Art Deco cinema – which is the making of this "intriguing" destination; the food is "ordinary" going-on "unforgiveable", but lunch can be "good value".* / **Sample dishes:** pan-fried chorizo & red peppers; fillet of salmon with saffron cream; crème brûlée. **Details:** www.thedaffodil.co.uk; just off Suffolk Square; 9 pm; closed Sun; no smoking.

**Lumière**                     £ 50
Clarence Pde  GL50 3PA   (01242) 222200
*There's some "serious" cooking to be had at Lin and Geoff Chapman's small town-centre restaurant; one reporter noted "a welcome reduction in complexity" this year, but overall the standard of the food was a little less highly rated by reporters.* / **Sample dishes:** seared foie gras on dressed fine beans; monkfish medallion with smoked salmon rice; pecan tart with bourbon ice cream. **Details:** www.lumiere.cc; off the promenade on the inner ring; 8.30 pm; D only, closed Mon & Sun; no Amex; no smoking; booking: max 10; children: 6+.

**Mayflower**                   £ 32          ★
32-34 Clarence St  GL50 3NX   (01242) 522426
*This long-established Chinese is tipped for its "fresh-tasting" fare in "good quantities"; its menu offers "a large number of veggie options" ("including mock-duck pancakes").* / **Sample dishes:** garlic & chilli frogs legs; roast duck; toffee bananas. **Details:** www.themayflowerrestaurant.co.uk; 10 pm; no smoking.

**Le Petit Blanc**              £ 32          ✕
Queen's Promenade  GL50 1NN   (01242) 266800
*Fans insist it's "a good example of a chain restaurant that works", but too many reporters continue to find this Raymond Blanc-branded brasserie "formulaic" and "disappointing".* / **Sample dishes:** twice-baked Roquefort soufflé; tuna with pine kernel crust & red pepper relish; chocolate fondant with pistachio ice cream. **Details:** www.lepetitblanc.co.uk; 10.30 pm; no smoking.

### Ruby £ 30
52 Suffolk Rd  GL50 2AQ   (01242) 250909
*"Handy for those visiting the Ladies' College"* – a consistently
*"good"* Chinese. / **Details:** near Cheltenham Boys College; 11.30 pm.

### Storyteller £ 30 Ⓐ
11 North Pl  GL50 4DW   (01242) 250343
*"Small mark-ups on the wine"* – which you choose in a room
dedicated for that purpose – are the main attraction of this
conservatory-like joint; the food plays something of a supporting
rôle. / **Sample dishes:** home-cured tuna loin; sizzling duck with onions & beans;
chocolate mud pie. **Details:** www.storyteller.co.uk; near the cinema; 10 pm;
no Amex; no smoking.

---

## CHESTER, CHESHIRE 5–2A

### Albion Inn £ 18 Ⓐ
Park St  CH1 1RN   (01244) 340345
*"Step back in time"*, when you visit this *"delightful"* corner boozer
– claimed as the cradle of CAMRA – tucked away in a
characterful location near the Newgate; its culinary ambitions are
modest, but it offers *"all fresh food, home-cooked"*.
/ **Sample dishes:** casseroles & stews; bread & butter pudding.
**Details:** www.albioninnchester.co.uk; 8 pm; no credit cards; no smoking; need 6+
to book; children: 18+ only.

### Arkle
### The Chester Grosvenor £ 79
Eastgate  CH1 1LT   (01244) 324024
The *"Savoy of the North"* – an unusually grand city-centre hotel,
owned by the Duke of Westminster – has long offered some
of the stateliest city dining outside London; Simon Radley's food
is *"first-class"* and makes much use of *"luxurious ingredients"*,
but prices give nothing away. / **Sample dishes:** oxtail ravioli with
langoustine tails; duck with black fig sauce; basil blancmange with iced gingerbread.
**Details:** www.chestergrosvenor.co.uk; 9.30 pm; closed Mon & Sun; jacket required
at D; no smoking. **Accommodation:** 80 rooms, from £185.

### Francs £ 23
14 Cuppin St  CH1 2BN   (01244) 317952
*"Good French food at reasonable prices"* is the gist of pretty much
all reports on this *"always-reliable"* bistro; *"the prix-fixe offers
especially good value"*. / **Sample dishes:** smoked salmon, melon & avocado
salad; lamb's liver & bacon with mash; lemon tart. **Details:** www.francs.co.uk;
11 pm; no smoking area.

### Moules A Go Go £ 31 ★
39 Watergate Row  CH1 2LE   (01244) 348818
*"Good, reliable, fast, and with a real buzz"* – this very centrally-
located spot does 'just what it says on the tin' (in fact, rather
more, as a full brasserie menu is available); for top value,
seek out one of the 'deals'. / **Sample dishes:** goat's cheese & pear
bruschetta; Welsh beef sirloin; sticky toffee pudding.
**Details:** www.moulesagogo.co.uk; 10 pm; smoking in bar only.

**sign up for the survey at www.hardens.com**

## CHETTLE, DORSET 2–4C

**Castleman Hotel** £31 ★

DT11 8DB (01258) 830096

"Lovely food", "reasonably priced", makes this "slightly eccentric" country restaurant-with-rooms (in a small village) a consistently popular dining destination. / **Details:** www.castlemanhotel.co.uk; 9.30 pm; D only, ex Wed & Sun open L & D; no Amex; no smoking area. **Accommodation:** 8 rooms, from £80.

## CHICHESTER, WEST SUSSEX 3–4A

**Comme Ça** £47 𝔸★

67 Broyle Rd PO19 6BD (01243) 788724

The least enthusiastic report on this 20 year-old "French-influenced" favourite says that it's "always enjoyable" – "the food may not be Gordon Ramsay, but it's very good", the service is "efficient" and there's "a lovely terrace in summer". / **Sample dishes:** asparagus hollandaise; cured Scottish salmon; summer pudding. **Details:** www.commeca.co.uk; 0.5m N of city centre; 10.30 pm; closed Mon, Tue L & Sun D; no smoking.

## CHIGWELL, ESSEX 3–2B

**The Bluebell** £44

117 High Rd IG7 6QQ (020) 8500 6282

"A perfect local restaurant, offering top-quality fare at reasonable prices" – that's the invariable gist of commentary on this "oasis in a gastronomic desert"; the "wonderful Sunday lunch" is of particular renown. / **Sample dishes:** sauteed scallops; peach melba. **Details:** www.thebluebellrestaurant.co.uk; 12.30 am; closed Mon, Sat L & Sun D.

## CHILGROVE, WEST SUSSEX 3–4A

**White Horse** £44

High St PO18 9HX (01243) 535219

It's the "unbelievably great" wine list – "particularly good on the more traditional clarets and Burgundies" – which makes this South Downs boozer of note; "the food is now tertiary". / **Sample dishes:** crab & avocado salad; local seafood & game in season; home-made ice cream in a chocolate tower. **Details:** www.whitehorsechilgrove.co.uk; 8m NW of Chichester on B2141; 9.30 pm; closed Mon & Sun D; no Amex; no smoking. **Accommodation:** 8 rooms, from £95.

## CHINNOR, OXFORDSHIRE 2–2D

**Sir Charles Napier** £41 𝔸

Spriggs Alley OX39 4BX (01494) 483011

"In a quiet location high in the Chilterns" (off the M40), this "laid-back" (sometimes to a fault) converted inn has long been known as a "sophisticated" country bolt hole; the "eclectic" cuisine is "good but variable" and – as the helipad hints – "not cheap". / **Sample dishes:** pan-fried foie gras; fillet of bream with tiger prawns; chocolate fondant. **Details:** www.sircharlesnapier.co.uk; M40, J6 into Chinnor, turn right at roundabout, carry on straight up hill for 2 miles; 10 pm, 4pm Sun; closed Mon & Sun D; no smoking area; children: 6+ at D.

## CHIPPENHAM, WILTSHIRE                    2–2C

**Manor House
Bybrook Restaurant**                    £ 65        ★
Castle Combe  SN14 7HR   (01249) 782206
*The ambience can sometimes seem rather "hotel dining room",
but reporters are unanimous in their praise for the "memorable"
cooking (with often "excellent" service) at this 'Exclusive Hotels'
country house. / Sample dishes: chicken, artichoke & wild mushroom terrine;
smoked salmon & crayfish with horseradish potatoes; glazed lemon tart.
Details: www.exclusivehotels.co.uk; 9 pm, Fri & Sat 9.30 pm; no smoking.
Accommodation: 48 rooms, from £235.*

## CHIPPING CAMPDEN, GLOUCESTERSHIRE       2–1C

**Juliana's
Cotswold House**                        £ 61        𝔸★
Chipping Campden  GL55 6AN   (01386) 840330
*With its "trendified artworks and lighting", the main restaurant
of this Cotswold village hotel offers a "relaxing" and stylish
location, which is – for most reporters – "matched by excellent
food and service". / Sample dishes: Isle of Skye scallops; cannon of local lamb;
rhubarb & strawberry compote. Details: www.cotswoldhouse.com; 9.45 pm; D only,
ex Sun open L & D; no smoking. Accommodation: 30 rooms, from £205.*

## CHRISTCHURCH, DORSET                    2–4C

**FishWorks**                            £ 39        ★
10 Church St  BH23 1BW   (01202) 487000
*An outlet of the national fishmonger/café chain, praised in most
accounts for its "excellent choice of local seafood, cooked
to perfection". / Sample dishes: spaghetti with crab & chilli; grilled plaice with
black butter; lemon tart. Details: www.fishworks.co.uk; 10 pm; closed Mon & Sun;
no smoking.*

## CIRENCESTER, GLOUCESTERSHIRE           2–2C

**Tatyan's**                             £ 27
27 Castle St  GL7 1QD   (01285) 653529
*In an area surprisingly devoid of decent restaurants, this friendly
town-centre Chinese has a name locally for its "great food".
/ Details: www.tatyans.com; near junction of A417 & A345; 10.30 pm; closed
Sun L.*

## CLACHAN, ARGYLL & BUTE                 9–3B

**Loch Fyne Oyster Bar**                 £ 34        𝔸★
PA26 8BL   (01499) 600236
*The "seafood is as fresh as you'll find" at this famous veteran –
"smack bang on the loch" – which manages to be very "busy"
despite the fact that it is "in the middle of nowhere"; it is
no longer related to the chain of the same name.
/ Sample dishes: smoked haddock chowder; king scallops; ice cream.
Details: www.loch-fyne.com; 10m E of Inveraray on A83; 8.30 pm; no smoking.*

---

## CLAVERING, ESSEX                                    3–2B

### The Cricketers                                     £36
Wicken Rd CB11 4QT   (01799) 550442
*"Jamie's folks know a thing or two about good pub food"*, say fans
of Trevor & Sally Oliver's *"reliable"* inn; *"the only criticism is its
popularity"* – it can become *"cramped"* and crowded.
/ **Sample dishes:** *avocado pear & crabmeat; medallions of monkfish fillet in herbs;
chocolate cheesecake.* **Details:** *www.thecricketers.co.uk; on B1038 between
Newport & Buntingford; 9.45 pm; no smoking.* **Accommodation:** *14 rooms,
from £100.*

---

## CLAYGATE, SURREY                                    3–3A

### Le Petit Pierrot                    £38         ★
4 The Parade  KT10 0NU   (01372) 465105
*"Cosy and great value, but cramped"* – that's the package at this
*"intimate"* restaurant, where *"real French food is served with
flair"*. / **Sample dishes:** *pan-fried foie gras; guinea fowl with morel risotto; crème
brûlée.* **Details:** *9.30 pm; closed Sat L & Sun; children: 8+.*

---

## CLENT, WEST MIDLANDS                                5–4B

### Four Stones                        £30         ★
Adams Hill  DY9 9PS   (01562) 883260
A *"very high-quality"* Anglo-Italian, of all the more note for
surviving in a very thin area. / **Sample dishes:** *risotto rice with strips
of chicken, asparagus & spring onions; halibut steak; tiramisu.*
**Details:** *www.thefourstones.co.uk; 10 pm; closed Mon & Sun D; no smoking.*

---

## CLEVEDON, BATH & NE SOMERSET                        2–2A

### Junior Poon                                        £30
16 Hill Rd  BS21 7NZ   (01275) 341900
This smart Chinese restaurant, in an impressive Georgian building,
is *"a great find"*, for most reporters, thanks to its *"tasty"* food and
*"smooth"* service; the odd reporter, though, found it a bit
*"uninspired"*. / **Sample dishes:** *barbecued-spiced spare rib; steamed whole sea
bass.* **Details:** *www.juniorpoon.com; near Clevedon Pier; 10.30 pm; no smoking.*

---

## CLIPSHAM, RUTLAND                                   6–4A

### The Olive Branch                   £36         Ⓐ★
Main St  LE15 7SH   (01780) 410355
*"In a lovely Rutland village"* (*"just off the A1"*), this *"characterful"*
pub has won an enormous following with its *"superb"* cooking and
*"laid-back"* approach. / **Sample dishes:** *goat's cheese & sweet pepper
mousse; braised lamb mash; coconut ice cream.*
**Details:** *www.theolivebranchpub.com; 2m E from A1 on B664; 9.30 pm; no Amex;
no smoking area.*

## CLITHEROE, LANCASHIRE　　　　　　5–1B
**Inn at Whitewell**　　　　　　　£39　　　Ⓐ
Forest of Bowland BD7 3AT (01200) 448222
*Thanks not least to its "idyllic" location, this "cosy", "country-house-style" inn, in the Trough of Bowland, has achieved "great popularity"; it is generally "superbly run", but reports on a year which has seen renovations and extensions have been unsettled – hopefully a passing phase.* / **Sample dishes:** *goat's cheese cannelloni; grilled black pudding with lamb's kidneys; British & Irish cheeses.* **Details:** *9.30 pm; D only (bar meals only at L); no Amex; no smoking.* **Accommodation:** *23 rooms, from £96.*

## COBHAM, SURREY　　　　　　　3–3A
**La Capanna**　　　　　　　　£43
48 High St KT11 3EF (01932) 862121
*This barn-like Italian remains a popular local destination, but even some who see it as "a class act" concede that it's "on the expensive side".* / **Sample dishes:** *crab salad; veal & scallops with mushroom sauce; bread & butter pudding.* **Details:** *www.lacapanna.co.uk; 10.45 pm; smoking in bar only.*

## COCKERMOUTH, CUMBRIA　　　　7–3C
**Kirkstile Inn**　　　　　　　£27　　　★
Loweswater CA13 0RU (01900) 85219
*"An interesting choice of well-cooked local produce" helps ensure that this "out-of-the-way" pub (which sells its own-brew beers) "always seems to be busy".* / **Details:** *www.kirkstile.com; 9 pm; no Amex; no smoking; children: 18+.* **Accommodation:** *9 rooms, from £38.*

**Quince & Medlar**　　　　　　£35　　Ⓐ★
13 Castlegate CA13 9EU (01900) 823579
*An "excellent veggie restaurant", occupying a panelled, candlelit townhouse dining room – its rarity in this part of the world makes it all the more of a "gem".* / **Sample dishes:** *French onion tart; butternut squash & broad beans; spiced quince cheesecake.* **Details:** *www.quinceandmedlar.co.uk; next to Cockermouth Castle; 9.30 pm; D only, closed Mon & Sun; no Amex; no smoking; children: 5+.*

## COGGESHALL, ESSEX　　　　　　3–2C
**Baumann's Brasserie**　　　　　£35
4-6 Stoneham St CO6 1TT (01376) 561453
*"Consistently good" food – and "good value", too, especially from the set menus – makes this unpretentious brasserie a handy destination in an "out-of-the-way" location.* / **Sample dishes:** *Baltimore crab & corn cake; cappuccino ice cream-filled profiteroles.* **Details:** *www.baumannsbrasserie.co.uk; 9.30 pm, Sat 10.30 pm; closed Mon & Tue; smoking in bar only.*

## COLCHESTER, ESSEX　　　　　　3–2C
**The Lemon Tree**　　　　　　£27　　　Ⓐ
48 St Johns St CO2 7AD (01206) 767337
*This "busy bistro in unusual surroundings" – the town's Roman wall runs "right through it" – is consistently praised by reporters for its "solid" and "good-value" cuisine.* / **Sample dishes:** *pan-fried scallops & spicy chorizo salad; roast lamb with garlic & rosemary salsa; black cherry cheesecake.* **Details:** *www.the-lemon-tree.com; in town centre; 9.30 pm; closed Sun; no smoking.*

## COLERNE, WILTSHIRE                    2–2B

**Lucknam Park**                    £78      A★★
SN14 8AZ   (01225) 742777
"Consistent excellence" – not least of Hywel Jones's cuisine –
wins almost unanimous 'rave' reviews for this elegant but relaxed
hotel, occupying a fine Georgian house. / **Sample dishes:** spinach
cappuccino with truffled quails eggs; roast venison with game chips & spiced pears;
citrus sorbets with citrus jelly. **Details:** www.lucknampark.co.uk; 6m NE of Bath;
9.45 pm; D only, ex Sun open L & D; jacket & tie required; no smoking; children:
8+ at D. **Accommodation:** 41 rooms, from £235.

## COLSTON BASSETT, NOTTINGHAMSHIRE       5–3D

**Martins Arms Inn**                £42
School Ln  NG12 3FD   (01949) 81361
"A traditional real-ale posh country pub", in a "beautiful location",
and where the food is sometimes "exceptional"; prices, though,
can seem "ridiculous". / **Sample dishes:** roast scallops with leeks; seared sea
bass fillet; chocolate fondant. **Details:** 1.5 miles off A46; 9.30 pm; closed Sun D;
no smoking.

## COMPTON, SURREY                        3–3A

**The Withies Inn**                 £41       A
Withies Ln  GU3 1JA   (01483) 421158
Cynics proclaim this "great" and "luxurious" inn, in the Surrey
Hills, as a good place to take visitors – it "reinforces their views
about picturesque England, high prices and mediocre food";
supporters prefer to describe its style as "classic".
/ **Sample dishes:** pan-fried sardines with lemon; roast lamb with rosemary; treacle
tart & custard. **Details:** off A3 near Guildford, signposted on B3000; 10 pm, 3 pm
Sun; closed Sun D; no smoking.

## CONSTANTINE, CORNWALL                  1–4B

**Trengilly Wartha Inn**            £40       A
Nancenoy  TR11 5RP   (01326) 340332
"There's a sense of achievement" in finding this "delightful" rural
gastropub, which is of note for its "immense" wine list, which
is backed up by some "tasty" food – it attracts much
commentary, all positive. / **Sample dishes:** scallops in their shells with
linguine; shoulder of Cornish lamb; Valrhona chocolate pot.
**Details:** www.trengilly.co.uk; 1m outside village; 9.30 pm; D only; no smoking.
**Accommodation:** 8 rooms, from £80.

## COOKHAM, BERKSHIRE                     3–3A

**Bel & The Dragon**                £41
High St  SL6 9SQ   (01628) 521263
"Reliable, if a little expensive", this "cheerful" gastropub (part of
a small chain) is consistently praised by reporters; the "noisy,
wine-bar ambience" of the bar seems to be preferred to that
of the dining room. / **Sample dishes:** baby goat's cheese on filled mushroom;
sticky toffee pudding. **Details:** www.belandthedragon.co.uk; opp Stanley Spencer
Gallery; 10 pm; no smoking Sun.

### Cookham Tandoori £41 ★
SL6 9SL (01628) 522584
*"Top-end food, with the emphasis on innovation" and "great service" contribute to the all-round charms of this "sophisticated" subcontinental.* / **Sample dishes:** chicken with tandoori & garlic coriander; home-made crème brûlée. **Details:** www.spicemerchantgroup.com; 11 pm; smoking in bar only.

### Inn on the Green £46 𝔸
The Old Cricket Common SL6 9NZ (01628) 482638
*Garry Hollihead's leafily-located and fashionably-revamped inn continues to inspire remarkably little commentary; such as there is says it's "pricey" but "pleasant", with "friendly" service and "good" food.* / **Sample dishes:** dressed crab and smoked salmon; smoked rib of beef; strawberry soufflé. **Details:** www.theinnonthegreen.com; 10 pm; closed Mon, Tue–Sat D only, closed Sun D; no smoking area; booking: max 6 on Sat. **Accommodation:** 9 rooms, from £130.

### Maliks £36 𝔸★
High St SL6 9SF (01628) 520085
*"A posh Indian at posh prices, but very good" – this thoroughly "high-class" establishment, in a Tudor inn, attracts little but praise.* / **Sample dishes:** grilled chicken with peanut sauce; lamb made with chef's special recipe; cinnamon pear. **Details:** www.maliks.co.uk; 11 pm; no smoking area.

---

## CORBRIDGE, NORTHUMBERLAND 8–2B

### The Angel of Corbridge £34
Main St NE45 5LA (01434) 632119
*It's not the setting ("could be cosier") or the service (sometimes "amateurish and slow") which is making this modernised inn, "in a lovely wee village", ever more "popular" – it must be the "good food, in an area with such a low density of restaurants".* / **Sample dishes:** smoked salmon soufflé; roast guinea fowl; chocolate tart. **Details:** www.theangelofcorbridge.co.uk; 8.45 pm; closed Sun D; no smoking. **Accommodation:** 5 rooms, from £79.

### The Valley £29 ★
Old Station Hs NE45 5AY (01434) 633434
*"Even better if you travel by the 'Curry Train' from Newcastle" (order en route for service on arrival), this rural Indian restaurant inspires only positive reports.* / **Sample dishes:** grilled green pepper stuffed with spicy mixed vegetables; bhuna lamb or chicken; crushed fruit sorbet. **Details:** www.thevalleyrestaurants.co.uk; 10.30 pm; D only, closed Sun; smoking in bar only.

---

## CORSCOMBE, DORSET 2–4B

### Fox Inn £36 𝔸★
DT2 0NS (01935) 891330
*Under owner Clive Webb, this "exceptionally cosy" thatched pub has gone from strength to strength, thanks to its "friendly" service and its "mouth-watering" gastropub fare; the chef is apparently set to move on to pastures new in late-2005.* / **Sample dishes:** roast aubergines with tomato & Mozzarella; chicken with celery, red pepper & cream sauce; plum crumble. **Details:** www.fox-inn.co.uk; 5m off A37; 9 pm; no Amex; no smoking area; children: 5+. **Accommodation:** 4 rooms, from £80.

**sign up for the survey at www.hardens.com**

---

## CORSE LAWN, GLOUCESTERSHIRE     2–1B

**Corse Lawn Hotel**     £42
GL19 4LZ   (01452) 780771
*The Hine family's "reliable" and "professional" bistro is part of a Queen Anne house, overlooking the village green; it can sometimes seem "a little quiet".* / **Sample dishes:** *ravioli of crab with spinach & cucumber sauce; pigeon breasts with red wine; vanilla panna cotta with rhubarb sorbet.* **Details:** *www.corselawn.com; 5m SW of Tewkesbury on B4211; 9.30 pm; no jeans or trainers; no smoking; children: 6+ at D.* **Accommodation:** *19 rooms, from £105.*

---

## COVENTRY, WEST MIDLANDS     5–4C

**Thai Dusit**     £24
39 London Rd CV1 2JP   (024) 7622 7788
*It may not have the best position (by the ring road), but this long-established oriental is noted for its "consistently high standards" and "good value".* / **Details:** *11 pm; no Amex.*

---

## COWBRIDGE, VALE OF GLAMORGAN     2–2A

**Farthings**     £32
54 High St CF71 7AH   (01446) 772990
*"Good basic menus" (with some "amazing puddings") make this "busy" bistro popular with all reporters – that's not to say they find it perfect, but "it's the best of the bunch in these parts".* / **Sample dishes:** *French onion soup; wild boar & pheasant sausages; hazelnut & raspberry meringue.* **Details:** *10 pm; closed Mon D & Sun D; no Amex; no smoking area.*

---

## COWLEY, GLOUCESTERSHIRE     2–1C

**Cowley Manor**     £47     ★
GL53 9NL   (01242) 870900
*A "relaxed" country house hotel, where "efficient yet unobtrusive" staff offer an "extensive" menu that's "a good mix of fancy dishes and comfort food"; the place's contemporary decor is, in fact, its least highly rated feature.* / **Sample dishes:** *crab linguine; sea bass & spinach; vanilla & orange panna cotta with strawberry & mint salsa.* **Details:** *www.cowleymanor.com; 10 pm; closed Fri D & Sat; no smoking.* **Accommodation:** *30 rooms, from £230.*

---

## COWLING, WEST YORKSHIRE     5–1B

**Harlequin**     £34
139 Keighley Rd BD22 0AH   (01535) 633277
*"Excellent food and service" is the gist of most (if not quite all) reports on this small restaurant-cum-wine bar.* / **Sample dishes:** *calamari & chorizo salad; roast duckling with rhubarb compote; Yorkshire ginger sponge.* **Details:** *on A6068 towards Colne; 9.30 pm; closed Mon & Tue; smoking in bar only; children: 7+ at D.*

**sign up for the survey at www.hardens.com**    

## CRASTER, NORTHUMBERLAND 8–1B
### Jolly Fisherman £16
NE66 3TR  (01665) 576461
"An old and unspoilt coastal pub, with fantastic views"; there was
the occasional misfire this year, but most reports still praise the
simple fare on offer, such as "good fish soups, and crab
sandwiches and chips". / **Sample dishes:** crab soup with whisky; kipper pâté
with melba toast; blackcurrant crumble with custard. **Details:** near Dunstanburgh
Castle; 8 pm; L only; no credit cards; no smoking area; no booking.

## CRASWALL, HEREFORDSHIRE 2–1A
### Bulls Head £31  𝔸★
HR2 0PN  (01981) 510616
"A Black Mountains 'secret'", this Aussie-run inn is hailed by all
reporters for its "great beer" and its "lovely" food, but in
particular for its "wonderful" location. / **Sample dishes:** soup of the day;
blanche bait with crispy salad; sticky toffee pudding.
**Details:** www.thebullsheadpub.com; 9 pm; no Amex; smoking in bar only.
**Accommodation:** 3 rooms, from £60.

## CREIGIAU, CARDIFF 2–2A
### Caesars Arms £31  ★
Cardiff Rd  CF15 9NN  (029) 2089 0486
"Showing no signs of diminishing popularity", this rural
counterpoint to La Brasserie – where you similarly choose your
fish, seafood or steak at the counter – is "keeping up high
standards". / **Sample dishes:** fishcakes; white chocolate & blackcurrant
cheesecake. **Details:** beyond Creigiau, past golf club; 10 pm; closed Sun D; smoking
in bar only.

## CREWE, CHESHIRE 5–3B
### The Ranulph
### Crewe Hall £47  𝔸
Weston Rd  CW1 6UZ  (01270) 253333
"A 19th-century-spectacular country house, just 4 miles from the
M6 (J16)" – under new owners (Marston Hotels), it's emerging
as "peaceful" and "good-value" destination, especially for business
dining (or for afternoon tea). / **Sample dishes:** seared scallops with mint
purée; confit leg of ducking; cappuccino & chocolate tart with Bailey's ice cream.
**Details:** www.crewehall.com; 9.30 pm; closed Sat L & Sun D; no smoking; children:
7+ at D. **Accommodation:** 65 rooms, from £129.

## CRICKHOWELL, POWYS 2–1A
### The Bear £37
High St  NP8 1BW  (01873) 810408
"A very good old-style country hotel" (in fact, a 15th-century inn),
which numbers a "warm welcome" and "consistently good bar
food" (in a "real pub atmosphere") among its attractions;
the dining room menu is quite contemporary, but it's perhaps as a
classic "Sunday lunch" destination that the place really shines.
/ **Sample dishes:** tian of crab & spiced avocado salsa; steamed treacle sponge &
crème anglaise. **Details:** www.bearhotel.co.uk; 9.30 pm; D only, ex Sun open L only,
closed Mon; no smoking; children: 7+. **Accommodation:** 34 rooms, from £77.

### Nantyffin Cider Mill £33 A★
Brecon Rd NP8 1SG (01873) 810775
*"Reliable food with a Welsh slant" and a "beautiful" dining room come together to make this ever-popular gastropub "worth the detour", for most reporters.* / **Sample dishes:** chicken liver parfait; red mullet with saffron linguine & crab; Drambuie panna cotta with figs. **Details:** www.cidermill.co.uk; on A40 between Brecon & Crickhowell; 9.30 pm; closed Tue (& Sun D in winter); no smoking.

---

## CROSTHWAITE, CUMBRIA 7–4D

### The Punch Bowl £35
LA8 8HR (01539) 568237
*This famous inn changed hands towards the end of our survey year, and has subsequently been totally refurbished; a rating will have to await the next edition.* / **Sample dishes:** beetroot & goat's cheese tart; slow-cooked lamb with leek & white bean stew; chocolate & ginger tart with honey ice cream. **Details:** www.punchbowl.fsnet.co.uk; off A5074 towards Bowness, turn right after Lyth Hotel; 9 pm; closed Mon & Sun D; no Amex; no smoking. **Accommodation:** 3 rooms, from £75.

---

## CROYDON, SURREY 3–3B

### Banana Leaf £30 ★
7 Lower Addiscombe Rd CR0 6PQ (020) 8688 0297
*"In the wastelands of Croydon, a surprisingly good subcontinental"; its "superb" and "eclectic" south Indian fare is liked by all, but is particularly "excellent for veggies and vegans".* / **Details:** www.a222.co.uk/bananaleaf; near East Croydon station; 11 pm; no smoking area.

---

## CUCKFIELD, WEST SUSSEX 3–4B

### Ockenden Manor £58 A★
Ockenden Ln RH17 5LD (01444) 416111
*On most reports, this "classy" Elizabethan manor house makes a "top-notch" retreat, where "well-prepared" dishes are made from "high-quality" ingredients; the odd misfire, however, is not unknown.* / **Sample dishes:** truffle risotto; grilled beef with mustard sauce; apple fritters. **Details:** www.hshotels.co.uk; 9 pm; no jeans; no smoking. **Accommodation:** 22 rooms, from £155.

---

## CUPAR, FIFE 9–3D

### Ostlers Close £45 A★★
25 Bonnygate KY15 4BU (01334) 655574
*"A simply outstanding restaurant in a small market town" –* all reporters are united in praise of James Graham's "great" cooking, which, for a quarter of a century, has made inspired use of local produce. / **Sample dishes:** fillet of Pittenweem halibut; breast of corn-fed duck; upside-down apple & bramble oat crumble. **Details:** www.ostlersclose.co.uk; centrally situated in the Howe of Fife; 9.30 pm; closed Sun & Mon, Tue-Fri D only, Sat L & D; no smoking; children: 6+ at D.

### The Peat Inn £46 A★
KY15 5LH (01334) 840206
*This grand coaching inn – famous for its vast wine list – wins high praise for the "finesse" with which it handles "country produce"; occasional disappointments can be induced by "staff who seem to think they are doing you a favour".* / **Sample dishes:** roast scallops with truffle risotto; roe deer with wild mushroom cake; caramel dessert. **Details:** www.thepeatinn.co.uk; at junction of B940 & B941, SW of St Andrews; 9.30 pm; closed Mon & Sun; no smoking. **Accommodation:** 8 rooms, from £165.

### DALRY, AYRSHIRE 9–4B
### Braidwoods £45 A★★
Drumastle Mill Cottage KA24 4LN (01294) 833544
*This "delightful country restaurant" occupies two converted cottages and is run by a "charming and very talented couple" (Keith and Nicola Braidwood); feedback is limited, but all tends to support the proposition that it offers "some of Scotland's best cooking".* / **Sample dishes:** curried prawn & coriander soup; honey-glazed duck with spiced beetroot; raspberry crème brûlée. **Details:** www.braidwoods.co.uk; 9 pm; closed Mon, Tue L & Sun D; closed 2 weeks in Jan & Sep; no smoking; children: 12+ at D.

### DARTMOUTH, DEVON 1–4D
### New Angel £47
2 South Embankment TQ6 9BH (01803) 839425
*Surely Michelin didn't just watch the TV show before rushing to 'star' John Burton-Race's relaunch of this harbour-side site? – some reporters do applaud his "fine" modern cuisine and the "vibrant" atmosphere, but many others just find the place "chaotic" or "amateurish", and "expensive" too.* / **Sample dishes:** Dartmouth crab salad; lamb with root vegetable strudel & cherry jus; lime parfait with strawberries. **Details:** www.thenewangel.co.uk; opp passenger ferry pontoon; 10.30 pm; closed Mon & Sun D; no smoking area at L.

### DATCHWORTH, HERTFORDSHIRE 3–2B
### Coltsfoot Country Retreat £42 A★
Coltsfoot Ln, Bulls Grn SG3 6SB (01438) 212800
*"An old barn with tiled floors and exposed wood beams" forms the venue for dining at this stylish modern country hotel, which all reports hail as a "great find".* / **Sample dishes:** smoked chicken & ginger spring rolls; fillet of sea bass & asparagus with crayfish risotto; raspberry & Bailey's crème brûlée. **Details:** www.coltsfoot.com; 9.30 pm; closed Sun; no smoking; children: 12+ at D. **Accommodation:** 15 rooms, from £135.

### DAVENTRY, NORTHANTS 2–1D
### Fawsley Hall £52 A
NN11 3BA (01327) 892000
*The surroundings are "stately", but the style of this Elizabethan house, converted a few years back into an hotel, is "very friendly"; some reporters still recall its "bad start", culinarily speaking, but nowadays most rate a meal here as a "good-value" overall experience.* / **Sample dishes:** foie gras terrine with pickled cherries; herbed lamb with creamed shallots; raspberry soufflé with chocolate sorbet. **Details:** www.fawsleyhall.com; on A361 between Daventry & Banbury; 9.30 pm; no smoking. **Accommodation:** 43 rooms, from £130.

## DEAL, KENT                                    3–3D

### Dunkerley's                                £36
19 Beach St CT14 7AH   (01304) 375016
*Ian Dunkerly has run this now rather "old-fashioned" hotel dining
room for over a quarter of a century; the focus of the "varied"
menu is on fish that's "well presented and served".*
/ **Sample dishes:** *lightly-spiced smoked haddock; slow-cooked lamb shoulder with
rosemary & garlic; plum & apple crumble with crème anglaise.*
**Details:** *www.dunkerleys.co.uk; 9.30 pm; closed Mon L; no smoking.*
**Accommodation:** *16 rooms, from £100.*

## DEDHAM, ESSEX                                 3–2C

### The Boathouse                             £35        A★
Mill Ln CO7 6DH   (01206) 323153
*You can still hire rowing boats at this bar/restaurant – a former
boathouse in a "great location" on the River Stour – but it's listed
here as a "welcoming" and "spacious" eatery, where the food
is usually "very good"; super terrace for the summer.*
/ **Sample dishes:** *roasted fennel soup; char-grilled rib-eye steak; iced coffee terrine
with crushed biscotti.* **Details:** *www.dedhamboathouse.com; 9.30 pm; closed Mon &
Sun D; smoking in bar only.*

### Milsoms                                    £32        A
Stratford Rd CO7 6HW   (01206) 322795
*"The best local all-day rendezvous", this "buzzy" no-booking
bistro (an informal sibling to the famous Talbooth) is tremendously
popular (and can sometimes seem "chaotic"); even some fans,
though, fear that drifting standards and rising prices are beginning
to dent its appeal.* / **Sample dishes:** *prawn & crayfish cocktail; braised lamb;
chocolate brownie with pecan fudge sauce.* **Details:** *www.milsomhotels.com;
9.30 pm, Fri & Sat 10 pm; no smoking area; no booking.* **Accommodation:** *15
rooms, from £95.*

### The Sun Inn                                £33
High St CO7 6DF   (01206) 323351
*This "traditional" country inn attracts a fair amount of feedback,
largely to the effect that its food is usually "good" (and sometimes
"excellent").* / **Details:** *9.30 pm; no Amex; no smoking area.*
**Accommodation:** *4 rooms, from £70.*

### Le Talbooth                                £56        A
Gun Hill CO7 6HP   (01206) 323150
*If you can get a sunny-day table on the riverside terrace, it's hard
not to warm to the Milsom family's Constable Country fixture
of over 50 years' standing; at other times, doubts may come
to the fore – "unless you're paying for pomposity, it's simply not
worth it".* / **Sample dishes:** *crab, artichoke & lobster salad; tournedos of Scotch
beef with seared foie gras; assiette of chocolate desserts.*
**Details:** *www.milsomhotels.com; 5m N of Colchester on A12, take B1029;
9.30 pm; closed Sun D; no jeans or trainers; no smoking during dinner.*
**Accommodation:** *10 rooms, from £165.*

**sign up for the survey at www.hardens.com**

## DENHAM, BUCKINGHAMSHIRE                    3–3A

**Swan**                                      £ 36          *A*
Village Rd  UB9 5BH   (01895) 832085
*The food may not have been much more than "pleasant"*
*in recent times, but this gastropub in a "lovely" village has quite*
*a following – perhaps a new chef will produce cooking to match*
*its popularity. /* **Sample dishes:** *potted brown shrimps with melba toast;*
*pot roast chicken supreme with Jersey royals; croissant bread & butter pudding.*
**Details:** *www.swanindenham.co.uk; 10 pm; no smoking.*

## DERBY, DERBYSHIRE                          5–3C

**Darleys**                                   £ 43          *A*
Darley Abbey Mill  DE22 1DZ   (01332) 364987
*"Good river views" and – on occasion – "top-drawer" cooking win*
*much praise for this "attractive" restaurant; there's quite a feeling*
*that it's "overpriced" and "too full of itself", though – the result,*
*presumably, of being the grand fromage in "the Derby desert".*
*/* **Sample dishes:** *scallops with crispy crab risotto cakes; roast pork belly with black*
*pudding & mustard mash; spiced poached pears with cinnamon shortbread.*
**Details:** *www.darleys.com; 2m N of city centre by River Derwent; 9.30 pm; closed*
*Sun D; no Amex; no smoking.*

## DINTON, BUCKINGHAMSHIRE                     2–3C

**La Chouette**                               £ 45          ★
Westlington Grn  HP17 8UW   (01296) 747422
*As long as you take to the "wildly eccentric" Belgian proprietor –*
*and vice-versa – you'll probably enjoy a trip to this "consistently*
*excellent" restaurant, which attracts unanimous praise for its*
*"good food and impressive wine list". /* **Details:** *on A418 between*
*Aylesbury & Thame; 9 pm; closed Sat L & Sun; no Amex; no smoking.*

## DODDISCOMBSLEIGH, DEVON                     1–3D

**Nobody Inn**                                £ 32          *A*
EX6 7PS   (01647) 252394
*An "amazing" wine list ("both its size and quality"), "superb"*
*cheese, and "a huge choice of malt whiskies" have helped make*
*an enormous reputation for this "lovely" ancient inn, "in the back*
*of beyond" outside Exeter; the cooking plays second fiddle, which*
*some reporters think is "a shame". /* **Sample dishes:** *fillet with cream &*
*mustard sauce; quail stuffed with rice & apricots; crème brûlée.*
**Details:** *www.nobodyinn.co.uk; off A38 at Haldon Hill (signed Dunchidrock); 9 pm;*
*D only, closed Mon & Sun; no smoking; children: 14+.* **Accommodation:** *7 rooms,*
*from £40.*

## DORKING, SURREY                            3–3A

**Stephan Langton**                           £ 31          ★
Friday St, Abinger Common  RH5 6JR   (01306) 730775
*It has "an enchanting setting amidst the Surrey Hills", and this*
*"tucked-away" pub serves wonderful food, at "good prices";*
*the décor, however, is "awful". /* **Sample dishes:** *terrine of chicken liver;*
*roast cod, black beans, chorizo & salse verde; apricot & almond tart.* **Details:** *off*
*A25 at Wotton; 10 pm; closed Mon & Sun D; no Amex; no smoking.*

## DUBLIN, COUNTY DUBLIN, *ROI*            10–3D

*Though clearly not geographically within the ambit of a
guide called UK Restaurants, we have included a small
range of the best-known names in the Irish capital. These
tend to be 'destination' establishments. Visitors looking for
less expensive dining may like to bear in mind that,
like London's Covent Garden, the popular tourist area
of Temple Bar is generally best avoided by those in search
of decent value. All restaurants are no-smoking.*

### L'Ecrivain                          €102            ★
109a Lower Baggot St  D2  (01) 661 1919
*"Creative, top-quality food"* served *"with care and efficiency"*
again wins praise for Derry and Sally Anne Clarke's contemporary-
style venture; its location is *"very good for business"*.
/ **Sample dishes:** foie gras; roast Angus Irish beef fillet; berry truffle cake.
**Details:** www.lecrivain.com; opp Bank of Ireland; 11.30 pm; closed Sat L & Sun;
no Switch; no smoking.

### Jacob's Ladder                      € 65          Ⓐ★
4-5 Nassau St  D2   (01) 670 3865
*Nab a window seat if you can (they have views of Trinity Green),
when you visit Adrian Roche's "user-friendly" first-floor operation;
the accomplished modern cooking is generally "excellent".*
/ **Sample dishes:** roast quail with quails eggs; roast pigeon with lentils; passion fruit
brûlée with chilli & coconut sorbet. **Details:** www.jacobsladder.ie; beside Trinity
College; 10 pm; closed Mon & Sun; no Switch; no smoking.

### King Sitric                         € 76
East Pier, Howth   (01) 832 5235
*The MacManuses' long-established restaurant-with-rooms is found
in a pretty suburb at the end of the DART; it's long had a lofty
reputation, not least for seafood, and feedback (albeit modest
in volume) suggests that it "still lives up".* / **Sample dishes:** grilled
scallops with black & white pudding; poached fillet of turbot; iced hazelnut parfait
with passion fruit coulis. **Details:** www.kingsitric.ie; Howth Harbour across sea front
on top of far pier; 10 pm; closed Sat L & Sun; no smoking. **Accommodation:** 8
rooms, from E138.

### Mermaid Café                        € 58          Ⓐ★
69-70 Dame St  D2  (01) 6708236
*An "ideal restaurant" – this "unpretentious" corner spot,
near Temple Bar, offers a "really enjoyable" combination
of "good" wine, "excellent" 'mid-Atlantic' cooking and a "buzzy"
ambience.* / **Sample dishes:** quail with pistachio; corn-fed chicken with buffalo
Mozzarella; pineapple tarte Tatin with lemon, rum & raisin ice cream.
**Details:** www.mermaid.ie; near Olympia Theatre; 11 pm, Sun 9 pm; no Switch;
no smoking.

### Restaurant Patrick Guilbaud        €143            ★
21 Upper Merrion St  D2   (01) 676 4192
*"Beautiful food… lovely room… even the art on the wall is good"
– all-round satisfaction is the norm when it comes to the Irish
capital's grandest dining destination (whose wine list runs to many
hundreds of bins); the prices, though, are vertiginous.*
/ **Sample dishes:** lobster ravioli in coconut cream; venison with pumpkin cream &
black radishes; assiette gourmand au chocolat. **Details:** www.merrionhotel.com;
10.15 pm; closed Mon & Sun; no Switch; no smoking. **Accommodation:** 145
rooms, from E370.

**sign up for the survey at www.hardens.com**            205

### Roly's Bistro € 61 Ⓐ
7 Ballsbridge Terr D4 (01) 668 2611
"A very jolly and lively ambience" has long been the mainstay
of this famous Ballsbridge brasserie; to fans it's "reliable" and
a "class act" – to critics it "doesn't deliver", and "missing
something". / **Sample dishes:** salmon & crab seafood gratin; grilled fillet of Irish
beef with braised oxtail; almond, pear, blackberry crumble.
**Details:** www.rolysbistro.ie; near American Embassy; 10 pm; no smoking.

### La Stampa € 67
35 Dawson St D2 (01) 677 8611
Celeb-chef Jean-Christophe Novelli added this former ballroom
to his portfolio of interests in summer 2005; his record has been
patchy in recent years, so it's hard to predict whether he will
revive reporters' interest in this potentially beautiful space.
/ **Sample dishes:** pan-fried foie gras brioche; roast fillet of beef; chocolate fondant.
**Details:** www.lastampa.ie; off St Stephen's Green; midnight, Fri & Sat 12.30 am;
D only; no Switch; no smoking. **Accommodation:** 22 rooms, from EE200.

### Thorntons
### Fitzwilliam Hotel €120 ★
128 St Stephen's Grn D2 (01) 478 7008
Kevin Thornton's relocated temple of gastronomy is "expensive but
well worth it for the superbly cooked and presented food and
excellent service"; on the downside, its new "luxury hotel" site
(once Peacock Alley, long RIP) is as "dull" as the old.
/ **Sample dishes:** sauteed Dublin Bay prawns; braised suckling pig with roasted
turnips; blood orange soufflé with blood orange sorbet.
**Details:** www.thorntonsrestaurant.com; 10.30 pm; D only, ex Fri open L & D, closed
Mon & Sun; no smoking.

---

## DUFFTOWN, ABERDEEN 9–2C

### La Faisanderie £35
2 Balvenie St AB55 4AB (01340) 821273
This Gallic-influenced town-centre restaurant is tipped
as "wonderful" place delivering "very good food in an area they
live on chips and steak"; in light of very limited feedback, however,
we've left it unrated. / **Details:** 8.30 pm; closed Tue; no Amex; no smoking.

---

## DUNKELD, PERTH & KINROSS 9–3C

### Kinnaird House £67 Ⓐ★
Kinnaird Estate PH8 0LB (01796) 482440
This "elegant and friendly" Edwardian house by the River Tay
attracts surprisingly thin feedback, but all of it speaks of "state-of-
the-art cuisine", "very attentive" service and "beautiful
surroundings". / **Sample dishes:** terrine of foie gras & langoustine; pan-fried
John Dory; hot pear soufflé. **Details:** www.kinnairdestate.com; 8m NW of Dunkeld,
off A9 onto B898; 9.30 pm; closed Mon-Wed in Jan & Feb; jacket & tie required
at D; no smoking; children: 12+. **Accommodation:** 9 rooms, from £275.

## DUNVEGAN, ISLE OF SKYE　　　　　　9–2A

**The Three Chimneys**　　　　　£59　　A★★
Colbost IV55 8ZT　(01470) 511258
*"A remote culinary outpost that's well worth seeking out"* – Eddie
and Shirley Spear's *"stunningly-located"* crofter's cottage is hailed
as an *"exceptional"* destination, and a *"romantic"* one too
(*"especially if you stay"*). / **Sample dishes:** *carrot, orange & ginger soup;
black pudding with leek & potato mash; apple & almond tart.*
**Details:** *www.threechimneys.co.uk; 5m from Dunvegan Castle on B884 to Glendale;
9.30 pm; closed Sun L; closed part of Jan; no smoking; children: 8+ at
D.* **Accommodation:** *6 rooms, from £240.*

## DURHAM, COUNTY DURHAM　　　　　8–3B

**Bistro 21**　　　　　　　£41　　A★
Aykley Heads Hs DH1 5TS　(0191) 384 4354
*"Still the No. 1 place to go in a woefully under-served gem of a
city"*; those in search of *"well-prepared and tasty cuisine"* should
seek out this *"stylish"* riverside warehouse.
/ **Sample dishes:** *Cheddar & spinach soufflé; slow-cooked beef with polenta &
Parmesan crisps; profiteroles with pistachio ice cream.* **Details:** *near Durham Trinity
School; 10.30 pm; closed Sun; no smoking; booking: max 10.*

**Hide Café Bar & Grill**　　　　£33
39 Saddler St DH1 3NU　(0191) 384 1999
*This "lively" ("noisy") pizzeria has become something of a default
central rendezvous in a city which still offers little real competition.*
/ **Sample dishes:** *duck spring rolls; pizza with anchovies & roast peppers; sticky
toffee pudding.* **Details:** *www.hidebar.com; 9.30 pm; no Amex; no smoking area.*

**Pump House**　　　　　　　£42
Farm Rd DH1 3PJ　(0191) 386 9189
*Fans say this bistro – a former pumping station – is "always
welcoming", and offers "the best food round Durham City"; critics
may find it "overpriced".* / **Sample dishes:** *pan-roasted scallops; stuffed
monkfish; mixed berries & crème brûlée.*
**Details:** *www.thepumphouserestaurant.co.uk; 9.30 pm; no smoking.*

## EAST CHILTINGTON, EAST SUSSEX　　3–4B

**Jolly Sportsman**　　　　　£36　　★
Chapel Ln BN7 3BA　(01273) 890400
*"Hard to find, but worth it"* – *"good fresh food"* (and *"a vast
selection of wines, beers and malts"*) has won this *"lovely country
pub-cum-restaurant"*, by a river, a huge following; it can get
*"very busy"*. / **Sample dishes:** *pigeon pancetta; crispy duck; panna cotta.*
**Details:** *www.thejollysportsman.com; NW of Lewes; 9 pm, Fri & Sat 10 pm; closed
Mon & Sun D; no Amex; no smoking.*

---

## EAST GRINSTEAD, WEST SUSSEX 3–4B

**Gravetye Manor** £65 A★

Vowels Ln RH19 4LJ (01342) 810567
*"New owners have maintained continuity"*, at this famous
*"retreat"* – a *"beautiful"* Elizabethan house in *"glorious"*
countryside and gardens; after a decade at the stoves,
Mark Raffan's *"classic but light French cuisine"* is as good as ever
(or possibly better). / **Sample dishes:** quail, black pudding & lardon salad;
roast John Dory; panna cotta with rhubarb. **Details:** www.gravetyemanor.co.uk;
2m outside Turner's Hill; 9.30 pm; jacket & tie required; no smoking; children: 7+.
**Accommodation:** 18 rooms, from £170.

---

## EAST LINTON, EAST LOTHIAN 9–4D

**Drovers Inn** £33

5 Bridge St EH40 3AG (01620) 860298
*"A friendly but busy rural inn"*, where they brew their own ale; it is
praised for its high-quality *"classic pub meals"*.
/ **Sample dishes:** chicken liver pâté; beef stew with herb dumplings; raspberry trifle.
**Details:** 9.30 pm; no Amex; no smoking.

---

## EAST LOOE, CORNWALL 1–4C

**Trawlers** £40 ★

On The Quay PL13 1AH (01503) 263593
An American-born chef delivers *"delicious"* and *"very fresh"*
locally-caught fish as this *"cramped"* fixture, which has
*"a delightful setting overlooking the harbour"*.
/ **Sample dishes:** steamed mussels; fillet of John Dory; crème brûlée.
**Details:** www.trawlersrestaurant.co.uk; 9.30 pm; D only, closed Mon & Sun;
no Amex; no smoking.

---

## EAST WITTON, NORTH YORKSHIRE 8–4B

**Blue Lion** £36 A

DL8 4SN (01969) 624273
Is this *"beautiful old inn with big log fires"* in the Dales just
becoming a bit too popular for its own good? – many reporters
still find it a *"delightful"* destination, but there's also a fair amount
of feedback to the effect that it's *"over-rated"*.
/ **Sample dishes:** onion & blue Wensleydale tart; chicken with smoked foie gras
sauce; crème brûlée. **Details:** www.thebluelion.co.uk; between Masham & Leyburn
on A6108; 9 pm; D only, ex Sun open L & D; no Amex. **Accommodation:** 12
rooms, from £79.

---

## EASTBOURNE, EAST SUSSEX 3–4B

**Café Belge**
**The Burlington Hotel** £35 ★

11-23 Grand Pde BN21 3YN (01323) 729967
This *"interesting café/bar, with sea views"* (part of a small chain)
makes a *"value-for-money"* destination; it offers *"50 ways
of cooking mussels"* (plus other dishes) and *"a beer list to die for"*.
/ **Details:** www.cafebelge.co.uk.

---

**sign up for the survey at www.hardens.com**

## The Mirabelle
## The Grand Hotel                           £52        A★

King Edwards Pde  BN21 4EQ   (01323) 412345

*A "very grand" and "very traditional" seaside hotel dining room
with few obvious peers (locally or nationally); this year's reports
were much more encouraging, with Gerald Roser's cooking often
rated as "brilliant".* / **Sample dishes:** foie gras salad; roast wild sea bass &
scallops; caramelised lime cream with bitter orange sauce.
**Details:** www.grandeastbourne.co.uk; 10 pm; closed Mon & Sun; jacket or tie
required at D; no smoking; children: 12+ at D. **Accommodation:** 152 rooms,
from £165.

## Tiger Inn                                    £34         A

The Green  BN20 0DA   (01323) 423209

*In a "lovely village" near Beachy Head, this picturesque inn
is praised by all for its "atmospheric and cosy style – just how
a pub should be"; its "delicious home-cooked food" also generally
finds favour.* / **Sample dishes:** smoked salmon; sea bass with minted potatoes;
pecan pie & cream. **Details:** 9 pm; children: 14+.

---

EDENBRIDGE, KENT                                  3–3B

## Haxted Mill                                 £45        A★

Haxted Rd  TN8 6PU   (01732) 862914

*This "country gem" – a family-run former water mill – is an
especially "charming place to eat out on a summer's evening" but
also makes a "cosy" winter destination; its "very good" cooking
(specialising in fish and seafood) was consistently acclaimed this
year.* / **Sample dishes:** grilled oysters with spinach; roast rack of lamb; fig tarte
Tatin. **Details:** www.haxtedmill.co.uk; between Edenbridge & Lingfield; 9.30 pm;
closed Mon & Sun D; no Amex; no smoking.

---

## EDINBURGH, CITY OF EDINBURGH           9–4C

The options for eating out in Auld Reekie have improved
considerably in recent times. *Restaurant Martin Wishart* may
be the only restaurant in Britain's first rank, but, for those
willing to seek them out, there are quality operations of most
styles – if still with some emphasis on 'traditional' formulas –
and at most price-levels.

For sheer charm of the setting, the city has two remarkable
venues – the *Witchery by the Castle* (the best-known place
in town) and the *Vintners' Rooms*. Despite rather iffy cuisine,
two modern rooms-with-views – *The Tower* and the more
recent *Oloroso* – have also gathered quite a following.

For casual dining, Leith, and its waterside, remains the best
place to go for a range of fun and relatively inexpensive
options.

## Ann Purna                                    £23

44-45 St Patrick's Sq  EH8 9ET   (0131) 662 1807

*A long-running Southside Gujarati, "beloved of university types".*
/ **Sample dishes:** mixed pakora; gajjar halwa. **Details:** 10.30 pm; closed Sat L &
Sun L; no Amex or Switch; no smoking; children: 10+.

**sign up for the survey at www.hardens.com**

### The Atrium £ 47 &#x1D49;

10 Cambridge St EH1 2ED (0131) 228 8882

*Is this "the most over-hyped and over-priced restaurant in North Britain?"; Auld Reekie's seminal (1993) trendy venue may benefit from a "very romantic" and "relaxed" style, but takes substantial flak from reporters for its "tiny" portions of "uninteresting" cuisine.* / **Sample dishes:** courgette & Parmesan soup; roast duck with cabbage & bacon; marjoram crème brûlée. **Details:** www.atriumrestaurant.co.uk; by the Usher Hall; 10 pm; closed Sat L & Sun (except during Festival); no smoking.

### blue bar café £ 34

10 Cambridge St EH1 2ED (0131) 221 1222

*"Solid food, and handy for the theatres" – those are the attractions of this "noisy" upstairs sibling to the Atrium; it's not the hotspot it once was, however, and the odd reporter finds it "awful" nowadays.* / **Sample dishes:** char-grilled tuna niçoise; sea bream with tomato & courgette galette; apple tart with Calvados parfait. **Details:** www.bluebarcafe.com; by the Usher Hall; 10.30 pm, Fri & Sat 11 pm; closed Sun (except during Festival); no smoking area.

### Café Royal Oyster Bar £ 45 &#x1D49;

17a West Register St EH2 2AA (0131) 556 4124

*"Wonderful", "opulent" décor – just in the style the name might lead you to expect – is the high-point of a visit to this Victorian institution; the food plays a respectable supporting rôle.* / **Sample dishes:** natural oysters; hot chocolate fondant. **Details:** opp Balmoral Hotel; 9.30 pm; no smoking.

### Le Café St-Honoré £ 43 &#x1D49;

34 NW Thistle Street Ln EH2 1EA (0131) 226 2211

*"Variable food, but a good atmosphere" – an apt summary of the pros and cons on this "very Gallic" New Town brasserie.* / **Sample dishes:** carrot & ginger soup; sirloin steak with caramelised shallots; chocolate & fig steamed pudding. **Details:** www.cafesthonore.com; 10 pm; no shorts; no smoking area.

### Centotre £ 33

103 George St EH2 3ES (0131) 225 1550

*It may be "one of the best of Edinburgh's many bank-conversion restaurants", but Valvona & Crolla's spin-off in the New Town still has to live up to its parentage – while it's a reasonably competent Italian, it's not, on its own account, of any particular note.* / **Sample dishes:** goat's cheese with char-grilled aubergines; hot chocolate with chocolate & vanilla ice cream. **Details:** www.centotre.com; 10 pm; closed Sun D; no smoking.

### Creelers £ 40 ★

3 Hunter Sq EH1 1QW (0131) 220 4447

*This "unpretentious" outfit, just off the Royal Mile, is roundly praised by all reporters, not least for its "excellent seafood menu" – "presented, cooked and served to perfection".* / **Sample dishes:** langoustine prawns; cured & smoked shellfish; Scottish strawberries. **Details:** www.creelers.co.uk; 10.30 pm; no smoking area.

### Daniel's £ 30

88 Commercial St EH6 6LX (0131) 553 5933

*"Robust Alsatian cooking" and "friendly service" maintain the popularity of this hard-edged Leith bistro; lunch menus, in particular, offer "excellent value".* / **Sample dishes:** tarte flambé; duck; spicy ice cream terrine. **Details:** www.daniels-bistro.co.uk; 10 pm; no smoking area.

## David Bann £ 25 ★★

56-58 St Marys St EH1 1SX (0131) 556 5888

*This "upmarket" vegetarian five-year-old "has a nice dining room in a lovely part of Edinburgh"; all reporters applaud its "wide selection of interesting dishes" (and "good wine" too).* / **Sample dishes:** grilled polenta & goat's cheese curd; kaffir lime paneer croquettes; amaretto cheesecake. **Details:** www.davidbann.co.uk; 10 pm; no smoking.

## Duck's at Le Marché Noir £ 44

14 Eyre Pl EH3 5EP (0131) 558 1608

*Tucked-away in the New Town, Malcolm Duck's ambitious and well-established restaurant wins praise for the "high standards" of its Gallic cuisine; it provoked the occasional "disappointing" reports, though, this year.* / **Sample dishes:** salmon terrine with crab; Aberdeen Angus fillet of beef; white chocolate & sour cherry cheesecake. **Details:** www.ducks.co.uk; 10 pm, Fri & Sat 10.30 pm; closed Mon L, Sat L & Sun L; no smoking area.

## Dusit £ 31 ★

49a Thistle St EH2 1DY (0131) 220 6846

*"A tucked-away gem serving superb Thai food" – this New Town oriental is a "friendly" place, where "beautiful presentation" is a forte.* / **Sample dishes:** Thai pancake with coconut prawns; stir-fry with asparagus & mangetout; banana fritter with vanilla ice cream. **Details:** www.dusit.co.uk; 11 pm; no smoking area.

## First Coast £ 28

99-101 Dalry Rd EH11 2AB (0131) 3134404

*This "busy" bistro on the west of the city is hailed by all reporters as a "reliable" stand-by, thanks to its "good" (if "standard") food and its "great" service.* / **Sample dishes:** marinated squid, soy & sesame salad; Aberdeen Angus sirloin steak; Eton mess. **Details:** www.first-coast.co.uk; 10.30 pm; closed Sun; no smoking area.

## Fishers Bistro £ 34 A★

1 The Shore EH6 6QW (0131) 554 5666

*This very popular Leith waterfront bistro is almost invariably hailed by reporters for its "high-quality fresh fish", its "very good" service and its "relaxed" atmosphere.* / **Sample dishes:** red snapper with sweet potato & Parmesan rosti; monkfish & swordfish brochette; Turkish delight in brandy snaps. **Details:** www.fishersbistros.co.uk; 10.30 pm; no smoking area.

## Fishers in the City £ 34 A★

58 Thistle St EH2 1EN (0131) 225 5109

*This "haven for seafood-lovers", in a New Town warehouse-conversion, runs neck-and-neck in reporters' esteem with its older sibling, in Leith; it is very consistently praised for its "fine" food, "willing" staff and "informal" style.* / **Sample dishes:** squid & octopus salad; whole Dover sole topped with roast hazelnut; orange sorbet. **Details:** www.fishersbistros.co.uk; 10.30 pm; no smoking area.

## Forth Floor
## Harvey Nichols £ 44 A

30-34 St Andrew Sq EH2 2AD (0131) 524 8350

*The food may be "somewhat standard", but this "cosmopolitan" café is generally hailed as a "cool" and "enjoyable" destination, thanks not least to its "fantastic" city views.* / **Sample dishes:** cured salmon with buckwheat blinis; grilled sea bass; strawberry & Mascarpone tart. **Details:** www.harveynichols.com; 10 pm; closed Mon D & Sun D; no smoking area; booking: max 8.

## The Gallery Restaurant & Bar £ 29 A★

The Mound EH2 2EL (0131) 624 6580
*London caterers Searcy's have made a surprisingly decent job
of this new gallery dining facility, whose attractions include
"very good food" and a "superb view".* / **Details:** *10 pm; no Amex;
no smoking.*

## Garrigue £ 30 A★

31 Jeffrey St EH1 1DH (0131) 557 3032
*"A lovely family-run restaurant", in the Old Town, that serves
often-"excellent" food that's "true to its owners' Languedoc
origins".* / **Details:** *www.lagarrigue.co.uk; 9.30 pm; no smoking.*

## Glass & Thompson £ 24 A★

2 Dundas St EH3 6SU (0131) 557 0909
*If you're looking for a "glorious" coffee (and a light, "imaginative"
snack), this elegant New Town deli/café is one of the top tips
in town.* / **Sample dishes:** *roast vegetables; seafood platter; passion cake.*
**Details:** *L only; no smoking.*

## Hadrian's
## Balmoral Hotel £ 36

1 Princes St EH2 2EQ (0131) 557 5000
*This handily-located grand-hotel brasserie is variously described
as "corporate", "beautiful, but sterile" and "pretentious"... and
that's by its fans!; it delivers "good brasserie cooking", though,
and the prix-fixe dinner is "a bargain".* / **Sample dishes:** *saffron risotto
Milanese; sirloin steak with fries & green beans; orange & grapefruit in Sauternes
jelly.* **Details:** *www.thebalmoralhotel.com; 10.30 pm; no smoking area.*
**Accommodation:** *185 rooms, from £225.*

## Haldanes £ 47 ★

39a Albany St EH1 3QY (0131) 556 8407
*Impressive art adorns this "pleasant" New Town basement;
it attracts surprisingly little commentary, but all to the effect that
it offers "top-notch ingredients, superbly presented".*
/ **Sample dishes:** *baked goat's cheese soufflé; rack of Scottish lamb with wild
mushroom sauce; hot chocolate fondant.* **Details:** *www.haldanes.com; 9.30 pm;
no smoking.*

## Henderson's £ 22

94 Hanover St EH2 1DR (0131) 225 2131
*A "great city-centre cafeteria" – this New Town basement of over
40 years' standing still ("after all these years") delivers
"wholesome and tasty veggie fare"; admittedly the ambience
is pretty "lousy".* / **Sample dishes:** *vegetable soup; baked aubergine & tomato
with Mozzarella; banoffi pie.* **Details:** *www.hendersonsofedinburgh.co.uk; 11 pm;
closed Sun; no smoking.*

## Indian Cavalry Club £ 29 A★

3 Atholl Pl EH3 8HP (0131) 228 3282
*A "posh" and "interesting" Raj-style subcontinental, in a
"beautiful" building in the West End; with its "good range"
of "authentic" dishes, it's no surprise that it's "busy,
even midweek".* / **Sample dishes:** *king prawn pakora; chicken biryani;
mango & lychee ice cream.* **Details:** *between Caledonian Hotel & Haymarket
Station; 11.30 pm; no smoking area.*

**sign up for the survey at www.hardens.com**

## Kalpna £23 ★
2-3 St Patrick Sq EH8 9EZ (0131) 667 9890
*"Consistently excellent vegetarian dishes"* (with *"many unusual items"*) is the simple but satisfying 'offer' at this long-established Gujerati restaurant, near the University. / **Sample dishes:** paneer tikka; okra curry; spiced Indian rice pancake with chutney.
**Details:** www.kalpnarestaurant.com; 10.30 pm; closed Sun; no Amex or Switch; no smoking.

## La Partenope £34 ★
96 Daltry Rd EH11 2AX (0131) 347 8880
*"Now expanded, but still very busy and very Neapolitan"* – this Haymarket Italian is particularly praised for its *"fresh fish and seafood"*. / **Sample dishes:** sauteed shellfish; mixed grill meats; home-made cakes. **Details:** 11 pm; closed Mon L & Sun L; no smoking area.

## Loon Fung £21 ★
2 Warriston Pl EH3 5LE (0131) 556 1781
*"Always busy, even midweek"*, this long-established (and perhaps *"dated"*) Chinese seafood-specialist attracts only positive reviews.
/ **Details:** near Botanical Gardens; 11.30 pm, Fri & Sat 12.30 am; closed Sat L & Sun L.

## Malmaison £38
1 Tower Pl EH6 7DB (0131) 468 5000
A *"favourite"*, for some reporters, this Leith waterfront design-hotel dining room is rated at least *"a good stand-by"* by all who comment on it. / **Sample dishes:** black pudding & potato pancake with apple; roast lamb with minted peas & beans; crème brûlée. **Details:** www.malmaison.com; 10.30 pm. **Accommodation:** 100 rooms, from £129.

## Marque Central £33
Grindlay St EH3 9AX (0131) 229 9859
Near the Lyceum, an unpretentious establishment where *"the pre-theatre menu is particularly good value"*. / **Sample dishes:** smoked haddock fishcakes; corn-fed chicken with Parma ham & roast potatoes; chocolate pudding. **Details:** www.marquecentral.co.uk; 10 pm, Sat 11 pm; closed Mon & Sun; no smoking.

## Martins £47 ★
70 Rose St, North Ln EH2 3DX (0131) 225 3106
Martin Irons's New Town fixture, just off Rose Street, looks *"very unprepossessing"*, but is still generally (if not invariably) praised for its *"great but understated"* cooking and its *"superb"* service; the cheese-board is the stuff of legend.
/ **Sample dishes:** hand-dived Scottish scallops; Scottish sea fish; fruit sorbet terrain. **Details:** www.edinburghrestaurants.co.uk; 10 pm; closed Mon, Sat L & Sun; no smoking; children: 8+.

## Mussel Inn £28 ★
61-65 Rose St EH2 2NH (0131) 225 5979
*"Just the place when you're shopped-out!"*; *"great seafood, simply served"* makes this *"reasonably cheap, and very cheerful"* New Town bistro popular with all reporters – even one who notes that *"not everything is perfect"* says that *"you'll never find better or more plentiful mussels"*. / **Sample dishes:** smoked salmon Caesar salad; mussels with white wine; chocolate truffle torte. **Details:** www.mussel-inn.com; 10 pm; no smoking.

## Namaste £ 28 ★

15 Bristo Pl  EH1 1EZ   (0131) 225 2000

*The decor can seem "a bit rough and ready", but the cooking at this "small" Indian, near the University, is "great and genuine".* / **Details:** *11 pm.*

## North Bridge Brasserie
## The Scotsman £ 50

20 North Bridge  EH1 1YT   (0131) 556 5565

*Fans say it's "just what a brasserie should be", but this prominently-sited operation (in the former Scotsman building) is a touch "expensive" for what it is, and "surprisingly unatmospheric".* / **Sample dishes:** crabcakes with sweet chilli salsa; beef fillet with pepper sauce; mango délice & melon sorbet.
**Details:** www.thescotsmanhotel.co.uk; 10 pm; no smoking. **Accommodation:** 69 rooms, from £185.

## Number One
## Balmoral Hotel £ 71

1 Princes St  EH2 2EQ   (0131) 557 6727

*One of Auld Reekie's grander eating venues, in the basement of the famous hotel, offers food "of an extremely high standard" (as you might hope at the prices), at well-spaced tables which afford "real privacy"; apart from the "bargain lunch", though, commentary remains remarkably 'thin'.* / **Sample dishes:** roulade of crab & salmon with quail eggs; loin of venison; millefeuille of mango with coconut panna cotta. **Details:** www.thebalmoralhotel.com; 10 pm; closed Sat L & Sun L; smoking in bar only. **Accommodation:** 188 rooms, from £290.

## Off The Wall £ 53 ★

105 High St  EH1 1SG   (0131) 558 1497

*An "attractive" destination, on the Royal Mile, praised by all reporters for its "consistently good" cuisine, involving "quite simple" presentation of "first-class" ingredients.* / **Sample dishes:** terrine of rabbit confit; lamb with baby spinach & dauphinoise potatoes; coconut parfait. **Details:** www.off-the-wall.co.uk; 10 pm; closed Mon L & Sun.

## Oloroso £ 43 &#x1F49;

33 Castle St  EH2 3DN   (0131) 226 7614

*"A location to die for" (with views to match) has helped make this "hidden-away" spot perhaps the most "fashionable" restaurant in town; the "good-but-not-outstanding" food, however, can just seem "too expensive for what it is".* / **Sample dishes:** sweet potato & lime leaf soup; chump of lamb with fondant potato, pancetta & lentil jus; passion fruit parfait. **Details:** www.oloroso.co.uk; 10.15 pm; closed Sun (in winter only); no smoking.

## Original Khushi's £ 19

26-30 Potterow  EH8 9BT   (0131) 667 0888

*A veteran budget Indian of 50 years' standing; since a move to modern premises two years ago, feedback has become mixed – most reporters say it remains a "good staple", but there's a body of former fans who feel it's "markedly declined".* / **Sample dishes:** lamb karahi; tandoori mixed grill. **Details:** www.khushis.com; 11 pm; closed Sun L; no smoking area.

**Outsider**  £31 A★

15-16 George IV Bridge EH1 1EE
(0131) 226 3131

*For the young-at-heart, this "trendy", "bright" and "busy" restaurant (whose window seats have Castle views) is a "fun" spot that's "good value" too; critics sometimes complain that it's "not a 'wow' destination", but that isn't really its aim.*
/ **Sample dishes:** *steamed mussels; king prawns with pineapple & coriander dressing; apple tarte Tatin.* **Details:** *11 pm; no Amex; no smoking area; booking: max 10.*

**La P'tite Folie** £28

61 Frederick St EH2 1LH (0131) 225 7983
*"Decent French food" and "friendly service" – that's the simple package which makes this New Town bistro perennially popular.*
/ **Sample dishes:** *home-made chicken liver pâté; grilled rib-eye steak; selected fromages.* **Details:** *www.laptitefolie.co.uk; 11 pm; closed Sun L; no Amex.*

**Le Petit Paris** £29 ★

38-40 Grassmarket EH1 2JU (0131) 226 2442
*"A small corner of Paris" – with "steak/frites a speciality", and "little choice for veggies" – that is "strongly recommended" by almost all reporters; the new West End branch at 17 Queensbury Street (tel 226 1890) is "just as good".*
/ **Sample dishes:** *steamed mussels in blue cheese sauce; seafood in fish soup; crème brûlée.* **Details:** *www.petitparis-restaurant.co.uk; near the Castle; 11 pm; no Amex.*

**Point Hotel** £26

34 Bread St EH3 9AF (0131) 221 5555
*A reputation for "good value" precedes the dining area of this budget design-hotel, though some people feel its "compartmentalised layout lets it down".* / **Sample dishes:** *smoked chicken salad with pineapple salsa; courgette & broccoli frittata; champagne sorbet with raspberries.* **Details:** *www.point-hotel.co.uk; 9.30 pm; closed Sat L & Sun; no smoking.* **Accommodation:** *140 rooms, from £70.*

**The Restaurant at the Bonham** £39

35 Drumsheugh Gdns EH3 7RN (0131) 623 9319
*The "quietly opulent" dining room of this elegant townhouse hotel helps make it a "relaxed" haven; the cooking is well-rated too.*
/ **Sample dishes:** *scallops; fillet Aberdeen Angus beef; summer pudding.*
**Details:** *www.thebonham.com; off west end of Princes St; 10 pm; no smoking.*
**Accommodation:** *48 rooms, from £185.*

**Restaurant Martin Wishart** £60 ★★

54 The Shore EH6 6RA (0131) 553 3557
*Martin Wishart's "stupendous" and "quirky" cuisine – "the best in Scotland" – "goes from strength to strength", at this Leith's waterside dining room; "caring" service (led by Mrs W) helps enliven the rather "unatmospheric" setting.* / **Sample dishes:** *tortellini of asparagus, leek cream & white wine velouté; roast saddle of lamb; Armagnac parfait, poached pear, praline biscuit.* **Details:** *www.martin-wishart.co.uk; near Royal Yacht Britannia; 10 pm; closed Mon, Sat L & Sun; no smoking; booking: max 10.*

**sign up for the survey at www.hardens.com**

## Rhubarb
## Prestonfield Hotel                                   £52          A
Priestfield Rd  EH16 5UT    (0131) 225 1333
*For an experience which is "beyond decadent", it's hard to beat
this "romantic" and "pampering" country house hotel – now in
the hands of the 'Witchery' team – not far from the city; perhaps
unsurprisingly, "the food does not live up".* / **Sample dishes:** *pan-seared
scallops; roast fillet of Angus beef rossini; rhubarb desserts.*
**Details:** *www.prestonfield.com; 11 pm; no smoking; children: 12+ at D.*
**Accommodation:** *22 rooms, from £195.*

## The Shore                                            £37          A
3-4 The Shore  EH6 6QW    (0131) 553 5080
*"A superb little snug restaurant, with a lively bar and a great
ambience" – this longstanding fixture of the Leith waterfront
serves "good" enough food, but it's the overall 'package' which
wows its fans.* / **Sample dishes:** *steamed mussels; grilled salmon fillet in curry
spices; chocolate mousse.* **Details:** *www.theshore.biz; 10 pm; no smoking.*

## Skippers                                             £33         A★
1a Dock Pl  EH6 6LU   (0131) 554 1018
*"Tucked-away on the Leith waterfront", this well-known, "cosy"
bistro is "a little long in the tooth, but still charming for all that";
it won consistent praise this year, for its "friendly" style and
"excellent" fish.* / **Sample dishes:** *queen scallops & prosciutto gratin; finnan
haddie grilled with Brie; white chocolate & Bailey's pot.* **Details:** *www.skippers.co.uk;
10 pm; no smoking area.*

## Suruchi                                              £25          ★
14a Nicolson St  EH8 9DH    (0131) 556 6583
*"A crazy menu in 'Scottish'" has long been a feature of this
"superior" curry house (opposite the Festival Theatre), where the
food is "consistently good".* / **Sample dishes:** *haggis fritters; lamb jalfrezi;
chilli & chocolate ice cream.* **Details:** *www.suruchirestaurant.com; opp Festival
Theatre; 11 pm; closed Sun L; no smoking.*

## Sweet Melindas                                       £36          ★
11 Roseneath St  EH9 1JH   (0131) 229 7953
*"Really good fish" is a highlight at this "very friendly"
neighbourhood restaurant, which pleases almost all who report
on it.* / **Details:** *10 pm; closed Mon L & Sun; no Amex; no smoking.*

## Thai Lemongrass                                      £25
41 Bruntsfield Pl  EH10 4HJ   (0131) 229 2225
*The cooking can be "a bit hit-and-miss" (and sometimes "rather
overpriced" too), but this Thai two-year-old makes waves locally
with often "delicious" dishes and "friendly" service; it's "always
busy".* / **Details:** *11 pm; no smoking area.*

## Thai Orchid                                          £29
44 Grindlay St  EH3 9AP   (0131) 228 4438
*Fans hail this handily-located Thai, near Usher Hall, as a "superb
but busy destination", which "never disappoints".* / **Details:** *10.45 pm;
closed Sat L & Sun; no smoking.*

**sign up for the survey at www.hardens.com**

## The Tower
## Museum of Scotland
**£44**  A ✗

Chambers St  EH1 1JF   (0131) 225 3003

*"Trading too much on its view"*, this expensive top-floor dining room *"has gone downhill in recent times"*; *"seeing the Castle while you eat"*, however, *"can make the ordinariness of the rest of the experience worthwhile"*. / **Sample dishes:** grilled asparagus & serrano ham; roast Scottish venison saddle; chocolate caramel tart.
**Details:** www.tower-restaurant.com; 11 pm; no smoking.

## Valvona & Crolla
**£30**  A ★

19 Elm Row  EH7 4AA   (0131) 556 6066

*Over seven decades in the hands of the Contini family, this is "one of the best delis in Britain"; its "chaotic" and "noisy" adjoining café is "not cheap", but it has a huge following for its "fresh Italianate dishes" and its "interesting" selection of wines (available at retail prices plus corkage).* / **Sample dishes:** pumpkin tortellini; Italian spicy sausage pizza; lemon tart. **Details:** www.valvonacrolla.com; at top of Leith Walk, near Playhouse Theatre; L & afternoon tea only; L only; no smoking.

## Vintners Rooms
**£49**  A ★

87a Giles St  EH6 6BZ   (0131) 554 6767

*An ancient whisky warehouse on the way to Leith provides the "exquisite and romantic" location for this Gallic restaurant; the food – "improved" under the new owners – is "good" too.* / **Sample dishes:** terrine of foie gras with lobster; pavé of venison with chocolate sauce; chocolate fondant with home-made pistachio ice cream.
**Details:** www.thevintnersrooms.com; 10 pm; closed Mon & Sun; no smoking area.

## The Waterfront
**£34**  A ★

1c Dock Pl  EH6 6LU   (0131) 554 7427

*A minority nomination as the city's "best place for fish", this "bright" and "cheerful" Leith spot remains consistently popular under new ownership.* / **Sample dishes:** grilled sardines with Feta & chick peas; swordfish with hot & sour sauce; white chocolate & Bailey's cheesecake. **Details:** www.skippers.co.uk; near Royal Yacht Britannia; 10 pm, Fri & Sat 10.30 pm; no smoking area.

## The Witchery by the Castle
**£49**  A

Castlehill, The Royal Mile  EH1 2NF   (0131) 225 5613

*"Dark" and "splendidly Gothic", this Old Town veteran is "as sexy as hell" – a picture-perfect venue for a romantic dinner (or weekend); critics find the food "catastrophically expensive", but there's much solace to be found in the "telephone directory" wine list.* / **Sample dishes:** home-smoked venison fillet; roast monkfish with spiced pork breast; vanilla panna cotta with champagne rhubarb.
**Details:** www.thewitchery.com; 11.30 pm. **Accommodation:** 7 rooms, from £275.

---

EGHAM, SURREY  3–3A
## The Oak Room
## Great Fosters Hotel
**£56**  A ★

Stroude Rd  TW20 9UR   (01784) 433822

*"The menu and cooking continue to improve"*, says one of the supporters of the dining room of this *"lovely"* country house hotel; it enjoys a *"stunning"* Elizabethan setting, all the more notable for its proximity to Heathrow! / **Sample dishes:** foie gras; Scottish fillet; citrus soufflé. **Details:** www.greatfosters.co.uk; 9.15 pm; closed Sat L; no jeans or trainers; no smoking; booking: max 12. **Accommodation:** 52 rooms, from £150.

## ELIE, FIFE                                          9–4D

### Sangster's                              £41        A★
51 High St  KY9 1BZ   (01333) 331001
*"Serious cooking, beautifully presented and served"* is the
hallmark of ex-London chef Bruce Sangster's very popular two-
year-old, in a *"beautiful seaside village"*. / **Sample dishes:** *pan-seared
scallops; slow-cooked shoulder of lamb; vanilla panna cotta.*
**Details:** *www.sangsters.co.uk; 9.30 pm; closed Mon, Tue L & Sun D; no Amex;
no smoking; children: 12+ at D.*

## ELLAND, WEST YORKSHIRE                              5–1C

### La Cachette                            £26
31 Huddersfield Rd  HX5 9AW   (01422) 378833
*An "intimate bistro ambience"* – *"with lots of nooks and corners"*
– *helps win popularity for this favourite local; the food is "good"
too (with particular value to be had from the early-evening menu).*
/ **Sample dishes:** *plum tomato basil & Mozzarella salad; white chocolate panna
cotta.* **Details:** *9.30 pm; closed Sun; no Amex.*

## ELSTEAD, SURREY                                     3–3A

### Woolpack                               £29
The Green  GU8 6HD   (01252) 703106
*A "reliable" town-centre pub, whose "traditional" scoff
in "good portions"* – *including "the best-ever puddings"* –
*is generally approved.* / **Sample dishes:** *deep-fried white bait; steak & kidney
pie; fruit pavlova.* **Details:** *7m SW of Guildford, on village green; 9.30 pm; no Amex;
smoking in bar only.*

## ELSTOW, BEDFORDSHIRE                                3–1A

### St Helena's                            £49        A
High St  MK42 9XP   (01234) 344848
*"A well-balanced menu, nice presentation, friendly service and
a good wine list"* – *these are the sorts of simple virtues which
commend this prettily-located restaurant to all reporters.*
/ **Sample dishes:** *flat mushroom filled with white crab meat; brace of boned quail
with sausage meat; raspberries & strawberries.* **Details:** *off A6, S of Bedford; 9 pm;
closed Mon, Sat L & Sun; jacket & tie required; no smoking; children: 12+.*

## ELY, CAMBRIDGESHIRE                                 3–1B

### Old Fire Engine House                  £37        A★
25 St Mary's St  CB7 4ER   (01353) 662582
*"An Ely institution which has moved with the times"* – *the Jarman
family's quirky fixture near the cathedral continues to earn its
stripes with "homely" service and "first-class", "very traditional"
English cooking.* / **Sample dishes:** *herrings with dill in cucumber & yoghurt;
spinach & ricotta tart with mushroom Stroganoff; ginger ice cream.*
**Details:** *www.theoldfireenginehouse.co.uk; 8.45 pm; closed Sun D; no Amex;
no smoking area.*

## EMSWORTH, HAMPSHIRE                    2–4D

### Fat Olives                    £38    ★

30 South St PO10 7EH   (01243) 377914

*"An old fisherman's cottage on a pretty road leading down to the harbour" – it's pretty much "the perfect local restaurant" for all who comment on it. / Sample dishes: quail with parsnip tartlet & honey dressing; halibut; white chocolate panna cotta. Details: www.fatolives.co.uk; 10 pm; closed Mon & Sun; no Amex; no smoking; children: 8+.*

### 36 on the Quay                    £58

47 South St PO10 7EG   (01243) 375592

*Praise for Ramon Farthing's well-established restaurant-with-rooms – which enjoys beautiful harbour views – was thinner on the ground this year; even reporters who say the food's "very good" can also find it "overpriced", and doubters dismiss the whole formula as "stuck in a time warp". / Sample dishes: pan-fried mullet with pesto; scallops with chicken & goose liver sausage; lemon dessert. Details: www.36onthequay.co.uk; off A27 between Portsmouth & Chichester; 9.45 pm; closed Mon & Sun; no smoking. Accommodation: 5 rooms, from £90.*

## ENGLEFIELD GREEN, SURREY                    3–3A

### Edwinns                    £36

Wick Rd TW20 0HN   (01784) 477877

*An attractive branch of a (quality) chain, with "a rural location on the edge of Windsor Great Park"; it is consistently praised for its "honest cooking" and "good value". / Sample dishes: seafood gratin; lamb steak; sticky pudding. Details: www.edwinns.co.uk; 10 pm; closed Sat L & Sun D; no smoking.*

## EPSOM DOWN, SURREY                    3–3B

### Le Raj                    £36    ★

211 Fir Tree Rd KT17 3LB   (01737) 371371

*"Subtly-spiced" (rather "nouvelle") dishes make this grand subcontinental very popular with all reporters – even those not wowed by the service or setting. / Details: www.lerajrestaurant.co.uk; next to Derby race course; 11 pm; no smoking area.*

## ESCRICK, NORTH YORKSHIRE                    5–1D

### Sangthai                    £31

Church Cottage YO19 6EX   (01904) 728462

*In a small village near York, this pleasant oriental offers some "good" Thai cooking; there's alfresco seating for the summer. / Sample dishes: tiger prawns; coconut curry with peanuts & potatoes; Thai custard. Details: www.sangthai.co.uk; 10 pm; closed Mon, Tue-Thu & Sat D only; no smoking.*

## ESHER, SURREY                    3–3A

### Good Earth                    £41    ★

14-18 High St KT10 9RT   (01372) 462489

*A "smart, high-quality Chinese" of long standing, whose "consistent" standards are currently running at a particularly high level. / Sample dishes: spicy spare ribs; Mongolian lamb; toffee apples & ice cream. Details: www.goodearthgroup.co.uk; 11.15 pm; booking: max 12, Fri & Sat.*

**Sherpa** £ 23

132 High St KT10 9QJ (01372) 470777

"An original selection of dishes from Nepal and Tibet" has helped make this "airy", "relaxed" and "reasonably-priced" spot very popular locally. / **Details:** 11 pm; smoking in bar only.

**Siam Food Gallery** £ 36

95-97 High St KT10 9QE (01372) 477139

A small fan club says the food is "wonderful" – and the service "good" too – at this locally eminent Thai restaurant.
/ **Sample dishes:** Thai fishcakes; green curry with chicken & steamed coconut rice; deep-fried ice cream with mincemeat. **Details:** 11 pm; no smoking area.

---

ETON, WINDSOR & MAIDENHEAD 3–3A

**Gilbey's** £ 36 🄰

82-83 High St SL4 6AF (01753) 854921

A "very varied" and "good-value" wine list underpins the appeal of this "relaxed" wine bar (which has "a lovely rear conservatory") – for some reporters, it's a "classic of its kind"; the "variable" food doesn't seem to detract from the experience.
/ **Sample dishes:** pork chilli pistachio galantine; grilled fillet of black bream with new potato & watercress salad; toffee apple with brown bread ice cream. **Details:** www.gilbeygroup.com; 10 min walk from Windsor Castle; 10.30 pm; no Switch.

---

EVERSHOT, DORSET 2–4B

**Summer Lodge**
**Country House Hotel & Restaurant** £ 53 🄰

Summer Lodge DT2 0JR (01935) 482000

This 18th-century country house, complete with walled garden, is such a "lovely" setting that a visit is always "a delight"; under the new owners (Red Carnation Hotels), however, the cuisine has become "a bit inconsistent". / **Sample dishes:** pan-seared foie gras; roast loin of Dorset lamb with spring pea & potato foam; piña colada mousse. **Details:** www.summerlodgehotel.co.uk; 12m NW of Dorchester on A37; 9.30 pm; no smoking; children: 7+ at D. **Accommodation:** 24 rooms, from £185.

---

EVESHAM, WORCESTERSHIRE 2–1C

**Evesham Hotel** £ 37 🄰

Coopers Ln WR11 1DA (01386) 765566

"Every possible wine-making country... except France" features on the "extraordinary" ("verging on mad") wine list of John Jenkinson's delightfully "quirky" destination of over three decades' standing; the "average" cooking is rather beside the point.
/ **Sample dishes:** quail eggs with bacon; baked cod with thyme & red wine; dried fruit tart. **Details:** www.eveshamhotel.com; 9.30 pm; no smoking; booking: max 12. **Accommodation:** 40 rooms, from £118.

---

EWEN, GLOUCESTERSHIRE 2–2C

**Wild Duck** £ 41 🄰★

Drakes Island GL7 6BY (01285) 770310

"Proximity to the Royal Agricultural College" can make for a "somewhat boisterous atmosphere" at this "perfect country pub" (complete with "delightful courtyard garden"); "it's none the worse for that", though. / **Sample dishes:** pâté ploughman's; smoked salmon & egg tart. **Details:** www.wildduckinn.co.uk; 10 pm; smoking in bar only. **Accommodation:** 12 rooms, from £70.

---

**sign up for the survey at www.hardens.com**

EXETER, DEVON                                    1–3D

### Brazz                                        £34
10-12 Palace Gate EX1 1JA (01392) 252525
*Fans of this slightly flashy brasserie hail it as a "well-run" and "buzzy" spot that's "THE place to dine in Exeter"; results, though, can be "hit-and-miss". / **Sample dishes:** mushroom brioche; chocolate brownie. **Details:** www.brazz.co.uk; 10.30 pm, Fri & Sat 11 pm; closed Sun; smoking in bar only.*

### Double Locks                                 £22      A★
Canal Banks EX2 6LT (01392) 256947
*"A beautiful location" has long been a major draw to this "hidden" canalside spot ("the only quick way there is to cycle from Exeter's quay"); it serves a "varied and excellent-value" menu of "pub grub". / **Sample dishes:** garlic bread with Cheddar; turkey & mushroom pie; sticky toffee pudding. **Details:** www.youngs.co.uk; through Marsh Barton industrial estate, follow dead-end track over bridges to end of towpath; 9.30 pm; no Amex; no booking.*

### Herbies                                      £22
15 North St EX4 3QS (01392) 258473
*"Excellent" food is reported at this long-established veggie; it's a "cosy" place (but can seem "too hot and smoky for elderly diners"). / **Sample dishes:** houmous with garlic bread; mushroom sundried tomato; apple pie. **Details:** 9.30 pm; closed Mon D & Sun; no Amex; no smoking.*

### Hotel Barcelona                              £38
Magdalen St EX2 4HY (01392) 281000
*"Pretty good Italian-ish cuisine" is hailed by fans of the dining room of this "quirky" design-hotel; even some of them, however, say "it's not going to set the world on fire", and, for a minority of reporters, the whole experience is plain "disappointing". / **Sample dishes:** marinated sea bass with Parma ham; duck breast with raspberry & port sauce; chocolate fondant pudding. **Details:** www.aliashotels.com; 9.45 pm; no smoking; booking: max 8. **Accommodation:** 46 rooms, from £99.*

### Michael Caines
### Royal Clarence Hotel                         £53
Cathedral Yd EX1 1HD (01392) 310031
*The Gidleigh Park chef's city-centre hotel restaurant "should be superb, but isn't"; that's not to say it doesn't have any fans (who find it "faultless"), but the consistency of reports one would expect – particularly "at these prices" – is notable by its absence. / **Details:** www.michaelcaines.com; 10 pm; closed Sun; no smoking. **Accommodation:** 56 rooms, from £130.*

### St Olave's Hotel                             £43      A★
Mary Arches St EX4 3AZ (01392) 217736
*"A quiet haven in the heart of Exeter" – and "the city's best place to eat" – this old-fashioned (but recently revamped) "oasis" serves "lovely" food in "elegant" and "comfortable" surroundings. / **Sample dishes:** carrot & ginger soup; pan-fried fillet steak; rich chocolate mousse with home-made biscuits. **Details:** www.olaves.co.uk; 9 pm; no Amex; no jeans; no smoking. **Accommodation:** 15 rooms, from £105.*

---

## FARNHAM, DORSET                                      2–3C

**Museum Inn**                                    £39

DT11 8DE   (01725) 516261

*Fans say it's "just great", but there's a rather up-and-down element to commentary on this "pricey" gastropub; so-so service seems a particular bugbear. / **Sample dishes:** mini fishcakes with lemon butter; fillet of lemon sole; crème brûlée with raspberry sorbet.*
***Details:** www.museuminn.co.uk; 9.30 pm; no Amex; no smoking; children: 8+.*
***Accommodation:** 8 rooms, from £95.*

---

## FAVERSHAM, KENT                                    3–3C

**The Dove**                                    £41        A★

Plum Pudding Ln  ME13 9HB   (01227) 751360

*Feedback is limited, but reports tends to extol this rural boozer for its "friendly" style, "lovely" setting and "excellent" food.*
*/ **Sample dishes:** spring onion & crab risotto; duck with lentils & foie gras; baked chocolate pudding. **Details:** 9 pm; closed Mon, Tue D & Sun D; no Amex.*

**Read's**                                    £62        ★

Macknade Manor, Canterbury Rd  ME13 8XE
(01795) 535344

*The "cosy" new country-house setting – "far better" than when it occupied a converted supermarket! – seems to be suiting this long-established local favourite; fans are strongly of the view that it serves some of "the best food in Kent". / **Sample dishes:** fillet of locally smoked eel; saddle of Kentish lamb; ginger parkin.*
***Details:** www.reads.com; 9.30 pm; closed Mon & Sun. **Accommodation:** 6 rooms, from £150.*

---

## FERRENSBY, NORTH YORKSHIRE                          8–4B

**General Tarleton**                              £38        A★

Boroughbridge Rd  HG5 0PZ   (01423) 340284

*"Gone from strength to strength since breaking away from the Angel" – this large roadside gastropub (run by the Hetton legend's former head chef) is now creating an "outstanding" reputation in its own right. / **Sample dishes:** Jerusalem artichoke soup; tuna with butter bean mash & Parmesan crisps; lemon & ginger cheesecake.*
***Details:** www.generaltarleton.co.uk; 2m from A1, J48 towards Knaresborough; 9.30 pm; closed Sun D; no smoking. **Accommodation:** 14 rooms, from £97.*

---

## FLETCHING, EAST SUSSEX                              3–4B

**The Griffin Inn**                               £38        A★

TN22 3SS   (01825) 722890

*The "Platonic ideal" of a country inn – this "great" (and sometimes "crowded") rural boozer delivers "everything one could hope for from such a place", including "a restaurant that's superb, and bar food that's good at the price"; there is also a "gorgeous" new terrace. / **Sample dishes:** roast quail with lemon sage Mascarpone; wood-roasted Rye Bay lobsters with lime & chilli butter; lemon & grappa panna cotta. **Details:** www.thegriffininn.co.uk; off A272; 9.30 pm; closed Sun D (in winter only); no smoking. **Accommodation:** 8 rooms, from £85.*

## FOREST ROW, WEST SUSSEX                    3–4B

### Anderida Restaurant
### Ashdown Park Hotel                         £ 60
Wych Cross  RH18 5JR   (01342) 824988
*"Lovely forest views" add a "relaxing" air to a meal at this 'Elite Hotels' country house, whose "good kitchen" was praised in most reports. / Sample dishes: seared scallops with pak choy; thyme-marinated rump of lamb with couscous; banana parfait with mango bavarois.*
***Details:*** *www.ashdownpark.com; 9.30 pm; jacket & tie required; no smoking.*
***Accommodation:*** *106 rooms, from £165.*

## FORT WILLIAM, HIGHLAND                      9–3B

### Inverlochy Castle                          £ 85          Ⓐ
Torlundy  PH33 6SN   (01397) 702177
*Reporters award lofty ratings to Matthew Gray's cuisine at this storybook-grand Baronial pile, in the foothills of Ben Nevis – the view and the prices, it seems, are equally capable of inducing vertigo! / Sample dishes: wild mushroom tart with veal kidneys; roast duck with vanilla mash & pickled cherries; orange crème brûlée with lemon & lime sorbet.*
***Details:*** *www.inverlochycastlehotel.com; off A82, 4 m N of Ft. William; 9.15 pm; closed Jan & part of Feb; jacket & tie required at D; no smoking; children: 10 at D.* ***Accommodation:*** *18 rooms, from £290.*

## FOWEY, CORNWALL                             1–4B

### Fowey Hall                                 £ 47          Ⓐ★
Hanson Drive  PL23 1ET   (01726) 833866
*"A beautiful stately home-style dining room" – part of a 'Luxury Family Hotel' – with "surprisingly good food", "very helpful staff" and a "buzzy atmosphere". / Sample dishes: foie gras; sea bass; raspberry & basil soufflé. Details: www.luxuryfamilyhotels.com; on the main road next to the car park; 9.30 pm; no smoking area; booking: max 10.*
***Accommodation:*** *24 rooms, from £160.*

### The Q Restaurant
### The Old Quay House                         £ 43          Ⓐ★
28 Fore St  PL23 1AQ
(01726) 833302
*"Gorgeous river views" are often noted by fans of this "beautifully-located" restaurant-with-rooms; its menu may be relatively short, but all reports confirm that it's extremely "well executed". / Sample dishes: watercress soup; grilled rib-eye of Cornish beef.*
***Details:*** *www.theoldquayhouse.com; 9 pm; no smoking; children: 12+ at D.*
***Accommodation:*** *12 rooms, from £150.*

### Sam's The Other Place                      £ 35          ★
41 Fore St  PL23 1AQ   (01726) 833636
*"Excellent seasonal menus and fantastic friendly service" win enthusiastic – if limited – feedback for Sam Saxton's fish and seafood restaurant. / Details: 9 pm; closed Sun; no Amex; no smoking.*

**sign up for the survey at www.hardens.com**

## FOWLMERE, CAMBRIDGESHIRE 3–1B
**Chequers** £39 ★
SG8 7SR (01763) 208369
*Under new ownership, this "smart and well-run dining pub" seems largely unchanged, and it offers consistently "good" food in a "variety of eating areas".* / **Sample dishes:** seared pan-fried scallops; grilled peaches laced with amaretto. **Details:** on B1368 between Royston & Cambridge; 9.30 pm; no smoking area.

## FRITHSDEN, HERTFORDSHIRE 3–2A
**Alford Arms** £35
HP1 3DD (01442) 864480
*On most accounts, this "idyllically-located" pub on the village green is a "hugely and deservedly popular oasis in a gastro-desert" (and its "dining room is booked out months in advance at the weekend"); feedback is not entirely consistent, though, perhaps because the place sometimes seems just "too successful".* / **Sample dishes:** lamb's kidneys; smoked haddock with poached egg; lemon crème brûlée. **Details:** www.alfordarmsfrithsden.co.uk; near Ashridge College, by vineyard; 10 pm; no smoking; booking: max 12.

## GANTS HILL, ESSEX 3–2B
**Elephant Royale** £39
579-581 Cranbrook Rd IG2 6JZ (020) 8551 7015
*"Great cheesy cocktails" get diners in the mood at this locally eminent Thai restaurant (right on the A12), which is well worth knowing about in a thin area; it has a newer sibling, on the Isle of Dogs.* / **Sample dishes:** chicken mango salad; grilled chicken; chocolate mousse. **Details:** www.elephantroyale.com; 11.30 pm; children: 2+.

## GATESHEAD, TYNE & WEAR 8–2B
**Eslington Villa Hotel** £33 &#x24B6;
8 Station Rd NE9 6DR (0191) 487 6017
*A "beautifully-situated" and "relaxing" Victorian country-house hotel, where most (if not quite all) feedback speaks of "consistently high" culinary standards.* / **Sample dishes:** smoked haddock & chive risotto; pork & pancetta with sage & onion mash; British cheeses with quince jelly. **Details:** www.eslingtonvillahotel.com; A1 exit for Team Valley Retail World, then left off Eastern Avenue; 9.30 pm; closed Sat L & Sun D; no smoking. **Accommodation:** 18 rooms, from £79.50.

# GLASGOW, CITY OF GLASGOW 9–4C

Glasgow has quite a line in 'institutions'. The fame of two of them – the very Art Deco *Rogano* and the very '70s *Ubiquitous Chip* – is considerable (and you can expect to pay accordingly). *The Buttery* – the city's classic comfortable businessman's destination – is currently on top form. At less exalted price levels, such places as *Babbity Bowster* and *Café Gandolfi* are much treasured by the locals.

The city also has an extensive contemporary restaurant scene, whose current champion is arguably Conran's *étain*. Also of note is *Gamba* – a great destination for fish-lovers – and the quirky *Wild Bergamot* (renamed from Gingerhill).

At the lower price levels, many of the better choices are subcontinental.

## Amber Regent                                   £ 40
50 West Regent St  G2 2RA   (0141) 331 1655
*It can seem "overpriced", but this grand city-centre Chinese still
enjoys quite a local reputation, thanks to its "authentic" cooking
and "excellent" service. / **Sample dishes:** spring rolls; toffee apples.
**Details:** www.amberregent.com; 10.45 pm; closed Sun.*

## Ashoka                                          £ 25          ★
19 Ashton Ln  G12 8SJ   (0141) 337 1115
*'Ashoka' is a leading Glaswegian curry brand, and covers
a number of outlets, not all of which are under common
ownership – the most famous is the Ashton Lane branch, where
commentary is favourable across the board.
/ **Sample dishes:** vegetable & fish pakoras; death by chocolate cake.
**Details:** www.harlequin-leisure.co.uk; behind Hillhead station; 10 pm; closed Sun L;
no smoking.*

## Babbity Bowster                                 £ 31          𝔸
16-18 Blackfriar's St  G1 1PE   (0141) 552 5055
*This "lovely" (James Adam) pub (with upstairs restaurant) makes
a "brilliant" destination, thanks not least to its "sound and reliable
brasserie fare"; the Auld Alliance is something of a culinary
theme, but "the Scottish dishes are the ones to go for".
/ **Sample dishes:** poached Scottish oysters; chocolate terrine.
**Details:** www.babbity.com; 10.30 pm; D only, closed Mon & Sun.
**Accommodation:** 6 rooms, from £55.*

## Brian Maule at Chardon D'Or                     £ 53
176 West Regent St  G2 4RL   (0141) 248 3801
*Brian Maule trained at Le Gavroche, and diners attend his "quiet"
restaurant near Blythswood Square with high expectations;
most reporters do indeed hail his food as "faultless", but – "after
all the hype" – some leave very unimpressed.
/ **Sample dishes:** salmon with cucumber & dill dressing; coley with warm celery &
lentil salad; roast pears with caramel sauce. **Details:** www.lechardondor.com;
9.30 pm; closed Sat L & Sun; smoking in bar only.*

## The Buttery                                     £ 55          𝔸★
652 Argyle St  G3 8UF   (0141) 221 8188
*This "hushed temple to Victorian plutocracy" – an "old-
fashioned", panelled institution these days cut off from the city-
centre by the M8 – is mostly praised for its "excellent" cuisine;
popularity amongst expense-accounters, however, ensures that it's
no bargain. / **Sample dishes:** apple & beetroot pasta pave on a confit
of venison; cannelloni of venison with goat's cheese; vanilla panna cotta with
strawberries. **Details:** 9.30 pm; closed Mon, Sat L & Sun; smoking in bar only.*

## Café Gandolfi                                   £ 33          𝔸
64 Albion St  G1 1NY   (0141) 552 6813
*"Great character, and the grub doesn't let it down" –
this Merchant City veteran is known for its "lovely" woody interior,
but it also offers "reliable café food" (which includes
"outrageously good" coffee and "breakfasts to die for").
/ **Sample dishes:** smoked chicken & duck salad with grapefruit & mango; white
chocolate & raspberry pot. **Details:** www.cafegandolfi.com; near Tron Theatre;
11.30 pm; no smoking area; no booking, Sat.*

**sign up for the survey at www.hardens.com**

### Café India £26
171 North St G3 7DA (0141) 248 4074
*"A lot of superstars"* are allegedly part of the *"interesting"*
clientele which dines at this locally celebrated curry house, which,
say fans, offers *"great"* subcontinental cuisine.
/ **Details:** www.cafeindia-glasgow.com; next to Mitchell Library; midnight.

### Café Mao £28
84 Brunswick St G1 1TD (0141) 564 5161
A crowded joint in the Merchant City, serving simple but
*"interesting"* oriental-fusion fodder. / **Sample dishes:** fishcakes; lemon
grass & chilli tiger prawns; frozen yoghurt. **Details:** www.cafemao.com; 11 pm;
no smoking area.

### City Merchant £40
97-99 Candleriggs G1 1NP (0141) 553 1577
*"You get a good standard of cooking, but in a setting that's tightly-
packed and rather noisy"*, at this straightforward Merchant City
stalwart, specialising in seafood. / **Sample dishes:** pan-seared king
scallops; meringue nest with berry compote. **Details:** www.citymerchant.co.uk;
10.30 pm; closed Sun; no smoking area.

### Dakhin £31
89 Candleriggs G1 1NP (0141) 553 2585
This Merchant City yearling claims to be Glasgow's first south
Indian restaurant – reports are limited but encouraging.
/ **Sample dishes:** rasam; crêpe with vegetarian filling; kesari bhath.
**Details:** www.dakhin.com; 10.30 pm; no smoking.

### étain £48 A★
The Glass Hs, Springfield Ct G1 3JX (0141) 225 5630
*"The top restaurant in Glasgow"*, for many reporters;
this northerly Conran outpost – in an elegant space on an upper
floor of Princes Square Shopping Centre – is roundly praised for its
*"superb"* cooking, and its often *"flawless"* service.
/ **Sample dishes:** grilled breast of wood pigeon with endive compote; honey and
spice glazed duck leg confit; chocolate marquise with coffee sauce.
**Details:** www.conran-restaurants.co.uk; 11 pm; closed Sat L; no smoking.

### Firebird £30 A
1321 Argyle St G3 HTL (0141) 334 0594
An *"eclectic and informal"* gastropub-style operation, near the
Kelvingrove Art Gallery, offering an *"organic pizza and more"*
menu of *"good quality"*. / **Sample dishes:** tomato & basil bruschetta;
slow-braised duck; caramel shortcake. **Details:** www.firebirdglasgow.com; 10.30 pm;
no Amex; no smoking; children: 16+ from 8 pm.

### Gamba £50 ★
225a West George St G2 2ND (0141) 572 0899
*"Beautifully-cooked fish and seafood"* from a *"thoughtful"* and
*"varied"* menu – and *"attentive"* service too – have made a big
name for this *"sophisticated"* city-centre basement.
/ **Sample dishes:** cauliflower soup; whole-roasted sea bream; mango cheesecake
with coconut & raspberries. **Details:** www.gamba.co.uk; 10.30 pm; closed Sun;
smoking in bar only; children: 14+.

## Ichiban £18

50 Queen St  G1 3DS    (0141) 204 4200

*Fans claim this "consistent and enjoyable" noodle bar is "better than Wagamama"; there's another branch at 184 Dumbarton Road (tel 334 9222). / Sample dishes: assorted sushi; pork chop curry & rice; green tea. Details: www.ichiban.co.uk; 9.45 pm, Thu-Sat 10.45 pm; no smoking; need 10+ to book.*

## Kember & Jones £21

134 Byres Rd  G12 8TD    (0141) 337 3851

*For breakfast or lunch, this "good new deli" – or "fine food emporium", if you prefer – makes a pleasant destination, near the University. / Sample dishes: Mediterannean vegetable soup; Parma ham, rocket & melon salad; berry pavlova. Details: www.kemberandjones.co.uk; 7 pm; L only; no smoking.*

## Malmaison £46

278 West George St  G2 4LL    (0141) 572 1001

*This style hotel brasserie "doesn't feel like it's part of an hotel", and has long been a popular city-centre stand-by. / Sample dishes: pea & goat's cheese tartlet; roast cod fillet & white bean purée; tarte au citron. Details: www.malmaison.com; off P : H st. (blyswood Sq); 10.30 pm; smoking in bar only. Accommodation: 72 rooms, from £125.*

## Mother India £26    Ⓐ★

28 Westminster Ter  G3 7RU    (0141) 221 1663

*For "the best curry north of Bradford" (plus some other "slightly unusual" dishes), many reporters tip "Scotland's best Indian" (located south of Kelvingrove Park); the "fantastic" café (1355 Argyle Street, tell 339 9145) offers similarly "great" food "in 'tapas' portions". / Sample dishes: aubergine fritters; chicken tikka passanda; gulab jamon. Details: beside Kelvingrove Hotel; 10.30 pm, Fri & Sat 11 pm; closed Mon L, Tue L & Sun L.*

## Mr Singh's India £28

149 Elderslie St  G3 7JR    (0141) 204 0186

*"The kilt-wearing waiters are good-humoured about the many obvious jokes", at this "imaginative" Kelvingrove Park spot, where the cultures of Scotland and the subcontinent collide to good effect. / Sample dishes: king prawn with garlic spice; char-grilled lamb with Punjabi spices; mango sorbet with coconut ice cream. Details: www.mrsinghsindia.com; 10.30 pm, Sat & Sun 11.30 pm.*

## Number 16 £35    ★

16 Byres Rd  G11 5JY    (0141) 339 2544

*You get "very good food at extremely reasonable prices", at this tiny and cramped bistro, near the Dumbarton Road. / Sample dishes: hot cheese fritters with apple & port sauce; roast venison with spiced red cabbage; sticky toffee pudding. Details: 10 pm; no Amex; no smoking.*

## Paperinos £29    ★

283 Sauchiehall St  G2 3HQ    (0141) 332 3800

*"Excellent pizza and pasta" are among the key attractions of this "buzzy" city-centre Italian; post-survey, it opened a West End offshoot at 227 Byres Road (tel 334 3811). / Sample dishes: stuffed mushrooms; penne in home-made pesto with tomato & cream; lemon sorbet. Details: www.paperinos.com; 10.45 pm; no smoking area.*

### La Parmigiana £ 34 &#x1F4B2;

447 Great Western Rd  G12 8HH   (0141) 334 0686

*Limited feedback this year on this eminent Kelvinbridge Italian of long standing – it's all pretty positive, however, if with the qualification that it's "not cheap".* / **Sample dishes:** *lobster ravioli; fish & shellfish soup with bruschetta; lemon tart with cherries.* **Details:** *near Kelvinbridge station; 10.30 pm; closed Sun.*

### Red Onion £ 28

257 West Campbell St  G2 4TT   (0141) 2216000

*A private chef whose clients having included Tina Turner and the Bee Gees cooks at this new city-centre brasserie; an early reporter tips it as 'one to watch'.* / **Sample dishes:** *field mushroom bruschetta with rocket & pesto; char-grilled calf's liver, bacon, champ & black pepper sauce; apple tarte Tatin.* **Details:** *www.red-onion.co.uk; 10.30 pm; no smoking.*

### Roastit Bubbly Jocks £ 31 &#x24B6;★

450 Dumbarton Rd  G11 6SE   (0141) 339 3355

*A BYO policy and live music every Friday night add an informal air to this "weird but fun" operation in Partick; it's "great value", and often "packed".* / **Sample dishes:** *seafish chowder; roast haunch of venison; iced white chocolate strawberry parfait.* **Details:** *9.30 pm; no smoking.*

### Rococo £ 64

202 West George St  G2 2NR   (0141) 221 5004

*This "comfortable" venue (complete with "romantic, twinkling lights in the ceiling") doesn't attract a huge amount of feedback; none of it is negative, though, and oenophiles will find much of interest in its choice of over 400 wines.* / **Details:** *www.rococoglasgow.com; 10 pm; no smoking area.*

### Rogano £ 50 &#x24B6;

11 Exchange Pl  G1 3AN   (0141) 248 4055

*Thanks to its "beautiful '30s décor", this long-established seafood destination will forever be a "true institution", and supporters still find a visit a "fantastic" experience; for such a "pricey" place, though, the food can often seem "mediocre".* / **Sample dishes:** *melon & Parma ham salad; roast chicken with lemon & thyme risotto & pak choy; crème brûlée.* **Details:** *www.rogano.co.uk; 10.30 pm; no smoking.*

### Room £ 40

1 Devonshire Gdns  G12 0UX   (0141) 341 0000

*The trendy successor to Ramsay's Amaryllis, in a swanky boutique hotel, has inspired few reports – most of these tend to the conclusion that its "experimental"/retro food is "a real surprise" ("the staff much enjoyed explaining the fabbo Scotch egg"), but it can also seem "expensive for what it is".* / **Sample dishes:** *melon & Parma ham; monkfish thermidor; cheesecake.* **Details:** *www.roomrestaurants.com; 10 pm; no smoking; booking: max 8; children: none.*

### Sarti's £ 31 &#x24B6;

121 Bath St  G2 2SZ   (0141) 204 0440

*"The best pizza outside Italy", or "questionable if it's worth including in the guide any more"? – this "once-obligatory port of call" has become "frustratingly hit-and-miss" in recent times, though its "real Italian" ambience remains; there is also a branch at 42 Renfield Street (tel 572 7000).* / **Sample dishes:** *minestrone soup; four cheese pizza; tiramisu.* **Details:** *www.fratellisarti.com; 11 pm; no smoking area; no booking at L.*

## 78 St Vincent £39
78 St Vincent's St G2 5UB (0141) 248 7878
*This brasserie in an impressive former banking-hall makes a "reliable" city-centre stand-by (not least for breakfast); its cuisine is "competent, if not remarkable". / Sample dishes: rainbow trout with sweet pepper butter; halibut with braised fennel & rocket; white chocolate praline tart. Details: www.78stvincent.com; 2 mins from George Sq; 10 pm, Fri & Sat 10.30 pm; no smoking area.*

## Shish Mahal £26 ★
66-68 Park Rd G4 9JF (0141) 334 7899
*"One of Scotland's first, and still going strong" – this old-favourite curry house is still praised for its "fresh" and "reasonably-priced" cooking. / Sample dishes: lamb cutlets; king prawns; home-made gulab jamon with ice cream. Details: www.shishmahal.co.uk; 11 pm; closed Sun L; no smoking area.*

## Stravaigin £40 ★
28 Gibson St G12 8NX (0141) 334 2665
*"The best bar food in Glasgow" ("better than most restaurants") is hailed by the fans of Colin Clydesdale's popular hang-out near the University; there's a less commented-on restaurant in the cellar (where the "contemporary Scottish" combinations "can be inspired, but risk going over the top"). / Sample dishes: twice-cooked sticky duck; oven-roasted bream fillet; pink grapefruit & vanilla Mascarpone nutty filo stack. Details: www.stravaigin.com; 11 pm; closed Mon, Tue-Thu D only; no smoking pre 10 pm.*

## Stravaigin 2 £35
8 Ruthven Ln G12 9BG (0141) 334 7165
*Colin Clydesdale's West End Stravaigain-offshoot offers his hallmark "interesting" menu – from "comfort food to more exotic options" – that's consistently hailed as "well cooked, and well presented"; "great burgers" are a highlight. / Sample dishes: basil with spaghetti; lamb kebab, citrus couscous & warmed tortilla; kaffir lime leaf Mascarpone panna cotta. Details: www.stravaigin.com; 11 pm; no smoking pre 10 pm.*

## Thai Fountain £37
2 Woodside Cr G3 7UL (0141) 332 1599
*"Lots of fresh tastes" still make this classy "stalwart" a "top oriental" locally; even some fans, though, concede it's "not the cheapest". / Details: www.thai-fountain.com; 11 pm, Fri & Sat midnight; children: 7+.*

## Two Fat Ladies £34 ★
88 Dumbarton Rd G11 6NX (0141) 339 1944
*"You'd never guess it from the outside" ("it looks like a dive!"), but this "wee and cosy" spot, with its "very helpful" staff, has quite a reputation for "the best fish cooking locally"; it has no relation to the TV-gels. / Sample dishes: scallops with black pudding; monkfish with lime; crème brûlée. Details: www.twofatladies.5pm.co.uk; 10.30 pm; closed Sun L.*

## Ubiquitous Chip £45 Ⓐ

12 Ashton Ln  G12 8SJ  (0141) 334 5007

*This West End institution of 35 years' standing is increasingly "out of step with modern times" – even some fans concede "standards are excellent-to-disappointing", and critics find it plain "complacent"; the "interesting" décor and "very intriguing" wine list, however, are reliable attractions.* / **Sample dishes:** vegetarian haggis & neeps; Loch Fyne herrings with tapenade mash; Caledonian oatmeal ice cream. **Details:** www.ubiquitouschip.co.uk; behind Hillhead station; 11 pm.

## Wee Curry Shop £21 ★

Buccleuch St  G3 6SJ  (0141) 353 0777

*"The only problem is that it's too small"; this "tiny" and "individualistic" place – an offshoot of Mother India – offers "simple stuff", but always "manages to feel like a treat".* / **Sample dishes:** aubergine fritters; chilli garlic chicken; ice cream. **Details:** 10.30 pm; no credit cards; no smoking.

## The Wild Bergamot £45 ★★

1 Hillhead St  G62 8AF  (0141) 956 6515

*"Hard to locate, but well worth the effort", Alan Burns's first-floor restaurant – renamed from Gingerhill – is an "unexpected" delight for somewhere "above a shop" in the 'burbs (near Milngavie station); it's a 'one-man band' type of venture, though, and service can be "slow".* / **Sample dishes:** horseradish-infused white crab with peppered tuna; seared scallops with creamed lentils & potatoes; butter chocolate tart with coffee & cocoa bean crunch. **Details:** www.thewildbergamot.co.uk; 9 pm; D only, ex Fri & Sat open L & D, closed Mon & Tue; no Amex; no smoking; booking: max 12; children: 14+.

## GODALMING, SURREY 3–3A

### Bel & The Dragon £38 Ⓐ

Bridge St  GU7 3DU  (01483) 527333

*"A beautifully-restored former church" provides the setting for this "fun" chain operation, where "eclectic" (and "quite expensive") "pub grub" is served up by "friendly Antipodean staff".* / **Sample dishes:** smoked haddock & spring onion cake; vanilla panna cotta with strawberries. **Details:** www.belandthedragon.co.uk; 10 pm.

## La Luna £38 ★

10-14 Wharf St  GU7 1NN  (01483) 414155

*"A local Italian made good" – this trattoria-with-ambitions is going "from strength to strength", with many reports praising its "outstanding" food and often-"impeccable" service; the interior is quite "stylish" too.* / **Sample dishes:** scallops with boiled beans & risotto; roast hake fillet with black olive pesto; semi-fried amaretto with roast peaches. **Details:** 10 pm; closed Mon & Sun; no smoking area.

## GOLCAR, WEST YORKSHIRE 5–1C

### The Weavers Shed £44 Ⓐ★

Knowl Rd  HD7 4AN  (01484) 654284

*This "exemplary" restaurant-with-rooms (in an old mill) is hailed by most reporters not only for its "inspired" cooking (which makes much use of home-grown vegetables), but also for "some of the best service in the county"; the wine list is "very interesting" too, and "good value".* / **Sample dishes:** potted crab & avocado; rib-eye steak with potato wedges; sticky toffee pudding. **Details:** www.weaversshed.co.uk; 9 pm, Sat 10 pm; closed Mon, Sat L & Sun; no smoking. **Accommodation:** 5 rooms, from £85.

## GORING, BERKSHIRE                                    2–2D

### Leatherne Bottel                    £48        Ⓐ
Bridleway  RG8 0HS   (01491) 872667
"It is difficult to imagine a more beautiful setting" than that of this
"picturesque" Thames-sider; the food can sometimes be "great"
too, so it's a shame that a fair proportion of reporters find the
place "snooty", "overpriced" or "unwelcoming". / **Sample dishes:** flat
mushrooms on black olive toast; braised lamb shank with roast garlic gnocchi; sticky
toffee pudding. **Details:** www.leathernebottel.co.uk; 0.5m outside Goring on B4009;
9 pm; closed Sun D; children: 10+.

## GRANGE IN BORROWDALE, CUMBRIA          7–3D

### Borrowdale Gates Hotel             £46
Grange-in-Borrowdale  CA12 5UQ   (01768) 777204
Given a change of ownership, we don't think a rating
is appropriate for this hotel which has "one of the most beautiful
locations in England"; an early reporter on the new régime,
however, found the food "surprisingly modern and inventive".
/ **Details:** www.borrowdale-gates.com; 8.45 pm; no smoking.
**Accommodation:** 29 rooms, from £126.

## GRASMERE, CUMBRIA                         7–3D

### The Jumble Room                    £35        Ⓐ★
Langdale Rd  LA22 9SU   (01539) 435188
An "unusual" destination that's "informal in style, but offers a high
standard of food and wine", as well as "very good service".
/ **Sample dishes:** chilli beef with pak choy & sesame; asparagus & Gruyère rosti;
raspberry & white chocolate cheesecake. **Details:** www.thejumbleroom.co.uk;
9.30 pm; closed Mon & Tue; no Amex; no smoking.

### Lancrigg Country House Hotel       £37        Ⓐ★
Easedale Rd  LA22 9QN   (01539) 435317
Sheer consistency is the most impressive feature of the feedback
on the Whittingtons' "beautifully-located" country house hotel,
and its "very imaginative" vegetarian cuisine; the wine list –
"from fruit, kosher and organic to good-quality 'regular' stuff" –
also rates mention. / **Sample dishes:** Parmesan polenta & roasted peppers;
cauliflower & potato balti; redcurrant & cream cheesecake with chocolate curls.
**Details:** www.lancrigg.co.uk; 8 pm; no smoking. **Accommodation:** 13 rooms,
from £100.

### Wordsworth Hotel                   £50        ★
LA22 9SW   (01539) 435592
"Right in the middle of a tourist trap", near the poet's grave,
it's all the more worth knowing about this "surprisingly quiet"
hotel, whose cuisine is often hailed for its "good value".
/ **Sample dishes:** quail & pistachio ballentine; fillet of beef; citrus mousse with
lemon cured ravioli. **Details:** www.grasmere-hotels.co.uk; 9 pm; no smoking;
children: 8+. **Accommodation:** 37 rooms, from £105.

**sign up for the survey at www.hardens.com**

---

## GREAT BARROW, CHESHIRE 5–2A
### The Foxcote £32
Station Ln CH3 7JN (01244) 301343
*"A good selection of dishes"* is a highlight at this *"unfussy"*, rural
boozer – a popular culinary destination in these parts; service,
though generally *"efficient"*, has been rather up-and-down
in recent reports. / **Sample dishes:** battered haggis with mustard; Thai red
snapper with sticky rice; sticky toffee pudding. **Details:** www.thefoxcote.com; 10 pm;
closed Sun D; no Amex; no smoking.

---

## GREAT BEDWYN, WILTSHIRE 2–2C
### Three Tuns £32    A★
High St SN8 3NU (01672) 870280
*"A superb gourmet dining experience in a very interesting pub
setting"* – that's the deal at this winning boozer; (n.b. some major
building works were completed shortly before this guide went
to press). / **Sample dishes:** scallops with ginger, lime & coconut sauce;
Spanish-style rabbit; home-made tiramisu. **Details:** www.the-starr.co.uk; 9 pm; smoking in bar only.

---

## GREAT DUNMOW, ESSEX 3–2C
### Starr £54    A★
Market Pl CM6 1AX (01371) 874321
*"Outstanding food for this neck of the woods (even if it's jolly
expensive)"* is to be found at this *"upmarket"* age-old inn, on the
market square, where standards seem to be rising under the new
chef. / **Sample dishes:** crisp fried duck egg & asparagus; aged fillet of beef;
aniseed parfait. **Details:** www.the-starr.co.uk; 8m E of M11, J8 on A120; 9.30 pm;
closed Sun D; no jeans or trainers; no smoking. **Accommodation:** 8 rooms,
from £120.

---

## GREAT GONERBY, LINCOLNSHIRE 5–3D
### Harry's Place £75    ★★
17 High St NG31 8JS (01476) 561780
*"Tiny, but almost perfect"* – Harry Hallam's 10-seater is a pure
one-off that provides *"exceptional"* cooking and as *"intimate"*
a dining destination as you could ever hope to find.
/ **Sample dishes:** mushroom soup; roe deer fillet with black pudding & Madeira
sauce; cherry brandy jelly. **Details:** on B1174 1m N of Grantham; 9.30 pm; closed
Mon & Sun; no Amex; no smoking; booking essential; children: 5+.

---

## GREAT MILTON, OXFORDSHIRE 2–2D
### Le Manoir aux Quat' Saisons £112    A★★
Church Rd OX44 7PD (01844) 278881
*"You won't want to leave"*, after a visit to Raymond Blanc's
*"superb"* walled manor house (set in *"beautiful"* gardens) which
offers an unrivalled *"all-round experience"* – not least
*"sensational"* cuisine and *"staff who make you feel like a million
dollars"*; sadly, of course, it's also *"hideously expensive"*.
/ **Sample dishes:** quail egg ravioli with Parmesan & truffles; roast Trelough duck
with vinegar & tamarind sauce; pistachio soufflé with bitter cocoa sorbet.
**Details:** www.manoir.com; from M40, J7 take A329; 9.30 pm; no smoking.
**Accommodation:** 32 rooms, from £265.

---

---

## GREAT TEW, OXFORDSHIRE     2–1D

**Falkland Arms**     £29     Ⓐ
The Green  OX7 4DB   (01608) 683653
*"Beautiful inside and out", this "fantastic" village pub enjoys
a "wonderful" Cotswolds location; fans also extol its "great food,
beer and wines". / **Sample dishes:** grilled goat's cheese salad; slow-cooked
lamb shank; sticky toffee pudding. **Details:** www.falklandarms.org.uk;
A361 between Banbury & Chipping Norton; 8 pm; closed Sun D; no smoking;
children: 16+. **Accommodation:** 6 rooms, from £75.*

---

## GREAT TEY, ESSEX     3–2C

**The Barn Brasserie**     £33     Ⓐ
Brook Rd  CO6 1JE   (01206) 212345
*This "stunning" conversion of a centuries-old barn inspires mixed
reviews; fans often hail it as an "amazing" place (especially
"for groups"), but even they can decry its "Jekyll and Hyde
performance", and doubters just find portions "stingy" and wines
(in particular) "overpriced". / **Sample dishes:** grilled garlic mushrooms;
deep-fried chocolate ravioli with raspberries. **Details:** www.barnbrasserie.co.uk;
10 pm; smoking in bar only.*

---

## GREAT YELDHAM, ESSEX     3–2C

**White Hart**     £34
Poole St  CO9 4HJ   (01787) 237250
*This "impressive timbered inn" has a "lovely" location; it received
mixed reviews this year (during which time it changed ownership
and management), so we've left it unrated. / **Sample dishes:** wild
mushroom & pigeon salad; steamed venison & onion pudding; raspberry & amaretto
trifle. **Details:** www.whitehartyeldham.co.uk; between Haverhill & Halstead
on A1017; 9.30 pm; no smoking.*

---

## GRIMSTON, NORFOLK     6–4B

**Congham Hall**     £55     Ⓐ
PE32 1AH   (01485) 600250
*For a classic "country house" dining experience, a small band
of supporters tip this "tranquil" and "relaxing" establishment –
one of the longer-serving members of the Von Essen portfolio
of luxury hotels. / **Sample dishes:** pan-seared scallops; roast chump of lamb &
garlic potato purée; apple soufflé. **Details:** www.conghamhallhotel.co.uk; 9.15 pm;
no jeans or trainers; smoking in bar only; children: 7+ for D. **Accommodation:** 14
rooms, from £185.*

---

## GUERNSEY, CHANNEL ISLANDS

**Auberge**     £38     Ⓐ
Jerbourg Rd, St Martin's  GY4 6BH   (01481) 238485
*The "wonderful" setting – with distant views of St Peter Port –
contributes to the attraction of this trendy coastal restaurant;
considering the relatively small scale of operations, though, service
can be "slow" and the food unremarkable. / **Sample dishes:** pistou
soup with four cheese ravioli; fillet of beef; organic lemon tart with Guernsey cream.
**Details:** www.theauberge.gg; 9 pm; no smoking.*

**sign up for the survey at www.hardens.com**

### Da Nello £31 ★
46 Lower Pollet St, St Peter Port  GY1 1WF
(01481) 721552
*Most (if not quite all) reporters are persuaded by the attractions
of this spacious and intriguingly laid-out St Peter Port Italian
of over 20 years' standing, where the food is "consistently good".*
/ **Sample dishes:** balsamic onions with Mozzarella; veal with asparagus & lemon
sauce; champagne & fruit jelly. **Details:** 10 pm; no smoking area.

### La Frégate £40 ★
Les Cotils, St Peter Port  GY1 1UT   (01481) 724624
*"Very good" food is the gist of all commentary on this "discreet"
hotel dining room, on the outskirts of St Peter Port; despite its
"stunning view of Sark", the "very modern" setting itself can seem
rather "stark".* / **Sample dishes:** lobster bisque; pan-fried calf's liver; roasted
apple Tatin. **Details:** www.lafregatehotel.com; 9.30 pm; smoking in bar only.
**Accommodation:** 13 rooms, from £135.

---

### GUILDFORD, SURREY 3–3A
### Café de Paris £38
35 Castle St  GU1 3UQ   (01483) 534896
*It has recently expanded, so this now more obviously Gallic-
themed brasserie must be doing something right; doubters say it's
"not as good as it was", though, and its somewhat "snooty" style
disenchants some reporters.* / **Sample dishes:** fish terrine with sole sauce;
soft chocolate with crème anglaise. **Details:** www.cafedeparisguildford.co.uk;
10.30 pm, Fri & Sat 11 pm; closed Sun D; no smoking area.

### Cambio £42
2-4 South Hill  GU1 3SY   (01483) 577702
*Doubters say it's "over-hyped" locally, but this pre-eminent local
Italian of long standing is – after its move a couple of years ago –
still hailed as "consistently good" by most reporters.*
/ **Sample dishes:** black lasagne with crab; amaretto mousse.
**Details:** www.cambiorestaurant.com; by Guildford Castle; 10.30 pm, Fri & Sat
11 pm; closed Sun D; no smoking.

### The Thai Terrace £36 Ⓐ★
Castle Car Pk, Sydenham Rd  GU1 3RT
(01483) 503350
*"Super food and a splendid view" – especially "in summer when
the terrace is open" – have made a really big name locally for this
"sophisticated" and "deservedly busy" oriental; is it, however,
beginning to "rest on its laurels"?* / **Details:** 10.30 pm; closed Sun;
no Amex; smoking in bar only.

---

### GULLANE, EAST LOTHIAN 9–4D
### La Potinière £50 ★
Main St  EH31 2AA   (01620) 843214
*"As good as ever under the new management… perhaps even
better" – Keith Marley and Mary Runciman have made "a good
effort at filling the Browns' shoes" at this re-launched 'destination';
all of the (still relatively few) reports extol the "consistently top-
class" cuisine, and the "comprehensive" wine list.*
/ **Sample dishes:** Thai coconut soup with scallops; fillet of beef; passion fruit
mousse with coconut & banana frangipane tart. **Details:** www.la-potiniere.co.uk;
20m E of Edinburgh, off A198; 9 pm; closed Mon & Tue; Oct-Apr closed Sun D;
no Amex; no smoking.

## GULWORTHY, DEVON                    1–3C

### Horn of Plenty                    £ 45
PL19 8JD   (01822) 832528
There's no doubt that it has a "beautiful" rural location,
but reporters differ in their enthusiasm for this restaurant-with-
rooms; for fans, it's a "favourite", with "excellent" cuisine –
to critics "merely good food is unacceptably-priced" (and graced
with a "mystifying" Michelin star). / *Sample dishes:* smoked salmon &
crab; roast lamb with mint & pesto tagliatelle; cappuccino parfait & coffee meringue.
*Details:* www.thehornofplenty.co.uk; 3m W of Tavistock on A390; 9 pm; closed
Mon L; no smoking; children: 13+ at D. *Accommodation:* 10 rooms, from £120.

## HALIFAX, WEST YORKSHIRE             5–1C

### Design House                      £ 30
Dean Clough  HX3 5AX   (01422) 383242
"Beautiful décor" helps this "smart" (but, some feel, "clinical")
establishment in a converted mill to live up to its name;
its "simple" food, though, can seem "rather expensive" for what
it is. / *Sample dishes:* smoked salmon & saffron risotto; pork belly with noodles &
tempura vegetables; pear & cinnamon fritters.
*Details:* www.designhouserestaurant.co.uk; from Halifax follow signs to Dean Clough
Mills; 9.30 pm; closed Sat L & Sun; no smoking.

### Shibden Mill Inn                  £ 33
Shibden Mill Fold  HX3 7UL   (01422) 365840
A "favourite" destination for some reporters, this 17th-century inn
– with a "lovely setting" by a stream – is generally hailed for its
"good" food in "huge" portions. / *Sample dishes:* chicken liver & foie gras
tartlet; herb-studded St Austel sea bass; toffee & banana crumble with home-made
banana ice cream. *Details:* www.shibdenmillinn.com; off the A58, Leeds/Bradford
road; 11.15 pm. *Accommodation:* 12 rooms, from £85.

## HAMBLETON, RUTLAND                 5–4D

### Finch's Arms                      £ 30        Ⓐ
Oakham Rd  LE15 8TL   (01572) 756575
This cosy 17th-century inn enjoys a "wonderful location"
overlooking Rutland Water (and comes complete with a huge beer
garden and dining conservatory); for the most part, the food
is "interesting" and "pretty well-prepared", but in summer the
place gets "swamped". / *Sample dishes:* foie gras medallions; steamed beef
with marrow & thyme dumplings; panna cotta with glazed kumquats.
*Details:* www.finchsarms.co.uk; 9.30 pm; no Amex; smoking in bar only.
*Accommodation:* 6 rooms, from £75.

### Hambleton Hall                    £ 77       Ⓐ★
LE15 8TH   (01572) 756991
A "magnificent situation" (overlooking Rutland Water) adds lustre
to this "cosseting" and "opulent" country house hotel, whose
"superb" cooking and "exceptional" wine list are roundly praised;
it is, of course, "expensive", though, and its "conservative" style
may not appeal to all. / *Sample dishes:* langoustine cannelloni; roast pigeon
with foie gras ravioli & truffle sauce; pavé of white & dark chocolate.
*Details:* www.hambletonhall.com; 9.30 pm; no smoking. *Accommodation:* 17
rooms, from £220.

**sign up for the survey at www.hardens.com**

## HAMPTON COURT, SURREY　　　　　　3–3A

**Caffe La Fiamma**　　　　　　**£ 30**　　　Ⓐ
Hampton Court Rd　KT8 9BY　(020) 8943 2050
A *"dynamite" location, overlooking Bushy Park, helps win
recommendations for this Italian restaurant; its cooking is mostly
praised, but it can sometimes seem "heavy".* / **Sample dishes:** *prawns
with white wine sauce & mango salsa; pasta with seafood & white wine tomato
sauce; zabaglione.* **Details:** *www.clfuk.com; 11 pm.*

## HARLECH, GWYNEDD　　　　　　　4–2C

**Maes y Neuadd**　　　　　　**£ 40**　　　Ⓐ★
Talsarnau　LL47 6YA　(01766) 780200
*Overlooking Snowdonia, this "welcoming" and "comfortable"
establishment is "just what a country house should be", and its
"consistently sound" cuisine does nothing to let it down.*
/ **Sample dishes:** *mackerel with Waldorf salad; chicken with bacon & garlic risotto;
strawberry & mint délice.* **Details:** *www.neuadd.com; 3m N of Harlech off B4573;
8.45 pm; no smoking; children: 8+.* **Accommodation:** *16 rooms, from £141.*

## HAROME, NORTH YORKSHIRE　　　　8–4C

**Star Inn**　　　　　　**£ 43**　　　Ⓐ★★
YO62 5JE　(01439) 770397
*Andrew Pern's "classic English dishes with a twist" – in the
"cramped" bar or in the dining room – and wife Jacquie's
"immaculately-judged" service have made this "wonderfully cosy"
thatched tavern perhaps the country's most famous gastropub;
an "excellent food shop" is a recent addition.* / **Sample dishes:** *grilled
black pudding with pan-fried foie gras; roebuck deer with venison Bolognese;
steamed syrup sponge with boozy cherries.* **Details:** *www.thestaratharome.co.uk;
3m SE of Helmsley off A170; 9.30 pm; closed Mon & Sun D; no Amex; no smoking.*
**Accommodation:** *11, 8 in hotel, 3 as cottage rooms, from £120.*

## HARPENDEN, HERTFORDSHIRE　　　　3–2A

**Bean Tree**　　　　　　**£ 46**
20a Leyton Rd　AL5 2HU　(01582) 460901
*"A lovely old cottage in an area with plenty of money, but few
decent places to eat"; most reporters praise its "good cooking"
(and its "amazing, 200-bin wine list"), but there are also a few
doubters who decry its "pretentious" menu and "London prices" –
for top value, seek out the "good midweek deals".*
/ **Sample dishes:** *asparagus with tomato & mint sauce; steamed sea bass;
raspberry soufflé.* **Details:** *www.thebeantree.com; 9:30 pm, Sat 10:30 pm; closed
Mon, Sat L & Sun D; no smoking.*

**Chef Peking**　　　　　　**£ 28**
5-6 Church Grn　AL5 2TP　(01582) 769358
*In an area starved of culinary talent, this "much-better-than-
average local Chinese" is a "buzzy" venue with
a disproportionately large following in the area.*
/ **Sample dishes:** *satay chicken; ice cream.* **Details:** *just off the High Rd;
10.45 pm; no smoking area.*

**The Fox** £ 38
469 Luton Rd AL5 3QE (01582) 713817
*Its style may be "fairly typical", but this "light and airy" new gastropub is a dependably "high-quality" operation that's already acquired an impressive following among local reporters.*
/ **Details:** www.foxharpenden.co.uk; 9.30 pm; smoking in bar only.

---

HARROGATE, NORTH YORKSHIRE 5–1C

**Bettys** £ 31    Ⓐ
1 Parliament St HG1 2QU (01423) 877300
*"It's still a great trip" ("even the queue is entertaining"), say fans of this grand and famous teashop; thanks not least to its "London prices", though, some reporters feel it's a "visit-once" experience.*
/ **Sample dishes:** Yorkshire rarebit; fruit tart. **Details:** www.bettysandtaylors.co.uk; 9 pm; no Amex; no smoking; no booking.

**The Boar's Head** £ 46    Ⓐ★
Ripley Castle Estate HG3 3AY (01423) 771888
*"A cross between a country house hotel and a pub", this "wonderful" inn (in Ripley, just outside the town) is unanimously hailed as a "charming" place with "really good" food, in both the bar and the restaurant.* / **Sample dishes:** duck with summer vegetable risotto; rabbit with caramelised apples; hot strawberry soufflé. **Details:** www.boarsheadripley.co.uk; off A61 between Ripon & Harrogate; 9 pm; no smoking area. **Accommodation:** 25 rooms, from £125.

**Clock Tower**
**Rudding Park** £ 48    Ⓐ
Follifoot HG3 1JH (01423) 871350
*"You will want to return", say fans of the contemporary-style dining room of this impressive-looking country house (just outside the town); it attracts limited feedback, all of which says the food is well-accomplished.* / **Sample dishes:** asparagus soup; beef fillet & fondant potatoes; terrine of sorbets. **Details:** www.ruddingpark.com; 10 pm; no smoking. **Accommodation:** 49 rooms, from £170.

**Drum & Monkey** £ 35    ★
5 Montpellier Gdns HG1 2TF (01423) 502650
*A "very good and fresh" selection of "seafood classics" has long maintained the quirky appeal of this "busy" local Victorian institution; it is "cramped", but a recent refurbishment has somewhat brightened up the interior.* / **Sample dishes:** lobster délice; smoked haddock florentine; crème brûlée. **Details:** 10 pm; no Amex; no smoking; booking: max 10.

**Hotel du Vin et Bistro** £ 48
Prospect Pl HG1 1LB (01423) 856800
*A "comfy" outpost of the boutique-hotel chain; as usual, it's the "terrific" wine list which is the stand-out attraction – even by the standards of its sibling establishments, the food here is "average".*
/ **Sample dishes:** seared pigeon with roast pine nuts; roast rump of lamb; rhubarb jalousie with crème anglaise. **Details:** www.hotelduvin.com; 9.45 pm; no smoking area. **Accommodation:** 43 rooms, from £95.

**sign up for the survey at www.hardens.com**    

**Quantro**                                    **£ 33**                    ★
3 Royal Pde  HG1 2SZ  (01423) 503034
*"Well-prepared food", "knowledgeable" service and "very good
value for money" figure in most reports on this "pleasant"
restaurant (which is slightly more favourably rated than its Leeds
sibling). / **Sample dishes:** scallops & calamari; duck breast; Cointreau milk
chocolate bread & butter pudding. **Details:** www.quantro.co.uk; 10 pm,
Sat 10.30 pm; closed Sun; no smoking; children: 8+.*

**Rajput**                                     **£ 23**                    ★
11 Cheltenham Pde  HG1 1DD  (01423) 562113
*"Marvellous food", using "fresh ingredients", wins unanimous
bravos for "Harrogate's best Indian"; a "superior" but "friendly"
place, it's often hailed for its "excellent value". / **Details:** midnight;
D only, closed Mon; no Amex.*

**Villu Toots**
**Balmoral Hotel**                             **£ 34**
Franklin Mount  HG1 5EJ  (01423) 705805
*The modern dining room of a small hotel, which continues
to attract plaudits for its "outstanding lunchtime value".
/ **Sample dishes:** sauteed king prawns; pan-fried duck breast & potato fondant;
steamed chocolate pudding, hazelnut & caramel sauce.
**Details:** www.villutoots.co.uk; 9.30 pm; D only; no Amex; smoking in bar only.
**Accommodation:** 23 rooms, from £80.*

---

HARROW, MIDDLESEX                                          3–3A

**Golden Palace**                              **£ 28**                    ★★
146-150 Station Rd  HA1 2RH  (020) 8863 2333
*Recent expansion seems to have done little to dent the attraction
of this "outstanding" suburban Cantonese, which fans insist offers
"the best dim sum in the West" – as is so often the case, there's
a sense that dinner is less exciting. / **Sample dishes:** mixed starter; crispy
duck; toffee banana. **Details:** midnight; no smoking area; no booking, Sat & Sun.*

**Old Etonian**                                **£ 31**                    Ⓐ
38 High St, Harrow On The Hill  HA1 3LL  (020) 8422 8482
*"The most romantic view in north west London" makes the
terrace of this long-established bistro a prized destination on a
sunny day; some (but not all) reporters say the
Gallic/Mediterranean fare is "superb" too. / **Sample dishes:** crêpe aux
fruits de mer; fillet Dijon; lime cheesecake. **Details:** www.oldetonianrestaurant.com;
10.30 pm; closed Sat L & Sun D. **Accommodation:** 14 rooms, from £75.*

---

HARTLEPOOL, HARTLEPOOL                                     8–3C

**Krimo's**                                    **£ 31**                    ★
The Marina  TS24 0YB  (01429) 266120
*This "gem" on the marina inspires warm words from all who
report on it, not least for its "good food" and its "excellent
harbour views". / **Sample dishes:** penne arrabiata with chilli & olives; prime
sirloin steak; sticky toffee pudding. **Details:** www.krimos.co.uk; 9 pm; closed Mon &
Sun D; no Amex; no smoking.*

---

## HARWICH, ESSEX                                3–2D

**The Pier at Harwich**              **£ 40**        ★

The Quay  CO12 3HH   (01255) 241212

*Refurbished in recent times, this harbour-side hotel, with its "well-presented" dining room, is owned by the Milsom family (of Talbooth fame); it is unanimously well-reviewed, not least for its "plain-grilled seafood". / Sample dishes: goat's cheese; Harwich grilled lobster with béarnaise sauce; sticky toffee pudding. Details: www.milsomhotels.com; 9.30 pm; no smoking area. Accommodation: 14 rooms, from £95.*

---

## HASCOMBE, SURREY                              3–3A

**White Horse**                      **£ 38**        ★

The Street  GU8 4JA   (01483) 208258

*"Very good food in great countryside" – that's the deal at this "good-value" 16th-century inn. / Sample dishes: Thai fishcakes; roast rack of lamb; sticky toffee pudding. Details: 10 pm.*

---

## HASSOP, DERBYSHIRE                            5–2C

**Hassop Hall**                      **£ 40**       Ⓐ★

DE45 1NS   (01629) 640488

*For "grand Peak District dining", you're unlikely to do much better than this "wonderful" and "welcoming" country house hotel, whose restaurant offers "extremely good value". / Sample dishes: smoked chicken & avocado salad; grilled fillet steak; vanilla & dark chocolate mousse. Details: 9 pm; closed Mon L & Sun D; no smoking. Accommodation: 13 rooms, from £79.*

---

## HASTINGS, EAST SUSSEX                         3–4C

**The Mermaid Café**                 **£ 20**       ★★

2 Rock-a-Nore Rd  TN34 3DW   (01424) 438100

*"The freshest fish and brilliant chips" – "we've yet to discover better" – are "as good as ever" at this "incomparable" seaside café. / Sample dishes: prawn salad; skate & chips; spotted dick & custard. Details: 7.30 pm; no credit cards; no booking.*

---

## HATCH END, GREATER LONDON                     3–3A

**Rotisserie**                       **£ 32**        ★

316 Uxbridge Rd  HA5 4HR   (020) 8421 2878

*"Great grills in a buzzy atmosphere" – that's the whole deal, really, at this "consistently good" venture, now the sole survivor of a small former chain. / Sample dishes: sauteed scallops; on-the-bone sirloin; chocolate pudding. Details: www.therotisserie.co.uk; 10.30 pm; closed weekday L.*

**Sea Pebbles**                      **£ 24**        ★

348-352 Uxbridge Rd  HA5 4HR   (020) 8428 0203

*"A bustling chippie with a fantastic 'family' atmosphere"; its "consistently good" fish is praised by many reporters. / Sample dishes: calamari rings; deep-fried scampi & chips; bread & butter pudding. Details: 9.45 pm; closed Sun; debit cards only; need 10+ to book.*

**sign up for the survey at www.hardens.com**

## HATFIELD PEVEREL, ESSEX 3–2C

**Blue Strawberry** £35
The Street CM3 2DW (01245) 381333
*"Now improved after a period of slippage"*, this *"charming bistro"*
is hailed by reporters for its *"friendly and professional"* standards,
and its *"good value"*. / **Sample dishes:** English asparagus topped with
a poached egg; calf's liver & bacon on a horseradish & spring onion cake; crème
brûlée. **Details:** www.bluestrawberrybistro.co.uk; 3m E of Chelmsford; 10 pm; closed
Sat L & Sun D; smoking in bar only.

## HAWORTH, WEST YORKSHIRE 5–1C

**Weaver's** £35 𝔸
15 West Ln BD22 8DU (01535) 643822
*"Good-value British cooking"* (with *"high-quality local ingredients"*)
and *"helpful"* service impress most visitors to this *"Bronteland"*
fixture of over 20 years' standing, which occupies a former
weavers' shed. / **Sample dishes:** monkfish, scallops & prawns; seared pork with
wilted greens; sticky toffee pudding. **Details:** www.weaversmallhotel.co.uk; 1.5m W
on B6142 from A629, near Parsonage; 9.15 pm; closed Mon, Tue L, Sat L & Sun D;
no smoking. **Accommodation:** 3 rooms, from £80.

## HAYWARDS HEATH, WEST SUSSEX 3–4B

**Jeremy's at Borde Hill** £38 𝔸★★
Balcombe Rd RH16 1XP (01444) 441102
*"The South's best food outside London, and honestly-priced too"*;
the *"imaginative"* cooking at Jeremy Ashpool's *"lovely"* restaurant
simply *"never fails to impress"*; the setting is a particular *"delight
in summer"*, when you can dine 'en terrasse'. / **Sample dishes:** prawn
bisque; rabbit with bubble & squeak; apple & rhubarb tart.
**Details:** www.jeremysrestaurant.com; 10 pm; closed Mon & Sun D; no smoking.

## HAZLEWOOD, NORTH YORKSHIRE 5–3C

**Anise**
**Hazlewood Castle Hotel** £38
Paradise Ln LS24 9NJ (01937) 535354
This *"beautiful"* castle has long been *"the best place to eat
hereabouts"*, even if it's perhaps been of most note as a place
to stay or hold an event; as this guide went to press, it's closed its
previous restaurant (1086) and opened this more ambitious
(and more expensive) location, in the heart of the building.
/ **Details:** www.hazlewood-castle.co.uk; signposted off A64; 9.30 pm; closed Mon,
Tue-Sat D only, Sun open L & D; no smoking; children: before 7 pm only.
**Accommodation:** 21 rooms, from £140.

## HELMSLEY, NORTH YORKSHIRE 8–4C

**Feversham Arms Hotel** £47 𝔸★
YO62 5AG (01439) 770766
Simon Rhatigan's chic and romantic country inn inspires notably
consistent feedback – food *"of a very high standard"* features
in all reports, as does *"friendly"* and *"efficient"* service.
/ **Sample dishes:** asparagus salad; braised oxtail stuffed; lemon soufflé.
**Details:** www.fevershamarmshotel.com; 9.30 pm; no jeans or trainers; smoking
in bar only; children: 12+ at D. **Accommodation:** 19 rooms, from £130.

## HEMINGFORD GREY, CAMBRIDGESHIRE     3–1B

**Cock**     £35

PE28 9BJ   (01480) 463609

*In a "pretty village", "a refurbished pub and restaurant" where the specialities are fish and sausages; the food "can be variable", but reports are generally upbeat.* / **Sample dishes:** *duck parcel; braised pork fillet; sticky toffee pudding.* **Details:** *www.cambscuisine.com; 9 pm; no Amex; no smoking.*

## HENLEY IN ARDEN, WEST MIDLANDS     5–4C

**Edmunds**     £38    A★

64 High St B95 5BX
(01564) 795666

*"Very good" (and often "exceptional") food at "very reasonable prices" makes Andy Waters's "friendly" restaurant in a half-timbered house an undoubted "value-for-money" destination – "try getting in!"* / **Sample dishes:** *pan-fried sea scallops; fillet of lamb; poached pear with hazelnut cream & caramel sauce.* **Details:** *9.45 pm; closed Mon, Sat L & Sun; no Amex; no smoking; booking: max 6.*

## HEREFORD, HEREFORDSHIRE     2–1B

**Floodgates**
**Left Bank**     £38    A

20-22 Bridge St HR4 9DF   (01432) 349009

*"Great views of the cathedral and river" help make this "quality" brasserie in a modern development a pleasant place for a meal; feedback remains limited, however, with reporters' assessments of the food ranging from "flavoursome" to "over-complicated".* / **Sample dishes:** *fillet of Hereford beef; pot roast rump of kangaroo.* **Details:** *www.leftbank.co.uk; 10 pm; no smoking area.*

**La Rive at Castle House**
**Castle House Hotel**     £59    ★

Castle St HR1 2NW   (01432) 356321

*The dining room at this Georgian townhouse-hotel can seem "slightly sombre", but the food is "interesting", and seems to have been "improved" by new chef Claire Nicholls.* / **Sample dishes:** *Thai risotto with tempura frogs legs; Cajun-spiced cod, pak choy & lemon grass soubise; dark chocolate & orange parfait.* **Details:** *www.castlehse.co.uk; 10 pm; no jeans or trainers; no smoking.* **Accommodation:** *15 rooms, from £200.*

## HERSHAM, SURREY     3–3A

**Dining Room**     £34    A

10 Queens Rd KT12 5LS   (01932) 231686

*Doubters dismiss the cuisine as "formula old English fare", but this well-established spot – with its somewhat "wacky" decoration – remains "rather popular" with the locals; it has a large terrace for sunny days.* / **Sample dishes:** *tiger prawns, tomatoes, garlic & basil; lamb & mint pie; Caribbean coconut ice cream.* **Details:** *www.the-dining-room.co.uk; just off A3, by village green; 10.30 pm; closed Sat L & Sun D; no smoking area.*

## HERSTMONCEUX, EAST SUSSEX       3–4B
### Sundial       £ 50       A★
Gardner St BN27 4LA   (01323) 832217
*More consistent reports this year on the "interesting" cooking at M. Rongier's "excellent French restaurant"; Mme. R's "personal" service contributes much to the atmosphere.*
/ **Sample dishes:** beef carpaccio; rib of veal with wild mushroom sauce; shortbread biscuit with crème brûlée & rhubarb coulis. **Details:** www.sundialrestaurant.co.uk; centre of village; 9.30 pm; closed Mon & Sun D; no Amex; no smoking.

## HETTON, NORTH YORKSHIRE       5–1B
### The Angel       £ 41       A★★
BD23 6LT   (01756) 730263
*"It's worth the drive" to this famous "olde worlde" pub, which enjoys a "peaceful and beautiful" Dales setting; "meticulous attention" – to "the food, its presentation and the wine that goes with it" – creates a "really memorable" overall experience.*
/ **Sample dishes:** black pudding; rack of lamb; sticky toffee pudding. **Details:** www.angelhetton.co.uk; 5m N of Skipton off B6265 at Rylstone; 9 pm; D only, ex Sun open L only; no smoking. **Accommodation:** 5 rooms, from £120.

## HINTLESHAM, SUFFOLK       3–1C
### Hintlesham Hall       £ 55       A★
Dodge St IP8 3NS   (01473) 652334
*Perhaps stating the obvious, some reporters note that this famous country house hotel is "for special occasions" (and its style can seem "a little overawing" at first); if you don't mind the money, though, the overall effect can be "stupendous".*
/ **Sample dishes:** smoked haddock, mussel & roast vegetable salad; lamb chump; iced raspberry parfait. **Details:** www.hintleshamhall.com; 4m W of Ipswich on A1071; 9.30 pm; closed Sat L; jacket required at D; no smoking; children: 12+ at D. **Accommodation:** 33 rooms, from £150.

## HOLKHAM, NORFOLK       6–3C
### Victoria Hotel       £ 43
Park Rd NR23 1RG   (01328) 711008
*The "relaxed" and "chilled" approach of this "Bohemian" beach-facing pub has made it quite a 'destination' (especially for Londoners); one reporter Delphically observes, however, that "you need a sense of humour to eat here", and some reporters keenly feel that the place "doesn't live up to the publicity".* / **Sample dishes:** local crab; venison with creamed cabbage & chocolate sauce; white chocolate cheesecake. **Details:** www.victoriaatholkham.co.uk; 9.30 pm; no Amex; smoking in bar only. **Accommodation:** 10 rooms, from £110.

## HOLT, NORFOLK       6–3C
### Yetman's       £ 45       ★
37 Norwich Rd NR25 6SA   (01263) 713320
*"Haute country cooking", "home-brewed beers" and an "ever-hospitable" welcome all help commend Alison and Peter Yetmans' "cosy and low-ceilinged" restaurant to the "north-Norfolk second home crowd" (and, indeed, to all reporters).*
/ **Sample dishes:** Louisiana crabcakes with red pepper mayonnaise; char-grilled duck with spiced figs; passion fruit & mango bombe. **Details:** www.yetmans.net; on A148, 20m N of Norwich; 9.30 pm; D only, ex Sun open L only (open Sun D Jul & Aug); no smoking.

---

## HONITON, DEVON 2–4A

**Combe House Hotel & Restaurant** £45    𝔸★
Gittisham EX14 3AD (01404) 540400
This "near-perfect" Elizabethan manor house benefits from
a "glorious" location, and makes a very "romantic" destination;
the food generally measures up, but service can be "slow".
/ **Sample dishes:** home-made fennel & celery soup; roast rump of Devon lamb;
raspberry coulis. **Details:** www.thishotel.com; 9.30 pm; no Amex; no smoking.
**Accommodation:** 15 rooms, from £148.

---

## HORNDON ON THE HILL, ESSEX 3–3C

**The Bell Inn** £36    𝔸★
High Rd SS17 8LD (01375) 642463
"The menu changes regularly, and the standard is always high",
says one of the many fans of this "lovely" half-timbered inn; it can
get "very busy". / **Sample dishes:** sweet potato & garlic soup; roast duck with
stuffed squid & parsnips; apple crumble with praline ice cream.
**Details:** www.bell-inn.co.uk; signposted off B1007, off A13; 9.45 pm; smoking
in bar only; booking: max 12. **Accommodation:** 15 rooms, from £50.

---

## HORTON, NORTHANTS 3–2A

**The New French Partridge** £41    𝔸
Newport Pagnell Rd NN7 2AP (01604) 870033
Even some who say "it's difficult to fault the quality" of this rural
village restaurant can find it "a tad pricey"; critics just say it's
"pretty" but "pretentious". / **Sample dishes:** galatine of chicken; rack of
lamb, three-peppercorn crust with vegetable gâteau; raspberry brûlée.
**Details:** www.newfrenchpartridge.co.uk; on B526 between Newport Pagnell &
Northampton; 9.30 pm; closed Mon & Sun D; no smoking. **Accommodation:** 10
rooms, from £140.

---

## HOUGHTON CONQUEST, BEDFORDSHIRE 3–2A

**Knife & Cleaver** £35
The Grove MK45 3LA (01234) 740387
"A slightly out-of-place conservatory-restaurant attached to a
quaint village pub, offering an excellent range of fish" –
one reporter summarises the attractions of this "good but
expensive" destination; doubters, though, find it "dull".
/ **Sample dishes:** salt cod tortilla with black olive sauce; beef fillet; chocolate
marquise. **Details:** www.knifeandcleaver.com; off A6, 5m S of Bedford; 9.30 pm;
closed Sat L & Sun D; no smoking. **Accommodation:** 9 rooms, from £53.

---

## HOYLAKE, MERSEYSIDE 5–2A

**Lino's** £32    𝔸★
122 Market St CH47 3BH (0151) 632 1408
"A top Merseyside gastronomic experience, in terms of the sheer
quality of the cuisine and the friendly, knowledgeable staff" –
one reporter speaks for all on the Galantini family's "wonderful"
Anglo-French restaurant. / **Sample dishes:** bean cobbler cannellini; roast
duck; coffee & Tia Maria-soaked ladyfingers. **Details:** www.linosrestaurant.co.uk;
3m from M53, J2; 10 pm; closed Mon & Sun; closed Aug; no Amex.

---

**sign up for the survey at www.hardens.com**

## HUDDERSFIELD, WEST YORKSHIRE 5–1C

### Bradley's £28 A★
84 Fitzwilliam St HD1 5BB (01484) 516773
"Reliable", "interesting" and "good-value" – these are the
invariable themes in commentary on the cooking at this "busy"
but "friendly" town-centre bistro. / **Sample dishes:** chicken fritters with
peanut & lime dip; mango tart with caramel ice cream.
**Details:** www.bradleys-restaurant.co.uk; 10 pm; closed Sat L & Sun; no Amex;
no smoking area.

### Huddersfield Jumbo Buffet £16
70-76 John William St HD1 1EH (01484) 549201
The ambience may be "canteen-like", but this "buffet-style
Chinese" inspires a good number of reports with its good-value
food offer. / **Details:** 11 pm; no smoking area.

### Lounge 68 £34 A
68 John William St HD1 1EH (01484) 545454
"Ignore the fact it is frequented by footballers' wives and
Emmerdale stars", and this can be a stylish (if "noisy")
destination; quieter lunchtimes are notable for their "exceptional"
value. / **Sample dishes:** roasted meatballs with a spicy tomato sauce; double rib
of lamb with kidneys & salsa verde; white chocolate & Bailey's crème brûlée.
**Details:** www.lounge68bar.com; 10 pm; closed Sun; no smoking area.

### Nawaab £24 ★
35 Westgate HD1 1NY (01484) 422775
"Tasty" food (including some "excellent" specials) helps ensure
consistently favourable feedback on this town-centre
subcontinental. / **Sample dishes:** tandoori chicken pikka; diced chicken
in yoghurt; matka kulfi. **Details:** www.nawaab.net; between bus & railway stations;
11 pm; D only; no smoking area.

## HULL, KINGSTON UPON HULL 6–2A

### Cerutti's £44
10 Nelson St HU1 1XE (01482) 328501
This locally-celebrated fish restaurant, of over three decades'
standing, occupies a Georgian house "a stone's throw from the old
docks"; "inappropriate saucing" can mask some "very good"
ingredients, but, generally, praise is high for the place's
"unvarying" culinary standards. / **Sample dishes:** pan-fried scallops;
mini house selection. **Details:** www.ceruttis.co.uk; follow signs to the fruit market;
9.30 pm; closed Sat L & Sun; smoking in bar only.

## HUNTINGDON, CAMBRIDGESHIRE 3–1B

### Old Bridge Hotel £41 A
1 High St PE29 3TQ (01480) 424300
An "extremely interesting" wine list adds spice to a visit to this
"welcoming" hotel near the river, where the cooking is "reliable",
if perhaps a touch "uninspiring"; you can dine in the "formal"
dining room or more "lively" conservatory. / **Sample dishes:** garlic &
mushroom risotto with parsley; roast salmon with Swiss chard & mussels; lemon tart.
**Details:** www.huntsbridge.com; off A1, off A14; 10 pm; no smoking.
**Accommodation:** 24 rooms, from £125.

## Pheasant Inn £38 ★

Loop Rd PE28 0RE (01832) 710241

This popular "thatched pub" is part of the Huntsbridge group and, like its siblings, boasts a "marvellous" wine list and an "easy-going" charm; it offers some of the better food in the chain, and wins consistent praise for its "well-executed" and "good-value" fare. / **Sample dishes:** deep-fried Brie; lamb fillet; vanilla & lavender panna cotta with red fruits. **Details:** www.huntsbridge.com; 1m S of A14 between Huntingdon & Kettering, J15; 9.30 pm; no smoking area.

---

## ILKLEY, WEST YORKSHIRE 5–1C

## Bettys £30 A

32-34 The Grove LS29 9EE (01943) 608029

"The big queue is worth it", say fans of this famous "traditional tea room"; it's "expensive", of course, but for "Yorkshire curd tart, ginger biscuits or tarte au citron, it's in a class of its own".
/ **Sample dishes:** Swiss potato rosti; fruit tart. **Details:** www.bettysandtaylors.com; 5.30 pm; no smoking; no booking.

## The Box Tree £55

35-37 Church St LS29 9DR (01943) 608484

Simon Gueller has done good work at this famous "old-timer", and it's certainly "nice to see it rejuvenated"; reporters still find it a bit "overpriced", though, and – even if the place is clearly "on the up" – Michelin's 'instant' star does seem rather precipitate. / **Sample dishes:** hand-dived sea scallops with celeriac; lamb cutlet with shallot purée; passion fruit soufflé with banana nut milkshake. **Details:** www.theboxtree.co.uk; on A65 near town centre; 9.30 pm; closed Mon & Sun D; closed 2 weeks in Jan; no Amex; no smoking; children: 10+ at D.

## Far Syde £33

1-3 New Brook St LS29 8DQ (01943) 602030

The move to new premises does not seem to have been an unmitigated success for this popular local restaurant; it's still generally hailed as "reliable", but there's also some feedback to the effect that it's "resting on its laurels". / **Sample dishes:** seafood ravioli; breast of chicken; chocolate & cherry pudding. **Details:** www.thefarsyde.co.uk; 10 pm; closed Mon & Sun; no Amex; no smoking.

---

## ILMINGTON, WARWICKSHIRE 2–1C

## The Howard Arms £32 A★

Lower Grn CV36 4LT (01608) 682226

"You get very good food at this typical country pub in a beautiful Warwickshire village, with no fuss, no pretension and no clichéd 'gastropub' dishes" – one of many reports on this "excellent" destination says it all. / **Sample dishes:** twice-baked cheese soufflé with a Stilton glaze; beef, ale & mustard pie; apple, pear & fruit flapjack crumble. **Details:** www.howardarms.com; 8m SW of Stratford-upon-Avon off A4300; 9 pm; no Amex; no smoking; children: 8+ after 7 pm. **Accommodation:** 3 rooms, from £97.

## INVERNESS, HIGHLAND 9–2C

### Abstract
### The Glenmoriston
### Townhouse Hotel £58 A★

Ness Bank IV2 4SF (01463) 223777

*With its "good location on the banks of the River Ness" this ambitious newcomer (a recipient of the Ramsay 'Restaurant Nightmare' treatment) has unusually 'haute' aspirations for the Highlands; Loic Lefebvre's classically-rooted cuisine is "slightly pricey", but "superb"./ **Sample dishes:** foie gras ravioli; roasted pigeon fillet; pineapple soufflé with piña colada sorbet. **Details:** www.abstractrestaurant.com.*

### Rocpool £38 A

1 Ness Walk IV3 5NE (01463) 717274

*"A lovely setting by a river", "very polite and helpful" staff and an "interesting and eclectic menu" help commend this brasserie-style operation to the few reporters who comment on it; an hotel of the same name is opening nearby in late-2005. / **Sample dishes:** seared king scallops with black pudding; carved fillet of Scotch beef with rosemary & garlic; white chocolate cheesecake with glazed bananas. **Details:** www.rocpool.com; 10 pm; no Amex; no smoking.*

## IPSWICH, SUFFOLK 3–1D

### Baipo £28 ★

63 Upper Orwell St IP4 1HP (01473) 218402

*"A must if you find yourself in Ipswich" – this "hospitable" Thai restaurant offers an "adventurous" oriental menu done to a "very consistent" standard. / **Details:** www.baipo.co.uk; 10.45 pm; closed Mon L & Sun; no Amex.*

### Bistro on the Quay £33

3 Wherry Quay IP4 1AS (01473) 286677

*"Good bistro food" in a "good location" – an "up-and-coming area on the old docks/marina" – is making quite a name for this "lively" and "straightforward" operation. / **Sample dishes:** bang bang chicken with peanut sauce; chocolate Maltesers cheesecake. **Details:** 9.30 pm; closed Sun D; no smoking.*

### The Galley £41 ★

25 St Nicholas St IP1 1TW (01473) 281131

*A "cramped" but "neat" Turkish/Mediterranean bistro that's perhaps most enjoyable when you can avail yourself of its "great" alfresco dining possibilities. / **Sample dishes:** crispy Feta & parsley filo pastry; Norfolk smoked trout; Belgian chocolate délice. **Details:** www.galley.uk.com; 10 pm; closed Mon & Sun; no smoking area.*

### Il Punto £33 A★

Neptune Quay IP4 1AX (01473) 289748

*The candlelit tables at this "interesting" boat moored in the "fast-improving" docks are "fantastic for romance"; once you're onboard, everything is "very French", and the food is often "superb". / **Sample dishes:** home-made lobster & prawns ravioli; roast rack of lamb; iced apricot & pistachio nougat. **Details:** www.ilpunto.co.uk; 9.30 pm; closed Mon, Sat L & Sun; no smoking.*

**sign up for the survey at www.hardens.com**

**Trongs** £ 32 ★

23 St Nicholas St IP1 1TW (01473) 256833
*"Small, but perfectly formed", this "excellent" family-run Chinese attracts uniform praise, not least for its "attentive" and "friendly" service; "it can be full, even midweek", so book ahead.*
/ **Details:** *10.30 pm; closed Mon; no smoking.*

---

IRELAND, BEDFORDSHIRE 3–1A

**Black Horse** £ 37 Ⓐ★

SG17 5QL (01462) 811398
*It's not just because "there's no competition for miles, and miles, and miles" that this "excellent" gastropub is so "popular" – Tracy Buggins's food is "consistently good", and the service is "first-class".* / **Sample dishes:** *gambas with pancetta; cannon of lamb; white chocolate & Bailey's truffle cake.* **Details:** *www.blackhorseireland.com; 10 pm; smoking in bar only.* **Accommodation:** *2 rooms, from £55.*

---

ITTERINGHAM, NORFOLK 6–4C

**Walpole Arms** £ 35 Ⓐ★

The Common, Itteringham NR11 7AR (01263) 587258
*"Wonderfully inventive but simple food, perfectly executed" is winning an ever-bigger reputation for this "lovely old pub, in the middle of nowhere"; strongly approved by almost all who report on it, it gets "very busy".* / **Sample dishes:** *salad of squid; ham-wrapped pork with garlic mash; Italian chocolate & almond torte.*
**Details:** *www.thewalpolearms.co.uk; 9.30 pm; closed Sun D; no Amex; smoking in bar only.*

---

IVER, BUCKINGHAMSHIRE 3–3A

**The Swan** £ 36 ★

2 High St SL0 9NG (01753) 655776
*A modern gastropub in a 16th-century coaching inn – reporters hail both the "thoughtful modernisation" of the building and the "scrummy" cooking.* / **Sample dishes:** *risotto of scallops, red wine sauce, Parmesan; grilled chicken, spinach & wild mushroom ravioli; champagne-poached strawberries.* **Details:** *www.theswaniver.co.uk; 10 pm; closed Sun D; no smoking area.*

---

JERSEY, CHANNEL ISLANDS

**Bohemia** £ 57 Ⓐ★★

Green St, St Helier JE2 4UH (01534) 880588
*With "food that's second to none" (seafood especially), service that's "always great" and "a wonderful ambience", this exceptional two-year-old is emerging as a major gastronomic destination.* / **Sample dishes:** *velouté of Jersey white crab; confit of belly pork; summer berry flavours.* **Details:** *www.bohemiajersey.com; 10 pm; closed Sun; smoking in bar only.*

**Longueville Manor** £ 74 Ⓐ★

Longueville Rd, St Saviour JE2 7WF (01534) 725501
*This grand (Relais & Chateaux) country house hotel has long had a lofty culinary reputation, and – on limited feedback – was again praised this year for its "very attentive" service and "excellent" cuisine.* / **Sample dishes:** *foie gras terrine; brill & calamari with aromatic noodles; mint & white chocolate soufflé.* **Details:** *www.longuevillemanor.com; 9.30 pm; no smoking area.* **Accommodation:** *31 rooms, from £230.*

**sign up for the survey at www.hardens.com**

## JEVINGTON, EAST SUSSEX                    3–4B

### Hungry Monk                    £ 44          Ⓐ
Long Jevington Rd  BN26 5QF   (01323) 482178
*"Good eating in a desert" – its cuisine may not set the world
on fire, but this cutely-housed '60s-veteran is worth knowing about
(not least as the self-proclaimed birthplace of Banoffi pie).*
/ **Sample dishes:** crab & avocado tian; lamb with Moroccan-spiced crust &
butternut squash; baked chocolate & raspberry Alaska.
**Details:** www.hungrymonk.co.uk; 5m W of Eastbourne; 9.30 pm; D only, ex Sun
open L & D; no smoking; children: 5+.

---

## KENILWORTH, WARWICKSHIRE                    5–4C

### Bosquet                    £ 47          ★★
97a Warwick Rd  CV8 1HP   (01926) 852463
*"Formerly very good, now superb" – the Lignier family's small
Gallic restaurant celebrated its quarter-century with cracking
reports; the "classic" cuisine is "excellent, and beautifully
presented", and service is "friendly" too.* / **Sample dishes:** watercress
soup with caviar; roast veal with chive & cream sauce; blueberry & almond tart.
**Details:** www.restaurantbosquet.co.uk; 9.30 pm; closed Mon, Sat L & Sun; closed
Aug; no smoking.

### Simply Simpsons                    £ 47          ★
101-103 Warwick Rd  CV8 1HL   (01926) 864567
*"A sister to the top-class Simpson's" – this "smart" bistro
"has maintained standards" since the main operation moved
to Brum; the style is "more relaxed" nowadays, "and all the better
for it".* / **Sample dishes:** haddock, cod & salmon fishcakes; breast of corn-fed
chicken; crêpes Suzette. **Details:** www.simplysimpsons.com; 9.30 pm, Fri & Sat
10 pm; closed Mon & Sun; no smoking.

---

## KIBWORTH BEAUCHAMP, LEICESTERSHIRE           5–4D

### Firenze                    £ 34          Ⓐ★
9 Station St  LE8 0LN   (0116) 2796260
*Leno and Sarah Poli's "lovely 'nouvelle' Italian" wins enthusiastic
endorsements for its "very good" cooking – some of "the best
in Leicestershire".* / **Sample dishes:** tomato Mozzarella salad with basil
dressing; rib-eye steak with creamed onions & pancetta; rich chocolate pudding with
almonds & apricots. **Details:** www.firenze.co.uk; 10 pm; closed Mon & Sun;
no Amex; no smoking area.

---

## KILLIECRANKIE, PERTH & KINROSS               9–3C

### Killiecrankie House Hotel           £ 42          Ⓐ
PH16 5LG   (01796) 473220
*One of the proprietors "was the chief-buyer for Oddbins" and the
"diverse" wine list at this Victorian country house hotel has
"good vintages, no rubbish and reasonable prices" – it also
somewhat overshadows the cooking.* / **Sample dishes:** seared scallops;
fillet of Highland venison; dark chocolate mousse flan with red wine syrup.
**Details:** www.killiecrankiehotel.co.uk; 8.30 pm; no Amex; no smoking; children: 10.
**Accommodation:** 10 rooms, from £158.

**sign up for the survey at www.hardens.com**

---

### KILLIN, PERTHSHIRE 9–3C

**Ardeonaig Hotel & Restaurant** £51    𝔸
South Loch Tay Side FK21 8SU (01567) 820400
*"A stylish country inn, with a South African ambience" (and a wine list to match), which benefits from a "superb lochside location" and "friendly and unobtrusive service"; the food seems to play something of a supporting rôle. / **Sample dishes:** braised oxtail; chocolate pudding with a liquid centre. **Details:** www.ardeonaighotel.co.uk; 9 pm; no Amex; smoking in bar only; children: 12+.*

---

### KINCLAVAN, PERTH & KINROSS 9–3C

**Ballathie House** £57    𝔸★
PH1 4QN (01250) 883268
*"A very attractive location", overlooking the Tay, is only part of the attraction of this grand country house hotel, which – despite the odd misfire – was generally praised by reporters for its "well-presented" food. / **Sample dishes:** truffle-roasted squab pigeon; seared scallops with chilli polenta & pesto; glazed passion fruit tart. **Details:** www.ballathiehousehotel.com; off B9099,take right from 1m N of Stanley; 8.45 pm; no jeans; no smoking. **Accommodation:** 42 rooms, from £178.*

---

### KINGSTON UPON THAMES, SURREY 3–3B

**Ayudhya** £30    ★
14 Kingston Hill KT2 7NH (020) 8549 5984
*"Inexpensive, but much above-average" – this Thai restaurant is consistently praised by reporters for its "fresh, nicely-presented dishes". / **Sample dishes:** chicken satay; spicy mixed seafood; banana fritters. **Details:** www.ayudhya-kingston.com; 11 pm, Mon & Sun 10.30 pm; closed Mon L; no Amex; no smoking area.*

**Frère Jacques** £33    𝔸
10-12 Riverside Walk KT1 1QN (020) 8546 1332
*"A lively French restaurant with lovely views of the Thames" (near Kingston Bridge); all reviewers agree that its "straightforward" Gallic cuisine comes at "reasonable" prices (the 'Rapide' menu being especially good value). / **Sample dishes:** smoked salmon; liver; crème brûlée. **Details:** www.frerejacques.co.uk; next to Kingston Bridge and the market place; 11 pm; no smoking area.*

---

### KINGSTON, SURREY 3–3A

**Riverside Vegetaria** £26    ★
64 High St KT1 1HN (020) 8546 7992
*The "interesting" vegetarian menu (from "Indian and Caribbean to less spicy dishes") comes in "generous portions" at this Thames-side spot; it is consistently praised by all reporters. / **Sample dishes:** organic carrot & coriander soup; aubergine & spinach gratin. **Details:** www.rsveg.plus.com; 10 mins walk from Kingston BR; 11 pm; no Amex; no smoking; children: 18+ ex L.*

**sign up for the survey at www.hardens.com**

## KINGUSSIE, HIGHLAND 9–2C

**The Cross** £ 48 Ⓐ★

Tweed Mill Brae, Ardbroilach Rd PH21 1LB
(01540) 661166

"Wonderful in every respect"; there isn't a huge amount
of feedback on this "friendly" restaurant-with-rooms in the
Cairngorms National Park – such as there is confirms it "never
disappoints". / **Sample dishes:** slow-roast pork belly & langoustines; rack of
lamb dauphinoise; hot chocolate fondant. **Details:** www.thecross.co.uk; head uphill
on Ardbroilach Rd, turn left into private drive after traffic lights; 8.30 pm; D only,
closed Mon & Sun; no smoking area; children: 9+. **Accommodation:** 8 rooms,
from £75.

## KIRKBY LONSDALE, CUMBRIA 7–4D

**Avanti** £ 32

57 Main St LA6 2AH (01524) 273500

"Above a lively bar", this stylish venture – with its "Mediterranean
atmosphere" and "innovative" menu – comes as something of a
surprise in a "Cumbrian market town". / **Details:** 10 pm; no Amex;
no smoking.

## KIRKHAM, LANCASHIRE 5–1A

**Cromwellian** £ 35 ★

16 Poulton St PR4 2AB (01772) 685680

"It may look like a tea room, but the food is far better than most
local restaurants" – this establishment of over 20 years' standing
is still praised for its "excellent, simple cooking". / **Sample dishes:** hot
potted shrimps in spiced brandy butter; fillet steak with Stilton; apple upside down
sponge pudding. **Details:** 9 pm; D only, closed Mon & Sun; no Amex;
no smoking area.

## KNIGHTWICK, WORCESTERSHIRE 2–1B

**The Talbot** £ 39

WR6 5PH (01886) 821235

A "favourite" pub-cum-microbrewery, next to a river – it has
a "pretty good restaurant", but is "worth a visit, for the speciality
beers alone". / **Sample dishes:** chicken liver parfait; slow roast shoulder
of lamb; white chocolate cheesecake. **Details:** www.the-talbot.co.uk; 9m from
Worcester on A44; 9 pm; no smoking area. **Accommodation:** 11 rooms,
from £75.

## KNOSSINGTON, LEICESTERSHIRE 5–4D

**Fox & Hounds** £ 31 Ⓐ

6 Somerby Rd LE15 8LY (01664) 454676

This "lovely" pub – in a charming, small village near Oakham –
has been "tastefully-modernised" and serves "simple", "high-
quality" food; 'Heat' readers will wish to know that the
chef/patron used to cook for Elton John. / **Sample dishes:** chicken liver
parfait, balsamic onions; grilled breast of chicken with creamy leeks & tarragon;
crème brûlée. **Details:** www.foxandhounds.biz; 9.30 pm; no Amex;
no smoking area.

---

### KNUTSFORD, CHESHIRE      5–2B

**Belle Époque**      £ 45     A

King St WA16 6DT (01565) 633060

*This rare and intriguing art nouveau building – perhaps Cheshire's only restaurant 'landmark' – could be so good; sadly, a number of reports tend to confirm the view that it's "lost the plot" in recent times. / **Sample dishes:** Tuscan spring salad; sea bass with red onion salsa; apricot fritters with Cointreau mousse. **Details:** www.thebelleepoque.com; 1.5m from M6, J19; 10 pm; closed Sat L & Sun D; no smoking area; booking: max 6, Sat. **Accommodation:** 6 rooms, from £80.*

---

### LACOCK, WILTSHIRE      2–2C

**At the Sign of the Angel**      £ 39     A

6 Church St SN15 2LB (01249) 730230

*"A good place to eat in a very pretty (National Trust) village"; this ancient inn offers "traditional" fare in an "unpretentious" manner. / **Sample dishes:** Stilton & walnut pâté; steak & kidney pudding; crème brûlée. **Details:** www.lacock.co.uk; close to M4, J17; 9 pm; closed Mon L; no smoking area. **Accommodation:** 6 rooms, from £105.*

---

### LANCASTER, LANCASHIRE      5–1A

**Bay Horse**      £ 37     ★

Bay Horse Ln LA2 0HR (01524) 791204

*"A useful recommendation for M6 travellers", this "very good gastropub" is unanimously hailed for the quality of Craig Wilkinson's "careful" and "reliable" cuisine. / **Sample dishes:** potted Morecambe Bay shrimps; braised lamb with ale & thyme sauce; lemon tart & lemon fruit ice. **Details:** www.bayhorseinn.com; 0.75m S of A6, J33 M6; 9 pm; closed Mon & Sun D; no Amex; smoking in bar only.*

**Pizza Margherita**      £ 22

2 Moor Ln LA1 1QD (01524) 36333

*"Still a happy place after all these years" – 27, to be precise – this pizzeria (owned by the sister of the founder of PizzaExpress) is "always welcoming", and "good value" too. / **Sample dishes:** garlic bread with cheese; pizza; dime bar crunch pie. **Details:** www.pizza-margherita.co.uk; 10.30 pm.*

**Simply French**      £ 29     A

27a St Georges Quay LA1 1RD (01524) 843199

*A bistro of ten years' standing, with a "nice location" on the river; the occasional reporter feels it's "average", but most applaud its "reliable" fare and "very friendly and casual" style. / **Sample dishes:** fig, asparagus & Mozzarella salad; grilled duck breast; Belgian white chocolate cheesecake. **Details:** www.quitesimplyfrench.co.uk; 9.30 pm; closed weekday L; no Amex.*

**Sultan of Lancaster**      £ 20     A★

Old Church, Brock St LA1 1UU (01524) 61188

*"Wonderful service and very good food" is the theme of all commentary on this "excellent curry house", atmospherically housed in a former Methodist chapel; "lovely lassis, etc" compensate for the absence of alcohol. / **Sample dishes:** onion pakora; tikka masala; coconut supreme. **Details:** www.sultanoflancaster.com; 11 pm; D only; no Amex.*

## LANGAR, NOTTINGHAMSHIRE          5–3D

**Langar Hall**          £ 44          Ⓐ
Church Ln  NG13 9HG   (01949) 860559
*"Imogen Skirving's entertaining personal service"* can add much
to a visit to the *"romantic"* dining room of her country house hotel
(which boasts a *"wonderfully bucolic setting"*); *"locally-sourced
ingredients"* help create *"good"* (if *"slightly pricey"*) dishes.
/ **Sample dishes:** asparagus & pea soup; roast duck; banana parfait with caramel
ice. **Details:** www.langarhall.com; off A52 between Nottingham & Grantham; 9 pm;
no smoking. **Accommodation:** 12 rooms, from £150.

## LANGHO, LANCASHIRE          5–1B

**Northcote Manor**          £ 63          Ⓐ★★
Northcote Rd  BB6 8BE   (01254) 240555
*"The best in the North West"*; Nigel Haworth's *"creative"* cuisine
– *"giving Lancashire produce star billing"* – remains the hallmark
of this *"charming and unpretentious"* restaurant-with-rooms,
in the Ribble Valley. / **Sample dishes:** black pudding & pink trout; lamb with
lemon marmalade & chive mash; apple crumble soufflé.
**Details:** www.northcotemanor.com; M6, J31 then A59; 9.30 pm; no smoking.
**Accommodation:** 14 rooms, from £140.

## LANGSHOTT, SURREY          3–3B

**Langshott Manor**          £ 59          Ⓐ
Ladbroke Rd  RH6 9LN   (01293) 786680
*Despite being only a few minutes from Gatwick, this Elizabethan
manor house hotel is of note for its "good all-round standards";
options include a "top-class restaurant" ("with all the trimmings
you expect at this price") and also a brasserie.*
/ **Sample dishes:** smoked salmon; grilled Scottish beef fillets with mashed potatoes;
assiette of Swiss chocolate. **Details:** www.langshottmanor.com, 9.30 pm;
no smoking. **Accommodation:** 22 rooms, from £190.

## LANGTON GREEN, KENT          3–4B

**The Hare**          £ 32          ★
Langton Rd  TN3 0JA   (01892) 862419
*This "beautiful village pub" occupies a large Edwardian building,
and its "well-cooked" cuisine "exceeds expectations"; "all ages are
catered for" too.* / **Sample dishes:** bacon, lentil & goat's cheese tart; seared
salmon with sweetcorn fritters; Malibu roulade with pineapple.
**Details:** www.hare-tunbridgewells.co.uk; on A264 to East Grinstead; 9.30 pm;
no Amex; no smoking area.

## LAPWORTH, WARWICKSHIRE          5–4C

**The Boot**          £ 36          Ⓐ
Old Warwick Rd  B94 6JU   (01564) 782464
*"An interesting menu"*, *"lots of choice"*, *"unobtrusive service"* and
*"very good-value lunch menus"* are among the pluses fans see
at this *"lovely"* (in a slightly *"Footballers' Wives"* way) canalside
pub. / **Sample dishes:** rustic bread with olive oil; chicken with goats cheese &
saffron; strawberry & mint crème brûlée. **Details:** www.thebootatlapworth.co.uk;
off A34; 10 pm; no Amex; smoking in bar only.

## LAUGHARNE, CAMARTHEN  4–4C

### Hurst House  £ 47  A★

East Marsh  SA33 4RS  (01994) 427417

"A bit of Notting Hill in west Wales", this "cool" and "chic" restaurant-with-rooms is "a special place" – even those who find it "eccentric" and "infuriating" also say it's "delightful". / **Sample dishes:** melon with blackcurrant sorbet; honey-roasted quail with wild rice & apricots; pecan & banana tart. **Details:** www.hurst-house.co.uk; 10 pm; no smoking area. **Accommodation:** 7 rooms, from £125.

## LAVENHAM, SUFFOLK  3–1C

### Angel  £ 31  ★

Market Pl  CO10 9QZ  (01787) 247388

A very popular gastropub – in a 14th-century inn, on the marketplace – where the cooking is universally hailed as "well-prepared and interesting". / **Sample dishes:** smoked salmon trout; duck's breast with juniper & mushroom sauce; sticky pudding. **Details:** www.lavenham.co.uk/angel; on A1141 6m NE of Sudbury; 9.15 pm; no smoking. **Accommodation:** 8 rooms, from £80.

### Great House  £ 38  A★★

Market Pl  CO10 9QZ  (01787) 247431

"Very good French-style food, using local produce, in a beautiful setting" – the key ingredients which make the Crépy family's half-timbered house a destination that "never disappoints". / **Sample dishes:** moules marinière; venison in red wine with duck foie gras sauce; saffron crème brûlée. **Details:** www.greathouse.co.uk; follow directions to Guildhall; 9.30 pm; closed Mon & Sun D; closed Jan; no Amex; no smoking. **Accommodation:** 5 rooms, from £96.

### Swan Hotel  £ 43

High St  CO10 9QA  (01787) 247477

This ancient inn – with its "amazing double-height medieval beamed dining room" – inspired unsettled reports in the year that's seen its transition to individual ownership; a proper appraisal of the new régime will therefore have to wait until the next edition. / **Sample dishes:** salmon & smoked haddock fishcakes; roast cannon of lamb; chocolate fondant with a chocolate orange sorbet. **Details:** www.theswanatlavenham.co.uk; 9.30 pm; no jeans or trainers; no smoking; children: not in main restaurant in evening. **Accommodation:** 51 rooms, from £140.

## LEEDS, WEST YORKSHIRE  5–1C

Especially as its city-centre restaurant scene is not large compared to, say, Manchester's, it's impressive how Leeds achieves occasional flashes of brilliance of a type which have tended to elude its larger rival. The long-term success story, *Pool Court at 42* (if not quite on top form of late) has in recent years been complemented by *No 3 York Place* and now by the extraordinarily accomplished *Anthony's*.

Otherwise, Leeds can offer something for most tastes, even if a number of places have reputations rather bigger than – reports suggest – the quality of their operation.

**sign up for the survey at www.hardens.com**  253

### Aagrah £24 ★

Aberford Rd LS25 2HF (0113) 287 6606
*"Consistent quality and a good range of dishes" is part of the package that makes this "modern" chain-outlet "a great Indian".*
/ **Details:** www.aagrah.com; from A1 take A642 Aberford Rd to Garforth;
11.30 pm; D only; no smoking area.

### Amigos £21 A

70 Abbey Rd LS5 3JG (0113) 228 3737
*"Sunny" staff contribute to the "you'd-think-you-were-in-Spain" vibe of this ever-popular tapas bar, near Kirkstall Abbey; now that it's licensed, you can no longer BYO.* / **Sample dishes:** meatballs
in chilli & tomato sauce; paella; Manchego cheese with apple.
**Details:** www.amigostapasbar.com; on A65 in Kirkstall; 11 pm; closed Sun;
no Amex.

### Anthony's £54 ★★

19 Boar Ln LS1 6EA
(0113) 245 5922
*"The best food in Leeds, possibly the country"; Anthony Flynn's "Yorkshire version of El Bulli" – the Spanish culinary cauldron where he was a 'stagiaire' – is making huge waves with its "molecular-without-being-silly" gastronomy; "immaculate" service helps take the edge off a dining room which is "too minimalist" for some tastes.* / **Sample dishes:** roast langoustine with fennel tea consommé;
roast duck with chocolate & olive oil bonbon; peanut ice cream in artichoke caramel.
**Details:** www.anthonysrestaurant.co.uk; 9.30 pm; closed Mon & Sun; no Amex;
no smoking area.

### Art's £33 A

42 Call Ln LS1 6DT (0113) 243 8243
*Still "the best place to while away an afternoon in Leeds city-centre" – this "bright" bar/café isn't trying to win any culinary awards, but offers "tasty food" in a "trendy" setting.*
/ **Sample dishes:** seared king scallops with risotto; sticky toffee pudding.
**Details:** www.artscafebar.co.uk; near Corn Exchange; 10 pm, Fri & Sat 10.30 pm;
no smoking area; no booking, Sat & Sun L.

### Bibis £43 A

Criterion Pl, Swinegate LS1 4AG (0113) 243 0905
*"What a place!" – the "glitzy" and "glamorous" Art Deco-style new premises of this local institution (of nearly 30 years' standing) have a style like "you only ever see in the movies"; the ambience is far too "frenetic" for some tastes, though, and the Italian food is no more than "not bad".* / **Sample dishes:** beef tomatoes with basil oil
dressing; pigeon & foie gras terrine; chocolate & amaretto cake.
**Details:** www.bibisrestaurant.com; 11.30 pm; no booking, Sat.

### Brasserie Forty Four £38

44 The Calls LS2 7EW (0113) 234 3232
*This perennially "fashionable" waterside brasserie "does most things well" and is "still buzzing, after all these years"; "the food doesn't scale the heights, but it's not meant to".*
/ **Sample dishes:** smoked Polish sausage; chocolate & amaretto fondue.
**Details:** www.brasserie44.com; 10 pm, Fri & Sat 11 pm; closed Sat L & Sun.

**sign up for the survey at www.hardens.com**

## Brio £36 ★
40 Great George St LS1 3DL (0113) 246 5225
*"Classy, slick, and friendly"*, this city-centre Italian is warmly
praised by all reporters for its *"gorgeous"* food; the pizzeria-
offshoot (at 28 The Headrow, tel 243 5533) is also popular –
*"better than any chain, and not expensive"*. / **Sample dishes:** seared
beef; sticky toffee pudding. **Details:** www.brios.co.uk; 10.30 pm; closed Sun.

## Bryan's £29
9 Weetwood Ln LS16 5LT (0113) 278 5679
*This famous chippy has inspired slightly lacklustre reports
in recent times; as we go to press, however, a total revamp
is nearing completion.* / **Sample dishes:** chicken goujons with spicy BBQ dip;
treacle sponge & custard. **Details:** off Otterley Rd; 9.30 pm, Sun 7 pm; no Amex;
no smoking; need 8+ to book.

## The Calls Grill £37
38 The Calls LS2 7EW (0113) 245 3870
*"A lovely canalside setting"* adds to the attraction of this
*"enjoyable"* brasserie, which offers *"simple, plain and well-
cooked"* dishes at *"reasonable prices"*. / **Sample dishes:** sauteed black
pudding with crispy bacon; Dover sole with citrus butter; caramel crème brûlée.
**Details:** www.callsgrill.co.uk; opp Tetleys brewery on waterfront; 10.30 pm; closed
Mon L, Sat L & Sun; no smoking; booking: max 6, Sat.

## Casa Mia Grande £35
33-35 Harrogate Rd LS7 3PD (0870) 444 5154
*Leeds's 'Casa Mia' Italian brand has grown like Topsy in recent
times, and now encompasses offshoots both at 10-12 Steinbeck
Lane and Millennium Square (same tel throughout); there is a
general feeling, though, that the empire is getting "too big for its
boots", and risks offering "poor value" all round.*
/ **Sample dishes:** smoked chicken salad with mango vinaigrette; honey-roast salmon
with spinach & lemon sauce; tiramisu. **Details:** www.casamiaonline.co.uk;
10.30 pm, Fri & Sat 11 pm; no smoking area.

## Darbar £34 A★
16-17 Kirkgate LS1 6BY (0113) 246 0381
*"Enter another world"*, when you visit this extraordinary city-
centre subcontinental – after the decidedly ordinary entrance,
its *"fantastic"* décor comes as a surprise, as does the *"great"*
food. / **Sample dishes:** mixed kebab platter; lamb with spinach; kulfi.
**Details:** www.darbar.co.uk; midnight; closed Sun; no smoking.

## Dare Café £19
49 Otley Rd LS6 3AB (0113) 230 2828
*This Mexican café in Headingley is of the type which makes
a classic "Sunday morning brunch destination"; it's "a friendly and
lively place that's always trying to improve".*
/ **Sample dishes:** tomato & Mozzarella salad; chicken fajitas; chocolate fudge cake.
**Details:** 10 pm; no smoking area.

### Dough Bakery £26
293 Spen Ln LS16 5BD (0113) 278 7255
*"Wholesome", "original" food and a welcoming atmosphere has made for some "great nights out" at this BYO bistro; as this guide goes to press, Wayne Newsome has sold out (but plans to remain at the stoves), and a refurb is planned – hence we've left it unrated. / **Sample dishes:*** rabbit & foie gras; organic pork with butter beans; hot chocolate fondant. **Details:** 9.30 pm; D only, closed Mon & Sun; no credit cards; no smoking.

### Flying Pizza £29
60 Street Ln LS8 2DQ (0113) 266 6501
*Even fans admit that it's "a bit flashy", but they insist that this locally (in)famous Roundhay pizzeria – full of "Hyacinth Buckets", and Sir Jimmy Saville – "does the business"; for doubters, though, it's just "living on its reputation". / **Sample dishes:*** rolled Italian ham with Mozzarella; chicken with farfalle in spicy tomato sauce; tiramisu. **Details:** www.theflyingpizza.co.uk; just off A61, 3m N of city centre; 11 pm, Thu-Sat 11.30 pm; no smoking area.

### Fourth Floor Café
### Harvey Nichols £34　　🅐
107-111 Briggate LS1 6AZ (0113) 204 8000
*One of the better Harvey Nics dining operations – the food, if "a bit expensive", is also "imaginative"; on some accounts, this is "the place to be seen" in Leeds, and certainly offers "plenty of people-watching". / **Sample dishes:*** smoked chicken with pears & Roquefort; rib-eye steak with sweet potato mash; passion fruit mousse. **Details:** www.harveynichols.com; 10 pm; L only, except Thu-Sat when L & D; no smoking area; no booking, Sat L.

### Fuji Hiro £17
45 Wade Ln LS2 8NJ (0113) 243 9184
*This "dependable" and "basic" noodle bar is "very popular" locally; for most reporters, it "never fails to satisfy". / **Sample dishes:*** dumplings; pan-fried noodles with vegetables. **Details:** 10 pm, Fri & Sat 11 pm; no credit cards; no smoking; need 5+ to book.

### La Grillade £33　　🅐
Wellington St LS1 4HJ (0113) 245 9707
*Leeds's "longest-established business restaurant" is a "typically Gallic" bistro – with its "candles and cellars and simple food", it reliably hits the spot. / **Sample dishes:*** French onion soup; char-grilled rib-eye steak; bread & butter pudding. **Details:** 10.30 pm; closed Sat L & Sun.

### Hansa's £23　　★★
72-74 North St LS2 7PN (0113) 244 4408
*"Wonderful", "delicately-spiced" cooking – "in a different league from a standard curry house" – has made Mrs Hansa Dabhi's Gujarati (vegetarian) destination popular for two decades now, and the ratings it attracts are currently on a high. / **Sample dishes:*** samosas; chicken curries; kulfi. **Details:** www.hansasrestaurant.com; 10 pm, Fri & Sat 11 pm; D only, ex Sun L only; no Amex; no smoking area; children: under 5s eat free.

**Leodis** £38

Victoria Mill, Sovereign St LS1 4BJ  (0113) 242 1010

*Fans insist this "pricey" canalside brasserie is "consistently good",
and praise its "terrific buzz"; doubters find it "really past its best",
though, in particular citing sometimes "snooty and slapdash"
service.* / **Sample dishes:** bacon & poached egg salad; steak & kidney sausages
with mash; chocolate nut brownie. **Details:** www.leodis.co.uk; 10 pm; closed
Sat L & Sun.

**Little Tokyo** £19 ★

24 Central Rd LS1 6DE  (0113) 2439090

*"Brilliant sushi", "great bento boxes" and "steaming bowls
of noodles" are the mainstay of this "tucked-away" Japanese,
which inspires many reports despite its backstreet location –
almost all to the effect that it's an all-round "gem".*
/ **Details:** www.littletokyo.co.uk; 10 pm, Fri & Sat 11 pm; closed Sun; no smoking;
need 8+ to book.

**Lucky Dragon** £27 ★★

Templar Ln LS2 7LP  (0113) 245 0520

*"A brilliant, long-established Chinese restaurant that just keeps
on getting better!"; this city-centre institution – "full of oriental
customers" – wins rave reviews for its "dim sum to die for"
(as well as its full meals).* / **Sample dishes:** sweet & sour chicken; fillet steak
Cantonese-style; prawn in chilli sauce. **Details:** 11.30 pm.

**Maxi's** £28

6 Bingley St LS3 1LX  (0113) 244 0552

*This "massive" Chinese restaurant is still hailed by some
as "the best in town"; as last year, though, there are a fair few
reporters who feel its standards are becoming "disappointing,
for a Leeds institution".* / **Sample dishes:** prawn toast with sesame seeds;
steak with ginger & spring onions; toffee bananas. **Details:** www.maxi-s.co.uk;
11.15 pm; no smoking area.

**Millrace** £35 ★

2-4 Commercial Rd LS5 3AQ  (0113) 275 7555

*Fans are hugely impressed by this "superb organic restaurant",
where the early-week menus, in particular, offer "exceptional
value for money"; the odd doubter, though, finds it rather "self-
important".* / **Sample dishes:** seared scallops; roast ham with smoked Cheddar
hash; triple chocolate cheesecake. **Details:** www.themillrace-organic.com;
near Kirkstall Abbey; 9 pm; D only; no Amex; no smoking.

**No 3 York Place** £46 Ⓐ★

3 York Pl LS1 2DR  (0113) 245 9922

*This "classy", contemporary brasserie in the city-centre offers
a winning all-round 'package' comprising "classic, Gallic-inspired
cooking", "top-notch" service and "a very good cellar"; get one
of the booths if you can.* / **Sample dishes:** lobster, mango & avocado salad
with basil oil; pig's trotter stuffed with ham hock; blood orange mousse.
**Details:** www.no3yorkplace.co.uk; 10 pm; closed Sat L & Sun; smoking in bar only.

**sign up for the survey at www.hardens.com**

### Pool Court at 42 £63
44 The Calls LS2 7EW (0113) 244 4242
*"Unbeatable food, beautifully presented"* has helped make this
canalside design-hotel dining room pre-eminent in Leeds for over
a decade; the *"unchanged"* décor can seem a little *"cold"*, though,
and a vociferous minority of critics finds the cooking
to *"lack panache"* nowadays. / **Sample dishes:** roast sea scallops; venison;
chilled pineapple & lemongrass soup. **Details:** www.poolcourt.com; 10 pm,
Sat 8.30 pm; closed Sat L & Sun; no Amex; no smoking; children: 3+.

### Quantro £35
62a Street Ln LS8 2DQ (0113) 288 8063
*"Good food with a twist"* helps inspire mostly warm feedback
on this Roundhay venture – an offshoot of a restaurant
in Harrogate; service can be *"indifferent"*, though, and the
occasional reporter finds the place *"pricey"* or *"pretentious"*.
/ **Sample dishes:** braised oxtail; venison with caramelised pear & dauphinoise
potatoes; soft dark chocolate pudding with lavender crème brûlée.
**Details:** www.quantro.co.uk; 10 pm; closed Sun; no smoking; children: 8+.

### The Reliance £26 🄰
76-78 North St LS2 7PN (0113) 295 6060
This *"shabby-chic"* bar near the Grand Theatre is consistently
popular as a *"cool"* destination (ideal for weekend breakfasts,
for example); *"good food"* (*"except for veggies"*) and/or
an *"interesting"* wine list also figure in most reports.
/ **Sample dishes:** sweet deep-fried calamari & whitebait; roasted pheasant; banoffi
pie. **Details:** www.the-reliance.co.uk; 10.30 pm; no smoking area; no booking.

### Room £41
Bond Hs, The Bourse Courtyard LS1 5DE (0113) 242 6161
This *"stylish bar/restaurant"*, near the Marriott Hotel, can deliver
some *"well-executed food"*; the ambience doesn't always gel,
though – it can be *"a bit lacking at lunch"*, or *"a cross between
a disco and a restaurant at night"*. / **Sample dishes:** prawn avocado
cocktail; chow mein; cheesecake. **Details:** www.roomrestaurants.com;
11pm (10pm Mon & Tue); closed Sun L; no smoking.

### Sala Thai £30 ★
13-17 Shaw Ln LS6 4DH (0113) 278 8400
Shame about the *"clinical"* ambience – this Headingley Thai
offers consistently *"tasty"* dishes, and *"wonderful"* service too.
/ **Sample dishes:** chicken satay; green curry chicken; Thai custard.
**Details:** www.salathaileeds.com; just off Otley Rd, near Arndale Centre; 11 pm;
closed Sat L & Sun; no smoking area.

### Salvo's £32 🄰★
115 Otley Rd LS6 3PX (0113) 275 5017
*"Consistently good value"* ensures a pretty much constant crush
at this *"buzzy and friendly"* Headingley Italian; perhaps the
opening of the new café two doors away (Salumeria) will take the
pressure off a place that risks becoming *"too popular for its own
good"*! / **Sample dishes:** cured Italian ham & salami; fillet steak; pears poached
in wine. **Details:** www.salvos.co.uk; 2m N of University on A660; 10.30 pm; closed
Sun; no smoking area; no booking at D.

**Sheesh Mahal** £19 ★

346-348 Kirkstall Rd LS4 2DS (0113) 230 4161

*"A queue outside the door" attests to the popularity of this Burley
subcontinental, whose cuisine comes "highly recommended"
by most reporters. / **Sample dishes:** prawn with tomato purée with mild
spices on a chapati; chicken breast with tomatoes, garlic, ginger & fried onions;
vanilla ice cream. **Details:** www.sheeshmahal.co.uk; next to Yorkshire TV centre;
midnight; D only; no smoking area.*

**Simply Heathcote's** £37

Canal Whf, Water Ln LS11 5PS (0113) 244 6611

*An "innovative slant on Yorkshire offal" ("101 things to do with
black pudding") are part of the "twists" on English cooking
at Paul Heathcote's "relaxed" canalside venture – one of the
better properties in this (Lancastrian) chef's portfolio!
/ **Sample dishes:** risotto of balsamic-roasted tomatoes; roast breast of duck with
deep-fried sage macaroni; bread & butter pudding. **Details:** www.heathcotes.co.uk;
off M621, J3, behind Granary Wharf; 10 pm, Sat 11 pm; no smoking.*

**Sous le Nez en Ville** £36

Quebec Hs, Quebec St LS1 2HA (0113) 244 0108

*This "marvellous basement bistro" has been a good city-centre
stand-by since 1991; the food is not much more than "reliable",
but the wines are "fabulous", and the "special-price early-bird
evening menu" is something of a local legend.
/ **Sample dishes:** tempura king prawns; fillet steak; bread & butter pudding.
**Details:** 10pm, Sat 11 pm; closed Sun; no Amex.*

**Sukhothai** £25 ★

8 Regent St LS7 4PE (0113) 237 0141

*"A fantastic, out-of-the-way purveyor of simple cuisine", which
offers "the best Thai food round Leeds". / **Sample dishes:** satay
chicken; roast duck; Thai custard. **Details:** www.thaifood4u.co.uk; 11 pm; D only,
closed Mon; no Amex; no smoking.*

**Tampopo** £25 Ⓐ★

15 South Pde LS1 5QS (0113) 245 1816

*Part of an impressive national chain, this "cheap" and "fast"
noodle-parlour delivers "a decent range of yummy Asian dishes",
with some emphasis on "healthy options". / **Sample dishes:** marinated
grilled beef; udon noodles, shredded leek, red pepper & seafood; ginger crème
brûlée. **Details:** www.tampopo.co.uk; 10.45 pm; no smoking; need 7+ to book.*

**Thai Edge** £42

7 Calverly St LS1 3DY (0113) 243 6333

*Fans insist "you get a real Thai experience" at this "nice-looking"
modern oriental, which inspires a fair volume of feedback; there
are a number of complaints, though, to the effect that it is
"way over-priced". / **Sample dishes:** stuffed squid; tenderloin cooked with
peppers & chilli; mango papaya sorbet. **Details:** www.thaiedge.co.uk; 11 pm;
no smoking.*

**Whitelocks Luncheonette** £19 Ⓐ✕

Turk's Head Yd, off Briggate LS2 6HB (0113) 245 3950

*Any visitor to Leeds should check out this extraordinary Victorian
pub and dining room – and its "traditional" fare – at least once;
"the brilliant ambience makes up for any other faults".
/ **Sample dishes:** crispy chicken strips; steak & Stilton pie; jam roly-poly with
custard. **Details:** 6.45 pm; no smoking in restaurant; children: 18+ only.*

**sign up for the survey at www.hardens.com**

## LEICESTER, LEICESTER CITY 5–4D

### Bobby's £ 20 ★
154-156 Belgrave Rd  LE4 5AT  (0116) 266 0106
*"Needs a lick of paint, but still good"*; this *"friendly"* Golden Mile
veteran – *"basically an Indian sweet shop, with a café attached"*
– serves *"beautifully done"* Gujarati veggie snacks that *"fill you
up for a fiver"*. / **Sample dishes:** deep-fried potato baskets; aubergine stuffed
with peanut & potato; caramelised ice cream. **Details:** www.eatatbobbys.com;
10 pm; no Amex; no smoking.

### Case £ 39
4-6 Hotel St  LE1 5AW  (0116) 251 7675
Leicester's perennially trendy in-place – a loft-style restaurant and
champagne bar near St Martin's – *"needs some competition"*;
some reporters still find the food *"imaginative"*, but too many say
it's *"overpriced"* and *"disappointing"*. / **Sample dishes:** smoked venison
salad with Brie & raspberry dressing; turkey escalope with roast polenta; selection
of miniature desserts. **Details:** www.thecase.co.uk; near the Cathedral; 10.30 pm;
closed Sun; no smoking area.

### Entropy £ 44
3 Dover St  LE1 6PW  (0116) 254 8530
Early reports on Leicester's new trendy hang-out, in a former
industrial unit, are not nearly as copious as we would like,
but they all tend to the view that it's a *"welcoming"* sort of place,
serving *"gourmet"* modern cuisine. / **Sample dishes:** terrine of pig's
head & foie gras; wild sea bass; tarte Tatin with lavender & vanilla ice cream.
**Details:** www.entropylife.com; 10 pm; closed Sun; smoking in bar only.

### Friends Tandoori £ 25 ★
41-43 Belgrave Rd  LE4 6AR  (0116) 266 8809
*"Freshly-spiced cooking that never disappoints"* helps underpin the
upbeat feedback on this large, *"traditional"* curry house – one of
the more comfortable spots on the 'Golden Mile'.
/ **Sample dishes:** samosas; chicken achari with pilau rice; kulfi.
**Details:** www.friendstandoori.co.uk; 11.30 pm; closed Sun; no smoking.

### Jones Cafe £ 32
93 Queens Rd  LE2 1TT  (0116) 270 8830
*"One of the best-value breakfasts, for veggies and meat-eaters
alike"*, especially on *"leisurely Sunday mornings"*,
or *"with children"* – the star feature at this café in Clarendon
Park. / **Sample dishes:** spinach ricotta ravioli; seared loin of lamb with roasted
sweet potato; black cherry parfait. **Details:** 9.30 pm, Fri & Sat 10 pm; closed
Sun D; no Amex; no smoking area.

### The Opera House £ 44 Ⓐ
10 Guildhall Ln  LE1 5FQ  (0116) 223 6666
A *"charming old building"* lends a *"lovely"* ambience to this
*"very intimate"* town-centre restaurant; it can seem
*"so pretentious"*, though, and doubters complain of *"mediocre"*
food and *"rip-off"* prices. / **Sample dishes:** twice-baked Cheddar soufflé;
fillet of Scotch beef fondant with wild mushroom sauce; brioche bread & butter
pudding with vanilla ice cream. **Details:** www.theoperahouserestaurant.co.uk;
10 pm; closed Sun; smoking in bar only.

## Shimla Pinks £28
65-69 London Rd LE2 0PE (0116) 247 1471
*This "busy and lively" outfit near the station is part of a once-notable, national Indian chain that attracts little interest from reporters nowadays; it wins consistent praise for its "friendly" style and "good" dishes. / Sample dishes: chicken shashlik; chicken tawa; ice cream. Details: www.shimla-pinks.com; opp railway station; 11 pm; closed Sat L; no smoking area.*

## Stones £36
29 Millstone Ln LE1 5JN (0116) 291 0004
*Some reporters find it "a bit self-consciously trendy", but this attractive city-centre hang-out (in a converted mill) has been much more consistent of late; its "partly-tapas" formula helps make it "a good place for lunch". / Sample dishes: chorizo; griddled marlin with Caribbean salad of plantain & yams; hot chocolate fondant with clotted cream sorbet. Details: www.stonesrestaurant.co.uk; midnight; closed Sun.*

## The Tiffin £28
1 De Montfort St LE1 7GE (0116) 247 0420
*A "buzzy" Indian, near the railway station, which offers a "great array of dishes" in "large" portions – critics, however, feel that they "lack inspiration". / Sample dishes: chilli-fried chicken; aubergine & tamarind curry; kulfi. Details: www.the-tiffin.co.uk; near railway station; 10.45 pm; closed Sat L & Sun; no smoking area.*

## Watsons £29
5-9 Upper Brown St LE1 5TE (0116) 222 7770
*In a former warehouse, this "open-plan" dining room is generally hailed for its "pleasing" menu and its "discreet" service – attributes that make it a "top business" recommendation hereabouts; the odd detractor, though, says the food is "dull". / Sample dishes: fish soup with rouille; salmon with wok-fried greens; strawberry millefeuille. Details: next to Phoenix Art Theatre; 10.30 pm; closed Sun; smoking in bar only.*

---

## LEIGH ON SEA, ESSEX 3–3C

## Boat Yard £44 Ⓐ
8-13 High St SS9 2EN (01702) 475588
*This "vibrant" modern venture has "a fantastic location on the estuary"; "it's a shame considering its potential", though, that "the food is very inconsistent, and service often bad". / Sample dishes: seared tuna with pickled vegetables; beef with green peppercorn sauce; chocolate tart with clotted cream. Details: www.theboatyardrestaurant.co.uk; near railway station; 10 pm; closed Mon, Tue L & Sun D; no Amex.*

---

## LEIGHTON BUZZARD, BEDFORDSHIRE 3–2A

## The Kings Head £60
Lvinghoe LU7 9EB (01296) 668388
*"Totally traditional and always reliable" – for its fans, this is "the perfect restaurant to be proposed to in, and re-visited for anniversaries"; doubters, though, can find it "on the stuffy side", and "not quite as good as it thinks it is". / Sample dishes: carpaccio of tuna; roasted rump of lamb; variety of French cheeses. Details: www.kingsheadivinghoe.co.uk; 3m N of Tring on B489 to Dunstable; 9.45 pm; closed Sun D; jacket & tie required at D; no smoking.*

## LEINTWARDINE, SHROPSHIRE 5–4A

**Jolly Frog** £39    🅐★
The Todden SY7 0LX (01547) 540298
*This "unfussy" former pub – which "feels like an old-fashioned French restaurant" nowadays – is "hard to fault"; "good fish" is a highlight.* / **Sample dishes:** seared king scallops with beetroot; monkfish with pancetta, spinach & wild mushrooms; white chocolate lasagne with lemon ice cream. **Details:** www.jolly-frog.com; 10.30 pm; closed Mon & Sun D; no Amex; no smoking.

## LEMSFORD, HERTFORDSHIRE 3–2B

**Auberge du Lac
Brocket Hall**  £60    🅐★
AL8 7XG
(01707) 368888
*"A divine lakeside setting opposite Brocket Hall" lends a "romantic" backdrop to this "oasis in the Herts desert" (though, "the interior lacks the charm of the terrace"); doubters find the style of the place "pretentious" and "pricey", but fans say JC Novelli's "assured" cuisine is "worth the expense".*
/ **Sample dishes:** foie gras terrine with Szechuan pepper; glazed pavé of turbot; crispy baked banana with crème caramel. **Details:** www.brockethall.co.uk; on B653 towards Harpenden; 10 pm; closed Mon & Sun D; no jeans or trainers; no smoking area. **Accommodation:** 16 rooms, from £185.

## LEWDOWN, DEVON 1–3C

**Lewtrenchard Manor** £49    🅐★
EX20 4PN (01566) 783256
*An "absolutely beautiful" setting helps create a "lovely", "intimate" ambience at this recently-refurbished Elizabethan country house hotel (part of the Von Essen group); its "labour-intensive" cuisine is rated somewhere between "very good" and "astonishing".* / **Sample dishes:** langoustine cappuccino with truffled leeks; sauteed liver with garlic mash & crispy bacon; apricot bread & butter pudding. **Details:** www.lewtrenchard.co.uk; off A30 between Okehampton & Launceston; 8.45 pm; closed Mon L; no jeans or trainers; no smoking; children: 8+. **Accommodation:** 14 rooms, from £150.

## LEWES, EAST SUSSEX 3–4B

**Circa
Pelham House** £30
BN7 1UN (01273) 471333
*Feedback is sparse but positive on this brasserie newcomer, whose food is simpler than its more established sibling; its "wonderful" location, in a smartly-converted townhouse scores higher than the "imaginative" cooking (and definitely better than the "amateurish" service).* / **Sample dishes:** twice-cooked pork belly; red-star beef fillet; vanilla panna cotta, candied fruits & saffron floss. **Details:** www.pelhamhouse.com; 9.30 pm; no Amex; no smoking. **Accommodation:** 23 rooms, from £110.

## Circa £36

145 High St BN7 1XT (01273) 471777

This "quirky" restaurant is known for its "uncompromising" Asian-Italian menu; perhaps it's no great surprise that cuisine which is "bizarre but wonderful" to some reporters just has "too many ingredients" for others. / **Sample dishes:** Thai buttnernut squash soup; bonito-smoked tiger prawns; vanilla panna cotta. **Details:** www.circacirca.com; 10 pm; closed Mon & Sun; no smoking area.

---

## LIDGATE, SUFFOLK 3–1C

### Star Inn £38 A★

The Street CB8 9PP (01638) 500275

Run by a "welcoming" Spanish family, and offering a "delicious and imaginative Iberian-orientated menu", this "friendly" and "atmospheric" place is certainly not your typical rural boozer; it makes a good find "way off the beaten track". / **Sample dishes:** baby squid; whole-baked sea bass; pavlova. **Details:** on B1063 6m SE of Newmarket; 10 pm; closed Sun D; no smoking.

---

## LIFTON, DEVON 1–3C

### Arundell Arms £46 ★

Fore St PL16 0AA (01566) 784666

Despite the modest name, this is quite a grand small hotel (owned for over 40 years by Anne Voss-Bark: a fly-fisher of some renown); feedback has waxed and waned over time, but current reports (if few in number) speak of "fabulous" meals. / **Sample dishes:** pan-fried sea scallops; casserole of monkfish & Cornish sea bass; quince apple panna cotta. **Details:** www.arundellarms.com; 0.5m off A30, Lifton Down exit; 9.30 pm; no smoking. **Accommodation:** 21 rooms, from £150.

---

## LINCOLN, LINCOLNSHIRE 6–3A

### Browns Pie Shop £31

33 Steep Hill LN2 1LU (01522) 527330

"Easy-going" and "informal", this "popular" and "cramped" medievally-housed restaurant can be a "romantic" place to eat ("if you get a seat downstairs"); its long menu is realised to a standard that's "good, if not great". / **Sample dishes:** Yorkshire pudding with spiced onion gravy; Bailey's cheesecake. **Details:** near the Cathedral; 10 pm; no smoking.

### Jew's House £39

15 The Strait LN2 1JD (01522) 524851

"Variable cooking" – "from sublime to moderate, all on the same occasion" – makes this occupant of a "lovely old building" difficult to recommend definitively; on a good day, though, it can seem "a great find". / **Sample dishes:** pancetta & black pudding; steak with wild mushroom jus; banana with Malibu & chocolate toffee sauce. **Details:** www.thejewshouse.co.uk; halfway down Steep Hill from Cathedral; 9.30 pm; closed Mon & Sun; no smoking.

**The Wig & Mitre** £35 ✗
30-32 Steep Hill LN2 1TL (01522) 535190
*This once-celebrated inn, by the cathedral, is a well-known
"haunt" hereabouts, thanks to its handy all-day opening; quite
a few former fans increasingly feel it's "lost its way", though,
with "no thought to the cooking" and "indifferent" service.*
/ **Sample dishes:** wild mushroom & Madeira soup; chicken in Parma ham with
pistachio & lemon stuffing; baked vanilla cheesecake.
**Details:** www.wigandmitre.com; between Cathedral & Castle; 11 pm; no smoking.

---

LINLITHGOW, WEST LOTHIAN 9–4C
**Champany Inn** £63 Ⓐ★
EH49 7LU (01506) 834532
*"The best steak this side of the Atlantic" (complemented by a
"most impressive wine list") is the culinary highlight of a trip
to this "well-appointed" inn; even fans, though, can find
it "overpriced".* / **Sample dishes:** marinated herring fillets; quail with bacon &
tarragon stuffing; chocolate marquise. **Details:** www.champany.com; 2m NE
of Linlithgow on junction of A904 & A803; 10 pm; closed Sat L & Sun; no jeans
or trainers; children: 8+. **Accommodation:** 16 rooms, from £125.

---

# LIVERPOOL, MERSEYSIDE 5–2A

Liverpool's appearance is being transformed. As in Brum,
however, developments in the culinary scene seem to be
lagging behind those in the architecture, and the restaurants
of any quality still tend to cluster along Hope Street (which
joins the two cathedrals). The street is home to the undoubted
top two restaurants in town – *60 Hope Street* and the upstart
*London Carriage Works* – and that ever popular stand-by,
the *Everyman Bistro*, is not far away.

There are quite a number of Chinese restaurants of some
interest – and a Chinatown – but the 'scene' could not in any
sense be said to rival Manchester's.

**L'Alouette** £40 Ⓐ
2 Lark Ln L17 8US (0151) 727 2142
*Fans say you "can almost imagine yourself on the Left Bank" –
no mean achievement in Sefton Park! – at this long-running local
favourite; the food, however, can seem "just too pricey for simple
brasserie cooking".* / **Sample dishes:** snails & frogs legs in garlic; steak with
Roquefort; lemon tart. **Details:** 10 pm; closed Mon.

**Casa Italia** £22
40 Stanley St L1 6AL (0151) 227 5774
*"Popular, unfussy and quick" – this "reasonably-priced" pizzeria,
in a former-warehouse, "remains a mainstay of the city's Italian
food scene".* / **Sample dishes:** smoked & cured meat platter; Ventresca
bacon & olive pizza; cassata. **Details:** www.thecasaitalia.co.uk; off Victoria St;
10 pm; need 8+ to book.

**Chung Ku** £25
Riverside Drive, Columbus Quay L3 4DB (0151) 726 8191
*"Lovely views across the Mersey" add interest to a visit to this
"very busy" Chinese restaurant; even fans can find the food
"pricey", however, or "not as good as they think it is".*
/ **Sample dishes:** pork & prawn dumplings; chocolate ice cream.
**Details:** www.chungkurestaurant.co.uk; 11.30 pm, Fri & Sat midnight.

**Ego**                                                    **£30**
Federation Hs, Hope St L1 9BS   (0151) 706 0707
*"For a quick meal before the Philharmonic", or for a "good-value
lunch", this Mediterranean bistro (part of a small chain) has its
uses; service, though, is sometimes "atrocious".*
/ **Sample dishes:** Andalucian chicken salad; roast salmon fillet with a langoustine &
spinach sauce; summer berries in wine jelly. **Details:** www.egorestaurants.com;
10.30 pm; smoking in bar only.

**Esteban Tapas Bar**                                      **£21**
40 Lark Ln  L17 8UU   (0151) 727 6056
*"Excellent tapas at good prices" ensure that this "lively" Lark
Lane bar-cum-restaurant is "always packed"; "you even have
to book during the week".* / **Details:** www.estebantapas.com; 10.30 pm;
no Amex; no shorts; no smoking area.

**Everyman Bistro**                                        **£22**            𝔸
5-9 Hope St  L1 9BH   (0151) 708 9545
*This "friendly" self-service bistro is a "long-standing Scouse
institution" (est. 1970), and its "varied" menu and "lively"
atmosphere continue to make it one of the best-known and best-
liked places in town.* / **Sample dishes:** chicken & wild mushroom pâté;
red chilli chicken with yellow rice; plum crumble. **Details:** www.everyman.co.uk;
midnight, Thu-Sat 2 am; closed Sun; no Amex; no smoking area.

**Far East**                                               **£19**
27-35 Berry St  L1 9DF   (0151) 709 3141
*"Many Scouse-orientals" at dinner evidence the attractions of this
cavernous Chinatown fixture (above an oriental cash-and-carry).*
/ **Details:** by church on Berry St; 11 pm; no smoking area.

**Gulshan**                                                **£25**            ★
544-548 Aigburth Rd  L19 3QG   (0151) 427 2273
*"Well-presented dishes at reasonable prices" win this
comparatively "sophisticated" subcontinental many nominations
as the "top Indian" in these parts.* / **Sample dishes:** chicken chat; chicken
green balti; kulfi. **Details:** www.gulshan-liverpool.com; 10.45 pm; D only;
no smoking area.

**Keith's Wine Bar**                                       **£16**            𝔸
107 Lark Ln  L17 8UR   (0151) 728 7688
*"Great cheap eats in a Bohemian atmosphere" is a formula that
keeps this long-standing Sefton Park institution "very popular" –
"you can't always get a seat"; the wine selection
is "very comprehensive" too.* / **Sample dishes:** grilled halloumi with pitta
bread; Spanish-style chicken with rice; sticky toffee pudding. **Details:** 10.30 pm;
need 6+ to book.

**London Carriage Works**              **£40**            𝔸★
40 Hope St  L1 9DA 9DA
(0151) 705 2222
*This "light and airy space, with high ceilings and big sofas" has
been a "stylish addition" to the city, and vies with its neighbour
60 Hope Street as the "cool" place in town; by a whisker,
reporters rate Paul Askew's cooking as "currently Liverpool's best".*
/ **Sample dishes:** smoked salmon platter; tempura tiger prawns with noodles &
sushi nori rolls; daily handmade specialities. **Details:** www.tlcw.co.uk; 10 pm;
no smoking area. **Accommodation:** 48 rooms, from £125.

**sign up for the survey at www.hardens.com**                      265

**Olive Press**                           **£30**
25-27 Castle St  L2 4TA   (0151) 2272242
A "pleasant" city-centre spot (part of the Heathcote empire)
which is popular for its "high-quality pizza, pasta and other
dishes". / **Details:** www.heathcotes.co.uk; 10 pm, Fri & Sat 11 pm;
no smoking area.

**The Other Place**                       **£33**    A★
141-143 Allerton Rd  L18 2DD   (0151) 724 1234
A characterful five-year-old providing "consistent" and "good-
value" cooking to a "nice mix of customers"; it also has a newish
offshoot (at 29a Hope Street, tel 707 7888) which "is good too".
/ **Sample dishes:** goat's cheese & red pepper spring rolls; grilled cod with
hazelnut & herb potato cake; passion fruit & coconut tart. **Details:** 9.30 pm; closed
Mon & Sun D; no Amex; no smoking area.

**Piccolino**                             **£30**
14a Cook St  L2 9QU   (0151) 236 2555
"A great new addition to the Italian ristorante scene", this city-
centre spot has instantly won quite a following; it does strike some
reporters as "a bit corporate and formulaic", but – considering it's
part of a group founded by the people originally responsible for
Est! Est! Est! – rather fewer than you might expect!
/ **Sample dishes:** king prawns with garlic & oil; sea bass with chopped tomatoes;
creamy ice cream, biscuit & chocolate sauce. **Details:** 11 pm.

**Pod**                                   **£24**    A★
137-139 Allerton Rd  L18 2DD   (0151) 724 2255
"An interesting range of tapas from Spain and around the world"
helps maintain the buzz of this popular Allerton destination –
at weekends, it can get "too full". / **Sample dishes:** chicken stuffed with
chorizo & coriander; sticky toffee pudding. **Details:** 9.30 pm; booking: max 6
at weekends.

**Puschka**                               **£33**    A★
16 Rodney St  L1 2TE   (0151) 708 8698
"Very good modern European cooking" and "a friendly
atmosphere" combine to make this "lovely small restaurant"
popular with all reporters; its funky offshoot café (nearby at 39
Hardman Street) also inspires favourable feedback.
/ **Details:** www.puschka.co.uk; midnight; closed Mon, Tue-Thu D only, Sun L only;
no smoking.

**Quarter**                               **£24**
7-11 Falkner St  L8 7PU   (0151) 707 1965
"Perfect for lunch, coffee or after-work meal and drinks" – such is
the appeal of this "easy-going" café operation from the 60 Hope
Street people. / **Sample dishes:** spinach, avocado & bacon salad; goat's cheese
with fettuccine pasta; apple pie & custard. **Details:** 11 pm; no Amex;
no smoking area.

**Sapporo Teppanyaki**                    **£47**
134 Duke St  L1 5AG   (0151) 705 3005
Reporters are divided over this "trendy" and "noisy" Japanese
venture; to fans, it offers an "entertaining" experience with
exemplary food – to detractors it's just "dreadful" and
"overpriced". / **Sample dishes:** deep-fried tofu; duck breast with raspberry;
banana tempura. **Details:** www.sapporo.co.uk; 10.30 pm.

**Simply Heathcote's** £ 37

Beetham Plaza 25, The Strand  L2 0XL  (0151) 236 3536
*Especially as an "excellent lunch stop" (and particularly
on business), this "lively" outpost of Paul Heathcote's brasserie
chain, near the Liver Building, is now winning more consistent
acclaim from reporters.* / **Sample dishes:** *grilled mackerel Caesar salad;
steak, ale & mushroom pie with creamed potatoes; lemon & lime posset.*
**Details:** *www.heathcotes.co.uk; 10 pm; no smoking.*

**60 Hope Street**  £ 45  A★

60 Hope St  L1 9BZ
(0151) 707 6060
*Despite tough competition from its new near-neighbour (London
Carriage Works), this "upmarket" joint remains the best-known
place in town; its good all-round standards include "dependable"
cooking that's "not over-priced".* / **Sample dishes:** *fishcakes with smoked
pepper aioli; lamb with crispy spinach risotto; peanut butter brûlée.*
**Details:** *www.60hopestreet.com; between the Cathedrals; 10.30 pm; closed Sat L &
Sun; no smoking.*

**Tai Pan** £ 23  ★

WH Lung Bdg., Great Howard St  L5 9TZ  (0151) 207 3888
*"Lovely oriental food" and "friendly service" are "let down" by the
"warehouse-style ambience" of this sprawling dining room, above
a supermarket.* / **Sample dishes:** *chicken satay; pork & green peppers in black
bean sauce; ice cream.* **Details:** *11.30 pm, Sun 9.30 pm.*

**Yuet Ben** £ 24  ★

1 Upper Duke St  L1 9DU  (0151) 709 5772
*Liverpool's longest-established oriental, by the Chinatown arch,
is "still the best"; service is "friendly" too.* / **Details:** *www.yuetben.co.uk;
11 pm; D only, closed Mon.*

**Ziba** £ 42

Hargreaves Building, 5 Chapel St  L3 9AG  (0151) 236 6676
*"Still not up to the standards of the old Ziba, despite the
prestigious setting"; it's sad that what was once Liverpool's best
all-rounder has been all but ruined by its transfer to the current
site, in an impressive Victorian club building.*
/ **Sample dishes:** *honey-marinated salmon; grilled salmon with tomato, chickpea &
chorizo stew; rich coffee tiramisu with tuile biscuit.* **Details:** *www.racquetclub.org.uk;
10 pm; closed Sat L & Sun.* **Accommodation:** *8 rooms, from £105.*

LLANDEGLA, WREXHAM 5–3A

**Bodidris Hall Hotel** £ 43  A

LL11 3AL  (0870) 729 2292
*The "lovely" manor house setting is the undoubted attraction
of this romantic hotel, but the food is generally thought to be
pretty "good" too.* / **Sample dishes:** *mosaic of fruits; lamb with leek & mint
mousse; raspberry bavarois.* **Details:** *www.bodidrishall.com; on A5104 from
Wrexham; 8.45 pm; no smoking; children: 14+.* **Accommodation:** *9 rooms,
from £99.*

**sign up for the survey at www.hardens.com** 267

## LLANDRILLO, DENBIGHSHIRE 4–2D
**Tyddyn Llan** £ 49 A★★
LL21 0ST (01490) 440264
The Webbs' small country house hotel is enthusiastically hailed
as a "Welsh gem" by all who comment on it – attractions include
"brilliant cooking, friendly service, comfy seats and, in winter,
a great fire". / Sample dishes: buffalo Mozzarella; fillet of steak; crème brûlée.
**Details:** www.tyddynllan.co.uk; on B4401 between Corwen and Bala; 9 pm; closed
Mon (Tue-Thu L by prior arrangement only); no Amex; no smoking; booking essential
Tue L-Thu L. **Accommodation:** 12 rooms, from £130.

## LLANDUDNO, CONWY 4–1D
**Bodysgallen Hall** £ 54 A★
LL30 1RS (01492) 584466
A new (late-2004) chef "has worked wonders", and the cooking
at this "magnificent" house (set in "lovely" gardens on a hill
outside the resort) now "matches up to the setting".
/ Sample dishes: roast tomato soup with pesto tortellini; roast chicken, foie gras &
mushroom terrine; chocolate & orange tart. **Details:** www.bodysgallen.com; 2m off
A55 on A470; 9.30 pm; no jeans or trainers; no smoking; booking: max 10; children:
6+. **Accommodation:** 35 rooms, from £175.

**Richards** £ 37
7 Church Walks LL30 2HD (01492) 877924
The team which took over this intimate bistro from the
eponymous Richard is "trying hard" – "it's not yet quite as good,
but may improve". / Sample dishes: salmon, halibut & spinach terrine;
pan-fried breast of chicken filled with Mozzarella; plum & almond tart.
**Details:** www.richards-restaurant.co.uk; 9.30 pm; D only, closed Mon & Sun;
no smoking.

**St Tudno Hotel** £ 47 ★
Promenade LL30 2LP (01492) 874411
This dining room of a "lavishly refurbished" hotel, near the pier,
offers cooking that's "very good indeed"; the place's "quiet"
atmosphere, however, can fail to inspire. / Sample dishes: terrine
of pork; pan-fried rump of Welsh spring lamb; chilled cappuccino mousse wrapped
in Belgian chocolate. **Details:** www.st-tudno.co.uk; 9.30 pm; no jeans or shorts;
no smoking area; children: 6+. **Accommodation:** 19 rooms, from £130.

## LLANGOLLEN, DENBIGHSHIRE 5–3A
**Corn Mill** £ 29 A
Dee Ln LL20 8PN (01978) 869555
This "huge former mill" has an ace location, above the River Dee,
at the heart of "the most beautiful valley in Wales";
most reporters praise the "simple" and "well-cooked" dishes,
but the odd cynic says the place's appeal "reflects the dire state
of eating elsewhere hereabouts". / Sample dishes: Caerphilly & leek
tartlet; poached salmon with cherry tomato, spring onion & celery; bread & butter
pudding. **Details:** www.brunningandprice.co.uk; 9.30 pm; no smoking area.

**Gales** £ 30 A
18 Bridge St LL20 8PF (01978) 860089
It's often "hard to get a table" at this "warm" and "friendly"
bistro, which is now heading for three decades in the same
ownership; feedback on the cooking tend to mixed, but all
reporters agree on the quality of the wine list.
/ **Details:** www.galesofllangollen.co.uk; 9.30 pm; closed Sun; no smoking area.
**Accommodation:** 15 rooms, from £60.

## LLANWDDYN, POWYS                      4–2D

**Lake Vyrnwy Hotel**                   £ 44        Ⓐ
Lake Vyrnwy  SY10 0LY  (01691) 870692
*"A lovely setting overlooking the lake" makes this "elderly" hotel,
in a large estate, something of a 'destination'; reviews were
uncharacteristically unsettled this year – let's hope new chef David
Green can restore the formerly high and consistent standards.*
/ **Sample dishes:** *Thai-spiced crab cakes with Asian coleslaw; loin of lamb with
parsley, garlic stuffing & rosemary jus; lime panna cotta with peppered strawberries.*
**Details:** *www.lakevyrnwy.com; on B4393 at SE end of Lake Vyrnwy; 9.15 pm;
no smoking.* **Accommodation:** *35 rooms, from £120.*

## LLANWRTYD WELLS, POWYS                4–4D

**Carlton House Hotel**                 £ 42        Ⓐ★
Dolecoed Rd  LD5 4RA  (01591) 610248
*Cooking of "the very highest standard" ("using rigorously-sourced,
largely local ingredients") is just one of the features of this
"friendly" and "relaxed" restaurant-with-rooms; "the wine list,
though not long, is an education" too.* / **Sample dishes:** *seared king
scallops; warm peppered beef salad; apple & calvados sorbet.*
**Details:** *www.carltonrestaurant.com; 8.30 pm; closed Mon L, Sat L & Sun;
no Amex; no smoking; booking: max 10.* **Accommodation:** *5 rooms, from £70.*

## LLYSWEN, POWYS                        2–1A

**Llangoed Hall**                       £ 59        Ⓐ★
LD3 0YP  (01874) 754525
*Sean Ballington (at the stoves since 2004) is "a chef to watch",
says one of the fans of Sir Bernard Ashley's country house hotel;
feedback is limited though, obliging us to rate the food more
conservatively than is possibly justified.* / **Sample dishes:** *butternut
squash velouté with smoked chicken; herb-crusted lamb with pea purée; seared
pineapple with tarragon sorbet.* **Details:** *www.llangoedhall.com; 11m NW of Brecon
on A470; 9.30 pm; jacket required at D; no smoking; children: 8+.*
**Accommodation:** *23 rooms, from £195.*

## LOCH LOMOND, DUNBARTONSHIRE          9–4B

**Cameron House**                       £ 78        ★
G83 8QZ  (01389) 755565
*Paul Tambourini's "imaginative" cuisine is winning renewed
acclaim for this stunningly-located lochside dining room; it's clearly
"very expensive" though, and – given the advantages of the
setting – the atmosphere can seem a touch "clinical".*
/ **Sample dishes:** *asparagus, leek & mushroom terrine; lobster & langoustine with
black olive pasta; banana tarte Tatin with pineapple sorbet.*
**Details:** *www.cameronhouse.co.uk; over Erskine Bridge to A82, follow signs to Loch
Lomond; 9.45 pm; D only, ex Sun open L & D, closed Mon & Tue; jacket & tie
required; no smoking; children: Not allowed.* **Accommodation:** *96 rooms,
from £245.*

## LOCHINVER, HIGHLAND 9–1B

**Albannach** £56 Ⓐ★

IV27 4LP (01571) 844407

We wouldn't expect a huge number of reports on the dining room of this small hotel, near the coast; the modest feedback we have received, though, hails the cooking as "fantastic".
/ **Sample dishes:** warm crab tartlet; pan-fried duck breast with foie gras; caramelised apple tartlet. **Details:** www.thealbannach.co.uk; 8 pm; D only, closed Mon; no Amex; no smoking; children: 12+. **Accommodation:** 5 rooms, from £210.

## LOCKSBOTTOM, KENT 3–3B

**Chapter One** £40

Farnborough Common BR6 8NF (01689) 854848

This popular venue has built a formidable reputation as a "classy" destination, offering "excellent-value" modern cuisine; it took more flak this year, though, from those who find it "pretentious".
/ **Sample dishes:** smoked goose, walnut & raspberry salad; provençale salmon; apple tart & thyme ice cream. **Details:** www.chaptersrestaurants.co.uk; 2m E of Bromley on A21; 10.30 pm; booking: max 12.

## LONG CRENDON, BUCKINGHAMSHIRE 2–2D

**Angel** £41 Ⓐ★

47 Bicester Rd HP18 9EE (01844) 208268

"The food lives up to the long-standing reputation" of this Chilterns pub, which also numbers a "lovely" atmosphere and "welcoming" staff among its attractions; "the fish is surprisingly good for somewhere so far from the sea". / **Sample dishes:** crispy duck & bacon salad; rack of lamb; raspberry & lemon tartlet. **Details:** 2m NW of Thame, off B4011; 9.30 pm; closed Sun D; no Amex; no smoking area; booking: max 12, Fri & Sat. **Accommodation:** 3 rooms, from £85.

## LONG MELFORD, SUFFOLK 3–1C

**Scutchers Bistro** £39 ★

Westgate St CO10 9DP (01787) 310200

"Good food, imaginatively served" (and "with more than a nod to current fashions") wins consistent praise for this "friendly", family-run restaurant. / **Sample dishes:** deep-fried tiger prawns; whole-grilled Dover sole; iced berries with white chocolate sauce. **Details:** www.scutchers.com; 9.30 pm; closed Mon & Sun; no smoking.

## LONGRIDGE, LANCASHIRE 5–1B

**The Longridge Restaurant** £39

104-106 Higher Rd PR3 3SY (01772) 784969

"Less formal and more relaxed than it used to be", the cottage-restaurant that kicked off star North Western chef Paul Heathcote's career often (but not invariably) delivers "memorable" dishes, with "local sourcing" much in evidence.
/ **Sample dishes:** herb polenta with char-grilled vegetables; crispy pork belly with spinach & red wine; iced apricot & gingerbread parfait.
**Details:** www.heathcotes.co.uk; follow signs for Jeffrey Hill; 10 pm; closed Mon & Sat L; no smoking.

## LOUGHBOROUGH, LEICESTERSHIRE 5–3D
**Thai House** £27
5a High St LE11 2PY (01509) 260030
A "noisy", "cheap and cheerful" town-centre oriental, where "everyone leaves happy". / **Details:** 10.30 pm; no Amex.

## LOWER ODDINGTON, GLOUCESTERSHIRE 2–1C
**The Fox Inn** £32  Ⓐ
GL56 0UR (01451) 870555
"Better standards" at this "very competent" (and "family-friendly") Cotswold gastroboozer make it look as if last year's investment in a new kitchen was justified. / **Sample dishes:** smoked haddock & watercress tart; braised lamb shank; steamed treacle sponge. **Details:** www.foxinn.net; on A436 near Stow on the Wold; 10 pm; no Amex. **Accommodation:** 3 rooms, from £68.

## LOWER WOLVERCOTE, OXFORDSHIRE 2–2D
**Trout Inn** £25  Ⓐ
195 Godstow Rd OX2 8PN (01865) 302071
"Arrive two hours early", if you want to beat the queues at this "charming" but "crowded" riverside pub (made famous by Inspector Morse); the "solid" food is rather an incidental attraction. / **Sample dishes:** salmon & broccoli fishcakes; beef & ale pie; profiteroles. **Details:** www.mbplc.com; 2m from junction of A40 & A44; 9.30 pm; no smoking; no booking; children: 18+.

## LUDLOW, SHROPSHIRE 5–4A
**The Cookhouse Café Bar**
**The Clive** £32
Bromfield SY8 2JR (01584) 856565
Perhaps because it isn't trying too hard on the cooking front, this "really enjoyable dining experience" is consistently praised by all who report on it. / **Sample dishes:** pan-roasted butternut squash & pumpkin seed salad; breast of chicken, pistachio & pine kernel mousse; apple tart with spicy almond crumble. **Details:** www.theclive.co.uk; 2m N of Ludlow on A49 to Shrewsbury; 9.30 pm; smoking in bar only. **Accommodation:** 15 rooms, from £70.

**Hibiscus** £58  ★★
17 Corve St SY8 1DA (01584) 872325
Claude Bosi's "vivid", "challenging" and "exciting" cooking was the 2nd highest-rated countrywide by reporters this year, and practically all feedback from his eminent (if perhaps slightly "sombre") manor house dining room is of truly "memorable" culinary experiences. / **Sample dishes:** white onion & lime ravioli with broad beans; roast turbot with tarragon & orange; chocolate tart with star anise. **Details:** www.hibiscusrestaurant.co.uk; 9.30 pm; closed Mon, Tue L & Sun; no Amex; no smoking; booking: max 14.

**Koo** £28  ★
127 Old St SY8 1NU (01584) 878462
"An excellent but slightly odd place" – Ludlow's 'only Japanese restaurant' (as it advertises itself) is consistently well reported on for its "very enjoyable" food. / **Sample dishes:** steamed vegetable dumplings; salmon with sweet white miso. **Details:** www.koo-ook.com; 9 pm; closed Mon & Sun; no smoking.

## Mr Underhill's £50 A★★

Dinham Wier SY8 1EH (01584) 874431

"Outstanding" food is "lovingly prepared by people who seem to enjoy their job", at Chris & Judy Bradley's "particularly welcoming" and "picturesquely-located" riverside fixture; it's "a great advertisement for no-choice, trust-the-chef menus". / **Sample dishes:** smoked haddock; duck with olives & honey; Italian bread & butter pudding. **Details:** www.mr-underhills.co.uk; 9 pm; D only, closed Mon & Tue; no Amex; no smoking. **Accommodation:** 9 rooms, from £105.

## Overton Grange £57

Hereford Rd SY8 4AD (01584) 873500

A majority of the (relatively modest) feedback on this formal Edwardian house tends to the view that the dining experience it offers suffers by virtue of being "over-ambitious". / **Sample dishes:** ravioli of lobster with mussel & basil sauce; cassoulet of quail & spanish white bean; chocolate raspberry cup with fennel bavarois. **Details:** www.overtongrangehotel.com; off A49, 1.5m S of Ludlow; 8.45 pm; no Amex; no smoking; children: 5 at D. **Accommodation:** 14 rooms, from £130.

---

## LUND, NORTH YORKSHIRE 5–1D
### Wellington Inn £36 A★

19 The Green YO25 9TE (01377) 217294

"A 'local' and a serious food place, all at the same time" – this "pleasant" inn is "the best choice for eating in East Yorkshire", for some reporters, and praised by all for its "consistent" culinary standards. / **Sample dishes:** Scottish seared scallops; local caught sea bass; assiette of lemon pudding. **Details:** 9.30 pm; closed Mon & Sun D; no Amex; smoking discouraged; children: 14+.

---

## LYDFORD, DEVON 1–3C
### The Dartmoor Inn £34 A★

Moorside EX20 4AY (01822) 820221

"A gem of a place", on "the edge of Dartmoor" – this "cosy" and "rambling" inn serves "interesting" and "consistently good" cuisine. / **Sample dishes:** artichoke purée tart; grilled mixed fish with courgette flower fritters; Bramley apple ice cream. **Details:** 9.30 pm; closed Mon & Sun D; no Amex; no smoking; children: 5+ at weekends. **Accommodation:** 3 rooms, from £125.

---

## LYDGATE, GREATER MANCHESTER 5–2B
### White Hart £42

51 Stockport Rd OL4 4JJ (01457) 872566

"Top-notch food all round and a cracking pint of real ale to boot!" – if that sounds good, look no further than this inn on the moors; "great home-made sausages" are a speciality. / **Sample dishes:** grilled tandoori chicken with cucumber yoghurt; calf's liver with pickled cabbage & thyme; lime & raspberry cheesecake. **Details:** www.thewhitehart.co.uk; 2m E of Oldham on A669, then A6050; 9.30 pm; no smoking. **Accommodation:** 12 rooms, from £110.

---

## LYME REGIS, DORSET 2–4A
### Fish Restaurant £

Cliff Cottage, Cobb Rd DT7 3JP (01297) 444111

This "unique" and accomplished fish venue is currently closed, due to major earthworks ('to stop Lyme slipping into the sea'); re-opening is scheduled for May 2007. / **Details:** www.thefishrestaurant.net; 0; no Amex; no smoking.

---

**sign up for the survey at www.hardens.com**

## LYMINGTON, HAMPSHIRE                    2–4D
### Egan's                                    £ 37        ★
Gosport St  SO41 9BE   (01590) 676165
*"Very good and reliable food"* at *"affordable"* prices ensures
a constant crush at John Egan's *"professional"* bistro.
/ **Sample dishes:** seafood tempura; rack of lamb with leeks; strawberries & ice
cream. **Details:** 10 pm; closed Mon & Sun; no Amex; no smoking; booking:
max 6, Sat.

### Gordleton Mill                          £ 40        🅐★
Silver St  SO41 6DJ   (01590) 682219
*"Superb, creative food"* is the gist of most feedback on this pretty
restaurant-with-rooms; with its *"beautiful"* tranquil location in the
New Forest, it is generally found to be *"worth a bit of a detour"*.
/ **Sample dishes:** Scottish salmon; roast rump of English lamb; raspberry cardinal.
**Details:** www.themillatgordleton.co.uk; 9 pm; closed Sun D; no smoking.
**Accommodation:** 8 rooms, from £125.

### Maine                                    £ 33        🅐
Ashley Ln  SO41 3RH   (01590) 672777
*"A good standard of cooking"*, an *"unusual"* wine list and
*"friendly"* service have made an immediate local hit of this *"fairly-
priced"* yearling, which benefits from a location in a former
chapel, *"tastefully-restored"* in *"New England style"* (*"hence the
name"*) . / **Sample dishes:** seared scallops with mint purée; line-caught sea bass,
spring onion salsa; lemon tart & clotted cream ice cream. **Details:** 9.30 pm; closed
Sun; smoking in bar only.

## LYNDHURST, HAMPSHIRE                     2–4C
### Le Poussin at Parkhill                    £
Beaulieu Rd  SO43 7FZ   (023) 8028 2944
This country house hotel is closed for refurbishment as this guide
goes to press, and the Aitkens family's 'first team' is currently
at their new Whitley Ridge property; the main focus is scheduled
to shift back here in 2007. / **Details:** www.lepoussin.co.uk; children:
8+ at D.

## LYTHAM, LANCASHIRE                       5–1A
### Chicory                                  £ 31        🅐★
5-7 Henry St  FY8 5LE   (01253) 737111
*"Outstanding food in a lively restaurant with excellent service"* –
a typical 'rave' review for this *"innovative"* three-year-old; it heads
up a mini-empire – also comprising a champagne bar (Flambé)
and a deli (Sweet Chicory) – all parts of which get the thumbs-up
from reporters. / **Details:** www.chicorygroup.co.uk; 9.30 pm; no Amex.

## MADINGLEY, CAMBRIDGESHIRE               3–1B
### Three Horseshoes                         £ 44
CB3 8AB   (01954) 210221
A *"lovely"* atmosphere has long made this rural pub a well-known
*"get-away from the hustle and bustle of Cambridge"*, not least for
undergrads with parents in tow; it's *"resting on its laurels"*, though.
/ **Sample dishes:** leek & morel tortellini with leek mousse; venison with star anise
noodles & pak choy; lemon tart with cherry vodka sorbet.
**Details:** www.huntsbridge.com; 2m W of Cambridge, off A14 or M11; 9.30 pm;
no smoking.

## MALMESBURY, WILTSHIRE                    2–2C

**The Old Bell Hotel**                    £ 44          A
Abbey Row  SN16 0AG   (01666) 822344
*"A nice surprise"; this "delightful" and "old-fashioned" (in all the best ways) hotel – the 'oldest in England' – goes out of its way to please today's travellers, not least with its "impeccable" service and "professional" cuisine.* / **Sample dishes:** *marinated Scottish salmon; roast rack of lamb; bread & butter pudding.* **Details:** *www.oldbellhotel.com; next to Abbey; 9.30 pm; no smoking; children: 8+ at D.* **Accommodation:** *31 rooms, from £125.*

## MANCHESTER, GREATER MANCHESTER  5–2B

Manchester has, by some margin, the largest restaurant scene outside London. For good European cooking, it was traditionally necessary, however, to head towards the south western suburbs – to the long-established *Moss Nook* (near the Airport), to West Didsbury's consistently impressive *Lime Tree* or to Altrincham's ambitious *Juniper*. The number of 'exceptions' to this rule is, however, growing, with such central restaurants as *Mont*, the *Establishment* and *Lounge 10* all maintaining high culinary standards.

The city-centre also boasts a very impressive range of oriental restaurants, including the most notable Chinatown in the UK outside London. The legendary *Yang Sing* – by far the best-known place in Manchester – is also the country's most famous Chinese restaurant outside London. And good places are springing up all the time, the latest being the new *Wings*. There are lots of Indian restaurants, too, mainly in the famed curry quarter of Rusholme. Some of them are quite good, but they remain, perhaps to a surprising extent, stuck in a pretty downmarket mould.

Western Europe's largest student population – bolstered nowadays by a growing army of young professionals resident in the city-centre – helps to support a growing number of places, such as *Kro*, which are fun and relatively affordable.

**Armenian Taverna**                    £ 27          ★
3-5 Princess St  M2 4DF   (0161) 834 9025
*This "consistent and friendly" family-owned fixture is praised by all reporters for its "reliable" Greek and Armenian cuisine; some feel the atmosphere of this city-centre basement is "fantastic" too.* / **Sample dishes:** *stuffed cabbage leaves; baklava.* **Details:** *11.30 pm; closed Mon; children: 3+.*

**The Assembly Rooms**                    £ 36
6 Lapwing Ln  M20 2WS   (0161) 445 3653
*Reporters debate whether this "lively" and "lavishly-decorated" Didsbury spot is better or worse than it was in its days as The Nose; if you're looking for the likes of "great burgers and chunky chips", however, it remains a popular stand-by.* / **Sample dishes:** *mini Australian pie floater; duck with Cumberland sausage; blueberry crème brûlée.* **Details:** *between Palatine Road & Withington hospital; midnight; no smoking.*

## The Bridge    £29    ★
53 Bridge St M3 3BW   (0161) 834 0242
*"Manchester's premier gastropub" – a "convivial" place, just off Deansgate – is winning a big name locally for its "British dishes with a twist"; its "unpretentious" charms inspire almost universal praise from reporters.* / **Sample dishes:** crab salad; Eccles cakes with double cream. **Details:** www.thebridgemanchester.co.uk; 9.30 pm; smoking in bar only.

## The Bridgewater Hall    £31    𝔸
Lower Mosley St M2 3WS   (0161) 950 0000
*The home of the Hallé is – especially by the standards of cultural-facility catering – "a stylish rendezvous, with good food".* / **Sample dishes:** shredded chicken salad; chocolate marquise. **Details:** www.bridgewater-hall.co.uk; 7.30 pm; openings affected by concert times; no smoking.

## Café Paradiso
## Hotel Rossetti    £33
107 Piccadilly M1 2DB   (0161) 200 5665
*A "strangely-designed" design-hotel brasserie, handy for Piccadilly station; pizzas and early-evening specials are particularly commended.* / **Sample dishes:** ox tongue with pickled beetroot & horseradish; pudding with crème fraîche. **Details:** www.aliasrossetti.com; 10 pm; no smoking; booking: max 8. **Accommodation:** 61 rooms, from £105.

## Cedar Tree    £23    ★
69 Thomas St M4 1LQ
(0161) 8345016
*"A not half bad Lebanese restaurant" in the Northern Quarter that's unlicensed but you can BYO; however, even though "the staff work hard", there can be "long waits".* / **Details:** 10 pm; no Amex; no smoking area.

## Choice    £37    𝔸
Castle Quay M15 4NT   (0161) 833 3400
*This "slick" warehouse-conversion has a "great" Castlefield location, and fans find its food "consistently good" too; this year's feedback was a bit up-and-down, though – perhaps it's "trying too hard to be trendy"?* / **Sample dishes:** pan-fried scallops on a Cheshire cheese scone; Eccles cake & chocolate black pudding. **Details:** www.choicebarandrestaurant.co.uk; 10 pm; smoking in bar only.

## Croma    £24
1 Clarence St M2 4DE   (0161) 237 9799
*"Chic" (going-on "glitzy"), this "great all-rounder" is a default central rendezvous for many Mancunians; its pizza menu makes a feature of "unusual" toppings, such as balti, Chinese duck, Cumberland sausage...* / **Sample dishes:** buffalo Mozzarella; fish lasagne; hot sticky toffee pudding. **Details:** www.cromamanchester.co.uk; off Albert Square; 11 pm; no smoking.

## Dimitri's    £28    𝔸
Campfield Arc M3 4FN   (0161) 839 3319
*A "terrific ambience" is the highlight at this "popular" and "lively" bar, just off Deansgate, which offers "classy" tapas in quite large portions; "if you can, sit 'outside', in the Victorian arcade".* / **Sample dishes:** chorizo salad; ribs with vegetable couscous; baklava. **Details:** www.dimitris.co.uk; near Museum of Science & Industry; 11.30 pm.

### Dukes 92 £22 Ⓐ

19-25 Castle St M3 4LZ (0161) 839 4642

*A relaxed boozer, with an attractive Castlefield location and simple food; feedback was limited this year, but very positive.*
/ **Sample dishes:** potato wedges; baked pizza; apple pie.
**Details:** www.dukes92.com; off Deansgate; 10 pm; no Amex.

### Eighth Day Café £17 ★

111 Oxford Rd M1 7DU (0161) 273 4878

*"Imaginative" but "unpretentious" cooking wins many fans for "Manchester's best vegetarian", near the University.*
/ **Sample dishes:** Armenian lentil soup; vegan pâté with pitta bread & salad; vegan chocolate cake. **Details:** www.eighth-day.co.uk; 7.30 pm; closed Sun; no smoking; no booking.

### Establishment £49 ★

43-45 Spring Gdns M2 2BG (0161) 839 6300

*This "sophisticated" yearling in an "imposing" former banking hall has proved itself to be "Manchester's best newcomer for some time"; it can seem "very expensive" by local standards, but the cooking "bears the hallmarks of real skill".* / **Sample dishes:** ham and spring vegetable consomme; pan-roasted squab pigeon with fondant potato; plum tarte tatin with almond cream. **Details:** www.establishmentrestaurant.com; 9.45 pm; closed Mon & Sun; smoking in bar only.

### Evuna £30

277 Deansgate M3 4EW (0161) 819 2752

*Where did it all go wrong? – though this tapas bar two-year-old is still of undoubted note for its "incredible" selection of wines, feedback on the food is all over the show: from "always excellent" to "very poor".* / **Sample dishes:** garlic prawns with chilli; sea bass baked in rock salt; Spanish cheesecake with Manchego. **Details:** www.evuna.com; 11 pm; closed Sun; no smoking area.

### Francs £31

2 Goose Grn WA14 1DW (0161) 941 3954

*"A pleasant surprise" for first-time visitors – this "consistent" Altrincham bistro of long standing is an ever-handy and "good value" stand-by.* / **Sample dishes:** salmon dauphinoise; chicken in coconut & lime; chocolate praline tartlet. **Details:** www.francs-altrincham.com; 10.30 pm, Fri & Sat 11 pm; no Amex; no smoking area.

### French Restaurant
### Midland Hotel £68 Ⓐ

Peter St M60 2DS (0161) 236 3333

*For "the ultimate 'retro' experience", it's hard to beat this "wonderful" dining room, and its "rich but reliable" cuisine – if you're looking for a "classical French restaurant", they don't come more Central Castings-perfect than this (well, not in England anyway).* / **Details:** www.themidland.co.uk; 10.30 pm; closed Mon D, Tue D & Sat L; no smoking. **Accommodation:** 303 rooms, from £165.

### Great Kathmandu £28 ★★

140 Burton Rd M20 1JQ (0161) 434 6413

*"Pretty average-looking, but wow!" – all reporters sing the praises of the "authentic" Nepalese cooking at this inauspicious West Didsbury spot; the setting is "too cramped when the place is busy" (which is to say usually) – perhaps a recent expansion will ease matters.* / **Sample dishes:** king prawns; Nepalese mixed masala; kulfi. **Details:** www.greatkathmandu.com; near Withington hospital; midnight.

## Green's £29 ★★

43 Lapwing Ln  M20 2NT   (0161) 434 4259

*Expansion has "lifted the standards" of this already very popular BYO West Didsbury veggie; now "livelier" than before, it has an ever stronger following, even among carnivores.*
/ **Sample dishes:** Feta, watermelon & cucumber salad; aubergine & potato curry; chocolate & honeycomb mocha pot. **Details:** 4m S of city centre; 10.30 pm; closed Mon L & Sat L; no Amex; no smoking.

## The Greenhouse £19

331 Great Western St  M14 4AN   (0161) 224 0730

*"You feel like you're in a living room", when you visit Robin Knight's "eccentric" venture in a Rusholme end-terrace; it offers a "vast" menu ("about 150 options") of "massive" dishes from a tiny kitchen – not everyone is impressed, but some people think "it's the best veggie ever".* / **Sample dishes:** houmous & pitta bread; peppers stuffed with cashews & pilau rice; knickerbocker glory.
**Details:** www.dineveggie.com; 9.30 pm, Sat 10 pm; closed Mon, Tue-Sat D only, Sun L & D, closed Aug; no Amex; no smoking.

## The Grinch £28 Ⓐ

5-7 Chapel Walks, off Cross St  M2 1HN   (0161) 907 3210

*"A fun place for a younger clientele"; "tasty pizzas" come especially highly recommended at this "buzzy" bistro, just of St Anne's Square.* / **Sample dishes:** crispy duck & Japanese cucumber salad; grilled chilli chicken Caesar salad; marshmallow ice cream & chocolate fudge sauce. **Details:** www.grinch.co.uk; 11 pm.

## Gurkha Grill £23

198 Burton Rd  M20 1LH   (0161) 445 3461

*"Some exquisite dishes" are regularly reported at this West Didsbury Nepalese; this year's feedback, however, was more mixed than usual.* / **Details:** www.gurkhagrill.com; midnight, Fri & Sat 1 am; D only.

## Jem and I £35 ★

School Ln  M20 6RD   (0161) 445 3996

*Jem O'Sullivan's "buzzy" Didsbury two-year-old seems to be building up a contented following, and on most (if not quite all) reports, "the confident and skilful cooking justifies such popularity".* / **Details:** 10 pm; closed Mon L; no Amex; no smoking area.

## Juniper £57 ★

21 The Downs  WA14 2QD   (0161) 929 4008

*Paul Kitching's Altrincham fixture – in a parade of suburban shops – offers a real "love-it-or-hate-it" experience; those who find his "experimental" cuisine "stunning" (and "entertaining") were more in evidence this year, but there remains a stubborn minority who just find the place "pretentious".* / **Sample dishes:** scallops with curried pea sauce; lamb with raisins & sweetbreads; lemon tart with Florida fruit cocktail. **Details:** www.juniper-restaurant.co.uk; 9.30 pm; closed Mon, Sat L & Sun; no smoking.

## Koh Samui £28 ★

16 Princess St  M1 4NB   (0161) 237 9511

*"The best Thai cooking for many miles around" makes this city-centre destination a "reliable winner"; "seafood a speciality".* / **Sample dishes:** seafood papaya salad; roast pork with chilli & sweet basil; sticky coconut rice with mango. **Details:** www.kohsamuirestaurant.co.uk; opp City Art Gallery; 11.30 pm; closed Sat L & Sun L.

### Koreana £25

40a King St West M3 2WY (0161) 832 4330
*This "cheap, cheerful and relaxed" family-run city-centre spot
is "always welcoming", and its, er, Korean fare is as "reliable"
as you would hope.* / **Sample dishes:** lemon ribs; soy bean casserole; Korean
rice cake with cream. **Details:** www.koreana.co.uk; 10.30 pm; closed Sat L & Sun.

### Kro Bar £25 Ⓐ

325 Oxford Rd M13 9PG (0161) 274 3100
*"The best breakfast in town", a "good choice of sandwiches and
hot meals" and "great hot chocolate" – these are the sort
of culinary attractions which make this "relaxing" café/bar,
near the University, popular at any time of day.*
/ **Sample dishes:** smoked fishcake; chicken patties; hot chocolate fudge cake.
**Details:** www.kro.co.uk; 9 pm; no Amex; children: 18+ only.

### Kro2 £27 Ⓐ

Oxford Hs, Oxford Rd M1 7ED (0161) 236 1048
*"Eating alfresco in Oxford Road shouldn't work, but it does",
and this "easy" café/bar remains a popular destination for
"good light meals"; it's "always busy".* / **Sample dishes:** roasted beef
chunks with potatoes & onions; grilled sirloin steak. **Details:** www.kro.co.uk/two;
10 pm; no smoking area.

### Lal Haweli £20 ★

68-72 Wilmslow Rd M14 (0161) 248 9700
*This "never disappointing" Rusholme Indian is – for one or two
reporters – "the pick of the Curry Mile".* / **Sample dishes:** king prawn
kebabs; chilli chicken; funky pie. **Details:** 1 am; no smoking area.

### Lead Station £26 Ⓐ

99 Beech Rd M21 9EQ (0161) 881 5559
*With its "good food" and its "relaxed atmosphere",
this "upmarket, pub-type brasserie" has established itself as the
default Chorlton rendezvous (especially for breakfast); it's "always
buzzing".* / **Sample dishes:** halloumi salad with lime & caper dressing; Spanish
lamb casserole with chorizo & mash; American cheesecake. **Details:** 9.30 pm;
no smoking; no booking.

### The Lime Tree £36 Ⓐ★

8 Lapwing Ln M20 2WS (0161) 445 1217
*A "great all-rounder" that's "always a pleasure"; as ever, this West
Didsbury stalwart wins lavish praise for its "consistently excellent"
brasserie cooking, its "high-quality" service and its "buzzy" style
that's "relaxed, without being too informal".* / **Sample dishes:** pan-fried
pigeon breast; venison medallions with bubble & squeak; Bailey's cheesecake with
honeycomb ice cream. **Details:** www.thelimetreerestaurant.com; 10.15 pm; closed
Mon L & Sat L; no smoking.

### Little Yang Sing £30 Ⓐ★

17 George St M1 4HE (0161) 228 7722
*Ratings increasingly support those who tout this "really good" and
"buzzy" Chinatown "favourite" as a "high-class rival to its better-
known big brother"; it serves "fantastic" food (including "dim sum
to die for").* / **Sample dishes:** mini spare ribs; fried fish fillet in chilli Szechuan
sauce. **Details:** www.littleyangsing.co.uk; 11.30 pm; no smoking area.

### Livebait £34

22 Lloyd St  M2 5WA   (0161) 817 4110

*"We feared a predictable chain, but found better"* – this handy *"central"* fish parlour attracts a lot of feedback, mostly praising its *"consistently good"* cooking; service, though, can be *"slow"*. / **Sample dishes:** *Mediterranean fish soup; lobster with new potato salad; panna cotta & strawberries.* **Details:** *www.santeonline.co.uk; 10.30 pm; no smoking area.*

### Lounge 10 £48  A★

10 Tib Ln  M2 4JB
(0161) 834 1331

*"A clairvoyant in the loo"* and *"loud"* live music are the sorts of *"quirky"* touches that can make a visit to this *"sexy"* city-centre spot quite an experience; you might expect the food to be secondary, but reporters almost unanimously hail it as *"very good"*. / **Sample dishes:** *Cornish squid risotto; bouillabaisse with saffron new potatoes; Scottish cranachan & raspberry milkshake.* **Details:** *www.lounge10manchester.co.uk; 11 pm; D only, closed Mon & Sun; children: 18.*

### Love Saves The Day £22  A

45-50 Oldam St  M4 1LE   (0161) 832 0777

You get *"a great NY deli-style experience"* (albeit *"with slower service"*), at this Northern Quarter café, which – with its *"welcoming"* atmosphere and *"eclectic"* customer base – retains its *"legendary"* local status. / **Sample dishes:** *Cheshire ham & cheese; meatballs & linguine; lemon & polenta cake.* **Details:** *www.lovesavestheday.co.uk; L only; no smoking.*

### The Lowry
### The Lowry Centre £30

Pier 8, Salford Quays  M50 3AZ   (0161) 876 2121

This striking Salford cultural centre was highly complimented this year as a *"classy experience"* that's *"good value pre-theatre and for lunch"* (and with *"great views of the Ship Canal"* too). / **Sample dishes:** *goat's cheese with sundried tomatoes; pan-fried chicken with cabbage chestnuts; vanilla panna cotta with strawberries & mint syrup.* **Details:** *www.thelowry.com; 7.30 pm; L only, D on performance nights only; no smoking.*

### The River Restaurant
### Lowry Hotel £47

50 Dearmans Pl, Dearmans Pl, Chapel Whf  M3 5LH
(0161) 827 4041

Rocco Forte may be a good hotelier, but some of his restaurants evoke the bad old Trust House days; some reporters do see 'Manchester's most fashionable venue' (its description) as *"an amazing treat"*, but it still attracts too many reports of the *"disappointing"*, *"over-rated"* and *"surely not five-star"* variety. / **Sample dishes:** *pistou soup with scallops; roast duck; praline crème brûlée.* **Details:** *www.thelowryhotel.com; 10.30 pm; no smoking area; booking: max 8.* **Accommodation:** *165 rooms, from £230.*

## Malmaison £37

Piccadilly M1 3AQ (0161) 278 1000

*Manchester has moved on, and this once-trendy outpost of the boutique hotel chain, by Piccadilly station, is increasingly overlooked nowadays; it can still make a "satisfactory" venue (as long as you like your music "very loud"). / Sample dishes: eggs Benedict; sea bream with asparagus; champagne & strawberry jelly.* **Details:** *www.malmaison.com; near Piccadilly Station; 11 pm; no smoking area.* **Accommodation:** *167 rooms, from £129.*

## The Market £38 Ⓐ

104 High St M4 1HQ (0161) 834 3743

*"How do they keep it up for 25 years?" – this "cosy", "retro" institution is again acclaimed by many reporters for its "very good food and good value" (and a "great" list of beers too); those who find it "quaint but average", however, are becoming more vociferous. / Sample dishes: potato ravioli with mint; Parmesan turkey; banana & passion fruit pavlova.* **Details:** *www.market-restaurant.com; 10 pm; closed Sun-Tue & Sat L.*

## Metropolitan £29

2 Lapwing Ln M20 2WS (0161) 374 9559

*This big West Didsbury gastropub has a strong name locally for its "very tasty" food (not least "excellent" burgers); it's a very "lively" and "busy" place (and strikes some as "brash"). / Sample dishes: Stilton fritters; pork & leek sausages with apple mash; sticky toffee pudding.* **Details:** *near Withington hospital; 9.30 pm; no smoking.*

## Le Mont
## Urbis Science Museum £51 ★

Cathedral Gdns M4 3BG
(0161) 605 8282

*"Wonderful views of the citiscape" – if not from the tables themselves! – add to the experience of visiting this "peaceful" dining room, atop a trendy museum; Robert Kisby's "imaginative" cooking is "first-rate" (although some locals may gripe about "southern-sized" portions). / Sample dishes: creamy white onion & cider soup; grilled & roast lamb; cinnamon poached pear with ice cream.* **Details:** *www.urbis.org.uk; 10.30 pm; closed Sat L & Sun; no smoking area.*

## Moss Nook £57 ★

Ringway Rd M22 5WD (0161) 437 4778

*Check out the website before choosing to dine at this "welcoming" suburban restaurant, of over 30 years' standing – its "OTT" Victorian styling (though "somewhat freshened" of late) is not to all tastes; the cooking is usually "rich" too (in every sense), but those who like it that way find it "excellent". / Sample dishes: twice-baked cheese & chive soufflé; beef with foie gras pâté & rosti; crème brûlée.* **Details:** *www.mossnookrestaurant.co.uk; on B5166, 1m from Manchester airport; 9.30 pm; closed Mon, Sat L & Sun; children: 11+.* **Accommodation:** *1 room, at about £120.*

## Mr Thomas's Chop House £33 Ⓐ★

52 Cross St M2 7AR (0161) 832 2245

*"Still flying the flag for British food" – this intriguing Victorian institution (an "excellent pub-style restaurant") is an ever-popular city-centre stand-by. / Sample dishes: black pudding, egg & smoked bacon salad; roast cod with bubble & squeak; jam sponge with custard.* **Details:** *www.tomschophouse.com; L only; no smoking.*

## Nawaab £ 15 ★
1008 Stockport Rd M19 3WN (0161) 224 6969
*This popular subcontinental restaurant re-located to Levenshulme
a couple of years ago, and its buffet-style formula wins it a good
number of nominations as a "top Indian"; (as this guide goes
to press, they plan to stop serving alcohol).*

## New Emperor £ 30
52-56 George St M1 4HF (0161) 228 2883
*"Very good dim sum" is the highlight at this gaudy Chinatown
stalwart, which fans say offers "extremely good value".*
/ **Sample dishes:** crispy duck; fish fillet in sweet & sour sauce.
**Details:** www.newemperor.co.uk; midnight.

## Obsidian
## Aurora Hotel £ 45
18-24 Princess St M1 4LY (0161) 238 4348
*It claims to be 'the perfect spot for Manchester's very own Carrie
Bradshaws', but Manhattan's finest would probably not
be impressed by the up-and-down performance of this self-
regarding basement yearling; one fan, however, acknowledging the
"weak start", insists the place is now "blossoming".*
/ **Sample dishes:** hand-dived scallops with ginger; roast duck breast with beetroot
chutney; chocolate muffin. **Details:** www.obsidianmanchester.co.uk; 10.30 pm.
**Accommodation:** 140 rooms, from £145.

## Olive Press £ 32 ★
4 Lloyds St M2 5AB (0161) 8329090
*"A quick, in-and-out place for really good pizza and pasta"; it's an
"airy" spot that generally "buzzes", though "atmosphere in the
evening can seem a bit lacking".* / **Sample dishes:** American pizza; white
chocolate cheesecake. **Details:** www.heathcotes.co.uk; 10 pm, Fri & Sat 11 pm;
no smoking area.

## The Ox £ 31
71 Liverpool Rd M3 4NQ (0161) 839 7740
*"Great Corrie star-spotting" and "down-to-earth" cooking win
praise for this Castlefield gastropub; gripes include that it's
"too busy" and "smokey".* / **Sample dishes:** salmon with coconut; pan-fried
chicken breast; bread & butter pudding. **Details:** www.theox.co.uk; 11 pm; closed
Sun D; no smoking. **Accommodation:** 7 rooms, from £45.

## Pacific £ 33 Ⓐ★
58-60 George St M1 4HF (0161) 228 6668
*You can go Chinese (ground floor) or Thai (above) at this
"very modern" (if "slightly bland") Chinatown spot; both options
are "equally good" – "excellent and consistent" standards have
made this place not only one of Manchester's most popular
places, but also one of the best.* / **Sample dishes:** steamed scallops
in garlic sauce; sizzling beef in black pepper sauce; toffee banana & ice cream.
**Details:** www.pacificrestaurant.co.uk; 10.45 pm; no smoking area.

**sign up for the survey at www.hardens.com**

## Palmiro £30 ★

197 Upper Chorlton Rd M16 OBH (0161) 860 7330
*This Whalley Grange Italian – which describes itself as a 'home-style River Café' – certainly doesn't lack ambition; its "risk-taking" cuisine can deliver "excellent" results, but even some fans admit to "occasional upsets". / Sample dishes: slow-roast tomato risotto; char-grilled sea bass; poached pears & caramel with polenta. Details: www.palmiro.net; 10.30 pm; D only, ex Sun open L & D; no Amex; no smoking area.*

## Pearl City £22

33 George St M1 4PH (0161) 228 7683
*This "everyday Chinese" in Chinatown is tipped as a good "cheap and cheerful" option, though its service could be improved. / Details: www.pearlcityrestaurant.co.uk; 1.30 am.*

## Pepper Restaurant £33

4 Warburton St M20 6WA (0161) 445 0448
*"Small" and "intimate" (and sometimes "crowded"), this Didsbury bistro offers "modern versions of old favourites". / Sample dishes: king prawns with smoked bacon; sea bass with lemon, Parmesan & chive mash; iced strawberry & raspberry mousse. Details: 10.30 pm; closed Mon & Sun D; no smoking.*

## Le Petit Blanc £31

55 King St M2 4LQ (0161) 832 1000
*It speaks volumes about this small national brasserie chain that its Manchester outpost – "formulaic" as it is – is the best of the breed; it has a handy location, too, and is especially popular as "a good stop for lunch". / Sample dishes: snail & spinach fricassée; roast chicken with braised leeks & morels; lemon tart with raspberry sorbet. Details: www.lepetitblanc.co.uk; 10.30 pm; no smoking.*

## Piccolino £30 🄰

8 Clarence St M2 4DW (0161) 835 9860
*"Very buzzy" and "atmospheric", this "slickly-run" city-centre Italian remains "in" with Manchester's movers and shakers (and is a top "people-watching" destination); "superb thin-crust pizzas" are a menu highlight. / Sample dishes: antipasto misto; lamb shank; chocolate nemesis. Details: www.individualrestaurant.co.uk; 11 pm.*

## Punjab Tandoori £20 ★

177 Wilmslow Rd M14 5AP (0161) 225 2960
*"A much higher standard of food than the Rusholme average" makes this "great-value" subcontinental popular with carnivores and veggies alike; the only real downside seems to be sometimes "slow" service. / Details: 11.45 pm.*

## The Restaurant Bar & Grill £34

14 John Dalton St M2 6JR
(0161) 839 1999
*"Competent" (if "unexciting") cooking is generally to be had at this would-be glamorous city-centre rendezvous, which maintains something of a "spot-the-stars" reputation locally. / Sample dishes: fried chilli squid with Thai noodle salad; crispy duck with Chinese greens, sesame & honey dressing; sticky toffee pudding. Details: www.individualrestaurants.co.uk; 11 pm; no smoking area; booking: max 8 at weekends.*

**sign up for the survey at www.hardens.com**

### Rhubarb £33 Ⓐ

167 Burton Rd M20 2LN (0161) 448 8887

*This West Didsbury hang-out is – most reporters say – a "gem", thanks to its "interesting" mix of dishes and its "seductive" ambience; it also attracts a few detractors, though, who say that "it had a good start, but the food is never better than average nowadays".* / **Sample dishes:** porcini mushroom risotto; pan-fried sea bass fillet with Mediterranean salsa; crème brûlée. **Details:** www.rhubarbrestaurant.co.uk; 10 pm; closed Mon, Tue–Sat D only, Sun open L & D; no Amex; no smoking.

### El Rincon £29 Ⓐ

Longworth St, off St John's St M3 4BQ (0161) 839 8819

*"Authentic tapas" and good wine contribute much to the success of this ten-year-old tapas bar; it's the "noisy" ambience, though – "like Madrid" – which makes it such an enduring hit.* / **Sample dishes:** prawns; grilled sea bass with lemon; cheesecake. **Details:** off Deansgate; 11 pm, Fri & Sat 11.30 pm.

### Sam's Chop House £35 Ⓐ★

Black Pool Fold, Chapel Walks M2 1HN (0161) 834 3210

*"Top for old-fashioned English food" (including "the best steak and kidney pudding in the world"), this "popular" Victorian-styled basement is also hailed for its "great atmosphere" and its "good range of wines and beers".* / **Sample dishes:** Morecambe Bay potted shrimps; Lancashire mutton hot pot; baked Eccles cakes. **Details:** www.samschophouse.com; 9.30 pm; closed Sun.

### San Carlo £42 Ⓐ

40 King Street West M3 2WY (0161) 834 6226

*"Well located", behind Kendals, this "welcome new Italian" is particularly praised for its "exciting array of fish and seafood", and its enjoyably "chaotic" ambience; as at the Birmingham original, though, service can be "complacent".* / **Sample dishes:** seafood salad; chicken breast with prawns; tiramisu. **Details:** www.sancarlo.co.uk; 11 pm; no smoking area.

### Sangam £16

9-19 Wilmslow Rd M14 5TB (0161) 257 3922

*"Consistently good curries" feature in most reports on this "friendly" Rusholme fixture, at the start of the Curry Mile.* / **Details:** www.sangam.co.uk; midnight; no smoking area.

### Second Floor Restaurant
### Harvey Nichols £42

21 New Cathedral St M1 1AD (0161) 828 8898

*"Plenty of people-watching" is a draw to this "minimalist" space on the second floor of the department-store; the cooking is "pricey" for what it is, though, and can "take ages".* / **Details:** www.harveynichols.com; 10.30 pm; closed Mon D & Sun D; smoking in bar only.

### Shere Khan £19

52 Wilmslow Rd M14 5TQ (0161) 256 2624

*This brightly-lit fixture of the Curry Mile is a well-known local destination – it serves "nothing new or groundbreaking", just "the classics" done to a "reliable" standard.* / **Sample dishes:** tandoori; mixed grill sizzler; rasmalai. **Details:** www.sherekhan.com; midnight, Fri & Sat 3 am; no smoking area.

### Simply Heathcote's       £37     ✗
Jackson Row, Deansgate   M2 5WD    (0161) 835 3536
A "trusted favourite", or "Manchester's worst"? – as ever,
the "minimalist" city-centre brasserie HQ of the North West's
'biggest' chef splits opinion; the place is most consistently tipped
as a rendezvous for business. / **Sample dishes:** grilled
herb crumpet; rump steak with onion rings & portobello mushrooms; bread & butter
pudding. **Details:** www.heathcotes.co.uk; near Opera House; 10 pm, Sat 11 pm;
no smoking.

### Stock       £43
4 Norfolk St   M2 1DW    (0161) 839 6644
This "smart" and "authentic" Italian, augustly housed in the
former Stock Exchange, has evident virtues as a business
destination; the food is "nothing special", though, and bills are
often thought to be "out of proportion". / **Sample dishes:** grilled
artichokes; steak with porcini mushrooms with cream & garlic; panna cotta.
**Details:** www.stockrestaurant.co.uk; 10.30 pm; closed Sun; no smoking.

### Tai Pan       £24    ★
81-97 Upper Brook St   M13 9TX    (0161) 273 2798
"Not the most glamorous restaurant around, but unmatched for
quality and variety" – one typical satisfied customer reports
on this shed-like Chinese, a little way from the city-centre; expect
"queues for Sunday dim sum". / **Sample dishes:** dim sum; king prawns
in black bean sauce; mango pudding. **Details:** www.taipanliverpool.com; 11 pm.

### Tai Wu       £20    ★★
44 Oxford St   M1 5EJ    (0161) 236 6557
"A huge and soulless place" – housed in a former cinema –
"that more than makes up for any lack of ambience with great
service and better Chinese food"; all reporters say it's "very good
value" – "half-price dim sum lunches (Mon-Thu)" and the "eat-
all-you-can buffet" (on the ground floor) are particularly praised.
/ **Details:** www.tai-wu.net.co.uk; 3.15 am; no smoking area.

### Tampopo       £25    ★
16 Albert Sq   M2 5PF    (0161) 819 1966
"Proper fast food" has made a huge hit of this "really good"
("better-than-Wagamama") noodle bar, which has a "great
location", near the Town Hall – for "canteen-style" eating,
it's "hard to beat". / **Sample dishes:** chicken satay; Singapore yellow noodles
with prawns & mild curry; ginger crème brûlée. **Details:** www.tampopo.co.uk;
11 pm; no smoking; need 7+ to book.

### That Café       £36    𝔸★
1031-1033 Stockport Rd   M19 2TB    (0161) 432 4672
"Imaginative" cooking (showing good "attention to detail") makes
this attractive outfit a "very surprising" find, in a down-at-heel bit
of Levenshulme. / **Sample dishes:** pan-fried squid & king prawn salad;
beef fillet with celeriac rosti; passion fruit tart. **Details:** www.thatcafe.co.uk; on A6
between Manchester & Stockport; 10.30 pm; closed Mon, Tue-Sat D only, closed
Sun D; no Amex; no smoking area.

### This & That       £ 5    ★
3 Soap St   M4 1EW    (0161) 832 4971
You get "very cheap curry, very quickly", at this "backstreet
canteen", in the Northern Quarter; it continues to attract
"a widely diverse clientele" with its "amazing-value" 'rice and
three' offer. / **Details:** 5 pm; closed Sat; no credit cards.

### Wing's

**£38**  A★★

1 Lincoln Sq  M2 5LN
(0161) 834 9000

*Fans are already hailing this "truly outstanding" Chinese newcomer as "a rival for the Yang Sing"; it occupies the smart city-centre site that was once The Lincoln (RIP), and has speedily established itself as "a good place to spot celebs".*
/ **Sample dishes:** fillet steak rolls; beef in peanut satay sauce.
**Details:** www.wingsrestaurant.co.uk; opp Manchester Evening News building; 10.30 pm, Fri & Sat 11 pm.

### Wong Chu
**£22**  ★

63 Faulkner St  M1 4FF   (0161) 236 2346

*"Few concessions to Western tastes" are in evidence at this "drab" but "interesting" Chinatown spot, where the cooking is "consistently of a high standard".* / **Sample dishes:** chicken & sweetcorn soup; roast pork with fried rice; coconut ice cream. **Details:** 11.30 pm.

### Yang Sing
**£30**  ★

34 Princess St  M1 4JY   (0161) 236 2200

*After almost three decades in business, Harry Yeung's Chinatown classic has made a name as "Europe's best Chinese restaurant"; much feedback continues to support this view, but the minority who "can't see what the fuss is about" grew more voluble this past year.* / **Sample dishes:** crispy spring rolls; pan-fried squid; custard tart.
**Details:** www.yang-sing.com; 11.45 pm, Fri & Sat 12.15 am.

### Zinc Bar & Grill
**£35**  ✗

The Triangle, Hanging Ditch  M4 3ES   (0161) 827 4200

*A Triangle outpost of Conran's stunningly dull brasserie chain; as at its London siblings, feedback is limited, and too often of the "never again" variety.* / **Sample dishes:** fried squid with chilli; lamb kebabs with bulgar wheat salad; lemon tart. **Details:** www.conran.com; 10 pm; no smoking.

---

## MANNINGTREE, ESSEX                                        3–2C

### Stour Bay Café
**£32**  ★

39-43 High St  CO11 1AH   (01206) 396687

*"Very good food, especially fish" features in all reports on this "terrific" little bistro, near the sea-front; it has "a useful wine list" too.* / **Sample dishes:** smoked eel & pancetta hash; local seafood; poached fruits in port with rum panna cotta. **Details:** www.stourbaycafe.com; 9.30 pm; closed Mon & Tue; no Amex; no smoking.

---

## MARKET HARBOROUGH, LEICESTERSHIRE          5–4D

### Han's
**£24**

29 St Mary's Rd  LE16 7DS   (01858) 462288

*This "above-average Chinese restaurant" is consistently well reported-on in this thinly-provided market town.*
/ **Sample dishes:** seafood & lettuce wraps; sizzling beef & black pepper; toffee apples & banana. **Details:** 11 pm; closed Sat L & Sun.

**sign up for the survey at www.hardens.com**

---

## MARLBOROUGH, WILTSHIRE 2–2C

### Coles Bar & Restaurant £41
27 Kingsbury St SN8 1JA (01672) 515004
*A local favourite, which can provide some "interesting" cooking – reports overall, however, are rather up-and-down.*
/ **Sample dishes:** *crispy fillet beef parcel; home-made merangue with thick organic cream.* **Details:** *www.colesrestaurant.co.uk; 10 pm; closed Sun; no Amex; smoking in bar only.*

### Harrow Inn £41 ★
Little Bedwyn SN8 3JP (01672) 870871
*It's the "terrific" choice of wines (especially Australian and Spanish) which has made this modestly-named establishment of particular note; the cooking, however, can be "very good" too.*
/ **Sample dishes:** *sashimi of monkfish & lobster; salt marsh lamb; fig & custard tart with coconut & rum ice cream.* **Details:** *www.harrowinn.co.uk; 9 pm; closed Mon, Tue & Sun D; no smoking.*

---

## MARLOW, BUCKINGHAMSHIRE 3–3A

### Compleat Angler £60 ✕
Marlow Bridge SL7 1RG (0870) 400 8100
*"I would never go again, even if someone else was paying the exorbitant prices" – a not-atypical report on this famous hotel dining room which, with its "barely average" food and "amateur" service, trades shamelessly on its "superb" riverside location.*
/ **Sample dishes:** *smoked haddock & potato terrine; roast duck with marinated white cabbage; Baileys & honey parfait.* **Details:** *www.compleatangler-hotel.co.uk; 10 pm; no smoking area.* **Accommodation:** *64 rooms, from £208.*

### Hand & Flowers £46 A★
West St SL7 2BP (01628) 482277
*This "traditional low-beamed pub" was turned into a "modern restaurant and bar" in early-2005, by Tom Kerridge, whose impressive CV includes a stint as head chef at Adlard's in Norwich; early reports are few, but all put the cooking somewhere between "interesting" and "wonderful".* / **Details:** *11 pm; closed Mon & Sun D; no jeans or trainers; no smoking.*

### Marlow Bar & Grill £34 A
92-94 High St SL7 1AQ (01628) 488544
*A "buzzing" and "friendly" establishment, where the menu caters "for everything from a snack to a blow-out"; its 'plain vanilla' charms impress all who report on it.* / **Sample dishes:** *fried chilli squid with Thai noodle salad; grilled fillet steak; chocolate pudding with Maltesers ice cream.* **Details:** *www.individualrestaurant.co.uk; 11pm; no smoking area.*

### Royal Oak £32 A★
Frieth Rd, Bovingdon Grn SL7 2JF (01628) 488611
*"Pub food much better than the average" and service "with its finger on the pulse" creates an enthusiastic following for this "gastropub that's worthy of the name"; rurally located up a hill outside of the town, it benefits from a "great garden".*
/ **Sample dishes:** *crispy duck & chorizo salad; roast lamb fillet; chocolate brownie & chocolate sauce.* **Details:** *www.royaloakmarlow.co.uk; half mile up from Marlow High Street; 10 pm; no smoking area.*

**The Vanilla Pod**  **£50** ★
31 West St  SL7 2LS
(01628) 898101
*Michael Macdonald's "inventive" and "perfectly-presented" cuisine
seems to be getting back on track, at his "tiny" but ambitious
three-year-old; no one raves about the ambience, though.*
/ **Sample dishes:** scallops with vanilla-poached pears; sea bass with Szechuan
sauce; bitter chocolate fondant. **Details:** www.thevanillapod.co.uk; 10 pm; closed
Mon & Sun; no smoking.

---

## MARTON, NORTH YORKSHIRE                8–4C

**The Appletree Inn**                  **£34**      ★
YO62 6RD   (01751) 431457
*"Imaginative" food "of a very high standard" wins enthusiastic
approval from most reporters for this "friendly" and "welcoming"
gastropub.* / **Sample dishes:** brûléed English goat's cheese; daube of beef with
horseradish cream; orchard gooseberry crumble. **Details:** www.appletreeinn.co.uk;
9.30 pm; closed Mon & Tue; no Amex; no smoking.

---

## MASHAM, NORTH YORKSHIRE                8–4B

**Black Sheep Brewery Bistro**            **£27**
Wellgarth  HG4 4EN   (01765) 680101
*On a good day, it can be "fun" to visit this "wonderful" rustic
dining room attached to a brewery, which offers some "lovely"
simple fare (with lots for veggies) and "great beer"; at busy times,
though, it can get "crowded" and "raucous".*
/ **Sample dishes:** Beaujolais pâté with sweet green pickles; lamb shank; treacle tart
with ice cream. **Details:** www.blacksheep.co.uk; 9.30 pm; Sun-Wed L only,
Thu-Sat L & D; no Amex; no smoking area.

**Samuel's
Swinton Park**                      **£54**      Ⓐ★
HG4 4JH   (01765) 680900
*This "breath-taking and beautiful" country house hotel (set within
200 acres of a much larger estate) attracts many rapturous
reviews, thanks not least to new chef Andy Burton's "highly
successful" cooking (which makes much use of home-grown
vegetables).* / **Sample dishes:** pressed pig's cheek, foie gras & green
peppercorns; saltimbocca of rabbit & ravioli of leg; rhubarb, crumble & custard.
**Details:** www.swintonpark.com; 9.30 pm; no smoking; children: 8+ at
D. **Accommodation:** 30 rooms, from £140.

---

## MEDBOURNE, LEICESTERSHIRE                5–4D

**Horse & Trumpet**                    **£42**      ★
12 Old Grn  LE16 8DX   (01858) 565000
*An ex-Inverlochy Castle chef/patron runs this modern restaurant-
with-rooms in a former village pub; his cooking is generally (if not
invariably) hailed as "fantastic", but even one or two fans feel
"the setting and service just don't live up to the food".*
/ **Sample dishes:** crab salad; breast of Gressingham duck; chocolate peanut ice
cream. **Details:** www.horseandtrumpet.com; 9.30 pm; closed Mon & Sun D;
no Amex; no smoking area; children: 12+ at D. **Accommodation:** 4 rooms,
from £75.

**sign up for the survey at www.hardens.com**

## MELBOURN, CAMBRIDGESHIRE                3–1B

**The Pink Geranium**                        **£ 48**
25 Station Rd  SG8 6DX   (01763) 260215
*Reports on this pretty and once-celebrated cottage have become
very mixed; the occasional fan says it "still impresses in every
way", but – on some recent accounts – the performance risks
becoming plain "amateur". / Sample dishes: smoked salmon; roast rack
of lamb; crème brûlée with raspberry coulis. Details: www.pinkgeranium.co.uk;
off A10, 2nd exit (opp church); 9.30 pm; closed Mon & Sun D; no smoking.*

**Sheene Mill**                        **£ 49**        A★
Station Rd  SG8 6DX   (01763) 261393
*TV-chef Steven Saunders's prettily-located operation, "overlooking
the river", strikes most reporters as "excellent in every way";
be prepared, though – it's "awash with info about how wonderful
Saunders is". / Sample dishes: Thai seafood salad of tiger prawns; roast rib-eye
of Angus beef; rich organic chocolate truffle cake. Details: www.sheenemill.co.uk;
off A10, 10m S of Cambridge; 10 pm; closed Sun D; jacket required; no smoking.
Accommodation: 9 rooms, from £95.*

## MELBOURNE, DERBYSHIRE                5–3C

**Bay Tree**                        **£ 44**        A★
4 Potter St  DE73 8HW   (01332) 863358
*"It has a great new look, but the food is as reliable as ever";
Rex Howell's "friendly" and "intimate" former coaching inn,
recently extended, is hailed by pretty much all reporters for its
"always-excellent" (if quite "expensive") cuisine, and its "informal
but attentive" service. / Sample dishes: seared beef fillets with Caesar salad;
milk chocolate & raspberry cheesecake. Details: www.baytreerestaurant.co.uk;
10 pm; closed Mon & Sun D; mainly non-smoking.*

## MELLOR, CHESHIRE                5–2B

**Oddfellows Arms**                        **£ 29**
73 Moor End Rd  SK6 5PT   (0161) 449 7826
*"An old pub, with modern food", offering a "lovely" setting and
"a good menu" – with fish and seafood especially commended –
"at fair prices"; there's no booking, though, and it's "often too
crowded". / Sample dishes: herrings with mustard sour cream; Catalan pork
tenderloin; frosted peach schnapps cheesecake. Details: 7m S of Stockport;
9.30 pm; closed Mon & Sun D; no Amex; no smoking.*

## MELMERBY, CUMBRIA                8–3A

**Shepherd's Inn**                        **£ 24**
CA10 1HF   (0870) 745 3383
*A spectacular view is a highpoint at this rural inn, which was little
commented-on this year, but always very favourably; it was in the
process of being sold as we went to press, hence we've left
it unrated. / Sample dishes: dill-marinated herrings; breaded wholetail scampi;
lemon cheesecake. Details: 9.45 pm weekends 9pm weekdays; no Amex;
no smoking area; no booking.*

**Village Bakery**                £24        ★★

CA10 1HE   (01768) 881811

*"We once came for breakfast... from Manchester"; fans are crazy for this "busy all-day" bakery Mecca – part of the set-up which supplies shops nationally, it is known for "home-made organic food at its best". / **Sample dishes:** breast & leg of chicken in a red wine & mushroom sauce; bread & butter pudding. **Details:** www.village-bakery.com; 10m NE of Penrith on A686; 4.45 pm; L only; no Amex; no smoking; need 6+ to book.*

---

## MERTHYR TYDFIL, MERTHYR TYDFIL        4–4D

**Nant Ddu Lodge**                £31

Brecon Rd   CF48 2HY   (01685) 379111

*"Surprisingly good food" is the gist of almost all commentary on the dining room of this family-run hotel/bistro/spa, south of Brecon. / **Sample dishes:** chicken liver & hazelnut pâté; braised lamb; sticky toffee pudding. **Details:** www.nant-ddu-lodge.co.uk; 6m N of Merthyr on A470; 9.30 pm; no smoking area. **Accommodation:** 31 rooms, from £90.*

---

## MICKLEHAM, SURREY        3–3A

**King William IV**                £28        ★

Byttom Hill   RH5 6EL   (01372) 372590

*"Dependable pub grub and lovely views" help make this "very consistent" inn popular with all who comment on it. / **Sample dishes:** garlic bread with Mozzarella & sundried tomatoes; steak & kidney pie; treacle tart. **Details:** www.king-williamiv.com; off A24; 9.30 pm; closed Sun D; no Amex; no booking in summer; children: 12+.*

---

## MIDDLESEX, GREATER LONDON        3–3A

**L'Orient**                £59        Ⓐ

58 High St   HA5 5PZ   (020) 8429 8488

*The menu may be a mélange – "Japanese, Chinese, Malay, Thai" – but it "works well", at this "warm-hearted" spot, housed in a Tudor building. / **Sample dishes:** smoked chicken with a chilli dipping; roast duck in coconut-flavoured green curry; glazed pineapple. **Details:** www.lorientcuisine.com; 11 pm; smoking in bar only.*

---

## MIDSOMER NORTON, SOMERSET        2–3B

**Moody Goose**
**The Old Priory Hotel**                £42

Church Sq   BA3 2HX   (01225) 466688

*Stephen Shore's "fantastic" cuisine long merited a better home than a downbeat Bath basement, but he moved to this new restaurant-with-rooms – in a medieval priory – too late in 2005 to figure in the survey; if he and his wife successfully translate the standards of their old venture, it should be well worth a trip. / **Sample dishes:** smoked haddock ravioli with goat's cheese; chicken with crayfish & artichoke mousse; passion fruit soufflé. **Details:** www.moody-goose.com; 9.30 pm; closed Sun; no smoking; children: 7+.*

---

## MILTON ERNEST, BEDFORDSHIRE    3–1A

**Strawberry Tree**    £ 53    ★

3 Radwell Rd  MK44 1RY   (01234) 823633

"Excellent cooking", imbued with "artful simplicity" – albeit from
a menu offering "limited choice" – makes this "eccentric" family-
run restaurant "an oasis in a dessert"; service can grate, though,
with the overall approach striking some reporters
as "too reverential". / **Details:** 9 pm; closed Mon, Tue, Sat L & Sun; no Amex;
no smoking.

---

## MILTON KEYNES, BUCKINGHAMSHIRE    3–2A

**Jaipur**    £ 26

599 Grafton Gate East  MK9 1AT   (01908) 669796

It can seem "expensive" – especially given the "vast" scale of the
enterprise – but the "well-spiced" food at this purpose-built Indian
generally satisfies. / **Sample dishes:** samosas; chicken tikka masala; rasmalai.
**Details:** www.jaipur.co.uk; 11.30 pm; no smoking.

---

## MORSTON, NORFOLK    6–3C

**Morston Hall**    £ 56    ★★

Main Coast Rd  NR25 7AA   (01263) 741041

"Quite simply the best dining experience of my adult life" –
fans are not shy in their praise for the "stylish" and
"sophisticated" (but no-choice) cuisine Galton Blackiston offers
at this "luxurious" but "unpretentious" hotel, near the coast.
/ **Sample dishes:** Milanese risotto with deep-fried leeks; roast lamb with buttery
mash; sticky toffee pudding. **Details:** www.morstonhall.com; between Blakeney &
Wells on A149; 8 pm; D only, ex Sun open L & D; no Amex; no smoking.
**Accommodation:** 7 rooms, from £105.

---

## MOULSFORD, OXFORDSHIRE    2–2D

**Beetle & Wedge**    £ 49    Ⓐ

Ferry Ln  OX10 9JF   (01491) 651381

A "fantastic setting by the Thames" – on the stretch that inspired
'The Wind in the Willows' – has long made it a "special"
experience to visit this riverside fixture; the hotel itself is for sale
as this guide goes to press, but the boathouse rôtisserie – which
has always outshone the main dining room – looks set to carry on.
/ **Sample dishes:** seared scallops; squid & prawns; meringue with red fruit.
**Details:** www.beetleandwedge.co.uk; on A329 between Streatley & Wallingford,
take Ferry Lane at crossroads; 9 pm.

---

## MOULTON, NORTH YORKSHIRE    8–3B

**Black Bull**    £ 46    Ⓐ★

DL10 6QJ   (01325) 377289

This "unchanging favourite" – where owner and chef have
60 years' experience between them – is "still the best pub-based
venue in the North East", for some reporters; "great seafood" is a
highlight – for preference, consume it in the "intimate" Pullman
railway carriage dining room. / **Sample dishes:** shellfish bisque; griddled
king scallops with black pudding; chocolate & amaretti terrine. **Details:** 1m S of
Scotch Corner; 10.15 pm; closed Sun; smoking in bar only; children: 7+.

---

**sign up for the survey at www.hardens.com**

## MUCH WENLOCK, SHROPSHIRE                    5–4B

### The Raven Hotel & Restaurant           £37
Barrow St  TF13 6EN   (01952) 727251
*"Happy" staff contribute to the "relaxing" feel of a visit to this
17th-century coaching inn, which offers "good food" and
"good value"; the odd reporter, though, finds the cooking "a bit
fussy".* / **Sample dishes:** fillet of Scottish salmon; pan-fried beef with black
pudding & sweet potato tian; cherry parfait with coconut tuiles.
**Details:** www.ravenhotel.com; 9 pm; no smoking. **Accommodation:** 14 rooms,
from £95.

## MYLOR BRIDGE, CORNWALL                     1–4B

### The Pandora Inn                        £33        Ⓐ
Restronguet Creek  TR11 5ST   (01326) 372678
*"Arrive by boat", best to appreciate this idyllically-located ancient
pub (which has a pontoon for sunny-day dining) – it "must be
tempting to rely on the location", says one reporter, but the
"quality" food and "helpful" service show no sign of doing so.*
/ **Sample dishes:** avocado, mango & smoked salmon salad; turbot with greens;
lemon ricotta cheesecake. **Details:** www.pandorainn.com; signposted off A390,
between Truro & Falmouth; 9 pm; no Amex; no smoking.

## NANT-Y-DERRY, MONMOUTHSHIRE               2–2A

### The Foxhunter                         £42      Ⓐ★★
Abergavenny  NP7 9DN   (01873) 881101
*"Extraordinarily good cooking" in a "lovely refurbished old pub" –
originally, in fact, a stationmaster's house – is proving a simple but
winning formula for the Tebbutts' accomplished four-year-old.*
/ **Details:** www.thefoxhunter.com; 9.30 pm; closed Mon & Sun; no Amex; smoking
in bar only.

## NAYLAND, SUFFOLK                           3–2C

### White Hart                            £36        ★
11 High St  C06 4JF   (01206) 263382
*This Constable Country restaurant-with-rooms, part-owned
by Michel Roux, has put in a much more consistent performance
of late, with all reporters now supporting the view that it offers
"remarkably good value".* / **Sample dishes:** rock fish soup; roast suckling pig
with sweet potato purée; sticky toffee pudding.
**Details:** www.whitehart-nayland.co.uk; off A12, between Colchester & Sudbury;
9.30 pm, Sat 10 pm. **Accommodation:** 6 rooms, from £92.

## NETHER ALDERLEY, CHESHIRE                  5–2B

### The Wizard                            £43      Ⓐ★
Macclesfield Rd  SK10 4UB   (01625) 584000
*"Consistently good food" is the gist of all reports on this "relaxed"
and "welcoming" former pub.* / **Sample dishes:** baby spinach, avocado &
Gorgonzola salad; herb-crusted cod with pea purée; rice pudding with stem ginger &
maple syrup. **Details:** www.racquetclub.org.uk; from A34, take B5087; 9 pm; closed
Mon & Sun D; no smoking area.

## NETHER BROUGHTON, LEICESTERSHIRE     5–3D
### Red House     £ 40
23 Main St LE14 3HB    (01664) 822429
*A trendified pub, hotel and restaurant that's generally hailed as a "relaxed" and "good-value" destination; the chef changed during the course of the reviewing year, so we think a proper appraisal should wait until the next edition. / **Sample dishes:** asparagus & Feta cheese; roast rump of lamb; summer pudding with yoghurt.
**Details:** www.the-redhouse.com; 9.30 pm; closed Sun D; no smoking.
**Accommodation:** 8 rooms, from £50.*

---

## NEW MILTON, HAMPSHIRE     2–4C
### Chewton Glen     £ 85    Ⓐ
Christchurch Rd BH25 6QS    (01425) 275341
*"Idyllic surroundings" in the New Forest and "smooth" service create a "dream" experience for devotees of this ultra-"plush" country house retreat; fans say its "rich" cuisine nicely rounds off the formula, but others feel it "could be a bit more ambitious". / **Sample dishes:** cheese soufflé; roast scallops; rhubarb & custard crumble with strawberry ice cream. **Details:** www.chewtonglen.com; on A337 between New Milton & Highcliffe; 9.30 pm; no smoking; children: 5+. **Accommodation:** 58 rooms, from £290.*

---

## NEWARK, NOTTINGHAMSHIRE     5–3D
### Café Bleu     £ 37    Ⓐ★
14 Castle Gate NG24 1BG    (01636) 610141
*This town-centre fixture remains a "top quality" regional "favourite" – the cooking is extremely "sound", but it's the "intimate" atmosphere and "good-value" prices that particularly underpin its success; nice courtyard in summer. / **Sample dishes:** sardines with saffron couscous; braised Aberdeen beef with baby carrots; lemon posset with champagne sorbet. **Details:** www.cafebleu.co.uk; 9.30 pm; closed Sun D; no Amex, no smoking area.*

---

## NEWBURY, BERKSHIRE     2–2D
### The Crab at Chieveley      £ 48    ★
Wantage Rd RG20 8UE
(01635) 247550
*"Superb and innovative" (albeit "pricey") cooking – including "the best seafood anywhere this far inland" – is earning a widespread reputation for this "cosy" inn (which has some "exquisite" themed bedrooms). / **Sample dishes:** creamed salt cod & sweet red pepper salad; cod chunk, salsify, buttered samphire & parsley sauce; hot chocolate fondant & Murphy's ice cream. **Details:** www.crabatchieveley.com; 9.30 pm, Fri & Sat 10 pm; no smoking in dining room. **Accommodation:** 10 rooms, from £140.*

---

## NEWCASTLE UPON TYNE, TYNE & WEAR     8–2B

Newcastle is a famously going-out kind of city (with most of the action centred around the Quayside). It has not traditionally been considered a great quality restaurant destination, but this seems to be changing fast, with outstanding openings such as *Black Door* and *Secco* now joining the likes of *Fisherman's Lodge* and *Treacle Moon*. Towards the cheaper end, *Pani's* and *Valley Junction 397* stand out.

### Barn @ the Biscuit £37
16 Stoddard St NE2 IAN (0191) 230 3338
*"Imaginative" but "eclectic" cooking – sometimes "variable",
but usually "competent" – and an "interesting" setting make this
local institution extremely popular; it is sadly no longer housed
in a barn, but its new site offers the "added delight" of an
en suite art gallery.* / **Sample dishes:** risotto with sun-brushed tomatoes &
basil pesto; chocolate tart with chocolate ice cream.
**Details:** www.thebiscuitfactory.com; follow Biscuit factory signs; 9:45 pm; closed
Sun D; smoking in bar only.

### The Black Door £54 A★★
32 Clayton Street West NE1 5DZ
(0191) 2616295

*This "wonderful" newcomer by St Mary's Cathedral – many of
whose staff, including the chef, worked at the old 21 Queen
Street – is hailed by early reporters as a simply "excellent" dining
experience, "from the first champagne cocktail to the perfect
cheese and petit fours".* / **Sample dishes:** crisp pork belly with seared
scallops; Northumberland beef and rosti potatoes; apple crumble parfait with
blackberry compote. **Details:** www.blackdoorrestaurant.co.uk; 10 pm; closed
Mon & Sun; no smoking.

### Blackfriars Café Bar £36
Friars St NE1 4XN (0191) 2615945
*Quite an "atmospheric" location (in a 13th-century refectory) and
"interesting" dishes make this a popular local stand-by; the food
is "good, rather than exceptional", but rarely disappoints.*
/ **Sample dishes:** black pudding & foie gras; wild sea trout with almond salad;
chocolate truffles with a passion fruit cream. **Details:** www.blackfriarscafebar.co.uk;
10 pm; closed Mon & Sun D; no Amex; no smoking.

### Café 21 £45
21 Queen St, Princes Whf NE1 3UG (0191) 222 0755
*Terry Laybourne's original venture – formerly called 21 Queen
Street – has long been the local "benchmark", known for
"fabulous food" and "good value"; it still has many fans, but the
complaints from those who say it's "not maintaining quality and
consistency" are becoming too loud to ignore.* / **Sample dishes:** grilled
gambas; roast sirloin of organic Aberdeen Angus beef; chocolate soufflé.
**Details:** 10.30 pm; closed Sun; no smoking area.

### Café Live £35
27 Broad Chare NE1 3DQ (0191) 232 1331
*An improving spin-off from Café 21, praised this year for its
"good" (if "unimaginative") cuisine, its "quick" and "friendly"
service, and its "great" Quayside location.*
/ **Details:** www.live.org.uk/information/CafeLive.php; 10.30 pm; closed Sun.

### Café Royal £31
8 Nelson St NE1 5AW (0191) 231 3000
*This "light and airy" ("but very crowded") grand café has been
almost too successful (and service can suffer); it has become the
city's top breakfast/brunch destination, and the Mediterranean
fare at other times is generally pretty good too.*
/ **Sample dishes:** crispy duck & watercress salad; beefburger; blueberry
cheesecake. **Details:** www.sjf.co.uk; 6 pm, Thu 8; L only, ex Thu open L &
D; no smoking.

## Fisherman's Lodge £61 ★
Jesmond Dene NE7 7BQ (0191) 281 3281
An "unparalleled location" – in the "beautiful parkland"
of Jesmond Dene – helps make this 'local-hero' fish restaurant
(the best-known location in town) a tranquil "oasis";
it's "very expensive", though, and not all reporters are convinced
that the place continues to improve, as it initially did, under its
new owners. / **Sample dishes:** assiette of crab; salmon with langoustine sauce;
chocolate ganache tart. **Details:** www.fishermanslodge.co.uk; 2m from city centre
on A1058, follow signposts to Jesmond Dene; 10.30 pm; closed Sun; no smoking;
children: 8+.

## Francesca's £18 &#x1D538;
Manor House Rd NE2 2NE (0191) 281 6586
A "brisk", "friendly" and "fantastically atmospheric" pizzeria
that's long been a local institution; "the recent extension means
less time queuing". / **Sample dishes:** garlic king prawns; mixed fish grill;
tiramisu. **Details:** 9.30 pm; closed Sun; no Amex; no smoking area; no booking.

## Heartbreak Soup £31
77 The Quayside NE1 3DE (0191) 222 1701
An "always varied" menu – with an "interesting mix of vegetarian,
Mexican and fish", not to mention some "lovely" Thai dishes –
wins consistent popularity for this "friendly" bistro, "handy for the
vibrant Quayside". / **Sample dishes:** Korean beef skewers; tandoori tempura
of monkfish; white chocolate baked cheesecake. **Details:** www.heartbreaksoup.com;
overlooking the River Tyne; 10 pm, Fri & Sat 11 pm; D only, closed Sun; no Amex
or Switch.

## King Neptune £31
34-36 Stowell St NE1 4XQ (0191) 261 6657
This Chinatown veteran has a pre-eminent local reputation,
not least for its seafood, and is "always busy"; the odd reporter,
though, finds it "over-rated". / **Sample dishes:** crispy duck pancakes;
chicken with Szechuan sauce; lemon sorbet. **Details:** www.kingneptune.biz;
10.45 pm.

## Malmaison Brasserie £41
Quayside NE1 3DX (0191) 245 5000
The recent refurbishment may strike some reporters as "awful",
but it does seem to have bucked up standards at this design-hotel
dining-room-with-a-view – previously dreadful, it is now merely
"run-of-the-mill". / **Sample dishes:** artichokes & asparagus; steamed sea bass
with radish & aubergine salad; English cheese platter. **Details:** www.malmaison.com;
10.30 pm; no smoking. **Accommodation:** 120 rooms, from £99.

## McCoys Rooftop at the Baltic
### Baltic £49 ✗
South Shore Rd NE8 3BA (0191) 440 4949
"Great views, but not good value for money" (so "a bit like the
Oxo Tower really") – reporters are pretty consistently of the view
that this top-floor arts-centre restaurant is "a disappointing barn
of a place". / **Sample dishes:** langoustine ravioli; braised pork wrapped in Parma
ham; chocolate bread pudding. **Details:** www.balticmill.com; 9.30 pm; closed Sun D;
no smoking.

## Pani's    £22    A★
61-65 High Bridge  NE1 6BX  (0191) 232 4366
*"Like stepping into Naples"*, this *"genuine"* and *"authentic"* café
has a huge fan club, thanks not least to its *"good Italian food
at reasonable prices"*. / **Sample dishes:** *bruschetta; chicken stuffed with
Dolcelatte; tiramisu.* **Details:** *www.paniscafe.com; off Gray Street; 10 pm; closed
Sun; no Amex; no smoking; no booking at L.*

## Paradiso    £35    A
1 Market Ln  NE1 6QQ  (0191) 221 1240
*"Excellent for a quick lunch or a more relaxed evening"*,
this *"cool"* and *"intimate"* destination remains a very popular
stand-by; the daytime menu, in particular, is *"a steal"*.
/ **Sample dishes:** *chicken brochette marinated in honey & ginger; lamb targine with
cumin; chocolate & rum mousse.* **Details:** *www.gustouk.com; opp fire station;
10.45 pm; closed Sun; no Amex; no smoking area.*

## Sachins    £28
Forth Banks  NE1 3SG  (0191) 261 9035
This *"long-established"* and *"reliable"* Punjabi restaurant is still
much-tipped locally as a *"top Indian"*; it strikes some reporters
as pretty *"standard"*, though. / **Details:** *www.sachins.co.uk; behind Central
Station; 11.15 pm; closed Sun.*

## Sale Pepe    £17
115 St George's Ter  NE2 2DN  (0191) 281 1431
A *"cheap and cheerful"* Italian, popular *"with students and
families"*. / **Details:** *10.30 pm; closed Sun.*

## Secco Ristorante Salentino    £41    A★
86 Pilgrim St  NE1 6SG
(0191) 230 0444
This *"glamorous"* and *"beautifully decorated"* yearling has been
an immediate hit, helped by its *"very attentive"* service and
*"sophisticated"* cuisine – it's *"surely one of the best Italians
outside London"*. / **Sample dishes:** *octopus with cannellini beans; strips
of pasta with buffalo Mozzarella.* **Details:** *www.seccouk.com; 10 pm; closed Sun;
no smoking.*

## Treacle Moon    £52    A★
5-7 The Side  NE1 3JE  (0191) 232 5537
Especially for *"an intimate dining experience"*, this *"romantic"*
Quayside fixture has made a name is some quarters as *"reliably
the best place in town"*; its *"eclectic mix of Mediterranean and
Far Eastern dishes"* is consistently highly rated.
/ **Sample dishes:** *brie & asparagus spring roll; chargrilled beef fillet with roast
shallots and dauphine potatoes; sticky fig & ginger pudding.*
**Details:** *www.treaclemoonrestaurant.com; beneath Tyne Bridge on Quayside;
10.30 pm; D only, closed Sun; smoking in bar only.*

## Valley Junction 397    £35    A★
Old Jesmond Stn, Archbold Ter  NE2 1DB  (0191) 281 6397
The food may be *"standard Indian"*, but it's *"done well"* at this
intriguing restaurant, in a former signal box; aperitifs are taken
in a railway carriage. / **Sample dishes:** *kebabs; salmon cooked with herbs;
Indian sweets.* **Details:** *www.valleyrestaurants.co.uk; near Civic Centre, off Sandyford
Rd; 11.15 pm; closed Mon, Fri L & Sun L; no smoking.*

**sign up for the survey at www.hardens.com**

**Vujon** £ 29
29 Queen St NE1 3UG (0191) 221 0601
"A posh Indian in a great Quayside location"; it serves
an "interesting range" of dishes, but the occasional reporter feels
"the realisation is not quite as good as it should be".
/ **Details:** www.vujon.demon.co.uk; 11 pm; closed Sun L.

---

NEWENT, GLOUCESTERSHIRE 2–1B

**Three Choirs Vineyards** £ 43 🄰
GL18 1LS (01531) 890223
"A wonderful setting overlooking the vineyard" makes a trip to this
"delightful" dining room rather an unusual experience;
its "rare mix" of fine English wines with "interesting" modern
cuisine (mostly) gets the thumbs-up from reporters.
/ **Sample dishes:** potato, celeriac, streaky bacon & wood pigeon terrine; seared
duck breast; sticky pear & ginger pudding.
**Details:** www.three-choirs-vineyards.co.uk; 9 pm; closed Mon L; no Amex;
no smoking. **Accommodation:** 8 rooms, from £95.

---

NEWICK, EAST SUSSEX 3–4B

**Newick Park**
**Newick Park Hotel** £ 54 🄰
BN8 4SB (01825) 723633
"A great venue for the right occasion"; this "formal" country
house hotel offers a classic dining experience of its type,
underpinned by some "competent" cooking.
/ **Sample dishes:** lobster & basil with crab soup; fillet steak with foie gras sauce;
caramelised apples with vanilla ice cream. **Details:** www.newickpark.co.uk; 8.45 pm;
jacket required at D; no smoking. **Accommodation:** 16 rooms, from £165.

---

NEWLAND, GLOUCESTERSHIRE 2–2B

**The Ostrich Inn** £ 33 🄰★
GL16 8NP (01594) 833260
A "very rustic" village pub that's winning wider support with its
"excellent and adventurous" menu at "reasonable prices"; service
is "cheery" too. / **Sample dishes:** pan-fried goat's cheese; rack of lamb with
garlic potato; chocolate amaretti pudding. **Details:** www.theostrichinn.com; 2m SW
of Coleford; 9.15 pm; no smoking area.

---

NEWPORT, NEWPORT 2–2A

**The Chandlery** £ 37 🄰
77-78 Lower Dock St NP20 1EH (01633) 256622
It continues to attract modest feedback, but all reports confirm
the high standards of this attractively-housed restaurant –
it's "very popular", thanks not least to its "consistently good" food.
/ **Sample dishes:** smoked chicken terrine; peach & almond tart with lemon curd ice
cream. **Details:** www.thechandleryrestaurant.com; at the foot of George St bridge
on the A48 (hospital side); 10 pm; closed Mon, Sat L & Sun; no Switch;
no smoking area.

**sign up for the survey at www.hardens.com**

## NEWTON LONGVILLE, BUCKINGHAMSHIRE    3–2A

**Crooked Billet**    £39

2 Westbrook End  MK17 0DF   (01908) 373936

*"An excellent variety of wines by the glass" is the special attraction of this old pub, which sometimes offers "imaginative" cooking too; the location, though, is sub-optimal – the place "sticks out like a thatched cottage on a council estate... which is more or less what it is".* / **Sample dishes:** *cream of pea soup; hazelnut & pistachio crusted chicken breast; fine apple tart & vanilla ice cream.* **Details:** *www.thebillet.co.uk; 10 pm; D only, ex Sun open L only; no smoking.*

## NEWTON-ON-THE-MOOR, NORTHUMBERLAND    8–2B

**Cook & Barker**    £33

NE65 9JY   (01665) 575234

*Handy for A1 travellers, an inn that's worth knowing about for "the best pub food in the area"; it's also "excellent with children".* / **Sample dishes:** *avocado, tandoori chicken & rocket salad; pot-roast lamb with bubble 'n' squeak; Belgian chocolate truffle cake.* **Details:** *12m N of Morpeth, just off A1; 9 pm.* **Accommodation:** *19 rooms, from £70.*

## NOMANSLAND, WILTSHIRE    2–3C

**Les Mirabelles**    £34    A★★

Forest Edge Rd  SP5 2BN   (01794) 390205

*This "excellent", "very French" restaurant, "in a lovely village" on the fringe of the New Forest, wins all-round rave reviews for its "superb" food, its "friendly" service and its "homely" atmosphere.* / **Sample dishes:** *smoked salmon mousse; lamb fillet; crème brûlée.* **Details:** *off A36 between Southampton & Salisbury; 9.30 pm; closed Mon & Sun; no smoking area.*

## NORDEN, LANCASHIRE    5–1B

**Nutter's**    £45    ★

Edenfield Rd  OL12 7TT   (01706) 650167

*In its "less homely" new premises, TV chef Andrew Nutter's eminent restaurant divides opinion – fans still praise his "outstanding" food and "lovely service from members of his family", but critics fear the approach is becoming "overblown" and smacks of "mass-catering".* / **Sample dishes:** *black pudding won tons; peppered fillet of lamb with lemon & black olive mash; cappuccino panna cotta.* **Details:** *www.nuttersrestaurant.com; between Edenfield & Norden on A680; 9.30 pm; closed Mon; closed 2 weeks in Aug; no smoking.*

## NORTH WALSHAM, NORFOLK    6–4D

**Beechwood Hotel**    £44    A★

Cromer Rd  NR28 0HD   (01692) 403231

*This "harmoniously extended" country house hotel doesn't inspire much commentary, but it's all to the effect that its pretty dining room offers a "great and varied menu".* / **Sample dishes:** *carrot, cumin & coriander soup; grilled lemon sole; selection of desserts.* **Details:** *www.beechwood-hotel.co.uk; 9 pm; no smoking; children: 10+ at D.* **Accommodation:** *17 rooms, from £120.*

## NORTON, SHROPSHIRE                    5–4B

### Hundred House                    £ 45
Bridgnorth Rd  TF11 9EE   (01952) 730353
"Nothing better till you hit Ludlow"; this "unpretentious"
gastropub in a fascinating old building offers "straightforward"
fare which – though "not exceptional" – is "among the best
options in the area". / *Sample dishes: shallot, fennel & goat's cheese tartlet;
wild boar with white bean casserole & chorizo; raspberry & meringue ice cream.*
*Details: www.hundredhouse.co.uk; on A442 between Bridgnorth & Telford; 9 pm;
no smoking area. Accommodation: 10 rooms, from £99.*

## NORWICH, NORFOLK                    6–4C

### Adlards                    £ 50        ★
79 Upper Giles St  NR2 1AB   (01603) 633522
Roger Hickman's "serious" but "nicely balanced" dishes, delivered
by "informal but attentive" staff, help maintain this eminent
townhouse-restaurant as a "firm favourite" for many reporters.
/ *Sample dishes: foie gras in cumin; veal with mash & roast parsnips; banana tarte
Tatin. Details: www.adlards.co.uk; near the Roman Catholic Cathedral; 10.30 pm;
closed Mon & Sun; no smoking.*

### Brummells                    £ 45        A★
7 Magdalen St  NR3 1LE   (01603) 625555
"Truly excellent food" and a "superb wine list" figure in most
(if not quite all) reports on this ambitious restaurant, prettily
housed in a 17th-century building; service is generally very good,
but seems to have its off-days. / *Sample dishes: seafood pancakes with
aniseed sauce; sea bass & leeks with prawn butter; stewed caramelised pears
in orange liqueur. Details: www.brummells.co.uk; 10.30 pm; smoking in bar only.*

### Tatlers                    £ 44
21 Tombland  NR3 1RF   (01603) 766670
"Good-value cooking" (from "local produce") helps make this
"well-located", buzzy bistro a popular stand-by; service is up-and-
down, though, and its acoustics can make it too "echoey" and
"noisy". / *Sample dishes: poached oysters; roasted saddle of lamb; English
strawberry & Mascarpone tart. Details: www.tatlers.com; near Cathedral, next to
Erpingham Gate; 10 pm; closed Sun; no smoking.*

### The Tree House                    £ 22        ★
14-16 Dove St  NR2 1DE   (01603) 763258
"A fantastic veggie eatery, with gorgeous healthy food" –
this quirky co-operative continues to go down well as an "ethical"
and "great-value" choice. / *Sample dishes: spicy tomato & lentil soup;
potato & cauliflower curry with rice; blueberry tofu cheesecake. Details: 9 pm;
L only Mon-Wed, closed Sun; no credit cards; no smoking; no booking at L.*

### Waffle House                    £ 20
39 St Giles St  NR2 1JN   (01603) 612790
"Even more of a Norwich institution than Delia!" – this "reliable"
destination serves "great, wholesome and tasty organic waffles"
and "very good coffee". / *Sample dishes: garlic mushrooms; ham, cheese &
mushroom waffle; banana & butterscotch waffle. Details: 10 pm; no Amex;
no smoking; need 6+ to book.*

## NOSS MAYO, DEVON                    1–4C

### Ship Inn                          £31    A★
PL8 1EW   (01752) 872387
*This "smart-casual" waterside inn is consistently hailed
by reporters as offering "very good food" in a "delightful" setting
– "well worth a detour".* / **Sample dishes:** smoked salmon; salad of Cornish
scallops with smoked bacon; sticky toffee pudding. **Details:** www.nossmayo.com;
9.30 pm; no Amex; no smoking; children: no children at D.

## NOTTINGHAM, CITY OF NOTTINGHAM  5–3D

First-time visitors might be surprised at the range of solid mid-
range dining destinations in Nottingham. It has perhaps been
in need of a real 'figurehead' in recent times: the relaunched
*Hotel des Clos* may well provide it. *Hart's* remains by far the
best-known local destination by quite a margin. The continuing
success of the trendy *World Service* is also impressive.

### Atlas                            £ 7    ★
9 Pelham St  NG1 2EH   (0115) 950 1295
*"Exquisite sarnies" and "delicious coffees" are among the
attractions which make this Mediterranean café/deli a "quick" but
"thoroughly satisfying" experience – it has a huge following among
local reporters.* / **Sample dishes:** ciabatta with tuna, basil & plum tomatoes;
home-made cakes. **Details:** L only; no smoking.

### Bluu                             £35
5 Broadway  NG1 1PR   (0115) 9505359
*The most commented-on member of a small national chain of hip
bar/restaurants – this "fashionably-located" former warehouse,
in the Lace Market, attracts consistent praise for its "tasty modern
cooking".* / **Sample dishes:** beef carpaccio; roast rump of Cumbrian lamb; lemon
posset. **Details:** www.bluu.co.uk; 10 pm; no smoking.

### Broadway Cinema Bar              £20
14-18 Broadway, Broad St  NG1 3AL   (0115) 952 1551
*A "funky" spot that's "always reliable for a light bite" (and "great
for veggies", too); for a cheap night out ("around £7 a head"),
its "great-value combined cinema and food ticket" is hard to beat.*
/ **Sample dishes:** vegetarian pâté; mudcakes. **Details:** 9 pm; no Amex;
no smoking area.

### Chino Latino
### Park Plaza Nottingham            £41
41 Maid Marian Way  NG1 6GD   (0115) 9477444
*Critics dismiss this oriental-Latin fusion joint as "a ghastly attempt
to be stylish, to ruthlessly mediocre effect"; most reporters are
more positive, though – even if they agree its "noisy bar/club
ambience" is "tacky", they say the food can be "superb".*
/ **Sample dishes:** duck wrapped in cucumber; three-sauce fillet; hot chocolate
fondant. **Details:** www.chinolatino.co.uk; 10.30 pm; closed Sun; no smoking.

### French Living £ 25
27 King St NG1 2AY (0115) 958 5885
*This "quirky" cellar bistro remains quite a local favourite,
with most reporters cherishing its culinary style – "cheap and
cheerful French cooking as some of us remember it from 30 years
ago".* / **Sample dishes:** *Burgundy snails; venison with peppered blueberry sauce;
crème brûlée with Tahiti vanilla.* **Details:** *www.frenchliving.co.uk; near Market
Square; 10 pm; closed Mon & Sun; no Amex; no smoking; booking: max 10.*

### Geisha £ 40     Ⓐ
3 Broadway NG1 1PR (0115) 9598344
*In its early days, this "beautifully-finished restaurant/bar/club",
which serves a "Japanese-esque" pan-Asian menu, has not
attracted very much feedback; one early convert says it's "under-
appreciated, perhaps because it's quite expensive".*
/ **Sample dishes:** *beef skewers; black cod; baked cheese fondant with passion fruit
sauce.* **Details:** *www.geishauk.com; 10 pm; closed Mon & Sun; no smoking;
children: 16+.*

### Hart's £ 48     ★
Standard Ct, Park Row NG1 6GN (0115) 911 0666
*"Cooking of the highest standard" has long made Tim Hart's
"smart" and professional brasserie by far the best-known place
in town; some find its "light and airy" setting a mite "clinical",
though, and a few reporters fear it's either getting "too slick"
or "resting on its laurels".* / **Sample dishes:** *courgette tart; veal with
spinach & Parmesan risotto; tarte Tatin with caramel ice cream.*
**Details:** *www.hartsnottingham.co.uk; near Castle; 10 pm; no smoking.*
**Accommodation:** *32 rooms, from £120.*

### Mem Saab £ 29
12-14 Maid Marian Way NG1 6HS (0115) 957 0009
*This "upmarket" subcontinental is still tipped as the "top Indian"
locally thanks to its "consistent" cuisine; under the new ownership,
some reporters, however, bemoan the "disappearance of some
of the more interesting dishes".* / **Sample dishes:** *chicken tikka; tandoori
salmon; home-made kulfi.* **Details:** *www.mem-saab.co.uk; near Castle, opposite Park
Plaza Hotel; 10.30 pm, Fri & Sat 11 pm; D only, closed Sun; no smoking.*

### Merchants
### Lace Market Hotel £ 41     Ⓐ
29-31 High Pavement NG1 1HE (0115) 958 9898
*With its "glamorous" and "romantic" looks, this design-hotel
dining room continues to benefit from its major 2004 make-over
(overseen by star designer David Collins); the food can be "tasty"
and "well presented", but it can also be "variable".*
/ **Sample dishes:** *aubergine, smoked Mozzarella & chorizo tart; tuna steak with
cherry tomato salad; vanilla & blackcurrant bavarois.*
**Details:** *www.merchantsnottingham.co.uk; 10.30 pm; closed Mon L & Sun;
no smoking.* **Accommodation:** *42 rooms, from £112.*

### Petit Paris £ 28
2 Kings Walk NG1 2AE (0115) 947 3767
*"Reliable" and "consistent" are terms usually present in reports
on this "useful" city-centre "stand-by", which is "convenient for the
theatres".* / **Sample dishes:** *smoked chicken & mushroom pancake; veal with
mushroom & brandy flambé; profiteroles with hot chocolate sauce.*
**Details:** *www.petit-paris.co.uk; near Theatre Royal; 10.15 pm; closed Sun;
no smoking.*

**Pretty Orchid**  £33

12 Pepper St NG1 2GH   (0115) 958 8344

*"Well-established" city-centre Thai, whose cooking is rated "good"
to "very good" by its small local fanclub. / **Sample dishes:** chicken
yakitori; stir-fried seafood with Thai chilli oil; sticky rice & mango. **Details:** 11 pm;
closed Sun; no Amex; no smoking.*

**Restaurant Sat Bains**  £77

Old Lenton Ln NG7 2SA
(0115) 986 6566

*What used to be Hotel des Clos is now owned by Sat Bains,
whose exciting cuisine has won much acclaim; it re-opened in May
2005 (just as the survey was closing), and feedback was too
limited for a definitive rating – early reporters, however, found the
cooking "superb and imaginative". / **Sample dishes:** roast scallops;
duck with apple & foie gras; apple tart with Granny Smith sorbet.
**Details:** www.hoteldesclos.com; 9.30 pm; D only, closed Mon & Sun; no smoking;
children: 8+. **Accommodation:** 8 rooms, from £129.*

**Royal Thai**  £24

189 Mansfield Rd NG1 3FS   (0115) 948 3001

*"A good-value lunch menu" helps commend this "pleasant"
Mansfield Road stand-by to all who comment on it. / **Details:** 11 pm;
closed Sun L; no smoking.*

**Saagar**  £28  ★

473 Mansfield Rd NG5 2DR   (0115) 962 2014

*"Always good food" – that's what keeps the punters going back
to this Sherwood Indian. / **Details:** 1.5m from city centre; midnight; closed
Sun L; no smoking area; children: 5+.*

**Siam Thani**  £28

16-20 Carlton St NG1 1NN   (0115) 958 2222

*"Gentle, calm and elegant service" is a highlight at this Lace
Market Thai, which is favourably reviewed by all reporters.
/ **Details:** www.siamthani.co.uk; 10.30 pm; closed Sun L; no smoking area.*

**Sonny's**  £35

3 Carlton St NG1 1NL   (0115) 947 3041

*Fans insist it's "getting back on form", but this long-established
city-centre brasserie continues to put in a real curate's egg of a
performance; perhaps the new chef will win back its place
in Nottingham's first team. / **Sample dishes:** scallops & black pudding with
lime & apple sauce; roulade of Cornish cod, Parma ham, pea & mint purée; lemon
curd tart. **Details:** www.sonnys.co.uk; near Victoria Centre; 10.30 pm;
no smoking area.*

**La Toque**  £44  ★

61 Wollaton Rd NG9 2NG   (0115) 922 2268

*Mattias Karlsson's serious Gallic venture delights its (largely local)
fans with "delicious and stylish cooking, professionally served";
the place is "pricey for Beeston", though, and a few critics find the
set-up a bit "pretentious" and "'90s". / **Sample dishes:** stuffed breast
of quail; roasted wild sea bass & compote of lobster; crème brûlée with rhubarb
clafoutis. **Details:** www.latoqueonline.co.uk; off A52 towards Beeston; 9.30 pm,
Fri & Sat 10 pm; closed Mon, Sat L & Sun; no smoking; children: 6+.*

**sign up for the survey at www.hardens.com**

### Victoria Hotel £ 20 ★

Dovecote Ln NG9 IJG (0115) 925 4049
*"An oasis of real ale and good food on the outskirts of the city" –
this "no-nonsense", "spit 'n' sawdust" pub (a former railway hotel,
by Beeston station) is "darned popular", thanks not least to its
"enterprising blackboard menu". / Sample dishes: herb-crusted rack
of lamb; Mars bar cheesecake. Details: www.victoriabeeston.co.uk; by Beeston
railway station; 8.45 pm; no Amex; no smoking area; no booking, Sun; children: 18 +
after 8 pm.*

### World Service £ 39 A★

Newdigate Hs, Castle Gate NG1 6AF (0115) 847 5587
*Despite the odd accusation that it is "pricey" or "hyped",
this "funky" venture, near the Castle, is highly rated by reporters
as a "sophisticated" destination, where "exceptional" staff deliver
"imaginative" and "appetising" modern cooking.
/ Sample dishes: grilled goat's cheese with Thai pickled onion; rack of lamb &
braised breast of lamb; pear & cinnamon tarte Tatin.
Details: www.worldservicerestaurant.com; 10 pm, Fri & Sat 10.30 pm; no smoking.*

---

OAKHAM, RUTLAND 5–4D

### Nicks
### Lord Nelson's House £ 41 A★

11 Marketplace LE15 6DT (01572) 723199
*An old building with "loads of atmosphere", on the market square,
is home to Nick Healey's "popular" local fixture, which serves
some "very decently-cooked food". / Sample dishes: roast goat's cheese
with poached pears; steak with rosti & caramelised onions; home-made bread &
butter pudding. Details: www.nelsons-house.com; 9.30 pm; closed Mon & Sun;
no smoking. Accommodation: 4 rooms, from £80.*

---

OAKMERE, CHESHIRE 5–2B

### Nunsmere Hall £ 66

Tarporley Rd CW8 2ES (01606) 889100
*This grand country house hotel, largely surrounded by a lake
is sometimes hailed as "the ultimate romantic dining rendezvous"
hereabouts; given the low volume of feedback, however, and the
fact that the chef changed towards the end of the survey year,
we don't think a rating is appropriate. / Sample dishes: seared,
hand-dived scallops; steamed fillet of turbot with Chinese spices; chocolate fondant.
Details: www.nunsmere.co.uk; off A49, 4m SW of Northwich; 10 pm; no smoking;
children: 12+. Accommodation: 36 rooms, from £195.*

---

OBAN, ARGYLL & BUTE 9–3B

### Ee-Usk (Fish Café)  £ 36 ★★

North Pier PA35 5QD
(01631) 565666
*Views differ on whether the surroundings are pleasingly "simple
and café-like" or a bit "cramped" and "basic", but all agree that
this waterfront venture offers some "exceptional" seafood.
/ Sample dishes: mussels with garlic butter; monkfish with mornay sauce & savory
mash; bread & butter pudding. Details: 9.30 pm; no Amex; no smoking area.*

**Isle of Eriska**  £ 48  A★

Ledaig  PA37 1SD  (01631) 720371

*"Lovely cooking in a great and remote highland spot"* –
this *"delicious time warp"* of a place (a castellated country house
on a small island) makes a *"formidably good"* destination.
/ **Details:** www.eriska-hotel.co.uk; 9 pm; jacket & tie required; no smoking; children:
high tea at 6. **Accommodation:** 22 rooms, from £260.

**Loch Melfort Hotel & Restaurant**  £ 35  A★

Arduaine  PA34 4XG  (01852) 200233

*"A great location"* (with *"lovely views"* of the loch for which its
named) and *"excellent food and wine"* are this gist of all
commentary on this waterside hotel. / **Sample dishes:** cream
of mushroom soup; roast saddle of Morayshire lamb with rosemary & garlic; baked
chocolate pudding. **Details:** www.lochmelfort.co.uk; 9 pm; no smoking.
**Accommodation:** 25 rooms, from £59.

OCKLEY, SURREY  3–4A
**Bryce's at the Old School House**  £ 39  ★

RH5 5TH  (01306) 627430

It's *"fairly old-fashioned"*, but this *"pleasant"* pub-cum-restaurant
has a widespread fanclub thanks to its *"interesting"* and *"good-
quality"* fish and seafood. / **Sample dishes:** king scallops & cucumber pickle;
steamed ginger & orange pudding with ice cream. **Details:** www.bryces.co.uk; 8m S
of Dorking on A29; 9.30 pm; closed Sun D in Nov, Jan & Feb; no Amex; no smoking.

ODIHAM, HAMPSHIRE  2–3D
**The Grapevine**  £ 38  ★

121 High St  RG29 1LA  (01256) 701122

This *"very friendly"* modern bistro attracts high praise from local
reporters for *"sensibly-priced"* cooking that *"punches out a lot
of flavour"*. / **Sample dishes:** pea soup with gremolata & fried garlic; salmon
in seaweed with linguine; caramelised lemon tart with orange sorbet.
**Details:** www.grapevine-gourmet.com; follow signs from M3, J5; 10 pm; closed
Sat L & Sun; no smoking.

OLD BURGHCLERE, BERKSHIRE  2–3D
**Dew Pond**  £ 41  ★

RG20 9LH  (01635) 278408

*"Why is it not in your guide?"*; perhaps because this *"cracking"*
country house restaurant, at the foot of Watership Down,
does not in fact attract a huge volume of feedback – such as
there is does indeed tend to support the view that the cooking
is *"excellent"*. / **Sample dishes:** Portland crab with gazpacho; saddle of roe
deer with wild mushrooms; assiette of chocolate. **Details:** www.dewpond.co.uk;
6m S of Newbury, off A34; 10 pm; D only, closed Mon & Sun; no Amex;
no smoking; children: 5+.

ONGAR, ESSEX  3–2B
**Smiths Brasserie**  £ 42  A★

Fyfield Rd  CM5 0AL  (01277) 365578

This *"large and airy conservatory-type fish restaurant"* is *"a little
expensive, but worth it for the freshest seafood around"*;
*"very popular"*, it's sometimes *"difficult to book"*.
/ **Sample dishes:** Mediterranean prawns; Atlantic cod & prawn fishcake; sticky
date & ginger pudding & custard. **Details:** www.smithsbrasserie.co.uk; left off A414
towards Fyfield; 10.30 pm; closed Mon; no Amex; children: 12+.

**sign up for the survey at www.hardens.com**

## ORFORD, SUFFOLK                                         3–1D
**Butley Orford Oysterage**                    £31              ★
Market Hill IP12 2LH   (01394) 450277
*"Doggedly Spartan, but good fish"; this "quaint" and "cramped"
seafood café of over 40 years' standing is "as good as ever",
but – with its "hard chairs and Formica tables" – still "not a place
to linger". / **Sample dishes:** smoked salmon pâté; hot smoked mackerel with
mustard sauce; chocolate trufito. **Details:** www.butleyorfordoysterage.co.uk; 9 pm;
Mon-Thu L only, closed Sun D in winter; no Amex; no smoking.*

**The Crown & Castle**                          £36
IP12 2LJ   (01394) 450205
*Reports on this attractively-located hotel were more consistent this
year, with most feedback praising its "wonderful food" and
"relaxed atmosphere"; one or two reporters, though, still scent
"too much hype". / **Sample dishes:** Trinity-potted brown shrimps; rump of
Suffolk lamb with rosemary mash; bitter chocolate soufflé cake.
**Details:** www.crownandcastle.co.uk; 9 pm; closed Sun D in winter; no Amex;
no smoking; booking: max 8; children: 8+ at D. **Accommodation:** 18 rooms,
from £90.*

## ORKNEY ISLANDS, ORKNEY ISLANDS
**The Creel**                                   £43              ★
Front Rd, St Margaret's Hope, South Ronaldsay  KW17 2SL
(01856) 831311
*A harbour-waterfront location "adds authenticity" to this fish
restaurant-with-rooms, which most reporters say is "well worth
a visit", thanks to Allan Craigie's "very good" cooking.
/ **Sample dishes:** crab bisque; supreme of cod; panna cotta.
**Details:** www.thecreel.co.uk; off A961 S of town, across Churchill barriers; 9 pm;
D only; closed Jan-Mar; no Amex; no smoking. **Accommodation:** 3 rooms,
from £90.*

## ORPINGTON, KENT                                        3–3B
**Xian**                                        £24              ★
324 High St  BR6 0NG   (01689) 871881
*"Spot-on" cooking and "attentive" service win invariable 'raves' for
this eminent Chinese; the only downside is that it's sometimes
"too busy for comfort". / **Details:** 11.15 pm, Fri & Sat 11.45 pm; closed
Sun L.*

## OSMOTHERLEY, NORTH YORKSHIRE                            8–4C
**Golden Lion**                                 £32
6 West End  DL6 3AA   (01609) 883526
*"A great pub in a great village" – a "busy" place, it serves up a
"small" but often "delicious" menu, and "good real ale".
/ **Sample dishes:** spaghetti with clams; pork & Parma ham with sage mash;
lemon & passion fruit pavlova. **Details:** 9.30 pm; no smoking area.*

## OTLEY, WEST YORKSHIRE                                   5–1C
**Korks**                                       £30              Ⓐ
40 Bondgate  LS21 1AD   (01943) 462020
*This "really cosy" wine bar-cum-brasserie is a popular local
destination, with a "varied" menu and a wine list that's above par.
/ **Sample dishes:** tandoori chicken; pork with cauliflower & turmeric jus; berry
pavlova. **Details:** www.korks.com; 10 pm; closed Sat L & Sun.*

## OUNDLE, NORTHAMPTONSHIRE 3–1A

### Falcon Inn £37 Ⓐ

Fotheringay PE8 5HZ (01832) 226254

"A pleasant place for family outings"; this ancient hostelry offers "a good menu and some nice wines"; "sit in the conservatory for a view of the church". / **Sample dishes:** Dorset crab tart; grilled rump of lamb with potato cake; bread & butter pudding. **Details:** www.huntsbridge.co.uk; just off A605; 9.30 pm; no smoking.

## OVINGTON, HAMPSHIRE 2–3D

### The Bush Inn £35 Ⓐ

SO24 0RE (01962) 732764

"A wonderful spot near the River Itchen" provides a "tremendous location" for this popular pub; sceptics accuse the cooking here of being "pricey" and "average", but fans insist that – though the menu is "limited" – it's "fresh and tasty". / **Sample dishes:** chicken liver pâté; rhubarb & ginger & lemon grass crumble. **Details:** www.wadworth.co.uk; just off A31 between Winchester & Alresford; 9.30 pm; closed Sun D; no smoking area.

## OXFORD, OXFORDSHIRE 2–2D

Especially for a city of such beauty and affluence, Oxford's restaurants are woeful. Some of them – such as Gee's – have notably attractive settings, but otherwise none of the European establishments is of any note whatsoever, and many of the city's best-known places would deserve a place in any rogues' gallery of underperformers. Those wishing to eat well will generally do best to eat Thai or Indian.

### Al Shami £24

25 Walton Cr OX1 2JG (01865) 310066

"Simple, unpretentious and good value", this "Spartan" Jericho Lebanese restaurant maintains a huge following; there's no denying, though, that a minority of reporters feel it "could try harder". / **Sample dishes:** falafel; Lebanese sweets. **Details:** www.al-shami.co.uk; 11.45 pm; no Amex; no smoking. **Accommodation:** 12 rooms, from £45.

### Aziz £30

228-230 Cowley Rd OX4 1UH (01865) 794945

"Not 100% consistent, but even at its worst better than anything else in Oxford" – still a fairly typical comment on this popular curry house; there's definitely a feeling, though, that "standards have been affected by opening the new branches in Burford and Witney". / **Sample dishes:** lentil cakes in tamarind sauce; green pumpkin in spicy sweet sauce. **Details:** www.aziz.uk.com; 10.45 pm; closed Fri L; no smoking area.

### Bangkok House £28 Ⓐ★

42a High Bridge St OX1 2EP (01865) 200705

This "ornately-carved" Thai once again (mostly) wins praise for its "lovely food" and "reasonable" prices. / **Details:** 10.45 pm; closed Sun; no smoking area.

### Bombay £ 20 ★
82 Walton St OX2 6EA (01865) 511188
*"Good food", "friendly staff" and "BYO" – three reasons to visit this Jericho curry house, which "can get very busy".*
/ **Details:** 11.15 pm; closed Fri L; no Amex.

### Branca £ 35
111 Walton St OX2 6AJ (01865) 556111
*Fans (and there are many) find this "friendly" Jericho Italian a "reliable" and "good-value" destination; service can be "leisurely", though, and doubters feel it's "much over-rated".*
/ **Sample dishes:** minestrone soup; linguine with tiger prawns & chilli; panna cotta with caramel & raspberries. **Details:** www.branca-restaurants.com; 11 pm; no smoking area.

### Browns £ 29 ✗
5-11 Woodstock Rd OX2 6HA (01865) 511995
*Some reporters claim the atmosphere is "still crazy after all these years", but this once great-brasserie is just the 'pits' nowadays – "when will people cotton on to how dreadful it has become"?*
/ **Sample dishes:** grilled goat's cheese salad; duck with plum relish; bread & butter pudding. **Details:** www.browns-restaurants.com; 11.30 pm; no smoking area; need 5+ to book.

### Café Coco £ 26 Ⓐ
23 Cowley Rd OX4 1HP (01865) 200232
*"A simple but good café/bar" that's unanimously hailed as a "lively", "relaxed" and "trendy" destination (and, unsurprisingly, "full of students").* / **Sample dishes:** houmous & garlic bread; sausage & ham pizza; banoffi pie. **Details:** 11 pm; no smoking; no booking.

### Cherwell Boathouse £ 35 Ⓐ✗
Bardwell Rd OX2 6ST (01865) 552746
*"The best setting in Oxford" (in summer) and an "extensive and reasonably-priced wine list" have long made this riverside restaurant of note; some reporters do claim the food has "improved", but, for too many, it's still "poorly conceived".*
/ **Sample dishes:** tian of crab & avocado light herb salad; sponge pudding. **Details:** www.cherwellboathouse.co.uk; 10 pm; no smoking.

### Chiang Mai £ 37 Ⓐ★
Kemp Hall Pas, 130a High St OX1 4DH (01865) 202233
*"Very good" Thai cooking and a "quaint setting in a very old building behind the High" have made this "reasonably-priced" oriental the city's best-known eatery – even those who feel it's "overhyped" concede "it's not at all bad"; a Winchester offshoot is planned.* / **Sample dishes:** steamed scallops; sticky rice with banana & nuts. **Details:** www.chiangmaikitchen.co.uk; 10.30 pm; no smoking area.

### Chutney's £ 29 ★
36 St Michael's St OX1 2EB (01865) 724241
*"Still the best curry house in town" – fans insist that there is now "clear blue water" between this "friendly" city-centre subcontinental and its local competitors.*
/ **Details:** www.chutneysoxford.co.uk; 11 pm; closed Sun.

**sign up for the survey at www.hardens.com**

### Cibo!                                              £26
4 South Pde  OX2 7JL   (01865) 292321
*Even a reporter who's not especially convinced by the charms
of this "bustling" Italian admits it's "a useful Summertown
alternative" – for its fans, it's simply "an oasis in a gastronomic
desert".* / **Sample dishes:** vegetable antipasti; home-made ravioli; home-made
panna cotta. **Details:** www.ilovecibo.co.uk; 10.30 pm; no Amex; no smoking.

### Edamame                                           £18           ★
15 Holywell St  OX1 3SA   (01865) 246916
*"A cheap and cheerful oasis in the culinary desert that is Oxford!"
– this "crowded" "hole in the wall" delivers "high-quality"
Japanese "home-cooking" at "very low prices"; "you'll likely have
to queue".* / **Sample dishes:** chicken kara-age; salmon teri with teriyaki sauce.
**Details:** www.edamame.co.uk; opp New College; 8.30 pm; L only, ex Fri & Sat open
L & D, closed Mon; no Amex; no smoking; no booking.

### Fishers                                           £36
36-37 St Clements  OX4 1AB   (01865) 243003
*"Could try harder" – that's the verdict on this popular and long-
established fish bistro; some do vaunt it as a "reliable" destination,
but others say it has become "very disappointing" of late.*
/ **Sample dishes:** tiger prawn brochette in coconut cream; char-grilled tuna steak;
sticky toffee pudding. **Details:** www.fishers-restaurant.com; by Magdalen Bridge;
10.30 pm; closed Mon L; no Amex; no smoking.

### Gee's                                             £40           𝔸
61 Banbury Rd  OX2 6PE   (01865) 553540
*Housed in a "delightful" Victorian conservatory, this "old-
favourite" is difficult to beat if you're looking for a "romantic"
destination; the food doesn't try too hard, but is at least "reliable".*
/ **Sample dishes:** king scallops with leeks; roast lamb with borlotti beans &
tapenade; chocolate soufflé with pistachio sauce.
**Details:** www.gees-restaurant.co.uk; 10.30 pm, Fri & Sat 11 pm; no smoking.

### Kazbah                                            £22           𝔸
25-27 Cowley Rd  OX4 1HP   (01865) 202920
*"Cool and atmospheric", this "Moorish tapas bar" is a popular
Cowley Road destination (not least as "a great place for a date").*
/ **Sample dishes:** anchovies cured in vinegar; chicken & olive tajine with lemon;
baklava. **Details:** 11 pm; no booking.

### The Lemon Tree                                    £41
268 Woodstock Rd  OX2 7NW   (01865) 311936
*Some reporters claim that this potentially "special" restaurant,
in a large North Oxford villa, is "back on form" under its new
owners; there's a very strong nay-saying element, though,
for whom it's just "flash", "loud" and "overpriced".*
/ **Sample dishes:** steamed mussels with saffron garlic & chilli; roast Blythburgh pork
belly. **Details:** www.thelemontreeoxford.co.uk; 1.5m N of city centre; 11 pm; closed
Mon L, Tue L & Wed L; smoking in bar only.

### Loch Fyne                                         £34
55 Walton St  OX2 6AE   (01865) 292510
*A much-trafficked branch of the national seafood chain; as usual,
reports range from "fabulous" and "reliable" to "patchy" and
"poor".* / **Sample dishes:** lobster bisque with garlic rouille; sea bass; crème brûlée.
**Details:** www.loch-fyne.com; 10 pm; no smoking area.

## The Nosebag £20 ★
6-8 St Michael's St OX1 2DU (01865) 721033
A "no-frills" self-service veggie café in the city-centre, praised
by all reporters for its "superb home-cooked food".
/ **Sample dishes:** smoked mackerel & chicken liver pâté; lamb & rosemary
casserole; strawberry & white chocolate cheesecake. **Details:** 10 pm; no smoking.

## The Old Parsonage £43 🅐
1 Banbury Rd OX2 6NN (01865) 310210
This "cosy and atmospheric" medieval townhouse – with its "old-
fashioned" and "club-like" interior – has a great location near the
city-centre; the "standard" food, however, "doesn't live up to the
promise of the setting". / **Sample dishes:** seared smoked salmon;
rare marinated beef & salad; cheesecake.
**Details:** www.oxford-hotels-restaurants.co.uk; 0.5m N of city centre; 10.30 pm;
no smoking. **Accommodation:** 30 rooms, from £155.

## Le Petit Blanc £34 ✕
71-72 Walton St OX2 6AG (01865) 510999
Some reporters do feel that this "noisy" Jericho brasserie
is "much improved under new management" (Loch Fyne); for far
too many, though, it's "unremarkable", and some see it as
a simple "rip-off". / **Sample dishes:** foie gras & chicken liver pâté; confit
of guinea fowl with wild mushrooms; 'floating island' dessert.
**Details:** www.lepetitblanc.co.uk; 11 pm; no smoking.

## Quod
## Old Bank Hotel £33 ✕
92-94 High St OX1 4BN (01865) 799599
Especially for lunch, this very central and "hustling" Italian has its
uses; with its "uninspiring" food, "indifferent" service and "bland"
décor, however, many reporters dismiss it as "all glitz and no-
substance". / **Sample dishes:** Mozzarella with oven-dried tomatoes; Atlantic cod
with mashed potatoes; lemon tart. **Details:** www.oldbank-hotel.co.uk; opp All Souls
College; 11 pm; no smoking area; no booking, Sun L. **Accommodation:** 42 rooms,
from £165.

## Randolph £46 ✕
Beaumont St OX1 2LN (0870) 400 8200
This "old-fashioned" hotel continues to languish in the hands
of Macdonald Hotels – the dining experience here is sometimes
dismissed as simply "dire". / **Sample dishes:** seared scallops; roast loin
of lamb; Bailey's parfait with coffee sauce. **Details:** www.macdonaldhotels.com;
opp Ashmolean Museum; 10 pm; no smoking. **Accommodation:** 151 rooms,
from £140.

## Saffron £25
204-206 Banbury Rd OX2 7BY (01865) 512211
The "unusual Indian/French fusion menu" (with the emphasis
"more on the former") generally gets the thumbs-up at this "airy"
North Oxford restaurant; it's "always busy", thanks not least to its
"very reasonable prices". / **Details:** 11.30 pm; no smoking area.

## Thai Orchid £26 🅐★
58a St Clements St OX4 1AH (01865) 798044
A "friendly" east-Oxford Thai ("with plenty of dark carved wood");
some reporters hail it as among the city's best, but others say it's
"only sometimes excellent". / **Sample dishes:** gadoog moo yang; Thai green
curry with chicken. **Details:** www.thaigroup.co.uk; nr Headington Park; 10.30 pm;
closed Sat L & Sun L; no smoking area.

### OXTON, WIRRAL                                    5–2A
**Fraiche**                                    £ 47      A★

11 Rose Mount  CH43 5SG   (0151) 652 2914
*The "outstanding" quality of Marc Wilkinson's cooking is hailed
in almost all reports on this "stunning" newcomer – by far the
most notable addition to the "Wirral scene" for many years.*
/ **Sample dishes:** *fillet of sea bream; Suffolk lamb; poached peach & thyme ice
cream.* **Details:** *9.30 pm; closed Mon & Sun; no Amex; no smoking.*

### PADSTOW, CORNWALL                                1–3B
**The Ebb**                                    £ 42      A★★

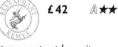

1a The Strand  PL28 8B5
(01841) 532565
*"Some say better than the Seafood" – it may not yet be quite
as famous, but Karen Scott's "innovative" but "unfussy" cuisine
is winning very high praise for this attractive and "personal" two-
year-old.* / **Sample dishes:** *seared scallops with sweet chilli dressing; whole-baked
sea bass; warm fruit soup with sorbet.* **Details:** *10 pm; D only, closed Tue; no Amex;
no smoking; children: 14+.*

**Margot's**                                    £ 36      A★★

11 Duke St  PL28 8AB   (01841) 533441
*"Rick Who?", ask fans of "the best fish restaurant in Padstow" –
a "gorgeous and totally unassuming front room", where Adrian
Oliver's cooking "never ceases to please".* / **Sample dishes:** *sardines
with watercress & radish salad; rack of lamb; saffron poached pears with shortbread.*
**Details:** *www.margots.co.uk; 9.30 pm; closed Mon L & Tue; closed Jan; no smoking.*

**Rick Stein's Café**                           £ 33      ★★

10 Middle St  PL28 8AP   (01841) 532700
*"The best value for money of all Stein's ventures"; this "buzzy"
and "welcoming" café – "simplicity itself" – serves "the freshest
and most delicious fish and seafood".* / **Sample dishes:** *salt & pepper
prawns; char-grilled steak with tomato & red onion salad; crème brûlée.*
**Details:** *www.rickstein.com; 9.30 pm; no smoking.* **Accommodation:** *3 rooms,
from £85.*

**Seafood Restaurant**                          £ 67      ★

Riverside  PL28 8BY   (01841) 532700
*For most reporters, "the best fish ever" justifies the trek to TV-
celeb Rick Stein's famous seafood Mecca – a "heaven-on-earth"
for true devotees, in "relaxed" (if "brightly-lit") premises by the
harbour; "astronomical" prices, though, are a source of some
complaint.* / **Sample dishes:** *hot shellfish; char-grilled sea bass & vanilla
vinaigrette; home-made vanilla ice cream.* **Details:** *www.rickstein.com; opposite
harbour master's car park; 10 pm; no Amex; no smoking; booking: max 14; children:
3+.* **Accommodation:** *13 rooms, from £115.*

**St Petroc's Hotel & Bistro**                  £ 44

4 New St  PL28 8EA   (01841) 532700
*Fans find it "as good as the 'Seafood', at a much lower price" –
and praise the "cheery", "well-informed" staff – but overall Rick
Stein's spin-off establishment attracts quite mixed reports;
it's undoubtedly "cramped", and can be "unbearably noisy".*
/ **Sample dishes:** *goujons of plaice with tartare sauce; sausage with a tomato
caper & shallot salad; gorgonzola with honey & walnuts.*
**Details:** *www.rickstein.com; 9.30 pm; no smoking.*
**Accommodation:** *10 rooms, from £110.*

**sign up for the survey at www.hardens.com**

### Stein's Fish & Chips £18 ★

South Quay  PL28 8BY  (01841) 532700
*"Excellent fish and chips justify the 40-minute wait", at Rick's year-old chippie; "seating is bench-style, or you can sit outside on the harbour wall". / **Sample dishes:** battered cod & chips.*
**Details:** www.rickstein.com; 11 pm; no Amex; no smoking.

---

### PARK GATE, HAMPSHIRE 2–4D
### Kam's Palace £32 A★

1 Bridge Rd  SO31 7GD  (01489) 583328
*"An unexpected find in bland suburbia", this "great" (and "OTT") Chinese restaurant includes "many orientals" among its large and satisfied clientele. / **Sample dishes:** deep-fried stuffed crab claws; stir-fried chicken with cashew nuts; ice cream. **Details:** 11 pm.*

---

### PARKGATE, CHESHIRE 5–2A
### Marsh Cat £27 A

1 Mostyn Sq  CH64 6SL  (0151) 336 1963
*"Good food, with a seafood bias" is one of the features that make it "a safe bet" to visit this "surprisingly good" bistro; in the evening, "there are lovely views, with the sun setting over the Dee estuary". / **Sample dishes:** Maryland crab cakes; seared sea bass, chorizo sausage & king prawns tagliatelle; nutty torte with raspberries.*
**Details:** www.marshcat.com; 10 pm; no smoking.

---

### PAXFORD, GLOUCESTERSHIRE 2–1C
### Churchill Arms £33

GL55 6XH  (01386) 594000
*"Varied food from a changing menu" recommends this "good gastropub" to many reporters – the year also saw a few reports, however, of the "disappointing" variety.*
*/ **Sample dishes:** spiced parsnip & celeriac soup; guinea fowl in Madeira & mushroom cream sauce; sticky toffee pudding. **Details:** www.thechurchillarms.com; off Fosse Way; 9 pm; no Amex; no smoking area; no booking. **Accommodation:** 4 rooms, from £70.*

---

### PEEBLES, SCOTTISH BORDERS 9–4D
### Halcyon £42 A★

39 Eastgate  EH45 8AD  (01721) 725100
*"A serious restaurant, at last befitting this lovely town"; this first-floor yearling – entered via an "unassuming entrance", and above a wine merchants – is a "pleasant" venue, which offers a "short but imaginative" menu realised to "excellent" effect.*
*/ **Details:** www.halcyonrestaurant.com; 9 pm; closed Mon & Sun; no Amex; no smoking.*

---

### PENSHURST, KENT 3–3B
### Spotted Dog £33 A

Smarts Hill  TN11 8EE  (01892) 870253
*"Super food, buzzy atmosphere, great views" – fans see little wrong with this "gem" of a country pub; it's the ambience, however – with "log fires in winter and tables outside in summer" – which is most prized. / **Sample dishes:** pan-fried scallops; rump of lamb; strawberry parfait with red berries & strawberry sorbet. **Details:** near Penshurst Place; 9.30 pm,; no Amex; no smoking area.*

---

**sign up for the survey at www.hardens.com**

## PENZANCE, CORNWALL                          I–4A

**The Abbey Restaurant**                       £45

Abbey St  TR18 4AR   (01736) 330680

*Some reporters do hail "great fish dishes" at this intriguingly-housed restaurant-with-rooms; overall, however, reports are strikingly variable, supporting those who say its style is "overdone" (and "vastly over-rated by Michelin and by local reviewers").* / **Sample dishes:** *courgette flowers with crab; roast fillet of sea bass; raspberry, peach & passion fruit pavlova.* **Details:** *www.theabbeyonline.com; 10 pm; closed Mon, Tue L, Wed L, Thu L & Sun; no Amex; smoking in bar only; children: 7+ at D.* **Accommodation:** *6 rooms, from £120.*

## PERTH, PERTH & KINROSS                      9–3C

**Let's Eat**                                  £34

77-79 Kinnoull St  PH1 5EZ   (01738) 643377

*Chef/patron Tony Heath's "creative and spirited" cooking has made this "relaxed" bistro a "welcome oasis" in this part of the world; it again achieved the highest grades from reporters, but – as its sale was being negotiated as this guide went to press – we've left it unrated.* / **Sample dishes:** *smoked salmon; herb-crusted lamb with rosemary jus; steamed ginger pudding with rhubarb.* **Details:** *www.letseatperth.co.uk; opp North Inch Park; 9.45 pm; closed Mon & Sun; no smoking.*

**63 Tay Street**                              £39        ★

63 Tay St  PH2 8NN   (01738) 441451

*It's not that easy to find fine dining in these parts, so – with its "classy contemporary Scottish food" and "consistently high all-round standards" – Jeremy and Shona Wares' "serious" (but welcoming) establishment is something of a beacon locally.* / **Sample dishes:** *smoked trout salad with lardons; date & fig pudding.* **Details:** *www.63taystreet.co.uk; on city side of River Tay, 1m from Dundee Rd; 9 pm; closed Mon & Sun; no smoking.*

## PETERSFIELD, HAMPSHIRE                      2–3D

**JSW**                                        £55        ★★

1 Heath Rd  GU31 4JE   (01730) 262030

*"Consistently inventive" cooking – offering "strong flavours, handled with sensitivity" – and "outstanding" service have made a big name for this small but "sophisticated and distinctive" establishment, in "a quiet corner of a little town".* / **Sample dishes:** *roast foie gras with shallot tarte Tatin; wild salmon; milk chocolate fondant.* **Details:** *9.30 pm; closed Mon & Sun; no Amex; no smoking; children: 7+.*

## PETWORTH, WEST SUSSEX                        3–4A

**Well Diggers Arms**                          £35

Lowheath  GU28 0HG   (01798) 342287

*"Vast portions of tasty, good and solid food" help live up to the name of this beautifully-located Georgian inn – an "unpretentious" place, with a style which is "eccentric" going-on "chaotic".* / **Sample dishes:** *French onion soup; roast duck; crème brûlée.* **Details:** *1m out of town on Pulborough Road; 9.30 pm; closed Mon, Tue D, Wed D & Sun D.*

## PHILLEIGH, CORNWALL                                 1–4B

### Roseland Inn                                       £32
TR2 5NB   (01872) 580254
*The year 2005 has seen a total change of régime at this "delightful" pub on the Roseland Peninsula – a rating and review will therefore have to wait until next the next edition.*
/ **Sample dishes:** coconut mussels; slow-roasted shoulder of lamb; baked cheesecake. **Details:** www.roseland-inn.co.uk; near King Harry ferry; 9.30; no credit cards; no smoking.

---

## PICKERING, NORTH YORKSHIRE                          8–4C

### White Swan                                £36              ★
Market Pl  YO18 7AA   (01751) 472288
*"Surprisingly good" food is the gist of most reports on this attractive inn; there is some feeling that "the bar has more ambience than the restaurant".* / **Sample dishes:** chicken liver & foie gras terrine; rack of lamb with aubergine & tomato caviar; grilled figs & amaretto cream. **Details:** www.white-swan.co.uk; 9 pm; no smoking. **Accommodation:** 21 rooms, from £139.

---

## PINNER, GREATER LONDON                              3–3A

### Friends                                            £45
11 High St  HA5 5PJ   (020) 8866 0286
*"Still flying the flag for quality Gallic cooking in Pinner"* – Terry Farr's cosy "gem" offers a "good", if "pricey", experience, and its new, "less twee" look seems to have done nothing to discourage *"a following of appreciative locals".* / **Sample dishes:** leek & goat's cheese strudel; lamb steak with bubble & squeak; Bramley apple crumble. **Details:** www.friendsrestaurant.co.uk; near Pinner Underground station; 9.30 pm; closed Mon & Sun D; no smoking.

### La Giralda                                         £26
66-68 Pinner Grn  HA5 2AB   (020) 8868 3429
*"Nothing ever seems to change", at this long-established, "traditional" Spanish restaurant; it retains a loyal local fan club, on account of its "good-value and consistency, in an area that's otherwise poorly served".* / **Sample dishes:** smoked salmon & prawns; half roast duckling, glazed apple rings; shortcake & strawberry cream. **Details:** A404 to Cuckoo Hill Junction; 10 pm; closed Mon & Sun D; no smoking area.

---

## PLOCKTON, HIGHLAND                                  9–2B

### Plockton Inn                                       £26
Innes St  IV52 8TU   (01599) 544222
*Confusingly, both an Inn and an Hotel bear the 'Plockton' moniker, and both are notable for "excellent" seafood; the establishment listed has its own smokery and serves real ales – the Hotel (tel 544274) has some "superb" harbour-views.* / **Sample dishes:** smoked seafood platter; sea trout with orange vinaigrette; sticky toffee pudding. **Details:** www.plocktoninn.co.uk; 9 pm; no Amex; no smoking. **Accommodation:** 14 rooms, from £36.

**sign up for the survey at www.hardens.com**

## PLUMTREE, NOTTINGHAMSHIRE                    5–3D

### Perkins                                    £31        𝔸
Old Railway Station  NG12 5NA  (0115) 937 3695
*"You almost expect to see the Railway Children", at this*
*"welcoming" bistro in a converted station, where staff "try hard";*
*some reporters tip it as "much improved of late" – others still find*
*the cooking "rather ordinary". / Sample dishes: seared wood pigeon*
*breast; steamed sea bass with asparagus spears; roast banana & toffee tart with ice*
*cream. Details: www.perkinsrestaurant.co.uk; off A606 between Nottingham &*
*Melton Mowbray; 9.45 pm; closed Mon & Sun D; no smoking area.*

## PLYMOUTH, DEVON                             1–3C

### Tanners Restaurant                         £43        ★
Prysten Hs, Finewell St  PL1 2AE  (01752) 252001
*One of the oldest buildings in town provides a "historic" setting for*
*the Tanner brothers' venture; the food is almost invariably hailed*
*as "very good", but the style of the place (characterised*
*as "Past Times-meets-Essex boy" by one reporter) can seem*
*"pretentious". / Details: www.tannersrestaurant.co.uk; 9.30 pm; closed Sun;*
*no smoking.*

### Thai Palace                                £37
3 Elliot St, The Hoe  PL1 2PP  (01752) 255770
*"Pleasant", "friendly" and "cosy" – this Thai restaurant's*
*consistent standards make it worth knowing about in this under-*
*provided part of the world. / Sample dishes: chicken satay; green beef*
*curry; raspberry pavlova. Details: www.thaipalace.co.uk; 11 pm; D only, closed Sun.*

## POOLE, DORSET                               2–4C

### Harbour Heights Hotel                      £44
73 Haven Rd, Haven Rd  BH13 7LW  (01202) 707272
*"You can't beat the view" – of the swanky Sandbanks peninsula –*
*from this "romantic" boutique-hotel dining room; the food is not*
*remarkable, but rarely disappoints. / Sample dishes: gratin of Shetland*
*scallops; Dorset Longhorn lamb; chocolate fondant.*
*Details: www.harbourheights.net; 9.30 pm; no smoking. Accommodation: 33*
*rooms, from £110.*

### Mansion House                              £39        𝔸★
Thames St  BH15 1JN  (01202) 685666
*Gerry Gooden is "a chef/patron with talent", and reporters are*
*"never disappointed" by the standards of his "stylish", "first-class"*
*Georgian townhouse (now an hotel); the "quieter" bistro*
*is sometimes preferred to the panelled main dining room.*
*/ Sample dishes: mackerel terrine; scallops with lentils & Indian spices; bread &*
*butter pudding. Details: www.themansionhouse.co.uk; follow signs for Ferry, turn left*
*onto quayside; 9.30 pm; closed Sat L & Sun D; smoking in bar only; children: 5+ at*
*D. Accommodation: 32 rooms, from £130.*

## PORT APPIN, ARGYLL & BUTE 9–3B

**Pier House Hotel** £36 A★★
PA38 4DE (01631) 730302
*"Watch the shellfish arrive, and then delight in the taste", at this "beautiful" hotel dining room, on the shore of Loch Linnhe – "a plain joy as a place to eat".* / **Sample dishes:** scallops with rice; beef Stroganoff; death by chocolate. **Details:** www.pierhousehotel.co.uk; just off A828 by pier; 9.30 pm; no Amex; no smoking. **Accommodation:** 12 rooms, from £65.

## PORTAFERRY, COUNTY DOWN 10–2D

**Portaferry Hotel** £39 A★
10 The Strand BT22 1PE (028) 4272 8231
*This "very civilised" dining room – overlooking Strangford Loch – continues to attract extremely positive reports, not least for its "wonderful" food and its "friendly" and "efficient" service.* / **Sample dishes:** goat's cheese, Parma ham & fig salad; salmon & champ with prawn cream; double chocolate torte. **Details:** www.portaferryhotel.com; on shore front, opposite ferry slipway; 9 pm. **Accommodation:** 14 rooms, from £95.

## PORTHMADOG, GWYNEDD 4–2C

**Yr Hen Fecws** £30 A★
16 Lombard St LL49 9AP (01766) 514625
*"Now established as one of North Wales's top places to eat", this "very friendly" restaurant-with-rooms pleases all who report on it; "beware the waiting list in summer though – you may have to book weeks in advance".* / **Sample dishes:** smoked salmon; sirloin steak with brandy & wholegrain mustard sauce; mocha fudge flan with coffee cream sauce. **Details:** www.henfecws.com; 9.30 pm; closed Sun; no Amex; no smoking. **Accommodation:** 7 rooms, from £57.

## PORTMEIRION, GWYNEDD 4–2C

**Portmeirion Hotel** £49 A★
LL48 6ET (01766) 770000
*It's not just the "heart-stoppingly beautiful" location – in the famous faux-Italian village, and with "wonderful estuary views" – which makes this hotel dining room a "stunning" and "romantic" destination; the service is "first-class", and the food is usually "great" too.* / **Sample dishes:** crab & smoked salmon potato cake; chicken & pancetta with wild mushroom tartlet; bread & butter pudding. **Details:** www.portmeirion-village.com; off A487 at Minffordd; 9 pm; no jeans or trainers; no smoking. **Accommodation:** 14 rooms, from £160.

## PORTRUSH, COUNTY ANTRIM 10–1C

**Ramore** £31 ★
The Harbour BT56 8D3 (028) 7082 4313
*"Creative fusion fare, in a busy wine bar environment with harbour views" – the features which make this "cheap and cheerful" destination so popular; "the only downside is that you can't book".* / **Sample dishes:** tortilla chips with guacamole; chilli fillet steak in pitta bread; tiramisu. **Details:** 10 pm; no Amex; need 10+ to book; children: before 8 pm only.

---

## PORTSMOUTH, HAMPSHIRE                    2–4D

**Lemon Sole**                              **£35**

123 High St PO1 2HW   (023) 9281 1303

*This "pick-your-own-fish" eatery (in business for over 30 years)
is generally hailed as a "reliable" and "fairly-priced" place, and –
though it attracts vocal minority criticism – merits mention in this
'thin' area.* / **Sample dishes:** *pan-fried scallops; grilled sea bass with home-made
chips; lemon & lime mousse.* **Details:** *www.lemonsole.co.uk; 10 pm; closed Sun;
no smoking area; booking: max 10 at Sat D.*

---

## POULTON, GLOUCESTERSHIRE                 2–2C

**The Falcon Inn**                    **£39**          A

London Rd  GL7 5HN
(01285) 850844

*"Charm and style without pretension" endear this three-year-old
gastropub to practically all reporters, even if the cooking "can be
a bit variable".* / **Sample dishes:** *mussels with leeks; char-grilled rib-eye steak;
treacle tart.* **Details:** *www.thefalconpoulton.co.uk; on A417 between Cirencester and
Fairford; 9.30 pm; no Amex; no smoking.*

---

## PRESTBURY, CHESHIRE                      5–2B

**White House**                             **£41**          ★

New Rd  SK10 4DG   (01625) 829376

*"Invariably top-rate" – this restaurant-with-rooms does not
disgrace its neighbours in this notoriously swanky village; (there
is the occasional doubter, however, who says the place "thinks
itself better than it is").* / **Sample dishes:** *steamed Welsh mussels; half-crispy
duckling; treacle tart with lemon.* **Details:** *www.thewhitehouse.uk.com; 2m N
of Macclesfield on A538; 10 pm; closed Mon L & Sun D.* **Accommodation:** *11
rooms, from £110.*

---

## PRESTON BAGOT, WARWICKSHIRE             5–4C

**The Crabmill**                            **£35**          A

B95 5DR   (01926) 843342

*Given its slightly "themey" style, reporters are generally impressed
by the "surprising quality and variety" (as well as the copious
quantities) of the dishes at this large modern rural inn; local
popularity is such that "your time at table may be limited".*
/ **Sample dishes:** *lamb's kidneys with apple & black pudding; duck breast;
chocolate tart with Bailey's cream.* **Details:** *www.thecrabmill.co.uk; on main road
between Warwick & Henley; 9.30 pm; closed Sun D; no smoking.*

---

## PRESTON, LANCASHIRE                      5–1A

**The Olive Press**                         **£33**          ★

23 Winckley Sq  PR1 3JJ   (01772) 886363

*"Good cooking" and "good value" – that's the gist of all
commentary on the Heathcote empire's town-centre pizzeria
(which is tipped as "particularly well geared up for business
visitors").* / **Sample dishes:** *spicy lamb meatballs; deep-fried prawns & squid;
tiramisu.* **Details:** *www.heathcotes.co.uk; 10 pm; smoking in bar only.*

---

**Winckley Square Chophouse** £ 36
23 Winckley Sq PR1 3JJ (01772) 252732
The first of Paul Heathcote's 'Simply Heathcotes' was always the best-rated member of that chain; after a "successful refurbishment" the same owner has now given it a new name and a new formula, and early reports are encouraging.
/ **Sample dishes:** black pudding with toasted herb crumpet; rump steak with onion rings & portobello mushrooms; bread & butter pudding.
**Details:** www.heathcotes.co.uk; 10 pm, Sat 11 pm; no smoking.

---

PRESTWOOD, BUCKINGHAMSHIRE 3–2A

**Polecat** £ 27
170 Wycombe Rd HB16 0HJ (01494) 862253
This roadside inn is a "crowded" place, with a "nice garden" and a lively atmosphere; it serves a wide selection of "good-value pub food" (including a decent choice for vegetarians).
/ **Sample dishes:** baked field mushrooms with melted cheese; walnut-crusted pork with spring onion salsa; coconut meringues with mango syllabub. **Details:** on A4128 between Great Missenden & High Wycombe; 9 pm; closed Sun D; no credit cards; no smoking area; need 8+ to book.

---

PRIORS HARDWICK, WARWICKSHIRE 2–1D

**Butchers Arms** £ 41
Church End CV47 7SN (01327) 260504
"Effervescent" service contributes much to the charm of this very popular inn, which has been owned by the same Portuguese family for over four decades; like the décor, the cuisine can seem "very conventional" ("complete with sweet trolley"), but it invariably seems to satisfy. / **Sample dishes:** mushroom & Stilton tart; beef Stroganoff; profiteroles. **Details:** www.thebutchersarms.com; 9.30 pm; closed Sat L & Sun D; smoking in bar only.

---

PURTON, WILTSHIRE 2–2C

**Pear Tree at Purton** £ 43 A★
Chruch End SN5 4ED (01793) 772100
"Very good, overall" – the tenor of all commentary on this "relaxed" and "friendly" gastropub, which offers some "lovely" food. / **Sample dishes:** creamed leek & smoked haddock broth; roast lamb with olive mash & pesto gravy; pear & hazelnut tart with fudge ice cream.
**Details:** www.peartreepurton.co.uk; 9.15 pm; closed Sat L; no smoking.
**Accommodation:** 17 rooms, from £110.

---

PWLLHELI, GWYNEDD 4–2C

**Plas Bodegroes** £ 54 A★
Nefyn Rd LL53 5TH (01758) 612363
A "wonderful" rural setting and "top-quality" cooking strongly commend this "romantic" country house hotel to most reporters.
/ **Sample dishes:** char-grilled monkfish salad; char-grilled rib-eye of Welsh black beef; oxtail & shallots; cinnamon biscuit of rhubarb & apple.
**Details:** www.bodegroes.co.uk; on A497 1m W of Pwllheli; 9.30 pm; closed Mon, Tue-Sat D only, closed Sun D; closed Dec-mid Feb; no Amex; no smoking.
**Accommodation:** 11 rooms, from £100.

**sign up for the survey at www.hardens.com**

## RAMSBOTTOM, LANCASHIRE                     5–1B

### Ramsons                                    £ 47      ★
18 Market Pl  BL0 9HT   (01706) 825070
*"Run with passion and verve" (and perhaps a hint
of idiosyncrasy), this Italian "gem" sweeps away most reporters
with its "lovingly-prepared" menu and its "exceptional range
of Italian wines". / Sample dishes: lobster & avocado salad; fillet of beef &
stir-fried raddicchio; pear & polenta pudding with Cambridge custard.
Details: www.ramsons.org.uk; 9.30 pm; closed Mon, Tue & Sun D; no Amex;
no smoking; booking: max 10.*

## RAMSGATE, KENT                              3–3D

### Surin                                      £ 26      ★
30 Harbour St  CT11 8HA   (01843) 592001
*"The palate is exercised to the extreme", at this "warm and
friendly" Thai/Cambodian/Laotian restaurant, near the harbour.
/ Sample dishes: Thai dumplings; green curry & thai noodles; banana fritters.
Details: www.surinrestaurant.co.uk; 11 pm; closed Mon L & Sun; mainly
non-smoking.*

## RAMSGILL-IN-NIDDERDALE, NORTH YORKSHIRE8–4B

### Yorke Arms                                 £ 58      A★★
HG3 5RL   (01423) 755243
*"The best food in North Yorkshire" is to be found "in the middle
of nowhere", at Frances and Gerald Atkins's "picture postcard"
inn, in the heart of the Dales; it's acclaimed by the many who
comment on it, not least for its "warm" but ultra-"professional"
service and its "real charm". / Sample dishes: lobster ravioli; lamb in
parsley crust; pear & butterscotch tart. Details: www.yorke-arms.co.uk; 4m W
of Pateley Bridge; 9 pm; no smoking. Accommodation: 14 rooms, from £120.*

## READING, BERKSHIRE                          2–2D

### Bel & The Dragon                           £ 42
Blakes Lock, Gas Works Rd  RG1 3DH   (0118) 9515790
*"Attractive" décor is central to the appeal of this "themed
pub/restaurant" (part of a small chain) in a former warehouse
(with riverside terrace); even some fans concede it's "not cheap",
though, and that "quantity can come at the expense of quality".
/ Sample dishes: grilled goat's cheese on niçoise salad; slow-roasted lamb
shoulders; sticky toffee pudding. Details: www.belandthedragon.co.uk; 10 pm;
no smoking area.*

### Forbury's                                  £ 46      ★
1 Forbury Sq  RG1 3BB
(0118) 957 4044
*"Consistently high levels of service and cuisine" have helped this
"formal" but "pleasant" new French restaurant – from a team
with a lot of 'serious' experience behind it – to win instant local
acclaim. / Sample dishes: Cornish lobster; roast wood pigeon with wilted
spinach & broad bean broth; mirabelle soufflé with a plum compote & almond
biscotti. Details: www.forburys.co.uk; 10 pm; closed Sun; no smoking area.*

### London Street Brasserie  £ 40
2-4 London St RG1 4SE   (0118) 950 5036
This "busy" riverside brasserie is head-and-shoulders above others
in the town in terms of the volume of commentary;
most reporters find it a "slick operation", but it's also sometimes
"a bit hit-and-miss". / **Sample dishes:** foie gras & duck terrine; sea bass with
baby squid & saffron dressing; Bakewell tart & custard.
**Details:** www.londonstbrasserie.co.uk; 10.30 pm; smoking in bar only.

---

### REED, HERTFORDSHIRE  3–2B

### The Cabinet at Reed  £ 42  𝔸★

High St SG8 8AH
(01763) 848366
"A wonderful and friendly eating experience in an out-of-the-way
corner of Hertfordshire" – thanks to its "great" and "distinctive"
cooking, this "simply and appropriately decorated dining pub"
is already making quite a buzz; it took on new owners in 2005,
but Paul Maguire remains at the stoves. / **Sample dishes:** apple,
Cheddar & onion marmalade egg roll; fillet of beef; banana tarte Tatin with
chocolate fudge sauce. **Details:** 9 pm; closed Mon; no smoking; children: 8+ at D.

---

### REIGATE, SURREY  3–3B

### La Barbe  £ 45  𝔸
71 Bell St RH2 7AN   (01737) 241966
"A good French brasserie experience" – that's really the whole
story on this "consistently good and reliable" local "favourite",
of over two decades' standing. / **Sample dishes:** roasted asparagus &
guinea fowl parcels; chicken, apple & cider casserole; strawberry charlotte with
blackcurrant sauce. **Details:** www.labarbe.co.uk; 9.30 pm; closed Sat L & Sun;
no smoking.

### Tony Tobin @ The Dining Room  £ 52
59a High St RH2 9AE   (01737) 226650
A good number of reports of "interesting" and "stylish" cooking
confirm the continuing attraction of TV-chef Toby Tobin's town-
centre restaurant; the vocal minority which scents decline,
however, will not go away. / **Sample dishes:** spiced chicken; chopped veal
with spinach, straw potato cakes & onion rings; honeycomb semifreddo with toffee
sauce. **Details:** www.tonytobinrestaurants.co.uk; 10 pm; closed Sat L & Sun D;
no smoking; booking: max 8, Fri & Sat.

---

### REYNOLDSTON, SWANSEA  1–1C

### Fairyhill  £ 47  𝔸★★
SA3 1BS   (01792) 390139
"Nothing is too much trouble", at this country house hotel, whose
remote Gower Peninsula location adds to its "romantic" appeal;
all reports on its dining room – which makes good use of local
produce – attest to the "fantastic" standards of food and wine.
/ **Sample dishes:** chilli & dill cured salmon; roast poussin with red cabbage;
steamed treacle pudding. **Details:** www.fairyhill.net; 20 mins from M4, J47 off
B4295; 9 pm; no Amex; smoking in bar only; children: 8+ at
D. **Accommodation:** 8 rooms, from £150.

**sign up for the survey at www.hardens.com**

---

## RIBER, DERBYSHIRE                                    5–3C

**Riber Hall**                          **£35**          Ⓐ
DE4 5JU   (01629) 582795
*"Lovely gardens"* add much to the experience of visiting this
Elizabethan country house hotel; the food – *"better than average,
if perhaps a bit bland"* – plays rather a supporting rôle.
/ **Sample dishes:** confit of duck leg; fillet of beef & braised oxtail; chocolate torte
with coconut ice cream. **Details:** www.riber-hall.co.uk; 9.30 pm; no smoking.
**Accommodation:** 14 rooms, from £72.50.

---

## RIPLEY, SURREY                                       3–3A

**Drakes**                              **£55**          ★★
The Clock Hs, High St   GU23 6AQ   (01483) 224777
Steve Drake's grandly-housed yearling *"just gets better and
better"*, and his cooking is on most accounts *"superb"*;
the downside is that the room has *"no atmosphere"* – no wonder
the place was so quickly awarded its Michelin star!
/ **Sample dishes:** lasagne of pork belly and langoustines; sea bass with passion fruit
sauce; figs in honey with lime jelly. **Details:** www.drakesrestaurant.co.uk; 9.30 pm;
closed Mon, Sat L & Sun; no Amex; no smoking; booking: max 6.

---

## ROADE, NORTHAMPTONSHIRE                              3–1A

**Roade House**                         **£43**          ★
16 High St   NN7 2NW   (01604) 863372
Rather living up to its name, this *"cosy"* restaurant-with-rooms
is *"an excellent place, just off the M1"*; it offers cooking
of *"consistent"* quality from a *"limited"* but *"imaginative"* menu.
/ **Sample dishes:** sun-dried tomato gnocchi with asparagus; baked fillets of plaice &
monkfish; compote of rhubarb. **Details:** www.roadehousehotel.co.uk; 9.30 pm;
closed Sat L & Sun; no smoking. **Accommodation:** 10 rooms, from £70.

---

## ROCK, CORNWALL                                       1–3B

**Black Pig**                           **£43**
Rock Rd   PL27 6JS   (01208) 862622
Star chef Nathan Outlaw led this unatmospheric two-year-old
to instant foodie stardom, but he left (to go to St Ervan Manor,
Wadebridge) as our survey was drawing to a close; we've
therefore held off on a rating of the new regime till next year.
/ **Details:** www.blackpigrestaurant.co.uk; 9.30 pm; closed Sun; no smoking.

---

## ROCKBEARE, DEVON                                     1–3D

**Jack in the Green Inn**               **£35**
London Rd   EX5 2EE   (01404) 822240
This *"capably-run pub-cum-restaurant"* is handily located for A30
travellers, and most reporters find it a *"consistently good"* and
*"welcoming"* option – the dining room is sometimes preferred
to the bar. / **Sample dishes:** smoked seafood mousse; roast pigeon with salsify &
pink peppercorns; rice pudding with pralines. **Details:** www.jackinthegreen.uk.com;
9.30 pm; no smoking.

---

**sign up for the survey at www.hardens.com**

## ROMALDKIRK, COUNTY DURHAM                    8–3B

**The Rose & Crown**                    £ 37          Ⓐ
DL12 9EB   (01833) 650213
This "relaxed" old coaching inn, in a "lovely village", inspires much
feedback for somewhere quite "remote"; the food's "not exciting,
but good". / **Sample dishes:** quails egg & bacon; baked plaice, scallops & oyster
mushrooms; lemon tart. **Details:** www.rose-and-crown.co.uk; 6m NW of Barnard
Castle on B6277; 9 pm; D only, ex Sun open L & D; no Amex; no smoking; children:
6+. **Accommodation:** 12 rooms, from £126.

## ROSEVINE, CORNWALL                    1–4B

**Driftwood**                    £ 49      Ⓐ★★
TR2 5EW   (01872) 580644
"In the nicest way, like a London restaurant parachuted into
Cornwall" – the dining room of this "wonderfully-located" modern
hotel inspires rapturous feedback on all aspects of its operation,
not least Rory Duncan's "fantastic" cooking. / **Sample dishes:** baked
chicken with soup; roast bass with smoked eel dill potato purée; banana brûlée with
rum & raisin ice cream. **Details:** www.driftwoodhotel.co.uk; 9.30 pm; D only;
no smoking; booking: max 6; children: 8+. **Accommodation:** 15 rooms,
from £160.

## ROWDE, WILTSHIRE                    2–2C

**George & Dragon**                    £ 39
High St  SN10 2PN   (01380) 723053
The new régime (since 2004) at this rural gastropub is praised for
"its attention to detail both in the kitchen and front of house",
and the "interesting" cooking that results; even a reporter who's
not especially impressed by the change-over concedes the new
team are "trying". / **Sample dishes:** seared scallops with black pudding;
steamed wild sea bass with soya & ginger; Eton mess. **Details:** on A342 between
Devizes & Chippenham; 9 pm; closed Mon & Sun D; no Amex; no smoking; booking:
max 8.

## ROWHOOK, WEST SUSSEX                    3–4B

**Chequers Inn**                    £ 29          ★
RH12 3PY   (01403) 790480
"A super country pub", where the "exceptional" menu includes
some "excellent seafood"; "enthusiastically run", it is also praised
for its "very good value". / **Sample dishes:** pan-fried scallops; crispy duck;
rich chocolate jaffa mousse with orange sorbet. **Details:** 9 pm; closed Sun D;
no Amex; no smoking.

## ROYAL LEAMINGTON SPA, WARWICKSHIRE      5–4C

**Emperors**                    £ 28      Ⓐ★
Bath Pl  CV31 3BP   (01926) 313666
"Every dish under the sun" (and in "good-sized portions" too)
adorns the menu of this "friendly" Chinese restaurant, whose
"fresh dishes using good ingredients" live up the the place's lofty
local reputation. / **Sample dishes:** sesame prawn toast; steamed sea bass with
ginger & spring onions; red bean pancakes. **Details:** 11 pm; closed Sun;
no smoking area.

### Thai Elephant £33

20 Regent St CV32 5HQ (01926) 886882

*"You eat in a mini-jungle"*, at this popular local oriental; it inspired relatively little feedback, but such as there was continues to praise its *"delicately-flavoured"* cooking. / **Details:** 10.30 pm; closed Sat L.

---

## RYE, EAST SUSSEX 3–4C

### Fish Cafe £35 ★

17 Tower St TN31 7AT (01797) 222210

This ambitious newcomer in an imposing brick building has been *"a welcome arrival"*, whether you choose to eat in the café or the restaurant; its cooking is generally hailed as *"good"* and *"reliable"* – otherwise, commentary is a little up-and-down.

/ **Details:** www.thefishcafe.com; 9 pm; no smoking; children: 12+ at D.

### Landgate Bistro £30 ★

5-6 Landgate TN31 7LH (01797) 222829

*"Same menu, same people, same quality, for 25 years"* – the *"cheerful"* charms of this long-established bistro continue to endear it to all who comment on it. / **Sample dishes:** spinach, pine nut & Parmesan tart; pigeon breast with red wine sauce; walnut & treacle tart. **Details:** www.landgatebistro.co.uk; below Landgate Arch; 9.30 pm; D only, closed Mon & Sun; no Amex; smoking in bar only.

---

## SALISBURY, WILTSHIRE 2–3C

### Jade £28 ★

109a Exeter St SP1 2SF (01722) 333355

*"Very good food for somewhere out of the big cities"* wins continued praise for this Chinese restaurant – again a top tip from locals for a decent meal hereabouts. / **Sample dishes:** spare ribs; lobster with ginger & spring onion; banana split. **Details:** www.jaderestaurant.co.uk; near the Cathedral; 11.30 pm; closed Sun; no Amex.

### LXIX £29

69 New St SP1 2PH (01722) 340000

For a *"not too expensive"* option (handily located by the cathedral), this modern bistro does have its advocates; its appeal, though, is undercut by iffy service and *"somewhat bleak"* décor.

/ **Sample dishes:** ginger roast salmon salad; steak with salad & fries; crème brûlée. **Details:** adjacent to Cathedral Close; 9.30 pm; closed Sun; no smoking area; children: 12+.

---

## SALTAIRE, WEST YORKSHIRE 5–1C

### Salts Diner £26 Ⓐ

Salts Mill, Victoria Rd BD18 3LB (01274) 530533

*"Surrounded by Hockneys in a converted mill"*, this is certainly a place to eat with a difference; it's *"pleasant"* and *"busy"* too, but the food is *"nothing to shout about"*. / **Sample dishes:** terrine of pork & pistachio nut; Yorkshire rib-eye steak; sticky toffee pudding. **Details:** 2m from Bradford on A650; L & afternoon tea only; no Amex; no smoking area.

## SAPPERTON, GLOUCESTERSHIRE 2–2C
**The Bell at Sapperton** £ 40 A★
GL7 6LE (01285) 760298
"A large and beautifully-furnished country pub" in an
"atmospheric" Cotswolds setting; it makes "commendable efforts
to make the most of local ingredients", and to good effect.
/ **Sample dishes:** pan-fried scallops; sticky toffee pudding.
**Details:** www.foodatthebell.co.uk; 9.30 pm; no Amex; no smoking area; no booking
at L; children: 10+ at D.

## SARK, CHANNEL ISLANDS
**La Sablonnerie Hotel** £ 33 A★
GY9 0SD (01481) 832061
A cottagey small hotel and restaurant, with a location which
is obscure even by Sark standards; just one reporter made the
trek this year, but the effort was rewarded with a "heavenly"
experience. / **Sample dishes:** baby courgette flowers with lobster mousse; saddle
of venison; chocolate tart. **Details:** www.lasablonnerie.com; 8.45 pm; closed
November to easter; no Switch; no smoking area. **Accommodation:** 22 rooms,
from £120.

## SAWLEY, LANCASHIRE 5–1B
**Spread Eagle** £ 28 A
BB7 4NH (01200) 441202
This "classy country pub" – with "fantastic views over the Ribble"
– is "very popular", and almost all reports confirm the quality
of its "attentive" service and its "consistent" and "well-priced"
cooking. / **Sample dishes:** smoked salmon; roast fillet of pork with apple purée;
bread & butter pudding. **Details:** www.the-spreadeagle.co.uk; NE of Clitheroe off
A59; 9 pm; closed Mon & Sun D; no Amex; no smoking.

## SAWSTON, CAMBRIDGESHIRE 3–1B
**Jade Fountain** £ 23
42-46 High St CB2 4BG (01223) 836100
A "friendly" Chinese "old-favourite", with quite a local following for
its "consistently yummy" cooking and its "interesting" choice
of dishes. / **Details:** 1m from M11, J10; 11 pm.

## SAXMUNDHAM, SUFFOLK 3–1D
**Bell Hotel** £ 30 ★
31 High St IP17 1AF (01728) 602331
"Amazing food" ("using a great selection of local and seasonal
ingredients") is the gist of almost all commentary on this
"revitalised" old hotel; we suspect this is one to watch.
/ **Details:** 9 pm; closed Mon & Sun; no Amex; no smoking. **Accommodation:** 10
rooms, from £70.

## SCARBOROUGH, NORTH YORKSHIRE 8–4D
**Lanterna** £ 40 ★
33 Queen St YO11 1HQ (01723) 363616
"Excellent local fish" is the menu highlight at this "first-class and
consistent" Italian, where "patient" staff sooth the impact
of décor some reporters find "awful".
/ **Details:** www.lanterna-ristorante.co.uk; 9 pm; D only, closed Sun; no Amex;
no smoking.

**Pepper's** £ 35 ★

11 York Pl YO11 2NP (01723) 500642

*The Smiths' "superb" townhouse-restaurant is praised by all reporters for its "beautifully-presented" dishes and its "friendly and attentive service"; they've been here for a decade now, but fans say the place is "always getting better".*
/ **Sample dishes:** *chicken liver & armagnac pâté; fillet of wild sea bass, roast asparagus & air-dried ham; apple crumble.* **Details:** *www.peppersrestaurant.co.uk; 10 pm; closed Sun; no Amex; smoking in bar only.*

---

SEAHAM, COUNTY DURHAM 8–3C

**Seaham Hall**  £ 68 Ⓐ★

Lord Byron's Walk SR7 7AG
(0191) 516 1400

*Fans say you get "the North's best cooking by far" – "served well and unobtrusively" – at this recently-converted country house hotel (which is most famous for its spa); perhaps inevitably, though, its style is a little too "posey" for some tastes.*
/ **Sample dishes:** *pan-fried foie gras; grilled lobster, gnocchi & giroles; apple tart.* **Details:** *www.seaham-hall.com; 9.30 pm; no smoking.* **Accommodation:** *19 rooms, from £195.*

---

SEAVIEW, ISLE OF WIGHT 2–4D

**Seaview Hotel** £ 41

High St PO34 5EX (01983) 612711

*New ownership a couple of years ago, a new manager early in 2005, and ongoing refurbishment must contribute to the impression of permanent revolution in reports on this "interestingly-located" hotel – in the circumstances, we've left it unrated until next year.* / **Sample dishes:** *hot crab ramekin; fillet of Isle of Wight beef; molten chocolate pudding.* **Details:** *www.seaviewhotel.co.uk; 9.15; no smoking.* **Accommodation:** *16 rooms, from £110.*

---

SEDGEFIELD, COUNTY DURHAM 8–3B

**Dun Cow** £ 30 ★

43 Front St TS21 3AT (01740) 620894

*"Friendly" and "efficient" service, and "home-made" food from "good ingredients" help win all-round support for the PM's local.*
/ **Sample dishes:** *freshwater prawns with lime dressing; medallions of pork with apple sauce; cheesecake.* **Details:** *www.landmarkinns.co.uk; 9.30 pm; no smoking area.* **Accommodation:** *6 rooms, from £60.*

---

SELLACK, HEREFORDSHIRE 2–1B

**The Lough Pool Inn** £ 36 ★

HR9 6LX (01989) 730236

*"An oasis in an area not renowned for its fine food", this "attractive old country pub" is run by ex-London restaurateur Stephen Bull; it's "informal" in style, but the "interesting" cooking (from a "locally-sourced and constantly-changing menu") is "worth a detour".* / **Sample dishes:** *butternut squash risotto; roast monkfish with curried red lentil salsa; ginger cake with brown bread ice cream.* **Details:** *9 pm; no Amex; no smoking; booking: max 8 at weekends.*

---

## SEVENOAKS, KENT — 3–3B

### Greggs — £37 — A★
28-30 High St TN13 1HX (01732) 456373
*This family-owned town-centre restaurant is much praised by locals as a "consistent" and "very enjoyable destination" – "charging London prices, the food needs to be good, and it doesn't disappoint".* / **Details:** www.greggsrestaurant.com; 9.30 pm; closed Mon & Sun D; no Amex; no smoking.

---

## SHEFFIELD, SOUTH YORKSHIRE — 5–2C

### Bahn Nah — £26
19-21 Nile St S10 2PN (0114) 268 4900
*A local-favourite Thai, which continues to attract only positive reviews.* / **Details:** www.bahnnah.co.uk; on A57 from Sheffield to Manchester; 10.30 pm; D only, closed Sun; no smoking.

### Candy Town Chinese — £25
27 London Rd S2 4LA (0114) 272 5315
*This large Chinese restaurant is 20 this year, and continues to win high ratings across the board from its local supporters.* / **Details:** 10 pm; no smoking.

### Kashmir Curry Centre — £15 — ★
123 Spital Hill S4 7LD (0114) 272 6253
*"For the price, unbeatable" – this "school dining hall"-like subcontinental delivers "copious" quantities of food, in a "basic" setting that's "part of the charm"; "bring in your beer from the pub opposite".* / **Sample dishes:** balti curries; chicken tikka jalfrezi; home-made kulfi. **Details:** midnight; D only, closed Sun; no credit cards; no smoking area.

### Marco @ Milano — £36
Archer Rd S8 0LA (0114) 235 3080
*"Generous and excellent" cooking has made quite a name for this Italian restaurant in a former police station; most commentary remains very upbeat, but recent reports also include a couple of 'disasters'.* / **Sample dishes:** aromatic crispy duck; lamb with Gorgonzola polenta; passion fruit crème brûlée. **Details:** 11.30 pm; D only, closed Mon & Sun; no Amex; smoking in bar only.

### Nirmals — £28
189-193 Glossop Rd S10 2GW (0114) 272 4054
*Mrs Nirmal Gupta's Indian veteran of almost a quarter century's standing "could use a face lift", and its service can be "overbearing at times"; even so, many (if not all) reporters say it's "worth it for the quality of food".* / **Sample dishes:** samosas; spinach with lamb; kulfi. **Details:** near West St; midnight; closed Sun L; no smoking area.

### Nonna's — £34 — A★
539-541 Eccleshall Rd S11 8PR (0114) 268 6166
*This "buzzing" Italian restaurant and coffee bar (recently extended) is "incredibly popular", and "deservedly so", with Sheffield's "posh crowd"; "real Italian ingredients" are used to create anything from a snack to a full meal.* / **Sample dishes:** chilli tuna carpaccio; polenta with Italian sausage & roast tomatoes; vanilla & lemon cream with plums. **Details:** www.nonnas.co.uk; M1, J33 towards Bakewell; 9.45 pm; no Amex; smoking in bar only.

## Rafters                                    £41        ★
220 Oakbrook Rd, Nether Grn  S11 7ED   (0114) 230 4819
*"Predictable, but good"* standards at this *"small"* and *"intimate"*
venture make it a *"pleasant"* destination for all who report on it.
/ **Sample dishes:** quail breast; grilled fillet of sea bass; raspberry tart with almond
cream & white chocolate sauce. **Details:** www.raftersrestaurant.co.uk; 10 pm;
D only, closed Tue & Sun; no smoking; children: 5+.

## Thyme Restaurant                          £36
32-34 Sandygate Rd  S10 5RY   (0114) 266 6096
*"As the Smith empire has expanded, there is perhaps less
attention to detail"*, at this still-eminent local Italian; if you want
*"really good food and fun service"*, reports suggest that the café-
offshoot (at 490-492 Glossop Road) is actually a much better bet.
/ **Sample dishes:** smoked salmon & haddock with cucumber gazpacho; fish &
chips; orange crème brûlée. **Details:** www.thymeforfood.co.uk; 9.30 pm;
no smoking.

## Zing Vaa                                   £30
55 The Moor  S1 4PF   (0114) 275 6633
*"Excellent dim sum"* wins particular praise for this long-
established Chinese restaurant, which all reporters agree is at
least *"a good stand-by"*. / **Details:** www.freespace.virgin.net/zingvaa.rest;
11pm, Fri & Sat 11.30 pm; no smoking area.

---

SHELLEY, WEST YORKSHIRE                       5–2C
### Three Acres                               £38      𝔸★★
Roydhouse  HD8 8LR   (01484) 602606
*"A lovely setting"* (by Emley Moor TV mast) is only part of the
appeal of this local *"institution"* – service is *"obliging"* and the
cooking (with *"excellent seafood"* a highlight) is *"way beyond
conventional pub food"*. / **Sample dishes:** Peking duck; confit of duck leg;
meringue with muscat poached fruits. **Details:** www.3acres.com; near Emley Moor
TV tower; 9.30 pm; closed Sat L; smoking in bar only. **Accommodation:** 20 rooms,
from £75.

---

SHEPTON MALLET, SOMERSET                      2–3B
### Charlton House                            £67
Charlton Rd  BA4 4PR   (01749) 342008
*Reports on this Mulberry-owned-and-decorated country house
were unsettled this year, perhaps unsurprisingly in the period
which saw the transition from one chef to another; in the
circumstances, we've left it unrated until the next edition.*
/ **Sample dishes:** linguini with sevruga caviar; cannelloni of lobster; chocolate pot
de crème. **Details:** www.charltonhouse.com; on A361 towards Frome; 9.30 pm;
no smoking. **Accommodation:** 17 rooms, from £155.

---

SHERE, SURREY                                 3–3A
### Kinghams                                  £38      𝔸★
Gomshall Ln  GU5 9HE   (01483) 202168
*"A lovely old cottage"*, where *"good modern cooking is served in a
traditional atmosphere"*; it particularly attracts commentary as a
lunch spot. / **Sample dishes:** seared scallops with pea & bacon patties; roast
lamb with sweet potato mash; chocolate pudding.
**Details:** www.kinghams-restaurant.co.uk; off A25 between Dorking & Guildford;
9 pm; closed Mon & Sun D; no smoking.

## SHINFIELD, BERKSHIRE                    2–2D

### L'Ortolan                    £75    ★

Church Ln  RG2 9BY
(0118) 988 8500

*After an uncertain start, chef Alan Murchison finally looks well
on the way to re-establishing this former rectory as a truly "great"
restaurant destination – it still, however, attracts surprisingly little
commentary.* / **Sample dishes:** *crab blinis & caviar; roast sea bass with Thai
shellfish; passion fruit tart with mango sorbet.* **Details:** *www.lortolan.com; J11 of
M4, take A33 -> Basingstoke, at first roundabout restaurant signposted; 9.30 pm;
closed Mon & Sun; no smoking.*

---

## SHIPBOURNE, KENT                    3–3B

### The Chaser Inn                    £30

Stumble Hill  TN11 9PE   (01732) 810360

*"As word spreads", this "large and buzzy" gastropub, with a
"nice garden", is becoming "very busy"; it offers a menu that's
"sizeable" but "well prepared".* / **Details:** *9 pm; no Amex; smoking
in bar only.*

---

## SHIPLEY, WEST YORKSHIRE                    5–1C

### Aagrah                    £24    ★

4 Saltaire Rd  BD18 3HN   (01274) 530880

*"Superb and unusual" food is hailed in pretty much all reporters
on this "consistently excellent" Indian – part of a chain that,
for its fans, is "the cream of Yorkshire".* / **Details:** *www.aagrah.com;
11 pm; no smoking area.*

---

## SHREWSBURY, SHROPSHIRE                    5–3A

### Cromwells Hotel                    £30

11 Dogpole  SY1 1EN   (01743) 361440

*This simple town-centre inn induced somewhat mixed feedback
this year – one or two reporters were "not impressed"; for the
most part, though, it was well rated for the "high standards" of its
"something-for-everyone" menu.* / **Sample dishes:** *avocado, Shropshire
blue & walnut salad; Thai green chicken curry; blackberry & apple crumble.*
**Details:** *www.cromwellsinn.com; opp Guildhall; 11 pm; smoking in bar only.*
**Accommodation:** *6 rooms, from £60.*

---

## SKENFRITH, MONMOUTHSHIRE                    2–1B

### Bell                    £41    🅐★

NP7 8UH   (01600) 750235

*"Interesting local produce" is mostly used to good effect at this
"gem" of an inn, in a "lovely" rural location by a river; a few
dissenting reporters, though, say the cooking has "lost its edge"
of late.* / **Sample dishes:** *carpaccio of tuna; pork tenderloin with shallot mash;
glazed lemon tart.* **Details:** *www.skenfrith.co.uk; on B4521, 10m NE
of Abergavenny; 9.30 pm; closed Mon (Nov-Mar only); no smoking; children: 8+ at
D.* **Accommodation:** *8 rooms, from £95.*

## SLEAT, ISLE OF SKYE                    9–2A

### Kinloch Lodge                         £ 53
IV43 8QY   (01471) 833333
"Slightly faded, but the food makes up for it" – Lord and Lady
Macdonald of Macdonald's small hotel in a former hunting lodge
offers cuisine which is "generally very good". / **Sample dishes:** locally
smoked haddock, lemon & parsley mousse; Isle of Skye crabmeat with spaghetti;
grape & ginger jellies with orange & grape compote.
**Details:** www.kinloch-lodge.co.uk; 9.30 pm; D only (closed weekdays in winter);
no smoking. **Accommodation:** 14 rooms, from £70.

## SNAPE, SUFFOLK                         3–1D

### The Crown Inn                         £ 30
Bridge Rd  IP17 1SL   (01728) 688324
Fans say you get "interesting food" and "bags of charm", at this
lively rural inn (and "very good value" too); after a difficult period,
feedback is becoming more settled. / **Sample dishes:** coarse game pâté;
scallops with lemon couscous & spiced sauce; sticky toffee pudding. **Details:** off A12
towards Aldeburgh; 9 pm; no Amex; no smoking; children: 14+.
**Accommodation:** 3 rooms, from £80.

## SNETTISHAM, NORFOLK                    6–4B

### Rose & Crown                          £ 35
Old Church Rd  PE31 7LX   (01485) 541382
A country inn, offering "solid" food – with fish a speciality –
in "either a traditional pub setting or the dining room"; recent
works have expanded the kitchen and added new
accommodation. / **Sample dishes:** smoked haddock; roast duck, sticky black
rice & sweet & sour cherries; strawberry pavlova.
**Details:** www.roseandcrownsnettisham.co.uk; 9.15; no Amex; no smoking
in restaurant. **Accommodation:** 11 rooms, from £85.

## SOLIHULL, WEST MIDLANDS                5–4C

### Beau Thai                             £ 28        ★
761 Old Lode Ln  B92 8JE   (0121) 743 5355
"A flag-bearer for oriental food" ("in an area dominated
by mediocre Indian restaurants"), this family-run Thai remains
notable for its "consistently high standards".
/ **Details:** www.beauthai.co.uk; 10 pm; closed Mon L, Sat L & Sun; mainly
non-smoking.

## SONNING ON THAMES, WOKINGHAM           2–2D

### The French Horn                       £ 70        Ⓐ
RG4 6TN   (0118) 969 2204
A "superb" riverside setting (with a "stunning" terrace) and
"good food from an unadventurous menu" (spit-roasted duck the
speciality) – that's the formula that's made the Emmanuel family's
"old-fashioned" but "brilliantly-managed" restaurant a major
Thames Valley destination for over 30 years. / **Sample dishes:** scallops
in bacon with creamed pea soup; rack of lamb; poached pear with chocolate sorbet.
**Details:** www.thefrenchhorn.co.uk; M4, J8 or J9, then A4; 9.30 pm; booking:
max 10. **Accommodation:** 21 rooms, from £150.

## SOUTHAMPTON, SOUTHAMPTON 2–3D

**Kuti's** £ 28 ★
37-39 Oxford St SO14 3DP (023) 8022 1585
*"Super Bangladeshi food prepared with real care and attention"*
has long made this *"reliable"* curry house the most notable spot
foodwise in an area with few competing culinary attractions.
/ *Sample dishes:* chicken mirch masala; garlic chicken; kulfi.
*Details:* www.kutis.co.uk; near Ocean Village; midnight.

**Oxfords** £ 37 Ⓐ
35-36 Oxford St SO14 3DS (023) 8022 4444
A *"large brasserie"* with a *"good buzz"*, *"welcoming"* staff and
*"very acceptable"* cooking; such is its all-round appeal that,
for some reporters, this is *"Southampton's best restaurant"*.
/ *Sample dishes:* seared scallops on a Parmesan & tomato tart; grilled corn-fed
chicken breast; raspberry crème brûlée. *Details:* www.oxfordsrestaurant.com;
10 pm; closed Sun; smoking in bar only; booking: max 10.

## SOUTHEND-ON-SEA, ESSEX 3–3C

**Pipe of Port** £ 30
84 High St SS1 1JN (01702) 614606
*"A pleasant surprise in a gastronomic dessert"*, this *"Dickensian"*
(in a '70s way) wine bar is noted for its *"consistently good food,
good wines and sensible prices"*. / *Sample dishes:* herrings with creamed
Stilton dressing; pork, plum & celery pie; lemon meringue pie.
*Details:* www.pipeofport.com; basement just off High Street; 10.15 pm; closed Sun;
no Amex; no smoking area; children: 16+.

## SOUTHPORT, MERSEYSIDE 5–1A

**Auberge Brasserie** £ 30
1b Seabank Rd PR9 0EW (01704) 530671
*"It may have lost some of its Gallic atmosphere since the
expansion, but the food's still of high quality"* – a representative
comment on this popular fixture. / *Sample dishes:* hot duck & apple
salad; lemon sole with prawn & dill mousse; chocolate & basil marquise.
*Details:* www.auberge-brasserie.com; 10.30 pm; no smoking area.

**Warehouse Brasserie** £ 32 Ⓐ
30 West St PR8 1QN (01704) 544662
*"Nothing fancy, but honest and well-cooked grub from
an enthusiastic team"* wins consistent praise for this *"friendly"*
and surprisingly *"contemporary"* brasserie; a regular says the
*"unusual"* dishes are best. / *Sample dishes:* Devon crab tartlets; grilled
halibut with savoy cabbage & smoked bacon; mini crème brûlée, ice cream &
cheesecake. *Details:* www.warehousebrasserie.co.uk; 10.15 pm; closed Sun.

## SOUTHROP, GLOUCESTERSHIRE 2–2C

**The Swan** £ 38 ★
GL7 3NU (01367) 850205
There are a fair number of reports on this *"up-and-coming"*
Cotswold gastropub *"in a beautiful village"*, where the *"attractive"*
menu is generally realised to *"great"* effect. / *Sample dishes:* crab
vinaigrette; breast of guinea fowl; hot chocolate fondant. *Details:* 10 pm.

## SOUTHWOLD, SUFFOLK                    3–1D

### The Crown                           £35
High St IP18 6DP   (01502) 722275
*"Adnams' enormous wine list"* and a *"lively"* ambience *(especially
in the bar)* remain key reasons to visit this famous old inn;
it's *"not what is was"*, though – service is increasingly
*"lackadaisical"*, and the food *"has lost its edge"*.
/ **Sample dishes:** *Norfolk crab with potato salad; cod tempura with sweet potato
chips; apple & cinnamon tart.* **Details:** *www.adnams.co.uk; 9.30 pm; no Amex;
no smoking; children: 5+ after 7 pm.* **Accommodation:** *14 rooms, from £58.*

### The Swan                           £41
The Market Pl IP18 6EG   (01502) 722186
*Standards seem to be on the up again at this "old-fashioned and
comforting" hotel, where the fixed-price dinner menu,
in particular, is praised for its "excellent value"; the splendid
Adnams wine list comes at "reasonable prices" too.*
/ **Sample dishes:** *seared tuna with niçoise salad; roast lemon chicken; caramelised
lemon tart.* **Details:** *www.adnams.co.uk; 9 pm; no Amex; no smoking; children:
5+ at D.* **Accommodation:** *42 rooms, from £130.*

## SOWERBY BRIDGE, WEST YORKSHIRE       5–1C

### Gimbals                            £35        A★
Wharf St HX6 2AF   (01422) 839329
*This bistro "gem" again wins all-round praise for its "lovely" food,
"excellent" service and "marvellous" value.*
/ **Sample dishes:** *Dolcelatte & mushroom open lasagne; mustard-glazed pork with
parsnip mash; bread & butter pudding.* **Details:** *9.15 pm; D only, closed Tue;
no Amex; no smoking.*

### The Millbank                       £33        A★
Millbank HX6 3DY   (01422) 825588
*The "ravishing", if "isolated", setting of this Pennine gastropub
makes for a dramatic backdrop to a meal; almost all reporters
find a trip here a "great" experience, in which "consistently good"
cooking plays no small part.* / **Sample dishes:** *pea soup with potato & ham
dumplings; loin of Yorkshire lamb with shepherd's pie; chocolate fondant cake.*
**Details:** *www.themillbank.com; 9.30 pm; closed Mon L; no Amex; smoking
in bar only.*

## SPARSHOLT, HAMPSHIRE                 2–3D

### Plough Inn                         £32
SO21 2NW   (01962) 776353
*A "popular" and beautifully-located inn, offering a "great range"
of "above-average" pub grub, including some "very good fish".*
/ **Sample dishes:** *grilled goat's cheese with herb croutons; pork fillet with
wholegrain mustard mash; roasted plum & almond tart.* **Details:** *9 pm, Fri & Sat
9.30 pm; no Amex; no smoking area.*

## SPEEN, BUCKINGHAMSHIRE                    3–2A
### The Old Plow                          £40        ★
Flowers Bottom Ln  HP27 0PZ   (01494) 488300
*"A tiny hamlet in a Chilterns valley"* is the bucolic location for
Malcolm and Olivia Cowan's converted pub (now a bistro and
grander restaurant); it was consistently praised this year for its
*"lovely"* service and *"superb"* cuisine. / **Sample dishes:** duck liver terrine;
roast duck breast; vanilla parfait with sorbet. **Details:** www.yeoldplough.co.uk;
20 mins from M40, J4 towards Princes Risborough; 9 pm; closed Mon, Sat L &
Sun D; no smoking.

## ST ALBANS, HERTFORDSHIRE                 3–2A
### Crêpes                                £26
15 Holywell Hill  AL1 1EZ   (01727) 846424
A dark little place, notable for its pancakes and its wines; limited
feedback confirms its continuing dependable standards.
/ **Sample dishes:** garlic mushrooms with French bread; crêpes Suzette.
**Details:** 9.30 pm; closed Mon, Tue-Fri D only, Sat & Sun open L & D; no Amex.

### La Cosa Nostra                        £24
62 Lattimore Rd  AL1 3XR   (01727) 832658
The odd reporter accuses this local veteran of *"complacency"*,
but it still wins many nominations as *"the best good-value Italian
in the area"*. / **Sample dishes:** grilled aubergine, rocket, tomato & red onion
salad; pasta quills in a bacon, onion & tomato sauce; tiramisu. **Details:** near railway
station; 10.30 pm; closed Sat L & Sun.

### Darcy's                               £38        ★
2 Hatfield Rd  AL1 3RP   (01727) 730777
*"A stylish town-centre restaurant, serving well-cooked food with
an Australian influence"*; over its three years in operation,
this *"lively"* and *"pleasant"* place has become by far the most
commented-on location in town. / **Sample dishes:** duck spring rolls;
chicken breast with Mozzarella & pesto; amaretti baked peaches & vanilla bean ice
cream. **Details:** www.darcysrestaurant.co.uk; 9.45 pm; smoking in bar only.

### St Michael's Manor                    £51        Ⓐ
Fishpool St  AL3 4RY   (01727) 864444
With its *"beautiful"* lake-view location, this country house hotel
particularly impresses with its *"peaceful"* charms; the cuisine,
says a cynic, *"doesn't try very hard, as, in a gastronomic dessert,
it doesn't have to"*. / **Sample dishes:** chicken boudin; wild boar; white
chocolate & lavender mousse. **Details:** www.stmichaelsmanor.com; nr Cathedral;
9 pm; no smoking. **Accommodation:** 22 rooms, from £180.

### Mumtaj                                £21        ★
115 London Rd  AL1 1LP   (01727) 843691
This *"buzzing local Indian joint"* is a 'destination' for those living
locally – all reports attest to its very high culinary standards.
/ **Details:** midnight; no smoking area.

### Sukiyaki                              £26
6 Spencer St  AL3 5EG   (01727) 865009
*"It doesn't look much"*, but *"a delightful Japanese lady owner"*
creates a *"convivial"* ambience at this *"very consistent"* oriental,
whose cooking wins universal approval from reporters.
/ **Sample dishes:** yakitori; agedashi dofu; ice cream. **Details:** 9.30pm; closed
Mon & Sun; no smoking area; children: no children after 7.30pm.

**The Waffle House**
**Kingsbury Water Mill**                    £ 20          Ⓐ
St Michael's St  AL3 4SJ   (01727) 853502
*"Average, but handy with kids"; this survivor from the early '80s
waffle craze offers "tasty" fodder and a "picturesque" setting
"by a stream, with ducks and so on"; "there's always a queue"
though, and service is "sometimes disappointing".*
/ **Sample dishes:** *chunky vegetable soup; ham, cheese & mushroom waffle;
banana & butterscotch waffle.* **Details:** *near Roman Museum; L only; no Amex;
no smoking; no booking.*

---

ST ANDREWS, FIFE                              9–3D
**Seafood Restaurant**                  £ 54          Ⓐ★
The Scores  KY16 9AB
(01334) 479475
*"Huge glass windows" and "a wonderful position overlooking the
sea" add drama to this striking modern structure – an "excellent"
("if expensive") place to eat "the freshest of fish".*
/ **Sample dishes:** *smoked salmon & gravlax terrine; baked fillet of halibut.*
**Details:** *www.theseafoodrestaurant.com; 9.30 pm; no smoking; children: 12+ at D.*

**Vine Leaf Garden**                    £ 38          ★
131 South St  KY16 9UN   (01334) 477497
*"A good choice of dishes" at "very reasonable prices" wins praise
for this "excellent small restaurant".* / **Sample dishes:** *roast figs stuffed
with Parmesan; Perthshire rack of lamb; brown sugar pavlova.*
**Details:** *www.vineleafstandrews.co.uk; 9.30 pm; D only, closed Mon & Sun;
no smoking.*

---

ST ERVAN, CORNWALL                            1–3B
**St Ervan Manor**                      £ 83
The Old Rectory  PL27 7TA   (01841) 540255
*When he was at the Black Pig at Rock, Nathan Outlaw made
a really big reputation for his "superb and very imaginative"
cooking; he moved to this 'luxury B&B' just as our survey was
drawing to a close, so a rating of his new gaff will have to wait
until next year.* / **Sample dishes:** *lobster risotto with tarragon & orange; duck,
vanilla potato & sauce prunes with lime; basil cream with olives & strawberries.*
**Details:** *www.stervanmanor.co.uk; 9 pm; closed Mon & Tue; no Amex; no smoking;
children: 14+.* **Accommodation:** *6 rooms, from £140.*

---

ST IVES, CORNWALL                             1–4A
**Alba Restaurant**                     £ 35          Ⓐ★
The Old Lifeboat Hs, Wharf Rd  TR26 1LF   (01736) 797222
*"Get a table at the window to enjoy the stunning harbour views"
from this former lifeboat shed; it's highly rated by reporters for its
"consistently professional" approach and "delicious" Gallic fish
and seafood dishes.* / **Sample dishes:** *tian of crab; sea bass, potato
vinaigrette; pudding with mint ice cream.* **Details:** *www.alba-restaurant.co.uk;
10 pm; no smoking.*

**Blue Fish**                           £ 40
Norway Ln  TR26 1LZ   (01736) 794204
*This arts-centre restaurant put in a more inconsistent
performance this year – the customary reports of "superb" food
were mixed in with the odd tale of "disappointing" results.*
/ **Sample dishes:** *figs & Mozzarella; chicken & goats cheese salad; home-made
cheesecake.* **Details:** *behind the Sloop Inn; 10 pm; no Amex; smoking in bar only.*

### Porthgwidden Beach Café £ 32 A★

TR26 1SL (01736) 796791

"Stunning sea views, good art, fantastic food, wonderfully friendly service and a brilliant children's menu" – what more could you ask of this "welcoming" and "unpretentious" venture, overlooking a small beach, which is particularly popular as a breakfast destination. / **Sample dishes:** crispy pancetta & roast beetroot salad; duck leg, braised lentils & string beans; brown sugar pavlova.
**Details:** www.porthgwiddencafe.co.uk; 10 pm; closed in Winter; no Amex; no smoking; booking: max 10.

### Porthminster Café £ 35 A★★

Porthminster Beach TR26 2EB (01736) 795352

"The perfect seaside restaurant"; reporters just can't find enough nice things to say about this "friendly" place, with "stunning" views, on a "beautiful" beach, and where the food (seafood especially, of course) is usually "fantastic". / **Sample dishes:** grilled scallops with tomato relish; grilled tronçon of brill with red wine sauce & potato hash; double chocolate tart. **Details:** www.porthminstercafe.co.uk; near railway station; 10 pm; closed Nov-Mar; no Amex; no smoking.

### The Seafood Café £ 32 ★

45 Fore St TR26 1HE
(01736) 794004

"The freshest of fish served in innovative ways" – you choose your piece from the cool-cabinets and select from "an array of wicked sauces" – wins acclaim for this operation which is "modern in both cuisine and décor". / **Sample dishes:** Cornish shellfish; catch of the day; sticky toffee pudding. **Details:** www.seafoodcafe.co.uk; map on website; 10.30 pm; no Amex; no smoking area.

---

## ST KEYNE, CORNWALL 1–3C

### The Well House £ 46 A★

PL14 4RN (01579) 342001

In its remote location, this quiet country house dining room comes as "a wonderful surprise", attracting consistently high ratings from all who mention it. / **Sample dishes:** ham terrine with pineapple tart; vanilla-seared bream with Swiss chard; pecan tart with coffee bean ice cream. **Details:** www.wellhouse.co.uk; half way between Liskeard & Looe off the B3254; 8.30 pm; no Amex; no smoking; booking essential; children: 8+ at D. **Accommodation:** 9 rooms, from £125.

---

## ST MARGARETS AT CLIFFE, KENT 3–3D

### Walletts Court £ 50

Westcliffe CT15 6EW (01304) 852424

On most reports, this "slick" but "relaxed" family-owned country house hotel (near the edge of the cliffs) remains a "delightful" destination, thanks not least to its "well structured menu featuring local produce". / **Sample dishes:** grilled squid with blackened green peppers; partridge stuffed with game parfait; crème brûlée with raspberries. **Details:** www.wallettscourt.com; on B2058 towards Deal, 3m NE of Dover; 9 pm; closed Mon L & Sat L; no smoking; children: 8+, no children after 8 pm. **Accommodation:** 17 rooms, from £119.

## ST MAWES, CORNWALL                    1–4B

### Hotel Tresanton                    £51            Ⓐ
27 Lower Castle Rd  TR2 5DR   (01326) 270055
*"A wonderful view and terrace"* is the highlight of the first-floor
dining room at Olga Polizzi's sleekly-designed seaside hotel;
when it comes to the cooking, some applaud its *"simplicity and
lack of fuss"* – perhaps that's another way of saying it's *"nothing
special"*. / **Sample dishes:** *gorgonzola & spinach tart; roast John Dory with
saffron gnocchi; honey fritters with lemon ricotta.* **Details:** *www.tresanton.com;
near Castle; 9.30 pm; booking: max 10; children: 8+.* **Accommodation:** *29 rooms,
from £220.*

### Idle Rocks Hotel                    £49            ✗
Harbourside  TR2 5AN   (01326) 270771
*"Abysmal"* service and *"uninteresting"* food have become
bugbears at this prominently-sited, harbour-side hotel – it was
well-rated last year, and some reporters feel it has been *"ruined"*.
/ **Sample dishes:** *lemon sole pouched with scallops; beef fillet with spinach;
rhubarb & orange.* **Details:** *www.idlerocks.co.uk; 9.15 pm; no jeans or trainers;
no smoking.* **Accommodation:** *33 rooms, from £138.*

### Rising Sun                    £39            ★
The Square  TR2 5DJ   (01326) 270233
*"Amazing fish"* is a highlight of the cuisine at the smart and
*"friendly"* pub-cum-restaurant, overlooking the harbour; by day,
the terrace is a popular location for bar lunches.
/ **Sample dishes:** *smoked salmon kedgeree; ballotine of duck; raspberry oatmeal
meringue.* **Details:** *www.risingsunstmawes.com; 8.45 pm; D only, ex Sun open L &
D; no Amex; no smoking.* **Accommodation:** *8 rooms, from £100.*

## ST MERRYN, CORNWALL                    1–3B

### Ripleys                    £50            ★
PL28 8NQ   (01841) 520179
*"Beautifully cooked and beautifully presented"* cooking and often-
*"exceptional"* service have made a big name locally for this
*"friendly"* fish-specialist, near Newquay Airport; the setting,
however, can seem *"cramped"*. / **Sample dishes:** *twice-baked goat's
cheese soufflé; roast monkfish with mussels & clam chowder; hot chocolate fondant
with banana ice cream.* **Details:** *9.30 pm; closed Sun & Mon, D only Tue-Sat;
no Amex; no smoking; booking: max 8.*

## ST MONANS, FIFE                    9–4D

### Seafood Restaurant                    £50            ★
16 West End  KY10 2BX   (01333) 730327
The location can seem *"unpromising"*, but this seaside restaurant
offers some *"superb"* and *"unfussy"* fish and seafood, as well
as *"great"* views. / **Sample dishes:** *crab leek & Parmesan tart; pan-seared
hand-dived scallops & green vegetable salad; peppered pineapple shortcake with
basil ice cream.* **Details:** *www.theseafoodrestaurant.com; 9.30 pm; closed Mon &
Sun D in Winter; no smoking.*

**sign up for the survey at www.hardens.com**

## STADDLEBRIDGE, NORTH YORKSHIRE 8–4C
**McCoys at the Tontine** £ 46
DL6 3JB (01609) 882671
*"Exceptional", "eccentric" and "always a delight", or "expensive",
"disappointing" and "in decline"? – opinions on this local
institution of 30 years' standing, remain deeply divided.*
/ **Sample dishes:** grilled black pudding with beetroot sauce; salmon & mussels with
langoustine butter; sticky toffee pudding. **Details:** www.mccoysatthetontine.co.uk;
junction of A19 & A172; 9.30 pm; bistro L & D every day, restaurant Sat D only.
**Accommodation:** 6 rooms, from £100.

## STADHAMPTON, OXFORDSHIRE 2–2D
**The Crazy Bear** £ 43 A
Bear Ln OX44 7UR (01865) 890714
*"A contemporary setting for an old-fashioned dirty weekend" –
that's how one reporter sees this "funky" and "truly kitsch"
theme-destination; curiously, the Thai cuisine ("of a reasonable
standard") is generally preferred to the English tucker also
on offer.* / **Sample dishes:** Roquefort soufflé with pears & walnuts; roast duck
with cider braised potatoes; chocolate cake. **Details:** www.crazybearhotel.co.uk;
10 pm; no smoking area. **Accommodation:** 12 rooms, from £120.

## STAITHES, NORTH YORKSHIRE 8–3C
**Endeavour** £ 35 A★
1 High St TS13 5BH
(01947) 840825
*"Exceptional" fish and other "excellent", "locally-sourced" dishes
again wins high praise for this small former fisherman's cottage,
in the middle of the town; the occasional reporter find such
plaudits overdone, though, saying it's "good but not special".*
/ **Sample dishes:** smoked haddock tartare; fillet of sea bass; sticky toffee pudding.
**Details:** www.endeavour-restaurant.co.uk; 10m N of Whitby, off A174; 9 pm;
D only, closed Mon & Sun; no smoking. **Accommodation:** 4 rooms, from £70.

## STAMFORD, LINCOLNSHIRE 6–4A
**The George Hotel** £ 44 A
71 St Martins PE9 2LB (01780) 750750
*The "warm" and "comforting", panelled main dining room of this
"lovely", "old-world" coaching inn is as suitable a setting as you'll
find for some "good old-fashioned cooking"; in summer, you can
also dine in the "pleasant" courtyard.* / **Sample dishes:** chicken & wild
mushroom sausage; pork & tarragon mustard in filo pastry; British cheeses.
**Details:** www.georgehotelofstamford.com; off A1, 14m N of Peterborough,
onto B1081; 9.30 pm; jacket & tie required; no smoking; children: 7+ at
D. **Accommodation:** 47 rooms, from £115.

## STANTON, SUFFOLK 3–1C
**Leaping Hare Vineyard** £ 36 A
Wyken Vineyards IP31 2DW (01359) 250287
*Notwithstanding "the occasional hiccup" (particularly when
it comes to service), this winery restaurant remains a very
satisfactory destination – the setting (a "huge timber-framed
barn") is "gorgeous", the wines are "very good", and the food
is generally of a "high standard".* / **Sample dishes:** Sussex lamb with
roasted potatoes & aubergine; oak-smoked chicken with wild mushroom risotto;
mango sorbet. **Details:** 9m NE of Bury St Edmunds; follow tourist signs off A143;
9 pm; L only, ex Fri & Sat open L & D; no Amex; no smoking.

## STAPLEFORD, LEICESTERSHIRE 5–3D
**Stapleford Park** £71     A
LE14 2EF   (01572) 787522
*Though all agree it's a "wonderful location", this famously
luxurious country house hotel and country club continues
to attract mixed reports as a culinary destination – prices are
dizzying, and some reporters feel they still "need to get the basics
right".* / **Sample dishes:** ceviche of red mullet; breast of duck & boulangère
potatoes; chocolate & raspberry cheesecake. **Details:** www.stapleford.co.uk;
4m from Melton Mowbray on B676; 9.30 pm; D only, ex Sun open L & D; jacket &
tie required; no smoking; children: 12+. **Accommodation:** 55 rooms, from £250.

## STATHERN, LEICESTERSHIRE 5–3D
**Red Lion Inn**  £32   A★
2 Red Lion St   LE14 4HS
(01949) 860868
*"More restaurant than pub", the "less famous sibling" of the Olive
Branch at Clipsham (located near Belvoir Castle) "hits all the right
notes", thanks not least to its "interesting and varied" menu;
"a good-sized terrace for the summer" plays a supporting rôle.*
/ **Sample dishes:** peppered beef salad with rocket & Stilton; Lincolnshire sausages
with sage mash & onion gravy; sticky toffee pudding.
**Details:** www.theredlioninn.co.uk; 9.30 pm; closed Sun D; no Amex; no smoking.

## STOCKBRIDGE, HAMPSHIRE 2–3D
**Greyhound** £44
31 High St   SO20 6EY   (01264) 810833
*This "ambitious" gastropub is undoubtedly "an oasis in a
gastronomic desert", and it is often praised for its "fine" cooking
(albeit at "restaurant prices"); a number of reporters, however,
note that its standards are ever more "variable".*
/ **Sample dishes:** terrine of honey and mustard glazed ham; fillet of Scotch beef;
mango parfait with toasted coconut ice cream. **Details:** 9.30pm; closed Sun D;
no Amex; no smoking area; booking: max 12. **Accommodation:** 8 rooms,
from £70.

## STOCKCROSS, BERKSHIRE 2–2D
**Vineyard at Stockcross** £77
RG20 8JU   (01635) 528770
*"The finest US wine list in Europe" is a stand-out attraction at Sir
Peter Michael's ambitious California-style restaurant-with-rooms;
John Campbell's modern cuisine is at long last beginning to show
some signs of measuring up – it still needs further attention,
though, as does the "patchy" service.* / **Sample dishes:** pressed
chicken & foie gras terrine; roast sea bass with butter bean purée; chocolate fondant.
**Details:** www.the-vineyard.co.uk; from M4, J13 take A34 towards Hungerford;
9 pm; no jeans; no smoking. **Accommodation:** 49 rooms, from £200.

## STOCKLAND, DEVON 2–4A
**The Kings Arms Inn** £30
EX14 9BS   (01404) 881361
*This thatched pub can be "worth searching out" for its "yummy"
cooking, but "the real star is John, the front-of-house manager" –
"it's just not the same on his nights off".* / **Sample dishes:** rack of lamb;
Calypso chicken with apricots & bacon. **Details:** www.kingsarms.net; 8.45 pm;
no Amex; no smoking area. **Accommodation:** 3 rooms, from £70.

## STOCKPORT, CHESHIRE 5–2B

**Arden Arms** £14    Ⓐ

23 Millgate SK1 2LX (0161) 480 2185
*"Very nicely prepared food in unspoiled surroundings"* and *"great locally brewed beers"* make this *"dingy but charming"* boozer – *"a recent runner-up for CAMRA Pub of the Year"* – popular with all who report on it. / **Details:** L only; no credit cards; no smoking area.

**Conti** £25    Ⓐ★

7 Market St SK12 2AA (01663) 765400
*"A great local Italian"*, run by *"lovely"* people, and offering a *"better-than-usual"* variety of interesting dishes.
/ **Sample dishes:** king prawns; tagliatelle in pesto sauce; chocolate fudge cake. **Details:** 9.30 pm; closed Mon; no smoking area.

## STOKE BRUERNE, NORTHAMPTONSHIRE 2–1D

**Bruerne's Lock** £36    Ⓐ

5 The Canalside NN12 7SB (01604) 863654
A pleasant inn with a *"perfect"* canalside location, and applauded for its *"good"* (if not ambitious) food. / **Sample dishes:** crab-smoked salmon with gazpacho dressing; chocolate & banana ravioli. **Details:** 0.5m off A508 between Northampton & Milton Keynes; 9.30 pm; closed Mon & Sun D; smoking in bar only.

## STOKE BY NAYLAND, ESSEX 3–2C

**The Crown** £29    ★

CO6 4SE (01206) 262346
*"Expensively revamped"* in recent times, this *"crowded"* gastropub offers *"reliable"*, *"middle-of-the-road"* cooking, mainly of *"traditional English"* dishes; *"decently-priced wine"* too.
/ **Sample dishes:** smoked trout with honey-roasted fennel; calf's liver with black pudding; poached pear pudding. **Details:** 9.30 pm; no Amex; no smoking area.

## STOKE BY NAYLAND, ESSEX 3–2C

**Angel Inn** £34

Polstead St CO6 4SA (01206) 263245
A *"blackboard menu filled with interesting goodies"* wins general support for this *"comfortable"* and *"relaxed"* gastropub; service in the Well Room (the *"only bookable part"*) can, however, be *"a let-down"*. / **Sample dishes:** mushroom & pistachio pâté; roast pork with apple mousse & red cabbage; raspberry bavarois. **Details:** www.horizoninns.co.uk; 5m W of A12, on B1068; 9.30 pm; no smoking area; children: in family room. **Accommodation:** 6 rooms, from £75.

## STOKE HOLY CROSS, NORFOLK 6–4C

**Wildebeest Arms** £34

Norwich Rd NR14 8QJ (01508) 492497
*"Back on form"*, this popular inn is hailed by pretty much all reporters for its *"enterprising"* menu, which is served in *"generous"* portions; it sometimes gets *"too busy"*.
/ **Sample dishes:** sautéed calamari with squid ink risotto; roast lemon & thyme pork fillet; passion fruit tart & rhubarb sorbet. **Details:** from A140, turn left at Dunston Hall, left at T-junction; 10 pm; no smoking area.

**sign up for the survey at www.hardens.com**    

## STOKE ROW, OXFORDSHIRE          2–2D

### The Crooked Billet          £ 40          𝔸★
Newlands Ln  RG9 5PU   (01491) 681048
*"There are bragging rights just for finding this place, it's so well hidden" – when you do truffle it out, the "very decent" fare at this "cosy" inn is almost invariably "a cut above".*
/ **Sample dishes:** home-cured gravlax salmon; chicken breast with mango & coconut; treacle tart & custard sauce. **Details:** www.thecrookedbillet.co.uk; on A4130; 10 pm; no Amex or Switch.

## STON EASTON, SOMERSET          2–3B

### Ston Easton Park          £ 62          𝔸
Ston Easton  BA3 4DF   (01761) 241631
*This well-known country house hotel induces surprisingly little feedback; such as there is does laud the cooking, but it's still the "charming" building and "fabulous" setting that cause the most rapture.* / **Sample dishes:** foie gras with apples; quail with goats cheese; banana souffle. **Details:** www.stoneaston.co.uk; 11m SW of Bath on A39; 9.30 pm; no smoking. **Accommodation:** 22 rooms, from £150.

## STONEHAVEN, ABERDEEN          9–3D

### Lairhillock Inn          £ 30          ★
Netherley  AB39 3QS   (01569) 730001
*This cosy pub-cum-dining room "continues to reach the highest standards" – "the beef here is arguably best in an area where good beef is the norm"; the inn also has a fine dining room (for which we received no comments) called Crynoch.*
/ **Sample dishes:** chunky seafood chowder; chicken stuffed with haggis; sticky toffee pudding. **Details:** www.lairhillock.co.uk; 7m S of Aberdeen; 9.30 pm; no smoking area.

### Tolbooth          £ 37
Old Pier Rd  AB39 2JU   (01569) 762287
*"A superb location overlooking a picturesque harbour" adds much to the enjoyment of a visit to this well-reputed seafood restaurant; feedback, however, remains inconsistent.* / **Sample dishes:** lobster mousse cannelloni; king scallops wrapped in Parma ham; chocolate coffee fondant. **Details:** www.tolbooth-restaurant.co.uk; 9.30 pm; closed Mon & Sun; no Amex; no smoking.

## STOURBRIDGE, WORCESTERSHIRE          5–4B

### French Connection          £ 31
3 Coventry St  DY8 1EP   (01384) 390940
*Feedback on this cosy, very Gallic outfit remains limited; such as there is says it "continues to provide great quality" in a thinly-provided area.* / **Sample dishes:** chicken liver, brandy & garlic pâté; baked pesto-crusted cod; brioche bread & butter pudding.
**Details:** www.frenchconnectionbistro.co.uk; 9.30 pm; closed Mon, Tue D & Sun; no smoking.

**sign up for the survey at www.hardens.com**          337

## STOW-ON-THE-WOLD, GLOUCESTERSHIRE    2–1C

### The King's Arms    £36    A★★
Market Sq  GL54 1AF   (01451) 830364
*Just occasionally, service is "too laid-back", but otherwise reports on meals at this impressive 500-year-old coaching inn are a hymn of praise, not least for the "excellent food and wine"; for best results, "book a table upstairs".* / **Sample dishes:** confit of duck; grilled black bream with rosemary & anchovies; almond torte with raspberries. **Details:** www.kingsarms-stowonthewold.co.uk; 9.30 pm; smoking in bar only. **Accommodation:** 10 rooms, from £70.

---

## STRATFORD UPON AVON, WARWICKSHIRE    2–1C

### Lambs    £34    A
12 Sheep St  CV37 6EF   (01789) 292554
*The practical attractions of this "stylish", "very pleasant" and "reasonably-priced" restaurant are vouchsafed by many reporters; pre-theatre pressure can make service "slow", but it's also "knowledgeable and charming".* / **Sample dishes:** grilled asparagus with free range poached egg & hollandaise; grilled rib-eye steak; lemon tart. **Details:** www.lambsrestaurant.co.uk; 10 pm; no Amex; no smoking; booking: max 12.

### The Oppo    £35    A
13 Sheep St  CV37 6EF   (01789) 269980
*A "stylish" and "buzzy" bistro that "gets you to the theatre on time"; the food is "reliable" and "tasty" too.* / **Sample dishes:** Greek salad with deep-fried halloumi; grilled Mexican chicken & avocado salad; sticky toffee pudding. **Details:** www.theoppo.co.uk; 10.15 pm, Sat & Sun 11.30 pm; no Amex; booking: max 12.

### Russons    £33
8 Church St  CV37 6HB   (01789) 268822
*"Always fine and reliable" – a town-centre restaurant that's useful pre-theatre, if a touch "unexciting" to hold the limelight on its own.* / **Sample dishes:** snails in garlic butter with spiced croutons; monkfish, salmon & bacon brochettes; sticky toffee cheesecake. **Details:** 9.30 pm; closed Mon & Sun; no smoking area; booking: max 8; children: 8+ after 7 pm.

### Thai Boathouse    £30    A
Swans Nest Ln  CV37 7LS   (01789) 297733
*No one doubts that this oriental restaurant has a "lovely" setting, "right on the river, opposite the theatre"; fans say the food lives up too, but there was also the odd "disappointment" reported.* / **Sample dishes:** chicken spring roll; sweet & sour chicken. **Details:** www.thai-boathouse.co.uk; 10.30 pm; closed Sat L; no smoking.

### Thai Kingdom    £28
11 Warwick Rd  CV37 6YW   (01789) 261103
*A "reliable" Thai stand-by, which continues to attract praise for its "polite" service and "good value".* / **Details:** 10.45 pm; smoking in bar only.

## STUCKTON, HAMPSHIRE                    2–3C
**Three Lions**                          £ 47      ★
Stuckton Rd  SP6 2HF   (01425) 652489
*The grannyish décor may not be to all tastes ("wear a blindfold"),
but this "deservedly popular" New Forest restaurant-with-rooms
more than compensates with its "classy" ("but unpretentious")
cooking, and its "charming" service.* / **Sample dishes:** crab bisque; roast
roebuck with ceps; hot chocolate pudding.
**Details:** www.thethreelionsrestaurant.co.uk; 1m E of Fordingbridge off B3078;
9.30 pm; closed Mon & Sun D; smoking in bar only. **Accommodation:** 4 rooms,
from £85.

## STUDLAND, DORSET                      2–4C
**Shell Bay Seafood**                    £ 43      🄰★
Ferry Rd  BH19 3BA   (01929) 450363
*"Perfectly-cooked fish, and wonderful views to match" –
the formula that proves invariably popular for this "simple
restaurant", overlooking Poole Harbour; "dine at sunset if you
can".* / **Sample dishes:** langoustine crevettes; char-grilled swordfish & marlin loins;
white chocolate & Bailey's American-style baked cheesecake.
**Details:** www.shellbayrestaurant.com; just near the Sandbanks -> Swanage ferry;
9 pm; closed Mon; no smoking; children: 12+ at D.

## STURMINSTER NEWTON, DORSET            2–3B
**Plumber Manor**                        £ 39      🄰★
DT10 2AF   (01258) 472507
*This "old-fashioned, luxury country house" – where the same
"convivial" family has offered "straightforward" English cooking for
over three decades – continues to be hailed as a "splendid"
retreat by all who comment on it.* / **Sample dishes:** chicken liver parfait;
salmon & sole roulade with a saffron & champagne sauce; lemon & ginger crunch.
**Details:** www.plumbermanor.com; off A357 towards Hazelbury Bryan; 9.30 pm;
D only, ex Sun open L & D; no smoking. **Accommodation:** 16 rooms, from £110.

## SUNDERLAND, TYNE & WEAR               8–2C
**throwingstones**
**National Glass Centre**                £ 26
Liberty Way  SR6 0GL   (0191) 565 3939
*"The only place in Sunderland for a meal or a snack" –
this strikingly-glazed museum café has a "stunning" location,
and the food it offers is generally "good".* / **Sample dishes:** roast
pepper & Mozzarella salad; salmon with rocket & orange salad; brandy snap with
toffee ice cream. **Details:** www.nationalglasscentre.com; A19 to Sunderland, follow
signs for National Glass Centre; 8.30 pm Fri & Sat; Mon-Thu L only, closed Sun D;
no Amex; no smoking.

## SURBITON, SURREY                      3–3B
**The French Table**                     £ 41      ★
85 Maple Rd  KT6 4AW   (020) 8399 2365
*"First-class" and "très français" – the quality of the cooking at this
"crowded" and "plainly-decorated" suburban fixture ("in the heart
of what estate agents call Surbiton Village") can come as quite
"a surprise".* / **Sample dishes:** mushroom cannelloni; pork stuffed with chorizo
mousse & endive; lemon curd ice cream. **Details:** www.thefrenchtable.co.uk;
10.30 pm; closed Mon, Tue & Sat D only, closed Sun D; no Amex; no smoking area;
booking: max 10, Fri & Sat.

**sign up for the survey at www.hardens.com**

**Joy** £24 ★

37 Brighton Rd KT6 5LR (020) 8390 3988

*"Innovative" cooking (with "very good" presentation) wins more-than-local acclaim for this "off-the-beaten-track" suburban subcontinental – after three years in business, it's "really beginning to find its feet".* / **Sample dishes:** king prawn; tandoori chicken platter; home-made ice cream. **Details:** www.joy-restaurant.co.uk; 11.30 pm; no smoking area.

**Lucia Lucia** £25 ★

282 Ewell Rd KT6 7AQ (020) 8399 1555

*Not only local reporters sing the praises of this "wonderful" new neighbourhood Italian; feedback is limited, but praise is fulsome for its "very tasty" cooking, and service that "goes out of its way to help".* / **Details:** www.lucialucia.co.uk; 11 pm; closed Sun; no Amex.

---

## SUTTON COLDFIELD, WEST MIDLANDS 5–4C

**Boathouse at Bracebridge** £39 🄰

Bracebridge Pool B74 2YR (0121) 308 8890

*A waterside dining room in a large park, where fish is the speciality; commentary is thin, but confirms it as a good all-rounder.* / **Details:** 9.30 pm, Sun 4 pm.

---

## SUTTON GAULT, CAMBRIDGESHIRE 3–1B

**Anchor** £36 🄰

Bury Ln CB6 2BD (01353) 778537

*A "superb" (if "desolate") fenland location ("surreal on a misty winter day") helps win much praise for this "timeless" canal-diggers' inn; it offers "tasty" and "unpretentious" fare, "often using fresh local produce".* / **Sample dishes:** Cornish crab salad; calf's liver with Bayonne ham; chocolate mousse. **Details:** www.anchor-inn-restaurant.co.uk; 7m W of Ely, signposted off B1381 in Sutton; 9pm, Sat 9.30 pm; no smoking area. **Accommodation:** 2 rooms, from £79.50.

---

## SUTTON GREEN, SURREY 3–3A

**Olive Tree** £38 ★

Sutton Green Rd GU4 7QD (01483) 729999

*"A former pub, now serving bar and restaurant meals", where the cooking ("specialising in fish") is invariably hailed as "very good".* / **Sample dishes:** crab & avocado with pink grapefruit; seared tuna with chilli & coriander; crème brûlée. **Details:** 9.30 pm; closed Mon D & Sun D; no Amex; no smoking.

---

## SUTTON-UPON-DERWENT, NORTH YORKSHIRE 5–1D

**St Vincent Arms** £30 🄰★

Main St YO41 4BN (01904) 608349

*The setting may retain a "country-pub feel", but – thanks to food "of restaurant quality" and a wine list which includes over a dozen champagnes (for example) – this is a destination "very much a cut above your average local".* / **Details:** 9.30 pm; no smoking in dining room.

**sign up for the survey at www.hardens.com**

## SWANSEA, SWANSEA                                    1–1D

**La Braseria**                              £32          Ⓐ
28 Wind St SA1 1DZ   (01792) 469683
*"Swansea's equivalent to Cardiff's Champers" (different
ownership these days) is a rustic 'Spanish bodega' with a similar
choose-at-the-counter formula; it is rated well for ambience,
but took flak this year for "slow" service and "taking good
ingredients and wrecking them".* / **Sample dishes:** *devilled chicken livers;
halibut Mornay; crème caramel.* **Details:** *www.labraseria.com; 11.30 pm; closed
Sun; need 6+ to book; children: 6+.*

**Morgans**
**Morgans Hotel**                            £46
Somerset Pl SA1 1RR   (01792) 484848
*Service which is "variable"-going-on-"poor" is noted in many
reports on this airy dining room of a "flashy" boutique-hotel;
the food attracts more favourable commentary, but even here
there's a feeling the place "should aim higher".*
/ **Sample dishes:** *salmon & crab potato cakes; roast tenderloin of pork with
bubble & squeak; pot au chocolat with ice cream.* **Details:** *www.morganshotel.co.uk;
9 pm; no smoking.* **Accommodation:** *20 rooms, from £100.*

**Patricks**                                 £35
638 Mumbles Rd SA3 4EA   (01792) 360199
*"The best restaurant hereabout" – a brasserie-with-rooms, on the
Mumbles – benefits from a "wonderful" seaside location;
its cooking is rated "excellent" by many reporters, but others say
it's only "OK".* / **Sample dishes:** *Feta sorbet with char-grilled watermelon;
sesame-crusted pork with satay sauce; cappuccino & chocolate terrine.*
**Details:** *www.patricks-restaurant.co.uk; in Mumbles, 1m before pier; 9.50 pm;
closed Sun D; no smoking.* **Accommodation:** *8 rooms, from £105.*

## SWINTON, SCOTTISH BORDERS              8–1A

**Wheatsheaf Inn**                           £39          ★
Main St TD11 3JJ   (01890) 860257
*In the middle of nowhere, a pub whose "friendly" new
management are establishing something of a reputation for "really
tasty and inventive cooking", using "locally-sourced ingredients".*
/ **Sample dishes:** *smoked haddock Scotch egg; roast rack of border lamb; toffee &
honeycomb parfait.* **Details:** *www.wheatsheaf-swinton.co.uk; between Kelso &
Berwick-upon-Tweed, by village green; 9 pm; Closed Sun D Dec-Jan; no Amex;
smoking in bar only.* **Accommodation:** *7 rooms, from £98.*

## TADCASTER, NORTH YORKSHIRE            5–1D

**Aagrah**                                   £24          ★
York Rd LS24 8EG   (01937) 530888
*"Good and dependable" ("especially the buffet") – this classic
Indian is an outlet of Yorkshire's pre-eminent subcontinental chain.*
/ **Details:** *www.aagrah.com; 7m from York on A64; 11.30 pm; D only;
no smoking area.*

## TAPLOW, BERKSHIRE                    3–3A

### Terrace
### Cliveden House                    £ 72      𝔸
Cliveden Rd SL6 0JF   (01628) 668561
*If you're looking for "total decadence" and "real pampering",
it can be simply "magical" to dine in the former library of this
grandest of the Thames Valley palazzi; the food does not figure
greatly in reports, but seems to do little to detract from the
"wonderful dining experience".* / **Sample dishes:** *asparagus soup;
pan-roasted fillet of turbot with a galette of fennel & thyme.*
**Details:** *www.clivedenhouse.co.uk; 9 pm; jacket & tie required at D; no smoking;
children: 18+.* **Accommodation:** *39 rooms, from £335.*

### Waldo's
### Cliveden House                    £ 77      𝔸
Berry Hill SL6 0JF   (01628) 668561
*The surveying year which has seen the arrival of new chef Daniel
Galmiche (ex-L'Ortolan) in the grand basement dining room
of this Italianate palace inspired solidly high ratings – but few
accounts of rapture – from reporters.* / **Sample dishes:** *smoked salmon;
roast fillet of duck with Szechuan pepper; fig tartlet with honey ice cream.*
**Details:** *www.clivedenhouse.co.uk; M4, J7 then follow National Trust signs; 9.30 pm;
D only, closed Mon & Sun; jacket & tie required; no smoking; booking: max 6;
children: 12+.* **Accommodation:** *39 rooms, from £335.*

## TARPORLEY, CHESHIRE                 5–2B

### Swan                             £ 37      ★
50 High St CW6 0AG   (01829) 733838
*It may look "rather ordinary from the outside", but this prettily-
located coaching inn serves up "high-quality local produce,
expertly cooked".* / **Sample dishes:** *pan-seared scallops; stuffed loin of lamb
with a minted potato purée; Baked Alaska.*
**Details:** *www.theswanhotel-tarporley.co.uk; in centre of High St; 9.30 pm;
no smoking.* **Accommodation:** *19 rooms, from £81.*

## TAUNTON, SOMERSET                   2–3A

### The Castle Hotel                  £ 61
Castle Grn TA1 1NF   (01823) 272671
*"Seriously good English food" is hailed by most (if not quite all)
who reported on this famous hotel's grand dining room this year –
of its nature, the cooking's rather on the "safe" side, but it rarely
disappoints.* / **Sample dishes:** *scrambled duck & smoked eel; Brixham scallops
with celeriac; bitter chocolate tart with steeped cherries.*
**Details:** *www.the-castle-hotel.com; follow tourist information signs; 9.45 pm; closed
Sun D; no smoking.* **Accommodation:** *44 rooms, from £180.*

### Willow Tree                       £ 40      𝔸★
3 Tower Ln TA1 4AR
(01823) 352835
*"Excellent use of local produce" (including "superb fish") is one
of the features that so endears Darren Sherlock's "lovely" little
restaurant to all who comment on it.* / **Sample dishes:** *roast pigeon with
bacon & chestnut mushrooms; sauteed medallions of monkfish; hot chocolate
fondant with date & Pedro Ximenez ice cream.*
**Details:** *www.willowtreerestaurant.co.uk; 10 pm; D only, closed Sun & Mon;
no Amex; no smoking.*

## TEFFONT EVIAS, WILTSHIRE 2–3C

### Howards House Hotel £54
SP3 5RJ (01722) 716392
A "lovely", if quite "formal", hotel, in a village house set in a
"lovely" garden, by a small river; the food inspires less
commentary than the setting, but is always well rated.
/ **Sample dishes:** fillet of John Dory; fillet of Aberdeen Angus beef; English
strawberry soufflé & strawberry ice cream. **Details:** www.howardshousehotel.com;
9m W of Stonehenge off A303; 9 pm; closed Mon L & Fri L; no smoking.
**Accommodation:** 9 rooms, from £145.

## TETBURY, GLOUCESTERSHIRE 2–2B

### Calcot Manor £52 &#x1F170;
GL8 8YJ (01666) 890391
Many reporters find the contemporary-style dining room of this
"wonderful" (and "child-friendly") hotel a "great" all-round
destination; as in the less formal 'Gumstool Inn', however,
feedback is not 100% consistent. / **Sample dishes:** scallops with spiced
couscous; roast pork with lardons & red onion; bread & butter pudding.
**Details:** www.calcotmanor.co.uk; junction of A46 & A4135; 9.30 pm; no jeans
or trainers; no smoking area; children: not at D. **Accommodation:** 30 rooms,
from £185.

### Priory Inn  £30 &#x1F170;★
London Rd GL8 8JJ
(01666) 502251
"Just a fantastic experience" – all early reporters sing the praises
of this "really friendly" and "laid-back" gastropub-with-rooms,
and its "great" and "adventurous" cooking.
/ **Details:** www.theprioryinn.co.uk.

### Trouble House Inn £40
Cirencester Rd GL8 8SG (01666) 502206
The food at this popular gastropub is "wonderful, sometimes",
and the place continues to inspire many reports; even one great
fan, though, is amongst those who suffer "occasional
disappointments". / **Sample dishes:** wild mushroom casserole; lemon sole with
braised leeks & mussels; white chocolate cheesecake with lemon ice cream.
**Details:** www.troublehouse.co.uk; 1.5m from Tetbury on A433 towards Cirencester;
9.30 pm; closed Mon; closed 2 weeks in Jan; no smoking area; booking: max 8;
children: 14+ in bar.

## THORNBURY, GLOUCESTERSHIRE 2–2B

### Thornbury Castle £57 &#x1F170;★
Castle St BS35 1HH (01454) 281182
"Very expensive, but probably worth it"; this landmark hotel in a
full-blown Tudor castle (a Von Essen property) attracts consistently
upbeat reviews, particularly for its "amazing" ambience.
/ **Sample dishes:** pan-fried scallops; fillet of local beef with braised oxtail & tongue;
assiette of coconut dessert. **Details:** www.thornburycastle.co.uk; near intersection
of M4 & M5; 9.30 pm, Sat 10 pm; no smoking. **Accommodation:** 25 rooms,
from £140.

## THORNHAM, NORFOLK 6–3B
**Lifeboat Inn** £32 A
Ship Ln PE36 6LT (01485) 512236

*"An old smugglers' inn"*, with *"thick walls and open fires, nestled amongst the dunes on the North Norfolk coast"*; it has quite a name for its food, but even some fans fear it's now *"too successful for its own good"*. / **Sample dishes:** Thai crab cakes with capsicum chutney; lemon sole with prawns; fruit crumble.
**Details:** www.lifeboatinn.co.uk; 20m from Kings Lynn on A149 coast road; 9.30 pm; D only, ex Sun open L & D; no Amex; no smoking. **Accommodation:** 14 rooms, from £78.

## THORPE LANGTON, LEICESTERSHIRE 5–4D
**Bakers Arms** £35 A
Main St LE16 7TS (01858) 545201

*"Cosy"* and *"always buzzing"*, this thatched inn offers your classic *"English pub/restaurant ambience"*; the food is *"consistently good"* and *"reliable"*, if perhaps just a touch *"predictable"*.
/ **Sample dishes:** mussels; sea bass with sweet potato mash; chocolate tart with caramelised bananas. **Details:** near Market Harborough off the A6; 9.30 pm; D only, ex Sat open L & D & Sun open L only, closed Mon; no Amex; no smoking area; children: 12+.

## TITLEY, HEREFORDSHIRE 2–1A
**Stagg Inn** £39 ★
HR5 3RL (01544) 230221

*"You can chat with the local farmers at the bar, or dine like the squire"* at this *"laid-back"* rural gastropub, which is *"beautiful outside as well as in"*; ex-Gavroche chef Steve Reynold's cooking is often *"gorgeous"* too. / **Sample dishes:** local organic trout tartar; rack of lamb with rosemary & goat's cheese; caramelised passion fruit tart with mango sorbet. **Details:** www.thestagg.co.uk; on B4355, NE of Kington; 9.30 pm; closed Mon & Sun D; closed 2 weeks in Nov; no Amex; no smoking area. **Accommodation:** 6 rooms, from £80.

## TODMORDEN, WEST YORKSHIRE 5–1B
**The Old Hall Restaurant** £38 A★
Hall St OL14 7AD (01706) 815998

Simply *"the best all-round restaurant"* – Nick and Madeleine Hoyles' historically-housed town-centre *"favourite"* incites universally adulatory reports, not least for its *"brilliant"* food and *"caring"* service. / **Sample dishes:** filo parcel of black pudding; roasted pork fillet; Yorkshire parkin with ginger sauce & rhubarb ice cream. **Details:** 15 mins from M62; 9 pm; closed Mon, Tue L, Wed L, Sat L & Sun D; no Amex; smoking in bar only. **Accommodation:** 3 rooms, from £80.

## TOPSHAM, DEVON 1–3D
**Darts Farm Café** £14
Clyst St George EX3 0QH (01392) 875587

*"Good ingredients used well"* – not least to create some *"very fresh fish 'n' chips"* – is part of the *"rough and ready"* formula which wins only praise for the eating possibilities at this rural retail complex. / **Sample dishes:** filled baguette; prime sirloin steak in a panini bread; apricot & raspberry tart. **Details:** www.dartsfarm.co.uk; 5 pm; no Amex; no smoking.

**La Petite Maison** £ 40

35 Fore St  EX3 0HR  (01392) 873660

*"Fine food"* and *"easy-going service"* are the invariable themes of commentary on this unpretentious local destination.

/ **Sample dishes:** *tian of crab; Devon duck breast; lemon tart.* **Details:** *10 pm; closed Mon & Sun; no Amex; no smoking.*

---

TORCROSS, DEVON 1–4D

**Start Bay Inn** £ 24 ★

TQ7 2TQ  (01548) 580553

*"A massive range of incredibly fresh fish"* is the culinary draw to this *"honest"* and *"enjoyable"* pub; it gets *"packed"* and *"noisy"*, but has a *"stunning location"*, by the quay, overlooking the beach. / **Sample dishes:** *scallops in garlic butter; whole Dover sole; gooseberry toffee crunch with clotted cream.* **Details:** *www.startbayinn.co.uk; on beach front (take A379 coastal road to Dartmouth); 10 pm; no Amex; no smoking area; no booking.*

---

TORQUAY, DEVON 1–3D

**No 7 Fish Bistro** £ 39 ★

Beacon Ter  TQ1 2BH  (01803) 295055

A *"friendly"* family-run bistro of long standing whose fish cooking *"continues to be outstanding"*. / **Sample dishes:** *hot shellfish platter; tempura special; brandy snap basket with amaretti.* **Details:** *www.no7-fish.com; 9.30 pm; D only Sun-Tue, closed Sun & Mon in Winter.*

**Orestone Manor** £ 48 ★

Rockhouse Ln  TQ1 4SX  (01803) 328098

A modernish country house hotel, in a *"superb setting"* (overlooking the sea, on the rural fringe of the resort); its cuisine is praised by all reporters, some of whom say it's *"very, very good"*. / **Sample dishes:** *pan-fried duck breast; roast lamb with sweet carrot purée; bread & butter soufflé.* **Details:** *www.orestone.co.uk; 9 pm; no smoking.* **Accommodation:** *12 rooms, from £135.*

---

TRELOWARREN, CORNWALL 1–4B

**New Yard Restaurant** £ 42 Ⓐ

Mawgan  TR12 6AF  (01326) 221595

A *"wonderful setting"* – *"in the old stables of an ancient estate, deep in the heart of the Lizard"* – adds much to a visit to this restaurant, where Cornishman Greg Laskey makes much use of local ingredients; it induced limited feedback – most of it adulatory, but also the odd duff report.

/ **Sample dishes:** *locally-reared smoked ham; millefeuille of poached fish; champagne jelly with elderflower sorbet.* **Details:** *9.15 pm; closed Sun D; no Amex; smoking in bar only.*

---

TRING, HERTFORDSHIRE 3–2A

**Forno Vivo** £ 29 Ⓐ

69 High St  HP23 4AB  (01442) 890005

*"Authentic"* cooking and a *"brilliant"* atmosphere combine to make this (wood-burning) pizzeria, in a former post office, an unusually good destination of its type. / **Sample dishes:** *bruschetta al pomodoro; pizza Forno Vivo; cristatina di limone.* **Details:** *www.fornovivo.com; 10.30 pm; no Amex; no smoking.*

**sign up for the survey at www.hardens.com**

## TROON, SOUTH AYRSHIRE 9–4B

**Lochgreen House** £ 44 ★
Lochgreen Hs, Monktonhill Rd  KA10 7EN  (01292) 313343
*A recently-extended Edwardian golf-hotel, "designed to impress
rich tourists and high-powered business people"; its "perfectly-
cooked and impressively-presented" fare makes it a very "safe"
choice.* / **Sample dishes:** *scallops with celeriac & mustard oil; horseradish-crusted
lamb with rosemary noodles; hot chocolate & cherry pudding.*
**Details:** *www.costleyhotels.co.uk; 9 pm; no smoking.* **Accommodation:** *43 rooms,
from £205.*

## TROUTBECK, CUMBRIA 7–3D

**Queen's Head** £ 30  Ⓐ
Townhead  LA23 1PW  (01539) 432174
*"A stunning location" helps ensure this impressive Lakeland inn
remains a "very busy" destination; most (if not quite all) reporters
say the food is "excellent" too.* / **Sample dishes:** *wild mushroom, Stilton &
black olive terrine; supreme of chicken with mash; sticky toffee pudding.*
**Details:** *www.queensheadhotel.com; A592 on Kirkstone Pass; 9 pm; no Amex;
no smoking area; booking: max 8, Fri & Sat.* **Accommodation:** *14 rooms,
from £85.*

## TUNBRIDGE WELLS, KENT 3–4B

**Hotel du Vin et Bistro** £ 41  Ⓐ
Crescent Rd  TN1 2LY  (01892) 526455
*A generally well commented-on outpost of the boutique-hotel
chain; fans say it offers "good food in a great location", in addition
to the "superb" wine list which is the group's hallmark.*
/ **Sample dishes:** *salt cod brandade with peppers; chicken with creamed leeks &
black pudding; pineapple crème brûlée.* **Details:** *www.hotelduvin.com; 9.45 pm;
booking: max 10.* **Accommodation:** *36 rooms, from £89.*

**Thackeray's House** £ 52
85 London Rd  TN1 1EA  (01892) 511921
*While numerous supporters again hail Robert Phillips's cooking
at this villa-restaurant as "delicious", a number of former fans feel
the venture has "lost its edge" in recent times – let's hope that
now Hengist (same owners) is open, the place will get back
on track.* / **Sample dishes:** *scallop & herb pansotti; pan-fried fillet of wild
halibut & sauteed mangetout; Mascarpone & chocolate mousse with coffee & pecan
cake.* **Details:** *www.thackerays-restaurant.co.uk; near Kent and Sussex hospital;
10 pm; closed Mon & Sun D; no smoking.*

## TUNSTALL, LANCASHIRE 7–4D

**Lunesdale Arms** £ 27  Ⓐ★
LA6 2QN  (01524) 274203
*"A nicely feminine feel to the decorations" adds a slightly unusual
air to Emma Gillibrand's "increasingly popular" (and "lively")
gastropub; the cooking is "good", and it places "strong emphasis
on local products".* / **Sample dishes:** *tomato bruschetta with pesto; lime &
lemon grass chicken; cappuccino mousse.* **Details:** *www.thelunesdale.com; 15 min
from J34 on M6 onto A683; 9 pm; closed Mon; no Amex; no smoking.*

## TURNBERRY, SOUTH AYRSHIRE 7–1A

**Westin Turnberry Resort** £75 Ⓐ

KA26 9LT (01655) 331000

*"The restaurant is nearly as good as the golf!"* at this grand
sporting hotel (with two world-class courses), where the window
seats in the dining room offer marvellous sea views; the ambience,
however, tends to eclipse both the food and the service.
/ **Sample dishes:** oak-smoked Scottish salmon; seared monkfish with basil polenta;
chef's choice soufflé. **Details:** www.turnberry.co.uk; A77, 2m after Kirkswald turn
right, then right again after 0.5m; 10 pm; closed Sun L, ex for holidays; no smoking.
**Accommodation:** 221 rooms, from £220.

## TURNERS HILL, WEST SUSSEX 3–4B

**Alexander House** £58 Ⓐ

East St RH10 4QD (01342) 714914

Set in *"very pleasant"* and extensive grounds, this grand country
house hotel is consistently well-rated by reporters for its
traditional-ish cuisine (even if the odd sceptic still finds
it *"overpriced"*). / **Sample dishes:** goat's cheese ballotine with curry lentils;
braised shank of lamb with cream potatoes; glazed coconut custard on macaroon
with caramel sauce. **Details:** www.alexanderhouse.co.uk; off the M23 J10, follow
signs to E. Grinstead and Turners Hill, on the B2110; 9 pm; no jeans; no smoking;
children: 7+. **Accommodation:** 18 rooms, from £145.

## TYN-Y-GROES, CONWY 4–1D

**Groes Inn** £43 Ⓐ

LL32 8TN (01492) 650545

A *"great setting"* helps win praise for this *"very attractive old inn"*
(probably North Wales's oldest) as a *"wonderful"* destination;
it serves a *"good choice"* of *"home-cooking"*. / **Sample dishes:** crispy
black pudding, bacon & red onion salad; braised knuckle of lamb; bread & butter
pudding. **Details:** www.groesinn.com; on B5106 between Conwy & Betws-y-coed,
2m from Conwy; 9 pm; no jeans; no smoking area. **Accommodation:** 14 rooms,
from £95.

## TYNEMOUTH, TYNE & WEAR 8–2B

**Sidney's** £29 Ⓐ★

3-5 Percy Park Rd NE30 4LZ (0191) 257 8500

*"A small and friendly restaurant with a brilliant lunchtime menu"*
– that's long been the view on this popular spot, which was on the
point of recruiting a new chef as this guide went to press.
/ **Sample dishes:** French black pudding; lamb with garlic purée, roasted
aubergines & basil jus; Bailey's bread & butter pudding. **Details:** www.sidneys.co.uk;
9.30 pm; closed Sun; no smoking.

## ULLINGSWICK, HEREFORDSHIRE 2–1B

**The Three Crowns Inn** £30 Ⓐ

HR1 3JQ (01432) 820279

We wish we got more reports on this remote half-timbered inn –
such feedback as there is confirms that it offers an *"imaginative"*
menu in a *"lovely"* setting. / **Sample dishes:** crab & mussel tart; grilled
calf's liver & pancetta; date & pecan pudding. **Details:** www.threecrownsinn.com;
1.5m from A417; 9.30 pm; closed Mon; no Amex; no smoking.

**sign up for the survey at www.hardens.com**

## ULLSWATER, CUMBRIA     7–3D
**Sharrow Bay**     £ 53    𝔸★
CA10 2LZ (01768) 486301
*"Of its kind, simply the best – not bad after 57 years!"; under
new owners (Von Essen), the UK's original country house hotel
"continues to excel", particularly for a romantic escape; it offers
"unrivalled Lakeland views", "truly marvellous" service and
"fantastic" food in "huge" quantities.* / **Sample dishes:** fried calf's liver;
Scottish fillet steak with seared foie gras; fig tart with goat's cheese & rosemary ice
cream. **Details:** www.sharrowbay.co.uk; on Pooley Bridge Rd towards Howtown;
8 pm; no smoking; children: 13+. **Accommodation:** 26 rooms, from £340.

## ULVERSTON, CUMBRIA     7–4D
**Bay Horse**     £ 45    𝔸★
Canal Foot LA12 9EL (01229) 583972
*A "wonderful surprise" – this "pub-sounding but restaurant-
seeming" place is hidden away at "the seaward end of a hideous
road by a chemical works"; once you're there, you find a "candlelit
dining room", with "a great setting overlooking Morecambe
Bay"… and "great food" too.* / **Sample dishes:** chilled tomato &
redcurrant soup; guinea fowl with grape & chestnut stuffing; Irish coffee meringues.
**Details:** www.thebayhorsehotel.co.uk; after Canal Foot sign, turn left & pass Glaxo
factory; 8 pm; closed Mon L; smoking in bar only; children: 12+.
**Accommodation:** 9 rooms, from £110.

## UPPER SLAUGHTER, GLOUCESTERSHIRE     2–1C
**Lords of the Manor**     £ 75
GL54 2JD (01451) 820243
*Opinions vary on the new regime at this Cotswold destination;
fans say "the new chef has brought it back on course" and laud
it as "a great place for a break" – sceptics, though, rail at
"unsatisfying" food and "poor" service (and don't like its whole
style much either).* / **Sample dishes:** quail ravioli with morels; roast John Dory
with Parma ham & foie gras; pistachio soufflé. **Details:** www.lordsofthemanor.com;
2m W of Stow on the Wold; 9.30 pm; no jeans or trainers; smoking in bar only;
children: 7+ at D. **Accommodation:** 27 rooms, from £160.

## WADDESDON, BUCKINGHAMSHIRE     3–2A
**Five Arrows**     £ 38
High St HP18 0JE (01296) 651727
*"All the Rothschild wines" feature on the list of this grand inn
on the family's estate, where the (improving) cuisine is generally
now hailed as "reliable".* / **Sample dishes:** beetroot & cumin soup;
Moroccan lamb stew with cardamom rice; bourbon mousse with mango & raspberry
coulis. **Details:** www.waddesdon.org.uk; on A41; 9.30 pm; no smoking.
**Accommodation:** 11 rooms, from £85.

## WAKEFIELD, WEST YORKSHIRE     5–1C
**Aagrah**     £ 24    ★★
Barnsley Rd WF1 5NX (01924) 242222
*"The best branch of this high-quality West Yorkshire chain
of Indian/Kashmiri restaurants"; it is praised for its "beautiful
blends" of "fresh ingredients".* / **Details:** www.aagrah.com; from M1,
J39 follow Denby Dale Rd to A61; 11.30 pm; D only; no smoking area.
**Accommodation:** 13 rooms, from £40.

## Kaye Arms                    £ 34        A ★
29 Wakefield Rd  WF4 4BG   (01924) 848385
*"Top-class food", "excellent" service and an "exceptional wine list" make this "very pleasant country pub/bistro" popular with all of the many reporters who comment on it; it's been in the same hands for 35 years, so they must be doing something right.*
/ ***Sample dishes:*** *seared scallops with pea purée; Cheddar cheese soufflé with stuffed peppers; sticky banana pudding.* ***Details:*** *7m W of Wakefield on A642; 9.30 pm; no Amex; no smoking area; no booking on Sat; children: 14+ at D.*

---

## WAREHAM, DORSET                           2–4C

## Priory                       £ 49        A
Church Grn  BH20 4ND   (01929) 551666
*"Summer meals on the terrace by the river are especially good", at this "romantic", "civilised" and "comfortable" hotel; its afternoon tea is also hailed as "the best this side of the Ritz".*
/ ***Sample dishes:*** *seared scallops with rhubarb butter; lamb with herb polenta & roast garlic jus; ginger crème brûlée.* ***Details:*** *www.theprioryhotel.co.uk; 10 pm; no Amex; jacket & tie required; no smoking; children: 8+.* ***Accommodation:*** *18 rooms, from £140.*

---

## WARWICK, WARWICKSHIRE                      5–4C

## Saffron                      £ 25        ★
Unit 1 Westgate Hs, Market St  CV34 4DE   (01926) 402061
*"It may offer a wide range of curries, but this is a restaurant, not a curry house", and "its slightly weird shopping-precinct location just adds to the experience"; "outstanding service" likewise.* / ***Details:*** *www.saffronwarwick.co.uk.*

---

## WATERMILLOCK, CUMBRIA                      7–3D

## Leeming House Hotel          £ 47        A ★
Ullswater  CA11 0JJ   (01768) 486622
*This "cosy and friendly country house hotel" benefits from "a lovely position on the lake"; practically all reports suggest it offers accomplished cooking at "a fair price".*
/ ***Sample dishes:*** *smoked salmon; guinea fowl; chocolate extreme mousse.* ***Details:*** *www.macdonald-hotels.co.uk; near A592; 9 pm; no jeans or trainers; no smoking.* ***Accommodation:*** *41 rooms, from £180.*

---

## WATH-IN-NIDDERDALE, NORTH YORKSHIRE    8–4B

## Sportsman's Arms            £ 39        ★
HG3 5PP   (01423) 711306
*This "jewel" of over a quarter of a century's standing has a beautiful Dales location; on limited feedback, commentary on both service and ambience were a touch mixed, but esteem for Ray Carter's "locally-sourced" cuisine remains at a very high level.*
/ ***Sample dishes:*** *Camembert & goat's cheese; breast of Gressingham duckling; roasted plums with cinnamon & Mascarpone.* ***Details:*** *www.sportsmans-arms.co.uk; take Wath Road from Pateley Bridge; 9 pm; no Amex; no smoking.* ***Accommodation:*** *11 rooms, from £100.*

---

**sign up for the survey at www.hardens.com**

## WEST HALLAM, DERBYSHIRE 5–3C

### The Bottle Kiln £17
High Lane West  DE7 6HP   (0115) 932 9442
*"Good, if old-fashioned, cooking"* of the *"quiches and soups"*
variety makes this *"interesting"* art gallery annexe a handy stand-
by. / **Sample dishes:** home-made soup & bread; Stilton and apricot quiche; rum &
apple cake. **Details:** L & afternoon tea only, closed Mon; no Amex; no smoking;
no booking.

## WEST MALLING, KENT 3–3C

### Swan £37  𝔸★
35 Swan St  ME19 6JU   (01732) 521910
*"This was once a pub, but it's hard to see it as such nowadays"* –
whatever you call it, however, this *"buzzy"* outfit pleases reporters
with its *"very good"* fare. / **Sample dishes:** chicken & foie gras parfait;
slow-baked belly of pork & black eye beans; chocolate fondant.
**Details:** www.theswanwestmalling.co.uk; 10.30 pm; no smoking.

## WEST MERSEA, ESSEX 3–2C

### The Company Shed £14  ★★
129 Coast Rd  CO5 8PA   (01206) 382700
*Huge platters of "mind-blowingly fresh seafood"* – and at
*"absolute bargain prices"*, too – mean you may have to queue
(even if you arrive early) at Heather Howard's *"unique"*, *"spit-
and-sawdust"* sea-front shed; take your own bread, butter and
wine. / **Sample dishes:** fish platter. **Details:** L only, closed Mon; no credit cards;
no booking.

## WESTCLIFF ON SEA, ESSEX 3–3C

### Paris £44  𝔸★
719 London Rd  SS0 9ST   (01702) 344077
*Reports are few, but they all tend to support the view that
Matthew Locker's "professional" and "very friendly" restaurant
offers "a top dining experience"; frequent themed menus seem
to go down particularly well.* / **Sample dishes:** pressed terrine of overcoat
duck & foie gras; tournedos rossini; vanilla crème brûlée.
**Details:** www.parisrestaurant.net; on A13 into Southend; 10 pm; closed Mon &
Sun D; no smoking area.

## WESTERHAM, KENT 3–3B

### Tulsi £23  ★
20 London Rd  TN16 1BD   (01959) 563397
*"Great Indian food"* – *"time and time again"* – is the gist of all
commentary on this moderately trendy curry house.
/ **Sample dishes:** vegetable samosa; chicken curry; ice cream. **Details:** 11.30 pm;
no smoking area.

**sign up for the survey at www.hardens.com**

---

## WESTFIELD, EAST SUSSEX                                3–4C

**Wild Mushroom**                        £38        ★
Westfield Ln  TN35 4SB   (01424) 751137
*"First-class cooking of best-quality local produce"* earned very
positive reviews this year for Paul and Rebecca Webbe's *"rather
ordinary-looking"* former boozer. / **Sample dishes:** *foie gras & duck confit
terrine; pan-fried calf's liver with sage sauce; tropical fruit sorbets with jasmine syrup.*
**Details:** *www.wildmushroom.co.uk; 9.30 pm; closed Mon & Sun D; closed 3 weeks
in Jan; smoking in bar only.*

---

## WETHERBY, WEST YORKSHIRE                          5–1C

**La Locanda**                           £32
Wetherby Rd  LS22 5AY   (01937) 579797
*An "extensive" menu of food that's sometimes "really good"*
makes this *"always busy"* Italian worth knowing about; it's also
*"quite handy for the M1"*. / **Sample dishes:** *fried calamari with salad;
beef Stroganoff; chocolate fudge cake.* **Details:** *www.lalocanda.co.uk; 11 pm;
no smoking area.*

---

## WEYBRIDGE, SURREY                                   3–3A

**Colony**                               £31
3 Balfour Rd  KT13 8HE   (01932) 842766
*"It hasn't changed for 25 years"* – this long-established, upmarket
Chinese restaurant may sometimes seem *"dull"*, but its virtues
include consistently *"good"* cooking. / **Sample dishes:** *spring rolls & crispy
seaweed; toffee apples.* **Details:** *on A317; 10.30 pm.*

---

## WEYMOUTH, DORSET                                    2–4B

**Perry's**                              £36        ★
4 Trinity Rd, The Old Harbour  DT4 8TJ   (01305) 785799
*This "excellent" and "unpretentious" fish restaurant is highly
praised by all reporters; you get "lovely views" too ("…as long
as you get the upstairs window seat").* / **Sample dishes:** *smoked
haddock & potato soup; fillet of beef with parsnip mash; coffee cheesecake.*
**Details:** *www.perrysrestaurant.co.uk; 9.30 pm; closed Mon L & Sat L; closed Sun D
in Winter; no smoking.*

---

## WHALLEY, LANCASHIRE                                 5–1B

**Three Fishes**                         £30
Mitton Rd  BB7 9PQ   (01254) 826888
*As a new part of the Northcote Manor operation, this "no-
nonsense" gastropub has found an instant local following,
and fans extol its "superb traditional Lancashire food"; doubters,
however – who say it's "rather too pleased with itself, and has yet
really to deliver" – are more numerous than one might hope.*
/ **Sample dishes:** *ribs; deep-fried haddock with marrowfat pea & tartar sauce;
chocolate & orange pudding.* **Details:** *www.thethreefishes.com; 9 pm; no smoking.*

**sign up for the survey at www.hardens.com**

## WHITBY, NORTH YORKSHIRE 8–3D

### Magpie Café £26 ★★
14 Pier Rd YO21 3PU (01947) 602058
*"Incomparably fresh fish cooked in the world's best batter"* have
made this *"cramped"* chippie one of the best-known eateries
in the UK; *"are the queues longer?"*, though, *"it gets sooooooo
busy"*. / **Sample dishes:** grilled tuna with fritters; cod & chips; sticky sultana loaf.
**Details:** www.magpiecafe.co.uk; opp Fish Market; 9 pm; no Amex; no smoking;
no booking at L.

### Trenchers £21 ★
New Quay Rd YO21 1DH (01947) 603212
*Whether this palatial, "modern" chippie is "every bit as good
as the Magpie"* remains hotly debated by reporters (it scores
fractionally lower) – all agree, however, that the *"traditional fish
'n' chips"* are *"top-class"*, and *"with no queues"*!
/ **Sample dishes:** smoked salmon; halibut with chips & salad; sticky toffee pudding.
**Details:** www.trenchersrestaurant.co.uk; opp railway station, nr marina; 9 pm;
no Amex; no smoking; need 7+ to book.

### The White Horse & Griffin £38 Ⓐ
Church St YO22 4BH (01947) 604857
*A bistro attached to a "quaint" hotel in an "interesting" building;
it serves "hearty portions" of traditional dishes "with a twist" –
these please most reporters, but doubters find them "average"
or "too expensive".* / **Sample dishes:** gravlax & goat's cheese mousse;
monkfish wrapped in Parma ham; Swiss chocolate fondue.
**Details:** www.whitehorseandgriffin.co.uk; centre of old town, on Abbey side of river;
9 pm; no Amex; no smoking area. **Accommodation:** 10 rooms, from £60.

## WHITCHURCH, HAMPSHIRE 2–3D

### Red House Inn £33 Ⓐ
21 London St RG28 7LH (01256) 895558
*This Californian-owned rural boozer (with a pleasant garden)
inspired somewhat mixed feedback this year; however, even one
reporter who said "it's not as good as it was" still rated the
cooking as "very good", and some reporters feel it's plain
"marvellous".* / **Sample dishes:** Parmesan-crusted langoustine; fillet steak
in bacon with Stilton sauce; lemon tart & strawberry coulis. **Details:** 9.30 pm;
no Amex; no smoking; children: 12+ at D.

## WHITLEY, WILTSHIRE 2–2B

### The Pear Tree Inn £38 Ⓐ★
Top Ln SN12 8QX (01225) 709131
*This "quaint" boozer is almost "more a restaurant these days" –
whatever its designation, the arrival of Stephen Perry at the stoves
has made the food more "memorable".* / **Sample dishes:** grilled pear &
goat's cheese salad; grilled lamb cutlets with pan-fried polenta; lemon semifreddo.
**Details:** 9.30 pm; no Amex; smoking in bar only. **Accommodation:** 8 rooms,
from £90.

## WHITSTABLE, KENT                                   3–3C
### Crab & Winkle                                     £ 34
South Quay, Whitstable Harbour  CT5 1AB
(01227) 779377
*New owners were completing a major revamp of this popular fish
restaurant as this guide went to press – hopefully this will instil
more consistent standards than those reported in this year's
survey.* / **Sample dishes:** *oysters; vegetable paella; lemon tart.*
**Details:** *www.crab-winkle.co.uk; 8.45 pm; no Amex; smoking in bar only.*

### Sportsman                                         £ 36      ★★
Faversham Rd, Seasalter  CT5 4BP   (01227) 273370
*"In the middle of nowhere, but worth a trip", this coastal pub
is praised for its "fantastic" food by all of the (fairly numerous)
reporters who comment on it – it "justifies a visit, even just for the
oysters with hot sausage".* / **Sample dishes:** *crab salad; roast rack of lamb;
tayberry & almond tart.* **Details:** *8.45 pm; closed Mon & Sun D; no Amex;
no smoking area; children: not allowed in main bar.*

### Wheeler's Oyster Bar                              £ 31      Ⓐ★★
8 High St  CT5 1BQ   (01227) 273311
*The Victorian setting is "tiny" (as well as "quaint"), but this "one-
off" BYO dining room – the original of what went on to be the
chain – has a huge reputation for its "fabulous" fish and seafood;
"book well ahead".* / **Sample dishes:** *skate ravioli; baked cod with spinach &
curried mussels; date & chocolate sponge.* **Details:** *7.30 pm; closed Wed; no credit
cards; no smoking.*

### Whitstable Oyster Fishery Co.                     £ 45      Ⓐ★
Horsebridge  CT5 1BU  (01227) 276856
*"A wonderful view of the bay" and an "excellent old-world feel"
are key features of this "fun" beach-side institution; its "super
seafood" better lived up to reporters' expectations this year,
and service also seems to be on the mend.* / **Sample dishes:** *rock
oysters; char-gilled mackerel with roast tomato sauce; chocolate truffle cake with
raspberries.* **Details:** *www.oysterfishery.co.uk; 9 pm, Sat 10 pm; closed Mon
(& Sun D Sep-May).* **Accommodation:** *32 rooms, from £55.*

## WHITTLESFORD, CAMBRIDGESHIRE                       3–1B
### Tickell Arms                                      £ 48
1 North Rd  CB2 4NZ   (01223) 833128
*"Wonderful tales of the late Baron" add to the "quirky" nature
of this camp rural inn, known to generations of varsity folk;
devotees say it's "exceptional all round" – those who don't 'get it',
can find the experience "disappointing, amateur and expensive".*
/ **Details:** *9 pm; closed Mon & Sun D; smoking in bar only.*

## WILMINGTON, EAST SUSSEX                            3–4B
### Giant's Rest                                      £ 28
The Street  BN26 5SQ   (01323) 870207
*This is officially a 'druid-friendly' pub (handy in these parts),
but it's also "perfect for a Sunday lunch after a refreshing
Downland walk"; the food has no fancy aspirations, but comes
"highly recommended" too.* / **Sample dishes:** *avocado & prawns;
home-made fishcakes; fruit crumble.* **Details:** *www.giantsrest.co.uk; from A22
at Polegate take A27 towards Lewes, after 2m left at crossroads; 9 pm; no Amex;
no smoking; booking: max 12.*

---

## WILMSLOW, CHESHIRE · 5–2B

**Chilli Banana**
**Kings Arms Hotel** · £31
Alderley Rd  SK9 IPZ  (01625) 539100
"South Manchester's best Thai" occupies a "noisy" dining room behind a pub, and offers a good "cheap and cheerful" experience. / **Details:** www.chillibanana.co.uk; 10.30 pm; closed Mon, Tue-Thu D only; no smoking.

---

## WINCHCOMBE, GLOUCESTERSHIRE · 2–1C

**5 North Street** · £40 · ★
5 North St  GL54 5LH
(01242) 604566
Marcus Ashenford is a chef of undoubted talent, and his (and his wife's) "small" and "cramped" two-year-old is undoubtedly "trying really hard"; the cooking is often "brilliant", but it can also sometimes be "inconsistent". / **Sample dishes:** roast scallop with sauteed foie gras; chump of lamb with haggis; chocolate brownie. **Details:** 9 pm; closed Mon, Tue L & Sun D; no smoking.

**Wesley House** · £54 · 𝔸★
High St  GL54 5LJ  (01242) 602366
"Imaginative and well-presented" dishes contribute to the positive views which all reporters hold on this "romantic", half-timbered inn. / **Sample dishes:** red snapper terrine with saffron potatoes; seared duck with pickled apples & calvados cream; iced toffee & pistachio parfait. **Details:** www.wesleyhouse.co.uk; next to Sudeley Castle; 9 pm; closed Sun D; no smoking. **Accommodation:** 5 rooms, from £150.

---

## WINCHESTER, HAMPSHIRE · 2–3D

**Chestnut Horse** · £37 · 𝔸★
Easton Village  SO21 IEG  (01962) 779257
It may be in a "remote" village, but this "outstanding" pub is "always full", thanks to its "always-dependable" cooking and its notably "friendly" service. / **Sample dishes:** crab; sticky toffee pudding. **Details:** 9.30 pm; no Amex; no smoking.

**Hotel du Vin et Bistro** · £43 · 𝔸★
14 Southgate St  SO23 9EF  (01962) 841414
"The first of the chain and still the best"; the "buzzy" original of the boutique-hotel group delivers an all-round-good package of "characterful" surroundings, "well-cooked" bistro food and – of course – "interesting" wine. / **Sample dishes:** moules marinière; salmon pavé with mussel ragoût; lime panna cotta. **Details:** www.hotelduvin.com; 9.45 pm; no smoking; booking: max 10. **Accommodation:** 23 rooms, from £109.

**The Chesil Rectory** · £66 · ★
1 Chesil St  S023 0HU  (01962) 851555
"Excellent, if rather pricey", this Tudor building is a venue that strikes some as tailor-made for romance; its cooking is invariably hailed by reporters as being of a high standard, if in a style that can seem "a bit '80s". / **Sample dishes:** foie gras with sauternes jelly; lamb shoulder with saddle cooked pink with morels; chocolate fondant with Bailey's ice cream & pistachios. **Details:** www.thechesilrectory.co.uk; 9.30 pm; closed Mon, Tue L, Wed L, Thu L, Fri L & Sun; no smoking.

**sign up for the survey at www.hardens.com**

## Wykeham Arms £ 34 Ⓐ
75 Kingsgate St SO23 9PE (01962) 853834
The "friendly" and "very traditional" charms of this "iconic"
boozer – which has managed to retain a "superb", "real old-pub"
atmosphere – win it many fans; the food is "always reliable" too –
"book early if you want to eat in the restaurant".
/ **Sample dishes:** mushroom, walnut & Stilton pâté; roast monkfish with red
onion & cherry tomato salad; orange & maple cheesecake. **Details:** between
Cathedral and College; 8.45 pm; closed Sun D; no smoking; booking: max 8;
children: 14+. **Accommodation:** 14 rooms, from £95.

---

## WINCHMORE HILL, BUCKINGHAMSHIRE 3–2A

## Plough £ 36
The Hill HP7 0PA (01494) 721001
The popular gastropub moved into new ownership in early 2005
– initial reports are up-and-down, but a proper appraisal will have
to wait for next year's survey. / **Sample dishes:** blue cheese & chive risotto;
roasted cod fillet with mussel risotto; lemon rice pudding. **Details:** off A404,
between High Wycombe and Amersham.; 9.30 pm; closed Mon & Sun D;
no smoking.

---

## WINDERMERE, CUMBRIA 7–3D

## Gilpin Lodge £ 59 Ⓐ★
Crook Rd LA23 3NE (01539) 488818
"Perhaps the best in Cumbria" – the dining possibilities of this
"romantic" hotel (in an Edwardian country house) seem,
if anything, to have improved under new chef Chris Meredith;
"you can tell the place is family-run by the service and the
attention to detail". / **Sample dishes:** smoked haddock pavé; roast lamb with
truffled potato & garlic sauce; Greek yoghurt sorbet. **Details:** www.gilpinlodge.com;
9.15 pm; no smoking; children: 7+. **Accommodation:** 14 rooms, from £220.

## Holbeck Ghyll £ 64 Ⓐ★
Holbeck Ln LA23 1LU (01539) 432375
"Thoughtful" food, prepared "with flair", helps make this
"wonderfully-located" country house hotel above Windermere
a simply "idyllic" dining location for most reporters; prices are
"very high", though. / **Sample dishes:** veal ravioli with morels; salmon with
tomato fondue; pear & praline parfait. **Details:** www.holbeckghyll.com; 3m N
of Windermere, towards Troutbeck; 9.30 pm; no smoking; children: 8+ at
D. **Accommodation:** 21 rooms, from £190.

## Jerichos £ 42 ★
Birch St LA23 1EG (01539) 442522
"Unpretentious" but "very professional" – this "friendly" town-
centre operation is hailed by all reporters for its "good" going-on
"exceptional" standards. / **Sample dishes:** smoked haddock, spring onion &
Cheddar risotto; pork tenderloin with roast parsnips & Madeira jus; butterscotch
toffee crème brûlée. **Details:** www.jerichos.co.uk; 9.30 pm; D only, closed Mon;
no Amex; no smoking; children: 12+.

### Samling £66 A★★
Ambleside Rd LA23 1LR (015394) 31922
The "superb" gastronomic menu – "every course a new experience, and wonderfully presented" – is a highlight at this "stylish" country house hotel, which enjoys a "wonderful setting overlooking Windermere". / **Sample dishes:** free range guinea fowl; Gloucestershire old spot; caramelised apples & yoghurt with saffron ice cream. **Details:** www.thesamling.com; take A591 from town; 9.30 pm; no smoking. **Accommodation:** 11 rooms, from £195.

---

## WINDSOR, WINDSOR & MAIDENHEAD 3–3A

### Al Fassia £29 ★
27 St Leonards Rd SL4 3BP (01753) 855370
"Fast growing out of its cramped premises", this friendly Moroccan "maintains high standards", and is a very popular local destination; book ahead. / **Sample dishes:** chicken & almond filo parcels; lamb stew with sweet prunes; Moroccan desserts. **Details:** 10.30 pm, Fri & Sat 11 pm; closed Sun; no smoking area.

### Spice Route £36
18a, Thames St, Boots Pas SL4 1PL (01753) 860720
An "excellent range of quality dishes" can make it an "enlightening" experience to visit this "innovative" ("Indian-fusion") subcontinental. / **Sample dishes:** potato cakes in spiced chick peas; prawns in coconut cream sauce; lychee-ginger ice cream with apple spice topping. **Details:** www.spice-route.co.uk; 11 pm; smoking in bar only.

---

## WINKFIELD, BERKSHIRE 3–3A

### Cottage Inn £35
Winkfield St SL4 4SW (01344) 882242
"A huge menu of traditional British food and daily specials" wins consistent acclaim for this "cramped" and "friendly" spot; it may have a "pub ambience", but it's still "always best to book". / **Details:** www.cottage-inn.co.uk; 9.30pm; closed Sun D. **Accommodation:** 10 rooms, from £75.

---

## WINKLEIGH, DEVON 1–2D

### Pophams £35 A★
Castle St EX19 8HQ (01837) 83767
There's "nothing quite like it": this quirky, 10-seat outfit of 20 years' standing; unsurprisingly, feedback is modest in volume, but all of this year's reporters were totally satisfied with the accomplished cuisine. / **Sample dishes:** baked goat's cheese with spicy chutney; lamb in puff pastry with mushroom pâté; orange tart with apricot sauce. **Details:** off A377 between Exeter & Barnstaple; open only Thu & Fri L; closed Feb; no credit cards; no smoking; children: 16+.

**sign up for the survey at www.hardens.com**

---

## WINTERINGHAM, N LINCS          5–1D

### Winteringham Fields        £77
DN15 9PF    (01724) 733096

*After 18 years, the Schwabs retired from this 16th-century manor house in August 2005, selling it on to Colin and Rebecca McGurren (but with all staff, not least chef Robert Thompson, remaining); it won the UK's very highest food-rating in this year's survey, but – in the light of such a profound change – a rating seems inappropriate.* / **Sample dishes:** pancake of scallops & sevruga caviar; squab with boudin noir; dark chocolate tart. **Details:** www.winteringhamfields.com; 4m SW of Humber Bridge; 9.30 pm; closed Mon & Sun; no smoking; booking: max 8. **Accommodation:** 10 rooms, from £135.

---

## WOBURN, BEDFORDSHIRE          3–2A

### Birch        £38
20 Newport Rd   MK17 9HX    (01525) 290295

*"Good, well-presented food" at "middle-range prices" helps make this "friendly" family-run former pub a "pleasant" destination for all reporters; in a thin area, it has acquired quite a following.* / **Sample dishes:** smoked duck, orange & chicken terrine; roast halibut steak; espresso panna cotta. **Details:** www.birchwoburn.com; 9.30 pm, Sat 10 pm; closed Sun D; no jeans; no smoking in dining room; booking: max 12, Fri & Sat.

### Market Place        £39    Ⓐ
19 Market Pl   MK17 9PZ   (01525) 290877

*A "quirky" and "buzzy" restaurant, in a somewhat Californian style which comes as a bit of a surprise in these parts; it generally wins approval for its "good" standard of cooking.* / **Sample dishes:** asparagus tempura; organic beef fillet with mushrooms; cheesecake with mango & passion fruit. **Details:** www.marketplacewoburn.co.uk; 9.30 pm; closed Mon & Sun D; no Amex; no smoking.

### Paris House        £74    Ⓐ
Woburn Pk   MK17 9QP   (01525) 290692

*The "dreamy parkland setting" adds much to the appeal of this grand Tudor-style restaurant, which fans find a simply "perfect" dining destination; even supporters may concede that it's not entirely consistent though, and doubters just say it's stuck "in a time warp".* / **Sample dishes:** confit of crispy duck; monkfish in tomato & basil sauce; hot raspberry soufflé. **Details:** www.parishouse.co.uk; on A4012; 9.30 pm; closed Mon & Sun D; no smoking area.

---

## WOLVERHAMPTON, WEST MIDLANDS      5–4B

### Bilash        £38
2 Cheapside   WV1 1TU   (01902) 427762

*Refurbishment has been a mixed blessing for Sitab Khan's town-centre Bangladeshi – lower ratings support a reporter who says "the food's still good, but, since the redecoration, prices seem too high".* / **Sample dishes:** stuffed prawn; Bengali milk curd with rice pudding. **Details:** www.bilash-tandoori.co.uk; opp Civic Centre; 11 pm; closed Sun; no smoking area.

---

**sign up for the survey at www.hardens.com**       

## WOODBRIDGE, SUFFOLK                           3–1D
### Captain's Table                           £30          ★
3 Quay St IP12 1BX   (01394) 383145
*"A sound menu" ("strong in fish") – "very well prepared" and
"professionally presented" – makes this "slightly formal"
restaurant an "always-reliable" destination; on a nice day, you can
sit in the walled garden.* / **Sample dishes:** *twice-baked spinach soufflé;
slow-roast duck with red wine sauce; hot toffee pudding.*
**Details:** *www.captainstable.co.uk; 100 yds from theatre; 9.30 pm, Fri & Sat 10 pm;
closed Mon & Sun D; closed 2 weeks in Jan; no credit cards; no smoking.*

### Galley                                     £34          A★
21 Market Hill IP12 4LX   (01394) 380055
*"A timbered building on the market square" provides the "great
setting" for this "welcoming" newcomer, whose "imaginative",
"Turkish-influenced" cuisine is praised by all reporters.*
/ **Sample dishes:** *crispy braised belly of pork; Aberdeen Angus ribeye steak; yoghurt
with pine nuts & currants.* **Details:** *www.galley.uk.com; 10 pm; no Amex;
no smoking.*

### Riverside                                  £36          A★
Quayside IP12 1BH   (01394) 382587
*"Airy, light and very pleasant" – this "unpretentious" waterside
restaurant and theatre venue induces all-round satisfaction in all
who report on it.* / **Details:** *www.theriverside.co.uk; next to Woodbridge train
station; 9.15 pm, Sat 10 pm; closed Sun D; no smoking.*

### Seckford Hall Hotel                        £41          A
IP13 6NU   (01394) 385678
*It's been half a century in the same hands, but this "amazing"
Elizabethan manor house – with its "beautiful setting" –
continues to win general praise for "maintaining its standards";
the odd "disappointing" report, however, is not unknown.*
/ **Sample dishes:** *pan-fried tiger prawns; fillet of Scottish beef & home-cured foie
gras; strawberry & vanilla semifreddo with a compote of berries.*
**Details:** *www.seckford.co.uk; off the A12, signposted from last Woodbridge
roundabout; 9.30 pm; closed Mon L; no jeans or trainers; no smoking.*
**Accommodation:** *32 rooms, from £130.*

## WOODSTOCK, OXFORDSHIRE                       2–1D
### The Feathers Hotel                         £56
Market St OX20 1SX   (01993) 812291
*"Too much fuss", "too many waits" – these are the sort
of complaints which make this "comfortable" and potentially
"very pleasant" boutique-hotel hard to recommend with
confidence.* / **Sample dishes:** *confit of chicken; lemon sole with rocket soufflé;
nougat glacé with mango & chocolate sauce.* **Details:** *www.feathers.co.uk; 8m N
of Oxford on A44; 9 pm; closed Mon & Sun D; no jeans or trainers; no smoking.*
**Accommodation:** *20 rooms, from £135.*

## WORCESTER, WORCESTERSHIRE                     2–1B
### Angel Chef                                  £17
Angel Mall, Angel St WR1 3QT   (01905) 731131
*An "exciting" destination (well, by local standards), this budget
buffet-oriental is hailed for its "huge choice" of "great-value" fare.*
/ **Details:** *11 pm; no Amex; no smoking area.*

**sign up for the survey at www.hardens.com**

**Brown's** £ 52

24 Quay St WR1 2JJ (01905) 26263

*"Useful to know of hereabouts"* – this pleasantly-situated pumphouse-conversion on the river (no relation to the ghastly national chain) wins solid approval ratings for its *"good"* all-round standards (including some excellent *"fresh fish"*). / **Sample dishes:** Cornish crab; roast duck with minted pea mousseline; caramelised banana cake with caramel sauce. **Details:** near the Cathedral on riverside; 9.45 pm; closed Mon, Sat L & Sun D; no smoking.

**Glass House** £ 40 A★

Church St WR1 2RH (01905) 611120

*"Good food and cheerful service"* make this intriguingly-housed city-centre restaurant (in an ancient schoolhouse) well worth knowing about; lunches can be *"a bit quick"*, but they still offer *"excellent value"*. / **Sample dishes:** wild musroom risotto; sea bass; espresso panna cotta. **Details:** www.theglasshouse.co.uk; 10 pm; closed Sun; no smoking.

---

WRESSLE, NORTH YORKSHIRE 5–1D

**Loftsome Bridge Coaching House** £ 31 ★

YO8 6EN (01757) 630070

Ratings for this ancient bridge-side inn are surprisingly 'light' in the atmosphere department, but it scores consistently well as a *"value-for-money"* dining destination. / **Sample dishes:** marinated chicken & bacon salad; pan-fried sirloin steak; freshly prepared sweets. **Details:** www.loftsomebridge-hotel.co.uk; 9.15; closed Sun D; no smoking. **Accommodation:** 17 rooms, from £65.

---

WREXHAM, WREXHAM 5–3A

**Pant Yr Ochan** £ 30 A

Old Wrexham Rd LL12 8TY (01978) 853525

*"Good pub food in a beautiful lakeside setting"* is a formula that makes this *"charming"* inn very popular locally – the style of cooking, however, is *"not especially imaginative"*. / **Sample dishes:** mushroom ravioli; red bream & olive potatoes with asparagus; apple tart with cider custard. **Details:** www.brunningandprice.co.uk; 1m N of Wrexham; 9.30 pm; no smoking area; booking: max 14; children: 16.

---

WRIGHTINGTON BAR, LANCASHIRE 5–1A

**High Moor** £ 33 A

8 High Moor Ln WN6 9PS (01257) 252364

*"Wonderful views"*, a *"great interior"* and cooking that's *"a cut above the rest"* induce consistent (if not hugely plentiful) feedback on this restaurant in a 17th-century building, overlooking the Lancashire Plain. / **Sample dishes:** melon, pineapple & orange cocktail; fillet of lamb; chocolate bread & butter pudding. **Details:** 9.30 pm; closed Mon; no smoking.

**Mulberry Tree** £ 44

9 Wood Ln WN6 9SE (01257) 451400

This *"old pub"* (*"a couple of minutes off the M6"*) has been *"well modernised in bistro style"* and you can eat in the bar or the restaurant; it's a *"classy"* joint – the chef came from Le Gavroche – but one which strikes the occasional reporter as *"not terribly friendly"*. / **Sample dishes:** pea & ham soup; baked cod with cheese & basil crust; rice pudding with apricots. **Details:** 2m along Mossy Lea Rd, off M6, J27; 9.30 pm; no Amex; no smoking; children: 14+.

## YARM, CLEVELAND                                    8–3C

### D P Chadwicks                                     £36
104b High St  TS15 9AU   (01642) 788558
"Excellent pizza", good burgers and "real chips" are the sort
of superior staples that make this modern brasserie a "great
local". / **Sample dishes:** Catalan seafood salad; calf's liver & bacon with onion
rings; baked cherry cheesecake. **Details:** www.chadwicksrestaurant.com; just after
Yarm Bridge; 9.30 pm; closed Mon & Sun; no Amex; no smoking; booking: max 12.

### McCoys in the Yarm                               £34
44 High St  TS15 9AE  (01642) 791234
This informal bistro above a store (owned by the McCoys
of Tontine fame) can become "busy" and "loud", but mostly wins
praise for its "well-cooked" dishes. / **Sample dishes:** smoked haddock
fishcakes; braised lamb with Spanish black pudding; Eton mess.
**Details:** www.mccoysinyarm.co.uk; off the A19; 10 pm; closed Sun;
no smoking area.

## YARMOUTH, ISLE OF WIGHT                            2–4D

### George Hotel                                     £59     A★
Quay St  PO41 0PE   (01983) 760331
The "wonderful" waterside location is not the only attraction
of this elegant 17th-century inn – again rated by reporters the
best place to eat on the island; there is both a brasserie
(with garden) and restaurant. / **Sample dishes:** trio of duck starters;
braised pork with Morteau sausage & parsnip purée; rum baba with Earl Grey syrup.
**Details:** www.thegeorge.co.uk; 9.30 pm; D only, closed Mon & Sun; no Amex;
children: 12+ in restaurant. **Accommodation:** 17 rooms, from £180.

## YATTENDON, BERKSHIRE                               2–2D

### Royal Oak Hotel                                  £41     A
The Square  RG18 0UG   (01635) 201325
This "authentic old inn" still seems to be striving to get back
to the destination-status it once enjoyed, but its boosters say that,
with its "enthusiastic" chef, it "deserves a wider clientele".
/ **Sample dishes:** red mullet, tapenade, artichokes & tomato vinaigrette salad;
neck of lamb; raspberry crème brûlée. **Details:** www.royaloakyattendon.com; 5m W
of Pangbourne, off B4009; 10 pm; no smoking; children: 6+. **Accommodation:** 5
rooms, from £130.

## YORK, CITY OF YORK                                 5–1D

### Abbey Inn                                        £33     A★
Byland Abbey  YO61 4BD   (01347) 868204
"A very acceptable alternative to the nearby Star at Harome"
(and "you don't have to book months in advance either") –
this "spectacularly-located" gastropub (overlooking the ruins
of Byland Abbey) has improved under new owners, and now offers
a menu that's "more restaurant-like" than before.
/ **Details:** www.bylandabbeyinn.co.uk; 9 pm; closed Mon L & Sun D; no Amex;
no smoking area. **Accommodation:** 3 rooms, from £95.

**sign up for the survey at www.hardens.com**

## Bettys £ 28 Ⓐ
6-8 St Helen's Sq  Y0I 8QP  (01904) 659142
*For fans, this famous "throwback to a bygone era" – the best-known branch of the Yorkshire tea-room chain – is "a delightful escape from the horrid modern world"; it attracts a fair few brickbats, though, for becoming ever more "complacent" and "expensive".* / **Sample dishes:** *Swiss rosti with bacon & cheese; Yorkshire curd tart.* **Details:** *www.bettysandtaylors.com; down Blake St from York Minster; 9 pm; no smoking; no booking.*

## Blue Bicycle £ 45
34 Fossgate  YO I 9TA  (01904) 673990
*"Private booths in the cellar" ("a former brothel!") help win a number of "romantic" nominations for this popular bistro; under its owners of the last two years, however, it risks becoming "very overpriced".* / **Sample dishes:** *mussels with rosemary; smoked haddock rarebits; sticky toffee pudding.* **Details:** *www.thebluebicycle.com; 9.30 pm; no Amex; no smoking; booking: max 8.* **Accommodation:** *2 rooms, from £150.*

## Café Concerto £ 33 Ⓐ
21 High Petergate  YO I 7EN  (01904) 610478
*"Lovely surroundings and views of the Minster" contribute to the all-round charms of this "whimsical" but "busy" café/bistro, which "can do for a quick coffee or full meal"; for the latter, it serves "filling" helpings of "comfort" dishes.* / **Sample dishes:** *tomato soup with pesto; satay beef stir-fry; strawberry & raspberry pavlova.* **Details:** *www.cafeconcerto.biz; by the W entrance of York Minster; 9.30 pm, Fri & Sat 10 pm; no Amex; no smoking; no booking at L.*

## City Screen Café Bar £ 20
Coney St  YO I 9QL  (01904) 541144
*"Lengthy waits" feature in too many reports on this otherwise enjoyable cinema-café – an "always busy" local stand-by; for those with time to invest, it has "lovely" views over the Ouse.* / **Sample dishes:** *Parma ham & Mozzarella salad; smoked salmon & scrambled eggs; lemon cheesecake.* **Details:** *www.picturehouses.co.uk; 9 pm, Sun-Tue 5 pm; closed Mon D, Tue D & Sun D; no Amex; no smoking area; no booking.*

## Masons Bistro £ 38
13 Fossgate  YO I 9TA  (01904) 611919
*"Simple cooking with a Mediterranean flavour" is winning wider support for this handily-located bistro, which is praised for its "large portions".* / **Sample dishes:** *vine leaves stuffed with Feta, spinach & pine leaves; pan-fried red snapper; cherry & kirsh clafoutis.* **Details:** *www.masons-bistro.co.uk; 9.30 pm; closed Mon; no smoking; booking: max 8.*

## Maxi's £ 25 ★
Ings Ln, York Business Pk  YO26 6RA  (01904) 783898
*"Popularity amongst Chinese families is an indicator of the quality" of this large oriental restaurant, located on the outer ring road – ratings for its "authentic" cuisine certainly run rings round those for the Leeds branch.* / **Details:** *www.maxi-s.co.uk; 11.30 pm; no smoking area.*

## Melton's                                    £ 38       ★
7 Scarcroft Rd  YO23 1ND  (01904) 634341
"A consistently good restaurant tucked-away in an
unprepossessing corner, just outside the city walls"; "very fair wine
pricing" adds to its attractions as a "gastronomic" destination –
let's hope that new chef Anni Prescot is keeping the flag flying!
/ **Sample dishes:** mussels with apple cider; roast Yorkshire beef with red wine jus;
home-made coconut ice cream with pineapple syrup.
**Details:** www.meltonsrestaurant.co.uk; 10 mins walk from Castle Museum;
9.30 pm; closed Mon L & Sun; no Amex; no smoking area.

## Melton's Too                                £ 26       ✗
25 Walmgate  YO1 9TX  (01904) 629222
"Still not quite right" – though it attracts a fair amount
of feedback, this spin-off bistro remains a pale shadow of its
namesake; a new chef has recently been installed, so perhaps
he will help perk things up. / **Sample dishes:** pork rillettes with Cumberland
sauce; Merguez sausage with couscous & lemon oil; Yorkshire curd tart.
**Details:** www.meltonstoo.co.uk; 10.30 pm; no Amex; smoking in bar only.

## Middlethorpe Hall                           £ 57
Bishopthorpe Rd  YO23 2GB  (01904) 641241
In a 200-acre estate on the fringe of the city, the dining room
at this Historic House hotel is by far the grandest place to eat
in these parts; it can seem "stuffy", though, and a number
of reporters feel the food "doesn't measure up to the splendour
of the setting". / **Sample dishes:** oxtail terrine with horseradish cream;
pike fillet with Bayonne ham; aniseed parfait with roast pears.
**Details:** www.middlethorpe.com; next to racecourse; 9.30 pm; jacket required;
no smoking; children: 8+. **Accommodation:** 29 rooms, from £175.

## Rish                                        £ 45
7 Fossgate  YO1 9TA  (01904) 622688
"This would be expensive in London – in York it's too much";
despite some reports of "excellent" cooking, the issue of price
dominates feedback on this Edwardian shop-conversion, where
an ex-Winteringham Fields chef risks "trying too hard".
/ **Sample dishes:** beetroot-scented gravlax; roast lamb with olive mash & salsify;
pear Bakewell tart with Calvados sorbet. **Details:** www.rish-york.co.uk; 10 pm;
no smoking.

## Tasting Room                                £ 41
13 Swinegate Court East  YO1 8AJ  (01904) 627879
This central two-year-old is "friendly", "personable" and "well-
intentioned", but risks "missing its mark" – the problem seems
to be that it can get "overstretched" by "trying to cover all the
bases from a light lunch to a full à la carte". / **Sample dishes:** seared
scallops & samphire; roast duck breast; white chocolate & lavender crème brûlée.
**Details:** www.thetastingroom.co.uk; 9.30 pm; no Amex; no smoking; children: 4+.

**MAPS**

**Overview**

10

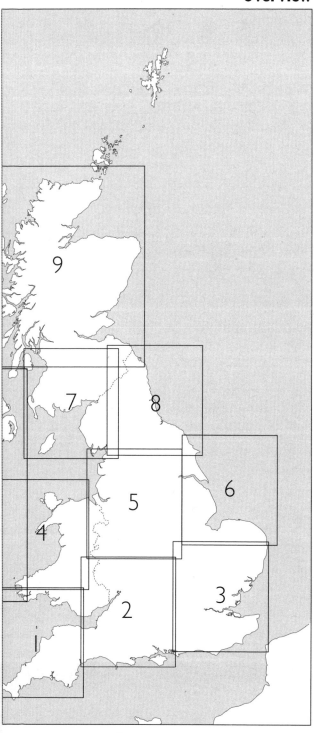

# Map 1

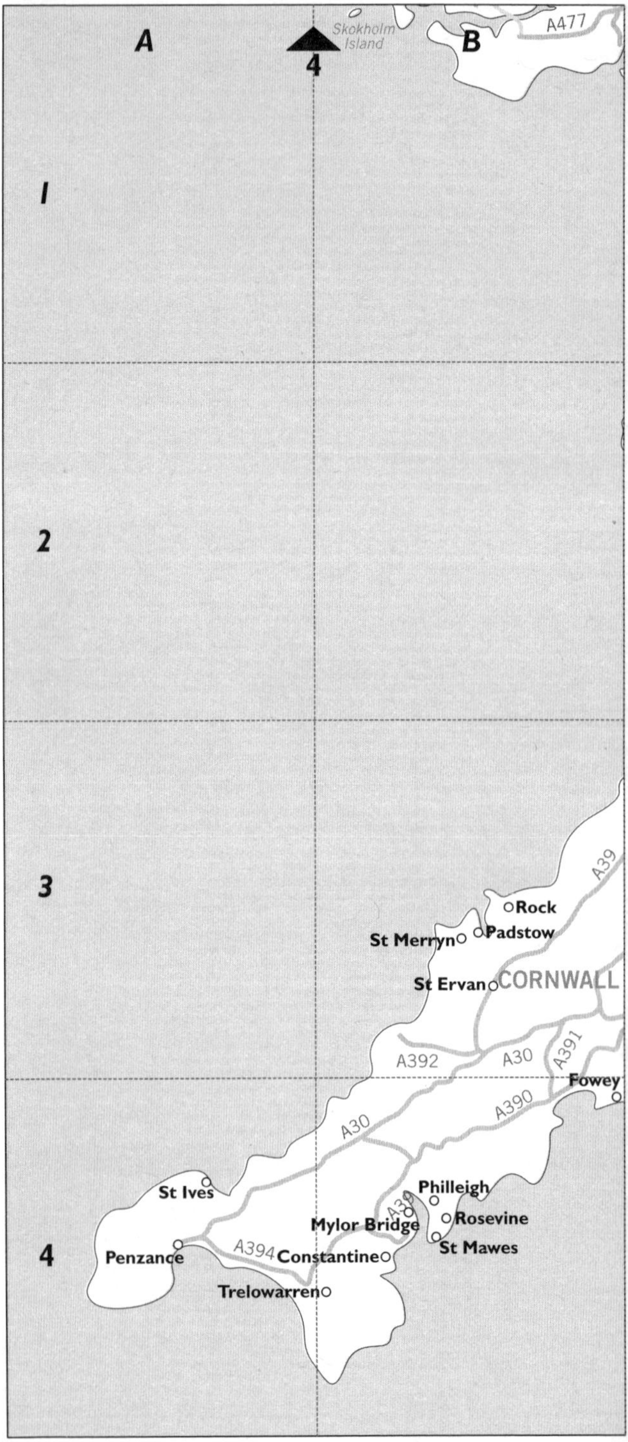

**A**

**B**

Skokholm Island

A477

**4**

**I**

**2**

**3**

○Rock

St Merryn○ ○Padstow

St Ervan○ CORNWALL

A39

A391

A392    A30

A30    A390

Fowey○

A30

St Ives○

Philleigh

Mylor Bridge○ ○Rosevine

Penzance○    A394  Constantine○    St Mawes

Trelowarren○

**4**

# Map 1

# Map 2

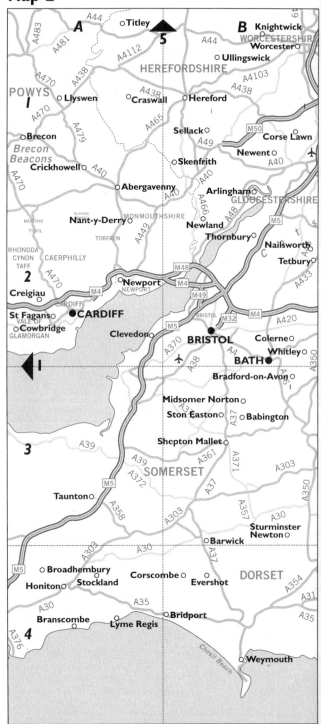

# Map 2

# Map 3

# Map 3

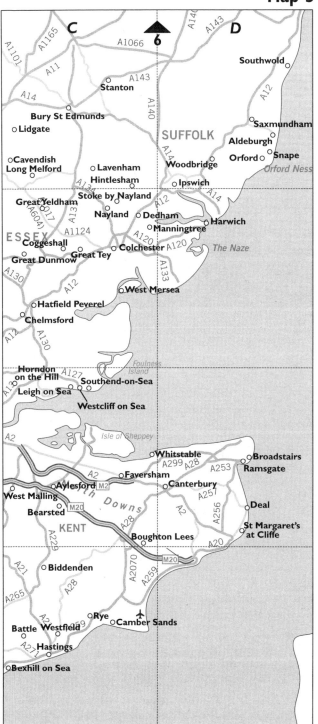

**Map 4**

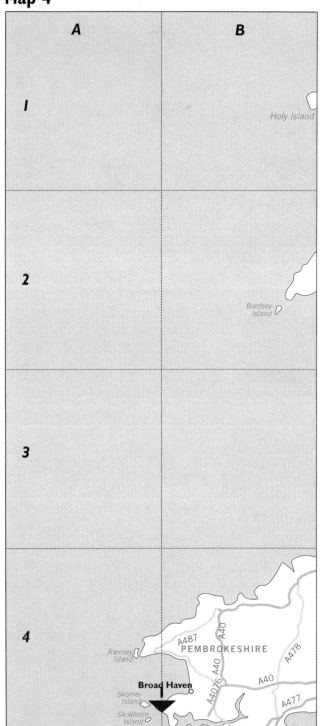

**Map 4**

# Map 5

# Map 5

**C** Harrogate

**8** A59

**D** A166

EAST RIDING OF YORKSHIRE

A59

A59

York

Addingham

Ilkley

A65

Wetherby

Sutton-upon-Derwent

Otley

Tadcaster

A61

A58

Escrick

Wressle

A19

A614

Saltaire

Shipley

Aberford

Lund

Haworth

A650

Bradford

**LEEDS**

M621

A1

A63

M62

Sowerby Bridge

Halifax

Elland

Brighouse

M62

Wakefield

M18

Winteringham

Huddersfield

Golcar

A62

M180

M181

A61

M1

Shelley

A629

A628

A616

SOUTH YORKSHIRE

A1(M)

A159

Bawtry

A631

A156

A57

A6

Sheffield

*Peak*

A57

M1

A1

A57

*District*

A619

A60

A614

Hassop

A622

Baslow

A619

Bakewell

DERBYSHIRE

Caunton

**6**

Birchover

NOTTINGHAM-

A617

A17

A6

SHIRE

Newark-on-Trent

Ashbourne

A38

A46

A1

A52

Riber

Hazlewood

A52

**NOTTINGHAM**

Great Gonerby

West Hallam

A52

A50

Derby

A6

Langar

Stathern

A516

Plumtree

Colston Bassett

A607

A518

A50

A515

Melbourne

Nether Broughton

A38

M1

Belton

A6

Loughborough

Stapleford

A444

A607

A606

RUTLAND

A50

A46

Oakham

M42

LEICESTERSHIRE

Knossington

Hambleton

Leicester

A47

A606

Sutton Coldfield

Thorpe Langton

A600

M6

Kibworth Beauchamp

M69

A6

Medbourne

**BIRMINGHAM**

M1

Market Harborough

R427

MIDLANDS

M42

A45

A4304

A14

A508

NORTHAMPTONSHIRE

Solihull

Coventry

M6

A43

Lapworth

Kenilworth

**2**

M42

M40

Henley-in-Arden

Warwick

A46

M45

A45

Preston Bagot

Royal Leamington Spa

Bishops Tachbrook

# Map 6

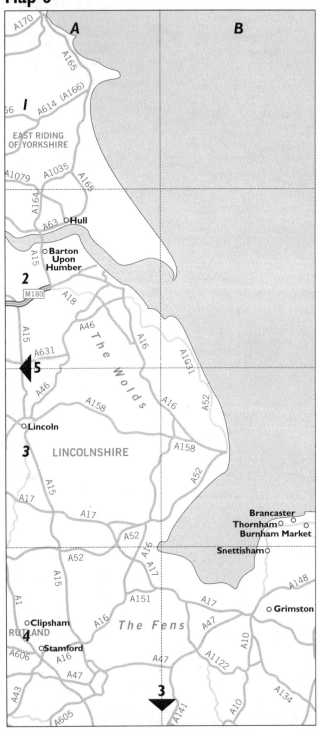

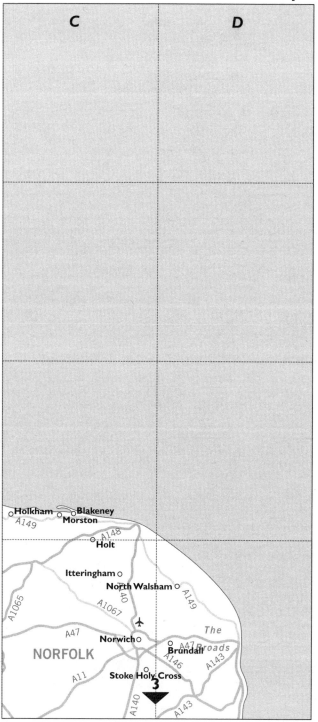

**Map 6**

C

D

Holkham   Blakeney
A149   Morston

A148
Holt

Itteringham

A140   North Walsham   A149

A1065   A1067

A47

The

A47   Broads

Norwich   Brundall   A143

**NORFOLK**   A146

A11   Stoke Holy Cross

A140   **3**   A143

# Map 7

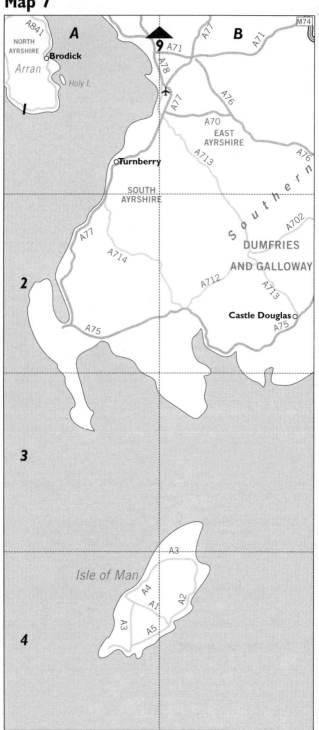

**Map 7**

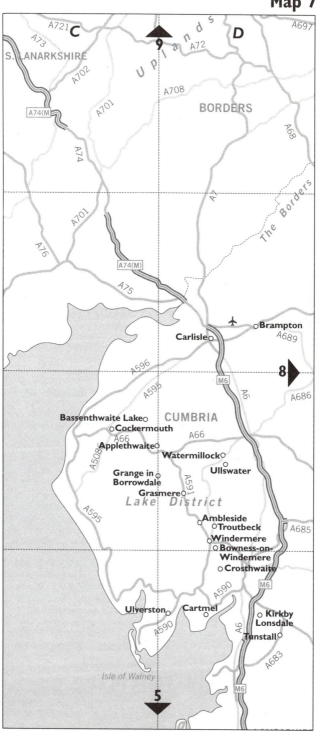

C

A721

A73

S. LANARKSHIRE

A702

A701

A74(M)

A74

A701

A76

A74(M)

A75

9

Uplands

A72

A708

BORDERS

A7

The Borders

D

A697

A68

Carlisle

✈

Brampton
A689

8

A686

A596

A596

Bassenthwaite Lake

Cockermouth

A66

Applethwaite

A508

A595

CUMBRIA

A66

Watermillock

Ullswater

Grange in Borrowdale

A591

Grasmere

Lake District

Ambleside
Troutbeck

Windermere

Bowness-on-Windemere

Crosthwaite

A685

M6

A6

M6

Ulverston

A590

Cartmel

A590

Kirkby Lonsdale

Tunstall

A6

A683

Isle of Walney

5

M6

# Map 8

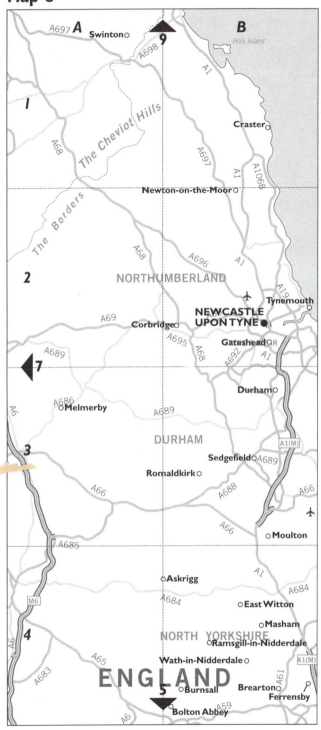

**Map 8**

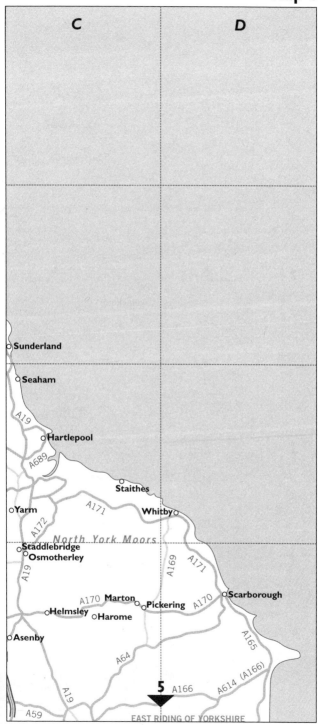

**C**

**D**

Sunderland

Seaham

A19

Hartlepool

A689

Staithes

Yarm

A171

Whitby

A172

*North York Moors*

Staddlebridge

Osmotherley

A19

A169

A171

Marton

A170

Pickering

A170

Scarborough

Helmsley

Harome

A165

Asenby

A64

A614 (A166)

**5** A166

A19

A59

EAST RIDING OF YORKSHIRE

# Map 9

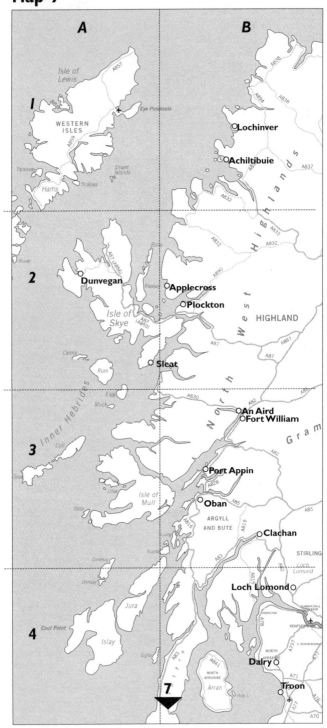

# Map 9

# Map 10

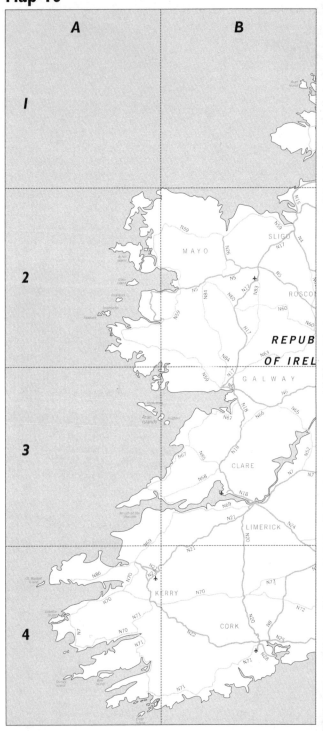

# Map 10

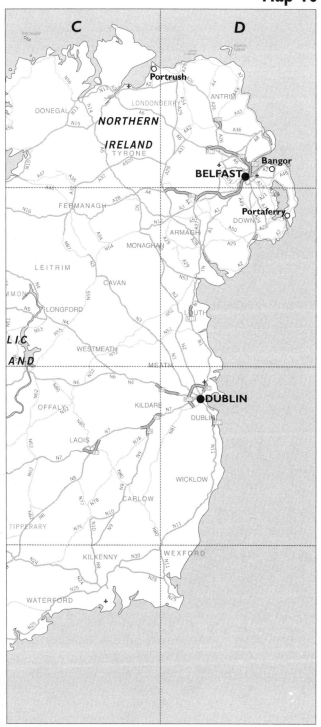

# ALPHABETICAL INDEX

# ALPHABETICAL INDEX

# ALPHABETICAL INDEX

# ALPHABETICAL INDEX

# ALPHABETICAL INDEX

# NOTES

# NOTES

# NOTES